Lectures on the Psychology of Women

Fourth Edition

Joan C. Chrisler
Connecticut College

Carla Golden
Ithaca College

Patricia D. Rozee
California State University at Long Beach

D0218334

WAVELAND

PRESS, INC.

Long Grove, Illinois

For information about this book, contact:
  Waveland Press, Inc.
  4180 IL Route 83, Suite 101
  Long Grove, IL 60047-9580
  (847) 634-0081
  info@waveland.com
  www.waveland.com

Contents

❖

Preface

——————— ❖ ———————

The three of us have known each other for a number of years, having met through feminist psychology conferences. In the summer of 1992, we were together in Atlanta, Georgia, at a meeting of the leadership of the Association for Women in Psychology. Our conversation eventually turned to our respective psychology of women classes, our favorite lectures, and whether or not we lectured from notes. As we each spoke with excitement about what we considered our best and most interesting lectures, one of us suggested (and the other two of us elaborated and encouraged the idea) that we might invite a number of different feminist psychologists to put into written form their "favorite" lectures to make a psychology reader to accompany psychology of women textbooks. It is from this idea and collaboration that this project grew. Our discussion ended with a frank talk about the pros and cons of the various textbooks we'd used, and we concluded that all of them could be improved if paired with a good collection of supplementary readings.

Lectures on the Psychology of Women is not meant to stand alone. It was designed to be a companion to the available texts on the psychology of women, psychology of gender, or gender-role development. We invited our authors to write about topics not normally covered or not covered extensively in the textbooks. Thus, the dual purposes of the lectures are to supplement the main text and to provoke classroom discussion. The lectures are short, and they are not intended to be comprehensive. It is up to the instructor to provide context and commentary.

The lectures are organized to follow the arrangement of topics in several of the standard textbooks, but each is independent of the others, so they can be rearranged and assigned in any order. Some may also be useful assignments for other women's studies or psychology courses.

Each lecture was written by an experienced teacher of the psychology of women. The lectures are written in an informal manner; the authors speak directly to the students on the students' level and address questions that students often ask. The authors involve their readers in the topics by asking questions and by suggesting ideas to consider or exercises to try. Some describe the authors' personal experiences with the topics; others present original data. None of the lectures has been previously published. All were prepared specifically for this collection.

The lectures also serve the purpose of exposing students to some of the experts in the field of feminist psychology. The work of many of the authors is cited in the psychology of women textbooks, so students may already be familiar with their names when they read their lectures, or they may be delighted to encounter their work in the text after having read their lectures. The informal tone of the lectures and the biographical statements and photographs are intended to give readers the feeling that they have been "introduced" to the authors.

Working on this book was more than a professional challenge or an intellectual exercise for us. It was a genuine pleasure to collaborate on this project with other feminist psychologists. We got to know each other much better during the time we spent preparing this book, and we've come to appreciate each other's (and each author's) unique strengths and skills. We're pleased with the results of our work, and we hope you'll enjoy reading *Lectures on the Psychology of Women* as much as we enjoyed editing it.

ACKNOWLEDGMENTS

We'd like first to thank the authors of the lectures for generously agreeing to contribute their ideas to our project, for their willingness to write (and rewrite) in a style other than the usual scientific one, and for responding graciously to our anxious prodding about deadlines. This book would obviously not exist without them!

Our thanks go to our students; we've probably learned almost as much from them as they've learned from us. Our students' needs and our desire to meet them were the inspiration for this book.

Thanks to the Association for Women in Psychology and Division 35 of the American Psychological Association, without whom there would be no organized field of the psychology of women, and without whose activities we would never have met and had the discussion that started this project.

We'd like to thank our colleagues in the Psychology and Women's Studies Departments at Connecticut College, Ithaca College, and the California State University at Long Beach. They provided the supportive atmosphere in which we worked on this project. Thanks to Nancy MacLeod, Sandy Nicolls, Jayde Pryzgoda, and Jennifer Smirlock for their assistance in the preparation of the manuscript.

We would also like to thank the following reviewers for their many helpful comments and suggestions: Joyce L. Carbonell, Florida State University; Suzanne M. Johnson, Dowling College; Ingrid Johnston-Robledo, SUNY Fredonia; Linda Kline, California State University at Chico; Shirley Ogletree, Texas State University at San Marcos.

Finally, we are grateful to Kate Russillo, our editor, for her enthusiastic embrace of our ideas and her vision for this project. Many others were supportive and always ready with helpful advice throughout the preparation of this manuscript.

Joan C. Chrisler
Carla Golden
Patricia D. Rozee

Introduction

❖

The works in this volume all have one thing in common: They are written by feminist psychologists, all of whom are active and committed teachers of the psychology of women. Because the emphasis is on feminist teachers and teaching, perhaps a definition would be appropriate. Webster's dictionary defines the word "feminist" as a person (either female or male) who believes in the economic, political, and social equality of women and men. Although all of the writers in this volume are feminists and teachers, they also differ in many ways. They represent a variety of racial, ethnic, and religious backgrounds. They are lesbian, bisexual, and heterosexual in sexual orientation. They were raised in working-class, middle-class, and wealthy families. They live and work in rural, suburban, and urban areas. But these authors are all alike in their belief in both the necessity and importance of gender equality, which includes a commitment to the elimination of all forms of inequality and domination, including sexism, racism, classism, and homophobia.

Certain perspectives on the world are common among feminists. Feminists are concerned with inequality at the personal, institutional, and cultural levels. Patricia Spencer Faunce (1985) described the feminist worldview from the personal perspective.

> Feminism is an advocacy system for women. Feminism insists that women must have personal autonomy and both the freedom to direct and the responsibility for directing all areas of their lives; they must decide for themselves what it means to be a woman; and they must define themselves as independent persons, separate from their relationships. Feminism fosters pride in being female, emphasizes the commonality of the female experience across cultural and socioeconomic lines, and develops a sense of community among women. Feminism holds that all roles are open to all people and that every woman is entitled to the opportunity to develop her potential fully. Feminism recognizes the culturally and experientially based perspective differences between women and men, assumes women and men are more alike than not, and insists that possible differences not be conceptualized in terms of "superiority/inferiority." Finally, feminism strives to equalize personal power, asserts that no person should have non-contractual dominion over another, and encourages equalitarian relationships. (p. 310)

The cultural and institutional aspects of feminism are emphasized by bell hooks (1981; cited in Ruth, 1995, p. 5), who defined feminism as

A commitment to eradicating the ideology of domination that permeates Western culture on various levels—sex, race, and class, to name a few—and a commitment to reorganizing U.S. society, so that the self-development of people can take precedence over imperialism, economic expansion, and material desires.

As you can see, feminism is a life philosophy, a worldview, a blueprint for justice. Feminists believe that, once we remove the patriarchal lens through which we are accustomed to viewing the world, we are free to organize our world according to our own priorities. The choices we make are then made with full knowledge of all available alternatives, rather than limited to the alternatives predetermined for us by a patriarchal culture. Once we know ourselves, we are in a better position to work toward changing the cultural and institutional power arrangements that keep women in their place.

The following are some other common feminist themes you will encounter in the readings in this book.

SOCIAL CONSTRUCTION OF GENDER

Feminists are interested in how gender is constructed by different societies and at different times in history. By "social construction," we mean that the biological reality of being born female or male is differentially embellished in varying cultural and situational contexts. The biological body is not born into a sociocultural vacuum; rather, it is influenced by all kinds of external factors or contexts: cultural expectations, life situations, institutional pressures, environmental events, and even the presence or absence of others. Thus, the biological female is shaped into a girl and then a woman by the culture and time into which she is born. For example, in the nineteenth century, middle-class and upper-class White women were expected to be frail and weak and to "swoon," or faint, regularly. This was considered very feminine and desirable. Today, however, if we met a woman who was frail and weak and fainted periodically, we would think she was ill! Indeed, we have since learned that those nineteenth-century fair damsels fainted because they were suffering from a lack of oxygen caused by too-tight corsets. Susan Basow discusses the socialization of women and girls and its impact on their social status in her chapter "Gender Socialization, or How Long a Way Has Baby Come?" Lisa Bowleg looks at the overlapping categories of race, class, and gender and how these factors differentially affect women's health status in her chapter "The Health Risks of Being Black, Latina, Woman, and/or Poor: Redefining Women's Health Within the Context of Social Inequality." Maureen C. McHugh addresses the social construction of gender and pathology in her lecture "A Feminist Approach to Agoraphobia: Challenging Traditional Views of Women at Home."

POWER

Feminists argue that it is impossible to examine the psychology of women without considering women's relative position in the power hierarchy. In general, women have less power and status than men. This is true all over the world. Worldwide, there is a clear preference for male children (Unger & Crawford, 1992); women are paid less than men for the same work and have fewer opportunities for advancement; men control the U.S. Congress and every state legislature; they hold the top positions in nearly all U.S. corporations, and they are the majority of the faculty in U.S. universities; women do nearly all the housework and childcare; women and their children make up the majority of poor people in this country; and violence against women has been characterized as pandemic. The pervasive power differences between women and men in our society, the oppression of women, and the institutionalization of androcentric (male-centered) values are discussed by Ruth S. Ostenson in her lecture entitled "Who's In and Who's Out: The Results of Oppression" and by Sandra Lipsitz Bem in her lecture "Transforming the Debate on Sexual Inequality: From Biological Difference to Institutionalized Androcentrism." The economic oppression of women is the topic of Deborah Belle's lecture "Poor Women in a Wealthy Nation." The misuse of power in the workplace is discussed by Faye J. Crosby in her chapter "Sex Discrimination at Work." The use of violence to enforce the social control of women is discussed by Patricia D. Rozee in her lecture, "Women's Fear of Rape: Causes, Consequences, and Coping"; by Geraldine B. Stahly in "Battered Women: Why Don't They Just Leave?"; and by Britain A. Scott in "Women and Pornography: What We Don't Know Can Hurt Us."

THE PERSONAL IS POLITICAL

"The personal is political" means that what at first appears to be a personal problem is really a social problem with a political solution (Faunce, 1985). We live in a society that tends to blame the victim for her own misfortune. "Victim blaming," as this is called, is a result of our tendency to examine a person's behavior out of context. It is easier to make internal attributions for someone's behavior than to consider all the possible situational factors that may have led to the behavior. For example, one of our students lost a promotion. The reason? Her boss thought she was not committed to her department because she was often late for work. The student explained that she was late because she had to deliver her two small children to daycare on her way to work. Because the daycare center did not open until 7:30 A.M. and the student had to be at work 20 miles away by 8:00 A.M., she often hit traffic and was delayed, so what initially looked like a personal problem, lack of commitment to the job, was actually a social problem, lack of quality childcare, which probably has a political solution—a national childcare policy. Diane M. Hall looks at mothering as a status variable in her chapter entitled "Feminist Perspectives on the Personal and Political Aspects of Mothering." Rhoda Olkin makes clear how the personal is political in her lecture "Women With Disabilities."

THE VALUE OF DIVERSITY

Feminists value the diversities among women, such as those based on race, ethnicity, religion, social class, sexual orientation, age, and physical ability. The consensus among feminist educators (*Proceedings of the Division 35 National Conference on Education and Training in Feminist Practice, 1993*) is that valuing diversity means being appreciative of and open to differences among and between women and recognizing the value of difference. This requires not only receptiveness to and respect for difference but the cultivation and nurturance of different perspectives. Psychology has often presented human experience as male, White, Christian, and heterosexual. But because of the importance of understanding the worldview of all women, we believe that these exclusionary practices must be challenged. Therefore, we have included a number of lectures that will expose the reader to the multiple perspectives of women: for example, Connie S. Chan's lecture "Asian American Women and Adolescent Girls: Sexuality and Sexual Expression"; Linda D. Garnets's lecture "Life as a Lesbian: What Does Gender Have to Do With It?"; Carolyn M. West's lecture "Mammy, Jezebel, Sapphire, and Their Homegirls: Developing an 'Oppositional Gaze' Toward the Images of Black Women"; Carla Golden's lecture "The Intersexed and the Transgendered: Rethinking Sex/Gender"; and Donna Castañeda's lecture "Gender Issues Among Latinas." Valuing diversity includes the consideration of multiple overlapping oppressions. Often, it is difficult for a Woman of Color to know whether discrimination is directed at her because she is a woman, an ethnic minority, or both. Angela R. Gillem discusses this issue in "Triple Jeopardy in the Lives of Biracial Black/White Women."

VALUING WOMEN AND WOMEN'S EXPERIENCE

Because ours is a society in which males and maleness are more valued than females and femaleness, it is important to feminist psychology to value women and women's experience. Women have long been silenced. Our contributions to society have not been recorded in history books, our experiences have not been heard or valued, and our stories have not been told. In fact, our reality has often been defined by men. For example, most of what was written early on about female sexuality, and even female orgasm, was written by men. If you are a woman, can you imagine writing a book about male orgasm? And without talking to any men about it? Such is the power of patriarchy to define and name. Recognizing and validating women's experience is discussed by Mary Gergen as she helps to reframe our views of aging in her chapter entitled "Positive Aging for Women."

Topics of interest to women, from women's experience, that have generally been ignored by traditional psychology include female friendships (Suzanna M. Rose, "Crossing the Color Line in Women's Friendship"); women's choices in parenting decisions (Nancy Felipe Russo, "Understanding Emotional Responses After Abortion"); and women in sports (Ruth L. Hall, "Sweating It Out: The Good News and the Bad News About Women and Sport").

*V*ALUES

An important theme in a feminist psychology of women is values. Each of us grows up with a sense of values instilled by our family, our peers, our social organizations, our community, even our city, state, region, and nation. Often, the values we hold dear are not conscious. Like a fish that is unaware that its evironment is wet, we are often unaware of how strongly our values influence our attitudes and behavior (Bem & Bem, 1976). As students of the social and behavioral sciences, we have been taught to assume that science is objective and value-free. In psychology we try to design our experiments with control groups, placebos, and double-blind methods to eliminate the effects of our values on the research process.

Nevertheless, feminist psychologists argue that science, including psychology, is not value-free. Psychology is people studying people; it is unlikely that we will be able to completely eliminate the bias infused by the values of the researchers. Our values influence every phase of the research process, from the initial question formulation, through the research design and analysis, to the interpretation.

For example, if scientists think that only women's moods are influenced by hormonal fluctuations, then they might design experiments that study only women. By not studying men and their mood fluctuations, scientists perpetuate the idea that women are controlled by their hormones and men are not. The scientists' own values would then have prevented them from examining mood fluctuations that may occur as a result of varying levels of testosterone in men. Because there is some evidence that the relatively higher levels of testosterone may be related to aggressive behavior in males, this is a serious omission. Joan C. Chrisler illustrates the limiting effects of androcentric values as she discusses "PMS as a Culture-Bound

Syndrome." Christine A. Smith's lecture "Women, Weight, and Body Image" confronts the effects of men's values on women's comfort with their own bodies.

INCLUSIVE LANGUAGE

There is no longer any doubt that the use of noninclusive, sexist, or male-biased language has negative psychological effects. Our language both contributes to and is limited by our conceptualization of the world. Although some people have argued that language is a trivial issue contrived by feminists, the same people are often very offended by "dirty" talk, swearing, and "improper" English. That is because they know that language is powerful.

English—and many other languages as well—use the terms "man" and "he" to describe the whole human race, women as well as men. Studies show, however, that people, from preschoolers through college adults, interpret the word "man" to mean males. For example, when research participants are asked to draw pictures of "early man," their drawings are virtually all of male human beings (Harrison, 1975). Thus, the word "man" is not inclusive of woman, as some have argued; it is not the generic "human" but, rather, the male human that is conceptualized. Little girls will opt out of careers described with such words as "police*man*" or "fire*man*" because they think these are "boy jobs," yet when the words "police *officer*" and "fire*fighter*" are used, the girls are more likely to see these as careers to which they might aspire. Thus, early in life girls are limited in their aspirations by their conceptualization of "man" to mean male (Unger & Crawford, 1992). Feminists see this as a barrier to equality. All the authors in this volume are cognizant of the power of language and are committed to changing language usage, both through example and through institutional changes, such as persuading textbook publishers to adopt inclusive language guidelines. Current American Psychological Association (APA) guidelines require the use of nonsexist language in all manuscripts submitted for publication in psychology journals.

GLOBAL STATUS OF WOMEN

The authors of this volume are concerned with the global status of women. In today's world, media, transportation, ecological, and economic factors have combined to result in an increased intertwining of the interests of the nations of the world. No longer is it possible to consider issues such as violence against women in the limited context of our own country. Instead, the global economy and political interests of nations affect the ways in which women are treated. In addition, the increasing immigration to the United States makes an understanding of other cultures imperative.

To understand gender, one must understand its different manifestations around the world. Thus, most lectures in this volume address the global implications of the topics.

THE VALUE OF SOCIAL ACTIVISM

Feminists value the collective actions of women, for women, to create social change. The current emphasis on engagement and community service learning has prompted many professors to include community service in their courses. In this way, many more women are becoming involved in women's issues in the community by working at shelters, hotlines, and after-school programs for girls' empowerment. We embrace the empowerment of women by both individual and collective actions. Women's collective power to change our status is vast. However, many women do not see either the need for such change or their own power to enact social change. We hope that you will understand both by the time you have finished reading this book.

REFERENCES

BEM, S. L., & BEM, D. J. (1976). Training the woman to know her place: The power of a nonconscious ideology. In S. Cox (Ed.), *Female psychology: The emerging self* (pp. 180–191). Palo Alto, CA: Science Research Associates.

FAUNCE, P. S. (1985). Teaching feminist therapies: Integrating feminist therapy, pedagogy, and scholarship. In L. B. Rosewater & L. E. A. Walker (Eds.), *Handbook of feminist therapy* (pp. 309–320). New York: Springer.

HARRISON, L. (1975, April). Cro-magnon woman in eclipse. *The Science Teacher,* pp. 8–11.

Proceedings of the Division 35 National Conference on Education and Training in Feminist Practice. (1993). Boston: Boston College.

RUTH, S. (1995). *Issues in feminism.* Mountain View, CA: Mayfield.

UNGER, R., & CRAWFORD, M. (1992). *Women and gender: A feminist psychology.* New York: McGraw-Hill.

Patricia D. Rozee
Carla Golden
Joan C. Chrisler

*S*ANDRA *L*IPSITZ *B*EM *is Professor of Psychology and Feminist, Gender, & Sexuality Studies at Cornell University, where she also served as Director of FGSS (formerly Women's Studies) for 10 years. Dr. Bem taught courses on the social construction of gender and sexuality at Cornell and Stanford from 1971 to 2003. She has been honored by several professional organizations for her many contributions to the literature on gender and sexuality.*

1

Transforming the Debate on Sexual Inequality

From Biological Difference to Institutionalized Androcentrism

❖

B ecause I am a feminist psychologist, I am frequently asked to lecture on the question, What biological sex differences are there, *really?* This question puts me in an awkward position because I not only don't have the answer to it; I don't even think it's the question we ought to be asking. I'll tell you why.

I begin with a single historical fact: Since the middle of the nineteenth century (and especially during times of intense feminist activity), Americans have been literally obsessed with the question of whether women and men are fundamentally the same as one another or fundamentally different from one another. In other words, the question of biological difference has been the focal point of almost all American discussions of sexual inequality.

This focus on biological difference came into being almost immediately after feminists such as Elizabeth Cady Stanton and Susan B. Anthony first started pushing to get women the most basic rights of citizenship, including the rights to vote, own property, speak in public, and have access to higher education. Threatened by these extraordinarily radical proposals for social change, antifeminists tried to argue against them by raising the specter of biological difference. I'll mention just three examples of this antifeminist stance, all by highly regarded scientists and scholars of the period. Paul Broca argued against higher education for women by claiming that their brains were too small. Edward Clarke argued against higher education by claiming that it would divert women's limited complement of blood from their reproductive

3

organs to their brains; hence, their reproductive organs would atrophy, and they would be unable to bear children. And finally, Herbert Spencer argued against giving women the right to vote on the grounds that they had too much maternal instinct to allow only the fittest in society to survive.

These nineteenth century arguments against women's equality, I should note, were heavily tinged with racism and classism as well as sexism. With educated White women beginning to have many fewer babies than uneducated women, and with the United States also experiencing a gigantic increase in the number of immigrants from eastern and southern Europe, the feminist proposals for social change were seen as threatening not just to male dominance but to White dominance. When G. Stanley Hall argued that higher education for women would spell "race suicide," it was not the suicide of the human race that he was worried about but the suicide of the White, or European, race.[1]

In response to all of this biological and antifeminist theorizing on the part of some of the most respected scientists of the nineteenth century, by the early twentieth century, many *feminists* were beginning to focus on the question of biological difference as well. I'll give but one example. Beginning in 1903, two of the very first women with PhDs in the new field of empirical psychology took it upon themselves to try to refute all this anti-woman theorizing by doing their own carefully controlled studies of male-female difference on a whole variety of intellectual and other abilities. They also began to publish a whole slew of review articles carefully compiling and evaluating the results of all the research on male-female difference then available.[2] Not only is this work by Helen Thompson Woolley and Leta Stetter Hollingworth recognized today as being among the best science of its time, it is also what started the century-old tradition of psychological research on sex differences, which tries to figure out once and for all what alleged sex differences really exist. Of course, the very existence of this research tradition is itself an example of the American obsession with biological sex difference.

Although our obsession with the question of biological difference died down somewhat after women finally got to vote in 1920, it exploded onto the scene again after the second major wave of American feminism in the late 1960s and early 1970s and has been with us ever since. This modern focus on whether males and females are fundamentally the same or fundamentally different is now so integrated into American culture that you can see it in almost any magazine article on women and men that you happen to pick up at your local supermarket. Here are just a few of the most popular of today's sex difference themes. There's the idea from sociobiology that male dominance (including even the so-called male predisposition to rape) is encoded in our genes. There's the idea from prenatal hormone theory

---

[1]For more on these and other biological theories from the nineteenth and early twentieth centuries, see Jordanova (1989), Russett (1989), and Sayers (1982).

[2]For more on this early feminist work in psychology, see Shields (1975a,b).

that in-utero testosterone is responsible for male aggression. There's the idea that some kind of a male math gene explains why males do better at mathematics. There's the idea that some difference in brain structure having to do with the corpus callosum makes males "right-brained" and females "left-brained." And finally, there's the idea from a popular stream of modern feminism that says females are naturally concerned about relationships and caring, whereas males are naturally concerned about autonomy and justice—and this is why we have such a hard time relating to one another.

There are two reasons I am beginning my lecture by pointing out that Americans organize almost all of their discussions about gender and sexual inequality around the issue of biological difference. First, I want to shift your angle of vision a little and have you focus—if only for a moment—on the *question* Americans are always asking instead of the *answer* to that question. Put somewhat differently, I want you to stop taking the focus on sexual difference for granted as something completely natural and unremarkable and instead begin to say to yourself, Why *is* this the question we are always asking? And even more important, Is there some *other* question we could or should be asking instead?

Second, I want to set the stage for my major argument, which is that Americans need to shift the focus of their discussion of sexual inequality from *biological difference* to *institutionalized androcentrism*. That is, we need to reframe our discussion of sexual inequality so that it focuses not on male-female difference per se but on how our androcentric (or male-centered) institutions transform male-female difference into female disadvantage.

My overall argument has two parts. First, I will argue that the focus on biological difference is based on a false assumption and hence is misguided both intellectually and scientifically. Next, I will argue that we need to accept at least a certain level of biological difference as given or axiomatic and thereby shift the starting point of our discussion from difference per se to society's situating of women in a social structure so androcentric that it not only transforms what is really just male-female difference into female disadvantage; it also disguises what is really just a male standard or norm as gender neutrality.

*T*HE FOCUS ON BIOLOGICAL DIFFERENCE IS MISGUIDED

The reason Americans have become so obsessed with the biology of sex differences is that for the past 150 years feminists have been saying that we need to change our society in order to make women more equal—and for that same 150 years, the society has been saying back that our biological differences may not even allow for the kind of equality that feminists like me are always advocating. Implicit in this response, however, is a *false assumption,* which is *that biology is a kind of bedrock beyond which social change is not feasible.* Not only is that assumption false in and of itself; it also leads to the misguided conclusion that the question of biological sex difference is urgent, both politically and scientifically. I disagree. As I see it, social change—or what I would rather call cultural invention—can so radically transform the situational context in which biology operates that the human organism can actually be liberated from what had earlier seemed to be its intrinsic biological limitations. Consider but three examples.

1. As a biological species, human beings require food and water on a daily basis, which once meant that it was part of universal human nature to live as survivalists. But now human beings have invented agricultural techniques for producing food, and storage and refrigeration techniques for preserving food, which means that it is no longer part of universal human nature to live as survivalists.

2. As a biological species, human beings are susceptible to infection from many bacteria, which once meant that it was part of universal human nature to die routinely from infection. But now human beings have invented antibiotics to fight infection, which means that it is no longer part of universal human nature to die routinely from infection.

3. As a biological species, human beings do not have wings, which once meant that it was part of universal human nature to be unable to fly. But now human beings have invented airplanes, which means that it is no longer part of universal human nature to be unable to fly.

As dramatically liberating as these three examples of technological innovation clearly are, the general principle that they illustrate is so mundane and noncontroversial that even sociobiologists would unhesitatingly endorse it. Simply put, *the impact of any biological feature depends in every instance on how that biological feature interacts with the environment in which it is situated.*

Of course, the question that immediately arises is the following: If this whole idea of biology interacting with the social context is right, then why have women and men played such different and unequal roles in virtually every society on earth? The biology-in-context answer is that, throughout human history, there have not only been certain indisputable and universal differences between men's and women's bodies, with only women being able to become pregnant and to breast-feed and with men, on average, being bigger and stronger. There have also been certain indisputable and universal features of the environment, with all cultures everywhere having no effective means of controlling fertility, no digestible substitutes for mother's milk, few technological instruments for extending the strength of the human body, and relatively little work that was mental rather than physical.

Now, in that sociohistorical context, the argument continues, the bodily differences between the sexes not only made it likely that most women would be either pregnant or breast-feeding during most of the years from menarche to menopause; they also made it likely that the culture would develop both a division of labor based on sex and an institutionalized system of male political dominance. In the current sociohistorical context, however, those very same bodily differences do not need to impact on people's lives in quite the same way.

But, of course, this biology-in-context answer then raises another question that is almost always presented as the ultimate challenge to modern feminism: If cultural invention has now so transformed the situational context of human life that the bodily differences between the sexes are no longer as functionally significant as they once were, then why is it that males and females continue to play such different—and unequal—roles in even a modern technological society such as our own, which has not only effective control over fertility and digestible substitutes for mother's milk but little or no labor for which the sex of the laborer is truly decisive? There is both a short answer to this question and a long answer, both of them historical.

The long answer is spelled out in my book *The Lenses of Gender: Transforming the Debate on Sexual Inequality* (Bem, 1993). The short answer is that women and men are both politically and economically unequal, even in the United States today, because *we live in an androcentric social structure that continues invisibly to transform what is really just a biological difference between males and females into a massive female disadvantage.* I'll shift in a moment to a discussion of what androcentrism is and how it works, but first I want to make one more point about biology. In particular, I want to answer the question that many of you are silently asking in your minds, which is, Do I really believe that all biology does in the context of sex and gender is produce male and female bodies? Put somewhat differently, do I really believe there are no biological differences between the sexes besides the very obvious differences in anatomy and physiology?

The truth is that I'm very much an agnostic with respect to this question. For all I know, there may well be a kernel of truth in Alan Alda's (1975) argument that men are more physically aggressive than women because they are suffering from prenatal "testosterone poisoning." There may also be a kernel of truth in Alice Rossi's (1985) argument that women are more maternal than men because of their female hormones. And there may even be a kernel of truth in Camilla Benbow's (1988) argument that males are better at higher mathematics than females because they have some special biological ability to reason mathematically.

But there are three related issues about which I am not at all agnostic, and about which I would not be very likely to become agnostic, even if it should turn out that human males and females differ biologically with respect to any number of specific abilities or predispositions:

1. There would be so much overlap between the sexes in all of these cases that the differences would pale into insignificance next to

the bigger and more obvious differences between male and female bodies. Even if they should someday be shown to have a biological component, these differences would thus add little or nothing to our understanding of why it is that women and men have virtually played such different—and unequal—roles in virtually every society on earth.

2. These biological differences would be so poorly matched to the requirements of the jobs that women and men currently hold in American society that they would again add little or nothing to our understanding of why American women and men currently hold the different—and unequal—positions that they do, so, yes, women might well turn out to be more biologically nurturant than men on the average, but that should make them psychiatrists, not secretaries. And, yes, men might also turn out to have a higher aptitude for mathematics than women on the average, but that would not explain why there are so many more women with a high aptitude for mathematics than there are women in careers *requiring* a high aptitude for mathematics. Stated more generally, no matter what subtle biological differences there may someday prove to be between women and men on the average, those differences will never justify the sexual inequality that has, for centuries, been a feature of human social life.

3. No matter how many subtle biological differences between the sexes there may someday prove to be, both the size and the significance of those biological differences will depend, *in every single instance,* on the situational context in which women and men live their lives. The feature of the situational context that I have focused on so far is the historically universal absence of modern technology. At least as important in the development of sexual difference and sexual inequality, however, is the male-centeredness that has resulted from the institutionalization of male political power in every single culture. And that feature of the environment I'll talk about now.

*A*NDROCENTRISM

The concept of androcentrism was first articulated in the early twentieth century by Charlotte Perkins Gilman, who wrote in *The Man-Made World; or, Our Androcentric Culture* (1911/1971):

> All our human scheme of things rests on the same tacit assumption; man being held the human type; woman a sort of accompaniment and subordinate assistant, merely essential to the making of people. She has held always the place of a predisposition in relation to man. She has always been considered above him or below him, before him, behind him, a wholly relative existence—"Sydney's

sister," "Pembroke's mother"—but never by any chance Sydney or Pembroke herself. . . . It is no easy matter to deny or reverse a universal assumption. . . . What we see immediately around us, what we are born into and grow up with, . . . we assume to be the order of nature. Nevertheless, . . . what we have all this time called "human nature" . . . was in great part only male nature. . . . Our androcentric culture is so shown to have been, and still to be, a masculine culture in excess, and therefore undesirable. (pp. 20–22)

Without actually using the term itself, Simone de Beauvoir brilliantly elaborated on the concept of androcentrism and integrated it more completely into a theory of sexual inequality in *The Second Sex* (1952). According to de Beauvoir, the historical relationship of men and women is not best represented as a relationship between dominant and subordinate, or between high and low status, or even between positive and negative. No, in all male-dominated cultures,

man represents both the positive and the neutral, as is indicated by the common use of *man* to designate human beings in general; whereas woman represents only the negative, defined by limiting criteria, without reciprocity. . . . It amounts to this: just as for the ancients there was an absolute vertical with reference to which the oblique was defined, so there is an absolute human type, the masculine. Woman has ovaries, a uterus; these peculiarities imprison her in her subjectivity, circumscribe her within the limits of her own nature. It is often said that she thinks with her glands. Man superbly ignores the fact that his anatomy also includes glands, such as the testicles, and that they secrete hormones. He thinks of his body as a direct and normal connection with the world, which he believes he apprehends objectively, whereas he regards the body of woman as a hindrance, a prison, weighed down by everything peculiar to it. . . . Thus humanity is male and man defines woman not in herself but as relative to him; she is not regarded as an autonomous being. . . . She is defined and differentiated with reference to man and not he with reference to her; she is the incidental, the inessential as opposed to the essential. He is the Subject, he is the Absolute—she is the Other. (pp. xv–xvi)

These quotations make androcentrism pretty clear, but let me describe it a few different ways and then give you some concrete examples to illustrate it. As I see it, *androcentrism is the privileging of males, male experience, and the male perspective.* There are many different ways to describe this privileging. For example, you could say that in the drama of human life males are treated as the main characters around whom all action revolves and through whose eyes all reality is to be interpreted, whereas the females are treated as the peripheral or marginal characters whose purpose for being is defined only in relation to the main—or male—characters. This goes along with Gilman's idea that women are always defined in relation to men. Or you could say that an androcentric viewpoint treats the male as if he were some kind of universal, objective, or neutral representative of the human species, in contrast to the female, who is some kind of special case—something different, deviant, extra, or other. This goes along with de Beauvoir's idea that man is the human and woman is the other.

There are lots of examples of androcentrism that you already know about even if you haven't ever thought to label them as such. In language, for example, there's the generic use of "he" to mean "he or she"; "he" is treated as universal, human, and genderless, and "she" is specifically female. In the Old Testament story of Adam and Eve, not only is Adam created first (in God's image) and Eve created (out of Adam) to be his helper, but if you recall, only Adam is explicitly given the power to name every creature on earth from his own perspective. And then, of course, there's Freud's (1925/1959) theory of penis envy, which treats the male body as so obviously being the human norm—and the female body as so obviously being an inferior departure from that norm—that the mere sight of the other sex's genitals not only fills the 3-year-old boy with "a horror of the mutilated creature he has just seen"; it also leads the 3-year-old girl to "make her judgment and her decision in a flash; she has seen it and knows that she is without it and wants to have it" (pp. 190–191).

Let me shift now to some examples of androcentrism that are both more modern and more pertinent to everyday life. As long as we've been talking about the presumed inferiority or otherness of the female body, let's begin with the U.S. Supreme Court's rulings related to pregnancy—in particular, the Court's rulings on whether employees can exclude pregnancy from the package of disability insurance benefits that they provide to their employees. The situation is this: An employer says its insurance benefits will cover you for every medical condition that keeps you away from work, *except* pregnancy and giving birth. Is this exclusion okay? The Supreme Court says yes. But why is it okay to exclude pregnancy if discrimination against women is now illegal? Because, says the Court, although such an exclusion may appear on the surface to discriminate against women, in actuality, it is gender-neutral.[3]

The Court has tried to argue this claim of gender neutrality in a number of different ways. First, says the Court, the exclusion doesn't divide people into the two categories of women and men but into the two categories of "pregnant women and nonpregnant persons." Second, "there is no risk from which men are protected and women are not. Likewise, there is no risk from which women are protected and men are not." And finally, "pregnancy-related disabilities constitute an *additional* risk, unique to women, and the failure to compensate them for this risk does not destroy the presumed parity of the benefits . . . [that accrue] to men and women alike."

There are some problems with the Court's reasoning here because, as I hope you see, it is androcentrically defining whatever is male as the standard and whatever is female as something "additional" or "extra." Justices Brennan, Douglas, and Marshall came within millimeters of exposing this androcentrism when they wrote in a dissenting opinion,

[3]All legal opinions quoted here can be found in the analyses of *Geduldig v. Aiello* (1974) and *General Electric Co. v. Gilbert* (1976), which appear in Lindgren and Taub (1988).

> By singling out for less favorable treatment a gender-linked disability pecu-
> liar to women . . . [while simultaneously giving] men . . . full compensation for
> all disabilities suffered, including those that affect only or primarily their sex,
> such as prostatectomies, circumcision, hemophilia, and gout, . . . the State . . .
> [is creating] a double standard for disability compensation.

Justice Stevens came even closer to exposing the Court's androcentrism
when he argued in his dissent,

> It is not accurate to describe the program as dividing "potential recipients
> into two groups—pregnant women and nonpregnant persons." . . . The clas-
> sification is between persons who face a risk of pregnancy and those who do
> not. . . . By definition, such a rule discriminates on the basis of sex; for it is the
> capacity to become pregnant which primarily differentiates the female from
> the male. . . .
>   Nor is it accurate to state that under the plan "[t]here is no risk from
> which men are protected and women are not. . . . If the word "risk" is used
> narrowly, men are protected against the risks associated with a prostate op-
> eration whereas women are not. If the word is used more broadly to describe
> the risk of uncompensated employment caused by physical disability, men
> receive total protection . . . against that risk whereas women receive only par-
> tial protection.

What is going on in these pregnancy cases should be clear. Just like
Sigmund Freud himself, the Court is androcentrically defining the male
body as the standard human body; hence, it sees nothing unusual or inappropriate about giving that standard human body the full insurance
coverage that it would need for each and every condition that might befall
it. Consistent with this androcentric perspective, the Court is also defining
equal protection as the granting to women of every conceivable benefit
that this standard human body might require—which, of course, does not
include disability coverage for pregnancy.

If the Court had even the slightest sensitivity to the meaning of androcentrism, there are at least two truly gender-neutral standards that
it would have surely considered instead. In set-theory terms, these are
(1) the *intersection* of male and female bodies, which would have narrowly
covered only those conditions that befall both men and women alike; and
(2) the *union* of male and female bodies, which would have broadly covered all those conditions that befall both men and women separately. In
fact, however, the Court was so blind to the meaning of androcentrism that
it saw nothing the least bit amiss when, in the name of equal protection, it
granted a whole package of special benefits to men and men alone.

Let me now move to a final example of an androcentric law that looked
gender-neutral to me until just a couple of years ago. This final example
has to do with our culture's legal definition of self-defense, which holds
that a defendant can be found innocent of homicide only if he or she perceived imminent danger of great bodily harm or death and responded to
that danger with only as much force as was necessary to defend against it.
Although that definition had always seemed to have nothing whatsoever

to do with gender and hence to be perfectly gender-neutral, it no longer seemed quite so gender-neutral once feminist legal scholars finally pointed out how much better it fit with a scenario involving two men in an isolated episode of sudden violence than with a scenario involving a woman being battered, first in relatively minor ways and then with escalating intensity over the years, by a man who is not only bigger and stronger than she is but from whom she cannot readily get police protection because he is her husband. The "aha" experience here is the realization that, if this woman and this situation had been anywhere near the center of the policymakers' consciousness on the day when they were first drafting our culture's supposedly neutral definition of self-defense, they might not have placed so much emphasis on the defendant's being in imminent danger at the particular instant when the ultimate act of self-defense is finally done.

Of course, it isn't only in the context of insurance and self-defense that the male difference from women is "affirmatively compensated" by American society whereas the female difference from men is treated as an intrinsic barrier to sexual equality. To quote Catharine MacKinnon (1987), who is perhaps the most distinguished feminist lawyer in the United States today:

> Virtually every quality that distinguishes men from women is . . . affirmatively compensated in this society. Men's physiology defines most sports, their needs define auto and health insurance coverage, their socially designed biographies define workplace expectations and successful career patterns, their perspectives and concerns define quality in scholarship, their experiences and obsessions define merit, their objectification of life defines art, their military service defines citizenship, their presence defines family, their inability to get along with each other—their wars and rulerships—defines history, their image defines god, and their genitals define sex. For each of their differences from women, what amounts to an affirmative action plan is [thus] in effect, otherwise known as the structure and values of American society. (p. 36)

Of all the androcentric institutions on MacKinnon's list that are typically thought of as gender-neutral, there is perhaps no institution more directly responsible for denying women their rightful share of the United States' economic and political resources than the structure of the American work world. Although that work world may seem to many Americans to be as gender-neutral as it needs to be now that explicit discrimination against women has finally been made illegal, in fact, it is so thoroughly organized around a worker who is not only presumed to be male rather than female, but who is also presumed to have a wife at home to take care of all the needs of his household—including the care of his children—that, as I've said several times already, it "naturally" and automatically ends up transforming what is intrinsically just a male-female difference into a massive female disadvantage.

Imagine how differently our social world would be organized if all of the workers in our workforce were women rather than men, and hence most of the workers in our workforce—including those at the highest levels of government and industry—were also either pregnant or responsible for childcare during at least a certain portion of their adult lives. Given such a workforce, "working" would so obviously need to coordinate with both birthing and parenting that institutions facilitating that coordination would be built into the very structure of the social world. There would thus not only be such things as paid pregnancy leave, paid days off for sick children, paid childcare, and a match—rather than a mismatch—between the hours of the workday and the hours of the school day. There would probably also be a completely different definition of a prototypical work life, with the norm being not a continuous 40 hours or more per week from adulthood to old age but a transition from less than 40 hours per week when the children are young to 40 hours or more per week when the children are older.

The lesson of this alternative reality should be clear. It is not women's biological and historical role as mothers that is limiting their access to economic and political resources in the United States. It is a social world so androcentric in its organization that it provides but one institutionalized mechanism for coordinating work in the paid labor force with the responsibilities of being a parent—namely, the having of a wife at home to take care of one's children.

Now, to people who don't yet appreciate either what androcentrism is or how it operates institutionally, the suggestion that we need to change our social institutions so that they are more accommodating to women or more inclusive of women's experiences seems completely wrong-headed. As they would surely describe it, it seems like a move away from gender neutrality and hence in the absolutely wrong direction of where this country ought to be going.

But, in fact, American institutions have been so thoroughly organized for so long from an androcentric perspective—that is, they have for so long been taking care of men's special needs automatically while women's special needs have been either treated as special cases or simply left unmet—that *the only way for them even to begin to approximate gender neutrality is for our society finally to begin giving women as complete a package of special benefits as it has always given to men and men alone.*

I want to end my lecture with an analogy that may help you see even more clearly that the gender problem in the United States today isn't about the difference between women and men; it's about the transformation of that difference into female disadvantage by an androcentric social structure that looks not only gender-neutral but even God-given, because we're just so used to it by now that we don't realize that it is, literally, *man*-made until that fact is forced upon us.

This analogy plays on another one of my own nonprivileged attributes, not my femaleness this time but my shortness. (I am only 4'9" tall.) Imagine, if you will, a whole community of short people just like me. Given the argument sometimes made in our society that short people are unable to be firefighters because they are neither tall enough nor strong enough to do the job, the question arises: Would all the houses in the community eventually burn down? Well, yes, if we short people had to use the heavy ladders and hoses designed by and for tall people. But, no, if we (being as smart as short people are) could instead construct lighter ladders and hoses usable by both tall and short people. The moral here should be obvious. It isn't short biology that's the problem; it's short biology being forced to function in a tall-centered social structure.

It should be clear that there are two related morals in both this final story and this whole lecture. The first moral is that, as important as the biological difference between the sexes may appear on the surface, the impact of that biological difference depends in every single instance on the environment in which it is situated. This interaction of biology and the situational context can be liberating, as in the case of antibiotics, refrigeration, airplanes, and baby formula. This interaction can also be discriminating, as in the case of women being disadvantaged—and men being advantaged—by a male-centered social structure.

The second moral is that, as familiar, comfortable, gender-neutral, and natural as our own culture's institutions may appear to be now that explicit discrimination against women has finally been made illegal, in fact, our institutions are so thoroughly saturated with androcentrism that even those that do not discriminate against women explicitly—like the definition of self-defense—must be treated as inherently suspect.

REFERENCES

ALDA, A. (1975, October). What every woman should know about men. *Ms.*, pp. 15–16.

BEM, S. L. (1993). *The lenses of gender: Transforming the debate on sexual inequality.* New Haven, CT: Yale University Press.

BENBOW, C. P. (1988). Sex differences in mathematical reasoning ability in intellectually talented preadolescents: Their nature, effects, and possible causes. *Behavioral and Brain Sciences, 11,* 169–232.

DE BEAUVOIR, S. (1952). *The second sex.* New York: Knopf.

FREUD, S. (1925/1959). Some psychological consequences of the anatomical distinction between the sexes. In E. Jones (Ed.), *Sigmund Freud: Collected papers* (vol. 5, pp. 186–197). New York: Basic Books.

GILMAN, C. P. (1911/1971). *The man-made world; or, our androcentric culture.* New York: Johnson Reprint.

JORDANOVA, L. (1989). *Sexual visions: Images of gender in science and medicine between the eighteenth and twentieth centuries.* Madison: University of Wisconsin Press.

LINDGREN, J. R., & TAUB, N. (1988). *The law of sex discrimination.* St. Paul, MN: West.

MACKINNON, C. A. (1987). Difference and dominance: On sex discrimination (1984). In C. A. MacKinnon (Ed.), *Feminism unmodified: Discourses of life and law* (pp. 32–45). Cambridge, MA: Harvard University Press.

Rossi, A. S. (1985). Gender and parenthood. In A. S. Rossi (Ed.), *Gender and the life course* (pp. 161–191). New York: Aldine.

Russett, C. E. (1989). *Sexual science: The Victorian construction of womanhood.* Cambridge, MA: Harvard University Press.

Sayers, J. (1982). *Biological politics: Feminist and anti-feminist perspectives.* New York: Tavistock.

Shields, S. A. (1975a). Functionalism, Darwinism, and the psychology of women. *American Psychologist, 30,* 739–754.

Shields, S. A. (1975b). Ms. Pilgrim's progress: The contributions of Leta Setter Hollingworth to the psychology of women. *American Psychologist, 30,* 852–857.

SUGGESTED READINGS

Bem, S. L. (1993). *The lenses of gender: Transforming the debate on sexual inequality.* New Haven, CT: Yale University Press.

Bem, S. L. (1994, August 17). In a male-centered world, female differences are transformed into female disadvantages. *Chronicle of Higher Education,* pp. B1–B3.

MacKinnon, C. A. (1987). *Feminism unmodified: Discourses on life and law.* Cambridge, MA: Harvard University Press.

Tavris, C. (1992). *The mismeasure of woman.* New York: Simon & Schuster.

RUTH S. OSTENSON is Professor Emerita of Psychology at Worcester State
College. Ms. Ostenson taught psychology of women at Worcester and at
Roxbury Community College. She draws on her own life experiences as
she writes about oppression and other topics.

2

Who's In and Who's Out

The Results of Oppression

———————— ❖ ————————

John Smith, age 40, White, happily married, with two kids, church-going (Christian), physically fit, good-looking, financially well off—who is this person? This is the most privileged member of our society, the individual who has power and advantages as a member of eight different dominant groups.

If we examine the constructs of modern American society, there are clear divisions between dominants and subordinates (Miller, 1986). Various groups have been viewed *historically* as unequal through the accident of birth: In other words, you are defined by the situation into which you are born. For example, were you born female or male? What is your racial or ethnic identification? Were you born into an economically impoverished environment, or were you born into an upper-class and privileged environment? Were you born physically challenged or physically able? In some cases, these divisions may not be entirely permanent. That is, you may attempt to change class membership, or at least economic level; you may choose to change religious affiliation; your physical ableness may actually be temporary; and so on.

According to Miller (1986), the dominants (those in power) label their subordinates as substandard, defective, and inferior. The preferred roles in the culture are reserved for the dominants, and they define the acceptable roles for the subordinates—for example, providing the services that dominants do not want to perform. In addition, the dominants determine the philosophy, values, and morality of the society (Miller, 1986).

It is possible, then, to identify specific areas of oppression in our society, where the dominant groups clearly have the power and the subordinate groups have been mistreated. Traditionally, subordination has served as the basis of oppression. These areas are sexism, racism, ageism, heterosexism, classism, ableism, anti-Semitism, and very possibly an eighth, sizism or looksism. (See Table 1.)

17

TABLE 1

Components of Oppression

Dominant Group	Subordinate Group	Oppression
Males	Females	Sexism
Whites	People of Color	Racism
Early and middle adulthood (i.e., "youthful" adults)	Children and elderly	Ageism
Heterosexuals	Lesbians, gay men, bisexuals, transsexuals, etc.	Heterosexism
Monied/upper class	Poor/working class	Classism
Able-bodied	Disabled	Ableism
Christian	Jewish	Anti-Semitism
"Physically attractive" (as defined by society's ideals)	Very tall, very short, very thin, fat, etc.	Sizism/looksism

Note: This is an imperfect list. You may care to make additions—political affiliation, individuals labeled mentally ill, etc.

Divisions are often blurred because a person's group membership may be mixed: for example, an African American working-class male or a White disabled lesbian. Being a subordinate in some areas may help to raise consciousness in areas where one is a dominant. It seems, however, that the individuals most resistant to change are those who are dominants on several fronts—such as John Smith, mentioned at the opening of this lecture.

When considering the common elements of subordination, it is important to remember that the experiences of individuals are unique and that groups and their members differ tremendously one from another. The purpose here is not to imply that the experiences of all subordinates are the same, but simply to identify some of the commonalities across a broad continuum of experiences. Ideally, a better understanding of any one of the "isms" can be derived by considering it in the context of other areas of oppression.

DEFINING OPPRESSION

Traditional definitions of any oppression include both prejudice and discrimination. Generally, a dominant individual or group expresses prejudice and discrimination toward a subordinate individual based on group membership or toward a subordinate group in general. Prejudice is defined as an unfairly negative *attitude* toward members of a particular group. (The root of the word actually means "to prejudge.") Discrimination, on the other hand, is a biased *action* toward members of a particular group. In an analysis of dominants and subordinates, I think it is important to include the issue of power because dominants generally have power over subordinates. Therefore, a preferred definition of any "ism" might be prejudice + discrimination + power. Consequently, it is difficult for any member of any subordinate group to truly demonstrate any "ism" because subordinates are not in powerful positions. A subordinate could clearly be prejudiced (that is, possess a negative attitude toward a member of the dominant group) but would find it difficult to truly discriminate because the individual is not usually in a position of political, social, or economic power and therefore is not able to engage systematically in a biased action toward a dominant. For example, some believe that it is not possible for a Person of Color in the United States to be truly racist toward a White person. An individual of Color may possess some biased attitudes but, not being in a privileged position in society, he or she cannot discriminate against a White person.

When considering the definitions of oppression, the distinction between individuals and institutions should be noted. A dominant individual may display prejudicial attitudes and discriminatory behavior toward a subordinate individual. Thus, we have individual cases of racism, ageism, heterosexism, etc. On the other hand, an institution such as a university, a corporation, a government agency, or an organization may enforce a particular practice or policy that is prejudicial and discriminatory. We have many examples of institutional racism, sexism, etc. The policy may or may not have been intended to be prejudicial and discriminatory; nevertheless, the effect is to restrict the opportunities of subordinates, with harmful consequences. For example, a corporation may hire only college graduates even though a BA is not entirely necessary for the job. People of color may have had fewer opportunities to acquire a college education. As a result, this company policy decreases the job opportunities for people of color. This is an example of institutional racism.

HOSTILITY

The power imbalance between dominants and subordinates may help to explain what Pharr (1988) labels "horizontal hostility." It is common for members of a subordinate group to express hostility in a horizontal direction—toward one's own kind. Clearly, this is safer than expressing hostility toward the oppressor. Consequently, there may be a fair amount of infighting among members of a subordinate group. Said Pharr (1988), "We may see people destroying their own neighborhoods, displaying violence and crime toward their own people, or in groups showing distrust of their own kind, while respecting the power of those that make up the norm" (p. 61).

The perception of vertical hostility is another factor that contributes to oppression. Dominants may believe that they are subject to hostility from those with lower status (subordinates), and the strength of this belief can interfere with their ability to learn about oppression. For example, men may fear false accusations of date rape or sexual harassment from women, and Whites may fear hostility from Blacks in the form of crime or verbal attacks. These perceived fears then get in the way of examining one's dominant status. Prominent media coverage of the exceptions tends to perpetuate these misconceptions. For example, the media may focus on the rare case of a false accusation of rape or the uncommon occurrence of Black-on-White violence (most crime occurs within—not between—races).

PRIVILEGE

In each area of oppression, the dominant group carries with it certain rights and privileges that are not necessarily available to subordinates. We can talk about male privilege, White privilege, youth privilege, heterosexual privilege, class privilege, able-bodied privilege, Christian privilege, and the privileges that go along with being physically attractive in our society.

These privileges consist of automatic assumptions that the dominant groups generally do not recognize. Obviously, it is easier to identify the privileges of those in power when you are out of power and do not have access to the same privileges. In general, most dominants are unaware of these rights and, in fact, are not particularly interested in becoming conscious of their privilege. As McIntosh (1991) pointed out, Whites are taught not to recognize their privilege; they are meant to be unaware of it. Let's assume, for example, that you are having a problem in a department store and ask to speak to "the person in charge." Most likely, this person will not be fat, extremely short, a person of color, disabled, very old or very young, obviously homosexual, etc.—the specific oppressions in operation vary from situation to situation. However, this is just one small example that illustrates the kind of assumptions we make without question. Clearly, there are invisible entitlements at work here.

Let us consider another example. Many heterosexuals do not understand and appreciate the many privileges that go along with being heterosexual. Such entitlements and assumptions include the legal and social benefits of marriage—public acknowledgment of one's union and the accompanying gifts and celebration, the right of the spouse to healthcare and inheritance, and so on. There are other automatic rights as well: being able to be affectionate in public without fear of harassment and an unquestioned right to have and raise children. We are starting to see changes in some of these areas, but these heterosexual privileges have been rooted in our society for centuries.

SELF-HATRED

One of the most damaging effects of being a member of a subordinate group is self-hatred. It is not unusual for a subordinate at times to feel depressed, to experience despair, and to consider suicide. This is often the result of the internalization of the dominant group's beliefs that those who are subordinates are substandard, defective, and inferior. There are numerous examples of this: The rate of depression in women is two to three times that of men (Matlin, 2000); lesbians and gay men are at greater risk for suicide than heterosexual women and men (Rofes, 1983); many older people experience a sense of despair when they grow old and are no longer considered valued members of society. It is no wonder, then, that movements for social change focus on increased self-esteem and belief in oneself. This is the basis for slogans such as Black Is Beautiful and Gay Pride.

PASSING

In our society, there is tremendous pressure on members of minority groups to assimilate, "to drop one's own culture and differences and become a mirror of the dominant culture. This process requires turning one's back on one's past and one's people" (Pharr, 1988, p. 62).

The pressure to assimilate may lead to a member of a subordinate group "passing" as a member of the dominant group. The term "passing" originally referred to "invisible blackness"—the ability of some light-skinned Blacks to assume new identities as White people and gain acceptance in a White world. This was most common between 1880 and 1925 (Williamson, 1980). I am suggesting that some form of passing takes place in every area of oppression among members of a subordinate group, although it is not generally viewed as such. It may be something as simple as a single act, which is quite temporary, or it may involve a complete change of identity, which has far-reaching consequences.

Passing may also be symbolic; that is, the subordinate group member tries to adopt or be accepted as having the same qualities, values, or personality characteristics as the dominant group. This is commonly labeled "identification with the oppressor" or "imitation of the dominants." An example of this is the Queen Bee syndrome (Matlin, 1987). A Queen Bee is a woman who has achieved considerable success in a male-dominated profession and does not support other women. She has, in essence, become "one of the boys" and has adopted the prevailing male standards for success. She believes, however, that she has reached her success entirely on her own without assistance from other women or the women's movement. She may even deny the existence of sexism in any appreciable way, as she believes that she has never experienced it personally. She is unaware or unwilling to accept the suggestion that the feminist movement may have at least helped her indirectly by paving the way for her success. (Does anyone ever really make it entirely on her own?)

Passing is often the result of deliberate effort on the part of a subordinate who wants to be assumed to be a dominant. It may also be inadvertent in the sense that others simply make assumptions based on general appearances without any effort put forth directly by the subordinate. The issue of passing seems to be more prevalent in the early stages of a social movement and seems to be a result of internalized oppression. It is not pathological. It is often a healthy response to a sick situation or, at least, a survival technique in a situation perceived to be dangerous. Unless it is temporary, passing is in some sense a denial of who one is and, consequently, is damaging to one's self-esteem. The emotional costs may be heavy. As a movement gains more rights and protections, and individuals can safely take more pride in their identities, the incidence of passing seems to be less common.

Because passing is often not emphasized when dealing with the issues of subordination, I have included examples for the eight areas of oppression cited previously. These various examples should underscore the importance of this phenomenon.

There are many cases in which women have assumed a male identity in order to gain acceptance. George Eliot, an English novelist (1819–1880), was born Mary Ann Evans. She was aware of the difficulties women authors encountered in publishing, so she chose to write under a man's name (Moffat & Painter, 1974). Judith Leyster (1609–1660) was a prolific Dutch painter, who is now considered to have achieved great excellence. From her death until 1893, however, her work was either ignored or credited to a male painter, Frans Hals (Hofrichter, 1993). Roberta Gibb Bingay, the first woman who tried to run the Boston Marathon in 1966, was officially rejected as an entrant, so she hid in the bushes at the start of the marathon and waited until about half of the runners had passed before entering the race. To disguise her sex, she wore a hooded blue sweatshirt at the start. In 1967, Kathrine Switzer officially entered the race by disguising her name. She entered as K. Switzer and, although unknown to the officials, she was the first woman to be issued an official number in the Boston Marathon (Hosler, 1980).

In the case of People of Color, there are many examples of individuals of mixed ancestry who were able to pass as White. Sometimes this involved a deliberate effort on the part of the individual as a survival strategy. "Light mulattoes would simply drop out of sight, move to an area where they were not known, usually north or west, and allow their new neighbors to take them as White" (Williamson, 1980, p. 100). In other cases, people simply made assumptions about the light-skinned individuals who "were often *de facto* white from silence" (Williamson, 1980, p. 101). This is a phenomenon that has affected many ethnic groups. A former student of mine who is Cuban told me that her family had changed their last name after immigrating to this country so as not to appear to be Cuban. She and her family easily assimilated. Some Asian American teenage girls are having plastic surgery done on their eyes so as to more closely resemble "White girls."

Women, especially in our society, are encouraged to look younger than their age and never to talk about how old they are. The idea here, of course, is to pass as younger than you are. In the United States, profitable industries promote products with "youthful" images in mind—cosmetics, hair products that cover up gray, diet products, and so forth. In addition, plastic surgery is becoming more commonplace, especially face-lifts and tummy tucks. A friend of mine recently showed me an advertisement she received in the mail from an organization called Prevention. The cover of the envelope states "Old Age Isn't Natural" and goes on to mention ways to reverse the aging process. Chanel ads advised professional women that it is a "smart career move" to fight signs of aging by using antiwrinkle creams (Faludi, 1991). People often tell me that I look "young for my age." Although this is meant as a compliment, I do not consider it as such. To me it is a denial of who I am. It does not acknowledge my full range of life experience and maturity and, as a 65-year-old woman, I do not care to pass as someone I am not.

It is interesting to note that Jamie Lee Curtis, well-known actress, author, and movie star, appeared in the September 2002 issue of *More* magazine in a photo layout designed to reveal her true physical appearance. She intentionally wanted the public to see her as she is naturally, without makeup and without all the efforts generally made to disguise the shape of her real body. It is a stark comparison of reality and the Hollywood fantasy with which we are so familiar. Feminists have praised this courageous and consciousness-raising act on the part of this 43-year-old mother of two.

With respect to heterosexism, the issue of passing seems to be a daily occurrence. Because lesbians, gay men, and bisexuals have no identifying physical characteristics, there is no way to make this distinction without a verbal acknowledgment. Many heterosexuals seem to be unaware of or simply to ignore the statistic that 10 percent of the population is gay. By this calculation, in a class of 40 students, there will be an average of 4 gay people present. I have been present at many gatherings where it is simply assumed that everyone present is heterosexual. Gay people may intentionally pass by wearing mainstream clothes and by keeping silent about their personal lives in order to gain social acceptance and compensate for feeling like an outsider. In some cases, it may be viewed as a necessary survival strategy. It is not unusual for many gay and bisexual professionals to appear to be straight during the workday and to assume their gay and bisexual identities once they arrive home. Thus, we have part-time passing on a continual basis.

In the case of classism, there is tremendous pressure in our society to "keep up with the Joneses," to buy the latest technology or gadget and to live beyond one's means—in other words, to pass as being more wealthy than we are. The easy availability of credit cards contributes to this phenomenon. Many individuals who are continually in debt are eventually forced into bankruptcy. There are other examples of passing that are more related to status, such as those individuals who try to appear to be monied or belonging to an upper class through having a certain dress style, using certain language, having certain mannerisms, driving the "right automobile," being seen in the "right places," living in a "desirable" neighborhood, and so on.

With respect to ableism, able-bodied individuals have historically simply ignored or overlooked those with disabilities. There is tremendous pressure on individuals with disabilities to pass whenever physically possible as not disabled. A deaf student whom I know was forbidden by her parents to learn sign language. Her parents also refused to learn sign language. She was deaf from birth but through extensive speech therapy acquired some language skills. She also communicated with written notes. According to the young woman, the family did not want to draw attention to themselves and appear to be "different," and as a result she had to rely on lip-reading. This presented a conflict for her, especially when she got involved with a young man who was fluent in American Sign Language (ASL). Rather than allowing her to use all possible resources, her parents were limiting her in the hope that she would appear to be "normal" and not disabled. Some individuals who experience hearing or sight loss refuse to wear hearing aids or glasses as long as they possibly can. Again, they are passing as able-bodied.

Franklin D. Roosevelt (1882–1945), the thirty-second president of the United States, offers another example of passing. He was paralyzed by polio at the age of 40 and lost the use of his legs. Although he was usually confined to a wheelchair, he was rarely photographed in it. Roosevelt's disability was well hidden from the American public, and he often passed as able-bodied.

During Hitler's regime, being able to pass as a gentile was the only hope for survival for many Jews. Many Jewish immigrants to this country had plastic surgery on their noses or changed their surnames. Again, this type of activity, although undertaken for protection and survival, is extremely damaging to one's sense of self because it involves a denial of one's heritage and ethnicity.

In the case of sizism/looksism, individuals who do not meet the physical ideals of our society suffer a great deal. There have been cases of job discrimination as well as personal rejections on many fronts. Overweight people are encouraged to dress in a way that disguises their true body shape (for example, vertical stripes and loose clothing) and to take advantage of liposuction and plastic surgery to change their body shape, breast size, or facial features. The idea here is to alter one's body permanently so as to pass as "physically attractive." In addition, we are encouraged to use a variety of cosmetics, hair dyes, and hair straighteners or permanents to achieve that impossible physical ideal.

IMPACT OF SUBORDINATION

The mistreatment and personal wounds of subordinates are quite evident. We as a society need to examine carefully how we deal with the issue of difference. Tavris (1992) pointed out that women are not the inferior sex, the superior sex, or the opposite sex. By the same token, no subordinate group is inferior, superior, or the opposite of a dominant group. As Miller (1986) suggested, the engagement of difference does not have to lead to difficulty and degradation. Differences are not deficiencies; diversity is not defectiveness. Someone who is different is not "more than" or "less than." We do not need to distrust or fear those who look or act differently from ourselves. A difference is simply a difference. Dealing with difference should be a source of growth. It provides us with the opportunity to interact with others unlike ourselves and to enrich our experiences and our lives greatly.

REFERENCES

FALUDI, S. (1991). *Backlash: The undeclared war against American women.* New York: Doubleday.

HOFRICHTER, F. F. (1993). *Judith Leyster: A Dutch master and her world.* Zwolle, Holland: Waanders.

HOSLER, R. (1980). The women of Boston. In R. Hosler (Ed.), *Boston: America's oldest marathon* (pp. 50–56). Mountain View, CA: Anderson World.

MATLIN, M. (1987). *The psychology of women.* New York: Holt, Rinehart & Winston.

MATLIN, M. (2000). *The psychology of women* (4th ed.). Fort Worth, TX: Harcourt Brace College.

MCINTOSH, P. (1991, Summer). White privilege: Unpacking the invisible knapsack. *New England Women's Studies Association Newsletter,* pp. 1–5.

MILLER, J. B. (1986). *Toward a new psychology of women* (2nd ed.). Boston: Beacon Press.

MOFFAT, M. J., & PAINTER, C. (1974). George Eliot (1819–1880). In M. J. Moffat & C. Painter (Eds.), *Revelations: Diaries of women* (pp. 218–224). New York: Random House.

PHARR, S. (1988). *Homophobia: A weapon of sexism.* Inverness, CA: Chardon Press.

ROFES, E. E. (1983). *"I thought people like that killed themselves": Lesbians, gay men, and suicide.* San Francisco: Grey Fox Press.

TAVRIS, C. (1992). *The mismeasure of woman.* New York: Simon & Schuster.

WILLIAMSON, J. (1980). *New people: Miscegenation and mulattoes in the United States.* New York: The Free Press.

SUGGESTED READINGS

EISLER, R. (1995). *Sacred pleasure: Sex, myth, and the politics of the body.* San Francisco: HarperCollins.

MCINTOSH, P. (1991, Summer). White privilege: Unpacking the invisible knapsack. *New England Women's Studies Association Newsletter,* pp. 1–5.

MILLER, J. B., & STIVER, I. P. (1997). *The healing connection: How women form relationships in therapy and in life.* Boston: Beacon Press.

PHARR, S. (1988). *Homophobia: A weapon of sexism.* Inverness, CA: Chardon Press.

DEBORAH BELLE is Professor of Psychology at Boston University, where she has been teaching courses on the psychology of women since 1984. She has published and lectured on women's experience of poverty, women's social networks and social supports, and the impact of economic inequality on women's emotional and physical health.

3

Poor Women in a Wealthy Nation

❖

The United States is such an extraordinarily wealthy nation that it sometimes seems as if everyone here must be rich. Certainly, television and magazine advertisements give the impression that for many U.S. women the most difficult problems in life have to do with choosing a shampoo or a new car, yet many U.S. women today live in poverty, and increasing numbers are hungry or homeless. In recent years, the United States has had the highest poverty rate among the wealthy nations of the world. Understanding U.S. women requires understanding the ways in which poverty and the threat of poverty affect our lives, even in this very wealthy nation. Although poverty is a severe problem for women around the globe, in this lecture I will only attempt to discuss the experience of poverty in wealthy nations such as ours.

My own concern with poor women deepened a quarter of a century ago, when I began doing research that explored the lives of 43 low-income women and their children through interviews and home observations. The Stress and Families Project was begun by the late Marcia Guttentag in 1976 to investigate the stresses that make low-income mothers the group at highest risk for the mental health problem of depression. The National Institute of Mental Health funded the study. The women's movement of the time created the political and social context in which such a study could actually be supported and carried out.

I came to this research from a comfortably middle-class background, and I was deeply shocked by what I found. It still amazes me that I live so close to women struggling to rear children in desperate poverty and that I know so little about their daily lives. It makes me angry that my nation and my community do so little to ease that desperation.

The Stress and Families Project was begun in a climate of optimism. In addition to its basic research goals, the study was designed to discover points at which government might intervene to protect women's mental health and the well-being of their families. We promised the women we worked with that our research would lead to more than just another book on a library shelf, that it would lead to real improvements in the lives of women. With political leaders as well as academic researchers on our project's advisory board, and with the encouragement of our funders at the National Institute of Mental Health, we planned to recommend and to work for political changes to make life less stressful for low-income women. From my current vantage point, it is hard to recapture the buoyant hopes of those earlier days. It is also hard to cope with the disappointment we experienced when our hopes, and the promises we had made, did not come to fruition.

Before I discuss the implications of poverty for women, I would like to review a few facts about the prevalence of poverty and economic hardship in this country. I find many of these realities quite upsetting, and I know that many of my students do as well. What is also remarkable to me is that many of these facts are not well known or widely discussed, in or out of the classroom. See how many of my facts and figures come as a surprise to you. Why do you think you did not know about such realities already? (Those of you interested in learning more in this area can read my paper in *Psychology of Women Quarterly* (2003) for complete citations of this material.)

*T*HE ECONOMIC STATE OF THE UNION—POVERTY IN THE UNITED STATES OF AMERICA

I grew up in the years following World War II, when the economic picture was brightening for most Americans. Strong unions and a strong economy helped to ensure that wages kept going up for workers, and the federal government provided some financial support to parents if they were unable to find jobs. Corporations prided themselves on fulfilling their responsibilities not only to their shareholders, but also to their workers and to their communities. Taxes fell most heavily on the wealthy and on corporations, so that average workers could keep most of their earnings. There were certainly serious problems in those decades: women were kept out of well-paid jobs and were paid less than men for the same work, and African Americans and other minority groups suffered discrimination not only by employers but also by government programs that were supposed to support all families. Despite these gross injustices, most families in the United States saw their real incomes rise dramatically in the postwar years. In fact, the poorest families saw their incomes rise the most.

In the 1970s, however, U.S. wages reached a peak and then generally stagnated or declined. Over the past three decades, the real purchasing power of U.S. wages generally has been lower than it was in 1973, and the value of the minimum wage has declined tremendously. (A minimum wage job used to support a family well above the poverty line. Today it does not.) Meanwhile, the costs of housing, healthcare, and education are much higher than they were a generation ago.

We are often told that women's wages are closing the gender gap and becoming closer to men's wages. Yet a woman who works full-time year-round earns only 77 cents for every dollar earned by a man who works full-time year-round. This earnings ratio has hardly budged for years, despite the antidiscrimination laws on the books and women's vastly increased education and work experience over the past generation (Murphy & Graff, 2005).

In order to make ends meet, U.S. workers now work more hours per year than workers in any of the other industrialized nations! And U.S. workers do all this extra work with less help from our government and from the companies we work for than workers elsewhere. In the other wealthy nations, workers typically benefit from lengthy paid vacations, subsidized childcare, paid parental leaves, and universal healthcare. Many U.S. workers have lost health insurance, retirement benefits, and paid sick leave in recent years, and more jobs now require work in the evening and weekend hours, when childcare is particularly hard to arrange. It has become harder than it used to be for most of us to feed our families, keep a roof over our heads, and ensure that our children are safe and secure.

Recent decades have also witnessed striking increases in the concentration of income and wealth in the United States, with corporate profits and chief executive pay at record levels. Chief executive officers, almost none of whom are women, earn 431 times as much as the workers at their corporations. The richest 1 percent of the population today owns more wealth than the bottom 95 percent (Wolff, 1998). Such economic inequalities are more pronounced in the United States than in any other wealthy country, and low-wage workers in the United States are less likely than those in other wealthy economies to move to high-wage jobs (Mishel, Bernstein, & Schmitt, 1999). The tax burden has also shifted, so that wealthy individuals, wealthy families, and corporations keep a much larger share of their pretax income than they did several decades ago, whereas the poor and the middle class pay at much higher rates. Many corporations disavow responsibility for their workers and the communities in which they are located, downsizing and relocating plants to take advantage of more desperate workers elsewhere, as well as threatening local governments with such actions in order to win concessions on taxes. Companies also invest billions in union-busting activities, even though many union-busting practices are illegal. Many politicians and their wealthy benefactors want to eliminate the estate tax, which taxes only the wealthiest 1 percent of us to provide services for all. We are returning to the tremendous disparities in wealth that characterized the Gilded Age, when great American dynasties lived in splendor, supported by the labor of millions of impoverished workers.

Just as these extremes of wealth and income reached new heights in the late 1990s, the U.S. government ended 60 years of guaranteed economic assistance to poor mothers and children, leaving such women with few options for economic survival beyond their own employment. (It strikes me that this timing was not coincidental, but more about that later.) Most of the women who once received welfare payments and now work for pay earn only about $7.00 per hour, and poverty has increased among working families. Other women have not been able to find jobs at all. Some have returned to violent husbands and boyfriends. Substantial and well-documented increases in demand at food banks and homeless shelters have also occurred. In the new millennium, hunger is increasingly a problem in the United States for poor women with children, especially poor Women of Color.

More than 37 million Americans today live below the poverty line, giving the United States a poverty rate of 12.7 percent. Nearly one-fourth of Black and Hispanic women live in poverty, and over one-fourth of women who head their own households are poor. Even these figures do not capture all of the economic hardship faced by U.S. women, because the official poverty line itself is extremely low and does not actually measure how much money people need to support themselves and their families. In 2004, a single mother with two children was considered poor only when her annual income fell below $15,219, and a two-parent, two-child family when its annual income fell below $19,157. Families with incomes even $1.00 higher than these thresholds were not poor, according to the U.S. Census. I can't imagine renting an apartment, feeding and clothing children, and paying for heat, electricity, and medical care on such an income. I have no idea how a mother with young children could pay for childcare, too, so that she could go to work to earn that money for her family. You might want to calculate the amount of money you think would be necessary to support an adult and two children in the city or town where you live.

It is not surprising that, when Americans are asked the minimum income necessary to make ends meet in their own communities, they produce numbers that are consistently and substantially higher than the official poverty threshold. And when social scientists compute the actual cost of living for families today, they also come up with figures far higher than the federal poverty line. Some people imagine that poor families typically receive help in paying for housing, medical care, and childcare. But most families with incomes below the poverty line pay the full cost of their own housing and childcare. Only about half receive food stamps to cut the cost of food or Medicaid to subsidize medical care. And today, 46 million Americans, more than one of every seven of us, have no health insurance at all.

THE IMPACT OF ECONOMIC HARDSHIP ON WOMEN'S WELL-BEING

We began our Stress and Families research with low-income women because earlier studies had shown that the mental health problem of depression afflicts women more than men but that not all women are at equal risk. Women who have low incomes and who care for young children are at greatest risk. This result had been found in the United States and in Great Britain, and it has since been found again and again. The low-income women my colleagues and I studied in the late 1970s reported a level of depressive symptoms similar to those of people who had recently suffered the death of a husband or wife, and half of the women in our study scored at a level that indicates severe depressive symptoms. Very similar results have been found in many studies since that time. Rates of major depression in low-income mothers are about twice as high as in the general population of women (Bassuk, Buckner, Perloff, & Bassuk, 1998). However, despite being at great risk for depression, poor women rarely receive mental health services of any kind (Coiro, 2001).

On the positive side, income gains to low-income mothers are associated with the alleviation of depressive symptoms, especially when these gains move women above the poverty line (Dearing, Taylor, & McCartney, 2004). Poor children also show a significant decrease in psychiatric symptoms, particularly conduct and oppositional defiant disorders, when their families gain income that moves the family out of poverty (Costello, Compton, Keeler, & Angold, 2003).

Why should poverty be so strongly associated with depression? Researchers have offered many plausible and overlapping explanations. For one thing, poor women are more likely than other people to experience frequent threatening and uncontrollable events in their lives, such as robberies, evictions, and illnesses, and such experiences have been found to raise the risk of depression. The mothers we interviewed told us, for instance, about a tremendous amount of crime and violence in their lives. More recently, Bassuk et al. (1998) found that 83 percent of the low-income mothers in their sample had been physically or sexually assaulted during their lifetimes. The onset of depression is also linked to the experience of humiliating or entrapping events, which are, in turn, more common among women experiencing financial hardship (Brown & Moran, 1997). Living in dangerous neighborhoods or inadequate housing, having burdensome responsibilities, being uncertain of one's future income, and experiencing other chronic conditions are even more stressful than acute crises and events and often set the stage for such crises. Impoverished women are at very high risk of experiencing just such noxious, long-term conditions (Brown, Bhrolchain, & Harris, 1975; Makosky, 1982). Recent research also demonstrates, not surprisingly, that going hungry because one doesn't have enough money to buy food is a significant predictor of depression among low-income women, even after controlling for other risk factors (Siefert, Heflin, Corcoran, & Williams, 2001).

One of the things that shocked me most in our research was the poor health of the women we studied. The women we were interviewing were close in age to those of us doing the interviewing, but their health problems often made them seem much older and more frail. Almost one-quarter of the women rated their health as poor or very poor, and among our 43 respondents, whose average age was 30, were cases of asthma, ulcers, colitis, tuberculosis, migraines, chronic colds, blindness, rheumatoid arthritis, recurring pneumonia, diabetes, high blood pressure, and obesity. As I now understand, the health problems of our research participants are not at all unusual among poor women. In fact, serious physical health problems are as strikingly associated with poverty as are mental health problems such as depression. Mortality itself is a strong correlate of income: Poor women die at much younger ages than women who are economically secure.

Poverty frequently damages women's important relationships, and this may well be one of the most crucial links between poverty and depression. Economic hardship tends to increase conflict between spouses, and the sympathy of the marital bond is often strained or broken by economic stress. Parents living below the poverty line are less likely to be happily married than those above the poverty line, and low-income women are less likely than middle-class women to turn to their husbands as confidants, particularly during the phase of the life cycle when there are young children at home. Divorce is more common among low-income families.

Poverty also makes it difficult to be a good mother. The needs of poor children for time with parents are at least as great as the needs of economically comfortable children, but poor parents typically are prevented by the draconian pressures of their jobs from responding to their children as they would like. Compared with economically secure parents, poor parents are more likely to be working multiple jobs, less likely to have any paid leave or flexibility in their jobs, and more likely to be working in the afternoon and evening hours, when children need help with homework (Heymann, 2000). Lacking reliable cars, and often living far from the places where they work, poor parents have more difficulty in getting to meetings at children's schools, and they often arrive home exhausted after a workday lengthened by hours of commuting on a complicated set of train and bus routes.

The poor mothers Edin and Lein (1997) studied generally wanted to have jobs, both to avoid the stigma of receiving welfare payments and to offer their children positive role models, yet these mothers also realized that paid employment carried serious risks for their children. Because most of the women who worked for pay could not afford health insurance or decent childcare, the mothers who chose to work "often had to trust their family's medical care to county hospital emergency rooms and their children's upbringing to the streets" (Edin & Lein, 1997, p. 5). To supplement wages and welfare payments too low to support their families, mothers sometimes turned to under-the-counter or illegal work. Such actions, other breaches of conscience that were necessitated by poverty, and the sense of being a "bad" mother, wife, or provider are the sort of experiences that low-income women point to as having triggered their depressions (Wolf, 1987).

Once depressed, women are likely to have even greater difficulties in being the kind of mothers they want to be. In the Stress and Families

Project, we found that, when the women were depressed, the children's requests for help, attention, or even food were frequently not granted and were often ignored. Instead of offering affection to their children, the depressed mothers tended to issue warnings, reminders, and commands. When their children misbehaved, the more depressed mothers tended to yell, to retaliate, and to use physical punishment, whereas the less depressed women in our study relied more on reasoning and removing privileges. In describing their own behavior, the mothers stated that caring for children was one of the very hardest things to do when they were depressed. Both the mothers and children obviously suffered at such times. Recent research reinforces this picture by showing that poverty diminishes parents' capacity for supportive, attentive, and consistent parenting and leads to more frequent use of physical punishment (McLoyd, 1990; Mistry, Vandewater, Huston, & McLoyd, 2002). Many of the same factors that put poor mothers at high risk for depression are also risk factors for the physical abuse of children.

Many poor women create mutual aid networks through which they care for each other in times of stress. Such networks are truly "strategies for survival" for many women, and support from family, friends, and other network members is associated with a reduced risk of depression among low-income mothers.

However, social networks can add to the stress that women experience, just as they can serve as sources of social support. Network members are themselves likely to be poor and stressed, so that considerable stress "contagion" is likely. Paying back the help that is received from family members and friends can be very time-consuming, and networks can actually make it more difficult to escape poverty. Poor women need social networks that promote upward mobility, as well as those that provide emotional and task support. Dominguez and Watkins (2003) found that some employment settings and social service agencies successfully connected low-income women with others outside their own immediate circles of family and friends, providing just the information, assistance, and encouragement women needed to leave poverty behind.

With limited resources at their disposal, low-income women engage in many active, thoughtful, and creative strategies to cope with the difficult problems they face. However, many of these coping efforts do not achieve their goals or do so only at great cost. Dill and Feld (1982) described one woman whose apartment in public housing was being ruined by leaking water. Public health officials declared the apartment unsafe, but the public housing authority never came to make repairs. The woman appealed to everyone she could find to listen to her case and even called in the local television station for an exposé. However, at the time she was interviewed, years after these efforts began, water continued to leak into her apartment. Another woman was worried about her son, who was dyslexic and emotionally disturbed. She tried and failed to get him an early learning abilities evaluation through his school and tried and failed to have him placed in a Big Brother program, in after-school daycare, and in a special school for the learning disabled. Unable to obtain the help she needed, through no failure of effort or imagination on her part, she felt guilty and inadequate as a mother and was increasingly concerned that her son's problems, left untreated, would only get worse.

Poor women's coping strategies must be understood in relation to their severely limited options and the dangers that threaten their children. Among the mothers Edin and Lein (1997) studied were some who occasionally did without necessities in order to pay for luxuries for their children. As Edin and Lein argued, "Although these items are not essential for a child's material well-being, a cable television subscription is a relatively inexpensive way for mothers to keep their children off the streets and away from undesirable peers. Likewise, buying a pair of expensive sneakers is insurance against the possibility that children will be tempted to steal them or sell drugs to get them" (p. 8).

Poor women are often so powerless in their dealings with employers, landlords, and government bureaucracies that their coping strategies are severely constrained and unsuccessful. (An unforgettable depiction of the powerlessness of contemporary low-wage women workers can be found in Ehrenreich's [2001] *Nickel and Dimed: On (Not) Getting By in America.*) Repeated coping failures may then lead to a woman's belief that problems cannot be overcome. In such a situation, it is hardly surprising that some women turn to ingesting drugs or alcohol, sleeping during the day, and using other strategies to dull the pain of terrible problems that cannot be overcome. Although many observers would criticize the apparent helplessness represented by the choice of such strategies, Fine (1983–1984) argued that such behaviors are also ways of taking control, given the impracticality and even the danger of more "active" problem-solving techniques for low-income women in many situations.

To add insult to injury, Americans are more likely than most other national groups to blame poverty on the poor themselves, ignoring the societal factors, such as discrimination, the high cost of living, and the lack of decently paid work, that precipitate so much poverty in this country. Those with higher incomes are particularly likely to believe that the economic system is fundamentally just, that there is plentiful economic opportunity for all, and that the causes of both poverty and wealth are internal to the persons who experience them. Such beliefs, which are also shared by many low-income people, make poverty a shameful and difficult experience. As a coping strategy, many low-income women do not identify with one another, and they emphasize their differences in order to retain a sense of individuality and separateness from this undesirable image.

The most stigmatized form of poverty involves reliance on government economic support, and women who receive welfare payments often describe experiences of humiliation, dehumanization, denigration, depression, and shame. Most of the welfare recipients interviewed in one recent study claimed that negative comments about people on welfare had been directed to them personally (Seccombe, James, & Walters, 1998). Even women themselves who receive welfare payments are not immune from sharing in the pervasive societal contempt for the "welfare mother." Seccombe et al. (1998) found that women who received welfare payments typically blamed societal factors or fate for their own economic situations but subscribed to popular notions of *other* welfare mothers as lazy and unmotivated.

It is easy to patronize poor women and to imagine that their problems are the result of laziness or lack of imagination. One of the women I worked with years ago, whom I will call Faye Eaton, lived in a neighborhood with a high crime rate, and I took many precautions to protect myself when I visited her. I traveled in daylight and, if possible, with a colleague. I did not carry a handbag, and I hid my tape recorder in a grocery bag to avoid becoming a target for robbery. I was alert to those I passed on the street. I always felt a strong sense of relief when I reached the relative safety of Faye's apartment and especially when I left Faye's neighborhood for the day after my interview or observation was complete. However, I usually enjoyed walking across the small, open park on the way from my bus stop to the Eaton apartment. The park looked uncared for, but at least it had green grass and a few fine old trees. I began to wonder why I never saw the Eatons or other families with children in the park, why everyone instead played in the housing project playground, where broken glass made the jungle gyms and swings dangerous. In my ignorance, I actually thought that perhaps Faye and the other parents might have overlooked the park in favor of the playground or been too lazy to go the small extra distance to take advantage of it. When I finally asked Faye why she didn't take her children to the park, she told me, "People get killed there. That's where the dope dealers hang out." This conversation and others like it showed me that the world around us offered Faye fewer options than seemed evident to a middle-class observer like me. The conversation also taught me not to walk through the park!

In talking with Faye, I was particularly interested in her relationships with friends, relatives, and neighbors. Before beginning the study, I had done a good bit of reading about social networks and social support, and I was eager to learn how our respondents' social networks might act as support systems for them. I believed that isolation from supportive ties was a grave danger but that involvement in relationships could lead to many advantages. Residential mobility I saw as a threat, because it tended to disrupt social ties, but staying in one apartment or one neighborhood seemed to promise many benefits.

One day while walking around the housing project with Faye, I asked her to tell me how long she had known each of the people we met. At one point, I turned to her and remarked with satisfaction, "You've known most of these people five or six years." To my way of thinking at that time, such stability augured well for the supportiveness of her social network. "Yeah," she said, "that's about how long it takes to get out of here." Her response opened my eyes to other implications of residential stability, which is not the same phenomenon in a public housing project as it is in a pleasant suburban town. I later discovered that, for the women in our study, living longer in a neighborhood was not associated with a more positive assessment of the neighborhood or with mental health advantages, as it was for women who had actively chosen their neighborhoods for positive reasons.

Faye took great joy in the happiness of others. One of my vivid memories is of her laughingly lifting her cousin in a great bear hug and whirling her around the floor in shared pleasure at some good news this woman had received. However, Faye was having serious problems with her physical health. She suffered from many symptoms of depression, and during a time shortly before the study she often drank enough to induce forgetfulness and dull her pain. Looking back on a year during which she completed a treatment program for her alcohol problem, she commented that her life is harder now "because I don't have the alcohol to blind me and help me to forget. I got to face reality, and it's horrible with no husband, no boyfriend, three kids, and the Welfare." As I became more aware of what she suffered, I tried to think through ways in which Faye's problems could be solved.

Perhaps a job was the solution, and, in fact, Faye often spoke longingly of her wish for employment, of her memories of a time before the children and before her marriage failed when she had enjoyed working. But what were her realistic options at this moment, without education beyond high school, without credentials or marketable skills, with responsibility for three preschool children, and without a coparent or convenient grandparent to help with their care? Virtually all the jobs she might have found would have paid less than the cost of the necessary daycare for her children, and she would also have lost the state-provided medical insurance on which she and her family depended. Further training could have opened up better employment options, but how could Faye afford the costs of training as well as childcare? In addition, her physical health was poor, as was that of many of the most stressed women in our study, and this further limited the types of employment that made sense for her.

If a job or job training were not possible at this time in her life, I wondered if she could at least improve her financial situation through help from other members of her family. But Faye had no one at all, in her entire family circle, with greater financial resources than she had. In fact, she had provided a temporary home in her small apartment for her brother, when his own apartment burned down, and for her mother, who moved up from the South so that Faye could nurse her when she became ill. Far from being able to look to others for financial help, Faye was further strained by helping out members of her family who were in even greater financial distress than she was. Most of Faye's friends were women in circumstances similar to her own, who were also struggling to make ends meet. The articles I had read on social support emphasized the advantages obtained through membership in a social network of mutual obligation and mutual assistance. Thinking about Faye Eaton's life made me aware of the stresses associated with such a network, particularly when one is called on to provide more economic and instrumental assistance than one receives.

I sometimes imagined myself poor like Faye Eaton, and my imaginings frightened me. I saw myself unable to buy the clothing and food my children needed, unable to live with them in a safe place. The more I learned about Faye's situation, the less hope I could see for improving it. Without relatives or friends with money or with clout and without advanced education or credentials, Faye had few resources to extricate herself from poverty, to put a stop to the continuous stresses that were eroding her mental health and her capacity to nurture her children.

Barbara Ehrenreich (2001) recently carried out my thought experiment in reality, taking on low-wage work and discovering through her own experiences how difficult it is to make ends meet, let alone attempting to escape from poverty. In Florida, Maine, and Minnesota, Ehrenreich took the highest-paid jobs she could find without relying on her advanced education and the best housing she could afford on that income. Her investigative forays into waitressing, housecleaning, and work as a nursing home aide, a hotel maid, and a Wal-Mart sales clerk show from the inside out how difficult life is for those confined to the low-wage service economy. She started her participant-observation with several advantages over most of those who do low-wage work involuntarily. She had no children or dependent relatives to support, she allowed herself a functioning car and an initial bank balance, and she began her study in good health, the result, she pointed out, of her previous middle-class privilege—decades of decent healthcare, a high-protein diet, expensive gym memberships, and work that was not physically damaging.

What are the greatest outrages Ehrenreich uncovered? That Wal-Mart demanded overtime work and then didn't pay overtime rates for it? (Lawsuits for unpaid overtime have been brought against Wal-Mart in more than 30 states.) That the housecleaning service charged its clients $25 per worker per hour and then paid its workers $6.65 each? That the nursing home was sometimes dangerously understaffed? Was it the humiliating drug tests, the denial of work breaks, the petty rules and regulations, the lack of control over work schedules, the debilitating work itself? Perhaps the ultimate outrage is that the jobs Ehrenreich performed at such cost left her and those she worked with teetering on the brink of homelessness. Or perhaps the worst outrage is that those of us who profit from the misery of these workers remain so maddeningly oblivious to their suffering.

> The "working poor," as they are approvingly termed, are in fact the major philanthropists of our society. They neglect their own children so that the children of others will be cared for; they live in substandard housing so that other homes will be shiny and perfect; they endure privation so that inflation will be low and stock prices high. To be a member of the working poor is to be an anonymous donor, a nameless benefactor, to everyone else. (Ehrenreich, 2001, p. 221)

*T*HE IMPACT OF ECONOMIC INEQUALITY

When I first began research with low-income women, I thought that most of their problems resulted from the material hardships they suffered—the dangerous neighborhoods, poor housing, and inadequate diets. More recently, I have come to believe that much of what is stressful in the lives of poor women results from the contrast between their own difficult situations and the opulence and extravagant consumption of those who surround them. I worry that the experience of poverty, homelessness, and hunger in our vastly wealthy society must damage poor women by conveying the community's lack of concern, despite its evident capacity to help. Herman (1992) recounted the experiences in psychotherapy of a Navy enlisted man who was rescued at sea after his ship was sunk during wartime. The officers were rescued first, even though they were already relatively safe in lifeboats, while the enlisted men hanging onto the raft had to wait; some of them drowned before help came. According to Herman (1992), the rescued man

> was horrified at the realization that he was expendable to his own people. The rescuers' disregard for this man's life was more traumatic to him than were the enemy attack, the physical pain of submersion in the cold water, the terror of death, and the loss of the other men who shared his ordeal. The indifference of the rescuers destroyed his faith in his community. (p. 55)

It is important to understand how impoverished women experience their communities and how they cope with the realization that they, too, are expendable.

A recent body of research suggests that economic inequalities are harmful to health. Among the industrialized nations, it is the most egalitarian societies, not the wealthiest societies, that have the longest-lived citizens (Wilkinson, 1996). The United States, which leads the industrialized world in income inequality, ranks behind 19 other nations in life expectancy, including Costa Rica, Greece, and Spain (Kawachi & Kennedy, 1999). Within the United States, those who live in states or cities with greater income inequality have poorer health and die younger than those who live where income is more equally distributed (Kaplan, Pamuk, Lynch, Cohen, & Balfour, 1996; Kennedy, Kawachi, Glass, & Prothrow-Stith, 1998). Where income is more equally distributed, mortality shows a weaker association with social class, and people from all social classes live longer than do people from comparable social classes in more unequal societies (Wilkinson, 1996).

Income inequality, measured at the state level, is strongly associated with women's risk for depression. Kahn, Wise, Kennedy, and Kawachi (2000) replicated the familiar finding that low income is a significant risk factor for both depressive symptoms and poor physical health among mothers of young children. In addition, they found that living in a state with high income inequality significantly increased the chances that women would report high levels of depressive symptoms and only fair or poor health. The effects were strongest for the poorest women, with high income inequality associated with a 60 percent greater risk of depressive symptoms and an 80 percent greater risk of fair or poor health among women already at risk because of their low family incomes.

Why does economic inequality have such effects? One answer may be that public priorities are skewed when the wealthy have enormous sums of money and the poor and the middle class have little. Money buys influence in the American political system; thus, it is probably not surprising that, as incomes for the wealthy have climbed, their tax rates have fallen. Meanwhile, programs for low-income families have been slashed. In U.S. states with high levels of income inequality, public spending for education and economic support for poor families are lower than in U.S. states where income is more equally distributed. It is not surprising that children in more unequal states are not as likely as children in more equal states to achieve well academically or to complete high school. Unequal states then spend more of their budgets on police, prisons, and healthcare (Kaplan et al., 1996). As a classic Tom Tomorrow cartoon put it, "If the poor don't like it, let them buy their own senators!" Or as Supreme Court Justice Louis Brandeis put it, "We may have democracy, or we may have wealth concentrated in the hands of a few, but we can't have both" (Lonergan, 1941, p. 4).

The wealth of the advantaged also creates a housing market that displaces those who cannot keep up with rapidly rising housing costs, fracturing communities and producing homelessness and the fear of becoming homeless. Many wealthy people isolate themselves in gated communities, while more than 2 million Americans, most of them poor, are sequestered in jails and prisons. (We imprison a larger percentage of our citizens than do any of the other industrialized countries.) In national surveys, the extent to which Americans express trust in each other has declined by approximately one-third during a recent 25-year period, a period in which income inequality in this country has also grown enormously. Cross-sectional analysis shows that, in U.S. states with high levels of income inequality, trust in others is far lower than in states where income is more equitably distributed (Kawachi, Kennedy, Lochner, & Prothrow-Stith, 1997).

FUTURE DIRECTIONS

Thinking about the lives of poor women makes me very angry, and I hope that it makes you angry, too. It seems unfair to me that so many women suffer so much while there is such incredible wealth all around us. Public policies that could reduce poverty, material hardship, and economic inequality would go a long way toward reducing the sorts of stresses that subject poor women to emotional problems, such as depression, and to physical health problems and early death. Enacting such policies is a daunting task yet one that holds out tremendous promise for improving the well-being of U.S. women.

Ironically, welfare "reform" has foreclosed for many women the only plausible route to real economic security. As a result of "reform," many women have been forced to leave colleges and serious vocational training programs to take dead-end minimum wage jobs that will never enable them to support their families at a decent level. Some states have redefined work requirements to include the possibility of higher education. Other states should follow their examples.

At this point in our history, U.S. society provides a unique laboratory in which to examine the mental health consequences of poverty and economic inequality. Nowhere else in the industrialized world does one find such high poverty rates, such stunning income and wealth inequality, and such ideological assurance that both the rich and the poor deserve their fates. Our priority, as psychologists and as citizens, must be to dismantle this laboratory.

REFERENCES

BASSUK, E. L., BUCKNER, J. C., PERLOFF, J. N., & BASSUK, S. S. (1998). Prevalence of mental health and substance use disorders among homeless and low-income housed mothers. *American Journal of Psychiatry, 155*(11), 1561–1564.

BELLE, D. (2003). Poverty, inequality, and discrimination as sources of depression among U.S. women. *Psychology of Women Quarterly, 27*(2), 101–113.

BROWN, G. W., BHROLCHAIN, M., & HARRIS, T. (1975). Social class and psychiatric disturbance among women in an urban population. *Sociology, 9*, 225–254.

BROWN, G. W., & MORAN, P. M. (1997). Single mothers, poverty, and depression. *Psychological Medicine, 27*, 21–33.

COIRO, M. J. (2001). Depressive symptoms among women receiving welfare. *Women and Health, 32*, 1–23.

COSTELLO, E. J., COMPTON, S. N., KEELER, G., & ANGOLD, A. (2003). Relationships between poverty and psychopathology: A natural experiment. *Journal of the American Medical Association, 290*, 2023–2029.

DEARING, E., TAYLOR, B. A., & McCARTNEY, K. (2004). Implications of family income dynamics for women's depressive symptoms during the first 3 years after childbirth. *American Journal of Public Health, 94*, 1372–1377.

DILL, D., & FELD, E. (1982). The challenge of coping. In D. Belle (Ed.), *Lives in stress: Women and depression* (pp. 179–196). Beverly Hills, CA: Sage.

DOMINGUEZ, S., & WATKINS, C. (2003). Creating networks for survival and mobility: Social capital among African-American and Latin-American low-income mothers. *Social Problems, 50*, 111–135.

EDIN, K., & LEIN, L. (1997). *Making ends meet: How single mothers survive welfare and low-wage work.* New York: Russell Sage Foundation.

EHRENREICH, B. (2001). *Nickel and dimed: On (not) getting by in America.* New York: Metropolitan Books.

FINE, M. (1983–1984). Coping with rape: Critical perspectives on consciousness. *Imagination, Cognition and Personality, 3*, 249–267.

HERMAN, J. L. (1992). *Trauma and recovery.* New York: Basic Books.

HEYMANN, J. (2000). *The widening gap: Why America's working families are in jeopardy and what can be done about it.* New York: Basic Books.

KAHN, R. S., WISE, P. H., KENNEDY, B. P., & KAWACHI, I. (2000). State income inequality, household income, and maternal mental and physical health: Cross-sectional national survey. *British Medical Journal, 321,* 1311–1315.

KAPLAN, G. A., PAMUK, E. R., LYNCH, J. W., COHEN, R. D., & BALFOUR, J. L. (1996). Inequality in income and mortality in the United States: Analysis of mortality and potential pathways. *British Medical Journal, 312,* 999–1003.

KAWACHI, I., & KENNEDY, B. P. (1999). Income inequality and health: Pathways and mechanisms. *Health Services Research, 34,* 215–227.

KAWACHI, I., KENNEDY, B. P., LOCHNER, K., & PROTHROW-STITH, D. (1997). Social capital, income inequality, and mortality. *American Journal of Public Health, 87*(9), 1491–1498.

KENNEDY, B. P., KAWACHI, I., GLASS, R., & PROTHROW-STITH, D. (1998). Income distribution, socioeconomic status, and self-rated health: A U.S. multi-level analysis. *British Medical Journal, 317,* 917–921.

LONERGAN, R. (1941). Brandeis' glorious career ended. *Labor, 23*(9), 4.

MAKOSKY, V. (1982). Sources of stress: Events or conditions? In D. Belle (Ed.), *Lives in stress: Women and depression* (pp. 35–53). Beverly Hills, CA: Sage.

MCLOYD, V. (1990). The impact of economic hardship on Black families and children: Psychological distress, parenting, and socioemotional development. *American Psychologist, 61,* 311–346.

MISHEL, L., BERNSTEIN, J., & SCHMITT, J. (1999). *The state of working America: 1998–1999.* Ithaca, NY: Cornell University Press.

MISTRY, R. S., VANDEWATER, E. A., HUSTON, A. C., & MCLOYD, V. C. (2002). Economic well-being and children's social adjustment: The role of family process in an ethnically diverse low-income sample. *Child Development, 73,* 935–951.

MURPHY, E., & GRAFF, E. J. (2005). *Getting even: Why women don't get paid like men—and what to do about it.* New York: Simon & Schuster.

SECCOMBE, K., JAMES, D., & WALTERS, K. B. (1998). "They think you ain't much of nothing": The social construction of the welfare mother. *Journal of Marriage and the Family, 60,* 849–865.

SIEFERT, K., HEFLIN, C., CORCORAN, M., & WILLIAMS, D. (2001). Food insufficiency and the physical and mental health of low-income women. *Women and Health, 32*(1/2), 159–177.

WILKINSON, R. G. (1996). *Unhealthy societies: The afflictions of inequality.* London: Routledge.

WOLF, B. (1987). *Low-income mothers at risk: The psychological effects of poverty-related stress.* Unpublished doctoral dissertation. Harvard University Graduate School of Education, Cambridge, MA.

WOLFF, E. N. (1998). Recent trends in the size distribution of household wealth. *Journal of Economic Perspectives, 12,* 3.

SUGGESTED READINGS

BELLE, D. (Ed.). (1982). *Lives in stress: Women and depression.* Beverly Hills, CA: Sage.

DODSON, L. (1998). *Don't call us out of name: The untold lives of women and girls in poor America.* Boston: Beacon Press.

EDIN, K., & LEIN, L. (1997). *Making ends meet: How single mothers survive welfare and low-wage work.* New York: Russell Sage Foundation.

HAYS, S. (2003). *Flat broke with children: Women in the age of welfare reform.* New York: Oxford University Press.

*F*AYE J. CROSBY *is Professor of Psychology at the University of California, Santa Cruz. She has been teaching courses on the psychology of women, gender studies, and feminism since 1975, first at Boston University, then at Yale University, Smith College, the Kellogg School of Management, and UC Santa Cruz. Her research centers on the social psychology of social justice with an emphasis on ways to diminish sex discrimination.*

4

Sex Discrimination at Work

---------- ❖ ----------

Imagine a small restaurant where John employs Martha. Martha waits on tables. John doubles as owner and chef. John takes all the profits and suffers all the losses of the business, but he pays Martha $13.50 an hour and allows her to keep all tips. Business thrives, and the small restaurant becomes a chain. Martha and 60 other waitresses now work for $15.00 an hour. Then, one day, John hires two male waiters at $17.50 an hour.

Now think of the consulting firm of Dewey, Hookem, and Howe. Louise Dewey, one of the principals in the firm, insists that all employees be available for impromptu staff meetings between 4 P.M. and 7 P.M. Except when they are traveling or visiting a client, every consultant in the firm is expected to arrive in the conference room with only 25 minutes' notice if the meeting occurs between 4 P.M. and 7 P.M.

Is John engaging in sex discrimination? How about Louise?

The answers to such questions are not possible without knowing a great deal more detailed information. In the case of John's restaurant, for example, one would need to know if the two male waiters had more experience than the 60 female waitresses or if they differed in some other meaningful way. In the case of the consulting firm, one would need to know detailed information about the pressures on the firm in order, for example, to separate spontaneous whim from business necessity.

One would also need a firm definition of sex discrimination. Even when people agree about the facts in a case, they may disagree about the principles. What strikes one person as being sex discrimination may not seem so to another.

Thanks to Virginia Lee Roberts and to Julie Dimmitt.

WHAT IS SEX DISCRIMINATION?

In the most basic sense, discrimination is simply a form of differentiation and is neither good nor bad in and of itself. Psychologists have studied, for example, the factors that allow a pigeon to distinguish between a round disc and an oval disc. If the round disc is associated with rewards, and the oval disc with punishments, the pigeon learns rapidly to make the differentiation or, in a technical sense, "to discriminate."

Discrimination, in the sense of differentiation, can serve useful purposes. You discriminate between your friends and strangers, and often to good effect. You discriminate between your life partner and a stranger, and that too may be quite appropriate as, for example, when you are deciding where to sleep for the night.

Discrimination can also be harmful. In everyday parlance, when we refer to discrimination, the connotation is negative. In the American legal system, (negative) discrimination is against the law.

Discrimination occurs whenever individuals from different groups are treated differently from each other wholly or partially as a function of their (different) group memberships. When People of Color and White people are treated differently from each other, ethnic or racial discrimination is said to occur. When women and men, or girls and boys, are treated differently from each other, sex discrimination is said to occur. When the different treatment of women and men occurs in the economic realm, we say that there is sex discrimination in employment.

Given that differential treatment is the central feature of the definition of sex discrimination, the question becomes: What is differential treatment? Are the waitresses at John's restaurant chain being treated differently than the waiters? Are the female consultants at Dewey, Hookem, and Howe being treated differently than the male consultants?

To answer the question about differential treatment, both social scientists and lawyers take into account the "inputs" as well as the "outcomes" that are associated with members of different groups in any situation. Outcomes include factors such as pay, praise, and promotions. Inputs include factors such as people's qualifications and efforts and aspects of their work assignments. Differential outcomes do not automatically signal sex discrimination; differences in the outcomes of men and women only spell sex discrimination if there are no justifying differences in inputs.

Let's return to the example of John's restaurant chain. If we find that the waiters earn more than the waitresses, but have equivalent qualifications and are assigned to the same shifts, then we must conclude that sex discrimination exists. But imagine that the waiters need to be on 24-hour call and to serve as "pinch hitters" when others are suddenly ill, whereas no such demand is made of the waitresses. Or imagine that the waiters both have long years of experience in the restaurant business, but the waitresses do not. When gender differences in inputs correspond to gender differences in outcomes, no one can claim sex discrimination.

As we shall see, much ink has been spilled—and thankfully so—over the question of what constitutes "outcomes" in the input/outcome ratio. Consider the consultants at Dewey, Hookem, and Howe. On the surface, the men and women are being treated exactly the same: Everyone, not just the women, is expected to be available for late afternoon meetings. But surface similarities can be misleading, especially in light of the current realities in America about the division of household and family labor. Requiring everyone to be available in the late afternoon places a much greater burden on women than on men. Unless it is justified by business necessity, treatment that is *prima facie* neutral, but disparate in impact, is against the law. To see why, just contemplate an organization that grants all of its employees paid medical leave for prostate cancer and denies all of its employees paid medical leave for uterine cancer.

Also much debated is the question of legitimate inputs. Conservatives have often argued that sex differences in compensation result more from the different choices that women and men make about productive and reproductive work than from differential treatment. According to many conservative scholars, women essentially select "freedom" in the form of "mothers' hours" over high wages and salaries. In respect to the Dewey, Hookem, and Howe example, a conservative scholar might note that anyone, man or woman, has the choice to work elsewhere where the demands are fewer and the rewards are also less. Such a scholar would not see it as appropriate to hold Dewey, Hookem, and Howe responsible for choices made by female employees. But liberal scholars across the disciplines note that the choices of any one individual are constrained by social norms and realities. Just as it does not make sense to blame a person born into poverty for choosing to live in a rat-infested house when other, cleaner houses exist, so it does not make sense, say the liberal scholars, to imagine that women's behavior is simply the result of free agency.

Complicated though it is to take into account various aspects of differential treatment (i.e., matching inputs and outcomes), the social scientific definition of sex discrimination is quite simple in one regard: At question is behavior, not attitudes, opinions, thoughts, or feelings. For the social scientist, unlike the everyday observer, discrimination is a matter of measurable behavior. Attitudes, opinions, thoughts, and feelings may be related to discrimination but, for the social scientist, they are not a necessary part of the definition of discrimination.

Far-reaching implications derive from the distinction between behaviors, on the one hand, and, on the other hand, attitudes, opinions, thoughts, or feelings. As shall be shown in the course of this lecture, discrimination can occur in the absence of negative feelings or prejudices, and even in the absence of unconscious prejudices. And hostility, stereotyping, or other forms of negative prejudice do not necessarily and automatically result in discrimination.

Gender Discrimination at Work

Social scientists distinguish between sex and gender. Sex is a matter of biology; gender concerns the societal expectations that accompany sex. In the law, gender discrimination is sometimes recognized as a form of sex discrimination (Rhode & Williams, in press). Gender discrimination, thus, occurs when an individual is underrewarded or punished at work for acting in ways that defy gender expectations or stereotypes. When a woman is penalized for acting like a man, or a man is penalized for acting like a woman, gender discrimination is said to occur.

The famous case of *Hopkins v. Price Waterhouse* reached the Supreme Court as *Price Waterhouse v. Hopkins* and was decided in 1989. The case concerned the way that the partners of a major accountancy firm had treated their associate, Ann Hopkins, when she was being considered for promotion to partner. Hopkins had been a high performer, bringing millions of dollars in new contracts to the firm. Yet she was judged to be unsuitable for promotion to partner status. Men with lower qualifications than Hopkins were promoted. During the trials, it was discovered that many of the male partners had voted against Hopkins because they deemed her to have acted in ways that were "unladylike." Hopkins was not mistreated because she was a woman; she was mistreated because she was a woman who acted in ways that challenged people's gender stereotypes. The Supreme Court ruled in favor of Hopkins. The Court thus considered gender discrimination as a form of (illegal) sex discrimination.

Men can also be punished for acting in ways that are inconsistent with society's expectations. Research shows that some men are subjected to harassment at work more than others. The men who are likely to be harassed are those who behave in "effeminate" ways. Men are much more likely than women to be harassed by a member of their own sex (Stockdale, 2005).

Sexual Harassment at Work

One specific type of sex discrimination has received a great deal of attention in the media: sexual harassment. Scholars have also devoted much attention to sexual harassment, and most large organizations now publish their policies against this type of harassment. The reason is simple: The law holds organizations responsible for the harassing behavior of its employees unless the organization can show that it took reasonable measures to prevent employees from harassing each other (or anyone else, such as a customer).

According to the published guidelines of the Equal Employment Opportunity Commission (EEOC), sexual harassment comprises "unwelcome sexual advances, requests for sexual favors, and other verbal or physical conduct of a sexual nature" in the workplace. Much controversy has surrounded the concept of "unwelcome." One way an employee can establish that a certain behavior is unwelcome is to notify the perpetrator, preferably in writing, that the behavior is unwelcome. (Written notification is generally better than oral notification because it may be easier for the victim to confront the perpetrator in writing than in person, and also, information about the unwelcome behavior can be presented more precisely through written communication. Some "harassment" occurs as a genuine misunderstanding between individuals.) If the victim has not notified the perpetrator, a behavior can still be deemed sexually harassing if a reasonable person would label it as sexual and harmful or offensive. For example, if a woman did not complain about lewd pictures—in part, perhaps, because she thought that the reactions to her complaints would be as lewd as the pictures, the courts may still find that the woman was subject to a hostile work environment because any reasonable person would expect not to be subjected to lewd pictures.

Sexual harassment exists in two major forms. What is known as *quid pro quo* harassment corresponds to what the media generally portray as sexual harassment. In *quid pro quo* harassment, a supervisor pressures a subordinate through, what the subordinate considers, unwanted behavior and indicates that some rewards or punishments will be attached to the subordinate's response. For example, a boss might promise a promotion to an employee in exchange for sexual favors or might threaten retaliation if the employee refuses to engage in certain sexual behaviors.

The second type of sexual harassment comes under the rubric of hostile work environment. A hostile work environment exists when employees' conditions of employment are threatened by inappropriate intrusions of sexual matters into the workplace. When, for instance, male workers post photos of explicit sexual acts on the workroom walls, presumably in order to embarrass female workers, a hostile environment exists. The men are not exonerated or exculpated by the claim that they were simply engaging in behavior that was satisfying to them and did not intend to cause embarrassment; nor are they released from responsibility if the women fail to complain. As long as a reasonable person would find the environment to be threatening, the men, and by extension the organization that employs them, would be held liable for sexual harassment. In addition, when a supervisor has a romantic and/or sexual relationship with a subordinate, the courts presume the existence of a hostile work environment for all other subordinates. Such a presumption is based in common sense. Knowing that your co-worker is having an affair with the boss can make you feel mighty gloomy about your own chances for career advancement, especially if you and the co-worker are in competition for a promotion.

One common misconception is that sexual harassment is always across the sexes. Legally such is not the case. Social science research shows that men at work are more likely to be sexually harassed by men than by women (Gutek & Done, 2001).

In Sum

The definition of sex discrimination is both simple and more complicated than one might expect. Sex discrimination concerns behavior or treatment. Intentions are relevant, but not essential. Yet judgments of differential treatment are often not simple.

*W*HAT CAUSES SEX DISCRIMINATION?

Social scientists have identified four main factors that contribute to sex discrimination (Crosby & Stockdale, in press). The same factors have been found to operate in other types of discrimination, including ethnic or racial discrimination (Crosby & Dovidio, in press). Sometimes the effects of different types of discrimination add together for individuals in a linear way, and sometimes the effects seem multiplicative. Virtually never do the effects cancel each other out, so that, for example, the Woman of Color is better off than the Man of Color or than the White woman in terms of discrimination.

First Factor: Hostile Prejudice

Virulent misogyny, or hatred of women, exists among certain sectors of American society. Just as one can still locate pockets of White supremacists or of Jew-hating Nazis, so can one still discover groups of men who make a point of telling the world, and the women in it, how much they dislike women. But today in the United States, social norm dictates that one not show overt prejudices against women.

Although virulent and outspoken misogynists may be few and far between today, many men—and women too—continue to harbor beliefs that women are inferior to men. Often now the negative attitudes are expressed in socially acceptable language. An employer might claim, for example, that he would hire women as top managers or executives if only he could find any who are qualified and who have "fire in the belly." Or he might rail against how affirmative action for women has raised company costs or lowered work quality. He might attribute a woman's success to luck, yet attribute the same type of success by a man to talent (Sabattani & Cross, in press).

Recently, researchers have developed an interesting mechanism for measuring people's preconceptions or prejudices. Developed by Greenwald and Banaji, the measurement device involves having people react as rapidly as they can to words shown on a computer screen (Banaji, 2001; Greenwald & Banaji, 1995; Greenwald et al., 2002; Greenwald, Nosek, & Banaji, 2003). The procedure is called the Implicit Association Test (IAT) because it uses reaction times (measured in milliseconds and largely outside of people's conscious control) to determine if people implicitly associate some descriptive words with men, whereas other words are associated with women. In the pairing of words, the faster the reaction time, the closer is the association.

Researchers have utilized the IAT to demonstrate that many people perceive women to be very nice—indeed, nicer than men—but that they also assume that women are not as well-suited for business as are men. High-achieving women are disliked and thought to be cold and hard. Meanwhile, most people think of housewives as sweet but childlike and basically incompetent (Cuddy, Fiske, & Glick, 2004).

If you wish to test your own implicit associations, you can self-administer an IAT test over the Web. A Google search reveals several websites, including Banaji's site (https://implicit.harvard.edu). Many people who visit the website are surprised to discover the extent of their preconceptions or prejudices of which they have not been consciously aware.

Second Factor: Benign Prejudice

Much more common than hostile sexism in the United States today is what social psychologists call "benevolent sexism." The benevolent sexist is someone who glorifies women but thinks that women require "special treatment." The "chivalrous man" who holds the front door of the house open *for* a woman (but not for a man) is often the same one who often refuses to open the office door *to* a woman (but does keep it open to a man). Carefully conducted surveys show that Americans say they like women generally more than they say they like men, but the same people also like women to conform to certain preconceptions (Glick & Fiske, in press).

Closely related to the phenomenon of benevolent sexism is a phenomenon known as the shifting standard (Biernat & Kobrynowicz, 1997). When people are considered for entry into an organization, women are often given the benefit of the doubt. For the purposes of forming a group, women are held to a lower standard than are men. For example, a woman who attained a job as a director in Company X might be considered for the job of vice president in Company Y, whereas a man would need to have attained the level of assistant vice president to be considered for the same job. Yet when the time comes to decide on merit, pay, promotion, or whom to keep in the group, women are held to a higher standard. Thus, when the board of directors of Company Y is deciding on compensation packets for the vice presidents, the women vice presidents may earn less than the men, even when their performance is superior. Men are not the only ones to practice shifting standards; so do many women (Biernat & Vescio, 2002).

Third Factor: In-Group Favoritism

Psychologists have demonstrated again and again that people like to form groups and tend to favor their own groups over others (Crosby & Dovidio, in press). The power of in-group favoritism has been shown by in-class demonstrations such as the one in which the teacher partitions the class into those with red buttons and those with blue ones. One well-known demonstration by a teacher named Jane Elliot involved splitting a class into blue-eyed and brown-eyed children. She then told the children that the blue-eyed students were superior. After a short time, the blue-eyed children decided that they disliked the brown-eyed children and believed in their own superiority.

How does in-group favoritism contribute to sex discrimination? If men and women keep themselves separate at work, then men may come to see other men as their in-group and women may see other women as their in-group. Research has confirmed that women and men at work tend, by and large, to compare their work situations to others of the same sex as themselves (Zanna, Crosby, & Lowenstein, 1987); it seems logical that they thus think of themselves as some sort of group or club. Often, those in positions of power (men) may not be as interested in keeping women out of good jobs as they are in bringing other men into their in-group. Discrimination in favor of men has the same effect as discrimination against women. Meanwhile, the women, comparing themselves only to other women, may not realize the extent to which they are underpaid.

Fourth Factor: Structures that Reinforce Disadvantage

It is also possible that women today can be disadvantaged relative to men even though no one harbors negative feelings, holds limiting stereotypes, or consciously favors men. So long as individuals engage in practices or have their behaviors shaped by structures that were first established by sexist people, individuals can unthinkingly or unknowingly engage in discriminatory behaviors based on sex.

An example may illustrate the point. Decades ago, the military assumed that pilots were men. When they created a piece of apparel known as the G-suit to help pump blood back to the brains of pilots who were experiencing a rapid loss of altitude, the military fitted the apparel to men's bodies. Some time later, women lobbied to be pilots and even to be pilots of expensive fighter planes. To see if the female body could regain consciousness as rapidly as the male body, the military conducted a series of tests in which they put women and men in G-suits and twirled them around in centrifugal motion machines. The military found that it took women longer than men to regain consciousness after a dip; but the military did not consider that the suits (proportioned to the male body where legs are shorter relative to the torso than in the case of the female body) might not fit the women as well as the men. Thus, by simply doing their job of gathering and analyzing data to make "informed decisions," the military researchers contributed to a discriminatory situation.

Consider another example. In Canada in the 1980s, school children were all sent home for lunch. Canadian women made little progress toward achieving high-status careers during this time. Once it was decided to keep children at school during the lunch hour, women made greater inroads into their professions. The school policy was not formed with the express purpose of harming women; nor was it changed with the express purpose of helping women's careers. In fact, most people just went about their business without thinking of the consequences of the policy for sexual equity at work. But, contemplated or not, the consequences were real.

HOW SEVERE IS SEX DISCRIMINATION?

Most scholars agree that there is less sex discrimination in the United States today than there was in the 1950s. How great has the change been? How much has the situation improved today? Opinions differ. Some conservatives believe that America has by now largely eradicated sex discrimination. Looking at the data, most scholars are less sanguine.

The number of women in today's paid labor market has certainly skyrocketed. In the 1950s, only about one-third of working-age women had jobs outside the home, but 50 years later, the percentage had doubled. By the beginning of the twenty-first century, one-half of the paid labor market was female (Bergmann, in press). Yet mere presence in the paid labor market is not a good indication of lessened discrimination. In fact, although most of us imagine that sex discrimination has been vanquished, the statistics show a surprising persistence of unequal treatment. Even now, four decades after the passage of major civil rights legislation, gross inequalities persist.

Sex Differences in Compensation

One straightforward way to assess sex discrimination is to see if there are differences in the levels of compensation given to men and women. Over the last few years, women's median weekly earnings have been about 80 percent of men's (Bergmann, in press). Differences in median wages (a form of "outcome") need to be evaluated in light of differences in relevant inputs, such as hours worked, persistence in the paid labor market, and nature of the job (or job title). At least one study has shown that, for some samples of workers, it is possible to nearly completely eliminate sex differences in pay by statistically adjusting for sex differences in job-relevant inputs (Stanley & Jarrell, 1998). However, different researchers using other techniques and other samples have not been able to reproduce the happy finding of minimal discrimination. Through the technique of multiple regression analyses, one set of researchers has determined that women reap fewer benefits from education, experience, and training than do men (Crosby, 2004). Indeed, one analysis showed that the typical woman at the end of the 1980s earned less than three-quarters of what she would have earned if she were a man, as determined by assessed competencies and experiences (Raudenbush & Kasim, 1998).

One of the most telling indicators is how the two sexes fare in given occupations. Female lawyers tend to earn less than male lawyers, and the longer the time since completion of law school, the greater is the gap. Similarly, female nurses earn 87 percent of what male nurses earn. Even male dishwashers earn more than female dishwashers—to the tune of about $2,000 a year (Bergmann, in press).

Sex differences in total compensation tend to be greater than sex differences in wages or salaries. Total compensation takes into account benefits. Within any job category, men may negotiate higher "perks" than do women. More important, many benefits come as a function of working full-time rather than part-time. Although there is no logical reason to distinguish between full-time and part-time work in terms of benefits, employers are legally allowed to withhold benefits from employees who work less than 20 hours a week. Part-time workers, two-thirds of whom are women, would greatly benefit if the law were changed to mandate that benefits, like wages, be calculated on a pro-rated basis for part-time workers.

Sex Differences in On-the-Job Treatment

More women than men are subjected to harassment on the job (Gutek & Done, 2001). All studies that include both women and men show that women are more likely to have been harassed on the job than men, and sometimes the differential is very great, with 75 percent of women reporting that they have suffered sexual harassment at some point in their work lives.

Sex-Segregated Job Markets

Occupations in the United States are largely coded by sex. Most occupations are either male- or female-dominated (Bergmann, in press). Consider childcare workers: 96 percent are women. Similarly, 98 percent of workers in secretarial positions are women, and three-quarters of all administrative staff positions are filled by women, a statistic that has not changed in 35 years. On the other hand, less than 10 percent of car salespeople are women, and women occupy less than one percent of skilled craftsperson jobs.

Within occupations that include both women and men, women tend to congregate in some specialties, and men in others. Many women lawyers concentrate on family law or public interest law, whereas men concentrate disproportionately on corporate law. Within medicine, male physicians are overrepresented among surgeons, whereas female physicians are overrepresented among pediatricians and family practitioners. In many occupations, as women enter the ranks, men leave. And as men leave, salaries fall. The American Psychological Association has noticed the "feminization" of psychology and the relative drop in earnings by those in the profession. The gap in earning between surgeons and pediatricians today is greater than it was 30 years ago when few women were physicians (Bergmann, in press).

Given the sex segregation of the labor force in general, it is no surprise that many organizations in the United States have a concentration of women in low-ranking positions and a concentration of men in high-ranking positions. Only 16 percent of Fortune 500 corporate officers are women. Only two percent of CEOs are women (Bergmann, in press).

WHAT CAN BE DONE TO LESSEN SEX DISCRIMINATION?

Attempts to lessen sex discrimination are obviously important. They are more likely to be successful if they take into account the dynamics of discrimination; of what, in other words, has caused the discrimination. Individual social actors—activists such as Betty Friedan, Gloria Steinem, Ruth Bader Ginsberg, Catherine McKinnnon, Andrea Dworkin, Ann Hopkins, and many more—can have a great effect on the lives of many people. Yet even the feminist heroines have an effect by working in concert with each other and with larger social groups and by aiming their sights at a group or societal level.

One way to lessen sex discrimination is to make people aware of, and then challenge, their preconceptions, assumptions, or prejudices. The famous consciousness-raising sessions of the 1970s and 1980s, in which groups of women would come together for reflection and discussion, were effective ways of helping women realize the nature and extent of their own self-limiting and sexist assumptions. Many a feminist will tell you that her life has been changed by participating in consciousness-raising work. An additional value of consciousness-raising groups is that they help women recognize the extent to which they suffer from discrimination. Numerous investigations have now shown that people have a difficult time appreciating that they themselves are subject to the same disadvantages that affect the group to which they belong (Crosby, Iyer, & Sincharoen, 2006). Thus, for example, women often know that women in general are the victims of discrimination; yet each woman imagines that the discrimination touches only other women and not herself. This phenomenon is known as the "denial of personal disadvantage" (Crosby, 1984).

Men also often need to recognize the depth and consequences of their sexist thinking, and when men learn how silly and harmful it is to assume certain gender differences to be true, they can become effective agents of social change. Unless, and until, men assume their fair share of the work at home, women will never obtain their fair share of the rewards at work.

Ultimately, it is not enough simply to change attitudes. Social changes are more important than changes at an individual level because the choices of individuals are constrained by social realities. Many Canadian women and men were seeking to create egalitarian family situations; but much more important than their individual hope was the reality of children's luncheon needs.

Laws can promote or impede social change. Several laws have helped greatly to decrease sex discrimination. Title VII of the Civil Rights Act of 1964 made it illegal to discriminate on the basis of sex. The establishment of affirmative action, and particularly the requirement that all federal contractors (who have more than 50 employees and who do more than $50,000 of business with the federal government) must be affirmative action employers, has produced measurable improvement in women's chances of being hired, promoted, and well paid. The Family and Medical Leave Act, passed by Congress in 1993, has also helped diminish sex discrimination by safeguarding the jobs of women and men who take a leave from work to give birth, adopt a child, or provide caregiving to a sick or elderly family member.

It is not just the laws of the land that make a difference; so do the policies of organizations. Family-friendly policies can help organizations reduce sex discrimination. Such policies include flextime, on-site childcare, and family leave. According to at least one study, family-friendly organizations also reap greater profits than other similar organizations who do not have family-friendly policies, probably because of increased employee loyalty (Catalyst, 2004).

Affirmative action is a policy that aims at reducing discrimination, yet it is widely misunderstood and does not enjoy acceptance among Americans. In fact, affirmative action in employment operates in a way that makes a great deal of sense and differs from the popular misconceptions.

Affirmative action in employment involves a two-step process. First, organizations monitor themselves to make sure that they employ women or People of Color in various job classifications in proportion to the available talent pool. The talent pools are determined in ways prescribed by federal regulation and by common sense. For example, the talent pool for the job of professor is national, whereas the talent pool for a clerical job is local.

If, and only if, the first step of the affirmative action program reveals a problem, then the organization moves to the second step of making corrections. Imagine that an organization determines that 20 percent of the talent pool for a certain type of job are women and that 18 percent of the people whom it employs in the job are women. No further action is required. But imagine that the organization finds that 35 percent of those qualified for the job are women and yet only 10 percent of those actually employed are women. Such a disparity reveals a problem.

If an organization finds that its utilization of women in designated job classifications falls far short of the availability of qualified women, the organization must make the necessary corrections if it is a federal contractor (that is, if it does business with the federal government). Only some remedies are legally permissible. An organization cannot, for example, fire the men it has already hired just because it discovers that it employs fewer women than it should. However, special outreach and mentoring efforts are almost always appropriate.

A great deal of research by economists has shown that women gain greater parity with men in organizations that have affirmative action programs than in those that do not. Organizations with affirmative action policies have been found to promote equality of the sexes at work more than do comparable organizations in similar sectors of the economy (Crosby, 2004).

Affirmative action may be a very effective regulation because it does not require that the aggrieved parties come forward on their own behalf (Crosby, Iyer, Clayton, & Downing, 2003). Indeed, it does not even require that the aggrieved parties be aware of their own disadvantage. As mentioned earlier, people who are disadvantaged on the basis of group characteristics, such as gender, tend not to be aware of their disadvantage. Having a person in the organization whose job it is to monitor discrimination and to propose and implement needed corrections helps the organization stay on track and thus helps situations improve even before the victims become aware of the extent of the problem.

*T*HE FUTURE?

Is it likely that we will ever completely eradicate sex discrimination? Perhaps not. Certainly, humans constantly attend to the dimension of sex, noticing, for example, who is male and who is female. If you doubt how deeply we care about assigning sex to people, reflect on how you feel the next time you perceive a person of indeterminate sex, such as the famous androgynous "Pat" on the television show *Saturday Night Live*. Humans assign meanings and attach significance to dimensions that they notice. As cold, hard information processors, humans leave a lot to be desired. And thus, it may be natural to "see" all sorts of sex differences where, in fact, none really exist. These perceived sex differences often serve as justifications for differential treatment of the sexes.

Yet even though we will probably never totally eliminate sex discrimination in employment, we can still hope that future generations will continue the forward march toward sex equity. Someday, women may truly be rewarded for their "inputs" or qualifications in roughly the same measure as men. And someday, too, girls and women may have the opportunities to acquire the same qualifications as boys and men. When such a day arrives, all humans will benefit from having expanded options to realize their full potential. Boys and men will trade in one type of advantage—the advantage that comes from discrimination—for another, broader, and more humane advantage—the advantage that comes from living fully in a just society; and girls and women will exchange one type of security—the security that comes from living in a hierarchical and constrained world—for the security that comes from knowing that one is equal to all others in the eyes of the law and the eyes of society.

REFERENCES

BANAJI, M. R. (2001). Implicit attitudes can be measured. In H. L. Roediger, III, J. S. Nairne, I. Neath, & A. Surprenant (Eds.), *The nature of remembering: Essays in honor of Robert G. Crowder* (pp. 117–150). Washington, DC: American Psychological Association.

BERGMANN, B. (In press). An economist looks at sex discrimination. In F. J. Crosby, M. S. Stockdale, & S. A. Ropp (Eds.), *Sex discrimination in employment: An interdisciplinary approach*. Boston: Blackwell.

BIERNAT, M., & KOBRYNOWICZ, D. (1997). Gender- and race-based standards of competence: Lower minimum standards but higher ability standards for devalued groups. *Journal of Personality and Social Psychology, 72*, 544–557.

BIERNAT, M., & VESCIO, T. K. (2002). She swings, she hits, she's great, she's benched: Implications of gender-based shifting standards for judgment and behavior. *Personality and Social Psychology Bulletin, 28*, 66–77.

CATALYST (2004). *The bottom line: Connecting corporate performance and gender diversity*. New York: Catalyst.

CROSBY, F. J. (1984). The denial of personal discrimination. *American Behavioral Scientist, 27*, 371–386.

CROSBY, F. J. (2004). *Affirmative action is dead; long live affirmative action*. New Haven: Yale University Press.

CROSBY, F. J., & DOVIDIO, J. F. (In press). Discrimination in America and legal strategies for reducing it. In E. Borgida & S. Fiske (Eds.), *Psychological science in court: Beyond common knowledge*. Boston: Blackwell.

CROSBY, F. J., IYER, A., CLAYTON, S., & DOWNING, R. (2003). Affirmative action: Psychological data and the policy debates. *American Psychologist, 58*, 93–115.

CROSBY, F. J., IYER, A., & SINCHAROEN, S. (2006). Understanding affirmative action. *Annual Review of Psychology, 57*, 586–611.

CROSBY, F. J., & STOCKDALE, M. S. (In press). Understanding sex discrimination. In F. J. Crosby, M. S. Stockdale, & S. A. Ropp (Eds.), *Sex discrimination in employment: An interdisciplinary approach*. Boston: Blackwell.

CUDDY, A. J., FISKE, S. T., & GLICK, P. (2004). When professionals become mothers, warmth doesn't cut the ice. *Journal of Social Issues, 60*, 701–718.

GLICK, P., & FISKE, S. T. (In press). Sex discrimination: The psychological approach. In F. J. Crosby, M. S. Stockdale, & S. A. Ropp (Eds.), *Sex discrimination in employment: An interdisciplinary approach*. Boston: Blackwell.

GREENWALD, A. G., & BANAJI, M. R. (1995). Implicit social cognition: Attitudes, self-esteem, and stereotypes. *Psychological Review, 102,* 4–27.

GREENWALD, A. G., BANAJI, M. R., RUDMAN, L. A., FARNHAM, S. D., NOSEK, B. A., & MELLOTT, D. S. (2002). A unified theory of implicit attitudes, stereotypes, self-esteem, and self-concept. *Journal of Personality and Social Psychology, 109,* 3–25.

GREENWALD, A. G., NOSEK, B. A., & BANAJI, M. R. (2003). Understanding and using the Implicit Association Test: An improved scoring algorithm. *Journal of Personality & Social Psychology, 85,* 197–216.

GUTEK, B. A., & DONE, R. S. (2001). Sexual harassment. In R. Unger (Ed.), *Handbook of the psychology of women and gender* (pp. 367–387). Hoboken, NJ: John Wiley & Sons.

RAUDENBUSH, S. W., & KASIM, R. M. (1998). Cognitive skill and economic inequality: Findings from the national adult literacy survey. *Harvard Educational Review, 68,* 33–68.

RHODE, D., & WILLIAMS, J. C. (In press). Legal perspectives on sex discrimination. In F. J. Crosby, M. S. Stockdale, & S. A. Ropp (Eds.), *Sex discrimination in employment: An interdisciplinary approach.* Boston: Blackwell.

SABATTINI, L., & CROSBY, F. J. (In press). Overcoming resistance: Attitudes and resistance. In K. Thomas (Ed.), *Diversity resistance: Manifestations and solutions.* Mawah, NJ: Erlbaum.

STANLEY, T. D., & JARRELL, S. B. (1998). Gender wage discrimination bias? A Meta-regression analysis. *Journal of Human Resources, 33,* 947–973.

STOCKDALE, M. S. (2005). The sexual harassment of men: Articulating the approach-rejection theory of sexual harassment. In J. E. Gruber & P. Morgan (Eds.), *In the company of men: Male dominance and sexual harassment* (pp. 117–141). Boston: Northeastern University Press.

ZANNA, M. P., CROSBY F. J., & LOEWENSTEIN, G. (1987). Male reference groups and discontent among female professionals. In B. A. Gutek & L. Larwood (Eds.), *Pathways to women's career development* (pp. 28–41). Beverly Hills: Sage Publications.

SUGGESTED READINGS

CROSBY, F. J., IYER, A., CLAYTON, S., & DOWNING, R. (2003). Affirmative action: Psychological data and the policy debates. *American Psychologist, 58,* 93–115.

CROSBY, F. J., STOCKDALE, M. S., & ROPP, S. A. (Eds.). (In press). *Sex discrimination in the workplace: An interdisciplinary approach.* Boston: Blackwell.

GUTEK, B. A., & DONE, R. S. (2001). Sexual harassment. In R. Unger (Ed.), *Handbook of the psychology of women and gender* (pp. 367–387). Hoboken, NJ: John Wiley & Sons.

STOCKDALE, M. S., & CROSBY, F. J. (Eds.). (2004). *The psychology and management of workplace diversity.* Boston: Blackwell.

RECOMMENDED INTERNET RESOURCES

Employment Standards Administration: http://www.dol.gov/esa
Implicit Association Test: https://implicit.harvard.edu

DIANE **M. HALL** is a Research Associate and Lecturer at the University of Pennsylvania. Dr. Hall has taught courses on the psychology of women since 2000 at the University of Pennsylvania. She is co-founder of the Caucus on Mothering Issues of the Association for Women in Psychology (AWP). Her clinical and research work explores the roles of race, gender, and development on adolescents in their romantic and interpersonal relationships and the roles of race and gender on marginalized individuals within institutions, such as schools.

5

Feminist Perspectives on the Personal and Political Aspects of Mothering

❖

MOTHERING: THE PERSONAL AND THE POLITICAL

"Changing the status of mothers, by gaining real recognition of their work, is the great unfinished business of the women's movement."

Ann Crittenden (2001, p. 7)

"Feminism cannot claim to give an adequate account of women's lives and to represent women's needs and interests if it ignores the issue of mothering."

Patricia DiQuinzio (1999, p. xi)

We have a tendency to think of motherhood as something personal, individual, and relatively private, which occurs within the domestic sphere of home. Yet it is important to realize that mothering is also situated within the larger social and political context and that this larger context has an impact on our private lives. When people in power hold stereotyped or biased views of other groups of people, they can influence policies and social structures that have a significant impact on the lives of individuals. In this lecture, I will provide some examples of the political aspects of mothering and their impact on the private lives of individual women. The feminist saying "The personal is political" certainly applies to mothering and is something I think about continually as the feminist mother of a son.

PUBLIC/CULTURAL IMAGES OF MOTHERS

Images of motherhood abound in our culture. Think about television commercials and print ads designed to sell billions of dollars worth of baby products (Fleming, 2002). Soft focus photography of nursing mothers abounds. This powerful and emotional image sends a very important message about mothering. It makes mothering look natural, peaceful, and easy. It also sends a message that "real" mothers are biological mothers (who else would be nursing an infant?). In addition, the majority of the actors/models are White. If a partner is portrayed, it is always a man. Therefore, the image of the nurturing mother is White and heterosexual. She also is not poor—how else could she buy all of these wonderful products for her child? We are bombarded by these images, and they form the basis for our assumptions about mothering: that it is natural, joyous, and completely fulfilling in and of itself.

We also have images of mothers of older children and mothers of adults. Think of how mothers are portrayed in television situation comedies or in films. Mothers often are portrayed as irrational, aggressive, and cruel (e.g., Doris Roberts in the role of Marie Barone on *Everybody Loves Raymond*). It is socially acceptable to laugh at them; in fact, we are meant to, because this portrayal is often the setup for the joke. It is perfectly acceptable to blame mothers for all sorts of woes (Caplan, 2000), and psychology has been particularly hard on mothers (Hook, 2004; Rice & Else-Quest, 2005). Although psychologists no longer blame mothers for causing their children's autism or schizophrenia, mothers certainly are blamed for all sorts of behavioral problems. Why aren't fathers held accountable in this way?

Images of fathers show them as "helping" the mother or as incompetent in caring for a child. For example, several years ago there was a commercial in which the father could not make lunch for his child without the benefit of individually wrapped, microwaveable hotdogs. These are powerful images that send the message that mothers really *should* be doing the nurturing and childcare. This is a slippery slope for women—if women are "naturally" more nurturing and innately better or more competent at childcare, then *of course* they should be doing the majority of it. Many women, some feminists included, have internalized this "natural" and romanticized view of motherhood without questioning it (hooks, 2000). After all, caring for children is a source of power and pride for women. To quote bell hooks (2000, pp. 135–136):

> On the negative side, romanticizing motherhood, employing the same terminology that is used by sexists to suggest that women are inherently life-affirming nurturers, feminist activists reinforce central tenets of male supremacist ideology. They imply that motherhood is a woman's truest vocation; that women who do not mother, whose lives may be focused more exclusively on a career, creative work, or political work, are missing out, doomed to live emotionally unfulfilled

lives. While they do not openly attack or denigrate women who do not bear children, they (like society as a whole) suggest that it is *more* important than women's other labor and more rewarding. They could simply state that it *is* important and rewarding.

THE PRIVATE AND PUBLIC/POLITICAL ASPECTS OF MOTHERING

Becoming a Mother

There is a pressure on women to have children, and women who say that they are ambivalent about or uninterested in having children are often viewed as "abnormal" or selfish. This pressure is so great that it has been called the "motherhood mandate" (Russo, 1976). The English language does not even have an easy way to designate women who do not have children; "childless" or "childfree" are often used. "Childless" sends the message that *with children* is the more "normal" status for a woman and that not having a child is a deviation. "Childfree" suggests that having children is a burden; that is, children are something from which we need to be freed. Heterosexually partnered women are often asked *when*, not *if*, they are going to have children. This takes a seemingly private issue and makes it public.

Making the decision *not* to become a mother has become a public issue in this country, although *how public* depends on a woman's socioeconomic status. For example, many women who decide to prevent or postpone becoming mothers by going on oral contraceptives are finding that pharmacists are refusing to fill their prescriptions (National Women's Law Center, 2005). This can create a serious burden on rural or low-income women who then have to travel to another pharmacy. Groups like the National Women's Law Center are treating this issue as a serious violation of women's reproductive rights and an obstacle to critical healthcare. Again, what seems to be a private issue is also political.

In the United States, childbirth is seen as a medical issue, and most children born in the United States are born in hospitals. Childbirth, therefore, is situated within a context of risk management and liability protection. Obstetricians and gynecologists pay some of the highest malpractice insurance premiums, which has led to a shortage of ob/gyns in some areas of the country (Robinson et al., 2005). In addition, concerns about possible malpractice suits can lead to increased medical intervention as a "prevention" measure, and many such interventions are not medically necessary (Wolf, 2003). For example, many hospitals conduct continuous fetal monitoring (i.e., they attach a device to the laboring woman to monitor the heart rate of the fetus, which does not allow the mother to move around or be comfortable), despite the American College of Obstetricians and Gynecologists' (ACOG) recommendation for intermittent monitoring (Coughlin, 2005).

A more serious medical intervention involves cesarean sections, also called C-sections. In 2004 in the United States, 29.1 percent of live births were via cesarean section, which is a 40 percent increase since 1996 (Martin, Hamilton, Menacker, Sutton, & Mathews, 2005). The World Health Organization (1985) recommends no higher than 10–15 percent for a cesarean section rate, and *Consumer Reports* magazine (2005) listed cesarean section number three on its list of "12 Surgeries You May Be Better Off Without." I do believe that some women and their babies medically require cesareans, and the surgery certainly has saved lives. I am happy we have this knowledge and technology available. However, we have higher rates of medical intervention than other countries do, yet we also have higher rates of infant mortality. In 2002, the United States ranked 28th out of 37 countries for infant mortality rates (March of Dimes, 2002). Some of the countries with *lower* rates were: Hong Kong, Singapore, the Czech Republic, Northern Ireland, Australia, Portugal, England, Canada, Greece, New Zealand, and Cuba. I see a problem when we use *more* medical and surgical intervention in childbirth and still have a high infant mortality rate.

Furthermore, many women who had a C-section for their first birth cannot find hospitals or birthing centers where they may deliver their subsequent babies vaginally (known as vaginal birth after C-section, or VBAC) because many physicians and hospitals no longer perform VBACs (American College of Obstetricians and Gynecologists [ACOG], 2004; Grady, 2004). This is despite research that shows that vaginal birth after C-section can be safer than a repeat cesarean (ACOG, 2004) and has more advantages for both the mother and baby (Buhimschi & Buhimschi, 2006). Some feminists have said that this issue is another example in which women are not able to make decisions about their own bodies (Kuhn, 2004). Denial of a woman's right to control her own medical care is both personal and political.

There are other ways of becoming a mother that are often overlooked in our culture. The first involves women who use reproductive technology, such as artificial insemination, to become mothers. Despite the pitfalls and horror stories depicted in television dramas, medical technology increasingly is making motherhood an option for many women who can afford it, including single women, lesbian women, and heterosexually partnered women with fertility problems. The availability of medical technology also has allowed two-mother lesbian families to be "planned lesbian families" (Golombok, 2000) and has resulted in a "lesbian baby boom" (Riley, 1988). The second overlooked means of becoming a mother is adoption. Hollywood has made adoption seem glamorous and relatively easy, but people who adopt would likely say otherwise, especially due to the uncertainty and waiting. If you do not know *if* a baby or child will be placed with you, let alone *when*, when do you buy a crib and car seat? What do you tell family, friends, coworkers, or your boss? How do you plan a leave from work? Becoming a parent, whether through childbirth or adoption, involves substantial changes in one's life. Adoption lacks the visible sign (i.e., pregnancy) that cues others to upcoming important changes in your life. The third overlooked way of becoming a mother is through partnership with someone who already has children, and this may or may not involve legal adoption. But it can certainly involve all of the baggage that comes with the word "stepmother" for heterosexually partnered women. For two-mother lesbian families, this may involve parenting a child that one of the women had through a previous relationship with a man, although the number of these families is expected to decline as women begin coming out at younger ages (Bos, van Balen, & van den Boom, 2005).

Mothering and Work

In 2003, women comprised 47 percent of the total labor force in the United States. This translates to more than 68 million women, including 79.2 percent of women with children under the age of 18 (National Partnership for Women and Families [NPWF], 2004a). A review of employment discrimination against women in the 40 years since the passage of the Civil Rights Act of 1964 revealed that gender discrimination persists as a significant problem for women (NPWF). There are two specific types of this discrimination: pregnancy discrimination and caregiver discrimination. For most pregnant women, their pregnancy usually becomes obvious after some time and is not something that can be hidden. The Pregnancy Discrimination Act of 1978, which is an amendment to Title VII of the Civil Rights Act, states that "discrimination on the basis of pregnancy, childbirth, or related medical condition constitutes unlawful sex discrimination" (Equal Employment Opportunity Commission [EEOC], 2006). Although discrimination against pregnant women is illegal, the problem is that many women do not know their rights and do not file complaints. Or a woman files a complaint, and it is handled within the workplace, often with the condition that the woman will not file a lawsuit and will not discuss the complaint further with anyone (Paul, 2006). This makes it difficult to gauge the size and scope of the problem of pregnancy discrimination. Despite this, in 2005, the Equal Employment Opportunity Commission received 4,449 complaints of pregnancy discrimination in the workplace (EEOC, 2006). Since 1992, there has been a 39 percent increase in the number of pregnancy discrimination charges filed with the EEOC, despite a simultaneous decrease in the birthrate by 9 percent (NPWF, 2004b).

The second type of discrimination involves workers who are family caregivers, which can include caring for children or for sick or elderly family members. Caregiving triggers gender stereotypes for both female and male workers. For example, a pregnant woman can trigger the stereotype that mothers ought to be at home caring for children and not working at a career. As a result, employers may overlook these women for promotions and raises. In some cases, women have lost their jobs after having become mothers (WorkLife Law, 2006). For men who engage in caregiving, the stereotype that men are not supposed to be the nurturers can mean that men are not able to access benefits available to them, such as the national Family Medical Leave Act, which allows for unpaid leave to care for any family member. In many states, it is *not* illegal for interviewers to ask job candidates if they are married or if they have children, and these questions are most often directed to women (Blades & Row-Finkbeiner, 2006). If women lie and say that they do not have children, they may get the job, but they cannot then ask for health coverage for their children. Widespread discrimination against mothers, whether legally allowed or not, is both political and personal.

Often there are changes in how women are perceived by their co-workers once they become mothers. In one study of these perceptions, employed mothers were compared to employed fathers and to employed men and women without children (Cuddy, Fiske, & Glick, 2004). Women workers who were mothers were perceived as warmer but less competent than women workers who did not have children. Working men who were fathers were perceived as warmer than men without children, but without a cost to their competency ratings. Because ratings of competence were found to be related to interest in hiring and promoting workers, working women who become mothers may pay a higher cost than men who become fathers.

Many families need a mother's income because of higher standards of living, higher costs of living, and because many families are headed by single mothers. Therefore, any negative impact on a woman's wages will affect millions of children (Barnett, 2004). You may have heard about the "wage gap," which describes the difference in pay men and women make for the same work. In 2004, women made on average 76.5 cents for every dollar made by men (National Committee on Pay Equity, 2006). Economists and sociologists are now discussing the "mommy gap" or "motherhood penalty," which refers to the gap in pay between women with and without children. Women who have one child earn anywhere from 3 to 7 percent less than women without children (Anderson, Binder, & Krause, 2002; Budig & England, 2001; Waldfogel, 1997). Note that this comparison is to other women wage earners and not to men wage earners. For women with two or more children, the gap increases to 15 percent (Anderson et al.). This increases the gap between male wage earners and female wage earners who are mothers to 60.5 percent; that is, mothers with two children earn on average 60.5 percent of what a man in a similar job earns regardless of how many children he has. What is even worse, the gap is getting larger over time, whereas the gender pay gap has slowly begun to decrease over time (Waldfogel, 1998). This "mommy gap" persists, even when researchers control for part-time work status, job experience, work effort, and time out of the labor market (Anderson et al.; Budig & England).

Some researchers believe that some of the gap is due to discrimination by employers against mothers (Budig & England, 2001). Researchers at Cornell University (Correll & Benard, 2005) conducted a study in which they created hypothetical job applications and asked undergraduates to evaluate each "applicant" as a job candidate. The application profiles were equivalent except that one profile included mention of the woman's status as a mother of two and as an officer in a parent-teacher association. When asked if they would hire the applicants, 84 percent of the women without children would be hired, compared with 47 percent of the women with children. In addition, if mothers were offered the job, they were offered approximately $11,000 less in salary compared to women applicants without children.

Economists have suggested that family friendly work policies, such as paid maternal leave and workplace flexibility, can help to raise the wages of mothers and close the "mommy gap" (Boushey, 2005a). In addition, economists have suggested a Pay Gap Tax Credit as a means of bringing the earnings of women up to those of men. The tax credit would equal the gender pay gap working women face (Boushey, 2004). Legalized economic strategies to even "the paying field" may be necessary as long as discriminatory attitudes about mothers who work outside the home persist.

Joan Williams (2000), a law professor who writes on family and work issues, has suggested that women workers hit the "maternal wall" long before they hit the "glass ceiling." The "glass ceiling" essentially limits the promotion of women into the higher echelons of the working world. The "maternal wall" is triggered when a woman: (1) becomes pregnant, (2) becomes a mother, or (3) begins working part time or on a flexible arrangement in order to accommodate caring for a baby (Williams & Segal, 2003). The "maternal wall" concept reflects the bias and stereotype that women who are mothers are not good workers or are not committed to work. The common perception is that women cannot be both good mothers and good workers at the same time. A good mother is expected always to be there for her children (Kobrynowicz & Biernat, 1997), whereas a good worker is expected always to be there for her or his employer (Williams, 2000). These are competing and impossible expectations for the mother who works outside the home. Studies (e.g., Bielby & Bielby, 1989) have shown, however, that women and men do not differ in their commitment to work when they have similar work status, and women identify with work as strongly as men do.

Another area that illustrates the public and private nature of mothering concerns the continued focus on women's desire to "have it all," that is, to have both a career and a family. No one discusses or even questions whether men can "have it all." Yet it seems that there are "news" pieces every week about women's struggles in this area. One popular theme involves stories about highly educated professional women "opting out" of work to become stay-at-home mothers (SAHMs), with the anecdotal experiences of several individuals being given as evidence of a "growing trend" (e.g., Story, 2005). In addition, these stories do not account for employment losses due to the recent recession. When researchers control for these losses, they find that the presence of children does *not* lead to decreased participation in the labor force for women (Boushey, 2005b). An economic analysis is useful for putting the issue of "work or home" into a larger context, but there are other important factors to consider as well.

The first factor is social class. Mothers who earn the minimum wage certainly do not have the option of staying home full-time with their children. The idea of choosing "home or work" is not something working class women have had the luxury of thinking about. In addition, there are different cultural messages and societal expectations for mothers that vary by social class. These messages exert a powerful influence on the "choices" women make and on how they feel about them. Middle- and upper-class mothers are criticized and called cold, uncaring, or selfish if they work outside of the home. They "allow strangers to raise their children" (i.e., they have their children in some form of paid childcare). Social policies and welfare reforms dictate that mothers on welfare *have* to get jobs, regardless of the hours, pay, or cost and availability of childcare. Why aren't we concerned about their children? Furthermore, social class is related to race, in that some races are disproportionately represented among the lower socioeconomic statuses. Many Women of Color have always worked outside of the home. To them, the idea of staying at home is an option for Whites. Finally, single mothers, as sole family wage earners, do not have the "choice" to "opt out." So when it makes the "news" that women are struggling with this issue of "choice," journalists are talking about a small group that is not representative of all women.

Another problem is that the "choice" facing women is presented as a dichotomous one—as though working full-time outside the home or staying in the home full-time to care for children are the only options. Many women work part-time outside of the home, with "part time" defined as fewer than 34 hours per week. However, having children does not significantly increase a woman's likelihood of working part-time (Boushey, 2005b). This may be due to the scarcity of part-time work, especially work that is interesting and well paid, the stigma in the workplace associated with opting for part-time work (i.e., part-time work implies to many that one is not committed to work), or the loss of benefits that can occur with part-time work (Williams & Cooper, 2004). In addition, the discussion about "choice" assumes that once a woman chooses an option, it is a relatively permanent choice. This assumes that women do not cycle in and out of the labor market (Hewlett & Luce, 2005). One concern for women who try to cycle in and out, however, is the ease with which they can reenter the labor market. In many specialized fields such as information technology, medicine, or academia, staying home even for a few years can make it difficult to return to a field that has changed dramatically due to advances in technology or knowledge in the area. Many "reentry women" also find that they are not able to earn wages similar to what they previously earned. The average amount of "time off" is 2.2 years, and taking this amount of time translates to an average 18 percent loss of earning power (Hewlett & Luce).

In addition to the "opting out" stories, the popular media would have you believe that mothers are at war with one another. Similar to the "opting out" stories, stories on the so-called "Mommy Wars" seem to be designed to sell copies, increase viewership, and so on. Most of the stories, whether in the *New York Times* or on *Good Morning America*, involve pitting mothers who work outside the home against mothers who stay home full-time to care for their children. Behind the "Mommy Wars" rhetoric is judgment about the good mother/bad mother dichotomy, with good mothers again being those women who put their children before everything else (i.e., full-time, stay-at-home mothers). This requirement that good mothers always be available, always be patient, and always be nurturing is an impossible standard for mothers and has been called "intensive mothering" (Hays, 1996).

What is the impact of the "Mommy Wars" on mothers? One study (Johnston & Swanson, 2004) showed that stay-at-home mothers were more likely to see only the worker role of full-time employed mothers, and they focused on stereotyped, superficial images of employed mothers (e.g., SUV-driving, coffee-drinking, briefcase-toting, suit-wearing), whereas employed mothers talked about stay-at-home mothers as persons with feelings (e.g., they talked about the rewards stay-at-home mothers might experience in seeing their children grow). At-home mothers were more critical of employed mothers, felt a need to justify their own mother identities, which suggests that they feel more threatened by the "Mommy Wars" rhetoric, and reported hearing more critical and unsupportive comments from their families. Because people tend to seek support from those who share similar contexts, at-home mothers may seek support from other at-home mothers (Johnston & Swanson). This further separates employed and stay-at-home mothers from one another. In addition, this dichotomy of working *or* mothering creates the idea that career and mothering are completely incompatible, suggests that mothering is not work, reinforces the notion that mothers must sacrifice everything for their children, and thereby creates thorny situations for women.

"Having It All"—The Realities?

Surveys consistently show that young women are thinking about how to work outside of the home *and* have a family (e.g., Hoffnung, 2004). As mentioned previously, most women who work outside of the home have children under the age of 18 (National Partnership for Women and Families, 2004a), and most women with children remain in the labor force (Boushey, 2005b; Cohen & Bianchi, 1999). Whenever I am asked whether it is possible for a woman to "have it all" or to achieve "family-work balance,"

I always respond that it is the wrong question to ask. A better question is: "What could our society do to ensure that women are able to have *both* a career and family if that is what they want?" The former question focuses on individual women making individual choices; it focuses on the *personal* but not the political context. This focus can lead individuals to feel angry, frustrated, depressed, guilty, and alone as they struggle in this area. The question about what we as a society can do to support families includes the larger context and makes the question a political one. When the question is framed in a broad manner, mothers feel less isolated and realize that theirs is a common struggle. A broad frame also allows for the possibility that social policy and structural changes can provide a solution, instead of each individual mother having to find a solution that feels to her like the "best option available." Williams and Cooper (2004) discussed the constrained choices available to American mothers, especially when compared to the choices available to families in European countries. They stated that "American mothers try to make the best choices they can from a limited pool of available options; then they describe the results as reflecting their true priorities" (p. 851).

Judith Warner (2006) recently addressed this "personal vs. political" aspect of mothering in a *New York Times* column entitled "Stressing Parenthood." In it she focused on the larger social context in which mothering occurs and took issue with writings and commentaries that call the voicing of concerns by parents "complaining" or "whining." The issue is not with parenthood itself, rather the problem is with the social context in which parenting occurs. She stated:

> Not having access to decent child care or affordable health care or good quality public education is not a matter of attitude. Neither is being frustrated that you can't ever make it home for a family dinner because you can't afford to work a decent schedule or to live close enough to work to make it home at a decent hour. Talking about these problems isn't a condemnation of parenthood; it's a condemnation of the way parenthood is being lived, in our culture, at this particular time. (p. 12)

So, what would women need in order to have both careers and families without feeling guilty or feeling as if they are sacrificing in one area for another? In terms of workplace options, there are many policies that could help mothers. Paid maternity leaves could reduce the "mommy pay gap" (Boushey, 2005a), which would then have an impact on a woman's lifetime earnings. In addition, revising the tax code to include a "pay gap tax credit" could eliminate the gender wage gap and bring women's earnings in line with men's earnings (Boushey, 2004).

We also need to reexamine our definition of the "ideal worker." Higher level jobs and access to them frequently involve working long hours each week. Workers in the United States work longer hours and have less vacation time than workers in any other industrialized country (Gornick & Meyers, 2003). Overworked employees are more likely to make mistakes, to be angry at their employers, and to resent co-workers (Galinsky et al., 2005). In addition, work hours in the United States are rarely flexible and they do not coincide with school hours for children. Work-family stress would decrease if parents had flexibility in their hours so that they could attend their children's school recitals, school functions, and athletic events. Research on workplace flexibility has shown that employees with flexibility are more committed to their companies, more likely to plan to stay at a place of employment, and more satisfied with their jobs (Galinsky, Brownfield, Backon, & Friedman, 2006).

More vacation time, which workers are actually encouraged to use, would allow working parents to spend more time with their children. Many employers offer very little sick leave, and often there is no flexibility to use sick time to care for a sick child. Most daycare centers do not allow children who are sick to attend. A working parent usually needs to stay home when a child is sick, and many employers are not flexible or understanding about an employee's absence for this reason.

Increased availability and affordability of health insurance and other benefits also would help mothers and families. Many mothers work part-time, and only 17 percent of part-time workers have health benefits through their employers (Williams & Cooper, 2004).

We need to find a way to reduce the stigma attached to the use of family-friendly policies and to reduce the perception that workers who have family responsibilities are not committed to work (Hewlett & Luce, 2005). We also need to reduce the demands on male employees. Policies and biases that do not allow men to assume caregiving roles force women into those roles whether they want to assume them or not (Williams, 2000). Careerbuilder.com (2003) conducted a survey in 2003 in which 40 percent of working fathers stated their willingness to be full-time, stay-at-home fathers *if* their partner earned enough money for them to live comfortably. This study was a bit more scientific than the "opting out" anecdotal reports, yet it garnered very little media attention.

The U.S. Census Bureau (2004) estimated that there were 5.4 million stay-at-home mothers and 98,000 stay-at-home fathers. If so many fathers are willing to stay home to care for children, why aren't more of them doing it? Earlier I discussed the social stereotype of the "good mother" and the expectation that good mothers will engage in intensive mothering. The flip side to this belief is that any other caregiver is just a substitute, and one that is second-best (Hays, 1996). This includes fathers. This assumption means that they will continue to be seen as "helping" to care for their children and "helping" in household tasks. It is going to be difficult to get parents and employers to consider fathers as primary caregivers if we continue to equate "good mother" with intensive mothering. In addition, we need to consider the context in which couples make decisions about who will stay home to care for the children, if this is an option they can afford. I will come back to this point.

Finally, we come to the issue of childcare. As a country, we are ambivalent about this issue, which leads to inadequate availability of care, low quality of much of the care that is available, and problems in regulating and subsidizing the cost of care (Williams & Cooper, 2004). This is in contrast to many European countries, which view childcare as a social investment; these countries frequently have public childcare centers for *all* children, not just for lower income children, which could improve the public perception of child care (Williams & Cooper).

In the United States, most families use one of six types of childcare: (1) parental care, which involves the child being cared for by a parent, guardian, or stepparent at home or at work; (2) relative care, which involves care by a relative, including siblings 15 years of age or older; (3) family daycare, which is care by someone who is a relative away from the child's home; (4) nanny or sitter care, which is non-relative care in the child's home; (5) formal daycare, which is care in a daycare center, nursery, preschool, or Head Start program; and (6) self-care or sibling care, which involves a child caring for him/herself or being cared for by a sibling younger than the age of 15 (Boushey, 2003). It is difficult to estimate the cost of paid daycare because data often include all types of paid care. One estimate published by the U.S. House of Representatives (2004) gives a range for paid daycare at $50–81 per week, depending on household income. Keep in mind that these are medians and include all types of paid care. Formal daycare is generally more reliable and higher quality care (Boushey, 2003) and the most expensive. In major cities in the United States, many parents who have their children in nationally accredited formal childcare centers full-time can pay $17,000 for an infant per year and $14,000 per year for a toddler.

Daycare centers often experience high rates of staff turnover. On average, childcare workers, over 98 percent of whom are women, earn $265 a week, which is less than amusement park attendants, car washers, and pest control workers (National Committee on Pay Equity, 2001). Such a low wage, which translates to $13,780 per year, sends a message about the value we place on childcare. And what is the impact of low wages and high staff turnover on the quality of care that children receive?

Now that I have covered some workplace changes that likely would help mothers, what do women need at home in order to freely make a choice about career and/or mothering? One issue that needs to be included in a discussion of women and mothering is housework. Domestic work in the home is important; someone has to make sure that clothes are clean and food is available. If these things are done, one can pursue other types of work. Although these tasks are important, and even essential, to the functioning of our economy, they certainly are not valued or rewarded psychologically or monetarily. In the first issue of *Ms.* magazine, Judy Syfers (1972) wrote a humorous and now classic essay entitled "Why I Want a Wife." After including a laundry listing of tasks related to childcare, house cleaning, socializing, and attending to the sexual and emotional needs of a partner, she concludes: "My God, who wouldn't want a wife?" (p. 56).

In *The Second Shift*, Arlie Russell Hochschild (1989) documented that women in dual-career households work a "second shift" when they come home and have to attend to household and childcare tasks. This shift, for the most part, was not shared by male partners. It probably will not be a surprise to learn that women still do the majority of housework in this country, although the number of hours spent doing house-work has declined due to reliance on purchased goods (e.g., take-out dinners), mechanical aids such as dishwashers, and lowered standards of acceptability of neatness (e.g., not ironing every day and not iron-ing everything). Although men in heterosexual couples are doing more housework than they once did, findings show that tasks are still segre-gated by gender; women do "core" tasks, and men do episodic tasks (Bianchi, Milkie, Sayer, & Robinson, 2000). For example, a woman may be more likely to cook dinner, and a man may be more likely to cut the grass. Dinner is needed every day and cannot be skipped for a few days, whereas cutting the lawn is only done seasonally and can be put off for a day or two.

In addition to negotiating the division of labor for domestic tasks, parents need to work out how they care for their children. No matter how egalitarian a couple is before they have children, many couples find that having a child marks a shift toward a more gender-based division of labor (e.g., Cowan & Cowan, 1998). Francine Deutsch (2001, p. 25), who has written extensively about egalitarian parenting, stated that "Cou-ples become equal or unequal in working out the details: who makes children's breakfasts, changes their diapers, kisses their boo-boos, takes off from work when they are sick, and teaches them to ride bikes." The choices couples make in each of these examples are influenced by their internalized images of motherhood and fatherhood, by social messages about the ways mothers and fathers are supposed to behave, and by gen-der stereotypes in the workplace (e.g., Is it considered acceptable for dad to take time off when a child is sick?). In one study, researchers (Milkie, Bianchi, Mattingly, & Robinson, 2002) looked at couples' ideals about pa-rental involvement in childcare and the actual amount of care parents believed they provided. Most participants stated that parenting should be shared between mothers and fathers. When asked about their *actual* involvement, however, mothers perceived fathers to be less involved than the fathers believed themselves to be. Large gaps between the ideal and actual level of father involvement were related to mothers feeling higher levels of stress and increased feelings that things were unfair in their households. Another study (Ross & Van Willigen, 1996) showed that mothers were more likely than fathers to be angry and that this anger increased with each child. The researchers hypothesized that there are two types of stressors associated with parenthood (i.e., economic strains and stress associated with childcare) and that social inequalities at home result in increased feelings of anger. Mothers are exposed to both of these stressors at higher levels than fathers. In fact, mothers in that study were angrier when there was more economic and childcare stress (e.g., arranging and paying for childcare).

Researchers have also looked at gender differences in the quantity and quality of free time in heterosexual couples. Married heterosexual women experience less "uncontaminated free time" than married men do, largely because mothers more often than fathers have sole responsibility for children during their "free time" (Mattingly & Bianchi, 2003). It is no surprise that women experience less benefit from their free time than men do. Married heterosexual fathers now spend more time in childcare activities than was the case in the past, although they still spend less time with children than mothers do (Sayer, Bianchi, & Robinson, 2004). Furthermore, single mothers do not differ from married mothers in the amount of time they spend with their children (Bianchi & Robinson, 1997). And there is no difference between employed mothers and full-time, stay-at-home mothers in the amount of time they spend with their children (Bianchi & Robinson). Despite popular belief, both mothers and fathers reported spending more time with their children in the 1990s than they did in the 1960s (Sayer et al., 2004).

Researchers (Sayer et al., 2004) looked at diary data collected in large national surveys over four decades and found that, in 1965, mothers reported spending 80 minutes per day on primary childcare (e.g., providing medical care, dressing a child, changing diapers) and 10 minutes on teaching and playing activities (e.g., talking, reading, playing). In 1998, mothers reported spending 95 minutes per day on primary childcare and 24 minutes on teaching and playing activities. They also looked at the time diaries of fathers and found that fathers reported spending 17 minutes per day on primary childcare in 1965 and 51 minutes in 1998. In 1965, fathers reported spending 7 minutes a day on teaching and playing activities, and this increased to 20 minutes per day in 1998. This increase in time spent with children has come during a time of increased maternal participation in the labor force, increased single parenting, and increased parental education (Sayer et al.), but also during a time of decreased family size. The researchers suggested that this increase in time spent with children, and in particular the increase in the time fathers spend on childcare, reflects a move toward the ideal of shared parenting.

All of these issues come together to provide the context in which women are making a "choice" about pursuing a career versus staying at home with children. So, are women choosing to stay home because they really want to and that is their first preference? Or are they staying home because they are facing workplace discrimination, lower wages due to a "mommy gap," lack of opportunities for promotion, inflexible and un-family-friendly policies and attitudes in the workplace, the high cost of childcare, which may or may not be of high quality, and work that is not personally fulfilling? Do heterosexual couples look at all of this and then decide it just makes more "sense" for the mother to stay home? Is this really a *free* choice? Crosby, Williams, and Biernat (2004, p. 678) had this to say:

> Concerning the conservatives' arguments that a mother's disadvantaged workplace position reflects personal choice rather than discrimination, feminist lawyers have responded that choice and discrimination are not mutually exclusive. That a slave chooses to obey his master rather than to attempt to break away tells us little about the slave's preferences for slavery over freedom . . . Similarly, mothers' choices are framed within a discriminatory system.

WHERE DO WE GO FROM HERE?

I believe that we must begin to challenge the images of mothers in our society. Who do we see as mothers? For the most part, we see White, middle-class, heterosexual women. We make mothers of Color, lower socioeconomic status (SES) mothers, adoptive mothers, stepmothers, lesbian mothers, and homeless mothers invisible through portrayals in the media, through our social policies, and through our discussions of the issues mothers face. We need all mothers to be visible in our culture. We need to challenge when mothers are being blamed automatically and without question, and we need to ask why it is acceptable to laugh at how mothers are portrayed.

We need to start working on better social policy that includes *all* families. We need better work policies that are family-friendly and that truly support mothers and families. We need to question gender bias in the workplace. We need more and better affordable childcare. We need to socialize children in such a way that they do not think about housework and nurturing as things that only women do.

Williams and Cooper (2004) proposed 19 different policy changes that would benefit mothers and families. Some of the suggested changes include limiting the workweek to 35 hours, as France has done (Gornick & Meyers, 2003), making family and medical leave paid, increasing subsidies for childcare and funding for after-school care, and giving employers tax incentives to adopt flexible workplace policies.

Attitudes toward women's expanding social roles have changed over the years, as both men's and women's attitudes have become more egalitarian. A survey (Radcliffe Public Policy Center, 2000) conducted in the year 2000 asked people about the importance of different characteristics of a job. For the first time, more men rated having a work schedule that allows for family time higher in importance (79 percent) than being challenged by work (76 percent), being paid a high salary (46 percent), or having a high-prestige job (27 percent). In addition, the majority of men and women (82 percent and 86 percent) believed that family-friendly work schedules are important. In a different survey (Bond, Thompson, Galinsky, & Prottas, 2003), 42 percent of men reported that women's appropriate role was to take care of the home and the children. The good news is that this was down from 77 percent of respondents in 1977.

DEFINING FEMINIST MOTHERING

I began this lecture with two quotes about mothering, feminism, and the women's movement. It is difficult to find a definition of "feminist mothering," although many feminist mothers have written about their experiences and how their identities as feminists have shaped how they are mothers to their children. How does an individual woman's identity as a feminist shape her views on mothering?

> Fiona Joy Green (2000) interviewed feminist mothers and described them this way: Driven by their feminist consciousness, their intense love for their children, and the need to be true to themselves, their families, and their parenting, feminist mothers choose to parent in ways that challenge the status quo. Within their domain of mothering, they actively engage their children in the skill of critical thinking . . . They use entertainment, the media, news, and the lived experiences of friends and acquaintances as instances to talk about the ways in which people are oppressed by racism, class bias, sexism, homophobia, and notions of ability . . . Feminist mothers believe that one of the biggest contributions they make to feminism is in raising children who are socialized and taught to be critically conscious. To effectively challenge patriarchy and other forms of domination, people must be aware that we belong to a community of humans who are oppressed, in various ways, because of interlocking systems that devalue and divide people from each other, thus creating fear and hatred. (p. 2)

For me, a feminist perspective on the issue of mothering also means that we focus on the collective efforts and experiences of mothers. We focus on framing our personal experiences as political issues, and we challenge the system to change. Systems-level change will reduce the isolation and guilt that many women feel and will finally allow mothers in this country to *freely* choose how to balance career and family.

With all of this, what is my own personal take on mothering? For me, the experience of being a mother is best explained in this way: The highs are higher than I thought they would be, and the lows are lower than expected. I adore my son, and he has brought great joy into my life. Yet I cannot make him my entire life, and I cannot sacrifice my sense of self to be *only* his mother. I love being *his mother*, yet I detest and resist the construction of motherhood in our society and the pressure and emotions it creates for me (e.g., guilt, worry that I am not doing it "right"). I resent having my goals, accomplishments, and competence called into question or overlooked because of my role as mother. I am Dr. Hall at work, yet I am often called "Mom" at his daycare center and at the pediatrician's office. I often have to remind the daycare and health-care staff that I have studied child psychology extensively, as they seem to assume that as a mother, I do not know much about children. I miss my pre-mothering days and the freedom I had, for example, the ability to sleep whenever I wanted and for as long as I wanted. And yet nothing would make me wish to go back to the time in my life before my son was born. Adrienne Rich (1976) first wrote about the complexity of motherhood as both an empowering and an oppressive experience for women.

Her words are still true today; motherhood is both an experience and an institution. The joy I feel with my son and my enjoyment in caring for him are private, empowering experiences. How much control I have in making decisions when it comes to my body and reproductive and birthing freedom, the questioning of my commitment or ability because of my role as a mother, and constraints such as the availability of high-quality, affordable childcare are part of the larger institution of our larger society and are oppressive and limiting.

I am lucky in that my male partner is an equal partner when it comes to parenting. He changes half the diapers, feeds our son breakfast each morning and dinner half the time, gives our son his baths each night, shares in discipline, and alternates time off with me when our son is sick or when the daycare is closed due to weather, staff training days, or holidays such as Columbus Day. How others think about the roles of mothers and fathers has also had an impact on him. For example, I needed to return to work before our daycare center had an open availability (after being on a waiting list since midway through my pregnancy). My partner asked his employer about taking time off from his job for three weeks, while I returned to work part-time for a few weeks, so that we could cover childcare until the daycare "spot" was open. My partner was told that the Family Medical Leave Act only applied to mothers who had given birth, which is incorrect. He had to be persistent to get the *unpaid* leave time that he was entitled to under the law. Another example is that we have had to tell the staff at the daycare center repeatedly that they should call my partner at work when they cannot reach me. In three years the staff has yet to do this. Apparently, they believe it is acceptable to interrupt me at work, but they hesitate to interrupt him.

My feminism informs my struggle as a mother. I hope that these struggles as a nontraditional couple help to inform others about the possible roles mothers and fathers can play. Because of my feminism, I think that raising a son to be aware of issues of discrimination and oppression is very important work. But it is not my only work. The choices I make for him, from the selection of a daycare center to the books and clothing I buy, are guided by my feminist principles. I am hopeful that feminist mothers can make a difference to society as a result of their mothering choices with their children and the values they instill in them. But individuals working in isolation from one another can only accomplish so much. What we need is another movement, this time focused on the needs of mothers and families. I think the time has come. I hope you will join me to make it happen.

REFERENCES

AMERICAN COLLEGE OF OBSTETRICIANS AND GYNECOLOGISTS (ACOG). (2004). Vaginal birth after previous cesarean delivery. *Obstetrics and Gynecology, 104,* 203–212.

ANDERSON, D. J., BINDER, M., & KRAUSE, K. (2002). The motherhood wage penalty: Which mothers pay it and why? *The American Economic Review, 92,* 354–358.

BARNETT, R. C. (2004). Women and work: Where are we, where did we come from, and where are we going? *Journal of Social Issues, 60,* 667–674.

BIANCHI, S. M., MILKIE, M. A., SAYER, L. C., & ROBINSON, J. P. (2000). Is anyone doing the housework? Trends in the gender division of household labor. *Social Forces, 79,* 191–228.

BIANCHI, S., & ROBINSON, J. (1997). What did you do today? Children's use of time, family composition, and the acquisition of social capital. *Journal of Marriage and the Family, 59,* 332–344.

BIELBY, W. T., & BIELBY, D. D. (1989). Family ties: Balancing commitments to work and family in dual-earner households. *American Sociological Review, 54,* 776–789.

BLADES, J., & ROWE-FINKBEINER, K. (2006). *The motherhood manifesto: What America's moms want and what to do about it.* New York: Nation Books.

BOND, J. T., THOMPSON, C., GALINSKY, E., & PROTTAS, D. (2003). *Highlights of the 2002 national study of the changing workforce* (No. 3). New York: Families and Work Institute.

BOS, H. M. W., VAN BALEN, F., & VAN DEN BOOM, D. C. (2005). Lesbian families and family functioning: An overview. *Patient Education and Counseling, 59,* 263–275.

BOUSHEY, H. (2003). *Who cares? The child care choices of working mothers* [Data Brief No. 1]. Washington, DC: Center for Economic and Policy Research.

BOUSHEY, H. (2004, April 20). The pay gap tax credit [Electronic version]. *Boston Globe.* Retrieved February 22, 2006, from http://www.cepr.net/columns/boushey/2004_04_20.htm

BOUSHEY, H. (2005a, April 6). *Family-friendly policies: Boosting mothers' wages.* Washington, DC: Center for Economic and Policy Research.

BOUSHEY, H. (2005b). *Are women opting out? Debunking the myth.* Washington, DC: Center for Economic and Policy Research.

BUDIG, M. J., & ENGLAND, P. (2001). The wage penalty for motherhood. *American Sociological Review, 66,* 204–225.

BUHIMSCHI, C. S., & BUHIMSCHI, I. A. (2006). Advantages of vaginal delivery. *Clinical Obstetrics and Gynecology, 49,* 167–183.

CAPLAN, P. (2000). *Don't blame mother: Mending the mother-daughter relationship.* New York: Routledge.

CAREERBUILDER.COM (2003). Careerbuilder.com survey shows 40 percent of working fathers willing to relinquish breadwinner role. Press release retrieved September 1, 2006, from http://www.careerbuilder.com/share/aboutus/pr/2003/061003.htm?cbRecursionCnt=1&cbsid=279d154f0b414e5ab4c6d11442450e8a-211892250-tr-4

COHEN, P. N., & BIANCHI, S. M. (1999, December). Marriage, children, and women's employment: What do we know? *Monthly Labor Review,* 22–31.

CONSUMER REPORTS. (2005, November 30). Twelve surgeries you may be better off without [Electronic version]. Retrieved February 27, 2005 from http://www.consumerreports.org/mg/free-highlights/manage-your-health/needless_surgeries.htm#citation2

CORRELL, S., & BENARD, S. (2005, August). *Getting a job: Is there a motherhood penalty?* Paper presented at the meeting of the American Sociological Association, Philadelphia, PA.

COUGHLIN, L. (2005). ACOG recommendations for fetal heart rate monitoring. *American Family Physician, 72,* 527.

COWAN, C. P., & COWAN, P. A. (1998). *When partners become parents: The big life change for couples.* New York: Basic Books.

CRITTENDEN, A. (2001). *The price of motherhood: Why the most important job in the world is still the least valued.* New York: Henry Holt and Company.

CROSBY, F. J., WILLIAMS, J. C. & BIERNAT, M. (2004). The maternal wall. *Journal of Social Issues, 60,* 675–682.

CUDDY, A. J., FISKE, S. T., & GLICK, P. (2004). When professionals become mothers, warmth doesn't cut the ice. *Journal of Social Issues, 60,* 701–718.

DEUTSCH, F. M. (2001). Equally shared parenting. *Current Directions in Psychological Science, 10,* 25–28.

DIQUINZIO, P. (1999). *The impossibility of motherhood: Feminism, individualism, and the problem of mothering.* New York: Routledge.

EQUAL EMPLOYMENT OPPORTUNITY COMMISSION (EEOC). (2006). Pregnancy Discrimination. Retrieved February 16, 2006, from http://www.eeoc.gov/stats/pregnanc.html

FLEMING, A. (2002). Baby goes buy buy. *Insight on the news.* Retrieved February 16, 2006, from http://www.findarticles.com/p/articles/mi_m1571/is_28_18/ai_90307302

GALINSKY, E., BOND, J. T., KIM, S. S., BACKON, L., BROWNFIELD, E., & SAKAI, K. (2005). *Overwork in America: When the way we work becomes too much.* New York: Families and Work Institute.

GALINSKY, E., BROWNFIELD, E., BACKON, L., & FRIEDMAN, D. E. (2006). *When work works: Workplace flexibility: A guide for employees.* Retrieved March 1, 2006, from http://familiesandwork.org/3w/tips/downloads/employees.pdf

GOLOMBOK, S. (2000). *Parenting: What really counts?* London: Routledge.

GORNICK, J. C., & MEYERS, M. K. (2003). *Families that work: Policies for reconciling parenthood and employment.* New York: Russell Sage Foundation.

GRADY, D. (2004, November 29). Repeat caesareans becoming harder to avoid. *New York Times.* Retrieved March 1, 2006, from http://www.ican-online.org/news/news.php

GREEN, F. J. (2000, Spring). Some realities of being a self-identified feminist mother [Electronic version]. *Birth Issues, 14*(4). Retrieved February 21, 2006, from http://www.asac.ab.ca/BI_spring00/selfidfem.html

HAYS, S. (1996). *The cultural contradictions of motherhood.* New Haven, CT: Yale University Press.

HEWLETT, S. A., & LUCE, C. B. (2005). Off-ramps and on-ramps: Keeping talented women on the road to success. *Harvard Business Review, 83*(3), 43–54.

HOCHSCHILD, A. R. (1989). *The second shift: Working parents and the revolution at home.* New York: Viking.

HOFFNUNG, M. (2004). Wanting it all: Career, marriage, and motherhood during college-educated women's 20s. *Sex Roles, 50,* 711–723.

HOOK, M. (2004, Winter). Blame it on mother! *Feminist Psychologist, 32,* 11.

HOOKS, B. (2000). *Feminist theory: From margin to center.* Cambridge, MA: South End Press.

JOHNSTON, D. D., & SWANSON, D. H. (2004). Moms hating moms: The internalization of mother war rhetoric. *Sex Roles, 51,* 497–509.

KOBRYNOWICZ, D., & BIERNAT, M. (1997). Decoding subjective evaluations: How stereotypes provide shifting standards. *Journal of Experimental Social Psychology, 33,* 579–601.

KUHN, J. (2004, Fall). Feminism and childbirth (part 1). *Feminist Psychologist, 31,* 9.

MARCH OF DIMES. (2002). International comparisons—infant mortality rates: 2002. Retrieved February 27, 2006, from http://www.marchofdimes.com/peristats/iim.aspx

MARTIN, J. A., HAMILTON, B. E., MENACKER, F., SUTTON, P. D., & MATHEWS, T. J. (2005). Preliminary births for 2004: Infant and maternal health. Hyattsville, MD: National Center for Health Statistics.

MATTINGLY, M. J., & BIANCHI, S. M. (2003). Gender differences in the quantity and quality of free time: The U.S. experience. *Social Forces, 81,* 999–1030.

MILKIE, M. A., BIANCHI, S. M., MATTINGLY, M. J., & ROBINSON, J. P. (2002). Gendered division of childrearing: Ideals, realities, and the relationship to parental well-being. *Sex Roles, 47,* 21–38.

NATIONAL COMMITTEE ON PAY EQUITY. (2001). Profile of the gender wage gap by selected occupations for the year 2000. Retrieved February 28, 2006, from http://www.pay-equity.org

NATIONAL COMMITTEE ON PAY EQUITY. (2006). The wage gap over time: In real dollars, women see a continuing gap. Retrieved February 28, 2006, from http://www.pay-equity.org

NATIONAL PARTNERSHIP FOR WOMEN AND FAMILIES. (2004a). Women at work: Looking behind the numbers: 40 years after the Civil Rights Act of 1964. Retrieved March 5, 2006, from http://www.nationalpartnership.org/portals/p3/library/CivilRightsAffAction/WomenAtWorkCRA40thAnnReport.pdf

NATIONAL PARTNERSHIP FOR WOMEN AND FAMILIES. (2004b). The pregnancy discrimination act: 25 years later—pregnancy discrimination persists. Retrieved February 27, 2006, from http://www.nationalpartnership.org/portals/p3/library/WorkplaceDiscrimination/Pregnancy25thAnnivFacts.pdf

NATIONAL WOMEN'S LAW CENTER. (2005, November). The pharmacy refusal project. Retrieved February 17, 2006, from http://www.nwlc.org/details.cfm?id=2185&section=health

PAUL, A. M. (2006, February 17). Pregnancy remains heavy load for working women. *Women's eNews.* Retrieved February 17, 2006, from http://www.womensenews.org/article.cfm/dyn/aid/2639

RADCLIFFE PUBLIC POLICY CENTER. (2000). *Life's work: Generational attitudes toward work and life integration.* Cambridge, MA: Radcliffe Institute for Advanced Study.

RICE, J. K., & ELSE-QUEST, N. (2005). The mixed messages of motherhood. In J. Worrell & C. D. Goodheart (Eds.), *Handbook of girls and women's psychological health* (pp. 339–349). Oxford: Oxford University Press.

RICH, A. (1976). *Of woman born: Motherhood as experience and institution.* New York: Norton.

RILEY, C. (1988). American kinship: A lesbian account. *Feminist Issues, 8,* 75–94.

ROBINSON, P., XU, X., KEETON, K., FENNER, D., JOHNSON, T. R. B., & RANSOM, S. (2005). The impact of medical legal risk on obstetrician-gynecologist supply. *Obstetrics and Gynecology, 105,* 1296–1302.

ROSS, C. E., & VAN WILLIGEN, M. (1996). Gender, parenthood, and anger. *Journal of Marriage and the Family, 58,* 572–584.

RUSSO, N. F. (1976). The motherhood mandate. *Journal of Social Issues, 32,* 143–154.

SAYER, L. C., BIANCHI, S. M., & ROBINSON, J. P. (2004). Are parents investing less in children? Trends in mothers' and fathers' time with children. *American Journal of Sociology, 110,* 1–43.

STORY, L. (2005, September 20). Many women at elite colleges set career path to motherhood. *New York Times,* pp. A1, A18.

SYFERS, J. (1972, Spring). Why I want a wife. *Ms.*, (1), 56. Retrieved on March 7, 2006, from http://www.cwluherstory.com/CWLUArchive/wantawife.html

U.S. CENSUS BUREAU. (2004). "Stay-at-home" parents top 5 million, Census Bureau reports. Press release retrieved September 1, 2006, from http://www.census.gov/Press-Release/www/releases/archives/families_households/003118.html

U.S. HOUSE OF REPRESENTATIVES (2004, January). *2004 Green book: Background material and data on programs within the jurisdiction of the committee on ways and means.* Retrieved March 1, 2006, from http://waysandmeans.house.gov/media/pdf/greenbook2004/section9.pdf

WALDFOGEL, J. (1997). The effect of children on women's wages. *American Sociological Review, 62*, 209–217.

WALDFOGEL, J. (1998). Understanding the "family gap" in pay for women with children. *Journal of Economic Perspectives, 12*, 137–156.

WARNER, J. (2006, July 16). Stressing parenthood [Electronic version]. *New York Times,* Section 4, p. 12. Retrieved September 1, 2006, from http://query.nytimes.com/gst/fullpage.html?sec=health&res=9C0CE7DB1F30F935A25754C0A9609C8B63

WILLIAMS, J. (2000). *Unbending gender.* Oxford: Oxford University Press.

WILLIAMS, J. C., & COOPER, H. C. (2004). The public policy of motherhood. *Journal of Social Issues, 60*, 849–865.

WILLIAMS, J. C., & SEGAL, N. (2003). Beyond the maternal wall: Relief for family caregivers who are discriminated against on the job. *Harvard Women's Law Journal, 26*, 77–162.

WOLF, N. (2003). *Misconceptions: Truth, lies, and the unexpected on the journey to motherhood.* New York: Doubleday.

WORKLIFE LAW. (2006). http://www.uchastings.edu/?pid=3624

WORLD HEALTH ORGANIZATION. (1985). Appropriate technology for birth. *Lancet, 2*, 436–437.

SUGGESTED READINGS

BLADES, J., & ROWE-FINKBEINER, K. (2006). *The motherhood manifesto: What America's moms want and what to do about it.* New York: Nation Books.

CRITTENDEN, A. (2001). *The price of motherhood: Why the most important job in the world is still the least valued.* New York: Henry Holt and Company.

DOUGLAS, S. J., & MICHAELS, M. W. (2004). *The mommy myth: The idealization of motherhood and how it has undermined women.* New York: Simon & Schuster.

WILLIAMS, J. (2000). *Unbending gender: Why family and work conflict and what to do about it.* Oxford: Oxford University Press.

RECOMMENDED INTERNET RESOURCES

Moms Rising: http://www.momsrising.org
Mothers Movement Online: http://www.mothersmovement.org.

*S*usan Basow *is Charles A. Dana Professor at Lafayette College, where she helped to found the Women's Studies program. Dr. Basow has taught courses on the psychology of gender since 1974 and is the author of the textbook* Gender: Stereotypes and Roles. *She has also published the results of many of her studies of gender issues in course evaluations and of women and their bodies.*

6

Gender Socialization, Or How Long a Way Has Baby Come?

❖

W hen I gave birth to my daughter in 1980, I was vigilant about protecting her from gender-restrictive messages. I monitored her presents (clothes, toys), books (changing pronouns to be gender balanced or non-stereotypic), and prohibited television except for a few PBS programs. It was an uphill battle, and I appreciated the few non-stereotypic products available. I was particularly happy to have *Free to Be. . . You and Me* in audiotape (Thomas, 1972), and my daughter and I endlessly listened to the brave exploits of Atalanta, related to William's desire for a doll, and laughed at the girly-girl whose insistence on "Ladies first!" led to her demise. I dreamed of how much easier future parents would have it as they tried to rear non-gender-stereotypic children. I was wrong. In this lecture, we will review the current research on gender socialization at different developmental stages. The overall conclusion: Despite some changes in messages aimed at girls, gender stereotypes are alive and well.

WHAT IS GENDER SOCIALIZATION?

The socialization of gender results from an interaction between social influences from parents, media, peers, and books, and the simultaneous development of a mental self-schema through which children organize their representations

I want to acknowledge the research contributions made to this chapter by Alexandra M. Minieri, Lafayette College class of 2007, through the auspices of our EXCEL Scholars Program.

of the world. As Bussey and Bandura (1999) noted in their review of the literature:

> Gender development is a fundamental issue because some of the most important aspects of people's lives, such as the talents they cultivate, the conceptions they hold of themselves and others, the sociostructural opportunities and constraints they encounter, and the social life and occupational paths they pursue are heavily prescribed by societal gender typing. (p. 676)

The major mode of influence through which gendered information is communicated to children is modeling, or vicarious learning (Bussey & Bandura, 1999). Children observe the outcomes experienced by others (e.g., parents; other adults; peers; characters in storybooks, films, and television) for "appropriate" and "inappropriate" behavior, and combine this information with what they are told directly about the likely consequences of behaving in a manner different from that expected for their sex. After having been exposed to many behavioral possibilities, children are most likely to perform those behaviors that produce valued outcomes. Because traditional gendered behavior is most highly rewarded, especially for boys, children will model same-sex individuals and their behaviors. The experience of observing the outcomes of others' gendered behavior as well as one's own, helps the child to form a gender schema, a cognitive framework that guides information processing and regulates behavior by defining what is appropriate and what should be avoided for the self-identified gender. Children's judgments are extremely categorical, so new information to which children are exposed from parents, other adults, the media, school, peers, and books will be sorted into the dichotomy of gender developed in the child's schema, thereby influencing his/her perception of self as well as of the world.

For example, my daughter was always physically beautiful. Strangers on the street as well as family members and friends repeatedly commented upon her beauty, frequently suggesting that she model or become "Miss America." What my daughter learned from this was not only that people liked *her* looks, but that looks were important for girls, something that brought a girl positive attention and power. To this day, she takes great pride in her appearance, and it is a core component of her sense of self as well as gender.

Let's now examine what other gender messages children receive during the early years of their development.

INFANTS AND TODDLERS

In the popular television show *Friends* from the 1990s, a baby boy is born to two of the characters, Ross and Carol. In one scene, Ross stares bewildered at his ex-wife as she enters his apartment carrying their infant son; his eyes are focused on the Barbie doll in the child's hand. After she leaves, Ross expresses his disappointment to his male friends and his son;

he suggests other toys to the young boy, such as a Monster truck. When the boy continues to embrace the Barbie, Ross finds a GI Joe action figure and creates an elaborate scenario to distract the boy in order to remove the Barbie. When Carol returns, she questions the change in toy, and Ross explains that the child would rather play with the "boy toys."

When a child is born, it is immediately labeled a "boy" or a "girl" based on its genitalia, a label that will define the expectations and responses of others throughout its life (Basow, 2006). Parents influence the gender identity of their children from the very beginning of development by the ways in which they structure the children's environment and react to the children's activities. Infants are highly attentive to modeling influences, so they easily will learn the ways they are expected to behave from reinforcing responses made by their parents, as Ross's child undoubtedly would. Although most research on parenting has focused on mothers, fathers also have an influence. In fact, as shown in the Ross example, fathers appear to enforce gender stereotypes even more than do mothers (Basow, 2006; Bussey & Bandura, 1999), perhaps because of their own stricter gendered upbringing or because they tend to interact less personally with their children.

Even when there is no objective difference in size or activity level, parents of newborn girls rate them as finer featured, weaker, softer, and more delicate than parents rate their newborn boys. In a study of mothers, Mondschein, Adolph, and Tamis-LeMonda (2000) found different expectations about their children's crawling abilities based on their child's sex despite the fact that the participating children began crawling at equivalent ages and were equally likely to have gone down playground slides and climbed up and down household stairs. Compared to the mothers of girls, mothers of boys expected their infants to be more successful at descending steep slopes and more likely to attempt risky slopes. Overall, mothers expected their daughters to fail when the probability of success was 100 percent, such as when crawling down a slope with a slight decline; in contrast, mothers expected their sons to succeed when the probability of success was 0 percent, such as when crawling down a very steep slope. The differences in the responses of the mothers reflect prevalent cultural stereotypes that girls are weaker, more timid, and not as motorically competent as are boys.

More direct studies of how mothers interact with their infants and toddlers confirm that these interactions differ for girls and boys. For example, when the speech and play behavior of mothers with infants between 6 and 14 months were examined, mothers were found to interact and converse more with their daughters than their sons (Clearfield & Nelson, 2006). Furthermore, the types of verbal behaviors differed; mothers of girls made more interpretations, and mothers of boys gave more instructions. For example, a mother might say to her daughter, "You're playing with the octopus; you like that, right?", whereas to her son she might just say, "That's an octopus." Reviews of the literature consistently find that mothers talk to their daughters more than to their sons (Bussey & Bandura, 1999; Leaper, Anderson, & Sanders, 1998). These maternal behaviors, not based initially on gender differences in the children's own behaviors, may eventually lead to gender differences in the children's relational and independent behaviors.

Parents provide toys for their children that function to define a child's appropriate role based on his or her specified gender. Sons are given more toys overall, especially educational materials, machines, vehicles, and sports equipment, whereas daughters are supplied with baby dolls, doll houses, domestic items, and room furnishings (such as bedspreads) with ruffles and floral motifs (Basow, 2006; Bussey & Bandura, 1999). These toys orient boys to occupations that are performed outside of the home and girls to future activities inside the home, especially domestic roles. Parents also indicate approval or disapproval for gender-related behavior through their facial and verbal expressions, as we saw in Ross's reactions to his son's doll. Infants and toddlers rely on these cues to determine which behaviors are acceptable. Gender-stereotyped play is apparent when children are between 15 and 35 months old, and boys' preferences are evident at an earlier age than girls' (O'Brien & Huston, 1985). Boys can be found playing with masculine toys (trucks, tools) more than either neutral or feminine toys (dolls), and girls, though not as exclusively, play most often with toys stereotyped for their own gender.

PRESCHOOL

Gender socialization messages increase during the preschool years as children are exposed to other socializing agents and forces besides their parents. In particular, the media (e.g., television commercials, cartoons), books, games/toys, as well as peers take up an increasing part of a child's life. Parents, of course, continue to exert gender socialization pressures. For example, parents of 3-year-old children worry that their sons, but not their daughters, are underweight, even when weights and body mass indexes are basically identical (Holm-Denoma et al., 2005). These same parents believe that their daughters, but not their sons, eat enough food, a belief that may lead to a struggle around food between parent and daughter that could eventually lead to disordered eating. Parents also interact with their sons and daughters differently, and both sexes learn to associate more contained forms of play that include imagination with girls and more active play with boys (Lindsey & Mize, 2001). Parents also are more likely to purchase gender-traditional toys than gender-nontraditional toys, even when the child requests a counter-stereotypical toy (Bussey & Bandura, 1999). This is especially true for boys, because the masculine gender role is stricter and more highly valued. Toy advertisements usually encourage such gender-stereotypic purchases. Girls are most likely to be depicted playing with dolls, doll accessories, makeup, kitchen paraphernalia, and other toy-analogs for domestic activities. Thus, I should not have been surprised that my daughter's friends brought her birthday presents when she turned 5 years old that consisted entirely of Barbie paraphernalia and a makeup set, despite the fact that she never expressed a desire for any of these items. All of these "toys" imply that girls should be concerned with appearance and caretaking, above all else. In contrast, boys in advertisements typically are depicted in more active play and provided with toy-analogs of construction, transportation, and military equipment (Rivers & Barnett, 2005). For example, in a Target circular during the 2005 holiday season, a young boy adorned in a Santa hat smiled widely on the cover while holding two video games and surrounded by electronic toys. No girls were in sight.

There is some variation in the gender messages transmitted by parents to children as a function of race/ethnicity and social class (Basow, 2006). For example, in interviews with 35 African American parents, Hill (2002) found that those from the middle class were more likely than their European American counterparts to transmit and to model messages about gender equality. In contrast, parents from working-class backgrounds, both African American and European American, tend to convey stronger messages about gender inequality and to be especially unlikely to encourage sons to engage in any traditional feminine activities.

Television is another powerful source of gender messages and gender socialization. Children begin watching television typically between 18 and 24 months, and viewing time increases during the preschool years (Bussey & Bandura, 1999). Content analyses of children's shows reveal that, although the representation of girls and women has improved since the 1970s, girls and women still are underrepresented in number and disproportionately portrayed in domestic roles and in terms of their relationships with others (Leaper, Breed, Hoffman, & Pearlman, 2002; Thompson & Zerbinos, 1995). Gender stereotypes are particularly notable in traditional adventure cartoons (e.g., *HeMan, Batman, Robotboy*), where male characters outnumber female characters 4:1, and comedies (e.g., *Tom and Jerry; Ed, Edd, and Eddy; Dexter's Laboratory*), where male characters outnumber female characters 2:1. Although there now are nontraditional adventure cartoons with a female character as the heroine and equal representation of male and female characters (e.g., *PowerPuff Girls, Dora the Explorer*), children (especially boys) prefer the traditional adventure cartoons. And even for the girls who watch nontraditional programs, traditional gender messages abound (Brown, 2003; Corcoran & Parker, 2004). For example, girls can be "tough" and "spunky" only if they're also cute, nice, and/or guided by a man. "Bad" girls are still mean and, of course, ugly. Such a contrast between "good" girls and "bad" girls frequently pits girls against each other, especially based on appearance and male approval.

Because children are most likely to attend to and identify with same-sex characters on television (Signorelli, 1990), how male and female characters in programs and commercials are portrayed matters a lot. For example, children who viewed a commercial with only boys playing with certain toys later labeled those toys as solely for boys (Pike & Jennings, 2005). This was especially true for male viewers. In contrast, when children were exposed to commercials that depicted only girls playing with the toys, a nontraditional scenario, they were more likely to claim that the toys were for both boys and girls. Unfortunately, commercials typically show a very traditional gender-stereotypic world (Ganahl, Prinsen, & Netzley, 2003).

Storybooks provide additional information to preschool-age children, especially because books usually are read numerous times. Like other socializing media, books provide role models from whom children learn what society deems acceptable for men and women in terms of behaviors and occupations. Despite an increase in the number of female characters in children's books since the 1970s, gender portrayals have remained stereotypical (Gooden & Gooden, 2001; Oskamp, Kaufman, & Wolterbeek, 1996). In general, male characters appear more frequently in the text, illustrations, and titles of children's books than female characters do, which sends a message to children that boys and men are more important than girls and women because they are more prevalent. Different adjectives are used to describe female and male characters; girls are often beautiful, frightened, worthy, sweet, weak, and scared, whereas boys are big, horrible, fierce, great, terrible, furious, brave, and proud. The traits used for male characters are potent and powerful whereas those of female characters emphasize weakness and passivity (Turner-Bowker, 1996). In terms of parental roles, fathers are dramatically underrepresented in children's books; they appear in fewer than one-half of the books examined in one recent study (Anderson & Hamilton, 2005). When present, fathers appear in one-half the number of scenes that mothers do, and they are less likely than mothers to be affectionate or caring. Children are given the clear message that the task of raising and caring for children is solely the responsibility of mothers.

Another significant problem related to children's books is that, whereas female characters may be presented in counterstereotypical ways, male characters rarely are, which implies that masculine behavior is the ideal to which everyone should strive (Diekman & Murnen, 2004). Yet when preschool children were exposed to gender-neutral or nonstereotypic books, they were more likely to view future occupations as appropriate for both men and women rather than for the stereotypic gender only (Trepanier-Street & Romatowski, 1999). This finding suggests that children could become less gender-stereotyped if exposed to more illustrations of this possibility. As it stands, girls tend to show more variability in masculine and feminine toy play before exposure to gender-counterstereotypic models and greater behavioral change after exposure (Green, Bigler, & Catherwood, 2004). Boys, however, are treated more harshly for counterstereotypic play than are girls. For example, parents of 5-year-old children viewed nontraditional play, such as truck play, from their daughters with a great deal of tolerance but were concerned if their sons showed any engagement in cross-gender behaviors, such as doll play (Sandnabba & Ahlberg, 1999). From these messages, boys recognize the lower status and value of feminine activities in relation to masculine activities and roles and have little motivation to change their behavior.

As the above findings suggest, peers also exert an influence on other preschoolers through their own behaviors and reactions. Boys worry more than girls about peer "punishment" for nontraditional-gendered behavior and, because of the restrictiveness of the masculine gender role, there are more possible role violations for boys than for girls (Bussey & Bandura, 1999; Raag, 1999). Preschool boys and girls thus often wind up playing with different toys as well as with same-sex peers; such actions are viewed more positively than cross-sex play by both peers and teachers (Colwell & Lindsey, 2005; Maccoby, 1998). Within same-sex groups, different norms develop. Tulviste and Koor (2005) found that boys use significantly more moral rules than do girls (e.g., a focus on what's "right"), probably because boys' play engenders more conflict than does girls' play. In contrast, girls use significantly more rules involving social conventions (e.g., "playing nice"). If boys and girls are forced to play together, they often adapt to the style of their partner. For example, preschool boys who are paired with girls often become more willing to seek agreement when dealing with girls than when dealing with boys (Holmes-Lonergan, 2003). Overall, however, gender differences become more pronounced with age, possibly because as children grow older they become more familiar with ways in which they believe boys and girls differ, so their schemas become more detailed with increased numbers of behaviors they associate with a specific gender.

GRADE SCHOOL

As children become older, peers become increasingly influential. When my daughter was a second-grader, she got a new lunchbox that had holographic space-suited people on it. We both thought it was "cool," but her peers taunted her that it was a "boy's" lunchbox and made fun of her mercilessly. It turned out that the characters were based on a television show, and all of the characters on the show were male. Suddenly, the cool lunchbox became uncool and was never used again. In such ways, gender boundaries are carefully monitored by "the gender police," with reinforcement for "appropriate" gendered behaviors and punishment for "inappropriate" ones.

Still, parents continue to convey gender messages, especially in the way they respond to their children's behaviors. For example, mothers tend to be more tolerant of injuries to sons than to daughters, and they focus more on safety issues with daughters and discipline issues with sons (Morrongiello & Hogg, 2004). In response to sons' misbehavior, mothers most often expressed anger, whereas disappointment and concern were the most common emotions expressed in response to daughters' misbehavior. Overall, girls are reinforced for nurturant, polite, and passive behaviors, whereas boys are expected to be adventuresome and independent (Bussey & Bandura, 1999). Children notice their parents' responses and utilize this information to help define not only what is acceptable behavior for themselves but also for boys and girls in general.

In many households, time spent watching television exceeds time spent with parents. This is especially the case when babysitters are present for long periods of time (Signorelli & Bacue, 1999). Unfortunately, there appears to be a direct correlation between the amount of time spent watching television and children's traditional gender views and their own gender conformity (Frueh & McGhee, 1975; Signorelli, 1990; Thompson & Zerbinos, 1995). Although the portrayal of female characters on television has improved since the 1970s—they are more assertive, competent, stronger, and prevalent—women still are represented predominantly in domestic roles in the television shows children watch with few opportunities to be represented outside of the home or in the workforce (Glascock, 2001; Signorelli & Bacue, 1999). When women are employed outside the home, they typically are depicted in female-dominated occupations such as nurses, secretaries, waitresses, and teachers. Another continuing trend is for the women on television to be younger and more conventionally attractive than the men, which suggests that women's value is in their subordination and appearance. Similar gender portrayals exist in television commercials; women are underrepresented and more likely to advertise household products, whereas the men have more status and credibility and are more likely to advertise nondomestic products (Bartsch, Burnett, Diller, & Rankin-Williams, 2000; Ganahl, Prinsen, & Netzley, 2003). One small improvement: women, who once comprised only 10 percent of voice-overs in commercials, now comprise 30 percent.

Television does have the potential to provide counterstereotypical messages, and such messages can impact viewers' gender attitudes. For example, Rosenwasser, Lingenfelter, and Harrington (1989) found that greater knowledge of television shows with nontraditional gender role portrayals, such as *The Cosby Show, Who's the Boss,* and *Growing Pains,* was correlated with more flexible gender role perceptions in second-graders. Other research indicates that extended exposure to nonstereotypical male and female characters on television resulted in children who were more accepting of men performing some housework and women having successful careers (Signorelli, 1990).

During grade school, children are exposed to a wide variety of activities. However, most boys and girls still engage predominantly in gender-stereotypical games and sports. For example, girls on the playground are most often seen playing hopscotch or on the jungle gym; they rarely participate in "shooting the hoop" competitions with their male peers. Since the passage of Title IX in 1973, girls' opportunities and participation in sports have increased tremendously, mainly on the high school and college level (National Women's Law Center, 2002). For example, between 1971 and 2001, high school girls' participation increased 847 percent! Despite these gains, boys still participate in sports more than girls do, and the choice of which sports are played remains gendered. The girls most likely to be involved in sports later in life, including varsity sports in college, are the ones who engage in stereotypically masculine play as a child. Unfortunately, these girls tend to be denigrated by their peers for doing so (Giuliano, Popp, & Knight, 2000).

Gender norms even affect what musical instrument a child chooses (Harrison & O'Neill, 2003). Boys, from kindergarten to fourth grade, prefer playing the drums, which produce a loud, "masculine" sound, whereas girls more often play the stereotypically softer and more delicate violin. However, when children are exposed to a counterstereotypic model, they are less likely to select a gender-typed instrument than are those exposed to a model playing a gender-stereotypic instrument (Pickering & Repacholi, 2001). As you might expect, boys were less influenced than girls by the manipulation.

The greater gender-role rigidity of boys' behaviors compared to girls' becomes even more noticeable when peers are present (Banjeree & Lintern, 2000; Blakemore, 2003). Boys who engage in cross-gender behaviors may be directly ridiculed or punished, whereas girls who engage in cross-gender behaviors more often are just ignored and allowed to continue to play. These differential reactions convey that masculine-type behavior and appearance are more socially acceptable than feminine-type behavior and appearance, which are the exclusive province of girls. Thus boys who engage in anything associated with girls are denigrated, whereas girls who engage in anything associated with boys are accepted or at least tolerated.

The school experience teaches children gender messages not only on the playground but also through the curriculum and the teachers' behavior. Teachers pay more attention to, and interact more with, male than with female students, and boys receive more praise and criticism from teachers from nursery school through elementary school (Basow, 2004; Sadker & Sadker, 1994). These patterns are most pronounced for European American students, as African American boys frequently are given even fewer opportunities to respond than are girls of any ethnicity (Ross & Jackson, 1991). Overall, however, boys tend to receive praise for academic success and criticism for misbehavior, whereas girls are praised for "tidiness and compliance" and criticized for academic failure (Bussey & Bandura, 1999). Selective reinforcement and punishment functions to increase or decrease behavior, respectively, so children may begin to view their abilities and others' expectations based on the responses of teachers. Bussey and Bandura's (1999) review of the literature suggests that differential teacher responses to boys and girls have shown little change over the past 30 years.

Textbooks are considered objective sources of information; thus, gender-stereotyping in such books teach children traditional roles as fact. A recent content analysis of grade school fiction textbooks published by

Silver Burdett Ginn and Macmillan/McGraw-Hill indicates that, although there was greater numerical equality of male and female characters in the stories contained in these textbooks in 1997 than in the past, the portrayal of gendered characters in the stories remained stereotypical (Evans & Davies, 2000). Boys and men were represented as aggressive, competitive, and assertive, three characteristics girls and women never possessed, which suggests to readers that such behaviors are inappropriate for girls. The infrequency of traditionally feminine traits in story characters (e.g., affectionate, emotionally expressive, and understanding) suggests to children that these behaviors are not acceptable or valuable for anyone. For example, in a book for fifth graders, a boy in one story wants to be in charge of a fair project. He is the biggest and raises his fist in the air toward everyone else to signify the consequences of arguing with him. Of course, no one did.

Educational software is another important source of information for children. In this realm as well there are significantly more male than female main characters, and the appearance of female characters is very stereotypic, which suggests to children that a woman's value is dependent upon her physical attractiveness (Sheldon, 2004). To the extent that counterstereotypical behavior is displayed, it is almost always displayed by female rather than male characters. For example, female characters in software programs may display competitive, explorative, and independent behaviors (along with a conventionally attractive appearance), but male characters rarely demonstrate nurturance, compassion, or emotional expressiveness. This imbalance again conveys the message that masculine behavior is more desirable than feminine behavior. The limited number of female characters with which girls can identify may inhibit them from engaging in computer play as often as boys do and might contribute to girls' lower self-efficacy and interest in computers.

Gender stereotypes also exist with respect to academic domains. Elementary school children consider girls to be more successful than boys in spelling and less successful than boys in mathematics, computer science, engineering, and the physical sciences (Heyman & Legare, 2004). This belief in girls' lesser competence in math and science makes girls less likely than boys to enroll in a math class in the future (Crombie et al., 2005). In contrast, a boy's future enrollment plans depend only upon his prior math grades. These beliefs in differential competencies of boys and girls not only influence future enrollment choices but also future career choices; thus enrollments lead to gender divisions in eventual occupations (Bussey & Bandura, 1999; Schmader, Johns, & Barquissau, 2004). For example, children express more happiness at the prospect of obtaining a gender-consistent than a gender-inconsistent occupation later in life (Levy, Sadovsky, & Troseth, 2000). Thus, gender stereotypes function to limit children's future occupational possibilities.

Although feminists over the past 30 years have critiqued the restrictiveness of gender messages for both boys and girls (e.g., AAUW, 2001; Basow, 2004), more programming has been aimed at helping girls to improve their self-confidence and math and science skills than at expanding options for boys. But many programs initially aimed to help girls also help boys as well, such as inquiry-based and interactive science instruction. Lately, however, concern has been expressed regarding how schools are failing boys (e.g., Sommers, 2000; Tyre, 2006); these concerns are based on findings that girls now are more likely than boys to do well in school, graduate high school, and attend college. Unfortunately, many of these recent critics imply that girls are doing so well because there is "a war against boys." What these writers neglect to note is that the boys who are being left behind are predominantly young Hispanic and African American boys, as well as those from low-income families. Their problems are better attributed to an overwhelmed educational system that has increased pressures on teachers and students while reducing breaks, and to boys' socialization experiences that increasingly fail to prepare them for an educational environment that requires the ability to listen, sit still, pay attention, utilize fine motor skills, and cooperate with peers (Jacobson, 2006; Koch, 2003; Warner, 2006).

SUMMARY: STILL A LONG WAY TO GO

Overall, the factors that influence the social construction of gender have not changed much over the last 30 years. Parents, especially fathers, still expect, perceive, and reinforce traditional gendered behavior in their sons and daughters, although role expectations for women and girls have expanded to include more physical and intellectual competencies. In popular and educational media, gendered depictions are still the norm, although girls and women have become relatively more prominent and can be found engaging in non-gender-stereotypical behaviors. Indeed, young women are becoming more androgynous (Twenge, 1997) in their personalities (i.e., combining both expressive and agentic traits) than young women from previous generations. Despite (or because) of this expansion of role expectations for girls, the emphasis on an attractive appearance remains strong. There is continuing pressure on girls and young women to be thin and sexy. Indeed, the emphasis on "sexiness" has filtered down to grade school dress and appearance (midriff-baring outfits, makeup). The general message to girls is that it's okay to be smart and talented as long as they are also pretty and nice, with the latter qualities more important than the former. In this sense, my daughter, now in her late 20s, is a good illustration of current socialization. She is compassionate, assertive, bright, ambitious, warm, and analytical. But what most people see and comment upon is still how beautiful and "feminine" she is.

In reviewing the gender socialization research over the last 30 years, however, the most remarkable conclusion is that socialization messages regarding masculinity have remained relatively static, if not become increasingly stereotyped. Combined with continued negative sanctions for boys who engage in "feminine" behaviors, the message is that boys and most things "masculine" are still superior to girls and most things "feminine."

Change is needed. Parents, both mothers and fathers, need to treat their daughters and sons more equally and encourage positive constructive behaviors, regardless of gender associations. That is, we need to raise sons and daughters who are kind, capable, empathic, assertive, interdependent, and responsible. To do this, both parents need to model and reinforce those behaviors. In addition, media exposure needs to be monitored and exposure to non-stereotyped programming encouraged. Most of all, parents need to help children critically evaluate the stereotypic and limited gender messages they inevitably will encounter from people as well as from programs.

Teachers, too, need to encourage the best qualities and abilities in all their students, regardless of gender, race, or class. Textbooks and programs should be chosen with care, and teachers need to be aware of and modify their own gender-discriminatory behaviors. Students need to see examples of positively rewarded nontraditional behavior for boys as well as for girls, and each student should receive the type of instruction from which they will most benefit.

In order for children to be exposed to non-stereotypic examples, corporations need to do more to make available and promote such examples. Certainly we need more inclusive portrayals of men and women, boys and girls, in the media (comics, television, books, films) and from the toy industry, the textbook industry, and the advertising industry. We especially need to see more examples of boys behaving kindly and a de-emphasis on outward appearance for girls.

The current gender socialization experience is one of slightly more role flexibility for girls and continued role restrictiveness for boys. If change does not occur, children will continue to have their behaviors, goals, and aptitudes limited by their gender. Individual change without systemic change will only go so far. We all must work for a society that maximizes the development of individuals. We still have a long way to go in rearing babies to develop to their maximum potential, "free to be" themselves rather than a cultural stereotype.

REFERENCES

AMERICAN ASSOCIATION OF UNIVERSITY WOMEN [AAUW]. (2001). *Beyond the "gender wars:" A conversation about girls, boys, and education.* Washington, DC: Author.

ANDERSON, D. A., & HAMILTON, M. (2005). Gender role stereotyping of parents in children's pictures books: The invisible father. *Sex Roles, 52*, 145–151.

BANJEREE, R., & LINTERN, V. (2000). Boys will be boys: The effect of social evaluation concerns on gender-typing. *Social Development, 9*, 397–408.

BARTSCH, R. A., BURNETT, T., DILLER, T. R., & RANKIN-WILLIAMS, E. (2000). Gender representation in television commercials: Updating an update. *Sex Roles, 43*, 735–743.

Basow, S. A. (2004). The hidden curriculum: Gender in the classroom. In M. Paludi (Ed.), *Praeger guide to the psychology of gender* (pp. 117–131). Westport, CT: Praeger.

Basow, S. A. (2006). Gender role and gender identity development. In J. Worell & C. Goodheart (Eds.), *Handbook of girls' and women's psychological health* (pp. 242–251). New York: Oxford University Press.

Blakemore, J. E. (2003). Children's beliefs about violating gender norms: Boys shouldn't look like girls, and girls shouldn't act like boys. *Sex Roles, 48,* 411–419.

Brown, L. M. (2003). *Girlfighting: Betrayal and rejection among girls.* New York: New York University Press.

Bussey, K., & Bandura, A. (1999). Social cognitive theory of gender development and differentiation. *Psychological Review, 106,* 676–713.

Clearfield, M. W., & Nelson, N. M. (2006). Sex differences in mothers' speech and play behavior with 6-, 9-, and 14-month-old infants. *Sex Roles, 54,* 127–137.

Colwell, M. J., & Lindsey, E. W. (2005). Preschool children's pretend and physical play and sex of play partner: Connections to peer competence. *Sex Roles, 52,* 497–509.

Corcoran, C. B., & Parker, J. A. (2004). Powerpuff Girls: Fighting evil gender messages or postmodern paradox? In J. L. Chin (Ed.), *The psychology of prejudice and discrimination* (vol. 3, pp. 27–59). Westport, CT: Praeger.

Crombie, G., Sinclair, N., Silverthorn, N., Byrne, B. M., DuBois, D. L., & Trinner, A. (2005). Predictions of young adolescents' math grades and course intentions: Gender similarities and differences. *Sex Roles, 52,* 351–367.

Diekman, A. B., & Murnen, S. K. (2004). Learning to be little women and little men: The inequitable gender equality of nonsexist children's literature. *Sex Roles, 20,* 373–385.

Evans, L., & Davies, K. (2000). No sissy boys here: A content analysis of the representation of masculinity in elementary school reading textbooks. *Sex Roles, 42,* 255–270.

Frueh, T., & McGhee, P. E. (1975). Traditional sex role development and amount of time spent watching television. *Developmental Psychology, 11,* 109.

Ganahl, D. J., Prinsen, T. J., & Netzley, S. B. (2003). A content analysis of prime time commercials: A contextual framework of gender representation. *Sex Roles, 49,* 545–551.

Giuliano, T. A., Popp, K. E., & Knight, J. L. (2000). Footballs versus Barbies: Childhood play activities as predictors of sports participation by women. *Sex Roles, 42,* 159–181.

Glascock, J. (2001). Gender roles on prime-time network television: Demographics and behaviors. *Journal of Broadcasting & Electronic Media, 45,* 656–669.

Gooden, A. M., & Gooden, M. A. (2001). Gender representation in notable children's picture books: 1995–1999. *Sex Roles, 45,* 89–101.

Green, V. A., Bigler, R., & Catherwood, D. (2004). The variability and flexibility of gender-typed toy play: A close look at children's behavioral responses to counterstereotypic models. *Sex Roles, 51,* 371–386.

Harrison, A. C., & O'Neill, S. A. (2003). Preferences and children's use of gender-stereotyped knowledge about musical instruments: Making judgments about other children's preferences. *Sex Roles, 49,* 389–400.

Heyman, G. D., & Legare, C. H. (2004). Children's beliefs about gender differences in the academic and social domains. *Sex Roles, 50,* 227–239.

HILL, S. A. (2002). Teaching and doing gender in African American families. *Sex Roles, 47,* 493–506.

HOLM-DENOMA, J. M., LEWINSOHN, P. M., GAU, J. M., JOINER, T. E., JR., STRIEGEL-MOORE, R., & OTAMENDI, A. (2005). Parents' reports of the body shape and feeding habits of 36-month-old children: An investigation of gender differences. *International Journal of Eating Disorders, 38,* 228–235.

HOLMES-LONERGAN, H. A. (2003). Preschool children's collaborative problem-solving interactions: The role of gender, pair type, and task. *Sex Roles, 48,* 505–517.

JACOBSON, J. (2006, July 7). Report disputes notion that boys' academic performance is in decline. *Chronicle of Higher Education,* p. A35.

KOCH, J. (2003). Gender issues in the classroom. In W. M. Reynolds & G. E. Miller (Eds.), *Handbook of psychology: Educational psychology* (vol. 7, pp. 259–281). New York: Wiley.

LEAPER, C., ANDERSON, K. J., & SANDERS, P. (1998). Moderators of gender effects on parents' talk to their children: A meta-analysis. *Developmental Psychology, 34,* 3–27.

LEAPER, C., BREED, L., HOFFMAN, L., & PEARLMAN, C. A. (2002). Variations in the gender-stereotyped content of children's television cartoons across genres. *Journal of Applied Social Psychology, 32,* 1653–1662.

LEVY, G. D., SADOVSKY, A. L., & TROSETH, G. L. (2000). Aspects of young children's perceptions of gender-typed occupations. *Sex Roles, 42,* 993–1006.

LINDSEY, E. W., & MIZE, J. (2001). Contextual differences in parent-child play: Implications for children's gender role development. *Sex Roles, 44,* 155–176.

MACCOBY, E. E. (1998). *The two sexes: Growing up apart, coming together.* Cambridge, MA: Harvard University Press.

MONDSCHEIN, E. R., ADOLPH, K. E., & TAMIS-LEMONDA, C. S. (2000). Gender bias in mothers' expectations about infant crawling. *Journal of Experimental Child Psychology, 77,* 304–316.

MORRONGIELLO, B. A., & HOGG, K. (2004). Mothers' reactions to children misbehaving in ways that can lead to injury: Implications for gender differences in children's risk taking and injuries. *Sex Roles, 50,* 103–118.

NATIONAL WOMEN'S LAW CENTER. (2002). *The battle for gender equity in athletics: Title IX at thirty.* Washington, DC: Author.

O'BRIEN, M., & HUSTON, A. C. (1985). Development of sex-typed play behavior in toddlers. *Developmental Psychology, 21,* 866–871.

OSKAMP, S., KAUFMAN, K., & WOLTERBEEK, L. A. (1996). Gender role portrayals in preschool picture books. *Journal of Social Behavior and Personality, 11,* 27–39.

PICKERING, S., & REPACHOLI, B. (2001). Modifying children's gender-typed musical instrument preferences: The effects of gender and age. *Sex Roles, 45,* 623–643.

PIKE, J. J., & JENNINGS, N. A. (2005). The effects of commercials on children's perceptions of gender appropriate toy use. *Sex Roles, 52,* 83–91.

RAAG, T. (1999). Influences of social expectations of gender, gender stereotypes, and situational constraints on children's toy choices. *Sex Roles, 41,* 809–831.

RIVERS, C., & BARNETT, R. C. (2005). Holiday toys sell girls on primping and passivity. *Women's E-news.* Retrieved November 23, 2005, from http://www.womensenews.org/article.cfm

ROSENWASSER, S. M., LINGENFELTER, M., & HARRINGTON, A. F. (1989). Nontraditional gender role portrayals on television and children's gender role perceptions. *Journal of Applied Developmental Psychology, 10,* 97–105.

ROSS, S. I., & JACKSON, J. M. (1991). Teachers' expectations for Black males' and Black females' academic achievement. *Personality and Social Psychology Bulletin, 17,* 78–82.

SADKER, M., & SADKER, D. (1994). *Failing at fairness: How our schools cheat girls.* New York: Scribner.

SANDNABBA, K., & AHLBERG, C. (1999). Parents' attitudes and expectations about children's cross-gender behavior. *Sex Roles, 40,* 249–263.

SCHMADER, T., JOHNS, M., & BARQUISSAU, M. (2004). The costs of accepting gender differences: The role of stereotype endorsement in women's experience in the math domain. *Sex Roles, 50,* 835–850.

SHELDON, J. P. (2004). Gender stereotypes in educational software for young children. *Sex Roles, 51,* 433–444.

SIGNORELLI, N. (1990). Children, television, and gender roles: Messages and impact. *Journal of Adolescent Health Care, 11,* 50–58.

SIGNORELLI, N., & BACUE, A. (1999). Recognition and respect: A content analysis of prime-time television of characters across three decades. *Sex Roles, 40,* 527–544.

SOMMERS, C. H. (2000). *The war against boys: How misguided feminism is harming our young men.* New York: Simon & Schuster.

THOMAS, M. (1972). *Free to be . . . you and me.* [Sound recording.] New York: Arista.

THOMPSON, T. L., & ZERBINOS, E. (1995). Gender roles in animated cartoons: Has the picture changed in 20 years? *Sex Roles, 32,* 651–673.

TREPANIER-STREET, M. L., & ROMATOWSKI, J. A. (1999). The influence of children's literature on gender role perceptions: A reexamination. *Early Childhood Education Journal, 26,* 155–159.

TULVISTE, T., & KOOR, M. (2005). 'Hands off the car, it's mine!' and 'the teacher will be angry if we don't play nicely': Gender-related preferences in the use of moral rules and social conventions in preschoolers' dyadic play. *Sex Roles, 53,* 57–66.

TURNER-BOWKER, D. M. (1996). Gender stereotyped descriptors in children's picture books: Does 'curious Jane' exist in literature? *Sex Roles, 35,* 461–488.

TWENGE, J. M. (1997). Changes in masculine and feminine traits over time: A meta-analysis. *Sex Roles, 36,* 305–325.

TYRE, P. (2006, January 30). The trouble with boys. *Newsweek,* pp. 44–52.

WARNER, J. (2006, July 3). What boy crisis? *The New York Times,* p. A14.

*S*UGGESTED READINGS

BASOW, S. A. (2006). Gender role and gender identity development. In J. Worell & C. Goodheart (Eds.), *Handbook of girls' and women's psychological health* (pp. 242–251). New York: Oxford University Press.

BUSSEY, K., & BANDURA, A. (1999). Social cognitive theory of gender development and differentiation. *Psychological Review, 106,* 676–713.

MACCOBY, E. E. (1998). *The two sexes: Growing up apart, coming together.* Cambridge, MA: Harvard University Press.

THOMAS, M. (1972). *Free to be . . . you and me.* [Sound recording.] New York: Arista.

RUTH L. HALL *is Professor of Psychology at The College of New Jersey. Dr. Hall has taught courses on the psychology of women since 1987 and introduced a course on the psychology of Women of Color at TCNJ. She maintains a private practice in clinical psychology and consults frequently to agencies and organizations in her areas of expertise: women, People of Color, and sport psychology.*

7

Sweating It Out

The Good News and the Bad News
About Women and Sport

—————— ❖ ——————

Contrary to popular belief, the female athlete is not an oxymoron. Yes, we
sweat, we grunt, we get dirty, and we use our bodies to excel in athletics.
Yes, we participate in sports on recreational and on competitive levels. And
yes, we hear more about women as professional soccer, basketball, tennis, and golf
players as well as medal-winning Olympians. Why do so many girls decide not to
participate in sports or to leave athletics in their early teens? What are the messages
to girls that influence their decision to remain in or abandon sport? What's gender
got to do with it?

American culture ignores or minimizes sport participation of women and
girls. Many associate women in athletics with cheerleaders and supporters of male
athletic events. Women can cheer and jeer but are not always encouraged to enter
the athletic field. The implicit message is that participation in athletics is not for
girls and women. But teamwork, camaraderie, and competition are not inherently
for men only. Why should it be a problem when women use their bodies for other
than sexual purposes?

Women in sport is both good and bad news. The good news is that thousands
of girls and women are involved in sport, love to compete, and enjoy using their
minds and bodies as athletes. Sport provides an opportunity to work with other
girls and women, to excel in something, to learn or hone a skill, to become physically fit, to receive educational scholarships, and to compete. The bad news is that
many girls and women have not had the opportunity to participate in athletics,
have not been encouraged to do so, or have been warned that athletics will take
away from their "femininity." Of course, some girls and women just don't like
sport. That's OK, but look what they're missing!

My lecture will focus on the psychosocial aspects of sport, rather than on performance enhancement.[1] I will begin with a discussion of women's athletics as a legal issue and the role of feminism. Second, I will discuss some misconceptions about girls and women who participate in sport and how the media reinforce and perpetuate many myths. Third, I will discuss why girls initially participate in sport, why they remain in sport, and why they leave. Last, I will address two relevant and understudied areas of sport that are in need of further investigation: the role of homophobia in sport and women athletes of color.

HISTORY OF TITLE IX

"Women athletes are not responsible for the elimination of men's sports."
Women's Sports Foundation (WSF) (1997)

In 1972, an amendment of the Higher Education Act, Title IX, made it illegal to deny access to any federally funded educational institution's programs based on sex (Boutilier & SanGiovanni, 1983; Carpenter & Acosta, 2005, Nelson, 1991). The final revisions and mandated application of Title IX occurred in 1979. These additional funds made sport more available to high school girls and college women; as a result, more girls and women became active sport participants. Essentially, financial support provided uniforms, equipment, scholarships, coaching, and the opportunity to play against other teams.

This victory was relatively short-lived. In 1984, a subsequent ruling diluted Title IX. The *Grove City v. Bell* Supreme Court decision made it legal to limit equity in federal funding to the specific programs that received the funds. That is, if the institution did not use federal dollars in athletic and physical education departments (even if federal funds were supporting other programs within the institution), the monies allocated for athletic departments did not have to be equitable for men's and women's sport. However, the Civil Rights Restoration Act of 1988 completely reinstated Title IX, so that it serves once again as a legal document protecting women athletes. In the first 30 years after Title IX was passed, more than 2.8 million girls and 150,916 collegiate women have begun to participate in sport, an 847 percent and 403 percent increase, respectively. Before Title IX, only 30,000 women were involved in interscholastic sports (WSF, 2002b) and 295,000 girls in high school athletics.

The year 2007 marked the 35th anniversary of Title IX. Even with the increased involvement of women, true equity escapes us (Carpenter & Acosta, 2005, 2006; WSF, 2006a). According to the data collected by the Women's

---

[1]Performance enhancement is the development of skills that improve the execution of a sport or exercise program. These skills include goal setting, concentration, imagery, and relaxation. Performance enhancement also addresses how to handle "choking," burnout, and athletic injuries.

Sports Foundation (WSF, 2006a), women's college programs receive 43 to 45 percent of athletic scholarship money and comprise 43 percent of all college athletes, depending on the division (NCAA, 2004; WSF, 2006a). The budgets of women's programs are also less than the men's budgets. For example, at the college level (with the exception of Division I-AAA), 60 percent or more of recruiting costs are incurred by men (NCAA, 2004).

On Division I teams male coaches receive higher salaries than female coaches, regardless of whether they coach male or female teams (Jacobson, 2001; NCAA, 2004). Men's athletic teams in Division I and II institutions average 10 more competitions per sport per season than women's teams within the same divisions (NCAA, 2004). Carpenter and Acosta (2006) stated that, at the collegiate level, female coaches comprise 2 percent of the coaches on men's teams and 42.4 percent (the lowest percentage since the passage of Title IX) of the coaches on women's teams. The statistics are just as abysmal for head athletic trainers (27.4 percent), sport information directors (12.1 percent), and athletic administrators (35.2 percent or 1.21 women per school). It is interesting to note that women coached 90 percent of women's collegiate teams 30 years ago. With increased visibility and more attractive employment opportunities, more men are now interested in coaching women's teams. The end result is that women coaches have access to fewer coaching jobs (WSF, 2005b, Carpenter & Acosta, 2006). In essence, as the coaching salaries increase, the number of women coaches decreases.

Title IX is invaluable but remains unenforced in many institutions. The Women's Sports Foundation (WSF, 2002a) said it all when it stated that lawsuits generated by players and parents of players have to be filed to bring attention to the absence of a school's compliance. Why? Because the Office for Civil Rights (OCR) has not done its job to ensure that Title IX is upheld. The WSF stated that "not one institution has had its funding withdrawn because it is in violation of Title IX" (WSF, 2002b, p. 4). A startling 80 percent of college programs are not in compliance with Title IX (WSF, 2005a). Even though this is the case, there is a blacklash as some men's teams believe that they, not women, are being discriminated against when Title IX is enforced (WSF, 2002a). Donna Lopiano (2002), director of the Women's Sports Federation, stated that it is ridiculous to believe that men are "entitled" to participate in athletics and women are "permitted" to participate. Advocacy groups such as the Women's Sports Foundation are needed to serve as watchdogs for gender equity in sport.

The impact of Title IX is significant as it protects the rights of women athletes and provides opportunities for women to participate in sport in larger numbers. However, some women who should be sources of support did not fully embrace the swell of athletic opportunities for women: The relative absence of mainstream feminist support for women athletes is evident. Clearly, feminists were involved in opening the doors for women athletes. Feminists rallied around the Title IX controversy and a woman's right to participate in athletics. However, once the doors began to open, the incentive to integrate feminism and athleticism seemed to diminish. The problem seems to stem from sport being a male-identified (rather than male-dominated) activity. "It just makes us more like men," one feminist said. Another offered ignorance, "The only part of my body that I was encouraged to use was from the neck up." Is feminism so fragile that fighting for the rights of women athletes is too marginal? Does a focus on less "divisive" topics, such as sexual assault, child abuse, and battering, make us seem more "feminist"? Acknowledging and appreciating the differences among women is a tenet of feminism and doing so will not destroy the bond between women. Actually, it will make us stronger.

MYTHS AND MISINFORMATION

The world of women's athletics is filled with myths and lore—myths perpetuated by gender-role stereotypes, misinformation, fear, and the lore of successes and triumphs of our heroines! How many of you have heard of Danika Patrick (2005 Indy 500 Rookie of the Year), Althea Gibson and Billie Jean King (tennis greats), and Arthur Ashe and Pete Sampras (tennis stars)? Babe Dedrickson (all-around great woman athlete) and Lance Armstrong (cyclist)? Kobe Bryant and Lisa Leslie (NBA and WBNA top players)? Can you name a "great" in women's golf (LPGA) or men's golf (PGA)? Members of your institution's men's and women's varsity teams? Do you notice any patterns to your knowledge or lack of it? I would imagine that the number of male athletes you can name far surpasses the number of women athletes.

Ignorance, misinformation, and the lack of visibility of women in sport frequently obscure women's sport history. As a consequence, many girls and women may erroneously conclude that sport and athletics are not viable options for them. These myths and misconceptions about female athletes begin in childhood and gain momentum with puberty and womanhood. Society clearly reinforces the persistence of the myths in Table 1. It is our responsibility to dispel the myths that surround girls and women who participate in athletics and to provide the misinformed with accurate information.

BRING IN THE REINFORCEMENTS! THE ROLE OF THE MEDIA

When we examine the media, we are examining some negative factors that compromise women's participation in sport (Cohen, 2001). The media recognize and support women athletes marginally at best. It is important to recognize that the media coverage of women's sports has increased

TABLE 1

Myths About Women in Sport

Myths	Facts
1. Girls will get hurt if they participate in sports.	You can get hurt wearing high heels! Seriously, all athletes run the risk of getting injured, and girls are no different.
2. Sport are for boys.	By whose criteria?
3. Girls aren't good at sport.	The standards seem to be more related to opportunity than anything else (WSF, 2002a). Girls are smaller than boys and should have equipment that complements their build (Eccles & Harold, 1991).
4. Girls will never be as good as boys in sport, so why bother?	As the opportunity for girls increases, so does their participation. Our goal is not to compete with boys but to excel as girls. In fact, more women are trying out for collegiate sports (Parrillo, 2002).
5. Sport make girls masculine.	Sport participation tones you, reduces the risk of heart disease, and enhances your self-esteem. Does this sound masculine to you?
6. Boys don't like girls to play sport.	Lots of women athletes date and are in committed relationships with men. Who wants to be involved with a guy who compromises your love for sport? Would you have problems with his interest in sport? Some men can't handle being beaten by a woman in sport.
7. The proper role for girls in sport is cheerleading and supporting the boys.	Girls and boys can both play sports and both cheer! Yes, there are male cheerleaders too. Are they feminine?
8. Only lesbians play sport.	Lesbians are in every profession, occupation, avocation, and activity. It's no different in sport. No activity or interest can determine your sexual orientation (Nelson, 1991, 1998).
9. Supporting women athletes is a financial disaster.	Fully 93 percent of NCAA college football teams lose money annually (WSF, 1997). Is that a waste or a disaster (Lopiano, 2002)? With the exception of 15 NCAA Division I schools, football budgets were larger than all women's sports combined (WSF, 2005b).

incrementally, but it is by no means equitable to the coverage of men's sports. For example, newspaper and magazine coverage of the performance of women athletes is minimal. Women sportscasters numbered 127 in 2003 (AAFLA, 2005b; WSF, 2005b). Of the sports journalists at the 2004 Olympic Games, 16.6 percent were women. Televised coverage of women's sport increased from 5 to 8.7 percent from 1989 to 1999 (WSF, 2002b) and dropped to 6.3 percent in 2004 (AAFLA, 2005). With the exception of women's tennis, some track events, the LPGA, NCAA, basketball during Sweet 16, WNBA, softball playoffs and finals, and beach volleyball, the media have virtually no coverage of women athletes. For those of us without cable television, television coverage is even more limited. Actually, 90 percent of television coverage of sport is about men (Lupiano, 2002).

The public's exposure to any sport and its players is highly correlated to access to media coverage. Women's golf is a prime example of both the amount of coverage and the image projected by the media of women athletes (Oglesby et al., 1998). Though many believe that most men and women identify more with a woman's golf game, women still do not receive the visibility in the media. Existing media accounts often depict the female golfer as feminine, attractive, and heterosexual rather than talented (Young, 1989). The influence of advertisers, whose interest is selling products, contributes to the objectification of women athletes. In fact, qualities that enhance women's visibility in sport have little to do with performance and more to do with appearance and controversy (Boutilier & SanGiovanni, 1983; Schell, 2002). Positive changes are occurring, however: The visibility of Danika Patrick (Secret deodorant) and golf sensation Michelle Wie (Nike and Sony) are recognition that female athletes are good salespeople and that 81 percent of the purchasing power of sport-related apparel and equipment is purchased by women. Even though there are more women garnering sponsorships, their remuneration does not compare with that given to men. Why do so many women in the WNBA have another job in their off season? While the WNBA salaries range from $31,200 to $89,000, the NBA salaries range from $385,277 to $15,355,000! Quite a difference, wouldn't you say?

The Amateur Athletic Foundation of Los Angeles (AAFLA) has conducted four studies on the coverage of women athletes on the three major networks, ESPN, and Sports Center. Their first study was in 1989. They found that men received 92 percent of televised air time. The good news was that descriptors of women athletes were more positive. Overall, women's sports is taken more seriously. The bad news was that women's sports coverage has fallen from 8.7 percent in 1999 to 6.3 percent, of which 42.4 percent is women's tennis. On the printed page, *USA Today* provided more information about women athletes than other print publications (Kort, 1991). The WSF (2005b) reported that two independent studies of four newspapers' coverage of women ranged from 3.5 to 11 percent, still extremely low, and there is an exceptional amount of room for growth in the amount and the type of media coverage.

Not much has changed since ABC sport producer Eleanor Sanger Keyes (1991) stated that women were referred to by their first names most of the time; among men, African Americans were referred to by their first names. Both male and female commentators called women "girls" and men "men." Keyes also stated that the commentary during professional tennis tournaments implied that men won because of skill and women won because of a weakness in their opponent. In essence, the media do little to support women's athletic endeavors but do a sterling job of reinforcing the stereotype that women, with rare exceptions, are either not particularly good at (or not interested in) athletics (Keyes, 1991; Kort, 1991; Theberge, 1991).

Changes continue to occur with the increased visibility of women reporters and commentators (e.g., Robin Roberts, Hannah Storm). However, of the 416 *Sports Illustrated* covers since 1997, 29 were of women and of this number, eight covers were their swim suit editions (WSF, 2005b). But we're still climbing a steep slope. Let's bear in mind that the audience of women and girls watching sport is growing (WSF, 1997), and we need to keep the pressure on for more coverage of women's sport. We need more visibility for women's sport on television and in newspapers and magazines. Sadly, magazines like *Real Sports* are only available online. With the folding of seven professional leagues (such as WUSA in 2005), the market for attracting advertisers is problematic. Magazines such as *Real Sports* provide a positive view of women athletes. Academically, we need more journal articles and conference presentations that address girls and women in sport.

THE NARROW PARAMETERS OF ACCEPTABLE SPORT PARTICIPATION: A SHIFTING TECTONIC PLATE

Some sports are seen as appropriate for women, but others are seen as taboo. Even though more women and girls are participating in more team sport, society continues to perceive individual sport as more feminine than team sports (Boutilier & SanGiovanni, 1983; Sage & Loudermilk, 1979), and we permit women to compete if they remain feminine (Birrell, 1983). The implication is that tennis, figure skating, track, and gymnastics are fine for women, but basketball, rowing, rugby, softball, and field events such as the shot put are not. Mathes (1978) suggested that sport using more "masculine" skills are less desirable for women than those emphasizing delicacy and gracefulness. She noted that sport that are aesthetically pleasing or use light objects, such as racquets, are "more feminine" than those that involve body contact or require the application of force or the movement of heavy objects, such as boats (Snyder & Spreitzer, 1973). Women's successes in professional basketball (WNBA) is breaking the boundaries. In fact, 2006 was the 10-year anniversary of the WNBA! Sadly, women's softball will not be included in the 2012 Olympic Games, but beach volleyball will continue as an Olympic event. Also, women's wrestling was added to the Olympic venue in 2004. Even so, the rules about what physical activities are acceptable and unacceptable for girls and women remain. Just ask any girl or boy about which sport are for girls and which ones are for boys!

The continued confinement of women and girls to particular sport indicates that the social construction of gender influences the choice of sport for girls and boys, as well as for women and men. Even so, girls and women are pursuing a wider range of sports. We're gaining momentum. There's no stopping us.

SOCIALIZATION OF GIRLS AND WOMEN

The Sporting Goods Manufacturers' Association (SGMA, 2000) study of youth sports participation found that fun was the primary reason that girls participate in sport, followed by being in shape, getting exercise, enhancing skills, and honing a skill in which they have achieved some success. Similar results were found in the Athletic Footwear Association's (1990) survey. It also discovered that sports participation decreased with age for both boys and girls and that dating, watching television, and socializing with friends were the primary reasons for discontinuing sport. Out of 12 reasons for sport participation, winning ranked last for girls. For boys, winning was eighth. Girls' second and third reasons for remaining in sport were staying in shape and exercise, respectively. For boys, skill enhancement and participation in an activity in which they possessed skills were their second and third choices. Even though fun is essential to sport participation for both boys and girls, supplemental enhancers for sport participation vary with gender: Girls focus on appearance, and boys on skill enhancement (Greendorfer, 1987).

Both boys and girls begin to drop out of sport during adolescence but at disproportionate rates—according to Lupiano (2002), the drop-out rate for girls is six times that of boys in early adolescence. For adolescents, regardless of gender, the importance of peer acceptance increases exponentially in adolescence. Adolescents' participation in activities mirrors their desire to achieve social approval within their identified social network. If the environment for a young woman is nonsupportive of her participation in sport, she may decide not to participate in a sport.

An adolescent's environment includes family (nuclear and extended), friends, and classmates, and each environment influences her participation in athletics. The primary motive for an adolescent girl's participation in sport is parental interest (WSF, 2005b). The absence of parental support is expressed in a variety of ways: showing an overt lack of interest (for example, not attending her games), stating that she will outgrow her interest in sports, offering support only for her participation in cheerleading or other "feminine activities," or being unwilling (rather than unable) to purchase the proper equipment. Her friends may resent the time that she relegates to athletics and withdraw their support. The person whom she is dating may not support her involvement in sport and may suggest that she choose between the relationship and her sport. These issues may not influence male athletes in the same manner because sport involvement is a given for boys.

Schools may collude in the process as well and relegate equipment discarded by the boys' teams to the girls' teams (such equipment is tailored to the male body and usually a poor fit for girls and women) rather than purchasing appropriate equipment. Girls' time on the practice field may be at the least opportune times. Girls' teams may not have access to the same resources (assistant coaches, number of games, transportation, etc.) as boys' teams. And girls' teams may be the first cut in a budget crunch.

The additive effect of these events may discourage girls from sport participation. However, we persevere. In 2004, 2.9 million high school girls and 4 million high school boys participated in sport (Wilson, 2005). Not only does 1 in 2.5 girls participate in high school sport, but girls are also participating in a wider range of sport (e.g., ice hockey, football, wrestling, baseball). Unfortunately, the WSF (2006a) stated that the percentage of girls who participate in sport drops steadily in high school (from 30.6 percent to 17.3 percent over the four years). Clearly, we need to provide an environment that is more conducive to girls' continuing with sport.

WHAT DOES THE RESEARCH SAY? THE EARLIER, THE BETTER!

Gender role and gender-role expectations can keep girls and women away from athletics; thus, sport remains a male-dominated field (Gill, 1986; Harris, 1979; Nelson, 1991). Men—the gatekeepers of sport—conduct most of the research and focus on male athletes. Their conclusions assume that the traits, personality, and motivational factors of women athletes are identical to those of men and, therefore, separate studies for women or data that include both men and women are not necessary (Duda, 1991). Granted, the similarities between men and women are greater than their differences, but the fact remains that women need to serve as their own reference point (Gilligan, 1982; Harris, 1979; Hill-Collins, 1991). As the studies of the Sporting Goods Manufacturers' Association (SGMA, 2000) and the Athletic Footwear Association (1990) attest, women seem to be motivated by different factors than men. However, Allison (1991) suggested that to overemphasize gender differences does a disservice to women athletes.

Eccles and Harold (1991) conducted a longitudinal study and found that, even in elementary school, boys and girls see sport as something males are better at and more likely to do. Both girls and society place a glass ceiling on girls' sport ability and access to sport experiences. Eccles and Harold believe that, when girls see sport as attainable and acceptable, their participation will increase. The need to provide girls with support for and access to athletic participation is critical. If girls do not participate in sport by age 10, there is only a 10 percent chance that they will be active in sport at 25 (WSF, 2005b).

It seems obvious that we may actually prevent girls and women from choosing to participate in sport. Perhaps the arbitrary social construction of gender contributes to the low participation of girls and women in sport (Lenskyj, 1986). In her summary of studies on gender-role conflict and female athletes, Allison (1991) made the following observations: Many studies on female athletes are based on the Sage and Loudermilk (1979) instruments and constructs, which suggest that gender-role conflict for women athletes is the salient issue. A few studies (Anthrop & Allison, 1983; Sage & Loudermilk, 1979) suggest that both perceived and experienced gender-role conflict is relatively low (20 to 30 percent). Given the increasing number of women in sport, the percentages of girls and women "in conflict" seem to be diminishing. Allison acknowledges the existence of gender labeling and sport activity, but she believes that research design exacerbates this construct. She suggests that there is a difference between the recognition of and the internalization of gender stereotypes. We do not need to use men as the reference point or to believe that to be an athlete is to be male.

Dorothy Harris (1979), a pioneer sport psychologist, suggests that women who continue to participate in sport are women who are stronger and less influenced by societal stereotypes. The experiences of professional businesswomen support her position. Bunker (1995) conducted a survey of women executives in Fortune 500 companies that still rings true today (WSF, 2005b). Bunker states that 86 percent described themselves as tomboys when they were growing up. Furthermore, one of the most important skills that they learned from sport was how to handle victory and defeat. Their only regret is that they missed the opportunities that Title IX now provides for girls and women. The WSF (2005b) reported that 82 percent of women executives state that their sport experiences helped them in their jobs. Also, women executives are twice as likely as the general population to exercise regularly. Business leader and entertainer Oprah Winfrey touts the benefits of exercise all the time! We can conclude that sports and fitness training contribute not only to the physical well-being of professional women, but also to their careers.

THE CONSEQUENCES OF HOMOPHOBIA

"If there's a powerful woman out there in the world and she comes out, it's suddenly, 'Oh, no wonder, she's a dyke.'"
                        Ingrid Sischy, editor-in-chief of Interview

Rotella and Murray (1991) suggested that homophobia (the irrational fear of same-sex sexual orientation in oneself or in others) is harmful to everyone, gay or straight: "Individuals in sport have had a very difficult time openly addressing the issue of homophobia, seemingly preferring to avoid it or pretend it does not exist (men like to pretend it is only in women's sports, whereas women like to pretend it is only present in other women's teams)" (p. 361). Homophobia has the potential to prevent many women from participating in athletics. Homophobia also inhibits many lesbians and bisexual women athletes from coming out to themselves, to their teammates, or to their coaches (Griffin, 2001; Krane, 2001; WSF, 2001). Of course, lesbian and bisexual women are active in all levels of sport and athletics. Martina Navratilova and Billie Jean King are two athletes who are well known to us all. Sheryl Swapes (WNBA superstar) came out in 2005. Many heterosexual women are accomplished athletes as well, including Chris Evert Lloyd Mills, Venus Williams, Michelle Wie, Danika Patrick, and Jackie Joyner-Kersee. Clearly, any correlation made between athleticism and sexual orientation is misleading.

Still, homophobia compromises team cohesion and unity by emphasizing something other than the goal to pursue optimal performance in all athletes. It is an athlete's ability to perform, not her sexual orientation, that counts! To use people's sexual orientation against them, for any reason, is an unnecessary distraction and destructive to the team and to its members. Martina Navratilova stated:

> The thing in sport that really pisses me off is that women athletes have to prove to the world that they are not lesbians. I was asked the question forever, even before I knew I was gay. They wouldn't ask a male that. The male *athletes, the writers* protect them. They don't want to shatter the myth, "My God, we can't have a gay football player." It's a macho sport. But the women they attack immediately. (Kasindorf, 1993, p. 35)

Being a feminist and an athlete is especially suspect for women. As one female athlete stated, "To be an athlete and a feminist is the kiss of death in sport. Everyone then assumes that you are a lesbian." Clearly, not all strong women and great athletes are lesbians, and not all lesbians are great athletes or strong women, yet the lesbian label often accompanies a powerful or athletic woman.

Coaches who are lesbian face discrimination and fear being fired. Lesbian amateur and professional athletes may lose sponsorships, lose their jobs, or be relegated to riding the bench due to their sexual orientation. Rumors of a coach (especially an unmarried woman) being lesbian are frequently used in recruiting by heterosexual coaches to influence a recruit's selection of a college. Consider the consequences that occurred for Billie Jean King. King's affair with a woman (who attempted to sue her for damages) cost her several major endorsements and probably her position as the commentator for televised women's tennis tournaments (Lenskyj, 1986). Penn State women's basketball coach Rene Portland (Brownsworth, 1991; Lipsyte, 1991) allegedly had an unspoken policy not to allow lesbians on her team and to bench those lesbians who came out. When sources disclosed Portland's alleged policy, Penn State established a university policy that prohibited discrimination based on sexual orientation. Stories about lesbians benched or losing scholarships and coaching positions abound. It sounds like the witch hunts in the military, and the "Don't ask, don't tell" policy is followed by many closeted athletes and coaches. The biggest homophobic fear is that lesbians will recruit straight women to become lesbians; as if anyone else can determine your sexual orientation. No one can make you gay, straight, or bisexual—either you are or you aren't!

Heterosexism provides the basis of our definition of sexuality in the United States. Chodorow (1994) stated that, if we use heterosexuality's gender-role stereotypes as the basis for homosexuality, gay men are feminized and lesbians masculinized. Pharr (1988) suggested that homophobia is a weapon used to keep women in their traditional gender roles, in and outside of athletics. At what age do we begin to pathologize women who are tomboys (Lenskyj, 1986)? According to Bunker, tomboys become quite successful adults! Think about it: If girls and women did not fear being called lesbians, no one would be concerned! Athletic participation stretches these arbitrary gender-role boundaries and allows all of us choices based on interest and ability rather than some arbitrary parameters and limitations. What better place to find powerful women than athletics?

WOMEN ATHLETES OF COLOR

Basically, when we talk about women and girls in sport, we are implicitly talking about White women, and when we talk about race, the focus is on Men of Color (Anderson, 1992; Lee & Rotella, 1991). The literature has marginalized Women of Color, in the psychological literature, as well as in the sport psychology literature (Hall, 2001).

Even though accessibility to resources, including those for sport participation, is an issue for many Women of Color (WSF, 2003a), sport have been an oasis for many Girls of Color. The Women's Sports Foundation (WSF, 2005b, 2005c) reported that involvement in sport kept many students in school. Athletes of Color did better academically than their non-athlete counterparts but confronted a glass ceiling in obtaining athletic scholarships. Furthermore, within sport, Women of Color are often shuttled into particular sport (track and basketball for African American women) and particular positions within the sport. Lopiano (2001) stated that "positional tracking" is evident in sport: "An African American woman is underrepresented in skill/outcome control positions. She is also the setter in volleyball or the point guard in basketball" (p. 1).

In addition, Women of Color are not the primary recipients of the boom in women's sport. Suggs (2001) reported that the greatest growth for girls and women in sport were in golf, lacrosse, soccer, and rowing, sport that require access to large, grassy areas (available in the suburbs) and parents with the financial resources (for club membership and coaching) to begin a child's exposure to a sport at an early age. Whereas the number of girls and women participating in these growing sport has doubled (or more), the percentage of women on track and basketball teams has increased only 26 percent. The WSF (2005b) reported that in the 1990s, the number of African American women in collegiate sport remained relatively consistent (13.9 to 15.6 percent), whereas the number of Latina (3 percent), Asian (1.8 percent), and international (7 percent) women rose, and the number of Native Americans remained small. The increase in women athletes therefore has been in the number of White women in sports. So what? Well, opportunities for many Women of Color to be exposed to and participate in a wider diversity of sports at an early age result in fewer Girls of Color in grade school and high school able to compete with girls who have had the chance to do so. Opportunities for "walk-ons" (individuals who enter a sport at the collegiate level with no formal training in the sport) to be asked to join a team are not realistic: How can someone "take up" soccer at 18 and compete with young women who have been playing since they were in elementary school? Early exposure and access to coaches and training facilities is critical to participation on the collegiate level. Involvement in sport and exercise is critical for Women of Color. Girls and Women of Color, especially African American and Latina girls and women, are the least likely to exercise and are at the greatest risks for problems exacerbated by a sedentary lifestyle, including obesity, heart disease, diabetes, and hypertension (Hall, 1998, in press). Sabo and Snyder (1993) suggested that athletics is also important for professional Women of Color. The report stated that, although Women of Color were less likely than White women to participate in sports and fitness training, "Women of Color were more likely to believe that sports and fitness help to advance careers and to tap into business networks" than were White women (p. 2). For a variety of reasons, we need to increase the opportunities for Girls and Women of Color to participate in sport.

Furthermore, the number of Women of Color who are coaches, administrators, and teachers remains small (Corbett, 2001; WSF, 2005b), and the greatest opportunities are in African American schools and historically African American colleges and universities (HBCUS) (Corbett, 2001). Ironically, the same schools offer less opportunity for women to participate in sport (Suggs, 2001) and allocate fewer financial resources to women's teams. The WSF (2005b) reported that there were the 165 African American female coaches at HBCUS and three female athletic directors.

Additional literature is emerging that addresses the role of culture and racism in sport (Brooks & Althouse, 2000). My study on racial identity and women athletes (Hall, 1993) found that Black players' experiences in cross-racial interactions either affirmed racial pride or reinforced omnipresent racism within our culture (that is, reinforced the feeling of being alienated or stereotyped). Moreover, Suggs (2001) and Hall (2001) indicated that, when Women of Color were in a significant minority on a team, they tended to report feelings of isolation, an additional source of stress. White players did not differ significantly in their racial identity with their team's racial composition; for them, cross-racial interactions either proved to be educational or fulfilled their stereotypical view of Blacks. It is essential that the impact of culture and racism on the self-concept of Women of Color be researched further. The results will be useful to determine the role of cultural differences in team cohesion and interpersonal communication. Women of Color are more than the recipients of oppression, and we desperately need literature to address the psychosocial forces that may compromise their athletic experience.

POSITIVE ASPECTS OF SPORT FOR WOMEN

What does participation in athletics offer women? It's a way to get back in touch with our bodies, to use them, and to keep them fit. Physical activity reduces the risk of breast cancer and osteoporosis (Lupiano, 2002; WSF, 2005b). Sport is a natural for women: Participating in sport reinforces our sense of sisterhood, interdependence, and cooperativeness. It also teaches discipline, concentration, goal setting, team building, fitness, leadership, and determination. Participation in sport increases the self-esteem and self-confidence of girls and women (Lopiano, 2002; WSF, 2005b). Girls who participate in sport are less likely to get pregnant and more likely to graduate from high school. Regular exercise decreases the likelihood of health-related problems, including obesity, hypertension, and diabetes (Hall, 1998, in press). Most of all, it's fun! Athletics also teaches risk taking, persistence, empowerment, and assertiveness. Athletes have experience in putting loss and failure into perspective, in increasing self-efficacy through skill development, and in using preparation and training as roads to mastery. And yes, sport has the potential for great comebacks.

WHAT DO WE NEED TO DO?

We need to provide girls and boys with supportive athletic environments that include emotional support and access to quality coaching, facilities, and equipment. We *must* demand that our schools have a viable physical activity program, from elementary school through high school. The absence of physical education programs in many schools is pathetic. Federal law making physical education mandatory would be an investment in our children's healthy future. With the obesity epidemic in American children, doesn't it make sense to have physical activity as a part of one education system? Besides, it's fun! We need to let girls know when they're young that athletics is a viable option and to offer them the opportunity to participate regardless of socioeconomic status, race, or ethnicity.

If girls don't begin a physical activity before they are 10, there is only a 10 percent chance that they will be physically active as adults (WSF, 2005b). By exposing girls to sport, we will increase girls' feelings of competence in their present abilities and in their careers as adults. The more girls participate in sport, the more we will dispel myths and reinforce the literature that shows the power and relevance of sport in the lives of girls and women. Also, movies such as *Bend It Like Beckham* provide girls with a feeling that sports are available to them. *Billie Jean King: A Portrait of a Pioneer* (HBO, 2006) is inspiring.

Women athletes provide wonderful role models for all of us. We need more role models and greater visibility of women athletes of all races and ages. We need to offer women greater opportunities for athletic competition as adults. At present, there is a growing but limited future for a profession in sport for women. There are many more professional opportunities for men. We need posters, ads, and information about women athletes of all races. We need to confront homophobia, sexism, classism (yes, classism!), and racism in sport as well. We need more research on women's sports, and we should demand that magazines and journals include articles about girls and women in sport. Also, we need more coverage of women's athletic events in the news—both on radio and television. We need to examine sexism within sport organizations (Roper, 2002). We need to approach more grant sponsors to target and sponsor researchers who study girls and women's sport and exercise participation.

We need more programs available to girls, regardless of socioeconomic status or race, that expose them to opportunities to engage in athletics of all kinds. The Chicago Project, the Vespers rowing program in Philadelphia, the Arthur Ashe National Junior Tennis League, the Tiger Woods Foundation (golf), and Tina's Program are examples of programs that expose urban youth, in particular, to sporting opportunities.

In closing, remember that National Girls' and Women's Sports Day is February 4. Make February 4 a memorable day by inviting a woman athlete or coach to speak at your institution. Sponsor a community event for girls and women to participate in various athletic activities on your campus. Get your athletic, physical education, and women's studies departments (among others) to participate. Put posters of women athletes in the library, dormitories, and campus center display cases. Insist that your library purchase books on women and sport. Call radio and television stations and demand that they cover women's sport on a regular basis. Get involved in your own health and fitness. Share the good fortune that athletics can bring to all our lives!

*R*EFERENCES

ALLISON, M. T. (1991). Role conflict and the female athlete: Preoccupations with little grounding. *Journal of Applied Sport Psychology, 3,* 49–60.

Amateur Athletic Foundation of Los Angeles. From http://www.aafla.org

ANDERSON, M. B. (1992). Questionable sensitivity: A comment on Lee and Rotella. *Sport Psychologist, 7,* 1–4.

ANTHROP, J., & ALLISON, M. (1983). Role conflict and the high school female athlete. *Research Quarterly, 54,* 104–111.

ATHLETIC FOOTWEAR ASSOCIATION. (1990). *American youth and sports participation.* North Palm Beach, FL: Author.

BIRRELL, S. (1983). The psychological dimensions of female athletic participation. In M. A. Boutilier & L. SanGiovanni (Eds.), *The sporting woman* (pp. 49–92). Champaign, IL: Human Kinetics.

BOUTILIER, M. A., & SANGIOVANNI, L. (Eds.). (1983). *The sporting woman.* Champaign, IL: Human Kinetics.

BROOKS, D., & ALTHOUSE, R. (2000). *Racism in college athletics: The African-American athlete* (2nd ed.). Morgantown, WV: Fitness Information Technology.

BROWNSWORTH, V. A. (1991). Penn State basketball coach accused of anti-lesbian policy. *Philadelphia Gay News, 15*(21), 1.

BUNKER, (2005, February). Personal communication.

CARPENTER, L. J. & ACOSTA, R. V. (2005). *Title IX.* Champaign, IL: Human Kinetics.

CARPENTER, L. J. & ACOSTA, R. V. (2006). *Women in intercollegiate sport: A longitudinal, national study twenty-nine-year update, 1977–2006.* West Brookfield, MA: Acosta/Carpenter, Athletic Training/SID. Retrieved April 29, 2006, from http://webpages.charter.net/womeninsport/AC_29YearStudy.pdf

CHODOROW, N. (1994). *Femininities, masculinities, sexualities: Freud and beyond.* Lexington: University of Kentucky Press.

COHEN, G. L. (Ed.). (2001). *Women in sport: Issues and controversies* (2nd ed.). Newbury Park, CA: Sage.

CORBETT, D. R. (2001). Minority women of color: Unpacking racial ideology. In G. L. Cohen (Ed.), *Women in sport: Issues and controversies* (2nd ed., pp. 291–312). Oxin Hill, MD: AAAPERD Publications.

DUDA, J. L. (1991). Editorial comment. *Journal of Applied Sport Psychology, 3,* 1–7.

ECCLES, J. S., & HAROLD, R. D. (1991). Gender differences in sport involvement: Applying the Eccles expectancy-value model. *Journal of Applied Sport Psychology, 3,* 7–35.

GILL, D. L. (1986). *Psychological dynamics of sport.* Champaign, IL: Human Kinetics.

GILL, D. L. (2001). Feminist psychology: A guide for our journey. *Sport Psychologist, 15,* 363–372.

GILLIGAN, C. (1982). *In a different voice: Psychological theory and women's development.* Cambridge, MA: Harvard University Press.

GREENDORFER, S. L. (1987). Gender bias in theoretical perspectives: The case of females' socialization into sport. *Psychology of Women Quarterly, 11,* 327–340.

GRIFFIN, P. (2001). Heterosexism, homophobia and lesbians in sport. In G. L. Cohen (Ed.), *Women in sport: Issues and controversies* (2nd ed., pp. 278–290). Newbury Park, CA: Sage.

HALL, R. L. (1993, August). *Racial identity and racial composition of women's varsity basketball teams.* Paper presented at the meeting of the American Psychological Association, Toronto, Canada.

HALL, R. L. (1998). Softly strong: African American women's use of exercise in therapy. *Psychotherapy Patient, 10*(3/4), 81–100.

HALL, R. L. (2001). Shaking the foundation: Women of color in sport. *Sport Psychologist, 15*, 386–400.

HALL, R. L. (in press). On the move: Exercise, leisure activities, and midlife women. In V. Muhlbauer & J. C. Chrisler (Eds.), *Women over 50: psychological perspectives.* New York: Springer.

HARRIS, D. V. (1979). Female sport today: Psychological considerations. *International Journal of Sport Psychology, 10,* 168–172.

HBO. (2006, April 26). *Billie Jean King: Portrait of a Pioneer.*

HILL-COLLINS, P. (1991). *Black feminist thought: Knowledge, consciousness and the politics of empowerment.* New York: Routledge.

JACOBSON, J. (2001, June 8). Female coaches lag in pay and opportunities to oversee men's teams. *Chronicle of Higher Education,* p. A38.

KASINDORF, J. R. (1993, May). Lesbian chic: The bold, brave new world of gay women. *New York,* pp. 30–37.

KEYES, E. S. (1991, February). *Respondent: Gender stereotyping in sports media.* Paper presented at the Annual Kathleen Ridder Conference, Smith College, Northampton, MA.

KORT, M. (1991, April). Making waves. *Women's Sports and Fitness,* pp. 56–61.

KRANE, V. (2001). One lesbian feminist epistemology: Integrating feminist standpoint, queer theory, and feminist cultural studies. *Sport Psychologist, 15*, 401–411.

LEE, C. C., & ROTELLA, R. J. (1991). Special concerns and considerations for sport psychology: Consulting with black student athletes. *Sport Psychologist, 5,* 365–370.

LENSKYJ, H. (1986). *Out of bounds: Women, sport, and sexuality.* Toronto, Ontario: Women's Press.

LIPSYTE, R. (1991, May 24). Gay bias moves off the sidelines. *The New York Times,* p. Bll.

LOPIANO, D. (2001). *Gender equity and the Black female in sport.* Retrieved from http://www.womenssportsfoundation.org/cgi-bin/iowa/issues/disc/article.html?record=869

LOPIANO, D. (2002). *Gender equity in sports: Whose responsibility is it?* New York: Women's Sports Foundation.

MATHES, S. (1978). Body image and sex stereotyping. In C. Oglesby (Ed.), *Women and sport: From myth to reality* (pp. 59–73). Philadelphia: Lea & Febiger.

NCAA. (2004). *2002–2003 NCAA gender-equity report.* Indianapolis, IN: Author.

NELSON, M. B. (1991). *Are we winning yet? How women are changing sports and sports are changing women.* New York: Random House.

NELSON, M. B. (1998). *Embracing victory: Life lessons in competition and compassion. New choices for women.* New York: William Morrow.

OGLESBY, C. O., GREENBERG, D., HALL, R. L., HILL, K., JOHNSTON, F., & RIDLEY, S. (Eds.). (1998). *Encyclopedia of women and sport in America.* Phoenix, AZ: Oryx Press.

PARRILLO, R. (2002, July 26). Paterno weighs in on female kicker for Penn State. *Philadelphia Inquirer.*

PHARR, S. (1988). *Homophobia: A weapon of sexism.* Little Rock, AR: Chardon.

REAL SPORTS, The magazine. Retrieved June 6, 2006, from http://www.realsports mag.com/mag/index.html?PHPSESSID=f453belc43a9b61ddda41a5dd39e1605

Roper, E. A. (2002). Women working in the applied domain: Examining the gender bias in applied sport psychology. *Journal of Applied Sport Psychology, 14,* 53–65.

Rotella, R. J., & Murray, M. (1991). Homophobia, the world of sport and sport psychology consulting. *Sport Psychologist, 5,* 355–365.

Sabo, D., & Snyder, M. (1993). *Miller Lite report on sports & fitness in the lives of working women.* New York: Miller Brewing Company.

Sage, G. H., & Loudermilk, S. (1979). The female athlete and role conflict. *Research Quarterly, 50,* 88–96.

Schell, L. A. (2002). *(Dis)empowering images? Media representations of women in sport.* Retrieved from http://www.womenssportsfoundation.org/cgi-bin/iowa/issues/edia/article. html?record=881

Snyder, E. E., & Spreitzer, E. (1973). Family influences and involvement in sport. *Research Quarterly, 44,* 249–255.

SGMA. (2000). *The SGMA report 2000: Sports participation in America.* North Palm Beach, FL: Author.

Suggs, W. (2001, November 30). Left behind: Title IX has done little for minority female athletes, while White women have made significant gains. *Chronicle of Higher Education,* pp. A35–A37.

Theberge, N. (1991). A content analysis of print media coverage of gender, women and physical activity. *Journal of Applied Sport Psychology, 3,* 36–48.

Wilson, W. (Ed.). (July, 2005). *Gender in televised sports: News and highlights shows, 1989–2004.* Amateur Athletic Foundation of Los Angeles. Retrieved from http://www.aafla.org

WSF. (1989). *Minorities in sports. The effect of varsity sports participation on the social, educational, and career mobility of minority students.* New York: Author.

WSF. (1997). *Women's sports facts.* New York: Author.

WSF. (2001). *Homophobia in women's sports.* Retrieved from http://www.womens sportsfoundation.org/cgi-bin/iowa/issues/media/article.html?record=880

WSF. (2002a, June 17). *Response to National Wrestling Coaches Association Title IX suit against the education department.* Retrieved from http://www.womenssports foundation.org/cgi-bin/iowa/issues/media/press.html?record=894

WSF. (2002b). *Title IX at 30: Athletics receive C+.* New York: Author.

WSF. (2002c). *Women's sports and fitness facts and statistics.* New York: Author.

WSF. (2003a). *The Women's Sports Foundation Report: Title IX and race in intercollegiate sport.* Author. Retrieved from http://www.WomensSportsFoundation.org

WSF. (2005a, June 16). *Department of Education creates huge Title IX compliance loophole: The foundation position.* Author. Retrieved from http://www.womens sportsfoundation.org/cgi-bin/iowa/issues/disc/article.html?record=1009

WSF. (2005b, October). *Women's sport and fitness facts and statistics (Compiled by the Women's Sports Foundation, Updated 10/05).* Author. Retrieved May 31, 2006, from http://www.womenssportsfoundation.org/binarydata/WSF_Article/pdf_file/191.pdf

WSF. (2005c, November 30). *The Women's Sports Foundation Report: The status of health and physical activity in Chicago Hispanic girls.* Author. Retrieved from http://www.WomenssportsFoundation.org

WSF. (2006a, February). *State of women's sports. Executive summary.* Author. Retrieved from http://www.womenssportsfoundation.org/cgi-bin/iowa/issues/history/article.html?record=1168

Young, P. (1989, April 10). Belles on the ball (LPGA). *Maclean's,* pp. 68–69

SUGGESTED READINGS

Brooks, D., & Althouse, R. (2000). *Racism in college athletics: The African-American athlete* (2nd ed.). Morgantown, WV: Fitness Information Technology.

Griffin, P. (1998). *Strong women, deep closets: Lesbians and homophobia in sport.* Champaign, IL: Human Kinetics.

Nelson, M. B. (1998). *Embracing victory: Life lessons in competition and compassion. New choices for women.* New York: William Morrow.

Oglesby, C. O., Greenberg, D., Hall, R. L., Hill, K., Johnston, F., & Ridley, S. (Eds.). (1998). *Encyclopedia of women & sport in America.* Phoenix, AZ: Oryx Press.

CHRISTINE A. SMITH is Assistant Professor of Psychology at Antioch College. Dr. Smith has taught courses on the psychology of women since 1991 at Lewis and Clark College, Carlow College, Minnesota State University, and Ball State University. Her research interests are women's body image, feminist self-labeling, and gender collective self-esteem.

8

Women, Weight, and Body Image

❖

Every time I teach psychology of women, every time I look at a "women's magazine," every time I watch television, I am reminded that Western culture (and increasingly any culture with Western influences) is obsessed with thinness, and with women's thinness in particular. Weight concerns (eating disorders, health issues, body image) seem to have reached a frenzy with the general population, with the media, among psychiatrists and psychologists, and with feminists. The literature on body image and eating disorders has grown exponentially in the past decade. This lecture will deal with several issues and will examine them from a feminist psychological perspective. What are the feminist and psychological explanations for eating disorders and body image disturbance? Why is the current ideal a thin one? What is the meaning behind the current standard of beauty? Finally, what is the impact on women to strive toward the current ideal, which is perpetually young and perpetually thin, and unobtainable for most and eventually all women?

PERSPECTIVES ON WOMEN AND WEIGHT

Beliefs about what is attractive or erotic varies from one culture to another and from one historical period to another. What is beautiful? In some cultures, facial scarring is attractive; in others, drooping breasts. What is currently beautiful for women in Western culture? If one looks at the media—television, movies, magazines—one sees models who are tall and very thin; they are wrinkle-free and have small hips and waists, medium to large breasts, and European features. Women throughout the world are literally bombarded with Western images of this unrealistically slim, eternally young ideal woman. Weights for Miss America winners have consistently decreased since the 1950s, as have weights for fashion models and *Playboy* centerfold models (Garner, Garfinkel, Schwartz, & Thompson, 1980; Owen & Laurel-Seller, 2000; Wiseman, Gray, Mosimann, & Ahrens, 1992). These are women who represent ideal female beauty in our society—and they are getting thinner. Marilyn Monroe, who was a sex symbol in the 1950s, would be considered large by today's standards. Some of the current models bear a striking resemblance to Twiggy, who was popular in the 1960s, another period in which the body ideal was extremely thin.

Lori Irving (1990) found that women see the media as the main source of pressure to be thin. A study of women's magazines showed that 78 percent of the covers contained some message about body appearance, 94 percent showed a thin woman on the cover, and many of the articles suggested that losing weight or "changing the appearance of one's body will lead to better relationships, stronger friendships, and happier lives" (Malkin, Wornian, & Chrisler, 1999, p. 652). Who wouldn't want to lose weight if these are the rewards?

Large women are often treated very poorly in Western society. Individuals often attribute negative characteristics to large people, and more so to large women. People are less likely to want to associate with large people (see Jackson, 1992, for a review). A substantial volume of research demonstrates that fat people are discriminated against in a variety of areas, including healthcare (Hebl & Xu, 2001; Johnson, 2005), psychotherapy (Davis-Coelho, Waltz, & Davis-Coelho, 2000), college admissions (Rothblum, Brand, Miller, & Oetjen, 1990), financial support from parents (Crandall, 1991), and job applications (Rothblum, Miller, & Garbutt, 1988; see Solovay, 2000, for more information). There is extreme pressure on people, especially women, to be thin. Large women are evaluated more negatively than large men (Oliver, 2006; Stake & Lauer, 1987). Because being physically attractive is more important for women (Wade, 2000), being, or perceiving oneself to be, fat can result in negative consequences, such as social rejection and poor self-esteem for women (Stake & Lauer, 1987), especially for White women (Hebl & Heatherton, 1997).

What is the result of this societal pressure on women to be thin? Numerous studies have found that women are obsessed with thinness and unhappy with their weight, and that more similarities than differences exist across ethnic groups (Shaw, Ramirez, Trost, Randall, & Stice, 2004). For example, Thompson and Sargent (2000) found that 40 percent of their sample of White and Black women were highly concerned about their weight, 63 percent saw their ideal figure as smaller than their own, and 59 percent of Black women and 72 percent of White women thought that they were overweight (although only about 13 percent in both groups were actually overweight). Smith and Krejci (1991) found that one-third of their sample of Hispanic, Native American, and White public high school girls were "always terrified of weight gain," and 22 percent were "never satisfied with body shape." Rosen and colleagues found that 70 percent of the Native American women in their sample were trying to lose weight

(Rosen, Shafer, Dummer, Cross, Deuman, & Malmberg, 1988). Asian women also desire to be thinner (Barnett, Keel, & Conoscenti, 2001), as do Mexican American women (Cachelin, Monreal, & Juarez, 2006). Some research suggests that social class also may impact body image. Wang, Byrne, Kenardy, and Hills (2005) found that adolescent girls from high socioeconomic status (SES) families perceived themselves as larger than their ideal to a greater extent than did those from lower-SES backgrounds. Although underweight women tend to be most satisfied with their size, it seems that even they worry about their weight (Thompson & Sargent, 2000). Women are generally more dissatisfied than men with their appearance because they believe their bodies are too fat (Fallon & Rozin, 1985; Forbes, Adams-Curtis, Rade, & Jaberg, 2001).

As a result of feeling overweight, women are going to great lengths to avoid body fat. Hesse-Biber (1989) found that 59 percent of college women in her survey were using extreme and unhealthy measures, such as fasting, vomiting, and using laxatives to control their weight. Rosen and colleagues (Rosen et al., 1988) found similar percentages in their sample of Chippewa women and girls. It is estimated that as many as 11 percent of young women suffer from some type of eating disorder (Herzog & Copeland, 1985), which also includes preoccupation with food and extreme fear of becoming fat. In populations where thinness is mandatory—for example, dancers and models—eating disorders have been found to be common (Anshel, 2004; Garner & Garfinkel, 1978; Pierce & Daleng, 1998).

Because of the emphasis placed on women's attractiveness, women with physical disabilities may be particularly vulnerable to body dissatisfaction. Many of the women in a study by Taleporos and McCabe (2001) reported that their disabilities made them feel physically and sexually unattractive.

Although women of all ethnicities and sexualities have expressed dissatisfaction with body size, the results of a number of studies have suggested that body dissatisfaction may be lower for non-White, older, and nonheterosexual women. For example, Altabe (1998) found that European American and Hispanic American women showed more body dissatisfaction than African Americans and Asian Americans. Perry, Rosenblatt, and Wang (2004) found that White adolescents had smaller body ideals than either Hispanic or African American girls.

Several studies have found that lesbians are more comfortable with their bodies than are heterosexual women, even though they tend to weigh more (Bergeron & Senn, 1998; Brand, Rothblum, & Solomon, 1992; Morrison, Morrison, & Sager, 2004). Sari Dworkin (1988) cautioned us to remember that lesbians have been socialized in the same culture as heterosexual women; therefore, we should not be surprised to find that lesbian and heterosexual women share the same body image concerns. Her concern is supported by other studies that show that lesbians have levels of body dissatisfaction similar to those of heterosexual women (Beren, Hayden, Wilfley, & Streigel-Moore, 1997; Heffernan, 1996).

As Western images have spread throughout the world, the Western image of beauty has increasingly become the ideal. When Western images became widely available on Fiji television, girls' body image decreased and disordered eating increased as they sought to emulate television characters (Becker, Burwell, Herzog, Hamburg, & Gilman, 2002). In a study of 12 countries, researchers found that people in more Westernized countries, such as Italy, Spain, France, and Germany, reported more body dissatisfaction than those in non-Western countries, such as India, Iran, and Ghana (Jaeger et al., 2002). When women emigrate from non-Western to Western cultures, they often take on the decreased body satisfaction and increased disordered eating of their new culture (Chamorro & Flores-Ortiz, 2000; Jaeger et al, 2002).

In one study, Stevens and Tiggemann (1998) found that body dissatisfaction did not vary with age, and, in a study of Swiss women aged 30–75, 71 percent wanted to be thinner, although 73 percent of them were within the normal weight range (Allaz, Bernstein, Rouget, Archinard, & Morabia, 1998). Unfortunately, it seems that body dissatisfaction and weight preoccupation can be found in all groups of women. There is one fascinating exception: Old Order Amish. In a recent study, young Amish women and average-sized Amish women were not dissatisfied with their body size (Platte, Zelten, & Stunkard, 2000). Thus, it appears that separation from Western culture and its media has benefits!

The medical community, and even some psychologists, tend to view eating disorders and negative and distorted body images as diseases, which can only be diagnosed, treated, and "cured" by a medical professional (Bordo, 1993). Those with eating disorders are seen as abnormal or mentally ill, and the problem is attributed to the individual rather than to some external source. Indeed, much of the research on eating disorders and treatment is done by doctors, usually psychiatrists.

Certainly, poor eating patterns can result in health problems that require medical attention; however, eating disorders and negative body image may not be caused by physiological problems but by cultural and social pressures to be thin. Some psychologists and feminists argue that these eating disorders and negative body image may be symptoms of a larger "disease"—namely, the patriarchy—which has an underlying fear of women's power (Chernin, 1981; Freedman, 1986; Frost, 2001; Wolf, 1991). Although the overt social message may be "Thinner is fitter is stronger," the effect of the current emphasis of extreme thinness—a nearly unattainable goal for many women—is to keep women's self-esteem low and create a passive and readily exploitable group that will not fight the patriarchal structure (Freedman, 1986). Wolf (1991) maintains that "a cultural fixation on female thinness is not an obsession about female beauty but an obsession about female obedience" (p. 187).

Maybe feminists are overreacting or being paranoid. After all, beauty has "always" been important to women. Women have bound their feet, removed their ribs, and bound their breasts in order to maintain then current standards of beauty. Women have always adorned themselves and wanted to be beautiful and have performed harsh actions to be beautiful. Rodin and Streigel-Moore (1984, as cited in Rodin, Silberstein, & Streigel-Moore, 1984) found that weight and body image were the central determinants of women's physical attractiveness. Rubin (1979) found that, when women were asked to describe themselves in a way that would give a good sense of who they are, they consistently described their bodies, rather than their roles or careers. Women aren't doing anything nearly as extreme these days as binding their feet and, besides, thin is healthier, right? But given some estimates that between 1 and 3 percent of young women have a diagnosed eating disorder (Pearson, Goldklang, & Streigel-Moore, 2002), that at least 20 percent of college women engage in disordered eating (Mintz & Kashubek, 1999), that yo-yo dieting is unhealthy and can lead to health problems (see Ernsberger and Koletsky, 1999, for a review), and that individuals have genetically set weights, which their bodies will seek to maintain (Bennett, 1995), thin is not necessarily healthy. Women are going to extremes to lose weight, and many are suffering from anorexia nervosa and bulimia, negative body image, and low self-esteem because they have not met and cannot meet body ideals.

Many feminist theorists have examined the issue of disordered eating and body image. However, much of the focus in mainstream psychology and medicine, such as psychiatry, has been on diagnosis and treatment and on psychological factors within the individual or family that may have caused the problem (Foulkes, 1996; Jackson, 1992). The medical community has very often interpreted the causes and origins as medical or biological (for example, chemical disorders in the brain) rather than examining cultural influences, such as the extreme pressure to be thin in our society. Less focus has been on contributing factors, outside of mental disorders. The issue of mental disorders is an important one. What person in her right mind would starve herself to death? Women get labeled as masochistic or mentally ill for performing beauty rituals, but if they don't buy into the beauty ideal, if they don't try to make themselves beautiful and thin, they are still seen negatively, because they have failed to conform or have challenged the role that has been set up for them. What woman in her right mind wouldn't try to be beautiful?

The emphasis on mental disorders was most apparent in 1987, when the revised *Diagnostic and Statistical Manual of Mental Disorders*, put out by the American Psychiatric Association, added body dysmorphic disorder. This disorder has three aspects: dissatisfaction with appearance of the body, preoccupation with this aspect of appearance, and exaggeration of this defect. Fitts, Gibson, Redding, and Deiter (1989) found that 36 percent of college-aged women report strong agreement with all three aspects, with 85 percent reporting strong dissatisfaction, 60 percent strong preoccupation, and 57 percent strong exaggeration. Does this mean that over one-third of college women have a mental disorder regarding their body image? Women tend to exaggerate descriptions of huge thighs and stomachs. Does this mean that they have body dysmorphic disorder? Women internalize the message to be thin, that they must get rid of the areas that make them "fat," and then when they do, they are told that they have a mental disorder. Instead of examining social and cultural factors that might be contributing to these problems of distorted body image and problem eating, these behaviors are seen as abnormal, and women who have such concerns are seen as deviant or mentally ill, yet at least one study (Fitts et al., 1989) suggests that body image distortion and preoccupation may not be abnormal or infrequent at all.

HEALTH ISSUES

A number of authors (Campos, 2004; Gaesser, 2002; Oliver, 2006; Seid, 1989) have argued that the medical community promotes thinness by emphasizing the hazards of obesity but ignoring the health hazards that can be associated with thinness and dieting. One of the most common arguments against obesity (or just about any appearance of "excess" body fat) is that it is unhealthy. However, maintaining oneself in a state of semi-starvation, which is what it would take for most women to achieve the ideal body (Rodin et al., 1984; Wolf, 1991) cannot be considered to be healthy behavior. Also, few men are in weight-loss programs, even though there is evidence that abdominally-localized fat (the apple shape more common to men than women) is linked to increased risk of cardiovascular disease, diabetes, hypertension, and cancer (see Rodin, 1992, for a review of this literature).

Glenn Gaesser, an exercise physiologist, performed an extensive review of the medical literature on weight and weight loss. According to Gaesser (2002), fat can actually reduce the risk of certain diseases, such as lung cancer and osteoporosis, in both women and men. In addition, thigh and hip fat in women appears to provide protection against cardiovascular disease as well as certain kinds of diabetes. Gaesser's argument is not that fat is healthier than thin but that metabolic fitness is more important than fatness. He argues that individuals can be physically fit at almost any weight.

However, the belief that thinner equals healthier may be so ingrained in the minds of medical professionals that they find it difficult to acknowledge the substantial data that do not support their beliefs. An example of this research is a study by Sorley, Gordon, and Kannel (1980), who found that obesity did not affect mortality rates until women were at least 110 percent over their average weight. Also, the weight standard used by many physicians and researchers is the U.S. Metropolitan Life Insurance Company Table, which is based on life insurance applicants in 1959, most of whom were White middle- and upper-class men of Eastern European descent. These tables were never valid for women, especially non-White, working-class women (Rothblum, 1990). Reuben Andres (1980), former Clinical Director of the National Institute on Aging, found that the best weights for optimum longevity are 20 to 30 percent above the Metropolitan Life Insurance Company standards, and worst longevity is associated only with weight extremes: the very thinnest and very heaviest of the population (see Ernsberger and Koletsky, 1999, for an extensive review of the literature on weight and health). Physicians also fail to recognize that dieting can result in inadequate nutrition, fatigue, apathy, heart palpitations, bone loss, depression, loss of sexual desire, and sudden death from cardiac arrhythmia (Ciliska, 1990; National Institutes of Health, 2003). As Drs. Jerome Kassirer and Marcia Angell (1998) wrote in the New England Journal of Medicine, "the cure for obesity may be worse than the condition" (p. 53).

Because of the medical community's insistence that thin equals healthy, the emphasis on thinness has been argued by both medical professionals and laypeople from a health point of view, which gives the impression of a "serious" concern, rather than from the "superficial" point of view of aesthetics. Hence, a woman should be thin because it is healthier, not because Western society sees it as more attractive. Because thinness is equated with health, women may be rewarded for starving themselves, or engaging in unhealthy behavior such as purging, or using laxatives, as long as the end result is a thin body.

But why has thinness been especially emphasized for women if it is a health risk for both sexes? Attractiveness is more important for women (Wade, 2000), and unattractive men are evaluated more favorably than unattractive women. Thinness is currently associated with physical attractiveness, and physical attractiveness and its pursuit are integral to the feminine gender role (Rodin et al., 1984). Certainly, thinness is paramount to women's attractiveness (Coward, 1985; Wolf, 1991). And what is beautiful is thin.

FEMININITY AND POWER

Attractive women are perceived as more feminine than unattractive women (Jackson, 1983; Tiggemann & Kenyon, 1998). Some studies suggest that high femininity corresponds with more negative body image (Forbes et al., 2001; Joiner & Kashubeck, 1996). Research by Brown, Cross, and Nelson (1990) has suggested that college women who have engaged in bulimic behaviors tend to be more traditionally feminine than nonbulimic women. Thus, beauty and the pursuit of it are part of the traditional feminine role, in which most (if not all) of us have been socialized to various degrees.

However, many women who are not traditionally feminine are also concerned about their bodies and may engage in unhealthy eating behaviors and strive toward a thin ideal. Because women have traditionally had access to few avenues of achievement, beauty may be one socially acceptable form of achievement for women, because it is part of the traditional feminine role. Rodin et al. (1984) suggested that, "in striving to be thin and beautiful, a woman may be both feminine, thus pleasing society, and experience a sense of agency and control" (p. 292). Garner and Garfinkel (1978) suggested that adolescent women may confuse weight loss with personal accomplishment and achievement. But is this confusion—or is it a very real and safe form of achievement? The issue of control will be addressed again later, because for women, gaining control of their weight is often linked to gaining control of their lives.

As women achieve more and gain in power, attractiveness may become even more important, as seems to be the case currently. Certainly, powerful women are often seen negatively (Masser & Abrams, 2004). Powerful women threaten those who want to maintain the patriarchy. By being thin, a high-achieving woman may believe she is maintaining her feminine identity (Rodin et al., 1984). It may be a way of saying to society, "Don't worry, I don't want to be a man. See how feminine I look?" Thus, by conforming to social expectations, the powerful woman may be seen as less threatening.

The issue of fear of women's power is an important one. What both Black women and White women report disliking most about their bodies are those features that are unique to women: rounded hips, thighs, and stomachs (Munter, 1992; Thomas & James, 1988). Women with eating disorders often express a desire to lose all evidence of their womanly bodies, so in their attempts to obtain the ideal body, women are removing their unique physical characteristics to obtain a body that is not womanly but childlike. And many feminist theorists believe that it is not a coincidence that the beauty ideal is childlike. Children are weak and nonthreatening, unlike powerful women (Chernin, 1981). In early 1993, *Newsweek* published a review of the new popular models (Leland & Leonard, 1993), who were "boyish" and "waiflike." This new image of women was deemed to be liberating because frailness and weakness meant women no longer have to work out to be attractive. But a waif does not ask for equal pay or day-care for her children. A waif is an innocent child, nonthreatening, powerless. A more recent image (late 1990s) is what has been deemed "heroin chic"; the models, who are emaciated and have hollowed-out cheeks, look as if they are suffering the effects of heroin addiction. Far from being an improvement over the waif look, heroin chic may be seen as a more extreme version of it. Looking as if one is addicted to heroin is hardly a healthy or an empowering image for women to emulate. Although these images are from the 1990s, the images have not changed much since the beginning of the twenty-first century.

Susan Bordo (1993) discussed how the body reflects certain values and is a reflection of an individual. We seek to create a body that projects who we are, what our values are, so what a body looks like, how it is shaped, has a meaning in our culture. What meanings might a thin body represent? A thin body might represent weakness, malleability, conformity to patriarchy. It may also represent achievement and control.

In the 1920s, the 1960s, and the current period, the beauty ideal has been extreme thinness. The First Wave of the feminist movement in the United States peaked in 1920, when women gained the right to vote. The Second Wave began in the 1960s, after the publication of *The Feminine Mystique* (Friedan, 1963). Finally, a Third Wave of feminism seemed to have emerged in the 1990s. Is it a coincidence that a thin, restrictive beauty ideal—one that reduces women to looking like waifs and heroin addicts—occurred during the same periods that women sought to gain power and control?

HOW THE MESSAGE WORKS

If the ideal is childlike thinness, how can women be convinced that this is desirable and obtainable? Women must be convinced that their self-worth is based on their beauty, that their bodies are inadequate, and that their inadequacy is because they have womanly bodies—large hips, round stomachs. A more childlike, less curvaceous body is therefore more beautiful, more desirable. This message comes at a time when women's weights have increased, due to better nutrition (Garner & Garfinkel, 1978).

In actuality, nothing is wrong with women's bodies. What is wrong is that unrealistic and unnatural standards are set up for women, standards that define beautiful women as unnaturally thin, with narrow hips, large breasts, smooth skin—and a society that values what a woman looks like more than who she is or what she does. These are not characteristics of most women's bodies. They are characteristics of prepubescent girls' bodies and men's and boys' bodies with large breasts. The standards also have European features, are able-bodied, and are eternally young. Hence, Women of Color, disabled women, and older women are excluded from "real" beauty, although all are still expected to be thin. In addition, as Liz Frost (2001) pointed out, any sign of "imperfection" is seen as unnatural and problematic. But the message must be that there is something wrong with you, not with the standards. If women fail to internalize the message, it will not serve its ultimate goal: to keep women weak. As Rita Freedman (1988) succinctly stated in her book *Beauty Bound*, "A constricted body in turn dictates an equally constricted life" (p. 78). Thus, what is presented to women is only one standard of beauty: a young, able-bodied woman who is thin almost to the point of emaciation with European features. Occasionally, Women of Color are presented, but they still have all that is "required," including European features and light skin. If beauty is presented in different sizes, ages, colors, and features, then women might think that there are many ways to be beautiful, and they might resist conforming.

The second step is to convince women that this desirable body is attainable. Part of the myth of beauty is that any woman can attain it if she can control herself (Seid, 1989; Wolf, 1991). Large women are seen as personally responsible for their size and as lacking in willpower (Crandall & Martinez, 1996). Body size is one area that women are told they can control, even though 90 percent of dieters regain the weight they lost and may actually *gain* weight as a result of dieting (Chrisler, 1989). Advertisements for various weight-loss programs emphasize that anyone (although the commercials target women) can lose weight if he or she controls his or her eating habits. Chernin (1981) argued that women get the message that, if they can control their weight, they can control their lives. Because women have not been able to control much of their lives, the message that women can take control of anything is a powerful one for them: Job discrimination, violence against women, misogyny—will all cease to exist in her life if only she can control her weight. Orbach (1979) suggested that, by being thin, women can gain control over both traditionally feminine goals, such as attracting men, and traditionally masculine goals, such as competing successfully in the workplace. Hence, this issue of control that women often lack in their lives becomes transferred to control of their bodies. If women can control their bodies, they may think they can control other aspects of their lives.

Fredrickson and Roberts (1997) constructed their objectification theory to describe how women are socialized to adopt an outsider's gaze. Women learn to be evaluated as objects and, thus, come to feel detached from their personal identities. As a result, women become preoccupied with their appearance. Instead of rejecting unrealistic body standards, women feel shame when they compare themselves with the standards and judge their own bodies as inadequate. In an ingenious test of this theory, women and men wore either a bulky sweater or a swimsuit while solving math problems. Women (but not men) wearing a swimsuit did significantly worse on the problems, which suggests that body shame can actually consume women's mental resources (Fredrickson, Roberts, Noll, Quinn, & Twenge, 1998).

Not only must women control their weight, but they should also control any signs of aging. The body must be a thin, youthful one. Numerous products are offered to eliminate wrinkles and prevent "signs of aging." Naomi Wolf (1991) wrote a scathing review of the cosmetics industry, which feeds into the fear of aging many women have. As she noted, these false claims have received few objections from the U.S. Food and Drug Administration, which is responsible for monitoring claims of drugs and cosmetics, yet women spend $20 billion a year on these products, which do not work, in hopes of holding back aging. In addition, according to the American Society of Plastic and Reconstructive Surgeons, over 10 million cosmetic surgery procedures were performed in 2005 (an increase of 775 percent from 1992), over 85 percent of those procedures were done on women. The most common procedure is Botox treatment for temporary wrinkle reduction (American Society of Plastic and Reconstructive Surgeons, 2005). Women who seek these "anti-aging" treatments realize that a woman's worth is still determined by her beauty; as women age, they are perceived as "losing their looks." If the goal is to create a childlike innocence, signs of years of gaining wisdom and experience, signs such as laugh lines around mouth or eyes, are not considered to be beautiful (Sontag, 1979). In fact, they may be seen as threatening by those who seek naive, easily exploitable, nonthreatening women.

Capitalism also plays a role in convincing women that the current body ideal is desirable and attainable. In a capitalist society, it is profitable to create a problem and then offer a product to solve that problem. If cellulite were considered desirable, or at least nonproblematic, there would be no need to go to the gym to remove it or buy diet food to reduce fat. If short eyelashes, cellulite, wrinkles, or gray hair is a "problem," one need only purchase a product or service and the problem can be solved. Again, the message is that women can control their bodies.

What happens to women (eventually, all of us) who do not achieve the ideal body? When individuals repeatedly try to achieve something they are led to believe they can control, and they repeatedly fail, their self-esteem suffers. And this is exactly what our obsession with thinness has done to women. Many studies have demonstrated that women with negative body images have low self-esteem (Davison & McCabe, 2006; Forbes et al, 2001; Pliner, Chaiken, & Flett, 1990). Irving (1990) found that women who were exposed to advertisements with thin models had significantly lower self-esteem than women exposed to larger-sized models. This loss of self-esteem was evident in the laboratory after participants were shown only a few photographs. Jones (2001) demonstrated that when girls compare themselves to models they tend to feel dissatisfied with their bodies, and Cattarin, Thompson, Thomas, and Williams (2000) found that women who saw models that represented the thin and attractive cultural ideal became more anxious, more depressed, and less satisfied with their appearance than did women who saw models who were more average in attractiveness and thinness. What happens when women everywhere are exposed to thousands of these thin models?

By emphasizing that anyone can maintain an unattainable ideal, and that to be valued as a woman you must be beautiful, women blame themselves for not being able to attain that ideal, rather than seeing the ideal as unrealistic. Women feel like failures. And because they do not look like the ideal, they dislike their own bodies and, therefore, themselves. Their self-esteem suffers because they are labeled as failures, by themselves and by a culture that demands thinness (as well as youth) in women.

It is to the advantage of the patriarchal power structure to keep women's self-esteem low. A woman with high self-esteem does not tolerate pay inequity, sexual harassment, and the lack of safe and affordable childcare. As Wolf (1991) stated, "the beauty myth generates low self-esteem for women and high profits for corporations as a result" (p. 49). A patriarchal social system can maintain itself only if women are controlled and subordinated. As women gain access to some power structures, the system becomes threatened. By generating self-hatred in women, the system can guarantee that women will not question the system or rise up against it. Also, if women are preoccupied with themselves and channeling all their energies into their bodies, they don't have the time or energy to fight for equal pay, for an end to violence against women, or for reproductive rights, so women will be unwilling or unable to fight misogyny or oppose the patriarchal system.

An unrealistic beauty ideal also creates hatred between women. If beauty is the goal, and it is, then women will be jealous of other women who have reached the goal that they themselves cannot reach. They will be jealous of women who are valued by society. Certainly, one of the prime goals of beauty is to be pleasing and valuable to men. However, if the only goal of the beauty standards were to be pleasing to men, women would strive to be only as thin as men find desirable. But some studies suggest that women, especially White women, overestimate the extent to which men value thinness (Demarest & Allen, 2000; Fallon & Rozin, 1985). And Streigel-Moore, Tucker, and Hsu (1990) found that lesbian college students (who would, presumably, have less interest in being pleasing to men) had levels of body image dissatisfaction and disordered eating similar to those of a comparison group of heterosexual college women. Hence, there is more to the emphasis on thinness than being aesthetically pleasing to potential male partners.

Beauty is also an arena of competition for women. Women actively compete to be more beautiful than other women, constantly scrutinizing themselves and comparing themselves with other women. This is one area where ambition, a traditionally masculine attribute, is acceptable. Beauty is not only an acceptable ambition for women—it is expected. Women who do not attempt to (or are perceived as not attempting to) fit the beauty ideal are often stigmatized. Because being "overweight" is seen as a sign of weakness in Western society, women who are large are often scorned for daring to reject the thin ideal (even though they may actually desire a thin body) (see Tenzer, 1989, for examples). Feminists have traditionally been criticized for challenging and defying standard images of beauty (see, for example, Richardson, 1982). Chapkis (1986) discussed the challenge feminists have made to the beauty ideal, suggesting (as I do) that feminist defiance to the beauty ideal will lead to liberation from it. Women who defy the beauty ideal are directly challenging the ideal set up for them, and such women are threatening to those who seek to minimize women's power. Ojerholm and Rothblum (1999) suggested that women's challenge to the beauty ideal may be more threatening to the patriarchy than any specific feminist political action. Note a statement by conservative Rush Limbaugh, suggesting that women are feminists because they are too ugly to get a man. Feminists are often perceived as unattractive because it is "unattractive" to challenge the patriarchy to those who seek to keep women weak.

The beauty ideal is being actively challenged by feminist psychologists, not only through theory but also through direct action. Susan Tenzer (1989) discussed a form of group therapy, Fat Acceptance Therapy, aimed at liberating women from the social pressure to be thin, leading to a gain in power and self-esteem. Joan Chrisler (1989) argued that feminist therapists should not counsel clients to lose weight unless their weight proposes health risks. Because weight loss can damage health as well as self-esteem because most diets don't work (and to counsel clients to do something they are unlikely to succeed at is harmful), therapists should instead work on enhancing client self-esteem and feelings of personal power. Myrna Frank (1999) challenged us to be *culture-wise* parents, to raise girls who will resist cultural definitions. Hence, it is true that feminism is a threat to the beauty ideal, because the beauty ideal is a threat to women.

*C*ONCLUSION

Recognizing the impact of social standards of weight and body image is of great importance in efforts to empower women. And discussions of eating disorders and body image are incomplete without recognizing why these standards exist and why such pressures are put upon women. This lecture has sought to address the specific messages women receive about weight and body image as symptoms of a larger disease, one that seeks to keep women weak. Until the messages are recognized for what they are—attempts to suppress women—women will continue to dislike their bodies and, therefore, themselves. These issues must be recognized as part of the backlash against feminism, which, as Susan Faludi (1991) documented, seeks to convince women that feminism is women's own worst enemy and has only resulted in more misery for women. This is a powerful and dangerous message, especially when so many women are striving for power but hating themselves. How these messages affect our self-esteem, our images of our bodies, and our attitudes toward ourselves cannot be addressed fully by feminists or psychologists without recognition of this backlash.

Nita McKinley (2004) studied women who endorse fat acceptance, and found that these women did not use body size as a means of self-acceptance. A growing movement of "health at every size" endorses acceptance and respect of a variety of body sizes and promotes health and well-being for all people. Indeed, it is fear of fat that increases body hatred and shame in women no matter what size they are. Thus, if women come to see their own worth as more than their body (size), and if we learn to respect women and men at every size, all of us will be happier, healthier, and stronger. Commit a radical act—love your body.

REFERENCES

ALLAZ, A., BERNSTEIN, M., ROUGET, P., ARCHINARD, M., & MORABIA, A. (1998). Body weight preoccupation in middle-age and ageing women: A general population survey. *International Journal of Eating Disorders, 23,* 287–294.

ALTABE, M. (1998). Ethnicity and body image: Quantitative and qualitative analysis. *International Journal of Eating Disorders, 23,* 153–159.

AMERICAN PSYCHIATRIC ASSOCIATION. (1987). *Diagnostic and statistical manual of mental disorders* (3rd ed., rev.). Washington, DC: Author.

AMERICAN SOCIETY OF PLASTIC AND RECONSTRUCTIVE SURGEONS. (2005). Retrieved from http://www.plasticsurgery.org/public_education/2005statistics.cfm

ANDRES, R. (1980). Effects of obesity on total mortality. *International Journal of Obesity, 4,* 381–386.

ANSHEL, M. (2004). Sources of disordered eating patterns between ballet dancers and nondancers. *Journal of Sport Behavior, 27,* 115–133.

BARNETT, H. L., KEEL, P. L., & CONOSCENTI, L. M. (2001). Body type preferences in Asian and Caucasian college students. *Sex Roles, 45,* 867–878.

BECKER, A. E., BURWELL, R. A., HERZOG, D. B., HAMBURG, P., & GILMAN, S. E. (2002). Eating behaviours and attitudes following prolonged exposure to television among ethnic Fijian adolescent girls. *British Journal of Psychiatry, 180,* 509–514.

BENNETT, W. I. (1995). Beyond overeating. *New England Journal of Medicine, 332,* 673–674.

BEREN, S. E., HAYDEN, H. A., WILFLEY, D. E., & STREIGEL-MOORE, R. H. (1997). Body dissatisfaction among lesbian college students: The conflict of straddling mainstream and lesbian cultures. *Psychology of Women Quarterly, 21,* 431–445.

BERGERON, S. M., & SENN, C. Y. (1998). Body image and sociocultural norms: A comparison of lesbian and heterosexual women. *Psychology of Women Quarterly, 22,* 385–401.

BORDO, S. (1993). *Unbearable weight: Feminism, Western culture, and the body.* Berkeley: University of California Press.

BRAND, P. A., ROTHBLUM, E. D., & SOLOMON, L. J. (1992). A comparison of lesbians, gay men, and heterosexuals on weight and restrained eating. *International Journal of Eating Disorders, 11,* 253–259.

BROWN, J. A., CROSS, H. J., & NELSON, J. M. (1990). Sex-role identity and sex-role ideology in college women with bulimic behavior. *International Journal of Eating Disorders, 9,* 571–575.

CACHELIN, F. M., MONREAL, T. K., & JUAREZ, L. C. (2006). Body image and size perceptions of Mexican American women. *Body Image, 3,* 67–75.

CAMPOS, P. (2004). *The obesity myth: Why America's obsession is hazardous to your health.* New York: Gotham Books.

CATTARIN, J. A., THOMPSON, J. K., THOMAS, C., & WILLIAMS, R. (2000). Body image, mood, and televised images of attractiveness: The role of social comparison. *Journal of Social and Clinical Psychology, 19,* 220–239.

CHAMORRO, R., & FLORES-ORTIZ, Y. (2000). Acculturation and disordered eating patterns among Mexican-American women. *International Journal of Eating Disorders, 28,* 125–129.

CHAPKIS, W. (1986). *Beauty secrets: Women and the politics of appearance.* Boston: South End Press.

CHERNIN, K. (1981). *The obsession.* New York: Harper & Row.

CHRISLER, J. C. (1989). Should feminist therapists do weight loss counseling? *Women & Therapy, 8,* 31–27.

CILISKA, D. (1990). *Beyond dieting: Psychoeducational interventions for chronically obese women—A non-dieting approach.* New York: Brunner/Mazel.

COWARD, R. (1985). *Female desires: How they are sought, bought, and packaged.* New York: Grove Press.

CRANDALL, C. S. (1991). Do heavyweight children have a more difficult time paying for college? *Personality and Social Psychology Bulletin, 17,* 606–611.

CRANDALL, C. S., & MARTINEZ, R. (1996). Culture, ideology, and anti-fat attitudes. *Personality and Social Psychology Bulletin, 22,* 1165–1176.

DAVIS-COELHO, K., WALTZ, J., & DAVIS-COELHO, B. (2000). Awareness and prevention of bias against fat clients in psychotherapy. *Professional Psychology: Research and Practice, 31,* 682–684.

DAVISON, T. E., & MCCABE, M. E. (2006). Adolescent body image and psychosocial functioning. *Journal of Social Psychology, 146,* 15–30.

DEMAREST, J., & ALLEN, R. (2000). Body image: Gender, ethnic, and age differences. *Journal of Social Psychology, 140,* 465–472.

DWORKIN, S. H. (1988). Not in man's image: Lesbians and the cultural oppression of body image. *Women & Therapy, 8,* 27–39.

ERNSBERGER, P., & KOLETSKY, R. J. (1999). Biomedical rationale for a wellness approach to obesity: An alternative to a focus on weight loss. *Journal of Social Issues, 55,* 221–259.

FALLON, A. E., & ROZIN, P. (1985). Sex differences in perceptions of body shape. *Journal of Abnormal Psychology, 94,* 102–105.

FALUDI, S. (1991). *Backlash: The undeclared war against American women.* New York: Crown.

FITTS, S. N., GIBSON, P., REDDING, C. A., & DEITER, P. J. (1989). Body dysmorphic disorder: Implications for its validity as a *DSM-III-R* clinical syndrome. *Psychological Reports, 64,* 655–658.

FORBES, G. B., ADAMS-CURTIS, L. E., RADE, B., & JABERG, P. (2001). Body dissatisfaction in women and men: The role of gender-typing and self-esteem. *Sex Roles, 44,* 461–484.

FOULKES, E. (1996). Eating disorders, families, and therapy. *Australian Journal of Psychotherapy, 15,* 28–42.

FRANK, M. L. (1999). Raising daughters to resist negative cultural messages about body image. *Women & Therapy, 22,* 69–88.

FREDRICKSON, B. L., & ROBERTS, T. (1997). Objectification theory: Toward understanding women's lived experiences and mental health risks. *Psychology of Women Quarterly, 21,* 173–206.

FREDRICKSON, B. L., ROBERTS, T., NOLL, S. M., QUINN, D. M., & TWENGE, J. M. (1998). That swimsuit becomes you: Sex differences in self-objectification, restrained eating, and math performance. *Journal of Personality and Social Psychology, 75,* 269–284.

FREEDMAN, R. (1986). *Beauty bound.* Lexington, MA: D. C. Heath.

FRIEDAN, B. (1963). *The feminine mystique.* New York: W. W. Norton.

FROST, L. (2001). *Young women and the body: A feminist sociology.* New York: Palgrave.

GAESSER, G. A. (2002). *Big fat lies: The truth about your weight and your health.* Carlsbad, CA: Gurze.

GARNER, D. M., & GARFINKEL, P. E. (1978). Sociocultural factors in anorexia nervosa. *Lancet, 2,* 674.

GARNER, D. M., GARFINKEL, P. E., SCHWARTZ, D., & THOMPSON, M. (1980). Cultural expectations of thinness in women. *Psychological Reports, 47,* 483–491.

HEBL, M. R., & HEATHERTON, T. (1997). The stigma of obesity in women: The difference is black and white. *Personality and Social Psychology Bulletin, 24,* 417–426.

HEBL, M. R., & XU, J. (2001). Weighing the care: Physicians' reactions to the size of a patient. *International Journal of Eating Disorders, 25,* 1246–1252.

HEFFERNAN, K. (1996). Eating disorders and weight concern among lesbians. *International Journal of Eating Disorders, 11,* 391–396.

HERZOG, D. B., & COPELAND, P. M. (1985). Eating disorders. *New England Journal of Medicine, 313,* 295–303.

HESSE-BIBER, S. (1989). Eating patterns and disorders in a college population: Are college women's eating problems a new phenomenon? *Sex Roles, 20,* 71–89.

IRVING, L. M. (1990). Mirror images: Effects of the standard of beauty on the self and body-esteem of women exhibiting varying levels of bulimic symptoms. *Journal of Social and Clinical Psychology, 9,* 230–242.

JACKSON, L. A. (1983). The perception of androgyny and physical attractiveness: Two is better than one. *Personality and Social Psychology Bulletin, 9,* 405–413.

JACKSON, L. A. (1992). *Physical appearance and gender: Sociobiological and sociocultural perspectives.* Albany, NY: State University of New York Press.

JAEGER, B., RUGGIERO, G. M., EDLUND, B., GOMEZ-PERRETA, C., LANG, F., MOHAMMAD-KHANI, P., SAHLEEN-VEASEY, C., SCHOMER, H., & LAMPRECHT, F. (2002). Body dissatisfaction and its interrelations with other risk factors for bulimia nervosa in 12 countries. *Psychotherapy and Psychosomatics, 71,* 54–61.

JOHNSON, C. A. (2005). Personal reflections on bias, stigma, discrimination, and obesity. In K. D. Brownell, R. M. Puhl, M. B. Schwartz, & L. Rudd (Eds.), *Weight bias: Nature, consequences, and remedies* (pp. 175–191). New York: Guilford Press.

JOINER, G. W., & KASHUBECK, S. (1996). Acculturation, body image, self-esteem, and eating disorder symptomology in adolescent Mexican-American women. *Psychology of Women Quarterly, 20,* 419–435.

JONES, D. C. (2001). Social comparison and body image: Attractiveness comparisons to models and peers among adolescent girls and boys. *Sex Roles, 45,* 645–664.

KASSIRER, J. P., & ANGELL, M. (1998). Losing weight—an ill-fated New Year's resolution. *New England Journal of Medicine, 338,* 52–54.

LELAND, J., & LEONARD, E. (1993, February 1). Back to Twiggy: The skinny on a surprising revolution in fashion. *Newsweek,* pp. 64–65.

MALKIN, A. R., WORNIAN, K., & CHRISLER, J. C. (1999). Women and weight: Gendered messages on magazine covers. *Sex Roles, 40,* 647–655.

MASSER, B. M., & ABRAMS, D. (2004). Reinforcing the glass ceiling: The consequences of hostile sexism for female managerial candidates. *Sex Roles, 51,* 609–615.

McKINLEY, N. (2004). Resisting body dissatisfaction: Fat women who endorse fat acceptance. *Body Image, 1,* 213–219.

MINTZ, L. N., & KASHUBEK, S. (1999). Body image and disordered eating among Asian American and Caucasian college students: An examination of race and gender differences. *Psychology of Women Quarterly, 23,* 781–796.

MORRISON, M. A., MORRISON, T. G., & SAGER, C. (2004). Does body satisfaction differ between gay men and lesbian women and heterosexual men and women? A meta-analytic review. *Body Image, 1,* 127–138.

MUNTER, C. (1992). Fat and the fantasy of perfection. In C. S. Vance (Ed.), *Pleasure and danger: Exploring female sexuality* (pp. 225–231). London: Pandora Press.

NATIONAL INSTITUTES OF HEALTH, TECHNOLOGY CONFERENCE PANEL. (2003). Methods for voluntary weight loss and control: Technology Assessment Conference Statement. *Annals of Internal Medicine, 119,* 764–770.

OJERHOLM, A. J., & ROTHBLUM, E. D. (1999). The relationship of body image, feminism, and sexual orientation in college women. *Feminism and Psychology, 9,* 431–448.

OLIVER, J. E. (2006). *Fat politics: The real story behind America's obesity epidemic.* New York: Oxford University Press.

ORBACH, S. (1979). *Fat is a feminist issue.* New York: Paddington.

OWEN, P. R., & LAUREL-SELLER, E. (2000). Weight and shape ideals: Thin is dangerously in. *Journal of Applied Social Psychology, 30,* 979–990.

PEARSON, J., GOLDKLANG, D., & STREIGEL-MOORE, R. H. (2002). Prevention of eating disorders: Challenges and opportunities. *International Journal of Eating Disorders, 31,* 233–239.

PERRY, A. C., ROSENBLATT, E. B., & WANG, X. (2004). Physical, behavioral, and body image characteristics in a tri-racial group of adolescent girls. *Obesity Research, 12,* 1670–1679.

PIERCE, E. F., & DALENG, M. L. (1998). Distortion of body image among elite female dancers. *Perceptual and Motor Skills, 87,* 769–770.

PLATTE, P., ZELTEN, J. F., & STUNKARD, A. J. (2000). Body image and the Old Order Amish: A people separate from "the world." *International Journal of Eating Disorders, 27,* 408–414.

PLINER, P., CHAIKEN, S., & FLETT, G. L. (1990). Gender differences in concern with body weight and physical appearance over the life span. *Personality and Social Psychology Bulletin, 16,* 263–273.

RICHARDSON, R. J. (1982). *The skeptical feminist.* London: Penguin Books.

RODIN, J. (1992). Determinants of body fat localization and its implications for health. *Annals of Behavioral Medicine, 14,* 275–281.

RODIN, J., SILBERSTEIN, L., & STREIGEL-MOORE, R. (1984). Women and weight: A normative discontent. *Nebraska Symposium on Motivation, 32,* 267–307.

ROSEN, L. W., SHAFER, C. L., DUMMER, G. M., CROSS, L. K., DEUMAN, G. W., & MALMBERG, S. R. (1988). Prevalence of pathogenic weight-control behaviors among Native American women and girls. *International Journal of Eating Disorders, 7,* 807–811.

ROTHBLUM, E. D. (1990). Women and weight: Fad and fiction. *Journal of Psychology, 124,* 5–24.

ROTHBLUM, E. D., BRAND, P. A., MILLER, C. T., & OETJEN, H. A. (1990). The relationships between obesity, employment discrimination, and employment-related victimization. *Journal of Vocational Behavior, 37,* 251–266.

ROTHBLUM, E. D., MILLER, C. T., & GARBUTT, B. (1988). Stereotypes of obese female job applicants. *International Journal of Eating Disorders, 7,* 277–283.

RUBIN, L. (1979). *Women of a certain age.* New York: Harper & Row.

SEID, R. P. (1989). *Never too thin: Why women are at war with their bodies.* New York: Prentice Hall.

SHAW, H., RAMIREZ, L., TROST, A., RANDALL, P., & STICE, E. (2004). Body image and eating disturbances across ethnic groups: More similarities than differences. *Psychology of Addictive Behavior, 18,* 12–18.

SMITH, J. E., & KREJCI, J. (1991). Minorities join the majority: Eating disturbances among Hispanic and Native American youth. *International Journal of Eating Disorders, 10,* 179–186.

SOLOVAY, S. (2000). *Tipping the scales of justice: Fighting weight-based discrimination.* Amherst, NY: Prometheus Books.

SONTAG, S. (1979). The double standard of aging. In J. H. Williams (Ed.), *Psychology of women: Selected readings* (pp. 462–478). New York: W. W. Norton.

SORLEY, P., GORDON, T., & KANNEL, W. B. (1980). Body build and mortality: The Framingham Study. *Journal of the American Medical Association, 243,* 1828–1831.

STAKE, J., & LAUER, M. L. (1987). The consequences of being overweight: A controlled study of gender differences. *Sex Roles, 17,* 31–47.

STEVENS, C., & TIGGEMANN, M. (1998). Women's body figure preferences across the lifespan. *Journal of Genetic Psychology, 159,* 94–102.

STREIGEL-MOORE, R. H., TUCKER, N., & HSU, J. (1990). Body image dissatisfaction and disordered eating among lesbian college students. *International Journal of Eating Disorders, 9,* 493–500.

TALEPOROS, G., & MCCABE, M. P. (2001). The impact of physical disability on body esteem. *Sexuality and Disability, 19,* 293–308.

TENZER, S. (1989). Fat Acceptance Therapy (F.A.T.): A non-dieting group approach to physical wellness, insight and self-acceptance. *Women & Therapy, 8,* 39–47.

THOMAS, V. G., & JAMES, M. D. (1988). Body image, dieting tendencies, and sex role traits in urban Black women. *Sex Roles, 18,* 523–529.

THOMPSON, B. (1994). *A hunger so wide and so deep: American women speak out on eating problems.* Minneapolis: University of Minnesota Press.

THOMPSON, S. H., & SARGENT, R. G. (2000). Black and White women's weight related attitudes and parental criticism of their childhood appearance. *Women & Health, 20,* 77–92.

TIGGEMANN, M., & KENYON, S. J. (1998). The hairless norm: The removal of body hair in women. *Sex Roles, 39,* 873–885.

WADE, T. J. (2000). Evolutionary theory and self-perception: Sex differences in the relationships between self-perceived physical attractiveness and sexual attractiveness, self-esteem, and body esteem. *International Journal of Psychology, 35,* 36–45.

WANG, Z., BYRN, N. M., KENARDY, J. A., & HILLS, A. P. (2005). Influences of ethnicity and socioeconomic status on the body dissatisfaction and eating behaviour of Australian children and adolescents. *Eating Behaviors, 6,* 23–33.

WISEMAN, C. V., GRAY, J. J., MOSIMANN, J. E., & AHRENS, A. H. (1992). Cultural expectations of thinness in women: An update. *International Journal of Eating Disorders, 11,* 85–89.

WOLF, N. (1991). *The beauty myth.* New York: William Morrow.

SUGGESTED READINGS

BROWNELL, K. D., PUHL, R. M., SCHWARTZ, M. B., & RUDD, L. (Eds.). (2005). *Weight bias: Nature, consequences, and remedies.* New York: Guilford Press.

EDUT, O. (Ed.). (2000). *Body outlaws: Young women write about body image and identity.* Seattle: Seal Press.

GAESSER, G. A. (2002). *Big fat lies: The truth about your weight and your health.* Carlsbad, CA: Gurze.

THOMPSON, B. W. (1994). *A hunger so wide and so deep: American women speak out on eating problems.* Minneapolis: University of Minnesota Press.

*C*ARLA GOLDEN *is Professor of Psychology at Ithaca College. Dr. Golden has taught courses on the psychology of women and gender since 1977 at Ithaca, Smith College, and the University of Pittsburgh's Semester at Sea Program. She has published and lectured widely on feminist psychoanalytic theories, the development of women's sexuality, and transgender issues.*

9

The Intersexed and the Transgendered

Rethinking Sex/Gender

————— ❖ —————

As a feminist psychologist, I've learned to see the world differently and to keep rethinking even the most obvious things. In this lecture, I am going to revisit the sex/gender issue and discuss some shifts in our thinking that have led us to see sex and gender differently than when we first started talking about it 30 years ago. To begin our inquiry, we need to look at how feminist psychologists have thought about sex and gender, and often still do. Many of us found it made sense to use "sex" to refer to the biological characteristics that distinguish *female* from *male* (i.e., chromosomes, gonads, hormonal mix, genitalia) and "gender" to refer to the social, psychological, and cultural definitions of *woman/feminine* and *man/masculine* (Unger, 1979).

SEX DISTINGUISHED FROM GENDER

In making the sex/gender distinction, feminist psychologists highlight the social construction of gender and emphasize that what it means to be a woman or a man (or feminine and masculine) has no fixed and universal definition, but depends on socially shared meanings that vary historically and culturally. The meaning of womanhood even differs for women living in the *same* time and place because we are all situated differently in terms of our race, ethnicity, social class, sexual orientation, and so on. Not all females are "feminine" or perfectly fit the cultural specifications of "womanhood," and similarly not all males are masculine. In fact,

137

it is evident that some women are "masculine" as defined by their culture and some men "feminine." It has become increasingly clear that many behavioral characteristics associated with masculinity or femininity exist along a continuum rather than in two distinct gender categories, such that any individual person may be more or less feminine and more or less masculine. Feminist psychologists recognize that gender is not dichotomous and further that sex and gender are not inevitably linked; one's sex does not necessarily predict one's gender. Being born female or male doesn't automatically determine one's behaviors, interests, or abilities, nor does it always coincide with a matched gender identity.

In most contemporary psychology of women textbooks, three conclusions can be identified. (1) Sex is biological, and gender is cultural. (2) Sex comes in dichotomous categories (female and male), whereas gender does not. Though we recognize two socially constructed gender categories (woman and man), we also acknowledge that gender is best conceptualized as existing along two continua, one that measures culturally defined femininity and the other culturally defined masculinity. (3) One's sex does not determine one's gender. What the culture has divided into "masculine" or "feminine" ways of acting are simply human behaviors, which all people are capable of expressing.

RETHINKING SEX

In the late 1980s and 1990s, theoretical developments in feminist studies along with the increasing visibility and articulate voices of intersexual and transgender activists worked together to bring about a rethinking of sex and gender and their relation to each other. Let me start with the lessons we learned from the intersexed. Previously called hermaphrodites, intersex infants are born with what have been described as "ambiguous" genitals (i.e., genitals that are not clearly male or female). This can mean the penis is so small and/or the clitoris so large that it is not immediately clear to the obstetrician or parents whether the newborn infant is female or male. Keep in mind that I am using "intersexuality" as an umbrella term that covers a set of different physical conditions that result in "ambiguous" genitalia, rather than as one particular medical condition. Included under the umbrella are conditions such as congenital adrenal hyperplasia, androgen insensitivity syndrome, partial androgen insensitivity syndrome, hypospadias, Klinefelter's syndrome, and progestin-induced virilization, among others (Blackless et. al., 2000). It should also be noted that the so-called ambiguous genitals of intersex infants do not themselves pose any medical risks, though some of the conditions that give rise to them might require medical attention and treatment. A description of these conditions can be found on the excellent website of the Intersex Society of North America (www.isna.org).

It is difficult to estimate the frequency of intersexuality in the population because it is so often surgically corrected and thereby rendered invisible. Still, it has been estimated that intersexuals may constitute as many as 1.7 percent of births (Fausto-Sterling, 2000), about the same frequency as people with cystic fibrosis or bright red hair in the U.S. population. Or put differently, a rate of 1.7 percent of births would amount to about 5,100 intersex individuals in a city of 300,000. Studies of the medical treatment of hermaphrodites in the late nineteenth century (Dreger, 1998) and of contemporary intersex infants (Kessler, 1998; Fausto-Sterling, 2000) have made clear that there is genital variation in nature. This research has called into question the existence of two, and only two, sexes and has led feminist psychologists to recognize that there is more diversity in biological sex than the dichotomous, two-box system of female and male suggests. Whether you focus on the sex chromosomes, gonads, hormonal mix, or external genitalia, there are not just two categories, but a range of variations in-between. Nor do the sex chromosomes, gonads, and genitals in a person always match.

A variety of medical case reports describe people who have XX chromosomes and ovaries who are born with a penis; people with XY chromosomes and testes who are born with a clitoris; people born with one ovary and one testis; and people with a penis (or a clitoris the size of a penis) *and* a vagina. There are many variations in-between what we think of as female (people with XX chromosomes, ovaries, and vulvas) and male (people with XY chromosomes, testes, and penises). The genitals of intersexuals are only ambiguous if they must be labeled as female or male (i.e., seen in terms of two nonoverlapping categories). If sex is not dimorphic, then the intersexed do not have ambiguous genitals but *variations* of the two more commonly known forms. In other words, what looks like ambiguity from the perspective of a two-sex categorization scheme is natural variation viewed from outside that scheme.

Suzanne Kessler's (1998) study of the "medical management" or surgical correction of intersex infants led her to argue that sex itself is a social construction rather than a biological given. When a child is born with "ambiguous" genitals, physicians often decide what sex the child is (or should be) based on the size of the genitals. She reported cases where genetic males born with penises smaller than 2.5 cm are sex reassigned as females (to be raised as girls) because it was decided that life as a boy/man with a small penis would be unthinkable. According to Kessler, physicians operate according to the formulation that "good penis equals male; absence of good penis equals female" (p. 26). This is quite literally the social construction of sex—that is, the creation of sex (genitals) according to the medical team's *idea* of what size penis a boy must have in order to be a successful male (see also Colapinto, 1997). This is not about discovering what the child's "true" sex is but about *creating* sex, based not on medical necessities or biological "facts" but on social value judgments. What is the "true" sex of an infant who has XY chromosomes and genital tissue that is/looks clitoral? What this question reveals is that the very idea of "true" (biological) sex that comes in only two forms is suspect. Sex reassignment of intersex infants erases their difference and renders intersexuality invisible.

Consider another case of the social construction of sex through the surgical treatment of variant genitals. The Intersex Society of North America (ISNA) publishes a newsletter called *Hermaphrodites with Attitude*. In one issue, a woman described her experience of having her enlarged clitoris surgically reduced at the age of 12, with no explanation from parents or physicians, and many years of subsequent complications from the surgery. She never understood what had happened to her until she gained access to her medical records at the age of 24 and discovered that she had been born with XY chromosomes, undescended testes, and a condition known as partial androgen insensitivity syndrome. At age 12 when her clitoris was surgically reduced, the surgeons also removed her testes. How could this happen?! At birth, her genitals looked "female" and so she was raised as a girl. At puberty, her genital tissue responded to the androgens being produced by her undescended testes; the effect was that her clitoris enlarged. There was no medical problem here, nor was her clitoris a problem for her; in fact, she enjoyed masturbating. But when her mother saw her big clitoris, she was alarmed and took her to a doctor, who, along with a team of experts proceeded to "treat" her by removing her testes and surgically reducing her clitoris. Not only did the physicians fail to convey what was happening, but they advised her parents not to tell her. When her mother asked if she should get her daughter counseling, they discouraged the mother from doing so. Unfortunately, this story is not that unusual. There are many similar stories, which you can read about in the books by Kessler (1998), Dreger (1998), and Fausto-Sterling (2000) and on the ISNA website. A documentary film titled *"Hermaphrodites Speak!"* covers the first known gathering of intersexuals who came together through the ISNA network. Among the many things we learn from such stories is that female genital mutilation is not something practiced only in other places. Surgery designed to create "normal-looking" genitals has been estimated to occur about five times a day in the United States (Coventry, 2000). You might be inclined to think the situations are different, but whether we are focusing on intersex "corrective" surgery or female genital cutting as practiced in other cultures, it's about infants and children being physically altered to fit cultural demands.

The medical management of intersexed infants and the surgical correction of their genitals reveal the extent of the social construction of sex. As more intersex people speak out and their stories are told in publications such as *Time Magazine* (Gorman and Cole, 2004), the *New York Times Magazine* (Weil, 2006), and on television programs (e.g., HBO's Middle Sexes), it becomes harder to ignore the conclusion that there is more diversity in sex than the two categories male and female suggest. The sex binary, which appears to be grounded in biology, is not any more real or objective (i.e., to be found in nature, in only those two forms) than the more obviously socially constructed categories of woman and man. When genital diversity is treated as a problem to be corrected, the variations in genitals are made invisible, and the idea of two and only two sexes is perpetuated. Recently, there have been some important changes in the medical management of intersex cases. In a "consensus statement" signed by 50 international intersex experts and published in the journal *Pediatrics* in 2006, it was agreed that parents of intersex infants should be discouraged from choosing surgery for their children. It further states that no good evidence exists that infant cosmetic genital surgery improves the quality of life of intersex infants (Lee, Houk, Ahmed, & Hughes, 2006).

Information on intersexuals has recently made its way into psychology of women textbooks (Lips, 2003). This challenge to the idea of two and only two sexes may not be well known, but it is not a brand new idea, either. In 1993, Anne Fausto-Sterling, Professor of Biology and Medicine at Brown University, argued that medical evidence leads to the conclusion that there are at least five sexes. Most of us have grown up believing that there are only two sexes, and this idea is so embedded in our thinking and our view of the world that we never question it. We don't even think of it as an *idea* but as truth, as reality, as the way things are. In this context, Fausto-Sterling's suggestion that there are at least five sexes is truly fantastic—and shocking. But just because something is hard to believe is not a reason not to consider it. At one time, most people found it impossible to believe that the earth is round, or that women can be brilliant scientists. As I said at the start of this lecture, feminist psychology is about seeing things differently, so I hope I've interested you in thinking about sex in a new way. Now, let's move on to gender, because it's not only our thinking about sex that has changed; concepts of gender have shifted as well.

*R*ETHINKING GENDER

Feminist psychologists have understood that gender is socially constructed, which is to say that "masculine" and "feminine" are culturally specific ideas (i.e., social constructs) about what is appropriate for women and men. These social constructs vary as a function of changing historical and cultural pressures, and thus our concepts of masculinity and femininity are shifting, not fixed and universal. Nonetheless, our language may lead us astray. Even though we understand masculinity and femininity to be social constructs and, as such, subject to change, our naming of them imparts a certain palpable and fixed reality. When gender is conceptualized in terms of masculinity and femininity, it is easy to think of it as something that exists *within* a person, almost as if it's something we *have* or something we *are*. A variety of psychological tests actually measure femininity and masculinity as core dimensions of one's personality. Psychological concepts such as *gender identity* and *gendered personality styles* also locate gender within the individual, which suggests that it is an internal disposition. But our understanding of gender in terms of a socially created (and then internalized) masculinity and femininity has shifted over the past 20 years.

Postmodern gender theorists have argued that gender is an accomplishment, something people work very hard at creating, even though they may not be conscious of doing so (Butler, 1990, 2004). In this conceptualization, gender is not something inborn, or even internal; it is what we present to others, like a performance in which an actor creates the impression he or she wishes to convey. In Judith Butler's words, gender is performative; "[one] executes it, institutes, produces and reproduces it, wears it, flaunts it, hides it, but always stylises it in one way or another. For gender is a...way of acting the body...." (1989, p. 256). The new emphasis is on *doing gender* rather than on *having (a) gender*. When a woman acts reserved or helpless, we might say she is "doing" gender. When a man acts tough and "macho," he is doing gender according to a widely available cultural script. Both are performing, and the consequence of the performance is that they are "read" as feminine or masculine (whether or not they happen to think of it that way). When we conceptualize gender as performance, as something we do based on culturally shared meanings of what it means when a person does those things, we begin to see it as something beyond the person, as a process rather than as an individual attribute.

Thinking about gender as performance has many radical implications. First, if gender is performed, then it can be performed in many different ways; there is no one right way. Second, one's sex is not necessarily relevant to one's gender performance. Most behaviors can be performed by persons of any sex. Third, performances by their nature are fluid; they can and do change. Thinking about gender as performance presents great possibilities for multiple gender expressions. And this is just what we see in certain segments of contemporary culture—many different performances, or diverse ways of doing gender. The community in which gender performance is most visible, most diverse, and hence most interesting to me is the transgender community. Gender, as expressed and theorized within this community, has informed feminist psychology by enriching our understanding of gender as performance.

THE TRANSGENDER COMMUNITY

Let me first define what transgender means, and then I'll give you some idea of the diversity that exists under the umbrella of the transgender community. "Trans" means *across* or *beyond*, and thus transgender means that which moves across or beyond gender (as it is defined by the culture). As applied to people, it refers to someone who moves across or beyond gender boundaries. Leslie Feinberg, who first used the term and continues to elaborate on it (1993, 1996, 1998), identifies as a transgendered person, as well as a "he-she," and a masculine female. Even as s/he travels around the country speaking and raising consciousness on transgender issues, s/he lives and passes as a man in daily life because s/he fears for her safety as an openly transgendered person. Kate Bornstein (1995, 1998), a genetic male and a self-described "gender outlaw," sees herself as beyond gender. In both her writing and speaking, she is emphatic that she is not a man, despite having lived as one for 37 years, and "probably not a woman either," though to look at her you would think she was. Riki Wilchins (1997, 2004) adopts the label "transgender" at the same time as she rejects it. She points out that transgender is not some natural fact or true identity but a political category that people like her are forced to take on when they construct their sex and gender according to their own definitions and desires.

You may be wondering at this point what's the difference between people who call themselves transsexuals and those who call themselves transgendered. The answer is that it's very much a question of chosen identity. The word "transsexual" has been around much longer and has been used by psychologists and psychiatrists to describe people whose gender is at odds with their biological sex (Benjamin, 1966). Feinberg, Bornstein, and Wilchins are politically active feminists who have self-consciously constructed their own identities as transgender. They have also used the term "transpeople" (or "trans" for short). Still, in writings from within the transgender community, one will see abundant references to FTMs (female to male transsexuals, also called transsexual males) and MTFs (male to female transsexuals, also called transsexual females) (Green, 2004).

Transsexuals and transgendered people are a diverse group, and the transgender activists previously cited do not speak for all transsexuals. Many transsexuals tell the story of being "trapped in the wrong body," a powerful metaphor that rests on the essentialist belief that there exist only two sexes and two corresponding genders, each of which is fundamentally different from the other (Griggs, 1998). If the gender doesn't match the body's sex, then the body is wrong (a trap) and must be altered. Some transsexuals are happy to make the transition into the "other" sex and then disappear, i.e., to be seen as regular males and females. Others make their gender difference a source of activism and education, so that variations in gender expression are more visible (Green, 2004) and to challenge the view that there are only "men" and "women" in the world.

This essentialist dichotomy shows up also in the diagnostic category of gender identity disorder (GID), which first appeared in the third edition of the American Psychiatric Association's *Diagnostic and Statistical Manual of Mental Disorders (DSM)* in 1980. It is perhaps not surprising that the narrative told by so many transsexuals resonates with the psychiatric diagnosis they must have if they want to be considered acceptable candidates for surgical and hormonal treatments. The specific criteria that one must meet in order to be given a diagnosis of GID are completely dependent on binary models of sex and gender—specifically, the belief that a person is either male *or* female, a man *or* woman; there is no beyond or in-between. The criteria also rest on the assumption that one's sex and gender must match, and if they don't, something is profoundly wrong and warrants a psychiatric diagnosis.

It is worth considering the diagnosis of gender identity disorder in greater detail as it is presented in the *DSM-IV* (American Psychiatric Association, 1994). The first diagnostic criterion is "a strong and persistent cross-gender identification" (p. 532), which can manifest itself in a number of different ways. The *DSM-IV* spells them out as follows:

> In adolescents and adults, the disturbance is manifested by symptoms such as a stated desire to be the other sex, frequent passing as the other sex, desire to live or be treated as the other sex, or the conviction that he or she has the typical feelings and reactions of the other sex. (p. 537)

The second criterion is "persistent discomfort with his or her sex or sense of appropriateness in the gender role of that sex" (p. 537). Again, the *DSM-IV* attempts to clarify exactly what this means:

> In adolescents and adults, the disturbance is manifested by symptoms such as preoccupation with getting rid of primary and secondary sex characteristics (e.g., request for hormones, surgery, or other procedures to physically alter sexual characteristics to simulate the other sex) or belief that he or she was born the wrong sex. (p. 538)

There are two additional criteria for diagnosis; one specifies that "the disturbance" is not related to intersexuality and the other that it causes "clinically significant distress or impairment" in the life of the person so diagnosed. In the section on differential diagnosis, it is noted that gender identity disorder is not the same thing as "simple nonconformity to stereotypical sex role behavior" and that it is distinguishable from this "by the extent and pervasiveness of the cross-gender wishes, interests, and activities" (p. 536).

From a feminist psychological perspective, the diagnosis of gender identity disorder is both problematic and suspect. Cross-gender interests and activities? Feminist psychologists had already established that interests and activities are not, and should not, be constrained by one's sex/gender. Just because trucks are marketed to boys doesn't mean that a girl who wants to play with them (even exclusively) has "cross-gender interests." Consider another symptom: the conviction that one has the typical feelings and reactions of the other sex. Is a woman who feels angry, or sexual, or aggressive, or ambitious having the feelings of the other sex? You might agree with me that these so-called symptoms are questionable. But what about the desire to physically alter one's sexual characteristics through hormones and surgery? That's pretty extreme and a legitimate criterion of mental disturbance, isn't it? It all depends on how you think about it. What about the large numbers of nontranssexual women (i.e., biological females who consider themselves to be women) who are both dissatisfied and preoccupied with their secondary sex characteristics to the point of undergoing breast augmentation or reduction surgeries; electrolysis; frequent shaving (or waxing) of legs, underarms, and "bikini" lines; weight-reduction regimens; hormone replacement therapy—all of which are designed to alter the natural female body. Such practices on the part of women reflect the nonconscious ideology that females are born—if not the wrong sex—the second sex, or "the never-good-enough-as-you-are" sex. Yet women who choose to change their bodies in these ways are considered quite normal in our culture!

Finally, consider the "clinically significant distress" that must be present for the person to receive a diagnosis of GID. As with any condition of difference in our culture, one can question whether the distress comes from the condition itself or from other people's reaction to the difference. If transsexuals are distressed (as required for a diagnosis of GID), is it because they have "cross-gender" identifications and interests, or because in a culture where sex and gender are dichotomized, we are intolerant of people who step outside the dichotomies? Suppose a person has a "sense of inappropriateness in the gender role of that sex"? So what?! What is the "appropriate gender role" of each sex, anyway?! As I have argued earlier in this lecture, each sex doesn't have one and only one appropriate gender role. Sex and gender aren't linked in any necessary or inevitable way. The diagnostic category of gender identity disorder, like so many other gender- and sexuality-related diagnoses, is highly problematic for feminists or anyone in the process of rethinking the meaning of sex and gender and their relation to each other.

The social constructionism of the transgender activists is more enlightening than the essentializing and pathologizing language of the *DSM*, so let me return to consideration of transgender issues as they emerge from *within* that community rather than from outside of it. One question that often arises has to do with the relative frequency of trans-sexualism in females and males. Early discussions of the topic pointed to a much lower frequency in biological females (Raymond, 1979). The *DSM-IV* offers no data on prevalence of the disorder but does suggest that in terms of those who seek sex-reassignment surgery, the ratio is 3:1 in favor of biological males. It is difficult to know with any certainty, but recent estimates made from within the transsexual community are that there are probably as many FTMs as there are MTFs (Califia, 1997; Green, 2004). In the past decade, numerous works have appeared that have broadened our exposure to females who cross and sometimes move beyond the gender divide. Jamison Green's (2004) *Becoming a Visible Man* details one such story. Holly Devor's (1997) book *FTM: Female-to-Male Transsexuals in Society* offers more than 600 pages of description and analysis of her interviews with 45 FTMs. Loren Cameron (1996) has produced an eye-opening set of photographs of FTMs under the title *Body Alchemy: Transsexual Portraits,* and a documentary film called *You Don't Know Dick*[1] features female to male transsexuals talking about their lives.

Trans people can be anywhere in the process of moving across or beyond gender, from being preoperative to postoperative to any of a number of places in-between, including nonoperative. In contrast to essentialist transsexuals, transgender activists talk about choosing their gender as well as making choices about what kinds of bodies they want. Their chosen gender may or may not correspond to their genitals. Apparently, more and more transsexuals are choosing not to have genital surgery not only because it's extremely expensive (and often results in subsequent complications), but also because it's increasingly seen as unnecessary (Bloom, 1994; Califia, 1997). The belief in two sexes/genders is challenged, to say the least, by women with breasts and penises and men with beards and clitorises!

Trans people are as heterogeneous a group as any other group of people. In addition to the diversities of thought, personality, and interests that you would find in any group, there are differences among them as they relate to sex, gender, and identity. Some specifically identify as transgender, or trans, whereas others do not. They have been variously described as gender benders, gender-variant people, or gender queers (Devor, 1989; Feinberg, 1998). Among them are those who consider themselves to be women, or men, or intermediate, or neither, or in-progress, or just "different" from what their culture dictates a man or woman should be. Some say they have chosen their gender; others say it was not a choice. Some have decided to have genital surgery, and others have decided against it. Some elect to change other parts of their bodies, and some do not. Their sexualities cover a broad range of possibilities. Their performance of gender reveals its multiplicity and range of complexity. And they are only one segment of the larger whole that makes up the transgender community.

If we understand transgender to mean across or beyond gender lines, then there are many more people who might claim (or be claimed for) membership in the transgender community. The International Foundation for Gender Education (founded in 1987) estimates that six percent of the U.S. population are cross-dressers, also known as transvestites (Garber, 1992). In the *DSM-IV,* transvestites are identified as heterosexual males who cross-dress. I wouldn't argue that we need to expand the criteria for inclusion in the *DSM,* but clearly there are some gay men (known as drag queens) as well as women (less well known, but referred to as drag kings) who don clothing not considered appropriate for their sex. According to the *DSM-IV,* transvestism is classified as a "fetish," which means that there is some sexual arousal that accompanies cross-dressing in men. Psychologists and others have doubted that there are parallels between

---

[1]This film is distributed by the University of California (at Berkeley) Extension Center for Media and Independent Learning.

men's and women's cross-dressing, believing that for women cross-dressing is more socially acceptable and has no related sexual component. Pat Califia (1997) disagrees, pointing to the discrimination, condemnation, and even violence directed toward biological females who cross-dress.[2] She also describes the sexual rush she feels when she is in male drag and notes that her conversations with other women suggest that this is not uncommon. Like transsexuals, cross-dressers constitute a diverse group of men and women with a range of identities and practices. Cross-dressers have existed across history (e.g., Joan of Arc, Mulan) and although some have attempted to claim them as trans people (Feinberg, 1996), it's not so easy to say how they thought of themselves. In contemporary times, cross-dressing carries many meanings, and people do it for different reasons. It may or may not be related to sexual orientation, or to transsexuality, and it may or may not include a sexual component. Whatever the case, the very notion of "cross" dressing warrants its inclusion under the umbrella of the transgender community.

In addition to transsexuals and cross-dressers, self-identified intersexuals belong within the transgender community. Intersexual activists are raising awareness about the harm done to infants and children who are subject to genital surgeries they do not need (Chase, 1998; Lee, Houk, Ahmed, and Hughes, 2006). A federal law passed in 1996 bans genital cutting in the United States, and although the law was aimed at halting the practice among recent immigrants from countries where female genital mutilation is widely practiced, intersexual activists are seeking ways to use the law to ban medically unnecessary intersex surgeries as well. Taking a stand against surgery is not a simple issue for the transgender community, which is hardly monolithic. Movement across and beyond gender lines can work in multiple and sometimes contradictory ways. While intersexual activists are organizing and calling for a halt to intersex surgery, transsexuals are fighting for the right to surgically alter their bodies. Although there is a difference in informed consent (infants can't give it), a feminist social constructionist like me resonates best to the idea of people keeping whatever bodies and genitals they have and performing gender in whatever way suits them. As I see it, the most progressive trend in the transgender community is the one that challenges the requirement that the sex of the body must match the gender of the performance. Unfortunately, however, there is tremendous violence perpetrated against transgender people, and for many the changing of bodies is a basic safety issue (Wilchins, 2004).

Intimate partners of intersexuals and transgendered people deserve inclusion within the transgender community. One shouldn't assume that intersexuals and transgender people are lonely and have difficulty

---

[2]The notion that women can wear men's clothing without negative social consequence is belied by the experience of Brandon Teena who, in 1995, was killed for a having a female body at the same time that s/he presented as a man. This true story was powerfully depicted in the film *Boys Don't Cry*, for which the actress who played Brandon Teena (Hilary Swank) won an Academy Award in 2000.

establishing meaningful sexual relationships with others. Nor should it be assumed that they will always or most often relate intimately with other people like them (Bornstein, 1995). Any person sexually involved with a man who has breasts or with a woman who has a penis is crossing gender boundaries regardless of their own particular body or identification. Barry Winchell, a U.S. soldier, was murdered in his barracks in 1999 for loving a transperson, Calpernia Adams (France, 2000). Their love story was movingly depicted in the film, *A Soldier's Girl*.

There are still others to be included. Lesbians, gays, and bisexuals might consider themselves part of a broadly defined transgender community. Through their partnerships, self-presentations, and ideas, many lesbians, gays, and bisexuals cross and go beyond conventional gender lines. For that matter, so do some heterosexuals. There are a diversity of ways to cross and go beyond gender boundaries, from the mundane to the more unusual. Consider the report of a 31-year-old "normal" married heterosexual male who requested breast enlargement (which was accomplished via estrogen treatment), so that he could experience more sexual pleasure in his nipples during sexual activity with his wife (Kremer & den Daas, 1990).

Finally, there are contemporary boys and girls who are gender nonconformists, sometimes aided and encouraged by feminist parents and teachers, all of whom might be included within the transgender community for expanding the possibilities of what gender means. Girls especially seem to me to be stretching the boundaries, moving in-between and beyond gender. In conversations with young girls, I have found the concept of "tomboy" to be on the wane. One 7-year-old whom I asked to point out the tomboys in her class said she wasn't sure about that, but she could identify the "really girly girls" and the "sometimes girly girls" and "the kid kids," a category that included both boys and girls.

*T*HE FLUIDITY OF GENDER

I hope by now your head is spinning with the dazzling diversity of gendered expressions and with a sense of possibility. It all started out so neat and clear, with sex being defined as biological and gender as a social construction. Then I presented information on the intersexed and suggested that sex wasn't so neatly packaged into two and only two categories and that gender wasn't something we *have* or *are* but a performance. This was followed by a necessarily brief reference to members (or potential members) of the transgender community. The people I have described may or may not consider themselves to be part of a transgender community. But the fact that they might not consciously think of themselves as part of a larger coalition of gender benders or gender performers doesn't stop us from seeing them that way. Performances are seen and interpreted by others, and those of us who are in the process of learning to see differently can learn a lot from other people's performance of gender. Probably most important is that they can help us to imagine the gender possibilities for *ourselves* and to see that gender is fluid—a process, a work-in progress, something not yet finished—not just for *them*, but for *all* of us.

What we can learn from the experiences and performances of those within the transgender community is that neither bodies nor genders are fixed and unchanging. This has led some feminist psychologists to question the notion that a stable and fixed gender identity is desirable or even possible. Research over the past decade on the fluidity of women's sexuality has shown that fixed sexual orientation categories don't adequately describe many women's experience of sexual desire and identity (Golden, 1996, 1997). In the same vein, it is possible that fixed gender identities don't capture the multiplicities of our gendered selves, either. Some psychologists have begun to challenge the longstanding claim of mainstream developmental psychologists that the developing child *must* attain a fixed gender identity, and that doing so is a sign of maturity. Virginia Goldner (1991) suggested that learning to tolerate the ambiguity and instability of gender categories is a more appropriate developmental goal than achieving a gender-unified and coherent sense of self. Robert May (1986) has argued that, in men, a fixed gender identity may be the result of an inhibition of gender ambiguities and contradictions and as such reflects an impoverishment of character rather than a mature developmental outcome. Sandra Bem (1993) argued that, in a gender polarizing and androcentric culture that requires men to repress any "feminine" tendencies, the security of their gender identity will be under constant threat; thus, men will work ceaselessly to prove their masculinity. Sarah Pearlman (1995) described gender identity *destabilization* as healthy and elaborated on the opportunities for creative self-expression that can arise from such destabilization of fixed gender identity in women. For the most part, however, these views are too radical to have reached the mainstream of developmental psychology texts.

CONCLUSION

There are at least five "sex/gender principles" that can be extracted from this lecture, and they are based on what we have learned from the intersexed and the transgendered, broadly defined. First, there exists a lot more diversity in biological sex than we have previously acknowledged; our belief in the existence of only two sexes is a social construct. Second, because both sex *and* gender are socially constructed and because they don't always match, it is no longer so useful to distinguish between them. It made more sense to do so when we thought that gender was a social construct and sex was a biological fact, but this is no longer so clear. Third, people can choose their gender, and this includes moving away from or beyond the gender that had been imposed upon them as children. What they choose may not correspond to their genitals, and what that means is that genitals need not be the central marker of our sex/gender. Fourth, identities are not necessarily fixed, stable, and coherent, and thus a fixed gender identity is neither necessary nor advantageous to mental health. Just as our age-related or ethnic identities can change over the life course, so, too, can our gender identities. Fifth, the possibilities for gender fluidity, as well as gender ambiguity and contradiction, are enormous, as demonstrated by the members of the broadly defined transgender community.

In my early days as a feminist, I used to think that, in order to achieve equality between the sexes, we would need to deemphasize gender by constantly refocusing attention away from the differences between women and men. But that strategy was frustrating because it wasn't all that effective. People still focused on the differences, despite a body of research demonstrating that there are more similarities than differences. That was before I realized that gender is a mode of performance and that *more* of it might be better than less. The more we do gender, the more we can stretch it and in the process diversify and multiply the possibilities. Rather than aiming for a gender-free utopia, my vision now is for a world that would be gender-full, where there would be so many different ways to be women, men, in-between, and beyond, that in the end the categories themselves would lose meaning and what we would be left with is a diversity of ways to be. And I don't just mean that the categories woman and man would lose meaning, but so, too, would all cultural constructs grounded in gender, and that includes femininity and masculinity as well as heterosexuality, homosexuality, and bisexuality. A world of multiple gender expressions, where bodies, selves, and desires can combine in all possible ways will be one where there is a lot to see, to be, to do, and to learn—and being female or male, woman or man will have little to do with it. If we take social construction theory seriously, we must remember that those possibilities aren't merely "out there" to be discovered; they are to be actively created by us. Gender is not just what the other presents; it is what we do and what we see. Feminism is, after all, about seeing differently.

REFERENCES

AMERICAN PSYCHIATRIC ASSOCIATION. (1994). *Diagnostic and statistical manual of mental disorders*. (4th ed.). Washington, DC: Author.

BEM, S. (1993). *The lenses of gender: Transforming the debate on sexual inequality*. New Haven, CT: Yale University Press.

BENJAMIN, H. (1966). *The transsexual phenomenon*. New York: Julian Press.

BLACKLESS, M., CHARUVASTRA, A., DERRYCK, A., FAUSTO-STERLING, A., LAUZANNE, K., & LEE, E. (2000). How sexually dimorphic are we? Review and synthesis. *American Journal of Human Biology, 12*, 151–166.

BLOOM, A. (1994, July 18). The body lies. *The New Yorker*, pp. 38–44, 46–49.

BORNSTEIN, K. (1995). *Gender outlaw: On men, women, and the rest of us*. New York: Vintage.

BORNSTEIN, K. (1998). *My gender notebook*. New York: Routledge.

BUTLER, J. (1989). Gendering the body: Beauvoir's philosophical contribution. In A. Garry & M. Pearsall (Eds.), *Women, knowledge, and reality* (pp. 253–262). Boston: Unwin Hyman.

BUTLER, J. (1990). *Gender trouble: Feminism and the subversion of identity*. New York: Routledge.

BUTLER, J. (2004). *Undoing gender*. New York: Routledge.

CALIFIA, P. (1997). *Sex changes: The politics of transgenderism*. San Francisco: Cleis Press.

CAMERON, L. (1996). *Body alchemy: Transsexual portraits*. San Francisco: Cleis Press.

CHASE, C. (1998). Hermaphrodites with attitude: Mapping the emergence of intersex political activism. *Journal of Lesbian and Gay Studies, 4,* 189–211.

COLAPINTO, J. (1997, December 11). The true story of John/Joan. *Rolling Stone,* pp. 54–73, 92–97.

COVENTRY, M. (October–November, 2000). Making the cut. *Ms. Magazine,* pp. 52–60.

DEVOR, H. (1989). *Gender blending: Confronting the limits of duality*. Bloomington: Indiana University Press.

DEVOR, H. (1997). *FTM: Female-to-male transsexuals in society*. Bloomington: Indiana University Press.

DREGER, A. (1998). *Hermaphrodites and the medical invention of sex*. Cambridge, MA: Harvard University Press.

FAUSTO-STERLING, A. (1993). The five sexes: Why male and female are not enough. *The Sciences, 33,* 20–25.

FAUSTO-STERLING, A. (2000). *Sexing the body: Gender politics and the construction of sexuality*. New York: Basic Books.

FEINBERG, L. (1993). *Stone butch blues*. Ithaca, NY: Firebrand Books.

FEINBERG, L. (1996). *TransGender warriors: Making history from Joan of Arc to Dennis Rodman*. Boston: Beacon Press.

FEINBERG, L. (1998). *TransLiberation: Beyond pink or blue*. Boston: Beacon Press.

FRANCE, D. (2000, May 28). An inconvenient woman. *The New York Times Magazine,* pp. 24–29.

GARBER, M. (1992). *Vested interests: Cross-dressing and cultural anxiety*. New York: HarperPerennial.

GOLDEN, C. (1996). What's in a name? Sexual self-identification among women. In R. Savin-Williams & K. Cohen (Eds.), *The lives of lesbians, gays, and bisexuals: Children to adults* (pp. 229–249). Fort Worth, TX: Harcourt Brace.

GOLDEN, C. (1997). Do women choose their sexual identity? *Harvard Gay and Lesbian Review, 4,* 18–20.

GOLDNER, V. (1991). Toward a critical relational theory of gender. *Psychoanalytic Dialogues, 1,* 249–272.

GORMAN, C. & COLE, W. (2004, March 1). Between the sexes. *Time Magazine,* pp. 54–56.

GREEN, J. (2004). *Becoming a visible man*. Nashville: Vanderbilt University Press.

GRIGGS, C. (1998). *S/he: Changing sex and changing clothes*. New York: Berg.

KESSLER, S. (1998). *Lessons from the intersexed*. New Brunswick, NJ: Rutgers University Press.

KREMER, J., & DEN DAAS, H. (1990). Case report: A man with breast dysphoria. *Archives of Sexual Behavior, 19,* 179–181.

LEE, P. A., HOUK, C. P., AHMED, S. F., & HUGHES, I. (2006). Consensus statement on management of intersex disorders. *Pediatrics, 118*(2), 814–815. Retrieved from www.pediatrics.org

LIPS, H. (2003). *A new psychology of women: Gender, culture, and ethnicity.* (2nd ed.). Mountain View, CA: Mayfield.

MAY, R. (1986). Concerning a psychoanalytic view of maleness. *Psychoanalytic Review, 73,* 175–193.

PEARLMAN, S. (1995). Making gender: New interpretations/new narratives. In J. Glassgold & S. Iasenza (Eds.), *Lesbians and psychoanalysis: Revolution in theory and practice* (pp. 309–325). New York: The Free Press.

RAYMOND, J. (1979, 1994). *The transsexual empire: The making of the she-male.* New York: Teachers College Press.

UNGER, R. (1979). Toward a redefinition of sex and gender. *American Psychologist, 34,* 1085–1094.

WEIL, E. (2006, September 24). What if it's (sort of) a boy and (sort of) a girl? *The New York Times Magazine,* pp. 48–53.

WILCHINS, R. A. (1997). *Read my lips: Sexual subversion and the end of gender.* Ithaca, NY: Firebrand Books.

WILCHINS, R. A. (2004). *Queer theory, gender theory.* Los Angeles: Alyson Books.

SUGGESTED READINGS

KESSLER, S. (1998). *Lessons from the intersexed.* New Brunswick, NJ: Rutgers University Press.

FAUSTO-STERLING, A. (2000). *Sexing the body: Gender politics and the construction of sexuality.* New York: Basic Books.

FEINBERG, L. (1998). *TransLiberation: Beyond pink or blue.* Boston: Beacon Press.

WILCHINS, R. (1997). *Read my lips: Sexual subversion and the end of gender.* Ithaca, NY: Firebrand Press.

*J*OAN C. CHRISLER *is Professor of Psychology at Connecticut College. Dr. Chrisler has taught courses on the psychology of women since 1979 at Connecticut and at Mercy College and St. Thomas Aquinas College. She has published extensively on issues of women and gender, especially on women's health, menstruation, weight, and body image.*

10

PMS as a
Culture-Bound Syndrome

❖

W hen I first began to study changes related to the menstrual cycle in the 1970s, so few studies existed in the literature that I could honestly say that I'd read every word ever written about premenstrual syndrome (PMS). The litera- ture has expanded so dramatically that no one could say that today. When I collected data for my master's thesis on the experience of PMS, most of the women who partici- pated in my study had never heard of it. "Do you mean cramps?" they would ask.

What happened? How did PMS go from a little-known experience of ten- sion in the few days preceding menstruation to a syndrome consisting of dozens of possible symptoms that occur during the weeks preceding menstruation—an experience so common that most women complain about it and an experience so well known that jokes about it appear everywhere? In this lecture, we'll consider the sociocultural and political meanings of PMS and how they contributed to its rise from relative obscurity to cultural icon in a mere 30 years.

*W*HAT IS PMS?

A variety of physiological and psychological changes have been associated with phases of the menstrual cycle. Those changes that occur premenstrually (usu- ally days 23 to 28 of the cycle) have been called premenstrual tension (Frank, 1931) or premenstrual syndrome (Dalton, 1977). The most frequently reported premenstrual change is fluid retention, particularly in the breasts and abdomen. Other symptoms have been classified as follows (Debrovner, 1982):

- *Psychological.* Irritability, depression, anxiety, lethargy, sleep changes, low morale, crying spells, hostility

- *Neurological.* Headaches, vertigo, backaches
- *Gastrointestinal.* Nausea, vomiting, constipation, increased craving for sweet or salty foods
- *Dermatological.* Acne

It has also been suggested (see Dalton, 1960a, b, 1968), although there is no scientific evidence for this, that premenstrual women have difficulty concentrating, poorer judgment, lack of coordination, decreased efficiency, and lowered school or work performance.

Although the data do indicate that women experience cyclic changes, it is difficult to know how common such changes are. Estimates of the prevalence of premenstrual symptoms, which depend on how the data were collected, have ranged from 2 percent (using the strictest criteria of a 30 percent change in intensity of selected emotional and physical experiences charted daily over three menstrual cycles) to 100 percent (using the loosest criteria, "Have you ever experienced a cyclic change in physiological or psychological state?"). Despite efforts by the Society for Menstrual Cycle Research, the National Institute of Mental Health, and the American Psychiatric Association to produce a standard definition, there is little agreement on how many symptoms must be experienced or how severe the symptoms must be in order to be classified as premenstrual syndrome. So many different definitions exist in the literature that results cannot easily be compared with each other. Even the timing of the premenstrual phase of the cycle is not clear. Some researchers have described it as five to seven days before the start of menstruation; others have described it as the time between ovulation and menstruation (about two weeks). The problem of estimates is made more complicated by the fact that premenstrual experience is highly variable and personal. All women do not experience the same changes, and the experience of any given woman may vary from cycle to cycle. In addition, PMS has been so frequently discussed in recent years that the results of surveys and questionnaire studies have undoubtedly been affected by a response bias in the direction of the cultural stereotype of the premenstrual woman.

What is the cultural stereotype of the premenstrual woman? You probably don't need me to tell you! A recent walk through a shopping mall turned up a bumper sticker ("A woman with PMS and ESP is a bitch who knows everything"), buttons ("It's not PMS, I'm psychotic," "It's not PMS, I'm always bitchy"), greeting cards ("Some special advice for the birthday girl—never cut your cake during PMS"), a calendar of cartoons about a woman with a particularly bad case of PMS ("Plagued by a raging hormonal imbalance, Melinda devours Hershey, Pennsylvania"), and several "humorous" books (*Raging Hormones: The Official PMS Survival Guide*, *PMS Attacks and Other Inconveniences of Life*, and *Hormones from Hell*). Over the years, my students have brought me cartoons from magazines and newspapers, greeting cards for every occasion, and even postcards that make fun of premenstrual women. There have been many references to PMS on television and in the movies. Do you remember the episode in which Roseanne was premenstrual on Halloween?

Karen Levy and I performed a content analysis (Chrisler & Levy, 1990) of 78 articles about PMS that were published in American magazines from 1980 to 1987. The articles described a confusing array of symptoms and contradictory treatment recommendations. No single symptom was mentioned in every article; 131 different symptoms were described, including sallow skin, feeling fat, and changes in the way one's perfume smells. Treatment recommendations included drinking wine and limiting alcohol intake, limiting fluid intake and drinking plenty of water, and limiting protein intake and eating a high-protein diet. Although no biochemical differences have yet been found between women who suffer from PMS and women who don't, the journalists implicated hormone levels as the cause of PMS. The menstrual cycle was referred to as the "cycle of misery," a "hormonal roller coaster," the "inner beast," and the "menstrual monster" (p. 98). The premenstrual and menstrual phases of the cycle were described as "weeks of hell," during which women are "hostages to their hormones," and premenstrual women were described as "cripples" and "raging beasts" (p. 98). Among the titles of the articles we read were "Premenstrual Frenzy," "Dr. Jekyll and Ms. Hyde," "Coping with Eve's Curse," "Once a Month I'm a Woman Possessed," and "The Taming of the Shrew Inside of You" (p. 97).

Cartoons about violent women and journalistic representations of frenzied, "raging beasts" could easily make one lose sight of the fact that women commit fewer than 5 percent of all violent crimes. How did this violent image of premenstrual women arise? In 1981, two court cases in Great Britain gained worldwide attention as Sandie Smith and Christine English, on trial for murder, were found guilty of manslaughter. They were given probation because the judges accepted pleas of diminished responsibility after Dr. Katharina Dalton testified that they had PMS. When she first began working on PMS in the 1950s, Dr. Dalton did not believe that it was a problem that affected large numbers of women. By the early 1980s, she would suggest that most women have PMS, although they might not know it (Rome, 1986). The British trials resulted in an explosion of media interest in PMS. Images of violent premenstrual murderesses merged with ancient images of women as dangerous beings who lured men to their doom, but now there was a "scientific" basis to women's hostility and duplicity—hormones—and everyone was talking about them. Sociologist Sophie Laws (1983) has noted that few people bothered to ask how it is possible that the hormones of millions of women could be out of balance.

IS PMS A DISEASE? AN ILLNESS? A SYNDROME?

A disease is defined (Thomas, 1989) as a pathological condition of the body that has clinical signs, symptoms, and laboratory findings that are specific to it and that allow us to discriminate it from normal or other pathological states of the body. PMS is not a disease. There are no laboratory findings that can discriminate PMS sufferers from nonsufferers. The symptoms of PMS are not specific to it; some are common in men and in premenarcheal girls and postmenopausal women. The only clinical sign specific to PMS is that it is generally followed by menstruation. However, there are many menstruating women who don't experience PMS, and some women who don't menstruate (for example, women who have had hysterectomies) do complain of PMS.

In medicine, it is common to distinguish between disease and illness. Diseases are tangible and have elements that can be measured. Illnesses are highly individual and personal. When we speak of illness, we are generally referring to psychological experiences such as pain, suffering, and distress. For example, a person with hypertension obviously has a disease (chronic high blood pressure) but lacks pain or suffering and, hence, is not ill (Thomas, 1989). A major problem in treating hypertension is that people often decide to stop taking their medication because they feel fine. People with mental illness, on the other hand, are obviously suffering but may not have evidence of disease; for example, there may be no measurable pathological changes in their bodies. PMS can be categorized as an illness. Those women who have severe symptoms are distressed and may be described as suffering. However, you should consider carefully the definition of an illness before you apply it to yourself. If you experience only a few premenstrual changes that can be described as mild or moderate, are you ill?

"Illness behavior" refers to "the way in which symptoms are conceived, evaluated, and acted upon by a person who recognizes some pain, discomfort, or other sign of malfunction" (Townsend & Carbone, 1980, p. 230). Illness behavior is significantly affected by society's definition of symptoms and malfunctions and by the roles and expectations society holds for individuals who experience them. Surveys of adults (Meigs, 1961; Siegel, 1963) indicate that at any particular time about 90 percent of the population is aware of some "symptom" that could be seen as clinically serious. Think about this for a moment. Scan your body. Do you have a muscle ache, a stuffy nose, a tickle in your throat, eye strain, a cut or bruise? If 90 percent of adults are experiencing symptoms right now, then statistically, at least, experiencing symptoms is normal. Being ill, you see, is a social process, which we may or may not decide to enter into when we experience a sensation that could be called a symptom.

Cultural images and social roles and stereotypes shape women to notice menstrual cycle–related changes and to label them as pathological rather than as normal. Thirty years ago, a woman who was experiencing tension or depression before her menstrual period would have thought to herself, "I'm tense (or blue) today." Now she thinks, "I have PMS." The modern woman engages in illness behavior; she feels ill, tells others that she's ill, and treats her illness (with Pamprin, a day off, etc.). In the past, she would have coped in other ways and considered her mood to be part of the normal ups and downs of life. The reason we (Chrisler & Levy, 1990) found 131 different symptoms in our analysis of magazine articles is that the menstrual cycle has become so salient as problematic that American women attribute almost any change to it. If a man has a headache, he may think of several possible reasons for it—work pressure, hunger, or too much beer last night. If a woman has a headache, she can make any of those same attributions, but she's unlikely to do so. Three weeks out of four, she'll probably attribute her headache to her menstrual cycle—same symptom, very different illness behavior.

A syndrome is a group of symptoms that are related to each other by some anatomical, physiological, or biochemical peculiarity (Thomas, 1989). This definition does not insist that a common cause be known, simply that the symptoms be related in some way. The menstrual cycle is the physiological or biochemical peculiarity that links the "symptoms" of PMS, which appear or are intensified during the premenstrual (luteal) phase. Thus, PMS can be said to meet the definition of a syndrome, although the "symptoms" may never be found to have a common cause.

WHAT IS A CULTURE-BOUND SYNDROME?

To understand PMS, we have to take an interdisciplinary approach. So far, we've considered evidence from psychology, sociology, and medicine. Now it's anthropology's turn. Anthropologists invented the term "culture-bound syndrome" to help them understand illnesses that occur in some societies but not in others. Examples of culture-bound syndromes include illnesses that result from voodoo, gypsy curses, and other "magical" spells. Until recently, the literature on culture-bound syndromes focused on illnesses in other societies that the Western anthropologists found mystifying because there was no measurable disease process involved. Members of highly technological societies such as ours expect that a biomedical cause and cure will ultimately be found for every illness. Now, however, anthropologists are suggesting that the illness behavior that surrounds conditions with which we are very familiar (for example, obesity and menopause) may constitute culture-bound syndromes.

A culture-bound syndrome is a constellation of symptoms that have been categorized as a dysfunction or disease in some societies but not in others. (See Table 1 for a list of requirements for culture-bound syndromes.)

TABLE 1

Defining Features of Culture-Bound Syndromes

A culture-bound syndrome is characterized by one or more of the following:

- It cannot be understood apart from its specific cultural or subcultural context.
- The etiology summarizes and symbolizes core meanings and behavioral norms of that culture.
- Diagnosis relies on culture-specific technology as well as ideology.
- Successful treatment is accomplished only by participants in that culture.

Corollaries

- Treatment judged as successful in one cultural context may not be understood as successful from another perspective.
- The symptoms may be recognized and similarly organized elsewhere but are not categorized as the same "disease."

Source: Based on Cassidy (1982) and Ritenbaugh (1982).

IS PMS A CULTURE-BOUND SYNDROME?

I believe that PMS is a culture-bound syndrome, and I'll try to convince you to agree with me. The best way to do this is to take the statements from Table 1 and discuss them one at a time. This way we can decide whether these statements, which appear to Westerners to describe voodoo and gypsy curses, describe PMS as well.

PMS cannot be understood apart from its specific cultural or subcultural context. In order to understand PMS, one must have, at the most basic level, a concept of menstruation as cyclic, which is necessary in order to anticipate it. Menstruation is a rare event in societies in which women are pregnant or lactating much of their adult lives. Therefore, members of those societies would not develop the same expectations of the menstrual cycle as members of more technologically advanced societies, and they would not have the familiarity with it to notice that certain changes are related to its events. There would thus be no PMS, merely a coping with individual symptoms as they emerged.

Emily Martin (1988) has argued that, in order to understand PMS, one must live in an industrialized society. Before industrialization, people worked in tune with natural rhythms—seasonal for farmers, circadian for skilled laborers. Now that most of us work at jobs in offices and factories that require sustained labor throughout the year and reward discipline of the mind and body, lapses in such discipline are noted. Symptoms on the Menstrual Distress Questionnaire (Moos, 1968) that involve lapses in discipline include "difficulty concentrating," "confusion," "lowered judgment," "decreased efficiency," and "lowered school or work performance." Martin (1988) has suggested that the women who complain of these "symptoms" may be less willing (as opposed to less able) to discipline themselves as usual when they are premenstrual.

Industrialization may contribute to the belief in many societies that one can and should exercise self-control in order to feel and behave the same way all the time. Our culture encourages people to believe that we can have more control over our lives and bodies than is actually possible (Brownell, 1991; McDaniel, 1988; Ussher, 2004). Premenstrual women often complain of feeling "out of control" because they are irritable, angry at someone, craving chocolate, or not inclined to work as hard as usual—experiences that are considered "normal" in children or men but "pathological" in menstruating women. Control is so important to us that being out of control is frightening (Ritenbaugh, 1982). This belief in control contributes not only to PMS but to eating disorders and compulsive exercise. But that's another lecture.

Finally, there would be no PMS without strong negative attitudes toward menstruation. Many studies (Brooks-Gunn & Ruble, 1986; Clarke & Ruble, 1978; Chrisler, 1988; Golub, 1981; Ruder, Finn, & Rotman, 1981) conducted in the United States have shown that both women and men hold negative attitudes toward menstruation. Americans are uncomfortable talking about menstruation and believe that the menstrual cycle has negative effects on women's personality, behavior, and physiology. The most popular measure of menstrual cycle effects is the Menstrual Distress Questionnaire (Moos, 1968), a title that clearly lets research participants know what kind of responses the researchers are expecting. Margie Ripper (1991) was frustrated in her attempts to study women's experience of the menstrual cycle, a neutral expression, which everyone kept hearing as "women's menstrual problems." Potential participants would sometimes say to her, "I'd be no use to you; I don't have any problems." In a study (Chrisler, Johnston, Champagne, & Preston, 1994) that specifically looked at positive experiences, participants were startled to learn that anyone thought that the menstrual cycle could be related to any experience that wasn't negative. Negative attitudes are not limited to the general public. A 1979 editorial in the *British Medical Journal* concluded: "There is nothing pleasant about menstruation. At best it is a physiological inconvenience. At worst it contributes to chronic ill health" (cited in Laws, 1983, p. 30).

PMS summarizes and symbolizes core meanings and behavioral norms of the culture. Among the core meanings and behavioral norms reflected in PMS are mind-body dualism, which contributes to our belief that people are not responsible for emotional or behavioral symptoms of disease (Ritenbaugh, 1982); individuals' need for control and fear of noncontrol; the raging-hormones hypothesis, which promotes the belief that women are emotionally unstable (McDaniel, 1988); and the industrialized society's preference for stability of affect and behavior. Because stability is so highly valued, changeableness, rhythmicity, and emotionality have come to be viewed as inherently "unhealthy" (Koeske, 1983).

PMS also reflects the behavioral norms of the feminine gender role. Women are expected to be soft-spoken, nurturing, patient, and kind. Any woman who is turned inward or otherwise unapproachable is thought to have something wrong with her (Chrisler & Johnston-Robledo, 2002). Blaming the "unfeminine" parts of one's personality or behavior on PMS can be a survival strategy for women in that it can allow women to hold onto a self-definition of "good/proper" women (Laws, 1983; Ussher, 2004). The premenstrual week is the only time of the month some women "allow" themselves to be angry (McDaniel, 1988) because they can attribute their anger to their hormones rather than to any of the many things in the world that could "legitimately" anger them. However, this strategy also works against women. There's nothing more frustrating than expressing anger about something only to hear others say, "She must be on the rag" or "That's PMS talking."

The menstrual cycle provides such a clear distinction between women and men that "its correlates, concomitants, accompaniments, ramifications, and implications have become intrinsically bound up with issues of gender equality" (Sommer, 1983, p. 53). In fact, PMS can be seen as a collection of negative beliefs about women's "nature," a nature that "requires" medical management and the protection of men, who are stronger and "healthier" than menstruating women (Zita, 1988). Don't miss the point: If women are emotionally unstable and inherently unhealthy, it's for their own good and the good of society that women's roles in public life are limited.

Diagnosis of PMS relies on culture-specific technology as well as ideology. To diagnose PMS, one must have a knowledge of hormones and their actions and accept the idea that hormones influence affect and be-havior. There are no reliable laboratory tests for PMS, but calendars, thermometers, hormone assay techniques, nutrient deficiency measures, and self-report questionnaires have been used in attempts to document its existence. Technology may be involved in the cause as well as the detection of premenstrual symptoms. Landers (1988) has suggested that PMS may be an iatrogenic disease (i.e., an illness caused by medical in-tervention) because it frequently begins or worsens when a woman is using an IUD or stops using oral contraceptives or after she has had a hysterectomy, a tubal ligation, or an abortion.

The ideologies on which the diagnosis of PMS relies include the raging-hormone hypothesis, an assumption that cyclic change is inher-ently pathological, an acceptance of stereotypical gender roles as accu-rate and appropriate descriptions of healthy behavior for women and men, and a social contract between the patient and physician (McDaniel, 1988) that allows patients to trust their physicians as experts who are able to make a diagnosis in a case in which the symptoms are so vague and numerous.

These ideologies are responsible for the fact that many women who experience premenstrual changes diagnose themselves as having PMS.

They then talk about PMS with their friends and thus contribute to giving PMS a legitimacy it doesn't deserve. Such self-diagnosis is dangerous for women because individual acts affect culture as well as being affected by it. When others hear women complaining about PMS, it reinforces these ideologies and persuades others that women cannot be trusted to do important work or to make decisions that have serious implications.

Successful treatment is accomplished only by participants in that culture. The act of being diagnosed has a therapeutic effect for many women who suffer from premenstrual changes, whether or not the symptoms are alleviated (Abplanalp, 1983; McDaniel, 1988). Women are accustomed to having their complaints dismissed by powerful others, and the diagnosis may represent one of the few times someone has listened to the women in a way that made them feel worthy of attention (Abplanalp, 1983). The use of the label PMS indicates that the physician and the patient accept society's standards and the cultural assumptions discussed earlier, which may, in a way, be comforting.

One of the characteristics that women who complain of PMS share is a strong placebo response (McDaniel, 1988). Many cures in Western medicine rely on pills, and patients are accustomed to expect relief from them. A placebo response is a good thing to exhibit if the problem is PMS because there is no effective treatment for it. Women often try a variety of treatments in search of relief or are advised to treat individual symptoms.

Women may be more likely than men to have external health locus of control—that is, to be less likely than men to think that they can affect their health by their own actions. Seeking treatment for PMS, then, can be empowering for women because they will have to be put in charge of their health and self-care. Women will be assigned such tasks as charting symptoms and taking their temperatures daily during the diagnosis phase and then advised to alter their diet, exercise regularly, and learn relaxation strategies. These tasks also have the advantage of causing them to focus on taking good care of themselves and directing their attention away from the people and institutions in their daily lives that make them feel tense, anxious, and depressed (McDaniel, 1988).

Women believed to have PMS are often advised to join self-help groups. Self-help and support groups have become very popular with many Americans in recent years, and one can find such a group for almost any medical or psychological disorder or social situation. People from other cultures would find it very odd to talk about such private matters with a group of strangers and to accept advice from untrained peers!

Treatment judged as successful in one cultural context may not be understood as successful from another perspective. The purpose of treating PMS is to help women to function more smoothly in their traditional, subordinate, "feminine" role "in an uncomplaining, cheerful way" (Rome, 1986, p. 147). Dalton has suggested that it is a woman's duty and obligation to be treated for PMS (Rome, 1986). Adherence to rigid gender roles may not be seen as a successful treatment even within subcultural contexts of our own society!

Progesterone therapy, which has never been approved by the FDA, has been a popular recommendation for PMS, especially in Great Britain. Side effects of progesterone include chest pain, yeast infections from vaginal suppositories, diarrhea and cramping from rectal suppositories, excessive drop in blood pressure from sublingual administration (Rome, 1986), continuous bleeding, amenorrhea, menses that are heavier or lighter than usual, dizzy spells, restlessness, gain or loss of weight, uterine cramps, and change in sex drive (Landers, 1988). Sometimes progesterone therapy simply displaces the symptoms to another phase of the cycle. Results of animal studies suggest that progesterone may be addictive and increase cancer risk (Landers, 1988). Thus, the original symptoms may be much milder than the side effects of the treatment. Is this a cure?

Probably the most serious treatment that has been used to alleviate PMS is hysterectomy plus oophorectomy—the surgical removal of the uterus and ovaries. It is unlikely that interfering so drastically with a woman's body and ending her fertility would be seen as a successful treatment in other cultures.

The symptoms of PMS may be recognized and similarly organized elsewhere but are not categorized as the same dysfunction or "disease." The symptoms associated with PMS are numerous and vague and have considerable overlap with those of other conditions. They could easily be recognized but organized differently. Many of the symptoms—headaches, backaches, irritability, tension, crying spells—are also associated with stress. It is agreed that stress worsens PMS, but perhaps stress actually causes these PMS "symptoms" just as it does in men.

None of the symptoms associated with PMS are unique to menstruation. What seems to be important to Western medicine is cyclicity, which is seen as instability. If cyclic or rhythmic changes were seen as normative or natural, then emotional, behavioral, and physiological changes would be accepted and expected. They would not be pathologized.

Thinking about our premenstrual experience in a different way would also change our illness behavior. Instead of considering yourself as "overreacting," consider yourself "sensitive" (Koeske, 1983). Changing your attributions about premenstrual changes would also make you feel better. If you know you are premenstrual, thinking "Water retention makes my tear ducts feel full" is probably more accurate than thinking "I am depressed and about to cry" (Koeske, 1983). Consider whether some of the changes associated with PMS should even be considered symptoms. If we lived in a society that preferred loose clothing such as robes or saris, then water retention might not even be noticed (Rome, 1986). In our weight-obsessed society, the small weight gain from premenstrual fluid retention is actively feared by many women. Probably only in the United States could an occasional urge to eat a candy bar or a salty snack be seen as a sign of a medical condition!

Most of the research on PMS is done by scientists in a few Western countries (Australia, Canada, Germany, Great Britain, the Netherlands, Sweden, and the United States), which share many common cultural beliefs. World Health Organization (WHO) surveys indicate that menstrual cycle–related complaints (except cramps) are most likely to be reported by women living in Western Europe, Australia, and North America. Women in India generally report no or mild symptoms premenstrually (Chaturvedi, Chandra, Gururaj, Beena, & Pandian, 1994; Prakash & Rao, 1982), and their attitudes toward menstruation are largely positive (Hoerster, Chrisler, & Rose, 2003). Data collected from women in Hong Kong (Chang, Holroyd, & Chau, 1995), Taiwan (Hsiao, Liu, Chen, & Hsieh, 2002), and mainland China (Yu, Zhu, Li, Oakley, & Reame, 1996) indicate that the most commonly reported premenstrual changes are fatigue, water retention, muscular tension, pain, and increased sensitivity to cold. Women in the United States do not report cold sensitivity, and women in China rarely report negative affect. The results of these studies support the idea that culture shapes which variations in mood and physical sensations are noticed and which cause concern. Further support for cultural influence comes from Paige's (1973) study of women in the United States. She found that the most severe menstrual complaints came from strict Catholics and Orthodox Jews who strongly adhered to the feminine gender role.

*W*HY HAS PMS BECOME SO SIGNIFICANT?

Why has PMS become so well known in the last 30 years? With hindsight, we can see how the development of interest in PMS coincided with the conservative political shift in the United States and Great Britain in the 1970s and 1980s. It is part of the backlash against feminists so clearly delineated by Susan Faludi (1991). In fact, now that the backlash has made it so unpopular to embrace feminism publicly, we may want to consider whether women's willingness to embrace PMS serves a similar function in facilitating resistance to sociocultural demands (Chrisler & Caplan, 2002). Whereas 30 years ago a woman might have said, "I refuse to diet, to achieve a perfectly clean house, and to stifle my anger because I will not collude with patriarchal demands," she now says, "I cannot lose weight, get all of my work done perfectly, and stay calm and happy all the time because I have PMS."

To understand the significance of PMS, one must consider who benefits from it. Women? To some extent, yes—if they can excuse behavior others disapprove of by suggesting it was caused by PMS. If physicians or others pay attention to women and take them seriously, women may be said to benefit from seeking help for PMS, yet the benefits to women are few and the drawbacks many. The existence of PMS encourages women to think of themselves as unstable and potentially ill for at least half of each month. It encourages men to think of us that way, too, which limits our opportunities for self-expression and career advancement. Now that the American Psychiatric Association has placed in the fourth edition of its *Diagnostic and Statistical Manual* a mental illness called premenstrual dysphoric disorder, there will be additional ways to stigmatize women and use PMS to our disadvantage.

Emily Martin (1987) has drawn attention to the historical importance of the waves of interest in PMS. Frank "discovered" premenstrual tension around 1930, during the depression, when the economic gains women made during World War I were slipping away. He (Frank, 1931) noted that premenstrual women engaged in foolish and ill-considered actions, and he worried about the consequences these actions might have in the workplace. When she began to study PMS during the 1950s, Katharina Dalton became part of a movement, whether she intended to or not, to convince women to become full-time housewives and leave their jobs to World War II veterans. In the late 1970s, when work on PMS again picked up speed, women had made enormous advances in work, school, and public life thanks to the women's liberation movement. Each time women advance, there's someone there to remind us that we can't go further because of our delicate health.

Who benefits from PMS? The physicians who treat the many women who seek relief from it benefit greatly from the widespread belief that PMS is a disease. Gynecologists and psychiatrists have been battling each other over who has the "right" to treat PMS. Medical researchers and other scientists who work in the biomedical model have benefited greatly from the interest in PMS, as they have been given government and corporate grants to find a cause and cure for PMS. Pharmaceutical companies sponsor research conferences and medical education seminars on PMS in the hope that some drug they can manufacture will be the long-awaited cure (Parlee, as cited in Tavris, 1992). If the publicity about PMS has convinced most women that they have a monthly illness, think what the profits could be on a drug millions of women would buy every month! The Eli Lilly Company was certainly thinking of this when it convinced the U.S. Food and Drug Administration to extend its patent on Prozac by demonstrating a new use for it: the treatment of premenstrual dysphoric disorder and possibly PMS. The company now markets its drug under its new name (Sarafem) in cute, feminine, pink and purple pills. Perhaps you've seen its advertisements in magazines and on television.

The greatest beneficiary of PMS is the status quo. PMS serves to keep women in their place; it is a form of social control. It's a culture-bound syndrome because it is only necessary in societies in which women have made major gains toward equality of rights and opportunities. If women are preoccupied with rhythmic changes in their bodies and emotions instead of preoccupied with winning political power, social institutions are safe. For example, women who are thought to have PMS are told to slow down the busy pace of their lives, sometimes in ways that can hurt their chances for successful careers. Self-help books advise women to tell their bosses about their PMS and tell them not to schedule important business meetings or travel during the second half of their menstrual cycles (Chrisler, 2001).

What do women learn from the label PMS? Karen Levy (1993) believes that it tells women that their problems are internal and individual; warns women not to express the entire range of their emotions because some of their feelings and behaviors are inappropriate; isolates women from the social, cultural, and environmental context of their lives by defining their experience as a medical problem; alienates women from each other and from their collective experience; and silences women from speaking out about the oppressive conditions of their lives.

HOW DO WOMEN FEEL ABOUT THE LABEL "PMS"?

An interesting new line of research consists of qualitative studies (e.g., focus groups, interviews, discourse analysis) of women's beliefs about, attitudes toward, and embrace of or resistance to the label "PMS." Most of the participants in these studies have been White women, as have most of the patients who have sought help from PMS clinics (Markens, 1996). Although African American and European American women have reported similar levels of premenstrual symptoms in community studies (e.g., Stout et al., 1986), African American women's apparent reluctance to seek medical services, and the scarcity of articles about PMS in magazines written for a Black audience (Markens, 1996), suggests that resistance to the label "PMS" may be greater in some ethnic and socioeconomic groups than in others. Perhaps women who have experienced discrimination that is class-, race-, language-, or sexual orientation–based are less willing to call attention to their female state or less able to believe that they can expect sympathy for their condition than are women who have experienced less (or less overt) discrimination in their lives (Chrisler & Caplan, 2002).

In a series of interviews with women patients recruited from a PMS clinic in England, Swann and Ussher (1995) found that their participants' views of PMS were very similar to those presented in popular culture. They firmly believed that PMS is biologically based, and they rejected situational attributions for their distress, which the researchers described as "romantic discourse" (e.g., "everything else in my life is fine, it's just my PMS") (p. 365). The participants adopted a "dualistic discourse" (p. 364) that parallels the notion found in popular culture that women with PMS are like Dr. Jekyll and Mr. Hyde—normally, they are kind and pleasant, but when they are premenstrual, they become monsters. One of their interviewees spoke of herself as being possessed by menstrual madness ("this thing that takes over me") (p. 364) that causes her to lose control of her emotions and actions. In this way, the menstrual monster, not the "real" self, is responsible for any interpersonal problems or other negative outcomes that derive from actions taken during the premenstrual phase.

More recent studies (Cosgrove & Riddle, 2003; Lee, 2002) of community samples of women with and without PMS show more ambivalence, and some resistance, yet beliefs similar to those previously mentioned. Lee (2002) found that women with negative attitudes toward menstruation were more likely to consider PMS to be an appropriate label for their personal experience and to believe that women's symptoms and feelings are not taken seriously without a medical explanation. Women with more positive attitudes toward menstruation were more critical of the label "PMS," even though most of them said that they did experience premenstrual symptoms to some extent. Some commented that the term disempowers women by subsuming their normal experiences under the umbrella of illness. A few spoke of "changes" rather than "symptoms," as many feminist writers do, in order to "own" both the problematic and the positive fluctuations they experienced. Cosgrove and Riddle (2003) also found the frequent use of dualistic discourse in their participants' accounts of their premenstrual experiences. It is interesting to note that the women in their study who resisted the label "PMS" often gave biomedical explanations of why they did not have it (e.g., "I'm just lucky that I have good genes").

These studies show the power of culture to drive attributions about the behavior of self and others. Before PMS was popularized in the early 1980s, women did experience some premenstrual changes that were bothersome, but they did not think of themselves as victims of a sort of menstrual madness that could turn them into someone else or make them lose control of themselves. The power of the biomedical discourse and cultural stereotypes are so strong that even women who resist labeling themselves with PMS may use the discourse to defend themselves rather than attack the discourse and the construct itself.

SOME ADVICE

Stop thinking of menstruation as negative. It has positive aspects, too. Talk about its benefits with your classmates (for example, its presence is a sign of good health, it is symbolic of our connection to other women, it represents biological maturity, it signifies our ability to bear children or lets us know we are not pregnant). Stop using negative slang to describe menstruation. My friend Ingrid Johnston-Robledo likes to refer to the menstrual period as AOW, or Affirmation of Womanhood. Try doing that; see how your friends react. Refer to your premenstrual experiences as "changes" rather than "symptoms." A change is a neutral thing. A symptom implies an illness.

Examine your attributions about unpleasant experiences. Never let someone get away with suggesting that your emotions are caused by hormones. Hormonal fluctuations don't make women angry or irritable, although they may intensify those reactions. There are always reasons for your anger, and it's those reasons, not your hormones, that should be discussed. Dalton (1977) noticed that women who live alone are less likely to suffer from PMS than women who live with men. That makes sense to me. After all, it's other people who make us irritable and tense!

The purpose of this lecture was not to suggest that premenstrual changes don't exist. They do, as many women know from personal experience. What I hope you'll do is think about whether your experience of these changes is serious enough to be considered an illness. In most cases, it won't be. And if it's not, don't stereotype yourself and other women by excusing your behavior or by attributing your feelings to PMS. Think about who benefits if you do.

REFERENCES

ABPLANALP, J. M. (1983). Premenstrual syndrome: A selective review. *Women and Health, 8*(2/3), 107–124.

BROOKS-GUNN, J., & RUBLE, D. N. (1986). Men's and women's attitudes and beliefs about the menstrual cycle. *Sex Roles, 14,* 287–299.

BROWNELL, K. (1991). Personal responsibility and control over our bodies: When expectation exceeds reality. *Health Psychology, 10,* 303–310.

CASSIDY, C. M. (1982). Protein-energy malnutrition as a culture-bound syndrome. *Culture, Medicine, and Psychiatry, 6,* 325–345.

CHANG, A. M., HOLROYD, E., & CHAU, J. P. C. (1995). Premenstrual syndrome in employed Chinese women in Hong Kong. *Health Care for Women International, 16,* 551–561.

CHATURVEDI, S. K., CHANDRA, P. S., GURURAJ, G., BEENA, M. B., & PANDIAN, R. D. (1994). Prevalence of premenstrual symptoms and syndromes: Preliminary observations. *National Institute of Mental Health and Neurosciences Journal, 12,* 9–14.

CHRISLER, J. C. (1988). Age, gender-role orientation, and attitudes toward menstruation. *Psychological Reports, 63,* 827–834.

CHRISLER, J. C. (2001). *How to regain your control and balance: The "pop" approach to PMS.* Unpublished manuscript.

CHRISLER, J. C., & CAPLAN, P. J. (2002). The strange case of Dr. Jekyll and Ms. Hyde: How PMS became a cultural phenomenon and a psychiatric disorder. *Annual Review of Sex Research, 13,* 274–306.

CHRISLER, J. C., JOHNSTON, I. K., CHAMPAGNE, N. M., & PRESTON, K. E. (1994). Menstrual joy: The construct and its consequences. *Psychology of Women Quarterly, 18,* 375–387.

CHRISLER, J. C., & JOHNSTON-ROBLEDO, I. (2002). Raging hormones? Feminist perspectives on premenstrual syndrome and postpartum depression. In M. Ballow & L. S. Brown (Eds.), *Rethinking mental health and disorder: Feminist perspectives* (pp. 174–197). New York: Guilford Press.

CHRISLER, J. C., & LEVY, K. B. (1990). The media construct a menstrual monster: A content analysis of PMS articles in the popular press. *Women & Health, 16*(2), 89–104.

CLARKE, A. E., & RUBLE, D. N. (1978). Young adolescents' beliefs concerning menstruation. *Child Development, 49,* 231–234.

COSGROVE, L., & RIDDLE, B. (2003). Constructions of femininity and experiences of menstrual distress. *Women & Health, 38*(3), 37–58.

DALTON, K. (1960a). Effects of menstruation on schoolgirls' weekly work. *British Medical Journal, 1,* 326–328.

DALTON, K. (1960b). Schoolgirls' behaviour and menstruation. *British Medical Journal, 2,* 1647–1649.

DALTON, K. (1968). Menstruation and examinations. *Lancet, 2,* 1386–1388.

DALTON, K. (1977). *The premenstrual syndrome and progesterone therapy.* Chicago: Yearbook Medical.

DEBROVNER, C. (1982). *Premenstrual tension: An interdisciplinary approach.* New York: Human Sciences.

FALUDI, S. (1991). *Backlash: The undeclared war against American women.* New York: Crown.

FRANK, R. T. (1931). The hormonal causes of premenstrual tension. *Archives of Neurology and Psychiatry, 26,* 1053–1057.

GOLUB, S. (1981). Sex differences in attitudes and beliefs regarding menstruation. In P. Komnenich, M. McSweeney, J. A. Noack, & N. Elder (Eds.), *The menstrual cycle: Research and implications for women's health* (pp. 129–134). New York: Springer.

HOERSTER, K. D., CHRISLER, J. C., & ROSE, J. G. (2003). Attitudes toward and experience with menstruation in the U.S. and India. *Women & Health, 38*(3), 77–95.

HSIAO, M-C., LIU, C-Y., CHEN, K-C., & HSIEH, T-T. (2002). Characteristics of women seeking treatment for premenstrual syndrome in Taiwan. *Acta Psychiatrica Scandanavica, 106,* 150–155.

KOESKE, R. D. (1983). Lifting the curse of menstruation: Toward a feminist perspective on the menstrual cycle. *Women and Health, 8*(2/3), 1–16.

LANDERS, L. (1988). *Images of bleeding: Menstruation as ideology.* New York: Orlando Press.

LAWS, S. (1983). The sexual politics of premenstrual tension. *Women's Studies International Forum, 6,* 19–31.

LEE, S. (2002). Health and sickness: The meaning of menstruation and premenstrual syndrome in women's lives. *Sex Roles, 46,* 25–35.

LEVY, K. B. (1993). *The politics of women's health care: Medicalization as a form of social control.* Mesquite, TX: Ide House.

MARKENS, S. (1996). The problematic of "experience": A political and cultural critique of PMS. *Gender & Society, 10,* 42–58.

MARTIN, E. (1987). *The woman in the body: A cultural analysis of reproduction.* Boston: Beacon Press.

MARTIN, E. (1988). Premenstrual syndrome: Discipline, work, and anger in late industrial societies. In T. Buckley & A. Gottlieb (Eds.), *Blood magic: The anthropology of menstruation* (pp. 161–181). Berkeley: University of California Press.

MCDANIEL, S. H. (1988). The interpersonal politics of premenstrual syndrome. *Family Systems Medicine, 6,* 134–149.

MEIGS, J. W. (1961). Occupational medicine. *New England Journal of Medicine, 264,* 861–867.

MOOS, R. H. (1968). The development of a Menstrual Distress Questionnaire. *Psychosomatic Medicine, 30,* 853–867.

PAIGE, K. E. (1973, September). Women learn to sing the menstrual blues. *Psychology Today,* pp. 41–46.

PRAKASH, I. J., & RAO, S. (1982). Prevalence of premenstrual symptoms in a college population. *Indian Journal of Clinical Psychology, 9,* 95–98.

RIPPER, M. (1991). A comparison of the effect of the menstrual cycle and the social week on mood, sexual interest, and self-assessed performance. In D. L. Taylor & N. F. Woods (Eds.), *Menstruation, health, and illness* (pp. 19–33). Washington, DC: Hemisphere.

RITENBAUGH, C. (1982). Obesity as a culture-bound syndrome. *Culture, Medicine, and Psychiatry, 6,* 347–361.

ROME, E. (1986). Premenstrual syndrome through a feminist lens. In V. L. Olesen & N. F. Woods (Eds.), *Culture, society, and menstruation* (pp. 145–151). Washington, DC: Hemisphere.

RUDER, FINN, & ROTMAN. (1981). *The Tampax report.* New York: Author.

SIEGEL, G. S. (1963). *Periodic health examinations: Abstracts from the literature* (Public Health Service Publication No. 1010). Washington, DC: U.S. Government Printing Office.

SOMMER, B. (1983). How does menstruation affect women's cognitive competence and psychophysiological response? *Women and Health, 8*(2/3), 53–90.

STOUT, A. L., GRADY, T. A., STEEGE, J. F., BLAZER, D. G., GEORGE, L. K., & MELVILLE, M. L. (1986). Premenstrual symptoms in Black and White community samples. *American Journal of Psychiatry, 143,* 1436–1439.

SWANN, C. J., & USSHER, J. M. (1995). A discourse analytic approach to women's experience of premenstrual syndrome. *Journal of Mental Health, 4,* 359–367.

TAVRIS, C. (1992). *The mismeasure of woman.* New York: Simon & Schuster.

THOMAS, C. L. (Ed.). (1989). *Taber's cyclopedic medical dictionary* (17th ed.). Philadelphia: F. A. Davis.

TOWNSEND, J. M., & CARBONE, C. L. (1980). Menopausal syndrome: Illness or social role—A transcultural analysis. *Culture, Medicine, and Psychiatry, 4,* 229–248.

USSHER, J. (2004). Premenstrual syndrome and self-policing: Ruptures in self-silencing lead to increased self-surveillance and blaming of the body. *Social Theory & Health, 2,* 254–272.

YU, M., ZHU, X., LI, J., OAKLEY, D., & REAME, N. E. (1996). Perimenstrual symptoms among Chinese women in an urban area of China. *Health Care for Women International, 17,* 161–172.

ZITA, J. N. (1988). The premenstrual syndrome: "Dis-easing" the female cycle. *Hypatia, 3*(1), 77–99.

*S*UGGESTED READINGS

FINGERSON, L. (2006). *Girls in power: Gender, body, and menstruation in adolescence.* Albany, NY: State University of New York Press.

KISSLING, E. A. (2006). *Capitalizing on the curse: The business of menstruation.* Boulder, CO: Lynne Rienne.

LAWS, S. (1990). *Issues of blood: The politics of menstruation.* London: Macmillan.

MARTIN, E. (1987). *The woman in the body: A cultural analysis of reproduction.* Boston: Beacon Press.

*N*ANCY FELIPE RUSSO *is Regents Professor of Psychology and Women's Studies at Arizona State University. Dr. Russo has taught the psychology of women since 1971. She served as President of the American Psychological Association's Division (35) on the Psychology of Women in 1989 and as the editor of the journal* Psychology of Women Quarterly. *In 1995, she received the American Psychological Association's Award for Distinguished Contributions to Psychology in the Public Interest.*

11

Understanding Emotional Responses After Abortion

———— ❖ ————

D
o you know at least one person who has had an abortion? Most people do. This is not surprising given that about 1.5 million legal abortions are performed every year in the United States. Worldwide, an estimated 22 percent of pregnancies are terminated by abortion (Alan Guttmacher Institute [AGI], 1999). Throughout history, abortion has been used by women of diverse ethnic, class, and cultural backgrounds to time, space, and limit their childbearing. Nonetheless, women's access to abortion continues to be controversial. Today, one in four women live in countries where abortion is severely restricted or prohibited by law. Even within countries where abortion is legal, there are profound disagreements about religious, moral, and ethical issues related to abortion, disagreements that fuel intense public debates over laws and policies aimed at restricting women's access to this medical procedure. Although I will not focus on these moral and philosophical issues here, it is important to remember that our discussion of abortion takes place in a highly charged political context (Russo & Denious, 2000, 2005).

These debates are not confined to religious, moral, and ethical issues. Perhaps you have come across some variation of the argument that access to abortion should be restricted because abortion creates psychological problems for women. This argument is shaping legislation around the world and has been found in areas as diverse as Scotland, Switzerland, New Zealand, and Central and Eastern Europe (David, 1999). In the United States, in an attempt to discourage women from choosing to terminate their pregnancies, laws have been passed in many states that force doctors to tell abortion patients that as a result of having an abortion, they may experience a variety of negative psychological symptoms, including guilt, anxiety, and depression—a "postabortion syndrome." Most recently, the claim that abortion damages mental health was a prominent feature in testimony in support of legislation to ban abortion in South Dakota (SD), with the ultimate goal to overturn *Roe vs. Wade* (SD Task Force to Study Abortion, 2005).

There is no scientific basis for such claims. The argument that abortion is "legal, but not safe for your mental health" was developed after the political forces that opposed abortion were unable to make a case for the negative impact of abortion on physical health. The risks of abortion range from 0.6–1.3 deaths per 100,000 abortions in countries where abortion is legal on broad grounds and is performed by licensed physicians. In contrast, the risks associated with childbirth range from between 6 and 25 per 100,000 live births in developed countries (AGI, 1999; Gissler et al., 2004).

Recently, research from Finland (Gissler et al., 2004) has been misrepresented as showing abortion is riskier than childbirth (Reardon, 2004). Examination of the actual findings, however, reveals that death from direct pregnancy-related causes for women giving birth was three times higher than the rate for women having an abortion (3.9 vs. 1.3 per 100,000, respectively). Examination of deaths occurring within a year of pregnancy outcome (birth vs. abortion), however, reminds us that many women seek abortion because of severe health problems: Women who had abortions were more likely to die from natural causes unrelated to pregnancy than women who gave birth (20.4 vs. 12.0 per 100,000). The findings underscore the strong link between violent circumstances and unwanted pregnancy: Women in the abortion group were much more likely to die from violent causes than other women (60.0 versus 9.6 per 100,000). Thus, where abortion is legal, it is difficult to argue that a pregnant women should choose childbirth over abortion out of concern for her physical health. How many of you have ever had a shot of penicillin? Your risk of death from that shot was higher than a woman's risk of death from having a legal first trimester abortion.

In contrast, the mortality rate is much higher in developing countries where laws are more often restrictive and abortions are performed clandestinely by an unqualified practitioner or by the woman herself. For example, in Latin America, the death rate is 119 per 100,000 abortions; in Africa, the figure is 680 per 100,000 abortions. According to the World Health Organization, approximately 30 percent of pregnancy-related deaths around the world result from unsafe abortion (AGI, 1999).

But what about women's risk for psychological problems after abortion? Science cannot resolve moral issues—those depend on values—but it can answer testable questions about how people think, feel, and behave. Unlike many of the moral and ethical questions posed in abortion debates, the question of whether or not the experience of abortion is traumatic for women's mental health *is* testable by scientific methods. I will describe findings in the scientific literature related to women's postabortion emotional responses and the factors that shape those responses. At the end of this lecture, you should have a clearer understanding of the nature of the research findings, and how they suggest that the argument itself may be undermining the mental health of women.

PSYCHOLOGICAL RESEARCH ON POSTABORTION EMOTIONAL RESPONSES

Whatever our opinion about the morality of abortion, psychologists have an ethical obligation to speak out when psychological findings are misrepresented, as currently happens all too often in abortion debates. Put most simply, contrary to the concerted efforts to convince the public of the existence of widespread and severe postabortion trauma, there is no credible scientific evidence for the existence of such trauma, even though abortion occurs in a highly stressful context, that of unwanted pregnancy. Although any individual piece of research may have specific flaws, the overwhelming body of well-designed scientific studies, which are based on diverse samples, methods, and measurements, is consistent: For the majority of women, freely chosen legal abortion is not found to have severe or lasting negative psychological effects, especially when the abortion was conducted during the first trimester of pregnancy (Adler et al., 1990, 1992; Posavac & Miller, 1990; Russo, 1992; Russo & Denious 2000; Schmiege & Russo, 2005).

Does this mean that women are always "mentally healthy" after experiencing an abortion? No. Women's postabortion psychological responses vary. But the *most important* factor to consider in understanding them is psychological status *before* becoming pregnant (Major et al., 2000). Pregnancy (wanted or unwanted) is a stressful life event, even for women who have no history of mental disorder. However, psychological problems during and after pregnancy most often are found in women who have a history of psychological disorders, regardless of how the pregnancy is resolved (Gilchrist, Hannaford, Frank, & Kay, 1995; Steinberg & Russo, 2006).

Psychological health before becoming pregnant is not the only factor shaping postabortion responses. Other factors that predict a woman's mental health after abortion include the quality of her healthcare, the pregnancy's meaning to the woman, her comfort with her decision-making process, difficulty in deciding to have an abortion, termination of a pregnancy that was originally wanted, abortion in the second trimester of pregnancy, feeling coerced to have the abortion, not expecting to cope well with the abortion, and limited or no social support for the abortion decision (Adler et al., 1990, 1992).

But arguing that abortion is a risky option has little meaning for a woman confronted with an unwanted pregnancy without comparing that risk to her alternatives: having the child and keeping it or having the child and relinquishing it for adoption. The destructive impact of unwanted childbearing on the woman, her family, and society is well-documented (Berk, Sorenson, Wiebe, & Upchurch, 2003; David, 1992; David, Dytrych, & Matejcek, 2003; Russo, 1992). Little is known about the psychological effects of adoption. What is known suggests that it can involve substantial distress, and the predictors of that distress appear to be *similar* to those that predict distress after abortion.

Abortion is confounded with unwanted pregnancy. Women who have unwanted pregnancies are more likely to suffer social and economic disadvantage, have ill heath, and experience violent circumstances, and such women are more likely to terminate those pregnancies than carry them to term. So it is never surprising to find a correlation between abortion and a negative health outcome when proper controls are lacking. The controversy is over the claim that abortion contributes to an increase in risk for negative health outcomes.

Despite the confounding of abortion and unwanted pregnancy, a number of recent studies that compare abortion vs. delivery without controlling for wantedness of pregnancy and other relevant variables are being cited as evidence for such a claim (e.g., Fergusson, Horwood, & Ridder, 2006; Cougle, Reardon, & Coleman, 2003; Reardon et al., 2003; Reardon et al., 2002). As would be expected, such studies have reported that women who have a history of abortion have, on average, poorer mental health profiles compared to other women.

If well-designed, such work might contribute to understanding factors that predict variation in mental health among abortion patients. For example, the studies mentioned above suggest that likelihood of exposure to violence is high among women who have abortions. However, these studies do not have the proper controls to address the issue of whether a pregnant woman will increase her mental health risks should she voluntarily choose to have an abortion to avoid an unwanted birth. Previous mental health problems, including the aftermath of previous and ongoing violence in one's life, do not go away whatever the chosen option.

In more well-controlled studies that have compared psychological responses following abortion and delivery of unplanned or unwanted pregnancy, the few differences found suggested positive effects to be associated with choice of abortion (Russo & Zierk, 1992; Zabin, Hirsch, & Emerson, 1989; Schmiege & Russo, 2005; Steinberg & Russo, 2006). For example, in the United Kingdom, a large prospective cohort study of 13,261 women who were identified as having an unplanned pregnancy found that risk for total reported psychiatric disorder was no higher after termination of pregnancy than after childbirth. Women with a previous history of psychiatric illness were most at risk for subsequent disorder after the end of their pregnancy, whatever its outcome. Women without previous history of psychosis had a lower risk of psychosis after having an abortion than after giving birth (Gilchrist et al., 1995).

So, risk for severe psychological disorder after termination of an unplanned pregnancy is generally low and comparable to that of giving birth. But what about psychological distress that is severe enough to require treatment but not so severe that a psychiatric diagnosis is required? A number of studies in the United States have used psychological tests to assess various symptoms of psychopathology. Such studies report that levels of psychological distress after abortion are typically low, averaging below the clinical cut-off scores that signal risk for clinical disorder. For example, Brenda Major and her colleagues (Major, Mueller, & Hildebrandt, 1985), found that abortion patients averaged scores of 4.17 on the short form of the Beck Depression Inventory immediately after the abortion, and 1.97 three weeks later. Scores below 5 on that scale are considered *nondepressed*. Similarly, Sarah Schmiege and I examined the relationship between first unwanted pregnancy and subsequent risk for clinical depression. When relevant variables were controlled, 25 percent of the abortion group compared with 28 percent of the delivery group fell into the high-risk category (the difference was not statistically significant; Schmiege & Russo, 2005; Russo & Schmiege, 2005, 2006).

So how do we explain the fact that there are many women who are depressed or anxious and who have had abortions? First, it should be kept in mind that at any particular moment in time a certain percentage of women in the U.S. population have psychological problems whether or not they have an abortion. In addition, we must remember that abortion occurs in the context of an unwanted pregnancy—a stressful and negative life event. A woman's responses after resolving her pregnancy reflect the coping resources—physical, psychological, social, and financial—she has for dealing with such negative events (Adler et al., 1990, 1992; Major et al., 1988, 2000).

Research that I conducted with my student Kristin Zierk confirmed that access to coping resources, not the experience of abortion, explains variation in women's postabortion emotional responses. Our study, which examined women's self-esteem as a measure of their well-being, was based on data from the National Longitudinal Study of Youth (NLSY), a national sample of 5,295 women aged 14–24 in 1979 who were interviewed annually for eight years (from 1979–1987). Our findings were incompatible with the assertion of the existence of severe and widespread negative effects of abortion. In fact, women who had one abortion had higher self-esteem than women who did not! We do not conclude from this finding that having an abortion increases self-esteem, however. The point of our research is the need to avoid making any conclusions about the effects of abortion unless the relevant variables—including preexisting mental health—are controlled and abortion is considered in context.

To understand the effects of abortion and childbearing in context, we examined the 1987 self-esteem of women who had no abortions before 1980, using multivariate statistical analyses to control for the effects of previous levels of self-esteem (measured in 1980), coping resources (education, employment, income, presence of spouse), abortion, and childbearing. What happened when previous levels of self-esteem, coping resources, childbearing, and abortion variables were all controlled? As hypothesized, the most important predictor of well-being in 1987 was well-being in 1980—that is, well-being *before* any abortions occurred. In addition, being employed, having a higher income, having more years of education, and bearing fewer children all continued to have significant and independent relationships to increased well-being. Abortion did not make a difference (Russo & Zierk, 1992). Subsequently, Amy Dabul and I analyzed the data separately for Black women and White women and found the pattern of results to be similar for both groups (Russo & Dabul, 1997). Sarah Schmiege and I then examined the relationship between first unwanted pregnancy on subsequent risk for clinical depression, which was measured in 1992 in the NLSY sample. As mentioned above, the difference between abortion and delivery groups was not statistically significant (Schmiege & Russo, 2005; Russo & Schmiege, 2005, 2006). This study corrected the invalid findings of an earlier report that had been based on miscoded data (Reardon & Cougle, 2002).

Analyses of the NLSY data have also revealed that—contrary to the stereotypes of abortion patients as seeking to avoid childbearing responsibilities and have carefree lifestyles—one out of three of the women who had had abortions had more than two children (Russo & Zierk, 1992). Women having abortions had larger family sizes and were more likely to have unwanted children than other women. We concluded that abortion becomes linked to women's well-being through its role in reducing stress by reducing family size and increasing women's access to resources (i.e., ability to become employed, attain more education, and earn a higher income).

Marriage did not make an independent contribution to the well-being of the women in these analyses, but we were unable to differentiate between happy and unhappy marriages. However, in later research, Jean Denious and I were able to shed additional light on the factors underlying the simple correlations found between having an abortion and various negative mental effects, including conflict between marriage partners.

Our analyses of data from a national survey of women's health showed that women who reported having had an abortion also reported higher levels of depressive symptoms than women who reported no history of abortion. But women who reported an abortion were also more likely to report a history of childhood physical and sexual abuse and to have had a violent partner than other women. When history of violence and partner experiences were controlled, the correlation between abortion and depression disappeared. We are not talking about statistically significant yet meaningless differences here. For example, nearly 50 percent of women who reported an abortion also reported being emotionally, physically, or sexually abused as compared to 26 percent of other women. Looking at the data another way, of women who reported experiencing *no* childhood abuse (emotional, physical, or sexual), only 9.2 percent reported having had an abortion. Among women who reported experiencing all three types of abuse, 34.5 percent also reported experiencing abortion. History of childhood abuse is thus indicated as a critical factor in understanding the preexisting mental health of women seeking abortions. Further, high proportions of women who reported having had an abortion also reported having had abusive and violent partners. Indeed, 20 percent reported experiencing some form of "physical" violence (e.g., being hit, kicked, pushed, grabbed, shoved); for women who had not reported an abortion, the figure was 11.4 percent (Russo & Denious, 2001).

To learn more about the relation of abortion on a first pregnancy to risk for subsequent anxiety disorders, including posttraumatic stress disorder (PTSD), Julia Steinberg and I (2006) analyzed data from the National CoMorbidity Survey, the "gold standard" of surveys on psychiatric epidemiology. Although we were not able to control for wantedness of pregnancy, the assessment of violence was sufficiently complete such that after the variables that predict unwanted pregnancy were controlled (including violence exposure), there was no relationship between abortion and PTSD (or generalized anxiety disorder or social anxiety disorder, for that matter). We also found that in particular, women with repeat abortions (which signal repeat unwanted pregnancies) were significantly more likely to have histories of rape, physical attack, or to have been held captive, kidnapped, or threatened with a weapon; 41.1 percent of women who reported repeat abortions reported experiencing at least one form of violence before becoming pregnant compared to 26.2 percent of women who reported no abortion.

Given these findings, would you be surprised to find a woman who has had an abortion to be depressed or to display symptoms of PTSD? No, for it is likely that she has had experiences with violence, and the long-lasting physical and mental health effects of victimization are well documented (Koss et al., 1994; Russo, 2006). The point is to understand the inappropriateness of automatically attributing a woman's symptoms to the experience of abortion and the need to explore the context in which her unwanted pregnancy occurred. In our studies, controlling for exposure to violence and other relevant aspects of the women's context fully accounted for any relationships found between abortion and mental health outcomes studied (Russo & Denious, 2001; Steinberg & Russo, 2006).

What about the argument that women may not be distressed after having an abortion but in the long run they will suffer a delayed posttraumatic stress disorder? Evidence of the quality of emotional responses after resolving an unwanted pregnancy is incompatible with such a diagnosis.

First, most women show a combination of positive and negative postabortion responses. However, positive emotions (relief and happiness) are more often experienced and experienced more strongly than negative emotions (shame, fear of disapproval, guilt, regret, anxiety, and depression). This is true both immediately after the abortion and in the months following (Adler, 1975; Kero, Högberg, & Lalos, 2004; Lazarus, 1985; Osofsky & Osofsky, 1972).

For example, in an early study, Nancy Adler (1975) studied positive and negative emotions expressed by women over two to three months after an abortion. Women rated how much they felt each emotion from 1 ("not at all") to 4 ("to a considerable degree"). Positive emotions were felt most intensely, averaging 3.96 on the 4-point scale. Ratings of negative responses clustered into two groups—internally based and socially based emotions—and ranged from an average of 2.26 for the emotions that were internally based (anger, anxiety, depression, doubt, and regret) to 1.81 for socially based emotions (fear of disapproval, guilt, and shame). In other words, most women have ambivalent feelings after having an abortion, but they are mostly satisfied, relieved, and happy. Focusing on negative feelings and building a portrait of negative emotional outcomes for abortion patients is a gross distortion of the reality of the experience for most women.

Research on the *timing* of the emotional responses also brings the reality of a "postabortion syndrome" into question. In considering the findings, keep in mind that studies of other life stressors suggest that women who show no evidence of severe negative responses after a stressful event are unlikely to develop subsequent significant psychological problems in conjunction with that event (Wortman & Silver, 1989).

Several studies have found that women's anxiety and depression levels are highest *before* their abortion, drop immediately afterward, and continue dropping for several weeks later until they are lower than they were *before* the abortion (Cohen & Roth, 1984; Major et al., 1985; Zabin et al., 1989). This is not the pattern found in response to traumatic events and is inconsistent with the idea that abortion is the primary source of psychic trauma. On the contrary, this pattern suggests that *it is the unwanted pregnancy that is the primary source of distress for abortion patients.*

Nonetheless, some people argue that a time period of a few months is too short for postabortion distress to emerge—given more time, postabortion syndrome will develop, just as posttraumatic stress syndrome identified in Vietnam veterans and rape victims has been found to develop over time (note: this argument does ignore the fact that Vietnam veterans and rape victims do not report being relieved and happy immediately after their traumatic experiences). Most studies of abortion patients have focused on early responses, with two years being the longest period of direct follow-up (Adler et al., 1990, 1992). However, recall that Kristin Zierk and I examined the well-being of women who were followed over eight years. Time since abortion was not related to well-being over that eight-year time period, even when the sample was split and women who had abortions more than seven years previously were examined (Russo & Zierk, 1992).

Finally, ask yourself, What exactly does it mean to say that the abortion experience *per se* is the "cause" of negative postabortion psychological responses? What about research that suggests that a woman's postabortion emotional problems can lie more in her situation than in her personal attributes? Recall that in the study by Nancy Adler (1975), negative emotions after abortion clustered into two categories: internally based and socially based. These emotions were found to stem from different sources. Internally based negative emotions were found to be related to the personal meaning of the pregnancy for the woman, whereas socially based negative emotions were related to the woman's social environment.

For example, when age was controlled, unmarried women experienced socially based negative emotions more strongly than married women.

Women who attended church more frequently were also more likely to express stronger socially based negative emotions. Then there is recent research on the effects of picketing on women seeking an abortion; the researchers found that exposure to intense antiabortion activity, experiencing attempts to block clinic entry, and being upset by demonstrators were all associated with greater depression after the abortion (Cozzarelli & Major, 1998). Such findings point to factors *other* than the abortion experience *per se* as determinants of postabortion emotional status and remind us that it is possible to make the experience of abortion a traumatic event by ostracizing women into feeling guilt and shame.

THE HARM OF CONSTRUCTING POSTABORTION SYNDROME

"Pregnant? Need Help? You Have Options"—this is the opening page of a website for a 24-hour telephone hotline connecting pregnant women with "pregnancy resource" centers across the country. According to a recent governmental investigation, the website does not say that only pro-life centers are represented and only nonabortion options will be counseled. Federally funded pregnancy resource centers often mask their pro-life mission in order to attract "abortion-vulnerable" clients, placing ads in the yellow pages under "abortion services" although they do not provide referrals to abortion services. Instead of providing medically accurate information, such pregnancy resource centers are often a source of false or misleading information about the physical and mental health risks of abortion; women are being told the psychological effects of abortion are "severe, long-lasting, and common" (Committee on Government Reform—Minority Staff, 2004, p. 4).

So what if anti-abortion activists try to deter women from seeking abortion by defining women's psychological responses after having an abortion as a mental disorder? You might argue that, if fear of death, severe legal penalties, and unsafe conditions have not deterred women from seeking abortion around the world, psychological problems in some distant postabortion future are probably not going to be much of a deterrent.

One problem is that the argument *can itself create psychological problems for women* by undermining their coping mechanisms. Experimental work has demonstrated that belief in one's ability to cope after the abortion is *causally* linked to postabortion emotional responses (Mueller & Major, 1989). The inaccurate portrayal of abortion as having widespread severe negative psychological effects could subvert women's mental health by undermining the positive coping expectancies that are associated with beneficial mental health outcomes after abortion. Social ostracism and harassment of women seeking abortion could also have harmful mental health effects, through inducing negative socially based emotions, undermining social support, and encouraging unwanted childbearing.

It is important to recognize that people do continually reconstruct and reinterpret past events in the light of subsequent experiences. Under stressful and tragic circumstances, ideas of punishment and retribution surface, even among people who do not consider themselves especially religious. As Jeanne Lemkau (1988) has observed, under stressful conditions such as infertility, infant death, or catastrophic illness, which are associated with depressed mood and cognitive distortions, it is possible for a woman to make highly idiosyncratic causal connections to an earlier abortion as well as other events in her life history.

Such connections and their associated feelings need to be explored in therapy without prejudging their underlying causality. All people can experience sadness or depressed mood at times. But if a woman is severely anxious or depressed, or has other symptoms of psychological distress, it is important that she see a qualified, licensed mental health professional (Lemkau, 1988; Rubin & Russo, 2004).

Because of their psychological, social, and environmental circumstances, women are at higher risk for depression than men (McGrath, Keita, Strickland, & Russo, 1990; Keyes & Goodman, 2006). One of the many factors that contribute to that higher risk is women's tendency to ruminate about things that bother them rather than to take instrumental action (Nolen-Hoeksema, 1990). Self-help groups can have many useful benefits. However, when a woman is clinically depressed, without professional guidance, talking to others who are sympathetic may perpetuate her depression, particularly if they prejudge the woman's problems and encourage her to misattribute their causes to having an abortion. It is thus possible for support groups that are not monitored by a qualified professional to contribute to prolonging clinical depression. Given that a history of mental disorder, intimate violence, and expectancies for coping are associated with emotional problems after an abortion, focusing on the abortion itself rather than exploring the problems that preceded the pregnancy could impede the therapeutic process.

In this context, consider the words of Anne Speckhard (1985), the person whose Ph.D. dissertation in sociology has been the foundation for constructing the myth of postabortion syndrome. She describes how pro-life groups program negative postabortion responses:

> In these social systems [pro-life and fundamental religious groups] subjects found members who allowed them to freely discuss their feelings of grief, guilt, loneliness, anger, and despair. . . . Members of these systems were not adverse to discussing the details of the abortion experience with particular reference to concern over pain that the fetus may have experienced and damage that may have occurred to the subjects' reproductive organs. (pp. 139–140)

Speckhard herself points out that as a result of their interactions with pro-life groups, the women in this sample increasingly came to view abortion as the taking of a life:

> They became increasingly angry about the way abortion had been explained to them. . . . Many learned a great deal from pro-life groups about fetal development which initially increased their guilt, grief, and anger. (pp. 140–141)

It is clear that these women were highly distressed, some even had hallucinations; a disproportionate number had very late abortions. How these women would have felt had they consulted a qualified and understanding mental health professional is unknown. What we can say is that neither their characteristics nor their experiences are typical of the majority of abortion patients (ironically, many apparently even had abortions when abortion was illegal).

In discussing the mental health risks of abortion and its alternatives, we must remember that even if a woman comes to accept and love a child who is born after an unplanned and unwanted pregnancy, *the importance of women's ability to space and limit the number of their children for physical and mental health should not be underestimated* (Russo & Horn, 1994). In particular, we do not sufficiently appreciate how important spacing children is for the physical and mental health of a woman and her family. Small childbirth intervals are associated with many negative health outcomes. It is estimated that avoiding birth intervals of less than two years would reduce the risk of low birth weight and neonatal death *5–10 percent* (Miller, 1991). Close child spacing intervals are also *predictive* of child abuse (Altemeier, O'Connor, Vietze, Sandler, & Sherrod, 1984; Zuravin, 1987, 1988).

Abortion's role in reducing stress from potentially close child spacing is also not sufficiently appreciated. Yet research that my students and I have conducted has shown that its role is substantial. Consider that in 1987, nearly half of abortion patients were already mothers. Nearly one in four of those mothers who sought an abortion had a child under two years of age (Russo, Horn, & Schwartz, 1992). Among such mothers 20 years of age or older, more than one out of five had a child under 2 years of age; among teenage mothers seeking abortion that year, the figure was two out of three. Abortion's role in limiting family size was also apparent. More than half of mothers seeking abortion had two or more children. These mothers obviously had multiple sources of stress in their lives. Unfortunately, the stressors were not matched by high levels of coping resources: 71 percent of these mothers were unmarried, and 39 percent had family incomes below the poverty line (Russo, Horn, & Tromp, 1993).

By the way, have you ever heard the claim that the increase in reports of child abuse after *Roe vs. Wade* is evidence that abortion contributes to child abuse? Be aware that the child abuse reporting system was not even instituted until after *Roe vs. Wade,* so such comparisons are inappropriate. In reality, two of the strongest predictors of child abuse are (1) having two or more children under age five, and (2) less than a 12-month spacing between infants. Others include low self-image, unemployment, crowding, and large family size (Altemeier et al., 1984; Murphy, Orkow, & Nicola, 1985; Russo, 1992; Zuravin, 1987, 1988).

Why is it important to enable families to control their size? One does not have to have concerns about population issues to recognize the value of enabling women to control their childbearing. Larger family size is associated with social, educational, and economic disadvantages, including child abuse, antisocial behavior, delinquency, and criminality. Intelligence and academic achievement of children is inversely correlated with family size, and these effects seem to hold even when social class is controlled (Russo, 1992).

The association between female powerlessness and family size remains after controlling for use of contraception, age, education, husband's occupation, and family income (Morris & Sison, 1974). Family size is also negatively associated with women's self-esteem, even if education, income, and previous level of self-esteem (before having children) are controlled (Russo & Zierk, 1992).

A final comment: A point that is often left out of discussions of the mental health implications of restrictive abortion policies is consideration of the psychological effects of a woman's death from abortion on her family (Friedl, 1991). The risk of death from a legal abortion may currently be less than that of a penicillin shot, but should abortion become illegal, the situation would change.

CONCLUSION AND IMPLICATIONS

In conclusion, bearing and raising a child is a private and personal decision considered by our society to require a deep, long-lasting commitment. When a child is unwanted, there are well-documented severe and negative health, social, and economic consequences for the child, the mother, her family, and society.

In contrast, having a legal abortion appears to be a relatively benign experience, particularly if it occurs in the first trimester. Postabortion syndrome is currently a myth—but it is a destructive myth that has the potential to become a reality through aggressive efforts to shame, ostracize, and intimidate abortion doctors and patients and to "brainwash" women into attributing their emotional problems to having an abortion. Effective strategies for enhancing a woman's mental health include fostering positive appraisals, promoting her feelings of personal control and self-efficacy, and increasing her actual control over her important life choices

(Major et al., 1990; Rubin & Russo, 2004). Understanding the mental health implications of abortion and its alternatives means recognizing that abortion currently plays a critical role in enabling women to space and limit their childbearing. Denying women access to that effective tool without providing a similarly effective alternative is not likely to be a successful strategy, but it may have far-reaching and profound consequences to women, their families, and society. Ironically, the burden of unwanted childbearing and its consequences will fall most heavily on those people least likely to have access to effective contraception or a voice in the making of the laws and policies affecting their reproductive alternatives—that is, women who are poor, ethnic minority, single, young (Forrest, 1987), or entrapped in violent relationships (Russo & Denious, 1998; Steinberg & Russo, 2006).

What do you see as policy implications of such findings? There are many. Under current conditions, the effects of public policies that restrict women's access to abortion will be profound, widespread, and destructive. Policymakers and the public must learn to understand the realities of women's lives and appreciate the meaning of unwanted pregnancy and abortion from pregnant women's viewpoints, which are diverse. Unless effective and acceptable alternatives to abortion are developed, women around the world will seek abortions to terminate unwanted pregnancies, whether or not safe and legal abortions are available. Developing such alternatives is absolutely essential, and is something most (but admittedly, not all) people agree with, whether they call themselves "pro-life" or "pro-choice."

Whatever our moral views on abortion, I hope that we will put women's mental health and scientific integrity above religious and political agendas. I call on all of us to work together to ensure that misinformation in the service of policy debates is not used to undermine women's mental health. I hope that we will also work to ensure that every woman who is having psychological problems can obtain help from a qualified mental health professional who supports her choices and does not prejudge the causes of her symptoms.

REFERENCES

ADLER, N. E. (1975). Emotional responses of women following therapeutic abortion. *American Journal of Orthopsychiatry, 45*(3), 446–454.

ADLER, N. E., DAVID, H. P., MAJOR, B., ROTH, S., RUSSO, N. F., WYATT, G. (1990). Psychological responses after abortion. *Science, 248*, 41–44.

ADLER, N. E., DAVID, H. P., MAJOR, B., ROTH, S. H., RUSSO, N. F., & WYATT, G. E. (1992). Psychological factors in abortion: A review. *American Psychologist, 47*, 1194–1204.

ALAN GUTTMACHER INSTITUTE. (1999). *Sharing responsibility: Women, society, and abortion worldwide.* New York: Author.

ALTEMEIER, W. A., O'CONNOR, S., VIETZE, P., SANDLER, H., & SHERROD, K. (1984). Prediction of child abuse: A prospective study of feasibility. *Child Abuse and Neglect 8*, 393–400.

BERK, R. A., SORENSON, S. B., WIEBE, D. J., UPCHURCH, D. M. (2003). The legalization of abortion and subsequent youth homicide: A time series analysis. *Analyses of Social Issues & Public Policy, 1*, 45–64.

COHEN, L., & ROTH, S. (1984). Coping with abortion. *Journal of Human Stress, 10*(3), 140–145.

COMMITTEE ON GOVERNMENT REFORM — MINORITY STAFF, SPECIAL INVESTIGATIONS DIVISION, UNITED STATES HOUSE OF REPRESENTATIVES (2004). *False and misleading health information provided by federally funded pregnancy resource centers.* Washington, DC: Author.

COUGLE, J. R., REARDON, D. C., & COLEMAN, P. K. (2003). Depression associated with abortion and childbirth: A long-term analysis of the NLSY cohort. *Medical Science Monitor, 9*(4), 105–112.

COZZARELLI, C., & MAJOR, B. (1998). The impact of antiabortion activities on women seeking abortions. In L. J. Beckman & S. M. Harvey (Eds.). *The new civil war: The psychology, culture, and politics of abortion* (pp. 81–114). Washington, DC: American Psychological Association.

DAVID, H. P. (1992). Born unwanted: Long-term developmental effects of denied abortion. *Journal of Social Issues, 48*, 163–181.

DAVID, H. P. (1999). Overview. In H. P. David (Ed.), *From abortion to contraception: Europe from 1917 to the present* (p. 322). Westport, CT: Greenwood Press.

DAVID, H. P., DYTRYCH, Z., & MATEJCEK Z. (2003). Born unwanted: Observations from the Prague Study. *American Psychologist, 58*, 224–229.

FERGUSSON, D. M., HORWOOD, L. J., & RIDDER, E. M. (2006). Abortion in young women and subsequent mental health. *Journal of Child Psychology and Psychiatry, 47*, 116–24.

FORREST, J. D. (1987). Unintended pregnancy among American women. *Family Planning Perspectives, 19*(2), 76–77.

FRIEDL, J. (1991). Jim Friedl. In A. Bonavoglia (Ed.). *The choices we made: twenty-five women and men speak out about abortion* (pp. 35–39). New York: Random House.

GILCHRIST, A. C., HANNAFORD, P. C., FRANK, P., & KAY, C. R. (1995). Termination of pre-gnancy and psychiatric morbidity. *British Journal of Psychiatry, 167*, 243–248.

GISSLER, M., BERG, C., BOUVIER-COLLE, M. H., & BUECKENS, P. (2004). Pregnancy associated mortality after birth, spontaneous abortion, or induced abortion in Finland, 1980–2000. *American Journal of Obstetrics and Gynecology, 190*(2), 422–427.

KERO, A., HÖGBERG, U., & LALOS, A. (2004). Well-being and mental growth— long-term effects of legal abortion. *Social Science & Medicine, 58*, 2559–2569.

KEYES, C. L. M., & GOODMAN, S. H. (Eds.). (2006). *Women and depression: A handbook for the social, behavioral, and biomedical sciences.* New York: Cambridge University Press.

KOSS, M. P., GOODMAN, L. A., BROWNE, A., FITZGERALD, L., KEITA, G. P., & RUSSO, N. F. (1994). *No safe haven: Male violence against women at home, at work, and in the community.* Washington, DC: American Psychological Association.

LAZARUS, A. (1985). Psychiatric sequelae of legalized first trimester abortion. *Journal of Psychosomatic Obstetrics and Gynecology, 4*, 141–150.

LEMKAU, J. P. (1988). Emotional sequelae of abortion: Implications for clinical practice. *Psychology of Women Quarterly, 12,* 461–472.

MAJOR, B., COZZARELLI, C., COOPER, M. L., ZUBEK, J., RICHARDS, C., WILHITE, M., & GRAMZOW, R. H. (2000). Psychological responses of abortion after first-trimester abortion. *Archives of General Psychiatry, 57,* 777–784.

MAJOR, B., COZZARELLI, C., SCIACCHITANO, A. M., COOPER, M. L., TESTA, M., & MUELLER, P. M. (1990). Perceived social support, self-efficacy, and adjustment to abortion. *Journal of Personality and Social Psychology, 59,* 452–463.

MAJOR, B., MUELLER, P., & HILDEBRANDT, K. (1985). Attributions, expectations and coping with abortion. *Journal of Personality and Social Psychology, 48*(3), 585–599.

MAJOR, B., RICHARDS, C., COOPER, M. L., COZZARELLI, C., & ZUBEK, J. (1988). Personal resilience, cognitive appraisals, and coping: An integrative model of adjustment. *Journal of Personality and Social Psychology, 74,* 735–752.

McGRATH, E., KEITA, G. P., STRICKLAND, B. R., & RUSSO, N. F. (Eds.) (1990). *Women and depression: Risk factors and treatment issues.* Washington, DC: American Psychological Association.

MILLER, J. E. (1991). Birth intervals and perinatal health: An investigation of three hypotheses. *Family Planning Perspectives, 23*(2), 62–70.

MORRIS, N. M., & SISON, B. S. (1974). Correlates of female powerlessness: Parity, methods of birth control, pregnancy. *Journal of Marriage and the Family, 36,* 708–712.

MUELLER, P., & MAJOR, B. (1989). Self-blame, self-efficacy, and adjustment after abortion. *Journal of Personality and Social Psychology, 57,* 1059–1068.

MURPHY, S., ORKOW, B., & NICOLA, R. (1985). Prediction of child abuse and neglect: A prospective study. *Child Abuse and Neglect, 9,* 225–235.

NOLEN-HOEKSEMA, S. (1990). *Sex differences in depression.* Palo Alto, CA: Stanford University Press.

OSOFSKY, J. D., & OSOFSKY, H. (1972). The psychological reaction of patients to legalized abortion. *American Journal of Orthopsychiatry, 42,* 48–60.

POSAVAC, E., & MILLER, T. (1990). Some problems caused by not having a conceptual foundation for health research: An illustration from studies of the psychological effects of abortion. *Psychology & Health, 5,* 13–23.

REARDON, D. (2004). Abortion is four times steadier than childbirth: New Studies unmask high maternal death rates from abortion. Retrieved May 3, 2004, from http://www.afterabortion.org/PAR/V8/n2/Finland.html

REARDON, D. C., & COUGLE, J. (2002). Depression and unintended pregnancy in the National Longitudinal Survey of Youth: A cohort study. *British Medical Journal, 324,* 151–152.

REARDON, D. C., COUGLE, J. R., RUE, V. M., SHUPING, M. W., COLEMAN, P. K., & NEY, P. G. (2003). Psychiatric admissions of low-income women following abortion and childbirth. *Canadian Medical Association Journal, 168*(10), 1253–1256.

REARDON, D. C., NEY, P. G., SCHEUREN, F., COUGLE, J., COLEMAN, P. K., & STRAHAN, T. W. (2002). Deaths associated with pregnancy outcome: A record linkage study of low income women. *Southern Medical Journal, 95*(8), 834–841.

RUBIN, L., & RUSSO, N. F. (2004). Abortion and mental health: What therapists need to know. *Women & Therapy, 27*(3/4), 69–90.

RUSSO, N. F. (1992). Psychological aspects of unwanted pregnancy and its resolution. In J. D. Butler & D. F. Walbert (Eds.), *Abortion, Medicine, and the Law* (4th ed.). New York: Facts on File Publications.

RUSSO, N. F. (2006). Violence against women: A global health issue. In *Proceedings of the 28th International Congress of Psychology, Beijing, 2004*. New York: Psychology Press (Taylor & Francis Group).

RUSSO, N. F., & DABUL, A. J. (1997). The relationship of abortion to well-being: Do race and religion make a difference? *Professional Psychology: Research and Practice, 28*, 23–31.

RUSSO, N. F., & DENIOUS, J. E. (1998). Understanding the relationship of violence against women to unwanted pregnancy and its resolution. In L. J. Beckman & M. J. Harvey (Eds.), *The new civil war: The psychology, culture, and politics of abortion* (pp. 221–234). Washington, DC: American Psychological Association.

RUSSO, N. F., & DENIOUS, J. E. (2000). The socio-political context of abortion and its relationship to women's mental health. In J. Ussher (Ed.), *Women's health: Contemporary international perspective* (pp. 431–439). London: British Psychological Society.

RUSSO, N. F., & DENIOUS, J. E. (2001). Violence in the lives of women having abortions: Implications for public policy and practice. *Professional Psychology: Research and Practice, 23*, 142–150.

RUSSO, N. F., & DENIOUS, J. E. (2005). Controlling birth: Science, politics, and public policy. *Journal of Social Issues, 61*, 181–191.

RUSSO, N. F., & HORN, J. (1994). Unwanted pregnancy and its resolution: Options, issues. In J. Freeman (Ed.), *Women: A feminist perspective* (5th ed., pp. 47–64). Mountain View, CA: Mayfield Publishing.

RUSSO, N. F., HORN, J., & SCHWARTZ, R. (1992). U. S. abortion in context: Selected characteristics and motivations of women seeking abortions. *Journal of Social Issues, 48*, 182–201.

RUSSO, N. F., HORN, J., & TROMP, S. (1993). Childspacing intervals and abortion among Blacks and Whites: A brief report. *Women & Health, 20*(3), 43–52.

RUSSO, N. F., & SCHMIEGE, S. J. (2005). Debates about our design are beside the point: The Reardon and Cougle findings are invalid and cannot be reproduced with properly coded data. *British Medical Journal.* Retrieved December 18, 2005, from http://bmj.bmjjournals.com/cgi/eletters/331/7528/1303

RUSSO, N. F., & SCHMIEGE, S. J. (2006). Depression and unwanted first pregnancy: Methodological issues, additional findings. *British Medical Journal.* Retrieved February 10, 2006, from http://bmj.bmjjournals.com/cgi/eletters/331/7528/1303

RUSSO, N. F., & ZIERK, K. L. (1992). Abortion, childbearing, and women's well-being. *Professional Psychology: Research and Practice, 23*, 269–280.

SCHMIEGE, S., & RUSSO, N. F. (2005). Depression and unwanted first pregnancy in the National Longitudinal Survey of Youth: Is there a link? *British Medical Journal, 331*, 1303–1308.

SOUTH DAKOTA TASK FORCE TO STUDY ABORTION. (2005). *Report of the Task Force submitted to the Governor and Legislature of South Dakota.* Pierre, SD: Author.

SPECKHARD, A. C. (1985). *The psycho-social aspects of stress following abortion.* Unpublished doctoral dissertation, University of Minnesota.

STEINBERG, J., & RUSSO, N. F. (2006). *Abortion and anxiety: What's the relationship?* Unpublished manuscript.

WORTMAN, C. B., & SILVER, R. C. (1989). The myths of coping with loss. *Journal of Consulting and Clinical Psychology, 57*, 349–357.

ZABIN, L., HIRSCH, M. B., & EMERSON, M. R. (1989). When urban adolescents choose abortion: Effects on education, psychological status, and subsequent pregnancy. *Family Planning Perspectives, 21*(6), 248–255.

ZURAVIN, S. J. (1987). Unplanned pregnancies, family planning programs, and child maltreatment. *Family Relations, 36,* 135–139.

ZURAVIN, S. J. (1988). Fertility patterns: Their relationship to child physical abuse and child neglect. *Journal of Marriage and the Family, 50,* 983–993.

*S*UGGESTED READINGS

BECKMAN, L. J., & HARVEY, S. M. (Eds.). *The new civil war: The psychology, culture, and politics of abortion.* Washington, DC: American Psychological Association.

BONAVOGLIA, A. (Ed.). (2001). *The choices we made: Twenty-five women and men speak out about abortion.* New York: Four Walls, Eight Windows.

HAMILTON, J., & RUSSO, N. F. (2006). Women and depression: Research, theory, and social policy. In C. L. M. Keyes & S. H. Goodman (Eds.), *Women and depression: A handbook for the social, behavioral, and biomedical sciences* (pp. 479–522). New York: Cambridge University Press.

LUNNEBORG, P. (1992). *Abortion: A positive decision.* New York: Bergen & Garvey.

RHODA **O**LKIN *is Professor of Clinical Psychology at the California School of Professional Psychology, Alliant University, and a researcher at Through the Looking Glass (Berkeley, California), where she is studying parents with disabilities. She writes frequently about disability issues, especially issues of families and graduate students.*

12

Women With Disabilities

❖

I've been writing about disability since I completed my dissertation in 1981. However, although I'm also a woman, until very recently I didn't write specifically about women with disabilities. When I asked myself why the delay in coming to this topic, I thought of two reasons. First, oppression as a person with a disability is so all-encompassing that there is little room for anything else. The discrimination associated with disability is not limited to one arena (e.g., work) or one venue (e.g., housing) but, rather, is pervasive and experienced in almost every facet of one's life. This includes problems with access to movies, restaurants, buses, employment, education, medical insurance and medical care, housing, and visits to other people's houses. The social stigma of disability is experienced with co-workers, students, peers, family, and medical service providers, as well as in dating and in applying for jobs (Olkin, 1999). Further, there is the assumption that people with disabilities are always the clients or consumers, never the teachers or providers. For example, I recently gave a talk in an auditorium that had a wheelchair lift down to the floor where the auditorium was located and a flat seating area with good sight lines to the stage that was reserved for wheelchairs. But the stage was inaccessible. The message was clear: People with disabilities are the audience, not the speakers. Discrimination and stigma based on disability are so pronounced that it is easy to overlook the additional stigma experienced as a *woman* with a disability.

The second reason it took some time to address my two identities as a woman and as a person with a disability has to do with how I've been shaped to respond to disability issues as they arise in professional and social situations. In so many arenas, I am the only person with a disability present. Disability has been called the hidden minority (Gliedman & Roth, 1980), in part because no one notices the absence of people with disabilities. Disability issues are overlooked unless someone with a disability points them out. I know that, if I am not in the room during a discussion, I can count on other women to bring up gender issues. But if I am not there to bring up disability issues, no one else will. Thus, I've been shaped to be the resident disabled person. Many people wear the gender hat, but usually I am the only one in the room wearing the disability hat. I'm forced to be the disability spokesperson, advocate, and educator.

Of course, disability occurs in the context of a person, someone with a gender, an age, an ethnicity, a sexual orientation, and a culture, and these various aspects of identity cannot be considered separately. I am never a disabled person in the abstract; I can only be a disabled, heterosexual, Jewish woman in my forties. When people respond to me, I can never know how much of their response is due to disability and how much to gender (and how much to my personality, my height, my clothes, my level of attractiveness, etc.). So, in some ways, I have only discussed disability from the vantage point of a woman with a disability.

These multiple parts of my identity are inextricable. They also are immutable. I cannot ask myself who I would be if I were not disabled. It is rather like asking who you would be if you weren't a woman (or man). For most women, being female is so fundamental to who they are that, if they weren't women, they wouldn't be themselves. That is how it is with disability.

COMMONALITIES IN THE WOMEN'S AND DISABILITY RIGHTS MOVEMENTS

Women's issues and disability issues overlap, and the women's movement and disability rights movement share some ideology and history. In this section, I will outline these similarities, and in the next section I will consider the differences.

Both gender and disability are considered social constructs. For disability, this means that a disability is defined by its social context; thus, it is not disabling in all times and places. A person who is deaf may be handicapped in one situation (e.g., going to the movies) but not in another (e.g., attending a play that is presented in both English and Sign Language). The person has not changed, but in one context the person is disadvantaged by the environment, and in the other context the person is not. As a social construct, neither feminine gender nor disability status is considered intrinsically inferior but, rather, as a condition disadvantaged by society. With reference to disability, a person in a wheelchair is not a problem because he or she cannot walk; rather, the flight of stairs with no alternate access (ramp or elevator) is the problem. Calling disability a social construct means that (a) what is disabling changes with the social context, and (b) the problem is not the person's disability but the mismatch between the person's capabilities and the environment.

The notion of a personal characteristic (gender or disability status) as a social construct has led to important distinctions in semantics. Language conveys politics. Think of the transformations in society that paralleled changes in the use of the word *girls* to *ladies* and then to *women*. Similarly, profound sociopolitical changes were mirrored in the change of the terms *Colored* to

Negro to *Black* to *African American*. For disability as well, terminology reflects how one constructs the idea of disability. Currently in disability studies, three terms are generally used: *impairment* (i.e., the physical or biological condition—for example, retinal myopathy), *handicap* (the ramifications of the impairment—e.g., blindness), and *disability* (i.e., the disadvantages that accrue to the person with the impairment because of stigma, discrimination, and lack of accommodations). My *impairment* is polio; my *handicap* is limited mobility and increased fatigue; my *disability* is the sum of the social, physical, economic, and legal barriers erected by society.

The women's and disability rights movements have some similarities. In initial phases of any civil rights movement, it can be important to emphasize similarities within the group, to be one cohesive group, and to overlook intragroup differences. In reality, this emphasis translates into ignoring more stigmatized subgroups (e.g., based on ethnicity or sexual orientation). For the women's movement, the push for cohesiveness really meant a focus on straight, White women, to the detriment of the issues particular to Women of Color and/or those who were lesbian or bisexual. For the disability rights movement, this insistence on cohesiveness meant more focus on those with physical disabilities. As a result, the specific needs of people with cognitive impairments, psychiatric disorders, developmental disorders, and/or sensory disorders were not addressed, nor were those of people with disabilities who were also of Color or gay/lesbian/bisexual. However, as movements receive public recognition and validation and gain some initial ground in legal and social changes, there is more room for consideration of intragroup differences. In this later phase, a movement becomes more inclusive as it embraces diversity within its ranks, though usually not without internal struggle and divisiveness. These struggles are often hidden from outsiders in the effort to present a united front. To emphasize the issues of *women* with disabilities implies that the disability rights movement has benefited men with disabilities and women with disabilities differentially. But, of course, it has, just as men and women without disabilities benefit differentially from social and legal systems. Most studies of people with disabilities have been about men with disabilities (Hanna & Rogovsky, 1991), and it wasn't until the late 1980s, with the publication of the first texts on women with disabilities (Deegan & Brooks, 1985; Fine & Asch, 1988), that the conjunction of gender and disability began to be considered seriously.

Another similarity between women and people with disabilities is the pressure to conform to majority norms. Many women initially wanted to be more like men (e.g., to work *and* have children), until the idea that women's values, abilities, skills, and methods were different but equally valuable gained prominence. Similarly, most of disability rehabilitation is founded on the idea of making people with disabilities function as much as possible as people without disabilities. Society puts great value on *overcoming* the disability (i.e., acting to the greatest extent possible as if the disability did not exist). It may seem peculiar to those unfamiliar with disability culture to think that disability norms can be seen as different but equally valuable, but this is now an established idea in the disability community. It has been referred to as substituting asset value for comparative value (Wright, 1983)—that is, we value a means in terms of how it achieves its goals, rather than in comparison with how others achieve the same goals. For example, I consider my scooter a way to achieve locomotion (a positive asset value), rather than an inferior means of mobility compared with walking (a negative comparative value). Coming genuinely to value the ways of one's own group (women or people with disabilities) is part of the growth of individuals and the basis for establishing community with others.

Both the women's and disability rights movements began as grassroots movements. Although each had early public spokespeople and national leaders (e.g., Gloria Steinem and Bella Abzug for women, Ed Roberts and Judy Heumann for disability), much of the work was local, individual, and in small groups, spread from person to person. Each movement promoted the notion of the personal as political. The early disability warriors were women: mothers of children with disabilities. It was the mothers who fought for their children's rights; ignored negative predictions from medical personnel; fought stigma and segregation in the schools; started local, state, and national organizations; published newsletters; battled school districts; and became legal advocates. For both women and people with disabilities, women did the major work of founding civil rights movements. These movements pressed for changes in laws, in institutional structures, and in people's attitudes, to make room in society to meet the needs of and welcome all of its citizens.

DIFFERENCES BETWEEN THE WOMEN'S AND DISABILITY RIGHTS MOVEMENTS

There are differences between the experience of gender and of disability and some conflicts between the two movements. One of the fundamental differences is that children with disabilities are not raised by or with other people with disabilities. And one disadvantage to mainstreaming (i.e., the placement of children with disabilities into regular classrooms) is isolation and the absence of disabled peers. Thus, role models, family members, and peer groups reflect back a nondisabled perspective. As a result, children may try to "pass" as nondisabled and in other ways distance themselves from other people with disabilities. As adults, they may continue to be separate from the disability community, either through ignorance of its existence, inability to access it, or rejection of it. Women with disabilities are not likely to partner with other people with disabilities (with the exception of those who are prelingually deaf, who are much more likely to marry another deaf person). Thus, for much of life, disability is an isolating experience, with little access to a community of peer understanding and support.

Another difference is who started the movements. As discussed earlier, the women's and disability rights movements were pushed forward by women. But for people with disabilities, it was their mothers who advocated for them, whereas in the women's movement, women advocated for themselves. This difference means that people with disabilities did not necessarily gain the political and advocacy skills and the communal comradery that the women's movement afforded its members. The women's movement made women more visible. The disability rights movement first made mothers of children with disabilities, rather than people with disabilities, more visible. There was a significant delay in history before people with disabilities themselves held protests, took leadership roles in organizations, and became visible on the nightly news.

There is a profound philosophical difference between the two movements, notably related to reproduction. The women's movement has been fighting for reproductive freedom. This implies endorsement of access to birth control, control over pregnancy and childbirth, genetic testing, abortion, and the option of adoption. The disability movement has been struggling for the basic right to be born and remain alive as people with disabilities. This difference is most visible over the issue of genetic testing, which, after all, has as its main purpose the identification of deformities and abnormalities (i.e., disabilities) in fetuses that will become people like us (i.e., people with disabilities). Given the devaluation of people with disabilities, the trend toward the prevention of births of babies with disabilities is a challenge to the existence of children and adults with disabilities (Parens & Asch, 2000). One key question is whether the *option* to identify genetic defects will become the *mandate* to have *in utero* diagnostic testing and whether the abortion of defective fetuses will become obligatory (e.g., if managed care would not cover medical costs of babies with disabilities who had been identified prior to birth and could have been aborted).

The women's movement is fighting for the right of mothers to work for pay. Women with disabilities are fighting for the right to be mothers. The basic rights of parents are compromised for people with disabilities when they encounter inaccessible obstetricians' offices, medical personnel unfamiliar with the interaction of disability and pregnancy, pressure to terminate pregnancies or give babies up for adoption, threats to custody through divorce and from child protective services, and the pervasive assumptions of inadequacy of parenting due to disability (Kirshbaum & Olkin, 2002). Several studies of middle-class women with visual or physical disabilities—most of whom were White and had a college, and sometimes graduate, education—indicate that threats to the right to be a mother are experienced even by those who are more privileged (Cohen, 1998; Conley-Jung & Olkin, 2001). This suggests that the rates of those who experience interference with mothering could be higher for Women of Color and those with less financial means. These differences in perspectives on parenting have put the two movements at odds. For the individual woman who may consider herself both a disability rights activist and a feminist, these differences can create conflict and ambivalence.

GENDER AND DISABILITY COMBINED: THE SYNERGY OF MINORITY STATUSES

The disadvantages experienced by women with disabilities are more profound than those experienced by nondisabled women of the same ethnicity or by men with disabilities of the same ethnicity. Gender and disability synergistically interact to compound the stigma, prejudice, and discrimination women with disabilities face. Table 1 outlines the position of women with disabilities (of different ethnicities) relative to nondisabled women and to men with disabilities. On every measure, women with disabilities fare the worst. They are less likely to marry, and if married, are more likely to be divorced or separated (Hanna & Rogovsky, 1991). They have less education, are least likely to be in the job market and to work full-time, and, not surprisingly, have the lowest mean monthly income and are more likely to live below the poverty line. They get less social security because social security benefits are tied to previous earnings. Thus, women with disabilities face multiple disadvantages above and beyond the limitations of their impairments or the discrimination they experience due to their gender.

Because they are *women* with disabilities, they have different experiences and face stigma and oppression differently than do men with disabilities. Both women and people with disabilities are seen as childlike and helpless, and the confluence of the two statuses of gender and disability augments this view of the woman with a disability. Women are more likely than men to internalize the negative cultural messages about and devaluation of disability. This makes them even more vulnerable to depression than other women. Depression complicates the recovery and rehabilitation process, increases length of hospital stay, and reduces independent functioning (Olkin, 1999).

There are many issues particular to women with disabilities. It is not that men with disabilities don't also face challenges, but the effects of two stigmatized statuses complicates and reduces options for meeting these challenges. Statistics relevant to employment and medical coverage have been cited previously. In this section, I will focus on the sociocultural obstacles women with disabilities face in daily life. Those that will be discussed here include dating and partnering, sexuality, pregnancy and childbirth, mothering, and divorce or unpartnering. It should be noted that children and women with disabilities experience more physical and sexual abuse than do their nondisabled peers (Kewman, Warschausky, Engel, & Warzak, 1997). This history of violence and abuse can, in turn, affect many areas of functioning, such as dating, sexuality, and parenting.

Dating and Partnering

Disability stigma is most acute in the romantic realm. Unfortunately, most people indicate that they would not marry a person with a disability

TABLE 1

**Comparison of Men and Women With and Without Disabilities
on Five Variables**

		Men	Women	Total
Education				
Less than high school	Nondisabled	–	–	9%
	Disabled	–	–	20%
High school only	Nondisabled	29.0%	30.0%	29.6%
	Disabled	25.6%	28.1%	26.8%
College degree	Nondisabled	17.6%	16.8%	17.2%
	Disabled	12.8%	15.2%	13.9%
Employment				
Employed	Nondisabled	84.8%	70.9%	77.8%
	Disabled	41.1%	34.2%	37.5%
Unemployed	Nondisabled	5.9%	6.5%	6.2%
	Disabled	–	–	13.7%
Income				
Median income	Nondisabled	$59,200	$54,800	$57,100
	Disabled	$27,600	$25,700	$35,000
≤ Poverty level	Nondisabled	7.8%	10.8%	10.2%
	Disabled	18.6–25.5%	23.3–30.8%	24.6–28.2%
Satisfaction with life				
Very satisfied	Nondisabled	–	–	61%
	Disabled	–	–	33%

Note: Data related to populations of persons with disabilities is more variable than for the nondisabled population, due to changes in definitions of disability used.

Sources: Data from the U.S. Census (2000, 2005); Survey of Income & Program Participation (2002); Harris Polls no. 56 (1998) & no. 58 (2000); Cornell University Rehabilitation Research and Training Center on Disability Statistics (2005).

(DeLoach, 1994; Olkin & Howson, 1994), and, as previously reported, women with disabilities are least likely to be married. Ostracization and rejection may have marked the early relationship experiences of a woman with early onset disabilities, and she may continue to feel undesirable as an adult. She may also have some skill deficits due to lack of practice (e.g., in how to make small talk or in how to handle sexual advances). Early learning coupled with the stigmatization of women with disabilities can make dating a difficult and painful issue for many women with disabilities.

Generally, a woman's level of comfort with her disability is more important in interpersonal relationships than is the extent of the disability. But all women with disabilities need methods to *contain* the disability— that is, to get people to see them as persons, not as disabilities, and to show others that the disability affects only a small portion of what a person can do. They will be called upon to decrease others' anxiety and to answer questions about the disability, while projecting a positive self-image, as they assess how much they like the other person. If women with disabilities do not feel like viable romantic partners, they are more likely to settle for unacceptable relationships and less likely to leave relationships that are not working well for them. But it is fundamental for their well-being that their partners can accept the disability.

Sexuality

There is quite simply a lack of information about sexuality and disability (Sipski & Alexander, 1997), and therefore much is still unknown. The little information that does exist is usually more about the mechanics of sex (e.g., positions, erections, colostomy bags) than about psychosocial factors. There is nothing written for two partners with disabilities, and very little is available for gay or lesbian partners with disabilities.

Sexuality is not just one thing, but an amalgam of many factors, including sex drive and desire; self-concept; body image; sexual functioning, acts, and behaviors; and interpersonal relationships. Disability has differential effects on each of these factors. Disability can affect sexuality through numerous routes, including physiology (e.g., sensation, mobility, energy, pain), psychology (e.g., self-concept, body image), and sociology (e.g., the relationship, the culture). There are many facets to consider just about physiology. These include sensation of erogenous and nonerogenous areas; blood flow; functioning of the central nervous system (CNS); muscle tone and mobility, flexibility, and spasticity; arousal; ability to experience erection or lubrication; capability of achieving orgasm, ejaculation, and conception; bladder and bowel control; medications; fatigue; and pain. It is important to list these factors because the effects of disability will differ for each.

There are many myths about disability and sexuality (Hwang, 1997; Rousso, 1982; Tepper, 1997). The first and most pervasive is that persons with disabilities are asexual, which is mirrored in the belief that it is unacceptable for people with disabilities to be sexual beings. The second myth is that people with disabilities are incapable of functioning sexually. This myth comes in part from the idea that *sex* equals *intercourse*. Although some disabilities may interfere with the ability to have intercourse, the absence of intercourse does not imply the absence of sexuality. The third myth is that persons with disabilities lack the skills and judgment necessary to behave in a sexually responsible manner, and thus must be sterilized or kept apart from potential sexual partners. The fourth myth is that, if a nondisabled person is attracted to a person with a disability as a romantic and sexual partner, then something is wrong with that nondisabled person or the nondisabled person is settling for an undesirable partner. The fifth myth is that the sexual functioning of women with disabilities is less affected by disability than is that of men with disabilities. Women are stereotypically seen as more passive in the sexual role, and those with disabilities also are seen as passive; thus, the two stereotypes complement each other. However, for men, the stereotype of disability passivity is at odds with the stereotype of masculinity as active; as a result, men with disabilities are viewed as experiencing difficulties in managing these two stereotypes. The lack of research on sexuality in women with disabilities compared with the amount of research on sexuality in men with disabilities perpetuates the idea that disability is less disruptive to the sexuality of women with disabilities than to that of men with disabilities. It is important to remember that the person with the disability may have internalized some or all of these myths.

Many nondisabled people think that their own sexual problems are unique, weird, and abnormal. Because people with disabilities are already labeled as abnormal, they are even more vulnerable to feeling deviant or damaged in their sexuality. This can lead women with disabilities to try to emulate the methods of sexual expression of nondisabled women, but these methods may not work for women with disabilities. Women with disabilities should be able to express sexuality in ways that are comfortable for them, even if they are not mainstream methods.

Of course, all the factors related to sexuality in general also apply to persons with disabilities. These include issues such as AIDS and other sexually transmitted diseases, safer sexual practices, birth control, sexual orientation, history of sexual and/or physical abuse, and substance use or abuse. These factors may be complicated by some types of disabilities. For example, birth control pills and implants cannot be combined with various medications used for some disabilities.

Pregnancy and Childbirth

Many disabilities are relevant in the decision to adopt, become pregnant, and choose a birth method. Unfortunately, there is not much literature to guide women in making these decisions. But anecdotal evidence suggests that even women with seemingly severe impairments (e.g., paraplegia) can negotiate pregnancy and childbirth successfully (Rogers & Matsumura, 1991). Fertility may be affected by disability, but it is just as likely that any fertility problems will be unrelated to the disability. The pregnant woman with a disability is likely to encounter antagonism toward the idea that she will be a mother. Further, she will find that obstetricians are not typically trained in disability. These two things mean that a woman has to trust herself to make pregnancy and birthing decisions.

Women with physical disabilities may experience increased fatigue beyond what is usual for them due to their disability or beyond what is typical for pregnant women. Changes in hormone levels can affect muscle weakness and pain. The additional weight in the third trimester may affect mobility (Rogers & Matsumura, 1991). It can be helpful for the woman with a disability to plan for these contingencies, so that the pregnancy can go more smoothly. But disability in and of itself does not make a pregnancy high-risk.

Labor and delivery can be affected by several aspects of disability, such as weakened stomach muscles, scoliosis, and pelvic deformity. Careful evaluation of the pros and cons of vaginal versus caesarian births should be undertaken. Pain medication and anesthesia also need careful analysis and should be discussed prior to beginning labor.

Parents with disabilities also have the option to adopt. Adoption agencies fall under Title III (Public Accommodations and Services Operated by Private Entities) of the Americans with Disabilities Act (1990); thus, agencies should be accessible to persons with disabilities and cannot discriminate on the basis of disability per se. However, because they are theoretically guided by the best interests of the child, agencies may engage in discriminatory practices.

Mothering

There are approximately 8 million families with children under 18 living at home in which one or both parents have a disability. At least 2 million of these families are single-parent families, usually with a mother with a disability as head of household. Such families often live below the poverty line, and they face multiple stressors (e.g., single parenting, financial strain, less access to accessible transportation and housing, fewer social supports), because women with disabilities are more likely to be unemployed and they have lower rates of marriage.

However, disability per se does not necessarily impose adversity on the family. Studies of mothers with disabilities from a disability culture perspective have demonstrated mothers' ingenuity in developing their own methods and adaptations in baby care and mothering (Cohen, 1998; Conley-Jung & Olkin, 2001; Kirshbaum & Rinne, 1985; Meadow-Orlans, 1995). For example, in one study (Kirshbaum, 1988), mothers with disabilities and their nondisabled partners were each videotaped while diapering their infants. Analysis of the videos demonstrated that the babies and mothers made a series of mutual adaptations in a reciprocal dance. Infants as young as 1 month differentiated between their disabled and nondisabled parents, and with the nondisabled parent they behaved "less cooperatively, exhibiting fewer adaptations" (Kirshbaum, 1988, p. 10). This and other studies suggest that there is no one right way to parent and that disability may alter the form, but not the substance, of mothering.

Concerns about custody are present for most women with disabilities, and these fears are not unfounded. For example, in a national survey of almost 1,200 parents with disabilities, about 15 percent of the parents reported attempts to remove their children (Toms-Barker & Maralani, 1997). In a study of more than 300 undergraduate psychology majors, 7 percent said they did not think that people with disabilities should be parents at all (Patterson & Witten, 1987). The stigma attached to disability poses a threat to the right to parent, and the legal rights of parents with disabilities, especially in custody decisions, are a fundamental issue for all parents with disabilities. For a woman contemplating separation or divorce from an able-bodied partner, the concern over custody can be enough to stop her from leaving the relationship. The fears about custody are magnified for a lesbian woman with disabilities. She is less likely than her able-bodied partner to be the birth parent, and her rights to adoption are curtailed. Protections for visitation and custody are reduced or nonexistent. Disability stigma magnifies the fears of lesbian mothers about losing their rights.

Separation and Divorce

There are numerous obstacles for women with disabilities who wish to leave a partner (Olkin, 2003). These can be thought of as falling into four main areas: (1) physical needs, (2) financial needs, (3) custody concerns, and (4) relationship issues.

Regarding physical needs, immediate survival can be an issue. Many partners provide personal assistance, perhaps in getting out of bed, in bathing, or in mobility, and women would need someone to replace this aid immediately. The partner also may perform household tasks (e.g., taking out the garbage, vacuuming, grocery shopping) that are difficult for women with some types of disabilities, and they would need to be able to hire help, to take on the tasks themselves, or to find someone else to help them. Women with disabilities may rely on assistive technology (e.g., wheelchair, automatic door opener) that tends to break or malfunction, and, if the partners provided repairs or assistance, they will need a new backup plan. These extra worries can complicate the consideration of leaving a relationship.

Financial needs can be tremendous barriers. The loss of the partner's income can present hardship, especially given the low mean income of women with disabilities. Given the unemployment rate among women with disabilities, a woman may be unemployed and unable to survive on government assistance alone. Medical insurance is often obtained through employment, and, even if she is working, the loss of insurance through her partner can be extremely problematic; she may not qualify for medical insurance on her own because of her preexisting condition. Housing modifications for accessibility are costly, and most people with disabilities pay for these out of pocket (Toms-Barker & Maralani, 1997). Affording her home by herself may not be possible; finding other accessible housing is difficult, costly, and physically taxing.

Relationship issues can be pronounced in leaving a partnership. A woman with a disability can feel physically vulnerable when alone, and she may fear even minor injuries that could exacerbate her level of impairment. Her parents may communicate their own protectiveness or fears about their daughter's ability to fend for herself. She may feel discouraged about her ability to attract a new partner and daunted by the idea of working out the mechanics of sex with a new person. If her disability onset was after the previous relationship began, she may have no experience in dating as a woman with a disability, much less as an older woman. She may have created a family of choice within the disability community (much as gay and lesbian couples do), and if the partner was part of this family, there can be side taking and loss of family relationships.

SUMMARY AND CONCLUSIONS

In numerous areas of experience, women with disabilities differ from nondisabled women or men with disabilities. The effects of being a woman and a person with a disability are not simply additive; rather, they interact synergistically. Unfortunately, in many ways this is to the detriment of women with disabilities, who experience greater disadvantage than that predicted by either their gender or their disability status alone. The two movements toward social change and civil rights for women and for people with disabilities have commonalities but also profound differences that can create conflict for women with disabilities. However, both the women's movement and the disability rights movement have much to offer women with disabilities, provided that each movement does not force women with disabilities to choose one identity over the other. Perhaps now that I've started writing about women with disabilities, these parts of my life will come together creatively. But for this to happen I must be allowed out of the disability box. The more nondisabled people educate themselves about disability and work for the advancement of civil rights for people with disabilities, the less burden there is on people with disabilities constantly to represent disability issues.

REFERENCES

COHEN, L. (1998). *Mothers' perceptions of the influence of their physical disabilities on the developmental tasks of children.* Unpublished doctoral dissertation, California School of Professional Psychology, Alameda, CA.

CONLEY-JUNG, C., & OLKIN, R. (2001). Mothers with visual impairments or blindness raising young children. *Journal of Visual Impairment and Blindness, 91*(1), 14–29.

DEEGAN, M. J., & BROOKS, N. A. (Eds.). (1985). *Women and disability: The double handicap.* New Brunswick, NJ: Transaction Press.

DELOACH, C. P. (1994). Attitudes toward disability: Impact on sexual development and forging of intimate relationships. *Journal of Applied Rehabilitation Counseling, 25,* 18–25.

FINE, M., & ASCH, A. (1988). *Women with disabilities: Essays in psychology, culture, and politics.* Philadelphia: Temple University Press.

GLIEDMAN, J., & ROTH, W. (1980, February 2). The unexpected minority. *New Republic,* pp. 26–30.

HANNA, W. J., & ROGOVSKY, B. (1991). Women with disabilities: Two handicaps plus. *Disability, Handicap & Society, 6*(1), 49–63.

HWANG, K. (1997). Living with a disability: A woman's perspective. In M. L. Sipski & C. J. Alexander (Eds.), *Sexual function in people with disability and chronic illness: A health practitioner's guide* (pp. 119–130). Gaithersburg, MD: Aspen.

KEWMAN, D., WARSCHAUSKY, S., ENGEL, L., & WARZAK, W. (1997). Sexual development of children and adolescents. In M. L. Sipski & C. J. Alexander (Eds.), *Sexual function in people with disability and chronic illness: A health practitioner's guide* (pp. 355–378). Gaithersburg, MD: Aspen.

KIRSHBAUM, M. (1988, June). Parents with physical disabilities and their babies. *Zero to Three, 8,* 8–15.

KIRSHBAUM, M., & OLKIN, R. (2002). Parents with physical, systemic, or visual disabilities. *Disability and Sexuality, 20*(1), 65–80.

KIRSHBAUM, M., & RINNE, G. (1985). The disabled parent. In M. Aurenshine & M. Enriquez (Eds.), *Maternity nursing: Dimensions of change* (pp. 645–669). Belmont, CA: Wadsworth.

MEADOW-ORLANS, K. P. (1995). Parenting with a sensory or physical disability. In M. H. Bornstein (Ed.), *Handbook of parenting. Vol 4. Applied and practical parenting* (pp. 57–84). Mahwah, NJ: Erlbaum.

OLKIN, R. (1999). *What psychotherapists should know about disability.* New York: Guilford Press.

OLKIN, R. (2003). Women with physical disabilities who want to leave their partners: A feminist and disability-affirmative perspective. *Women & Therapy, 26*(3/4), 237–246.

OLKIN, R., & HOWSON, L. (1994). Attitudes toward and images of physical disability. *Journal of Social Behavior and Personality, 9,* 81–96.

PARENS, E., & ASCH, A. (Eds.). (2000). *Prenatal testing and disability rights.* Washington, DC: Georgetown University Press.

PATTERSON, J. B., & WITTEN, B. (1987). Myths concerning persons with disabilities. *Journal of Applied Rehabilitation Counseling, 18,* 42–44.

ROGERS, J., & MATSUMURA, M. (1991). *Mother to be: A guide to pregnancy and birth for women with disabilities.* New York: Demos.

ROUSSO, H. (1982). Special considerations in counseling clients with CP. *Disability and Sexuality, 5*(2), 78–88.

SIPSKI, M., & ALEXANDER, C. J. (Eds.). (1997). *Sexual function in people with disability and chronic illness: A health practitioner's guide.* Gaithersburg, MD: Aspen.

TEPPER, M. (1997). Living with a disability: A man's perspective. In M. L. Sipski & C. J. Alexander (Eds.), *Sexual function in people with disability and chronic illness: A health practitioner's guide* (pp. 131–146). Gaithersburg, MD: Aspen.

TOMS-BARKER, L., & MARALANI, V. (1997). *Challenges and strategies of disabled parents: Findings from a national survey of parents with disabilities.* Oakland, CA: Berkeley Planning Associates.

WRIGHT, B. (1983). *Physical disability: A psychosocial approach* (2nd ed.). New York: Harper & Row.

*S*UGGESTED READINGS

FINE, M., & ASCH, A. (Eds.). (1988). *Women with disabilities: Essays in psychology, culture, and politics.* Philadelphia: Temple University Press.

OLKIN, R. (1999). *What psychotherapists should know about disability.* New York: Guilford Press.

OLKIN, R. (2003). Women with physical disabilities who want to leave their partners: A feminist and disability-affirmative perspective. *Women & Therapy, 26*(3/4), 237–246.

O'TOOLE, C., & BREGANTE, J. (1993). Disabled lesbians: Multicultural realities. In M. Nagler (Ed.), *Perspectives on disability* (pp. 261–271). Palo Alto, CA: Health Markets Research.

*L*ISA **B**OWLEG, *a social psychologist, is Associate Professor of Community Health and Prevention in the School of Public Health at Drexel University. She has taught courses on the Psychology of Women, Psychology of Sex and Gender, Psychology of Sexual Orientation and Sexual Identity, and Multicultural Issues at Drexel, Georgetown University, and the University of Rhode Island. Her current research interests include the effects of gender role norms and social discrimination on HIV risk and multiple minority stress and resilience in African American lesbian, gay, bisexual, and transgender (LGBT) people.*

13

The Health Risks of Being Black, Latina, Woman, and/or Poor

Redefining Women's Health Within the Context of Social Inequality

❖

Women's health. What's in a word, or in this case, two? So ubiquitous are the terms "women" and "health" that we rarely take the time to ponder precisely what they mean. Enter the words "women's health" in a search engine such as Google and a dizzying 219,000,000 hits appear. There you'll find links to the Office on Women's Health in the Department of Health and Human Services, the National Women's Health Resource Center, and *Women's Health* magazine, to name just a handful. But which women are encompassed by the term "women's health"? Although there are many health issues that have an impact on most women nationally and internationally, women are not a monolith. Indeed, the answer to the question "Which women?" changes markedly when we specify which women we mean: racial and ethnic minority women, poor women, young women, middle-aged women, old women, rural women, urban women, immigrant women, women who lack health insurance (who may or may not be poor or unemployed), women with physical or mental disabilities, lesbian or bisexual women, and so on.

As for health, almost 60 years ago, the World Health Organization defined health as "a complete state of physical, mental, and social well-being and not merely the absence of disease or infirmity" (World Health Organization, 2006). Thus, although health includes disease and illness, it also encompasses aspects of wellness and health promotion. The level of health—individual or population—is also critical to any discussion of health. Accordingly, in this lecture I apply a public health perspective to the topic of women's health by focusing on women as a population, rather than women as individuals.

Women's health encompasses a breadth of topics that includes, but is not limited to, birth defects, cancer (breast, cervical, colorectal, endometrial, ovarian, skin), diabetes, heart disease, HIV/AIDS, menopause, osteoporosis, pregnancy (prenatal care, maternal health), reproductive issues (infertility, sterilization), toxic shock syndrome, violence against women, and tobacco use (Centers for Disease Control and Prevention Office of Women's Health, 2002). Though a myriad of factors such as genetics, biopsychosocial determinants, access and quality of healthcare, and risk behaviors may explain many of these conditions, so does gender inequity (Murphy, 2003). In her article *Being Born Female Is Dangerous for Your Health*, Murphy argued that gender inequity often manifests as poor reproductive and mental health consequences for women (e.g., unwanted pregnancy, unsafe abortion, maternal mortality, sexually transmitted infections, depression, and psychosomatic symptoms). The notion that women literally "embody" sexism, racism, heterosexism, classism, and other forms of social inequality is derived from ecosocial theory (Krieger, 1999). This theory seeks to understand how people incorporate their social experiences into their biology from conception to death and how they express this embodiment in population distributions of health, disease, and well-being. Although issues of gender inequity and health (and reproductive health in particular) are especially acute for women in developing countries, women in the United States—Black, Latina[1], and White women, in particular—are the focus of this lecture. I have chosen to focus on women from these racial[2] groups because the health disparities among them are the starkest[3] (Institute of Medicine, 2003).

[1]Latino (male) or Latina (female) refers to people originating from or who share a Latin American heritage. Latinos/as are considered to be an ethnic group rather than a racial group because they can be any "race" (e.g., Black, White, Native American, multiracial).

[2]Social scientists have historically used the term *race* to denote phenotypic characteristics such as skin color or hair texture. Rather than being some essentialist or biological reality however, genetic evidence demonstrates that race is a socially constructed phenomenon (American Anthropological Association, 1998). That is, roughly 94 percent of genetic variation lies *within* so-called racial groups rather than between them. Thus, when I use terms such as *racial* or *race* in this chapter, I am referring to the collective sociopolitical history of racial oppression that groups such as Blacks and Latinos/as have experienced in the U.S.

[3]Often, research on racial and ethnic disparities in women's health focuses on Black, Latino/a, and White women only because the sample sizes for Asian American, Pacific Islander, and Native American women are often too small for data analysis. This was the case, for example, with the *2001 Kaiser Women's Health Survey* (Henry J. Kaiser Family Foundation, 2002).

The lecture is organized around two core themes. First, multicultural identities such as race, ethnicity, socioeconomic status (SES) (typically education, income, and occupational status), disability status, sexual orientation (to name just a few) and the power and privilege linked to these identities, shape what it means to be a healthy woman. These factors quite literally influence how long women stay healthy, how long they live, and how early or late they die. Second, social inequality (e.g., racism, sexism, heterosexism, ableism) and social structural factors (e.g., poverty, neighborhood environment) provide a richer and more contextualized understanding of women's health (and that of men, girls, boys, and transgendered people, for that matter) than the one we get when we use psychological theories that attribute health solely to individual thoughts, beliefs, and behaviors.

WOMEN'S HEALTH: A BRIEF TRIP DOWN MEMORY LANE

The bounty of information and resources on women's health that we enjoy today is a relatively recent phenomenon. Today, it seems so commonsensical as not even to warrant mention that women's health needs differ from men's. Yet, this has not always been appreciated. Historically, women and their health needs have been invisible in medical science, treatment, and research. When women were the focus of healthcare, the attention centered on their fertility and reproductive capacity; women's needs in and of themselves were simply not considered important. Consequently, many of the diagnoses and treatments for women are based on the findings of studies conducted predominantly with samples of middle-class White men (Centers for Disease Control and Prevention Office of Women's Health, 2002). This pervasive institutionalized sex discrimination sparked a groundswell of feminist activism and advocacy in the 1970s and beyond that continues today. The plethora of Google sites on women's health attests to this powerful legacy.

The Boston Women's Health Book Collective (1989) deserves much of the credit for bringing women's health needs to the forefront of national consciousness. Their 1973 book, *Our Bodies, Ourselves,* was simply revolutionary. The preface of the revised 1984 edition of *The New Our Bodies, Ourselves* describes the impetus behind the collective work: "In 1969, there was practically no women's health information easily available, and every fact we learned was a revelation" (Boston Women's Health Book Collective, 1984, p. xi). Other women's health activists and pioneers soon emerged. In 1983, for example, Byllye Avery founded the National Black Women's Health Project (now known as Black Women's Health Imperative), the only national organization devoted solely to education, research, and advocacy on the health of Black girls and women

(Black Women's Health Imperative, 2006). A decade later in 1993, Mary Hayashi founded the National Asian Women's Health Organization to advocate for the health needs of Asian American women and their families (National Asian Women's Health Organization, 2006). That same year, Dr. Michael Trujillo, then Director of the Indian Health Service, assembled a group of women to discuss the health and wellness needs of Native American women, and the National Indian Women's Health Resource Center (2006) was born with the mission to "assist American Indian and Alaska Native women in achieving and maintaining optimal health and cultural well-being for themselves, their families, and their communities."

WOMEN: DISEASE, ILLNESS, AND INJURY

The public health concepts of *morbidity* and *mortality* provide an important foundation for examining diseases and illnesses among women. Morbidity refers to the number of cases of disease that exist; mortality describes the number of deaths attributable to a particular disease or cause. Time for a pop quiz: What's the leading cause of death for women in the U.S.? Did you say, "Breast cancer?" This is understandable in light of the popularity of advertisements for breast cancer walks and runs such as the *Breast Cancer 3-Day*, *Race for the Cure*, and the *Avon Walk for Breast Cancer*. Breast cancer is included within the category of cancer, the second leading cause of death for women in the U.S., but it is not the leading killer; heart disease is. Table 1 presents the leading causes of mortality for women as of 2002, the latest year for which these data exist (Anderson & Smith, 2005). Combined, heart disease and cancer account for one-half of the diseases that kill women in the U.S.[4]

Perceived from a multicultural perspective, the causes of death for women in the U.S. are fairly consistent by race and ethnicity. In fact, though in some cases the rank order may differ, all of the racial groups share six of the top 10 leading causes of death. For example, although heart disease is the leading cause of death for White, Black, and Latina women, cancer is the leading cause of mortality for American Indian or Alaskan Native and Asian or Pacific Islander women. In other cases, there are diseases that

---

[4]Heart disease and cancer are the leading killers of all adults in the U.S., including men as well as women. This is noteworthy because although on the one hand men and women often have different healthcare needs, men and women's morbidity and mortality experiences are sometimes more similar than they are different. More important though is the recognition that racial and ethnic health disparities often provide more insight about gender and health than a mere focus on gender differences. A glimpse of most of the morbidity and mortality categories that affect adults in the U.S. will demonstrate that racial and ethnic minority women and men are often more disproportionately affected and often fare more poorly than White women and men. In short, morbidity and mortality experiences are mediated more by race, ethnicity, and socioeconomic status than gender.

TABLE 1

**10 Leading Causes of Death in the U.S. for Females,
All Ages**

Cause of Death	Percent
1. Heart disease	28.6
2. Cancer	21.6
3. Stroke	8.0
4. Chronic lower respiratory disease	5.2
5. Alzheimer's disease	3.4
6. Diabetes	3.1
7. Unintentional injuries	3.0
8. Influenza and pneumonia	3.0
9. Kidney disease	1.7
10. Septicemia	1.5

(Anderson & Smith, 2005)

affect one or more racial and ethnic groups, but not others. For instance, Black women of all ages are the only group of women for whom HIV disease appears in the top 10 causes of mortality (it ranks 10th). Similarly, Asian or Pacific Islander women are the only group for whom hypertension appears in the top 10 list (it ranks 10th). Chronic liver disease appears only for American Indian or Alaska Native women (it ranks seventh) and Latinas (it ranks 10th). Latinas are the only group for whom perinatal conditions, that is, complications near or shortly after childbirth, rank in the top 10 causes of death (it ranks eighth). Age also provides an important perspective by which to examine women's morbidity and mortality. Let's take the HIV/AIDS epidemic among Black women, the focus of much of my research, as an example. HIV is the leading killer for Black women in the 25 to 35 age group. By comparison, it is the fifth, seventh, and eighth cause of mortality for Latina, Native American, and White women, respectively.

Albeit interesting, multicultural perspectives reveal only part of the story of women's health. They tell us the *what*—the distributional pattern of the disease or condition by aspects such as sex, age, geographic region—but they do not tell us the *how* about women's health, that is, how it is that some conditions or diseases are not evenly distributed among the population of women. To learn the mechanisms by which health and wellness are embodied differently for diverse groups of women, we need to examine women's health through the prism of power, privilege, and social inequality. The HIV/AIDS epidemic among women in the U.S. provides a troubling example of the link between social inequality and disease.

REFRAMING HIV/AIDS AMONG WOMEN IN TERMS OF SOCIAL INEQUALITY

In the U.S., HIV/AIDS continues to vary widely among women, particularly those who are Black and Latina, and those who are poor. Although Black women represent just 13 percent of the female population, they account for 64 percent of women living with HIV/AIDS (CDC, 2006). Latinas, who represent roughly 12 percent of the female population, account for 15 percent of these cases. By comparison, White women account for roughly 75 percent of the female population, but account for just 19 percent of women living with HIV/AIDS.

HIV surveillance statistics report the epidemiology of HIV/AIDS by race and ethnicity, age, exposure category, sex, and geographic region, but not by socioeconomic status (SES). Thus, we tend to conceptualize the HIV/AIDS epidemic among women solely in terms of race and ethnicity. Closer examination reveals, however, that the epidemic is not randomly distributed among racial and ethnic minorities. Rather, those who live in urban and rural areas where poverty and substance abuse are pervasive bear the epidemic's greatest brunt. Numerous scholars have critiqued traditional psychological theories for failing to consider how sociocultural factors such as gender roles, relationship power, and social structural factors such as poverty and neighborhood environment increase women's risk for HIV (Amaro, 1995; Zierler & Krieger, 1997). Psychologist Hortensia Amaro (1995), in her classic article, *Love, Sex, and Power: Considering Women's Realities in HIV Prevention*, reminded us that, because sexual behaviors between men and women often occur "in the context of unequal power" (p. 440), the concept of gender oppression provides an important theoretical framework for understanding women's HIV risk. At one end of the power continuum is the use of nonaggressive persuasion to garner a woman's consent for sex with or without a condom; at the other extreme is male violence (or the threat of it) in response to a female partner's request for condoms.

Traditionally, public health officials have recommended that male condoms, when used correctly and consistently, are effective in preventing HIV transmission. But feminist scholars rightly caution that condom use is a gender issue with different meanings and consequences for men and women (Amaro, 1995). Amaro noted: "For men, the behavior is wearing the condom; for women, the behavior is persuading the male partner to wear a condom or, in some cases, deciding not to have sex when the male partner refuses to wear a condom" (p. 440). In their provocative article, *Reframing Women's Risk: Social Inequalities and HIV Infection*, Zierler and Krieger (1997) encouraged us to reframe women's HIV risk through the prism of social inequality. They made a compelling case for such a focus by noting, for example, how neighborhoods fraught with economic impoverishment, social decay, and boredom produce residents who are more susceptible to drug use for relief and stimulation. These neighbor-hoods become breeding grounds for drug trafficking and drug use, and, no surprise, higher rates of HIV infection.

WOMEN'S WELLNESS

Let's venture now into the province of wellness and health promo-tion, the other aspect of health. The Centers for Disease Control and Prevention's Office of Women's Health (2006) provides a variety of use-ful information in their publication *Tips for a Healthy Life for Women*. Among them are "eat healthy, maintain a healthy weight, get moving, be smoke free, get routine exams and screenings, get appropriate vacci-nations, manage stress, know yourself and your risks, be safe—protect yourself, and be good to yourself." Women who follow the majority of these tips are likely to be far healthier than women who do not, right? Right. The recommendations are unquestionably sound. Indeed, a mountain of data exists to show that heart disease, the leading cause of death for women of all ages, is associated with failing to limit one's intake of saturated fat, failing to exercise, and not monitoring one's health with routine exams and screenings. Accordingly, it makes sense for public health officials to encourage individuals to take steps that will reduce their risks for disease and injury, and promote their overall wellness.

Yet a closer examination using the prism of power, privilege, and social inequality demonstrates that individual health promotion behaviors that appear at first glance to be readily accessible to every woman are in fact accessible to relatively few. Simply put, the power of the individual to affect healthy behaviors is mediated by the extent to which social structural factors grant her easy access to health promotion practices. In other words, if you reexamine these tips using a social structural frame of analysis, you see that many of the tips are rife with middle-class assumptions. Femi-nist psychologist Bernice Lott (2002) has reflected poignantly about the classist assumptions that abound within the discipline of psychology: "Psychological theories are preoccupied with people who are like those who construct the theories, that is, those in the middle class (and prima-rily European Americans)" (p. 101). The classist assumptions underly-ing many of the healthy living tips for women attest that psychologists hold no monopoly on the belief that we all have equal access to health promotion resources.

Let's start with the first tip: "eat healthy." This tip recommends eat-ing five or more servings of fruits and vegetables daily and lowering one's saturated fat intake. The prevailing assumption underlying this tip is that women have ready access to food in general and, in particular, to fruits and vegetables and other foods that are low in saturated fat. The reality though is that some 12 percent of all U.S. households experience "food insecurity" at some point. Food insecurity refers to the lack of access at all times to the food needed to maintain an active healthy life due to poverty. The U.S. food insecurity profile for 2004, the latest year for which data are available, shows that households headed by single women accounted for the bulk of these households (33 percent), and Black (24 percent) and Latina (22 percent) households were far more likely than White (9 percent) households to experience food insecurity (Nord, Andrews, & Carlson, 2005). Food insecurity does not always mean being completely hungry, however. Some two-thirds of food insecure households avoided hunger by doing things such as reducing their food intake or reducing the variety of food in their diets. So where might fruits and vegetables fit into the budget of a food insecure household? Well, last week, I spent $3.99 for a 5-ounce packet of organic spinach at my local supermarket. Though my professor's salary exceeds the poverty rate considerably, I have to say that the cost of the spinach gave me pause. I had to think about whether I really wanted to outlay that much cash for a decidedly healthy, but crazily expensive food item. The relevant point here is not merely the cost of the spinach per se, but that I had the option to buy it or not; choice is one of the hallmarks of privilege. Although federal agricultural officials cite research that demonstrates that the prices for fruits and vegetables are low enough for even low-income families to afford (Reed, Frazao, & Itskowitz, 2004), they also acknowledge that low-income families were twice as likely as those with higher incomes not to purchase any fruits or vegetables in a given week. A $3.99 packet of spinach is not a matter of choice for most poor people. They simply cannot readily and routinely afford expensive food items such as fruits and vegetables.

Besides costs, there is also the issue of access to healthy food. Researchers have found that predominantly low-income neighborhoods have fewer supermarkets with smaller varieties of food items than are found in wealthier neighborhoods (Morland et al., 2002). Moreover, White neighborhoods typically have four times the number of supermarkets as do Black neighborhoods (Morland et al., 2002). As for eating fruits and vegetables, consumption of these food groups rises with the presence of each neighborhood supermarket (32 percent for Black neighborhoods; 11 percent for White neighborhoods) (Morland et al., 2002). Thus for poor women, those in rural areas, or those who live in predominantly racial and ethnic minority neighborhoods, eating healthy may be less a matter of individual choice than it is one of privilege. And in urban areas where supermarkets are scarce, stores that sell low-priced, high-calorie foods, such as bodegas, fast-food restaurants, and takeout shops, predominate. Mariana Chilton, a researcher who studies low-income women's access to food, noted that buying readily available food is a sound investment compared with trekking to another part of town (exacerbated if you're doing so on public transportation with children in tow) to purchase more nutritious fare:

> Three dollars will buy you a fast-food calorie bonanza. It has no nutritional value, but it's laden with fats and sugars and it fills you up for the whole day. Even if you *could* buy string cheese and apples instead, you'd be hungry again in a few hours (Chilton & Booth as cited in "Mapping the Gaps," 2006, p. 11).

The health ramifications of food insecurity are not only physical, but mental. Indeed, Chilton's research with poor Black women in inner-city Philadelphia demonstrates an inextricable link between food insecurity and poor mental health (Chilton & Booth, 2006). Women in the study described two kinds of hunger: "hunger of the body," the physically painful sensation of hunger due to lack of money to purchase food; and "hunger of the mind," feelings such as depression and hopelessness that may be psychological manifestations of the routine trauma and structural and interpersonal violence that many poor Women of Color experience.

And what about the directive to "get routine exams and screenings"? This too is excellent advice, but one that presumes access to heathcare. The harsh reality of access to healthcare in the U.S. tells a more disturbing tale: 45.8 million Americans, many of whom are employed full-time, lack health insurance (DeNavas-Walt, Proctor, & Lee, 2005). It is not surprising that Latinos/as (32.7 percent) and Blacks (19.7 percent) are disproportionately more likely than Whites (11.3 percent) to be uninsured. Nor is access to health insurance a guarantee for quality healthcare when you belong to a racial/ethnic minority group. In its landmark report, *Unequal Treatment: Confronting Racial and Ethnic Disparities in Healthcare*, the Institute of Medicine (2003) reviewed a large number of studies that demonstrated that, even when investigators controlled for insurance status and income, "racial and ethnic minorities experience a lower quality of health services and are less likely to receive even routine medical procedures than are White Americans" (p. 2). The consequences of these disparities are deadly. The report cited, for example, studies that showed that relative to Whites, Blacks and Latinos/as were less likely to receive appropriate diagnostic tests for cancer; HIV medication; maternal and child health services; care for cardiovascular disease, renal disease, and diabetes; and a dizzying list of other illnesses and conditions. In light of these disturbing factors, is it any wonder why the mortality rates for People of Color with these diseases far exceed those of Whites? Thus, in focusing on women's health it becomes important to shift women's health from solely an individualistic perspective, to one that helps explain better why many Women of Color, regardless of their health behaviors—whether they seek out routine exams and screenings, or not—fare worse in the nation's morbidity and mortality statistics than do White women.

Finally, let's examine the "manage stress" tip. A study sponsored in part by the American Psychological Association (APA) shows that most of us are stressed. More than one-half of adults who worked, and almost one-half (47 percent) of all Americans, said that they were concerned about stress (Stambor, 2006). The health consequences of stress are serious; those who reported stress were also likely to report hypertension, anxiety, depression, or obesity. Although stress undoubtedly affects men too, the study's findings suggest that stress is very much a women's health issue. The study shows that being the primary decision maker for health issues in the household, a role that some 73 percent of women in the survey said that they occupied (compared with 40 percent of men), was especially stressful. Not only do women's stress symptoms manifest differently from those of men (e.g., women are more likely than men to report feeling nervous, wanting to cry, or lacking energy), but women cope with stress in some ways that are harmful to their health. For example, 31 percent of the women surveyed said that they ate for comfort when stressed (compared with 19 percent of men), which, according to the survey, was associated with higher levels of the most commonly reported stress symptoms (i.e., fatigue, sleeplessness, lack of energy, nervousness).

A social structural analysis is useful in examining some of the gender differences in stress. In her classic book, *The Second Shift*, sociologist Arlie Hochschild (1989)documented that women employed outside the home devoted 15 hours longer each week to housework and childcare than did men. Now, you don't have to be a Nobel Laureate to imagine what the health consequences for women might be as a result of doing a double-shift almost daily. That this "second shift" has not changed for most women indicates that stress for women is intricately woven into the social fabric of the culture.

Indeed, shifting the perspective on stress management from an individualistic perspective to a social structural perspective highlights the role of social structural factors (e.g., institutionalized racism, classism, heterosexism, ableism) in fostering "mundane extreme environmental stress experiences" (MEES) (Pierce, 1975, p. 111) for members of historically oppressed groups. In stark contrast to the daily hassles of losing one's keys or missing the bus, MEES describes instances of "racism and subtle oppression [that] are ubiquitous, constant, continuing, and mundane as opposed to an occasional misfortune" (Pierce, 1975, p. 195). In their groundbreaking research on women's experiences of sexist events, for example, Klonoff and Landrine (1995) found that 99 percent of the women they surveyed reported that they had experienced a sexist event at least once in their lives; 97 percent had experienced one in the past year. The most commonly experienced sexist event was being forced to listen to a sexist or sexually degrading joke (94 percent), followed equally by sexual harassment (82 percent) and being called sexist names (82 percent). Further analyses demonstrated that Women of Color were more likely than White women to report having experienced more sexist events in their lifetimes as well as over the past year. The study showed no differences in the experience of sexist events by income or education, however. A later study showed that women who reported having experienced more sexist events were likely to report more psychiatric symptoms such as depression, anxiety, and somatic symptoms than did men or women with fewer sexist experiences (Klonoff, Landrine, & Campbell, 2000).

As for women with other or multiple stigmatized social identities (e.g., Women of Color, women who are lesbian or bisexual, women with mental or physical disabilities), stress is often mundane and unrelenting. Daily doses of stress have serious consequences for women's health because the cumulative impact of daily stress contributes more to illness than do the more rare events of catastrophes and major life changes (Kohn, Lafreniere, & Gurevich, 1991). An abundant literature base documents the deleterious health consequences of stress for populations such as African Americans (e.g., Clark, Anderson, Clark, & Williams, 1999); women (e.g., Klonoff & Landrine, 1995); gay, lesbian, and bisexual people (e.g., DiPlacido, 1998); women who are poor (Belle & Doucet, 2003); and people with mental and physical disabilities (Olkin, 1999). Yet, research on the experience of stress among people with intersecting stigmatized identities is scant. Several recurrent themes about MEES have emerged from my research with Black lesbians, a group that is buffeted by the threat or actuality of intersections of sexism, racism, and heterosexism. Many of these women's narratives recount with distressing repetition the invariable stressors of overt prejudice and discrimination (e.g., being the target of racist, sexist, and heterosexist remarks; being fired because they are lesbian; being rejected by family or religious community members because of their sexual orientation), more covert microaggressors (e.g., stares when they display affection publicly with other women), and dealing with the attributional ambiguity of not knowing whether the prejudice that they are experiencing is due to their race, sexual orientation, or sex (Bowleg, Brooks, & Ritz, 2006; Bowleg, Huang, Brooks, Black, & Burkholder, 2003).

An especially ironic twist of the "manage stress" tip is this: Several of the stress-relieving tips that women may do (e.g., venturing outdoors for a walk or jog; meeting with friends for social support) may actually increase stress. Take the fear of sexual violence, for example, one of the most omnipresent stressors for girls and women. If, like me, you have ever gone for a stress-relieving walk alone in the park armed with a cell phone, a self-defense whistle, and the conscious intent of keeping the volume on your iPod low enough to ensure that you hear someone who might walk up behind you suddenly, then you know what I mean. And if, while doing so, you pass, as I have, police-posted rapist alert signs on the trees and lampposts, then you know how harrowing such stress-relieving strategies can be. Or say that you are a woman with a physical disability who decides to relieve your stress by meeting a friend at a restaurant for social support. Rhoda Olkin (1999), a psychologist and disability activist, has recounted a litany of frustrations and stressors with which people with physical disabilities regularly contend. These include, but are not limited to, the experience of calling a restaurant prior to arrival to learn whether or not it is accessible, being told that it is, but arriving to learn that accessibility means entry through the rear near the dumpsters; learning that one can access the restaurant's dining room, but that the restrooms are accessible by stairs only; or that the access ramp to the restaurant is too steep to navigate in a wheelchair.

WOMEN'S HEALTH: A CONCEPT IN NEED OF REDEFINITION

The discipline of psychology, with its historic focus on the individual as the unit of analysis, highlights the role of individual behavior and behavior change in hindering or enhancing health. Consistent with this trend, the concept of women's health typically refers to behaviors in which women may engage (or not) that promote or decrease women's health. My charge in arguing that women's health be contextualized through the prism of social structural factors is not to negate the responsibility that individuals bear for enhancing their health. Rather, my central thesis is that attempting to understand women's health behaviors devoid of the context of social inequality (e.g., sexism, racism, heterosexism, ableism) and social structural factors (e.g., poverty, neighborhood environment) is folly. It is a simplistic and shortsighted approach to women's health, and the health of all people for that matter.

SUMMARY

My goal for this lecture is to encourage students of psychology to integrate into their thinking a focus on how social inequality and social structural factors influence health. The aphorism "context is everything" is as highly relevant to the topic of women's health as it is to, well, just about everything. At least two approaches are warranted. First, psychological theories on health can be expanded to incorporate much of the innovative transdisciplinary scholarship on health disparities. I echo Belle and Doucet (2003), who, in their article, *Poverty, Inequality, and Discrimination as Sources of Depression among U.S. Women,* posited that the implications of inequality and discrimination are not well understood in psychology. Indeed, there is much that psychologists can learn about health by venturing beyond psychology into disciplines such as public health, sociology, social work, women's studies, economics, and medicine. Second, social structural problems demand structural solutions. Although there are a myriad of structural strategies that could vastly improve women's wellness, I'll highlight briefly just three. If we want women to manage their stress better, there are a number of obvious solutions. Among them are reliable, trustworthy, and affordable state and local government and/or employer-provided childcare programs; flexible work schedules and job-sharing programs; and a concerted effort to change gender role norms to encourage men to assume their fair share of household and childcare responsibilities via strategies such as employer-covered paternity leave. If we want to encourage women to get regular screenings and exams, the need for a national single-payer health insurance system[5] seems stunningly self-evident. If we want low-income women to consume more fruits and vegetables, then state governments must use various zoning laws and tax-relief incentives to encourage supermarkets to build in low-income neighborhoods. The structural solutions are all readily conceivable and feasible; what's missing is the political will. Alas, it is far easier to blame individuals for their behaviors than to enact policy and legislative solutions that will ensure healthier lives for us all.

The grim reality about women's health in the U.S. is that we live in a country in which the quality and quantity of what it means to be a healthy woman (or man, girl, boy, or transgendered person for that matter) are predicated not solely on individual health behaviors and individualistic psychosocial factors (e.g., self-efficacy, stages of change, health beliefs, risk perception, locus of control), but on one's status in the social hierarchy. The inexorable facts are these: Being a woman who is poor and/or Black and/or Latina will, in the long run, predict your health outcomes more reliably than many of psychology's traditionally individualistic theories now do. Psychologists and others interested in women's health must redefine, reframe, reshape, and recontextualize women's health through the prism of social inequality and social structural factors. This redefinition is critical to improving the health of women in the U.S. Simply and gravely put: It is a matter of life and death.

*R*EFERENCES

AMARO, H. (1995). Love, sex, and power: Considering women's realities in HIV prevention. *American Psychologist, 50,* 437–447.

AMERICAN ANTHROPOLOGICAL ASSOCIATION. (1998, May 17). Statement on "race." Retrieved April 16, 2002, from http://www.aaanet.org/stmts/racepp.htm

ANDERSON, R. N., & SMITH, B. L. (2005). Deaths: Leading causes for 2002. *National Vital Statistics Reports, 53*(17), 67–70.

BELLE, D., & DOUCET, J. (2003). Poverty, inequality, and discrimination as sources of depression among U.S. women. *Psychology of Women Quarterly, 27,* 101–113.

BLACK WOMEN'S HEALTH IMPERATIVE. (2006). Overview. Retrieved April 14, 2006, from http://www.blackwomenshealth.org/site/PageServer?pagename=AB_overview

---

[5]Single-payer national health insurance describes a health insurance system in which one (i.e., a single) organization that is public (e.g., the federal government) or quasi-public structures and organizes the financing of health, but health delivery services are provided primarily by private organizations (Woolhandler, Himmelstein, Angell, Young, & Physicians for a National Health Program, 2003).

BOSTON WOMEN'S HEALTH BOOK COLLECTIVE. (1984). *The new our bodies, ourselves: A book by and for women.* New York: Simon & Schuster.

BOWLEG, L., BROOKS, K., & RITZ, S. F. (in press). "Bringing home more than a pay-check": The trials and tribulations of Black lesbians in the workplace. *Journal of Lesbian Studies.*

BOWLEG, L., HUANG, J., BROOKS, K., BLACK, A., & BURKHOLDER, G. (2003). Triple jeopardy and beyond: Multiple minority stress and resilience among Black lesbians. *Journal of Lesbian Studies, 7*(4), 87–108.

CENTERS FOR DISEASE CONTROL AND PREVENTION (CDC). (2006). CDC HIV/AIDS fact sheet: HIV/AIDS among women. Retrieved May 1, 2006, from http://www.cdc.gov/hiv/resources/factsheets/PDF/women.pdf

CENTERS FOR DISEASE CONTROL AND PREVENTION OFFICE OF WOMEN'S HEALTH. (2002). Women's health. Retrieved April 15, 2006, from http://www.cdc.gov/washington/overview/womenhea.htm

CENTERS FOR DISEASE CONTROL AND PREVENTION OFFICE OF WOMEN'S HEALTH. (2006). Tips for a healthy life for women. Retrieved April 14, 2006, from http://www.cdc.gov/od/spotlight/nwhw/tips.htm

CHILTON, M., & BOOTH, S. (2006). Hunger of the body and hunger of the mind: African American women's perception of food insecurity, health, and violence. *Journal of Nutrition Education and Behavior.*

CLARK, R., ANDERSON, N. B., CLARK, V. R., & WILLIAMS, D. R. (1999). Racism as a stressor for African Americans: A biopsychosocial model. *American Psychologist, 54,* 805–816.

DeNAVAS-WALT, C., PROCTOR, B. D., & LEE, C. H. (2005). *Income, poverty, and health insurance coverage in the United States: 2004* (Current Population Reports, P60–229). Washington, DC: U.S. Census Bureau.

DiPLACIDO, J. (1998). Minority stress among lesbians, gay men, and bisexuals: A consequence of heterosexism, homophobia, and stigmatization. In G. M. Herek (Ed.), *Stigma and sexual orientation: Understanding prejudice against lesbians, gay men, and bisexuals* (pp. 138–159). Thousand Oaks, CA: Sage.

HENRY J. KAISER FAMILY FOUNDATION. (2002). 2001 Kaiser Women's Health Survey: Women's health in the United States: Health coverage and access to care. Retrieved September 22, 2006, from http://www.kff.org/womenshealth/whp031004pkg.cfm

HOCHSCHILD, A. (1989). *The second shift.* New York: Penguin Books.

INSTITUTE OF MEDICINE. (2003). *Unequal treatment: Confronting racial and ethnic disparities in health care.* Washington, DC: National Academies Press.

KLONOFF, E. A., & LANDRINE, H. (1995). The schedule of sexist events: A measure of lifetime and recent sexist discrimination in women's lives. *Psychology of Women Quarterly, 19*(4), 439–472.

KLONOFF, E. A., LANDRINE, H., & CAMPBELL, R. (2000). Sexist discrimination may account for well-known gender differences in psychiatric symptoms. *Psychology of Women Quarterly, 24,* 93–99.

KOHN, P. M., LAFRENIERE, K., & GUREVICH, M. (1991). Hassles, health, and personality. *Journal of Personality and Social Psychology, 61,* 478–482.

KRIEGER, N. (1999). Embodying inequality: A review of concepts, measures, and methods for studying health consequences of discrimination. *International Journal of Health Services, 29,* 295–352.

LOTT, B. (2002). Cognitive and behavioral distancing from the poor. *American Psychologist, 57,* 100–110.

MAPPING THE GAPS. (2006). *Interaction: News from the Drexel University School of Public Health*. Philadelphia: Drexel University.

MORLAND, K., WING, S., ROUX, A.D., & POOLE, C. (2002). Neighborhood characteristics associated with the location of food stores and food service places. *American Journal of Preventive Medicine, 22*, 23–29.

MORLAND, K., WING, S., & ROUX, A. D. (2002). The contextual effect of the local food environment on residents' diets: The atherosclerosis risk in communities study. *American Journal of Public Health, 92*, 1761–1767.

MURPHY, E. M. (2003). Being born female is dangerous for your health. *American Psychologist, 58*(3), 205–210.

NATIONAL ASIAN WOMEN'S HEALTH ORGANIZATION. (2006). About NAWHO. Retrieved April 14, 2006, from http://www.nawho.org/about.html

NATIONAL INDIAN WOMEN'S HEALTH RESOURCE CENTER. (2006). Welcome to the National Indian Women's Health Resource Center. Retrieved April 17, 2006, from http://www.niwhrc.org

NORD, M., ANDREWS, M., & CARLSON, S. (2005). Household food security in the United States, 2004. Retrieved April 14, 2006, from http://www.ers.usda.gov/publications/err11/err11b.pdf.

OLKIN, R. (1999). *What psychotherapists should know about disability*. New York: Guilford.

PIERCE, C. M. (1975). The mundane extreme environment and its effects on learning. In S. G. Brainard (Ed.), *Learning disabilities: Issues and recommendations for research* (pp. 111–119). Washington, DC: National Institute of Education.

REED, J., Frazao, E., & ITSKOWITZ, R. (2004). How much do Americans pay for fruits and vegetables? *Agriculture Information Bulletin, 790*, 1–39.

STAMBOR, Z. (2006, April). Stressed out nation: Many Americans resort to unhealthy habits to help manage extreme stress, a new survey suggests. *American Psychological Association Monitor on Psychology*, pp. 28–29.

WOOLHANDLER, S., HIMMELSTEIN, D. U., ANGELL, M., YOUNG, Q. D., & PHYSICIANS FOR A NATIONAL HEALTH PROGRAM. (2003). Proposal of the Physicians' Working Group for Single-Payer National Health Insurance. *Journal of the American Medical Association, 290*(6), 798–805.

WORLD HEALTH ORGANIZATION. (2006). Constitution of the World Health Organization. Retrieved July 18, 2006, from http://www.who.int/about/en

ZIERLER, S., & KRIEGER, N. (1997). Reframing women's risk: Social inequalities and HIV infection. *Annual Review of Public Health, 18*, 401–436.

SUGGESTED READINGS

AMERICAN PSYCHOLOGICAL ASSOCIATION, Health Psychology Division 38. http://www.health-psych.org

NATIONAL WOMEN'S HEALTH RESOURCE CENTER. http://www.healthywomen.org

OFFICE OF RESEARCH ON WOMEN'S HEALTH, National Institutes of Health. http://orwh.od.nih.gov

OFFICE ON WOMEN'S HEALTH, The Centers for Disease Control and Prevention, U.S. Department of Health and Human Services. http://www.cdc.gov/od/spotlight/nwhw/default.htm

OFFICE ON WOMEN'S HEALTH, U.S. Department of Health and Human Services. http://www.4woman.gov/owh

CONNIE S. CHAN is Professor of Human Services and Co-Director of the Institute for Asian American Studies at the University of Massachusetts at Boston. Dr. Chan has taught interdisciplinary courses on Asian women in America at U. Mass, Wellesley College, and Harvard University since 1987. Her research and writing focuses on the intersection of gender, cultural, and sexual identity in bilingual and bicultural Women of Color in the United States.

14

Asian American Women and Adolescent Girls

Sexuality and Sexual Expression

❖

This lecture addresses the cultural factors that shape and influence sexual expression and sexual identity for Asian American adolescent girls and women. As a group that is bicultural and bilingual to varying degrees, Asian American females confront a sometimes conflicting and confusing set of social and cultural values from their own ethnic and family origin as well as from their exposure to the mainstream "American" culture.

How do Asian American adolescent girls and women make sense of these cues and these values? How do they experience their sexuality, and what models are available to them as they develop their sense of themselves as sexual beings? What is the interaction of these cultural factors upon the choices they make about their sexual expression and sexual identity?

My discussion of these cultural factors is based upon a review of the research in this area and upon my clinical experience working with Asian American teenagers, women, and their families.

Before any discussion of Asian cultural factors, it is important to note that Asians are a very diverse and heterogeneous population, with over 30 separate and distinct ethnic groups, each with its own values, languages, customs, and traditions. To consider combining these very different groups into a single term as "Asian" or "Asian American" requires a certain degree of generalization. This generalization is based upon two assumptions: (1) Asian groups share a common foundation of cultural values based upon the Confucian and Buddhist philosophies, which stress harmony with others, maintaining the family unit, and the importance of women's familial role as daughter, wife, and mother; and (2) Americans of Asian descent and immigrants from Asia share a similar experience. This experience is based upon a history of racism characterized by a host of exclusionary laws that institutionalized the prejudice against Asians in this country: laws that severely limited the numbers of Asians allowed into the United States, prohibited Asians from becoming American citizens, kept them from owning property (parents were frequently forced to register their property in the names of their American-born children), and outlawed marriage between Asians and White Americans.

Most non-Asians do not distinguish among the various Asian ethnic groups and, as a result, tend to treat all Asian Americans in the same manner without regard to individual or ethnic group differences. Although Americans of Asian descent in the United States vary from fourth-generation American citizens to recent immigrants and refugees, they still share a common experience in the reactions they receive from American society.

Although we have some similarities as Asian Americans, our personal assimilation and levels of acculturation are unique and very much influenced by individual and familial experiences—how long we have been in the United States, how much contact we have with hegemonic American culture, what languages we speak at home, how literate we are in English and/or an Asian native language—as well as social and economic factors.

SEXUALITY: A FOUNDATION FOR UNDERSTANDING THE CONCEPTS

With these considerations in mind, let's now look at what the literature provides in understanding the concept of sexuality and sexual identity. First, as Chinese American sociologist Alice Tsui (1985) pointed out, any open discussion of sexuality or sexual expression is unusual, as sexuality is a very sensitive subject in Asian culture. Even among one's closest friends, a discussion about sexuality is considered to be awkward and highly embarrassing at best, and at worst strictly taboo.

This extreme discomfort with open and direct discussion of sexuality is sometimes misconstrued as *asexuality*. Other times, it is thought that this discomfort means that Asians are extremely repressed about sex and sexual identity. Both perceptions, although common, are incorrect. Most Asian cultures are neither asexual nor extremely repressed. There is a long history of Asian erotica, both in literature and in art, as well as documentation of private expressions of sexuality and sexual interest in personal journals and in letters. However, what is presented in *public* is very different from what is presented in *private*.

The distinction between the public and private self is a very important concept in most Asian cultures. For women, the public self conforms to the expected gender and familial roles of a dutiful daughter, wife, and mother.

A woman is expected to behave in a way that is socially acceptable, and she tries to avoid actions that would bring shame upon herself and her family.

Sexuality, including discussing sexual matters, should only be expressed within the context of one's private self. The private self is never seen by anyone other than a woman's most intimate family and friends. In some cases, an Asian American woman may choose never to reveal her private self to anyone. The dichotomy between the public self and the private self is much more distinct in Asian cultures than in Western cultures.

Why is this private-public split so important in understanding sexuality in Asian cultures? Not only is there very little public expression of sexuality, but private expressions of sexuality may take very different forms than in Western culture. Sexual and erotic behavior may be expressed only in private or in far more subtle and indirect ways in a public setting. Subtle nuances, such as a change in the register of voices of two people having a conversation, minimal physical contact such as the brush of a hand against the other person, a quick glance with the meeting of an eye, and barely discernible language patterns that reflect affection might be misperceived as nonsexual in nature by Westerners. These subtle, very indirect expressions of sexuality may easily be missed by those who are unfamiliar with the cultural cues and norms—not only non-Asians but also Asian American girls who may not see any obvious sexual expression from their parents and other adults.

Lacking role models within their own families for appropriate sexual and erotic behavior, Asian American adolescent girls may search elsewhere for examples of appropriate sexual expression. They may observe non-Asian peers, watch movies and television, and seek out sexually explicit pictures and stories in magazines. Because most of these available models will be Western in culture, Asian American girls may feel caught between the Asian cultural expectation of suppression of sexual expression and the Western expectation of developing a comfort with one's sexual expression.

A SIAN CULTURAL EXPECTATIONS OF SEXUAL EXPRESSION

Let's look at Asian cultural expectations. Most Asian cultures take pride in their sense of propriety and good manners in all areas of interaction, including in sexual and general female-male interactions. Sexuality exists, but it is rarely allowed open expression; control of individual sexual gratification and expression is expected. This control is necessary because the Asian cultural system assumes that individual needs are not as important as family and community needs. Thus, suppression of sexual desire is expected, especially for girls and women, because they are not allowed to indulge in individual needs that might bring shame or dishonor to the family. Historically, in Asian cultures, a woman would not be allowed to express her own sexuality and her own desire for sexual activity. If women expressed or acted upon their sexual desires, the custom of arranged marriage based upon social class would be undermined. Traditionally, the value of a young woman to her family was her ability to receive a dowry payment for a suitable marriage. A young Asian woman would have to be pure and chaste to be suitable for an arranged marriage.

Even in modern times, any open expression of sexuality outside of marriage is strictly forbidden. Extramarital sexual activity of any kind would bring great shame not only upon the woman herself but, more important, upon her family, clan, and community. Asian adolescent girls and women are expected to remain not only virginal but devoid of sexual desire and expression until their marriages.

These rigid restrictions upon the public and open expression of sexuality should not be mistaken, however, as a denial of sexuality, even for females, within Asian culture. As Alice Tsui (1985) noted, sexuality is considered a very normal part of life and an integral part of one's existence. Though little conscious attention is paid to sexuality, much as one gives very little attention to the normal breathing process, an individual's sexuality is expected to "stay healthy." It is something that one keeps in check and monitors from time to time, but Asian culture does not allow for public sexual expression that might be considered inappropriate.

At first glance, this Asian perception of sexuality as a "very normal part of life" seems to be in contradiction to the reported sexually conservative behavior among Asian Americans, but the two views are actually compatible. Research on Asian American sexual expression, although sparse, does describe "conservative" sexual behavior. Erikson and Moore (1986) indicated that Asian American high school students were significantly less likely to talk about sexual matters than were their White, Latina/o, or African American classmates. Thus, what is seen as sexual conservatism may actually be suppression not of sexual desires but of overt verbal and behavioral expression of sexuality. The absence of sexual expression is likely caused by rigid behavioral and expressive restrictions in traditional Asian cultures. As noted by Hirayama and Hirayama (1986), social order and control of emotions and feelings are highly valued among Japanese Americans. Outward displays of emotion are strongly discouraged. In contrast to the Western concept of individualism and independence in one's actions, Asian cultures value family or group unity, especially for females. Children are taught to depend upon the family and to have the utmost respect for their parents' expectations of them. This restraint of emotion and respect for family gives the family a greater degree of control over teenage and adult children. As a result, sexual expression and behavior of adolescents and young adults may be influenced by family values and expectations far more in Asian families than in Western culture.

SEXUAL BEHAVIOR AMONG ASIAN AMERICAN YOUTH

Traditional cultural values such as strong disapproval of marital infidelity and a tendency toward what Erikson and Moore (1986) termed "sexually conservative behavior" may help to reduce the risk for HIV and other sexually transmitted diseases. We must be careful, however, not to confuse conservatism in the outward expression of one's sexuality with an absence of sexual activity or with the notion that this will result in less high-risk sexual behavior.

There are indications that, when Asian American youth have sex, they engage in high-risk sexual practices to the same degree as do non-Asian youth. Cochran, Mays, and Leung (1991) studied the sexual practices of 153 heterosexual Asian American college students, ages 18 to 25. Asian American students reported unprotected sexual intercourse to the same degree as non-Asian students. Cochran et al. (1991) found no difference between U.S.-born and Asian-born students in their sexual practices.

Another common assumption is that Asian American adolescents and young adults are less sexually active than their non-Asian American peers. There is some evidence, both in the research literature and in clinical experience, that this perception is accurate. Cochran et al. (1991) found that 47 percent of their sample population were sexually active. This finding was significantly lower than among European Americans (72 percent), African Americans (84 percent), and Latinas/os (59 percent). Nationally, 54 to 57 percent of White 19-year-olds report that they are sexually active. Cochran's study, therefore, supports the notion that either Asian American young adults are less sexually active than their non-Asian peers or they are less likely to report that they are sexually active.

This finding conforms to my clinical experience and the reports of other clinicians who work with an Asian American population. In my adolescent discussion groups, Asian-born girls, ages 15 to 18, frequently reported that they were responding to explicit demands from both their families and their peers to refrain from expressing their sexuality. They noted that their non-Asian classmates joked and teased about boyfriends and sometimes talked openly about having sex. Within their own Asian peer group, there was an explicit expectation that couples do not engage in sexual activity unless they are "very seriously" involved—that is, engaged or nearly engaged to be married. Until they were convinced of the existence of such a commitment, the Asian American girls tried to avoid sexual activity in their relationships, even if pressured by their boyfriends.

Moreover, Asian American adolescent girls expressed the strong desire to avoid and downplay expressions of their sexuality in any form. They dressed conservatively, used minimal makeup and nonsexual body language, and preferred to be with boys while in groups rather than alone, limiting sexual expression to kissing and holding hands rather than what they termed "bodily contact."

Adolescent Asian American girls also struggle with their own version of meeting the idealized American concept of female beauty. In a 2002 study of 40 Asian American teenage girls, I found this group to be significantly less satisfied with their physical appearance and body image than their non-Asian peers. The Asian American girls reported feeling smaller, shorter, and "less sexually attractive" than their White, Black, and Latina classmates. Their self-esteem and body image scores were lower than the standardized norm for teenage American girls, with the exception that they were more satisfied with their weight than the standardized norm score. These Asian-born 14- to 19-year-old girls also reported feeling vulnerable and insecure in the American social environment. They reported that they had had to learn to adapt to different social standards and expectations while still fulfilling their families' strict expectations of what is acceptable behavior for an Asian adolescent girl.

MEDIA IMAGES OF ASIAN AMERICAN FEMALES

An added burden, the Western media often eroticize and stereotype Asian women, particularly in visual media. The history of Western colonization of Asian countries and U.S. involvement in the Philippines, Japan, and China, as well as, more recently, in Korea and Southeast Asia have created the perception in the American public mind that Asian women are prostitutes and sexual objects. This perception has not been restricted to Western soldiers overseas but is portrayed and perpetuated through film and other media in the United States and Europe. Although Asian people were frequently depicted as teeming masses in war movies, Asian women, shown in relation to a Western man, were almost always eroticized as exotic sexual objects. Asian women have suffered from a cultural stereotype of being exotic, subservient, sexy, passive, and available. More recently, the advertisements of Asian women mail-order brides, pictures of sexy Asian women in stocking and perfume ads, and images of competent but beautiful Asian women newscasters and ice skaters have dominated (and limited) the public image of Asian women in the United States. Some adolescents struggle to model these images at the same time that they balance the cultural message from their families to downplay their appearance and sexuality.

JUGGLING CONFLICTING MESSAGES FROM TWO CULTURES

Feeling vulnerable in a country where behavioral expectations and beauty standards are different and having to juggle conflicting cultural demands poses a dilemma for many Asian American girls and young women. Social control of the expression of sexuality comes from three primary sources: (1) from the family, including parents, grandparents, and older siblings; (2) from the adolescent peer group; and (3) from the social environment, including school and community. The greater the influence of traditional Asian cultural expectations, the fewer the choices an Asian American female will believe she has in deciding how she will express her own sexuality.

Within traditional Asian culture, parents play the dominant role in an adolescent girl's understanding of what would be considered appropriate expressions of sexuality. Although open and frank discussion of these issues with parents is unusual, Asian American teenagers consistently report that they receive strong and direct messages from their parents if their appearance or behavior is considered overtly sexual in nature. The parental messages that these Asian American girls receive may not be very different from those expressed by non-Asian parents. However, the difference lies in the relatively greater risk faced by Asian American girls and women if they do not follow the proscribed behavioral, cultural, and gender-role expectations of appropriate sexual expression. Any deviation from the range of acceptable behaviors may result not only in punishment but also in strong expressions of disappointment and shame from family members.

An Asian American adolescent girl or woman who transgresses in the realm of sexual activity—such as being "caught" kissing, hugging, or petting in a car; having premarital sexual intercourse; engaging in homosexual physical contact; contracting a sexually transmitted disease; or getting pregnant—can expect to be openly punished and shamed within the family. Given the strong family ties, she might internalize some of the disappointment and shame expressed by family members. She may experience guilt, loss of self-confidence and self-esteem, and feelings of depression. These feelings may be expressed as physical ailments, irritability, eating disorders, lack of concentration, and withdrawal from emotional attachments and social activities.

Asian American adolescent girls may exhibit these classic symptoms of depression when struggling with the conflict between their desire to express their sexuality and a culture that restricts this expression. Western counselors and therapists frequently misunderstand this overwhelming sense of guilt and shame and the bind in which these young women find themselves. The counselors often mistakenly believe that the depression-like symptoms are an overreaction to familial disappointment or to one's own rigid superego or conscience. However, within the context of Asian American culture, reactions of this type are not uncommon among adolescent girls and young women. Rather than being characterological, the symptoms may be situational and based upon a feeling that she has no options and is caught in a no-win situation. A counselor should help a client in this situation to understand her familial, peer, and internal pressures and work toward identifying viable options, which may not satisfy all parties but will allow her to regain some sense of control and choice in her decisions.

First- and second-generation Asian Americans, both female and male, often feel an extra burden of meeting their family's expectations of the American dream and are caught in these transitional cultural norms. Given their parents' sacrifices to emigrate to the United States, first-generation

American-born teenagers often feel a greater burden to meet their family's expectations. They also feel a greater responsibility and guilt if they are unable to live up to these demands. They are in the difficult position of having to maintain the mother culture *and* assimilate into American culture. When these familial and cultural expectations clash, the transitional generation faces the difficult task of finding a comfortable way of integrating conflicting values.

During the teenage years, the struggle often focuses around sexuality and the expression of sexuality for Asian American girls and young women. Each individual finds her own solution to this conflict: Some live double lives, pretending to be dutiful daughters at home while engaging in more typically American behaviors when away from the family. Others do not risk family disapproval but follow family expectations. Still others, usually those who have been caught transgressing the gender expectations for "good girls," may rebel and assert their independence from family and traditional cultural norms.

How do Asian American adolescent girls and women make these decisions about their actions and their sexual expression? When they can begin to recognize the conflicting messages of their cultures, their peers, and their families, they may understand that they are caught in an intersection in which varying expectations of their sexual behavior clash. When they do begin to recognize the conflicting messages, then they can understand their bind. After that, they can make informed choices and anticipate the kinds of reactions they might receive to the expressions of sexuality that they choose.

LESBIAN AND BISEXUAL OPTIONS

There are many choices of sexual expression that an Asian adolescent girl or young woman might consider. Such choices include engaging in homosexual or bisexual activity. On first glance, this might appear to be outside the realm of appropriate behavior, but further examination may show that it is more plausible than it seems.

Given the traditional Asian cultural restrictions against open or public expression of sexuality, identification of *any* sexual identity (whether homosexual, heterosexual, or bisexual) may be unacceptable in traditional Asian cultures. For an Asian woman to identify as a lesbian or as a bisexual would make a private expression of sexuality into a public one. Thus, the expression of homosexuality or bisexuality may exist within private expression or even within private identification with a sexual identity, but public expression and public identification as lesbian, gay, or bisexual would be completely out of character with traditional Asian cultural values.

As a result, far fewer Asian American lesbians and bisexuals may openly identify as such. Indeed, there is a common perception that there are proportionately fewer Asian and Asian American lesbian, gay, and bisexual individuals than in the non-Asian population, but there may simply be smaller numbers of openly identified lesbian, bisexual, and gay Asian Americans because of the reluctance to have a public identification of sexuality of any kind. It can also be argued that an Asian American woman who identifies herself as a lesbian or bisexual would have a greater identification with Western cultural influences than with the Asian culture, which values the privacy of one's sexuality. Moreover, with only a minimal identity as an individual distinct from the identity as a member of a family, having a sexual identity may be literally inconceivable except to those who are much more acculturated into a Western identity.

My study of lesbian and gay Asian Americans (Chan, 1989) supports this concept. Much as Oliva Espin (1987) found that Latina lesbians preferred to be affirmed as both lesbian and Latina (see Castañeda, this volume), my study indicated that Asian lesbians felt strongly about keeping both their cultural and sexual identities, yet, if forced to choose between the two communities, respondents in my study identified more closely with the lesbian community. Although they felt marginalized and somewhat stereotyped within the lesbian community, Asian American lesbians reported feeling even more invisible and invalidated for their sexual orientation within Asian American culture and communities.

Ironically, the restrictions upon open expression of sexuality may actually create less dichotomization of heterosexual versus homosexual behavior. It may also create less rigidly defined sexual identities within Asian cultures. Instead, with the importance of the concept of private expression of sexuality, there could be more allowance of fluidity within a sexual behavior continuum. There may be less public expression but also less necessity for any definition or declaration of sexual orientation. And thus more exploration along the sexual identity continuum may be possible for Asian American girls and women.

At the same time, Asian American adolescent girls report that their parents never directly address the issue of homosexuality or bisexuality with them. However, the teenagers are exposed to both positive and negative images of openly lesbian, gay, and bisexual people in American society. Given this greater exposure to different sexual orientations, it is possible that Asian American females may experience relatively greater flexibility within their private explorations of sexuality but still have more limited restrictions upon their public expressions of sexuality. Within the private self, homosexual or bisexual activity may carry equal weight in comparison with heterosexual activity—after all, it is *sexual behavior* that must be expressed privately—and as a result, homosexual and bisexual behavior may not be as stigmatized as within Western culture.

This concept of the fluidity of sexual behavior does not necessarily mean that Asian cultures are less homophobic or that homosexuality is more tolerated within Asian communities. In fact, Asian American community standards of sexual expression may be *more* restrictive, because any public expression and identification of homosexuality and bisexuality are considered to be taboo.

Clinically, Asian American lesbians and bisexual women have reported that parents frequently have as much difficulty with acknowledging that their daughters are sexually active *at all* as with acknowledging that they are lesbian or bisexual. For some families of Asian lesbians and bisexual women, the issue of engaging in homosexual behavior may be avoided as parents focus primarily upon the taboo of the public expression of sexuality. Families then tend to expend their energy in condemning sexual activity and the inappropriate expression of one's sexual desires.

A case illustration (Chan, 1992, p. 122) may help to clarify this point. Sachiko, 22, is a Japanese American woman who identifies as a lesbian. She came out to her family shortly after becoming sexually involved with another woman. Refusing to accept or to even acknowledge her identity as a lesbian, Sachiko's parents were extremely upset that she was sexually active in any way. They declared that she would never be fit to be married or to be considered part of their family again. No matter how hard Sachiko tried to explain her sexual orientation or identity as a lesbian to her family, they refused to accept that she was anything but a sexually active un-married woman. By insisting on affirming her own identity, Sachiko was perceived by her parents as having willingly brought shame upon their family. The family forbade her to disclose her lesbian identity to others and tried to convince her to discontinue her relationships with women. Sachiko, however, asserted her independence and insisted on affirming her identity as an Asian American lesbian.

FINDING A BALANCE THAT MAY SHIFT OVER TIME

Sachiko and women like her may choose to assert their independence from cultural restrictions and to express their sexuality more openly. Other Asian American young women may choose to refrain from expressing their sexuality, making individual decisions based upon their cultural pressures and social environments. As a group, Asian American girls and women confront a variety of messages concerning their sexuality and face many restrictions on what is acceptable private and public sexual expression. The traditional Asian cultural influences place a greater demand to restrict open expression of sexuality, whereas mainstream American culture exerts pressure to be more individualistic and openly sexually expressive. At the same time, American culture places greater emphasis upon the dichotomy of choosing either a homosexual or a heterosexual orientation.

Asian American girls and women make sense of these many messages and develop their own sense of themselves as sexual beings in individual ways; each finds her unique balance between Asian and American cultural influences. As with any identity development, sexual identity development is an ever changing concept, which will integrate different aspects of both cultures over an individual's life span. For adolescent girls, the pressures of parental approval may loom largest and play the most important role in determining their expressions of sexuality. As they mature and become women, Asian American adolescents will develop their own sense of sexuality, which is less tied to their cultural and familial influences and is more reflective of their bicultural social environment.

REFERENCES

CHAN, C. S. (1989). Issues of identity development among Asian American lesbians and gay men. *Journal of Counseling and Development, 68,* 16–20.

CHAN, C. S. (1992). Cultural considerations in counseling Asian American lesbians and gay men. In S. Dworkin & F. Gutierrez (Eds.), *Counseling gay men and lesbians: Journey to the end of the rainbow* (pp. 115–124). Alexandria, VA: American Association for Counseling and Development.

COCHRAN, S., MAYS, V., & LEUNG, L. (1991). Sexual practices of heterosexual Asian-American young adults: Implications for risk of HIV infection. *Archives of Sexual Behavior, 20,* 381–391.

ERIKSON, P. I., & MOORE, D. S. (1986). *Sexual activity, birth control use, and attitudes among high school students from three minority groups.* Paper presented at the meeting of the American Public Health Association, Las Vegas, NV.

ESPIN, O. (1987). Issues of identity in the psychology of Latina lesbians. In Boston Lesbian Psychologies Collective (Eds.), *Lesbian psychologies* (pp. 35–51). Urbana: University of Illinois Press.

HIRAYAMA, H., & HIRAYAMA, K. (1986). The sexuality of Japanese Americans. *Journal of Social Work and Human Sexuality, 4,* 81–98.

TSUI, A. (1985). Psychotherapeutic considerations in sexual counseling for Asian immigrants. *Psychotherapy, 22,* 357–362.

SUGGESTED READINGS

CHAN, C. S. (1992). Cultural considerations in counseling Asian American lesbians and gay men. In S. Dworkin & F. Gutierrez (Eds.), *Counseling gay men and lesbians: Journey to the end of the rainbow* (pp. 115–124). Alexandria, VA: American Association for Counseling and Development.

CHAN, C. S. (1995). Issues of sexual identity in an ethnic minority: The case of Chinese American lesbians, gay men, and bisexual people. In A. D'Augelli & C. Patterson (Eds.), *Lesbian, gay, and bisexual identities over the lifespan* (pp. 87–101). New York: Oxford University Press.

COCHRAN, S., MAYS, V., & LEUNG, L. (1991). Sexual practices of heterosexual Asian-American young adults: Implications for risk of HIV infection. *Archives of Sexual Behavior, 20,* 381–391.

LIU, P., & CHAN, C. S. (1996). Asian American lesbians, gay men, and their families. In J. Laird & R. J. Green (Eds.), *Lesbians and gays in couples and families: A handbook for therapists* (pp. 137–152). San Francisco: Jossey-Bass.

*L*INDA **D.** *GARNETS* has been an Affiliated Professor in the Departments of *Psychology, Women's Studies, and Lesbian, Gay, Bisexual, and Transgendered Studies at UCLA since 1987, where she teaches courses on the psychology of the lesbian experience and the psychology of gender. She is nationally known for her publications and presentations on lesbian, gay, and bisexual psychology, including a co-edited special issue of the* Journal of Social Issues *on* "Women's Sexualities: Perspectives on Sexual Orientation and Gender" *and a co-edited anthology titled* Psychological Perspectives on Lesbian, Gay, and Bisexual Experiences.

15

Life as a Lesbian

What Does Gender Have to Do With It?

————— ❖ —————

I remember the first time I met a lesbian couple. I was beginning to think that I might really be a lesbian, so I wanted to meet some other people who were gay. I knew very few gay people, and I had numerous fantasies about how they were going to look and act. I vividly remember standing by my front door waiting for them to arrive and having every possible stereotype about them. I thought they were going to ride up on motorcycles and have greasy hair and tatoos. I was shaking. But when I opened the door, there stood two of the most ordinary-looking women. I thought they must be at the wrong apartment. At dinner, I shared how I expected them to look and act, and we all laughed at how different they were in reality from my stereotypes.

This story reminds us that, in the absence of interaction with lesbians, we rely on stereotypes about them. We have all heard these stereotypes: "Lesbians imitate men in dress and mannerisms." "Lesbians are unfit parents." "Lesbians are abnormal and sick." "Lesbians are always flaunting their sexuality." "Lesbian relationships are unhappy and dysfunctional." These myths label lesbians as alien, deviant, and flawed. Social stereotypes define lesbians largely in terms of characteristics that relegate us to unequal status and set us apart from heterosexuals.

Imagine someone asking a heterosexual person any of the following questions: "Is it possible your heterosexuality is just a phase you may outgrow?" "Why do you heterosexuals feel compelled to seduce others into your lifestyle?" "With all the societal support marriage receives, the divorce rate is spiraling. Why are there so few stable relationships among heterosexuals?" "Why do heterosexuals place so much emphasis on sex?" "Considering the menace of overpopulation, how could the

I am grateful to several colleagues who read and commented on earlier drafts of this article: Jacqueline Goodchilds, Douglas Kimmel, Barrie Levy, Anne Peplau, and Dorothy Semenow.

human race survive if everyone were heterosexual like you?" (Rochlin, 1980). Why do these statements sound so absurd? They assume that homosexuality is natural and superior to heterosexuality, a reversal of what most people actually believe. In fact, all of these questions are often asked about lesbians.

These stereotypes are used to deny lesbians full social participation and civil rights. The experiences of contemporary lesbians must be understood in the context of widespread prejudice against sexual minorities in our society (Herek, 2000). How is this accomplished? The twin culprits are heterosexism and sexual prejudice. *Heterosexism* is a pervasive set of attitudes akin to sexism and racism. It is defined as "an ideological system that denies, denigrates, and stigmatizes any nonheterosexual form of behavior, identity, relationship, or community" (Herek, 1990, p. 316). *Sexual prejudice* refers to "individual heterosexuals' negative attitudes toward homosexual behavior, people who engage in homosexual behavior, or who identify as gay, lesbian, or bisexual; and communities of gay, lesbian, and bisexual people" (Herek, 2004, p.17). This assumption that everyone is or should be heterosexual is epitomized by notions that "for every girl, there is a boy" and "all women are going to marry someday." If someone had told me growing up that "for every girl, there is a girl or a boy," it would not have taken me so long to discover the possibility that I am gay.

By assuming that all people are or should be heterosexual, heterosexism excludes the needs, concerns, and life experiences of lesbians. Lesbians remain excluded from lists of protected categories in most civil rights legislation. As of 2006, except in 17 states, no legal protection exists against overt discrimination against lesbians in employment, housing, or access to public accommodations. The 1992 campaigns in Oregon and Colorado asked voters to amend their state constitutions to forbid adoption of civil rights protections for gay people by any local or state governmental entity and to invalidate the phrase "sexual orientation" in any statute where it currently appeared. These statewide efforts were aimed at legislating gay men and lesbians out of existence.

In 1996, the U.S. House of Representatives passed the "Defense of Marriage Act," which defined marriage for federal programs as a legal union between a man and a woman. This act also allowed states the right not to recognize same-sex marriages performed in other states. As of 2006, 39 states have enacted laws to prevent the recognition of same-sex marriage; 17 of them have changed their state constitutions to ban same-sex marriage. Moreover, 6 states by statute and 11 states by constitutional amendment have banned other forms of partner recognition in addition to marriage, such as domestic partnership agreements and civil unions.

Such heterosexist bias perpetuates the invisibility of lesbian existence. For example, I am in a 22-year relationship that I know is a life partnership, but it has no legal status because same-gender marriages are illegal, except in Massachusetts. My partner and I cannot be jointly covered by insurance, inheritance laws, or hospital visitation rules, except in Vermont under the "civil union" arrangement and in 13 states where domestic partnership benefits can be registered with public authorities. A good friend of ours was dying, and the hospital would only let her partner of 12 years see her if she pretended to be her sister. She was not considered "immediate family" by the hospital's visitation rules.

When the existence of lesbians is recognized, heterosexism and sexual prejudice lead to institutional and personal hostility toward lesbians: We are hated and despised; we lose our jobs; we lose custody of our children; we face eviction from our homes, verbal harassment and physical attacks, alienation and rejection by our families, friends, and co-workers, and the burden of continually asserting our existence. Too often, people use stereotypes about lesbians to justify discrimination, harassment, and acts of violence. For example, in a recent case in Virginia, a lesbian couple lost custody of their son to the mother of one of the couple solely because they are lesbians and therefore considered "unfit mothers." Another memorable example occurred in 1988 when a lesbian couple was shot while backpacking on the Appalachian Trail. One woman died; the other was seriously injured. As the surviving member of the couple explained, "He shot from where he was hidden in the woods 85 feet away, after he stalked us, hunted us, spied on us. Later his lawyer tried to assert that our sexuality provoked him. He shot us because he identified us as lesbians. He was a stranger with whom we had no connection. He shot us and left us for dead" (Brenner, 1992, p. 12).

Heterosexism and sexual prejudice create a catch-22 situation for lesbians—between the fear of discrimination and harassment if we disclose our sexual orientation and the invisibility of our true selves if we don't (DiPlacido, 1998). Many lesbians opt for invisibility as a way to avoid stigma, discrimination, and violence. Because lesbians are diverse and not easily identifiable, most can "pass" as heterosexual. This invisibility of sexual orientation obscures the true diversity of lesbians and contributes to widespread misconceptions about the realities of our lives. Even when lesbians are open about their sexual orientation, we do not automatically invalidate stereotypes about ourselves because each individual can be discounted as an exception to the general pattern (Garnets & Kimmel, 2003).

In my first year of graduate school, after I had just come out, my professor in a psychopathology course invited in two gay men and two lesbians to talk about their lives. When they left the room, the professor spent the rest of the class pointing out each person's pathology and tying it to their being gay. This gave me a powerful message that what I was experiencing was sick and something I should hide.

The good news is that lesbians have shown great resilience in the face of social oppression. As individuals, we typically manage to form a positive sense of self and do not suffer from low self-esteem (Garnets & Kimmel, 1991). As members of groups, lesbians have worked together to form support networks and communities to facilitate a positive individual and group identity (D'Augelli & Garnets, 1995) and to combat heterosexism and homophobia (Rothblum & Bond, 1996).

The movement to full civil equality for gays and lesbians through civil marriage represents a major national and international effort to end second-class status, stigma, and discrimination against LGBs (lesbians, gays, and bisexuals). To date, the following forms of partner recognition of same-sex couples have been recognized in the United States and Canada. Civil marriage to same-sex couples was legalized in Massachusetts in 2004 and throughout Canada in 2005. Court decisions in Canada, starting in 2003, had already legalized same-sex marriages in eight out of ten provinces and one of three territories, whose residents comprised about 90 percent of Canada's population. Most legal benefits commonly associated with marriage had been extended to cohabiting same-sex couples since 1999. Connecticut (2005) and Vermont (2000) are the only states with civil union laws. Four states (Hawaii, California, Maine, and New Jersey) have enacted laws that give domestic partnerships varying degrees of protections. California's domestic partnership law, which took effect in January 2005, provides the broadest array of protections.

GENDER STEREOTYPES AND ANTILESBIAN STEREOTYPES

When we look more closely at the content of antilesbian stereotypes, we discover that it is tied to gender stereotypes, reflecting a link between heterosexism and sexism. The students who take my class in the psychology of the lesbian experience are always a mix of heterosexuals, gay men and lesbians, and bisexual men and women. During the first class, I invite the students to participate in an exercise in which they call out cultural stereotypes for each of the following terms: "masculine," "feminine," "gay man," and "lesbian." I then ask them to examine the four lists and see what they notice about the relationships among the concepts. "Masculine" is defined using words suggesting positive and powerful images (dominant, assertive, independent, etc.). "Feminine" is depicted with words denoting powerlessness (passive, submissive, dependent, etc.). The descriptors for "gay man" are on the powerless and feminine side (passive, sissy, nurturant, etc.). In contrast, the list for "lesbian" stereotypes suggests powerful and masculine images but with a heavy negative bias added in (butch, hairy, dominating, man haters, etc.).

This exercise consistently reveals that gender stereotypes are an important aspect of antigay stereotypes. Specifically, lesbians are believed to have characteristics that are culturally defined as nonfeminine. As one lesbian described, "I really put down masculine-acting women until I came out and realized that not all lesbians act that way and that many straight women do" (Troiden, 1989, p. 57).

Let us consider this frequently asked question: Can someone be a "real" man or a "real" woman and be gay? Obviously, a great deal depends on our definition of a "real" man or "real" woman. In our society, our masculinity or femininity constitutes a core part of our identities, and being a "real" woman means being heterosexual. Because lesbians violate the cultural mandate of heterosexuality, it is assumed we deviate from gender expectations as well (Hyde & Jaffee, 2000).

Lesbians' existence challenges basic assumptions about female role expectations. Stereotypes portray lesbians in relation to men. Lesbians are depicted as failed females who want to be men or who hate men. It is suggested that a woman becomes a lesbian because she has had bad sexual experiences with men or because she cannot get a man. Never mind that these stereotypes find no basis in the reality of lesbian experience but arise instead from sexist assumptions that define women only in relation to men. A woman without a man is seen as a failure as a woman, and a lesbian is seen as unable to relate to men.

Let's now examine how women's roles and status shape stereotypes about lesbians today. In general, women have less power, less money, fewer job opportunities, fewer social outlets, less social and economic independence, and greater constraints on their autonomy than men. Lesbians share with all women the institutional oppression of sexism, which includes access to fewer material resources. In addition, lesbians face a second kind of discrimination based on their sexual orientation, which includes denial of civil rights and the social stigma of homosexuality.

In this context, heterosexuality can be seen as an institution reflecting male power over women (Livingston, 1996). Men have markedly greater power, rights, and privileges than women. As a lesbian explained, "You have to drop a lot of options. Like economic security. Women don't usually have a lot of money" (Schneider, 1989, p. 128). Women's status and power in this context are linked to their relationships with and dependence on men. Lesbians experience their attractions to women in a social context that devalues both women and gay people.

These attitudes toward lesbians reflect a perceived threat to the traditional patriarchal power structure (Rothchild, 2005). Lesbians may be perceived as having greater power than heterosexual women because they live independently of men and do not depend on men for sexual, emotional, or financial support. As one lesbian stated, "You can't turn to men for typical things. You have to depend on yourself and on other women. Men tell you that you can't do things on your own, that you need a man. I don't need a man to help me with anything because I can do it myself. I may depend on other women, but it's not being dependent" (Schneider, 1989, p. 124). Lesbians' autonomy and self-sufficiency may be perceived as challenging both the female's subordinate status and the gender role that defines her identity only in terms of her relationship to men. In other words, "autonomous woman" becomes synonymous with "lesbian," leading to accusations toward independent heterosexual women that they are the most hated kind of women: lesbians. And lesbians are "accused" of not being women.

COMING OUT

Now let's discuss a central aspect of lesbian experience: forming and maintaining a positive lesbian identity. Women come to label and construct their own lesbian identity through a process known as "coming out." Coming out is a complex sequence of events through which individuals acknowledge, recognize, and label their sexual orientation and then disclose it to others throughout their lives. In order to form a positive lesbian identity, one must transform the cognitive category "lesbian" from negative stereotypes to positive labels. As one woman explained, "I knew what homosexual meant, it was an in-joke with the kids I knew. So-and-so's bent, queer, a pansy, etc. When you're faced with such negative views of gays, it is not surprising that you are filled with terror at the prospect of acquiring a label.... How could an ordinary girl like myself possibly be one of a group of sick people?" (Plummer, 1989, p. 206).

This transformation is followed by increased acceptance of the label and commitment to the identity as applied to oneself. Cass (1979) described the growth of self-acceptance in the following terms: "I might be gay, I'm different"; then "I probably am gay"; then "I'm proud I'm gay"; then "I am gay and being gay is one aspect of who I am."

Coming out is considered a rite of passage because forming a positive lesbian identity takes place against a backdrop of difference from the heterosexual mainstream, which, as previously discussed, brings with it not only invisibility but also the prejudice and discrimination directed at women and lesbians (Garnets & Kimmel, 2003). As a lesbian noted, "All around me were girls my own age who were dating guys, who seemed to be enjoying that, and my parents who are heterosexual. I was surrounded by all that. So I felt like there was a part of me that wasn't being acknowledged. That it didn't exist, and it made me feel alone and depressed" (Schneider, 1989, p. 123). Managing one's lesbian identity includes developing strategies to evade the stigma associated with homosexuality and to manage the boundaries between the heterosexual and the gay worlds (D'Augelli & Garnets, 1995).

Whenever lesbians meet, sooner or later we get around to telling our coming-out stories. It is a ritual that bonds and affirms our identity. Self-labeling as gay, accepting this label, self-disclosing, and feeling accepted by others have been found to be strongly related to psychological adjustment (Garnets & Kimmel, 1991).

Today, one can also speak about coming in: the realization of having entered into a community and the process of identifying with a larger group of gay and lesbian people (Petrow, 1990). The presence of a lesbian support system has been found to be associated with adaptive coping strategies and positive well-being (Garnets & Kimmel, 2003). Contemporary lesbian communities are composed of networks connected by social and/or political activities. Lesbian community organizations and activities serve as cultural centers, gathering places, and forums for the expression of lesbian culture.

The lesbian community has tried to define a uniquely lesbian cultural vision, which is expressed in music and literature and disseminated at national and regional music festivals and conferences (D'Augelli & Garnets, 1995).

Our lives are enriched by coming out and living openly as lesbians. As deMonteflores explained (1986, p. 79), coming out "requires an acknowledgment to ourselves of who we are. In this acknowledgment there is a profound self-affirmation." In the course of coming out, many lesbians successfully overcome the threats to psychological well-being posed by heterosexism. We learn to reclaim and value important aspects of ourselves. We recognize that we are not alone, and this leads to a building of community. Coming out appears to provide coping skills that lesbians can subsequently use to face other life challenges.

What role do gender socialization and status differences play in the coming-out experiences of lesbians? Gay men and lesbians are more similar in many respects to heterosexual members of their own gender than to each other (Peplau & Garnets, 2000). Lesbians and gay men experience the same social pressure to conform to gender expectations as do heterosexual men and women.

What it means not to be heterosexual is different for lesbians than for gay men. For example, in teaching the course "Psychology of the Lesbian Experience" for several years, I have observed that gay men and lesbian students are initially closely aligned; they feel bonded together by the fact that they experience discrimination because of their sexual orientation. As the class progresses, however, the alliances switch: The lesbian and heterosexual women find they have more in common, and the gay and heterosexual men experience greater similarities.

Coming-out experiences appear to follow different developmental patterns for women than for men (Savin-Williams & Diamond, 2000). During the process of coming out, lesbians are more likely than gay men to define themselves in terms of their total identity and not only their sexual behavior. For example, a lesbian in Sears's (1989) study defined a homosexual as a person who "has intimate love for a person of the same sex." Lesbians more frequently define their sexual identity in terms of affectional preferences (emotional quality or love between partners) or political choices (affirmation of solidarity with all women or breaking with certain traditional standards of behavior for women) than do gay men (Peplau & Garnets, 2000).

Likewise, before they come out, lesbians and gay men use different stigma-management strategies in order to avoid labeling themselves as lesbian or gay. Consistent with female role expectations, lesbians are more likely than gay men to avoid identifying as lesbian by minimizing the importance of sexuality. For example, lesbians more often report using the "special case" strategy to avoid identifying as gay. They romanticize sexual events and explain them in terms of intense love and feeling for a particular woman: "I never thought of my feelings and our love-making as lesbian. The whole experience was too beautiful for it to be something so ugly. I didn't think I could ever have those feelings for another woman" (Troiden, 1989, p. 49). In my own case, it wasn't until there was a "special woman," and then another "special woman," and then still another that I began to think that I might actually be a lesbian.

A predominant pattern for lesbians is to engage in sexual activity as a natural and logical outgrowth of a strong emotional and romantic attachment (Garnets, 2002). Realization of being in love with or in a relationship with a person of the same gender may serve as a catalyst for solidifying lesbian self-identification. In general, lesbians report having their first sexual experience with a woman in the context of their first meaningful relationship with a woman. One woman described her process of adopting a lesbian identity: "When I was 17, I fell in love with my partner and knew it was right for me though I had never heard the word lesbian. We lived together as lovers in a committed relationship for many years before I came out to myself and then to others and discovered a lesbian community" (Johnson, 1990, pp. 149–150).

These findings fit with data on heterosexual women who are less likely to view sexual acts as a revelation of their true sexual self and who report sexual fantasies and sexual enjoyment in terms of interest in romantic settings and committed partners (Peplau & Garnets, 2000).

SOCIOCULTURAL INFLUENCES ON LESBIAN SEXUAL ORIENTATION

It is all too easy for us to ignore the many powerful ways that cultural forces influence sexual orientation. Although passion and sexual desire are experienced as intensely personal and unique, they are, in fact, shaped by cultural beliefs about gender and sexuality, by kinship systems, by women's economic and social status, by whether or not sexual identities are recognized in a given culture, and by attitudes of acceptance versus rejection toward sexual minorities (Blackwood, 2000; Peplau & Garnets, 2000). For example, in some cultures, same-gender attachments are socially approved and widespread; elsewhere they are stigmatized and hidden. In some settings, same-gender relationships for women co-exist with heterosexual marriage; in other settings, women are more likely to form exclusive relationships with either a same-gender or other-gender partner.

For example, anthropological research shows that same-gender behavior and relationships are associated with a label such as "gay" in some cultures but not in others. Wekker (1999) described a widespread institution among Creole working-class women in Suriname called *mati*. Mati are women who engage in sexual relationships with men and with women, either simultaneously or consecutively, and who conceive of their sex acts in terms of behavior, not identity (Peplau, 1998). This socially accepted arrangement is made possible by the fact that most Creole women own or rent their own homes and are single heads of households. Wekker noted that mati challenge Western belief that one's sexual identity is "the core of our being" (p. 120). Elements assumed to be basic to the nature of sexual orientation may be unique to our culture and not necessarily related to sexual orientation in other social contexts (see Blackwood & Wierenga, 1999).

How do these findings about the important role of culture in shaping and defining the meaning of same-gender sexual and affectional behavior impact the lives of lesbians of color within the United States? Different cultural norms and traditions about gender roles, sexuality, and sexual orientation are integrated into the concept of family. Lesbians of color are often perceived as challenging the well-defined gender-role expectations for women in their families and within their ethnic communities. Clear distinctions made between male and female roles in certain cultures may increase the difficulty for lesbians to carve out a nontraditional role (Greene, 2000b).

For example, Latina lesbians challenge many aspects of the well-defined role of women in their cultures: submissiveness, virtuousness, respectfulness toward elders, interdependence, and the expectation to reside within their family until marriage (Espin, 1987). They are perceived as being too independent from the family and not sufficiently feminine. "Being a lesbian is by definition an act of treason against our cultural values.... To be a lesbian we have to leave the fold of our family, and seek support within the mainstream white lesbian community" (Romo-Carmona, 1987, p. xxvi). Latino/a communities are less aware of the existence of Latina lesbians than of Latino gay men. Generally, only the openly masculine, or "butch," types (that is, those violating gender roles) are recognized as lesbians (Espin, 1984).

Asian Americans often regard sex as a taboo topic and see homosexuality as a threat to marriage and continuity of the family line. Asian communities in the United States, regardless of assimilation, emphasize sharply delineated gender roles and negate or deny the possibility of lesbian existence. If acknowledged, lesbians are perceived as tarnishing the family honor by not being dutiful daughters, by rejecting the role of wife and mother, by rejecting passive reliance on and deference to men, and by rejecting submersion of identity within the family structure (Chan, 1997). As Lin (1978) explained:

> The Chinese are very reticent about sex and male-female relationships. Needless to say, female-female relationships (i.e., lesbian relationships) simply do not exist; it would be too shocking to the Chinese conscience to even acknowledge their existence.... I didn't even know the Chinese word for "homosexuality" until I was in my late teens. But I have always been aware of my "feelings" for other women since I was four or five years old. (p. 227)

In some cultures, it is so important to have a firm identity as a member of the culture or race that a violation of some aspect of the cultural norms may affect one's entire racial identity (as perceived by oneself or by others). For example, African American lesbians may receive negative sanctions for not promoting survival of their people through propagation of the race. Sexuality may be viewed as a natural and positive part of life, and there is relative flexibility in defining gender roles within the family. However, homosexuality is perceived by some African Americans as racial genocide (Greene, 2000a).

*L*ESBIAN RELATIONSHIPS

Now let's turn our attention to lesbian relationships. Researchers have investigated the experiences of lesbians by making comparisons among married, cohabiting heterosexual, gay male, and lesbian couples. The same-gender and cross-gender comparisons have provided an opportunity to examine the relative impact of gender and sexual orientation on the factors that characterize intimate sexual relationships of all kinds.

Some major findings about lesbian relationships show that lesbians and gay men bring to love relationships many of the same expectations, values, and interests as heterosexuals of the same gender. Lesbians are more likely than gay men to live with their primary partner and be in a steady relationship (Baldwin & Baldwin, 1997). We are more likely to prefer having sex only with partners we care about, view sexuality and love as closely linked, and desire sexual exclusivity (Peplau & Garnets, 2000). Lesbians place greater importance on emotional intimacy. We are more likely to value and have equality of involvement and equality in power than are gay men. These findings fit with data on heterosexual women. Women, regardless of sexual orientation, value emotional expressiveness, sexual exclusivity, and investment in and commitment to maintain relationships more highly than do men (Peplau & Spalding, 2000).

When people unfamiliar with lesbian relationships try to imagine one, they often resort to a heterosexual frame of reference, attempting to identify the person in the "male" role and the one in the "female" role. In fact, lesbian couples frequently adopt a peer-friendship model of intimate relationships. A lesbian remarked about the most significant factors in her 33-year relationship: "Compatibility. Similar likes in people and other interests. Becoming good friends as well as lovers. Mutual respect" (Johnson, 1990, p. 142). Partners in lesbian relationships show greater equality, reciprocity, and role flexibility than partners in heterosexual relationships. Most lesbian couples value power equality and shared decision making as a goal for their relationships (Peplau, 2003). One partner of a 15-year couple noted, "We don't have to have equal money or do equal things. We need to feel we have equal value, power, and rights in the relationship" (Johnson, 1990, p. 122). Another lesbian, in an 11-year relationship, stated, "We both are very independent and assume that we will share decisions and responsibilities equally" (Johnson, 1990, p. 123). These findings suggest that a gender-based division of labor is not necessary for relationships to function well.

To understand these findings, it is important to remember that there are no prescribed roles and behaviors to structure such relationships. Because society does not provide explicit or clear models of interaction, lesbian partners rely more on innovative processes for creating idiosyncratic rules, expectations, and division of labor in relationships. This approach may provide lesbians an opportunity for greater creativity in structuring relationships than is true for heterosexuals. Lesbians create intimate relationships based on models that may reduce traditional gender-role power imbalances found in heterosexual relationships.

My stepdaughter was married recently. She told me that she had sought out a relationship with a man who had the elements of reciprocity, equality, and friendship that she had observed between my life partner and me. She wished to avoid the power inequity and role restrictions that she had observed in many heterosexual relationships.

GENDER-ROLE FLEXIBILITY AMONG LESBIANS

In examining the impact of gender roles on lesbian identity and relationships, we saw that in many respects gay men are similar to heterosexual men and lesbians are similar to heterosexual women. However, lesbians are often encouraged or permitted by their deviance from accepted norms to explore androgynous gender-role behavior, independence, self-reliance, and educational and occupational options.

The fact that lesbians have no predetermined models about how to interact leads to greater potential for "normative creativity":

> By lacking clear rules about how to be lesbian and gay in the world, we have made up the rules as we go along.... Simply being lesbian or gay has been something we have had to invent for ourselves, since whatever roadmaps the dominant culture offered have been full of wrong turns and uncharted territories. (Brown, 1989, pp. 451–452)

They often create patterns of behavior, identity, and relationships that neither mirror nor duplicate heterosexual patterns.

Lesbians neither adhere rigidly to traditional gender roles nor consistently engage in cross-gender behavior. Frequently, lesbians adopt a nontraditional identity that includes nontraditional gender-role norms. Lesbians may be more androgynous than heterosexual women. Comparative studies of heterosexual women and lesbian women found lesbians to be more autonomous, spontaneous, assertive, sensitive to their own needs and fears, unconventional, self-confident, and inner-directed (Morgan & Brown, 1991).

These characteristics of lesbians find plausible explanations in that lesbian communities more readily accept behaviors that would be perceived by the larger society as violations of gender roles. Thus, lesbians often find support within the lesbian communities for flexibility and diversity in their identities as women.

These differences also reflect lesbians' social adaptation to their position in society in which they need to be self-reliant and provide for themselves. In the words of one lesbian, "You have to protect yourself. Straight women think, 'I have a man to protect me,' but for me, it's just me. You've got to stick up for yourself and survive every day—just having the strength and using it" (Schneider, 1989). As Morgan and Brown (1991) noted:

> From a practical standpoint as well as an ideological one, it makes sense that lesbians as a group would tend toward less gender-role stereotypic behaviors: When women choose to live independent of men, the many household maintenance activities that have traditionally been classified as "men's work" (including the role of breadwinner) still must be done, so gender-role flexibility is a reasonable and necessary adaptive response. (p. 278)

The experience of lesbians provides a unique opportunity to see the impact on identity, behavior, and relationships when the traditional patterns based on gender are reduced or removed. Because traditional roles and stereotypes may limit options for women, gender-role flexibility among lesbians may contribute to their constructing self-images different from heterosexuals. That is, lesbian self-identity may be freer from the bonds of restrictive gender-role constraints.

THE IMPACT OF ANTIGAY ATTITUDES

Fear of being labeled gay is a powerful socialization influence in our society and has negative consequences for both heterosexuals and homosexuals. Women and men who manifest characteristics inconsistent with those culturally prescribed for their gender, regardless of their sexual orientation, are likely to be labeled as gay (Kite & Whitley, 1998). A woman who does not conform to what is considered feminine runs the risk of being labeled a lesbian. A woman may be labeled a lesbian if she exhibits autonomous or self-assertive behavior, fights for her rights as a woman, enjoys the company of other women, works at a nontraditional job, or says no to violence. This is referred to as "lesbian baiting," which is defined as any attempt to control all women by accusing them of being lesbians because their behavior is not acceptable or appropriate to their gender role (Rothchild, 2005). As Gloria Steinem (1978) noted:

The lesson of my experience . . . is that sooner or later, all nonconforming women are likely to be labeled lesbians. True, we start out with the smaller punishments of being called "pushy" or "aggressive," "man-hating" or "unfeminine." But it's only a small step from those adjectives, whether bestowed by men or other women, to the full-fledged epithet of "lesbian." (p. 267)

Sexual prejudice affects heterosexuals, as well as gay men and lesbians, through its enforcement of traditional, rigid gender roles (Hyde & Jaffee, 2000). One significant function of the social stigma of homosexuality is to define limits of acceptable behavior for all men and women. Heterosexuals often restrict their gender-role behavior for fear of provoking the stigmatizing homosexual label. A heterosexual woman may avoid mentioning to friends that she is involved with a feminist organization on campus because she is afraid that they will think that she is a lesbian. Or a heterosexual woman may not confront a heterosexist remark for fear of being identified with lesbians. Or a heterosexual woman may avoid or hide her friendships with lesbians for fear of being labeled one herself.

Attempts to avoid the stigma of being labeled gay inhibit heterosexual men and women from forming close, intimate relationships with members of their own gender. As one heterosexual woman explained, "I've always been physically affectionate with my friends—hugging, kissing them on the cheek, walking arm in arm down the street. I've experienced people assuming we're lesbians because of what we're doing. I've been called "dyke" by people on the street when they saw us being physically affectionate. I've had some friends get nervous and push me off, not wanting to touch anymore" (Elize, 1992, pp. 105–106). Clearly, the interpersonal costs of heterosexism and sexual prejudice are high.

*C*ONCLUSION

We have discussed the ways that women's lives are enhanced by living openly as lesbians. Having an open identity as a lesbian across life contexts is related to positive self-esteem and to overall psychological adjustment. Lesbians often experience a sense of freedom from the bonds of gender-role constraints. This includes the ability to create new forms of relationships that reduce the power imbalances sometimes found in traditional heterosexual models and that rely instead on role flexibility, power equality, and shared decision making (Schwartz, 1994). As Adrienne Rich (1980) put it:

I think "coming out"—that first permission we give ourselves to name our love for women as love, to say, I am a lesbian, but also the successive "coming-outs" to the world . . . is connected with power, connects us with power, and until we believe that we have the right not merely to our love but to our power, we will continue to do harm among ourselves, fearing that power in each other and in ourselves. (p. xiii)

So, what does gender have to do with it? As we have seen, the life of a lesbian is inextricably bound with being a woman. Our status and socialization as women appear to shape our experience as lesbians. For example, sexual orientation is influenced by a wide range of sociocultural factors. Moreover, negative attitudes and stereotypes about lesbians are closely linked to negative attitudes and stereotypes about women's deval-ued status in society.

Recent evidence suggests that attitudes equating homosexuality with violation of what is normal for women may be changing (Herek, 2000). Changing gender-role expectations for all women may make it possible for lesbians to be seen as "real" women. This benefits lesbians because it reduces homophobic stereotypes and prejudice. Heterosexuals, too, profit from expanded definitions of acceptable behavior—definitions that entitle them to fuller self-expression without fear of being labeled gay. As Charlotte Bunch (1978) stated:

> The lesbian is most clearly the antithesis of patriarchy—an offense to its basic tenets. It is woman-hating; we are woman-loving. It demands female obedience and docility; we seek strength, assertiveness, and dignity for women. It bases power and defines roles on one's gender and other physical attributes; we operate outside gender-defined roles and seek a new basis for defining power and relationships. (pp. 181–182)

REFERENCES

BALDWIN, J. D., & BALDWIN, J. I. (1997). Gender differences in sexual interest. *Archives of Sexual Behavior, 26,* 181–210.

BLACKWOOD, E. (2000). Culture and women's sexualities. *Journal of Social Issues, 56*(2), 223–238.

BLACKWOOD, E., & WIERENGA, S. E., (Eds.). (1999). *Female desires: Same-sex relations and transgender practices across cultures.* New York: Columbia University Press.

BRENNER, C. (1992). Survivor's story: Eight bullets. In G. M. Herek & K. T. Berrill (Eds.), *Hate crimes: Confronting violence against lesbians and gay men* (pp. 11–15). Newbury Park, CA: Sage.

BROWN, L. (1989). New voices, new visions: Toward a lesbian/gay paradigm for psychology. *Psychology of Women Quarterly, 13,* 445–458.

BUNCH, C. (1978). Lesbian-feminist theory. In G. Vida (Ed.), *Our right to love: A lesbian resource book* (pp. 180–182). Englewood Cliffs, NJ: Prentice-Hall.

CASS, V. C. (1979). Homosexual identity formation: A theoretical model. *Journal of Homosexuality, 4*(3), 219–235.

CHAN, C. S. (1997). Don't ask, don't tell, don't know: The formation of a homo-sexual identity and sexual expression among Asian American lesbians. In B. Greene (Ed.), *Ethnic and cultural diversity among lesbians and gay men* (pp. 240–248). Thousand Oaks, CA: Sage.

D'AUGELLI, A. R., & GARNETS, L. (1995). Lesbian, gay, and bisexual communities. In A. R. D'Augelli & C. J. Patterson (Eds.), *Lesbian, gay and bisexual identities across the lifespan.* New York: Oxford University Press.

DeMonteflores, C. (1986). Notes on the management of difference. In T. Stein & C. Cohen (Eds.), *Contemporary perspectives on psychotherapy with lesbians and gay men* (pp. 73–101). New York: Plenum Press.

DiPlacido, J. (1998). Minority stress among lesbians, gay men, and bisexuals: A consequence of heterosexism, homophobia, and stigmatization. In G. M. Herek (Ed.), *Stigma and sexual orientation: Understanding prejudice against lesbians, gay men, and bisexuals* (pp. 138–159). Thousand Oaks, CA: Sage.

Elize, D. (1992). "It has nothing to do with me." In J. Blumenfeld (Ed.), *Homophobia: How we all pay the price* (pp. 95–113). Boston: Beacon Press.

Espin, O. (1984). Cultural and historical influences on sexuality in Hispanic/ Latin women: Implications for psychotherapy. In C. Vance (Ed.), *Pleasure and danger: Exploring female sexuality* (pp. 149–163). London: Routledge & Kegan Paul.

Espin, O. (1987). Issues of identity in the psychology of Latina lesbians. In Boston Lesbian Psychologies Collective (Eds.), *Lesbian psychologies: Explorations and challenges* (pp. 35–51). Urbana: University of Illinois Press.

Garnets, L. (2002). Sexual orientations in perspective. *Cultural Diversity and Ethnic Minority Psychology, 8*(2), 115–129.

Garnets, L., & Kimmel, D. (1991). Lesbian and gay male dimensions in the psychological study of human diversity. In J. Goodchilds (Ed.), *Psychological perspectives on human diversity in America* (pp. 137–192). Washington, DC: American Psychological Association.

Garnets, L. D., & Kimmel, D. C. (Eds.) (2003). *Psychological perspectives on lesbian, gay male, and bisexual experiences* (2nd ed.). New York: Columbia University Press.

Greene, B. (2000a). African American lesbian and bisexual women. *Journal of Social Issues, 56*(2), 239–249.

Greene, B. (2000b). Beyond heterosexism and across the cultural divide. Developing an inclusive lesbian, gay, and bisexual psychology: A look to the future. In B. Greene & G. L. Croom (Eds.), *Education, research, and practice in lesbian, gay, bisexual, and transgendered psychology* (pp. 1–45). Thousand Oaks, CA: Sage.

Herek, G. M. (2000). The psychology of sexual prejudice. *Current Directions in Psychological Science, 9,* 19–22.

Herek, G. M. (2004). Beyond "homophobia": Thinking about sexual prejudice and stigma in the twenty-first century. *Sexuality Research and Social Policy, 1*(2), 6–24.

Hyde, J., & Jaffee, S. (2000). Becoming a heterosexual adult: The experiences of young women. *Journal of Social Issues, 56*(2), 283–296.

Johnson, S. E. (1990). *Staying power: Long-term lesbian couples.* Tallahassee, FL: Naiad Press.

Kite, M. E., & Whitley, B. E., Jr. (1998). Do heterosexual women and men differ in their attitudes toward homosexuality? A conceptual and methodological analysis. In G. M. Herek (Ed.), *Understanding prejudice against lesbians, gay men, and bisexuals* (pp. 39–61). Thousand Oaks, CA: Sage.

Lin, Y. (1978). The spectrum of lesbian experience: Personal testimony. In G. Vida, (Ed.), *Our right to love: A lesbian resource book* (pp. 227–229). Englewood Cliffs, NJ: Prentice-Hall.

LIVINGSTON, J. (1996). Individual action and political strategies: Creating a future free of heterosexism. In E. D. Rothblum & L. A. Bond (Eds.), *Preventing heterosexism and homophobia* (pp. 253–265). Thousand Oaks, CA: Sage.

MORGAN, K. S., & BROWN, L. S. (1991). Lesbian career development, work behavior, and vocational counseling. *Counseling Psychologist, 19*(2), 273–291.

PEPLAU, L. A. (2003). Human sexuality: How do men and women differ? *Current Directions in Psychological Science, 12,* 37–40.

PEPLAU, L. A., & GARNETS, L. D. (2000). A new paradigm for understanding women's sexuality and sexual orientation. *Journal of Social Issues, 56*(2), 329–350.

PEPLAU, L. A., & SPALDING, L. R. (2000). The close relationships of lesbians, gay men, and bisexuals. In C. Hendrick & S. S. Hendrick (Eds.), *Close relationships: A sourcebook* (pp. 111–123). Thousand Oaks, CA: Sage.

PEPLAU, L. A., SPALDING, L. R., CONLEY, T. D., & VENIEGAS, R. C. (1998). The development of sexual orientation in women. *Annual Review of Sex Research, 10,* 70–99.

PETROW, S. (1990, May). Together wherever we go. *The Advocate,* pp. 42–44.

PLUMMER, K. (1989). Lesbian and gay youth in England. *Journal of Homosexuality, 17*(1–4), 195–223.

RICH, A. (1980). Foreword. In S. J. Wolfe & J. P. Stanley (Eds.), *The coming out stories* (pp. xi–xiii). Watertown, MA: Persephone.

ROCHLIN, M. (1980, October). Heterosexual questionnaire. *Association of Gay Psychologists Newsletter,* p. 4.

ROMO-CARMONA, M. (1987). Introduction. In J. Ramos (Ed.), *Companeras: Latina lesbians* (pp. xx–xxix). New York: Latina Lesbian History Project.

ROTHBLUM, E. D., & BOND, L. A. (Eds.). (1996). *Preventing heterosexism and homophobia.* Thousand Oaks, CA: Sage.

ROTHCHILD, C. (2005). *Written out: How sexuality is used to attack women's organizing.* New York: International Gay and Lesbian Human Rights Commission and Center for Women's Global Leadership.

SAVIN-WILLIAMS, R. C., & DIAMOND, L. M. (2000). Sexual identity trajectories among sexual-minority youths: Gender comparisons. *Archives of Sexual Behavior, 29,* 419–440.

SCHNEIDER, M. (1989). Sappho was a right-on adolescent: Growing up lesbian. *Journal of Homosexuality, 17*(1–4), 111–130.

SCHWARTZ, P. (1994). *Peer marriage: How love between equals really works.* New York: Free Press.

SEARS, J. T. (1989). The impact of gender and race on growing up lesbian and gay in the South. *National Women's Studies Association Journal, 1,* 422–457.

STEINEM, G. (1978). The politics of supporting lesbianism. In G. Vida (Ed.), *Our right to love: A lesbian resource book* (pp. 266–269). Englewood Cliffs, NJ: Prentice-Hall.

TROIDEN, R. (1989). The formation of homosexual identities. *Journal of Homosexuality, 17*(1–4), 43–73.

WEKKER, G. (1999). "What's identity got to do with it?" Rethinking identity in light of the mati work in Suriname. In E. Blackwood & S. E. Wierenga (Eds.), *Female desires: Same-sex relations and transgender practices across cultures* (pp. 119–138). New York: Columbia University Press.

SUGGESTED READINGS

BLACKWOOD, E., & WIERENGA, S. E. (Eds.). (1999). *Female desires: Same-sex relations and transgender practices across cultures.* New York: Columbia University Press.

GARNETS, L. D., & KIMMEL, D. (2003). *Psychological perspectives on lesbian, gay, and bisexual experiences.* New York: Columbia University Press.

GREENE, B. (1997). *Ethnic and cultural diversity among lesbians and gay men.* Thousand Oaks, CA: Sage.

PEPLAU, L. A., & GARNETS, L. D. (2000). A new paradigm for understanding women's sexuality and sexual orientation. *Journal of Social Issues, 56*(2), 329–350.

DONNA CASTAÑEDA *is Associate Professor of Psychology at San Diego State University. Dr. Castañeda has taught gender-related courses at San Diego State and at the University of California at Davis. Her work focuses on close relationships among Latinas/os, health promotion in Latina/o communities, and sexual risk behavior among Latina women.*

16

Gender Issues Among Latinas

❖

DIVERSITY AMONG LATINAS

As an undergraduate in the late 1970s and early 1980s looking for published work specifically focused on Latinas, I found very little. A silence regarding these women exists in the larger society that is reflected in their invisibility in the social science literature. But the situation is improving and certainly there is much more information available now than in the past. Much of this newer work has been done by Latinas themselves. I think one of the most important elements in this emergent literature is the emphasis on the diversity present among Latina women. Much of the available research deals with Mexican American women because they are the largest Latina group. There is, however, growing interest in and concern for distinctions in socioeconomic class, degree of Spanish language usage, sexual orientation, acculturation, and race both within and across differing Latina groups, such as Puerto Rican, Dominican Republican, Central and South American, and Cuban women.[1]

Each unique constellation of these elements has very different implications for the lived experience of individual Latina women. Consider the case of two women, one a Dominican Republican woman of African descent who has recently arrived in the United States to work in a factory in New York City, the other a woman who came from Mexico to the United States and has worked, married, and raised a family in the Central Valley of California (a largely agricultural region) over the last

Special thanks to Elida Lopez for helpful comments on this paper.
[1]For the purposes of this paper, the term "Latina" refers to women of Mexican, South American, Central American, Puerto Rican, Dominican Republican, or Cuban descent. It does not indicate immigration status. The terms "Latina/o" and "Latinas/os" refer to both women and men.

30 years. Both would be considered immigrants and Latinas, and although their lives would contain certain commonalities, their circumstances and experience would be quite different. U.S.-born Latinas would also have a different experience from that of these two women. Their first language is likely to be English; they may be second-, third-, or even fourth-generation Latinas; and their personal and cultural identity will be related to their experience of growing up in the United States rather than in a different country.

Even college-educated Latinas can come from differing backgrounds. At the university where I teach, there is a sizable Latina student population. Most of the women in my classes are the first in their families to attend college, and they tend to come from working-class backgrounds. However, there are some whose parents are professionals and who have a history of higher education in their families. Because the campus where I teach is located at the United States–Mexico border, many of the Latina students are bilingual, but even in this location there is still variability in Spanish-language ability among the Latina students, with some who speak Spanish fluently and others who do not.

A DEMOGRAPHIC PICTURE OF LATINAS

Before examining gender-related issues, I think it is helpful to have a clear demographic picture of Latinas in the United States. Latinas/os overall are the largest ethnic group in the United States. They make up 14 percent of the nation's total population, and, by 2050, they are projected to make up 24 percent of the total population. The largest group of Latinas/os in the United States is composed of persons of Mexican descent (64 percent), followed by persons of Puerto Rican (10 percent), Cuban (3 percent), Salvadoran (3 percent), and Dominican (3 percent) descent. The remainder (17 percent) is of some other Central American, South American, or Caribbean descent. Latinas/os have become more geographically dispersed over the last 15 years, but they still tend to be concentrated in certain areas. For example, approximately 49 percent of Latinas/os, primarily Mexicans, live in California and Texas. About one-half of the Dominicans in the United States live in New York City, and one-half of the nation's Cubans reside in Miami-Dade County, Florida (U.S. Census Bureau, 2005c). As a group, Latinas are considerably younger than non-Latinas; the median age of Latinas is 27 years, compared to a median age of 41 years for non-Latina White women (U.S. Census Bureau, 2005a, 2005b). The popular perception of Latinas/os is that they are primarily immigrants. Although immigration of Latinas/os to the United States increased more after 1990 than in any previous period, 60 percent of Latinas/os were born in the United States (Ramirez & de la Cruz, 2002).

A significant factor that affects the lives of Latinas is poverty. Almost one-quarter of Latinas (24 percent) are living below the poverty line, compared to 9 percent of White women. This number jumps to 37 percent for Latinas who are single parents, compared to 20 percent of White women who are single parents (U.S. Census Bureau, 2004a). The high rate of poverty among Latinas is related to gender and ethnic discrimination, lack of educational opportunities, and the type of employment in which Latinas are concentrated. For example, only 59 percent of Latinas have graduated from high school, compared to 90 percent of White women (U.S. Census Bureau, 2004b). Since 1977 the number of bachelor's, master's, and doctoral degrees awarded to Latinas has increased substantially, but the number of Latinas who have received college degrees is still small. Only 12 percent of Latinas have received a BA or higher degree. In 2002, of the 44,160 doctoral degrees awarded in the United States, only 2 percent (783) went to Latinas (U.S. Department of Education, 2003).

A smaller percentage of Latinas than non-Latinas (56 percent versus 74 percent) work in white-collar or pink-collar jobs. Latinas who work in these sectors tend to be concentrated at the low end of the pay scale, and few are in management and or professional positions. On the other hand, more Latinas (46 percent) than non-Latinas (26 percent) work in blue-collar or service sector jobs (U.S. Census Bureau, 2004c).

*W*HAT'S IN A NAME?

The labels Latinas use to describe themselves are important to understand. Because Latinas are a diverse group, a great deal of complexity surrounds the use of these labels. For example, women of Mexican descent in this country may call themselves Chicanas, Mexican Americans, Hispanas, Tejanas, Mexicanas, Spanish Americans, or Hispanics. Each of these terms has its own history and regional specificity. In addition, how an individual names herself can contain political connotations. Many times these political connotations lead to strong feelings about which term should be used to describe Latinas. For example, the term "Chicana/o" was appropriated by activists in the Chicana/o movement in the late 1960s and early 1970s as a term indicating pride in a Mexican heritage, particularly a pre-Columbian Indian heritage, and a rejection of the implicit assimilationist connotations of the term "Mexican American." Thus, a woman who uses this term to describe herself would also be understood to hold these values. On the other hand, the term "Hispanic" is often viewed as a politically conservative label. It was coined by the government to indicate all persons of Mexican, Caribbean, Central American, or South American descent in the United States. A woman who prefers this term to describe herself would be understood to hold politically conservative views regarding the role of ethnicity.

Currently, when referring to women of Mexican, Puerto Rican, Cuban, Dominican Republican, or Central and South American descent in the United States, the term "Latina" is preferred. Even though it glosses over the diversity among these groups of women, it is a term that originated among Latinas themselves, and it connotes a sense of community across the many Latina subgroups.

At times, the norms surrounding labels developed in academic circles can be at odds with those used by Latinas themselves. Zavella (1993), in describing how her New Mexican informants characterized their ethnic identity, found that these women often had difficulty trying to describe themselves with a single label. They typically had to contextualize their answers to her question about ethnic identity by explaining where they were from, where their parents were from, to whom they were related, their religion, and traditional family activities. Or, as one woman said in response to that question, "I don't know, I'm just me" (p. 64). When Zavella reported her results at a conference using the term that the women had themselves used, "Spanish American," her academic colleagues angrily objected to it because they thought it was too politically conservative and racially inaccurate.

Labels are seen as important indicators of individuals' sense of their own ethnic identity. However, to me it seems that one's ethnic identity can rarely be summarized in a one-word label. The region where one has grown up; family and community norms; whether one has a mixed heritage, such as Latina and European American; immigration status (even the region where an immigrant is from); how long one has lived in the United States, level of acculturation; and political outlook (that is, assimilationist versus nonassimilationist)—all of these go into one's sense of ethnic identification. Of course, there are commonalities among Latinas, but there are multiple Latina experiences, and these often defy simple categorization. In order to understand an individual's sense of ethnic identity, it is important to go beyond labels and understand an individual's personal history. When Latinas meet each other for the first time, the interactions often include finding out in either direct or indirect ways a woman's background, where she is from, where she has lived, her work, and her Spanish-language proficiency. This is one of the ways that Latinas themselves determine understandings of each other.

GENDER AND FAMILY ROLES

The first gender-related issue I want to talk about is gender and family roles among Latinas. In general, gender roles among Latinas/os have been depicted as highly stylized and male-dominated. Women are thought to be submissive to, and controlled by, their male partners. This stereotype, however, obscures the multidimensional and dynamic quality of gender roles among this group. There is no question, of course, that patriarchy and gender oppression exist in Latina/o families and societies. However, more recent research on gender roles stresses the heterogeneity within this group by including an analysis of class, urban-rural, region, and generational differences and how these internal differences impinge on gender roles within Latina/o families.

The stereotype of dominant male and submissive female roles in the family is not held up in research that includes the factors mentioned, and a more complex picture emerges. In one study (Hurtado, Hayes-Bautista, Burciaga Valdez, & Hernandez, 1992), both Latina/o women and men rejected a solely male-dominated family structure (that is, one where a wife should do whatever a husband wants, husbands should make all important decisions, only girls should do housework, and only men should provide for the family). The strength of this rejection varied by generational status. Among first-generation Latinas/os, fewer than half endorsed a husband-dominated family structure; the percentages continued to decline for second- and third-generation women and men, although women tended to reject this family structure more than men at all generational levels.

The Latina/o family has been undergoing, and continues to undergo, many changes in its structure and functions. Because of this, Latinas, like women from other cultural and ethnic groups, are attempting to redefine or create new roles and identities for themselves in relation to their male partners and families. For Latinas, such processes may contain costs and strains owing to expectations that limit their growth and autonomy, from both inside and outside the family. For example, one woman in my class described how both her immediate and extended family, after being generally supportive of her efforts to complete her college education, stepped up pressures for her to get married after she graduated. "*Now* why aren't you getting married, they say, as if there is something wrong with me." That she may want to follow a different path is never considered.

According to a study by Williams (1988), social class is an important factor that influences Latina women's ability to change gender roles and expectations for their behavior in the family. A key issue for working-class Mexican American women was the need to develop new social and personal identities separate from husbands, something they had never done before. Attempts to do this, however, caused strain with husbands who continued to insist on maintaining control over women's behavior and activities. These women used both direct and indirect techniques to negotiate this strain. For example, one woman who wanted to join co-workers at Friday evening "happy hours" encountered resistance from her husband. He believed that women who went to bars unaccompanied by their husbands were "loose." This woman persisted, however, and she convinced her husband to change his beliefs, thus allowing her to attend happy hours with co-workers. At other times, working-class women used indirect methods that avoided direct confrontations. For example, if they knew their husbands would object to their autonomous behavior, they may have done something first and then informed husbands of what they had done afterward.

Mexican American business and professional women, on the other hand, took for granted the notion of both public and private identities that did not rely on their husband's status. For these women, conflicting demands of children, work, and husbands were sources of strain. Each of these domains was important to these women, and they coped with conflicting demands by keeping separate, or compartmentalizing, their public and private identities. By doing so, business and professional women were able to give high priority to both family and work. On the other hand, there were still costs associated with being part of the public domain and having a career. Husbands and family continued to expect them to shoulder the greater share of housekeeping and childcare. As one woman said, "It's unfair. Women have to do things that they are expected to do, hold on to housekeeping responsibilities. We are supermoms. I teach, and as a mother I work all night" (Williams, 1988, p. 210). Furthermore, the few Mexican American women who had more prestigious careers and made more money than their husbands had to downplay these for the sake of their husbands. As Williams (1988) said, "One woman carefully avoided emphasizing her own career or monetary success because this made her husband feel threatened; he conceded that he had difficulty accepting his wife's role in having a successful career and being chief wage earner of the family" (p. 211).

A common factor that influenced the roles of both working-class and business and professional women in this study was discrimination in the community and in the workplace. Cultural traditions give men greater authority over women in the Mexican American community, and discrimination based on gender *and* ethnicity in the workplace constrained women's efforts at refashioning their work and public roles. In the workplace, these women encountered negative stereotypes of Mexican Americans that were expressed both subtly and directly. As one woman said, "They [Anglo Americans] do not care for Mexican Americans. They will call you anything" (Williams, 1988, p. 211). The business and professional women were more likely to experience more subtle discrimination, such as negative stereotypes that were carried into the workplace (for example, that Mexican Americans are less competent).

CLOSE HETEROSEXUAL RELATIONSHIPS

The development of close heterosexual relationships presents Latinas with dilemmas surrounding cultural maintenance, identity, and women's changing roles. In one instance, for example, Mexican American women pursuing a higher education who were strongly ethnically identified and who preferred Mexican American partners in close relationships experienced stress because of their perception that Mexican American men feared high-achieving women. As Gonzalez (1988) suggested, college-educated Mexican American women may "experience conflict as their behavior is changing more rapidly than their sex role attitudes and the attitudes of their male partners" (p. 378). This situation may be particularly pronounced for Latinas with advanced degrees. As a friend of mine who has a PhD told me, "Finding Latino men who are not afraid of talented and educated Latinas is really hard. They talk the talk, but when it really comes down to it they want to marry their secretaries."

Another study (Castañeda, 1993) identified a componential definition of romantic love among heterosexual Mexican American college students. Although women were as likely as men to indicate that trust, communication, shared values and attitudes, and honesty were part of a definition of love, they significantly differed in their likelihood of indicating mutual respect as part of a definition of love. Women were more likely to identify mutual respect as a component of romantic love than were men. Open-ended responses revealed that mutual respect meant a willingness for each partner to listen to the other and to consider the partner's opinions to be important and valid. For the women in this sample, unlike the men, these elements could not as readily be taken for granted in heterosexual relationships. As one woman in this study said, "We don't have to agree on everything but I want respect for my opinions and beliefs. I guess listening is important in a love relationship."

Heterosexual relationships for Latina women are arenas of both satisfaction and struggle, but the burden of adaption to changing gender-role expectations falls primarily on them. This situation is similar to the situation of all women who are struggling to develop nonoppressive heterosexual relationships, but the unique historical, cultural, and class conditions of Latinas may result in the development of different strategies in response to different conditions. For example, Latinas must navigate and balance changing gender expectations; meet the needs of partners, children, and other family members; uphold the cultural integrity of Latinas/os as a whole; and resist racism while also meeting their own needs for positive growth and validation in close relationships. Many Latinas I know express that they are not getting their needs met in their relationships with men. They are frustrated with the lack of understanding received from male partners, but there are few places to turn for help and advice. There are few models for successfully resolving these frustrations that are culturally consistent and personally satisfying. Instead, there is a strong model of female self-sacrifice, obedience, and caring for the needs of others in Latina/o cultures. Because of this, focusing on oneself and getting needs met in a mutually satisfying way can be difficult for Latinas. As one woman described this process, "since in the Anglo [European American] culture the Catholic church is not the predominant religious institution, women believe in the right to self-improvement. They do not only believe in it, but they struggle for it, whereas in our Latin American culture if a woman speaks out for her rights she is immediately branded, labeled" (Colindres, 1989, p. 77).

HETEROSEXUAL SEXUALITY AND LATINAS

There are a number of contradictory myths regarding Latina sexuality. First, there is the notion of the woman who remains chaste and virginal until married, unsullied by sexual desire of any kind. If a woman is married, she is viewed as a mother figure who is happy having many children, but who is not particularly interested in sex. Instead, she merely "submits" to a partner's sexual desires. (The partner being, of course, a "Latin lover" with insatiable sexual demands.) Finally, there is the myth of the "sexy señorita with smoldering eyes" who is always ready for sex. Certainly, there is little consciousness of Latina lesbian sexuality. None of these myths reflect the reality of Latina sexuality, but there has been no public or private vision of Latina sexuality in between or outside of these extremes. Latinas have few realistic or positive images of their sexuality reflected in the media, art, literature, or the Latina/o or non-Latina/o culture.

A small number of empirical studies of Latina sexuality exist in the literature, but they are limited in their scope and interpretive power. These studies have found that Latina (and Latino) university students tend to be less knowledgeable about sexuality (Padilla & O'Grady, 1987) and more conservative in their sexual behavior (Baldwin, Whiteley, & Baldwin, 1992; Padilla & O'Grady, 1987) and in their attitudes toward sexuality (Padilla & O'Grady, 1987) than European American students. This situation also appears to be the case among Latina adolescents (Padilla & Baird, 1991; Scott, Shifman, Orr, Owen, & Fawcett, 1988).

The picture is somewhat different when community samples of Latinas are studied. Latinas in drug treatment were found to be quite willing and able to broach the subject of condoms to their male partners and to convince them to use them (Kline, Kline, & Oken, 1992). In another study (Amaro, 1988), Latina women did not endorse the notion that the purpose of sexuality was solely reproduction. However, this sample expressed a high level of dissatisfaction with the quality of their current sexual relationships.

To date, the most interesting and provocative work on Latina sexuality is to be found not in the social sciences but in literature, art, and poetry (for example, Alarcon, Castillo, & Moraga, 1989; Trujillo, 1991). A common theme in this work is the historical repression of Latina sexuality within the family and larger Latina/o culture. This repression has served to silence women and leave them with inadequate knowledge of their own sexuality. Catholicism, and its pervasiveness in Latina/o culture, has played a central role in keeping Latinas from full knowledge of their sexuality. As Castillo (1991) wrote, "Sexuality for the Catholic woman of Latin American background has, at best, been associated with her reproductive ability (or lack of it) and otherwise, repressed" (p. 40). In Catholicism the Virgin Mary, and the qualities she embodies, is upheld as the model for all women to emulate. These qualities include self-abnegation, motherhood, and above all sexual purity. This model, which may not be articulated by individual women, is clearly implicated in the stress on virginity until marriage for women within Latina/o cultures. In addition, although the reality of Latina sexuality indicates otherwise (e.g., the rates of teen pregnancy and sexually transmitted diseases), Latinas are still subjected to cultural expectations that emphasize a double standard in which men's sexuality is positively viewed and encouraged, whereas that of women is negatively viewed and discouraged.

All of these factors, the myths, Catholicism, repression, and the double standard directly influence the development of sexuality among Latinas. In some cases, sexual enjoyment itself can be conflictual for Latinas. In order to see themselves as virtuous, some women may, as Espín (1985) said, "shun sexual pleasure" (p. 156) and "even express pride in their own lack of pleasure or desire" (p. 156).

Despite the greater restrictions on Latinas' expression of their sexuality, my experience has been that, given the appropriate context, Latinas have much to say about sexuality and will do so openly. In a study I did (Castañeda, 1985) to examine mediation of sexuality during menstruation among a sample of Mexican farm-working women (certainly a topic many would consider too "taboo" for this group!), I found that these women could easily speak about this topic. They also had much to say about related topics, such as birth control, courtship, and gender relations. Given a space to do so, Latinas can express a multiplicity of sexual views, forms, and experiences.

*L*ATINA LESBIANS

To a large extent, lesbianism is invisible within Latina/o communities. Lesbians and gay men are generally negatively viewed and may be ostracized by their families if their sexual orientation is known. Because of this, Latina lesbians may not be out about their lesbianism with family members, even if they are out in other contexts of their lives.

On the other hand, I have seen a number of instances where, even though it may not be openly acknowledged, a Latina's lesbianism may be tacitly accepted by her family and her community. This may be one way that lesbian women can, at least to a small extent, exist in Latina/o communities. In these cases, Latinas are able to maintain connections with their community, their family, *and* their lesbian identity.

Because Latinas/os grow up in a context that stresses family bonds and connection to community, to be ostracized from these is particularly distressing for Latinas. To live solely in a non-Latina context, even though it may be one where an individual Latina's lesbianism is accepted and validated, is generally not preferable. However, unlike Latina heterosexuals or non-Latina lesbians, Latina lesbians must often make the decision to separate two fundamental elements of the self: ethnicity and lesbianism. Such social and psychological compartmentalization can result in significant negative emotional consequences for some (Flores-Ortiz, 1995), and the decision can be fraught with ambivalence and even anger that this decision must be confronted. One Cuban woman described these feelings well by saying, "It is a very painful question because I feel that I am both, and I don't want to have to choose. Clearly, straight people don't even get asked this question and it is unfair that we have to discuss it" (Espín, 1987, p. 47).

Another factor that affects the experience of Latina lesbians is that a much larger percentage of Latinas are poor. To establish and live a lesbian lifestyle is much more difficult for a Latina lesbian who is also poor (Castillo, 1991). The lives of all poor women are more difficult than those of middle-class women, but when one is poor, subject to racism in the larger society, and part of a culture that censures lesbianism, (a culture in which even definitions of heterosexual Latinas' sexuality are obscured by myth), the options for expression of a lesbian identity are more restricted. Because of this, many Latina lesbians may opt for a heterosexual lifestyle by marrying and having children, and they may either not acknowledge their awareness of their lesbianism or practice it in secrecy. In addition, if one's lesbian identity is expressed, the alternatives available for safety, both physical and emotional, are also limited if one is poor and Latina.

Unfortunately, there is very little published information regarding Latina lesbian sexuality. As previously mentioned, the silence surrounding Latina lesbian sexuality has been broken with the publication of various literary works, but these represent the work of educated and highly articulate women. The sexual lives of Latinas outside this small circle are not well represented, particularly in the social sciences. How Latina lesbians create, define, and live out their sexuality; its commonalities and differences from non-Latina lesbian sexuality; and how that intersects with factors affecting lesbian and ethnic identity are important issues for future research.

SPOUSAL AND INTIMATE-PARTNER VIOLENCE

Now I would like to turn to the issue of spousal or intimate-partner violence. What I mean by this is violence that Latinas experience from a husband or boyfriend. Little research has been done on family violence in general among Latinas/os in the United States. Available data show that Latina women are less likely to be victims of homicide by a spouse or an intimate partner than either African American or White women (UCLA-CDS, 1985, cited in Sorenson & Telles, 1991). Conversely, other research has shown that Latinas/os report high rates of intimate-partner violence with rates that range from 17 to 23 percent for Latinas/os compared to 11 to 15 percent for Whites (Caetano, Schafer, & Cunradi, 2001; Straus & Gelles, 1990). When acculturation level, that is, the extent to which Latinas/os have adopted the values, attitudes, and behaviors of U.S. society, is considered, a more complex picture appears. In general, the pattern is that that greater acculturation is related to higher rates of intimate-partner violence, particularly for Latino men (Caetano, Schafer, Clark, Cunradi, & Raspberry, 2000; Sorenson & Telles, 1991). However, one study showed that Latinas/os who are in the medium-acculturated group show the highest rates of intimate-partner violence, followed by those in the high-acculturated and then low-acculturated groups. In fact, Latina/o couples with just one partner in the medium-acculturated group were at higher risk for intimate-partner violence than couples where both partners were in the low- or high-acculturated groups (Caetano et al., 2000), and this was true regardless of whether male-to-female partner violence or female-to-male partner violence was considered.

Differences in the extent of intimate-partner violence based upon acculturation level may exist for a number of reasons. Latinas/os higher in acculturation may have fewer of the traditional social support structures available to them, such as extended family, than less-acculturated Latinas/os and thus may experience greater stress in navigating differing cultural contexts. Those in the medium-acculturated group may find this process particularly stressful, which may lead to increased conflict in couples. When both partners in a couple are medium in acculturation they may have a lower "reservoir of resilience" to stress, which may facilitate violent responses (Caetano et al., 2000, p. 43). Differences in definitions and tolerance for intimate-partner violence based upon acculturation level may also play a role. For example, immigrant Latinas may be less aware that violence from a male partner should not be tolerated. At least one study showed that Latina/o couples were less likely than White or African American couples to agree on reports of male-to-female intimate-partner violence events (Caetano, Schafer, Field, & Nelson, 2002). In this case, Latinas reported fewer male-to-female intimate-partner violence events than did their male partners. Although acculturation was not assessed in this study, these results suggest the need to be especially careful in determining rates of intimate-partner violence among Latinas, as they may be less likely to report these experiences. Finally, U.S.-born Latinas/os show higher rates of drug and alcohol use than immigrant Latinas/os (Amaro, Whitaker, Coffman, & Heeren, 1990; Markides, Ray, Stroup-Benham, & Treviño, 1990), and alcohol is implicated in intimate-partner violence (Leadley, Clark, & Caetano, 2000).

SEXUAL ASSAULT

Another form of violence I want to talk about is sexual assault. The study of sexual assault among Latinas is, again, an area in which little research has been done. In one study (Sorenson & Siegel, 1992), using a community sample in Los Angeles that included both women and men, Latinas/os were found to have a lower overall prevalence of sexual assault, 8.1 percent, compared with 19.9 percent among non-Latinas/os. A previous study that included analyses by immigration status found that, although Latinas/os overall show a lower prevalence of sexual assault, the prevalence of sexual assault among U.S.-born Latinas/os, 11.4 percent, approaches that of U.S.-born non-Latinas/os, 16.2 percent (Sorenson & Telles, 1991). This study included both women and men, but within every ethnic, age, and education level women reported a higher prevalence of sexual assault than men. Although Latinas/os were not significantly different from non-Latina/os in likelihood to resist rape, to report specific emotional reactions to a sexual assault, to develop mental disorders due to the assault, or to talk to someone about the assault, they were less likely to talk to a psychotherapist about the assault than were non-Latinas/os (Sorenson & Siegel, 1992).

Looking at only women, Sorenson and Telles (1991) found that Latina women overall reported lower rates of sexual assault, 8.6 percent, than non-Latina women, 22 percent. Again, immigrant Latinas reported lower rates, 4.2 percent, than U.S.-born Latinas, 14.3 percent. However, when immigrant women were sexually assaulted, almost one-third of the time, 31 percent, the perpetrator was a husband or an intimate partner. This was the case among only 13 percent of non-Latina women.

The reasons for lower rates of intimate-partner and sexual violence reported by immigrant Latinas are still unclear. These data should not lead to a sense that these women are somehow "protected" or safer from violence than U.S.-born Latinas or non-Latina women. In many ways, these women are quite vulnerable. They live and work in some of the most unsafe areas of U.S. cities, they must use public transportation at all hours to travel to and from work, they work in conditions where they are susceptible to sexual coercion, and those who are in the United States illegally have little recourse for protection from the police or legal system. The high rate of sexual assault from husbands or intimate partners among immigrant women suggests that these women may be particularly vulnerable to violence within the family. In addition, researchers are increasingly understanding the role of sexual violence in migrant and refugee women's migration motivations and outcomes (Arguelles & Rivero, 1995). Migration to another country can be a survival strategy for women who have experienced sexual abuse and assault, exploitation, and domestic violence in their home country. For some women, migration is seen as a way to escape heterosexist oppression in their home country. The process of migration itself can expose women to sexual violence from strangers, employers, border and other law enforcement officials, and family members (Arguelles & Rivero, 1995).

SERVICES FOR LATINA VICTIMS OF VIOLENCE

Although rates of spousal and intimate partner violence and sexual assault among Latinas are important to understand, equally important is the development of appropriate and accessible services for Latinas who experience these types of violence. Many rape crisis centers and bat-tered women's shelters make efforts at outreach to Latinas, but these services are often underutilized by Latinas and those who may need help may not receive it. Such programs need to consider language, cultural, and economic issues that may impact their accessibility to Latinas in the community. For example, service agencies should have bilingual and bicultural staff persons, should understand that Latinas may believe sacrifice for the family and keeping the family intact is im-portant, that Latinas' economic dependence may make them less able to take action, and that Latinas may fear that the social stigma of rape or intimate partner violence, if it is known, will affect not only them but their family as well. Furthermore, immigrant women may fear deportation, incarceration, or sexual abuse if they take complaints to legal authorities (Arguelles & Rivero, 1995).

CONCLUSION

For Latinas, each of these topics intersects with other issues, such as poverty, the secondary status of Latinas/os in U.S. society, and man-dates for women's behavior derived from both Latina/o cultures and the larger U.S. society. These are all inseparable elements of the lived experience of Latinas. For Latinas, being poor is equally as oppressive as discrimination based on race and ethnicity, or being subjected to sex-ism either by Latino or non-Latino men. The limited number of Latinas in higher education, for example, is due not just to racism; it is also due to living and growing up in poor communities with inadequate schools and to the secondary status of women in Latina/o and non-Latina/o society. Researchers are only beginning to uncover how these elements interactively influence the development, mental and physical well-being, and behavior of Latinas.

The diversity inherent in the Latina population has been a thread running throughout this lecture. Latinas are from various countries of origin; they are workers, students, scholars, activists, mothers, lesbians, heterosexuals, immigrants, and nonimmigrants. There are factors that separate them from non-Latina women as well as ones that lead to internal divisions, such as skin color, level of acculturation, and coun-try of origin. Because of this diversity, and because they must essen-tially navigate two cultures, they cross multiple contexts, or "borders," everyday (Anzaldúa, 1990). At times, Latinas must cross borders that are alienating, even denigrating, such as when they must interact with health, mental health, or educational institutions that are hostile to them or prefer to exclude them. However, being able to work well in many contexts can also lead to greater strength and a more insightful understanding of oneself. Mainstream psychology has not yet been able to represent this reality adequately.

The notion of border crossing has a deep resonance for me each time I go home to visit my family. In a family of seven children, I have been the only person to go to college, and on top of that I went on to get a PhD. Each homecoming is like moving from one world into another, from one self to another. The transitions are now much smoother for me than in earlier years, but only after a process of coming to understand that at any point in time I am more than one person, one dimension.

Currently, gender meanings and gender relations among Latinas/os are in flux. Instead of using stereotypes to explain gender-related behavior, researchers are either questioning their veracity or even moving beyond them to develop explanatory frameworks that are in greater touch with the multifaceted experience of Latinas. As more researchers, particularly Latina researchers, become involved in the study of gender issues among Latinas/os, a more viable image of this group of women is emerging. Although the diversity and complexity of Latina lives present challenges to researchers, developing a psychology of Latinas can also lead to a more integrative and truly representative discipline of psychology.

REFERENCES

ALARCON, N., CASTILLO, A., & MORAGA, C. (Eds.). (1989). *Third woman: The sexuality of Latinas*. Berkeley, CA: Third Woman Press.

AMARO, H. (1988). Women in the Mexican-American community: Religion, culture, and reproductive attitudes and experience. *Journal of Community Psychology, 20*, 6–20.

AMARO, H., WHITAKER, R., COFFMAN, G., & HEEREN, T. (1990). Acculturation and marijuana and cocaine use: Findings from the HHANES 1982–1984. *American Journal of Public Health, 80*, 54–60.

ANZALDÚA, G. (1990). La conciencia de la mestiza: Towards a new consciousness. In G. Anzaldúa (Ed.), *Making face, making soul, haciendo caras: Creative and critical perspectives by feminists of color* (pp. 377–389). San Francisco: Aunt Lute Books.

ARGUELLES, L., & RIVERO, A. (1995). Violence, migration, and compassionate practice: Conversations with some Latinas we think we know. In J. Adleman & G. Enguídanos (Eds.), *Racism in the lives of women: Testimony, theory, and guides to antiracist practice* (pp. 149–160). New York: Harrington Park Press.

BALDWIN, J. D., WHITELEY, S., & BALDWIN, J. I. (1992). The effect of ethnic group on sexual activities related to contraception and STDs. *Journal of Sex Research, 29*, 141–167.

CAETANO, R., SCHAFER, J., CLARK, C. L., CUNRADI, C. B., & RASPBERRY, K. (2000). Intimate partner violence, acculturation, and alcohol consumption among Hispanic couples in the United States. *Journal of Interpersonal Violence, 15*, 30–45.

CAETANO, R., SCHAFER, J., & CUNRADI, C. (2001). Alcohol-related intimate partner violence among White, Black, and Hispanic couples in the United States. *Alcohol Research and Health, 25*(1), 58–66.

CAETANO, R., SCHAFER, J., FIELD, C., & NELSON, S. M. (2002). Agreement on reports of intimate partner violence among White, Black, and Hispanic couples in the United States. *Journal of Interpersonal Violence, 17*, 1308–1322.

CASTAÑEDA, D. (1985). *Mediation of sexuality during menstruation among Mexican farmworking women: An analysis of differing levels of variables.* Unpublished manuscript.

CASTAÑEDA, D. (1993). The meaning of romantic love among Mexican-Americans. *Journal of Social Behavior and Personality, 8*, 257–272.

CASTILLO, A. (1991). La macha: Toward a beautiful whole self. In C. Trujillo (Ed.), *Chicana lesbians: The girls our mothers warned us about* (pp. 24–48). Berkeley, CA: Third Woman Press.

COLINDRES, C. (1989). A letter to my mother. In N. Alarcon, A. Castillo, & C. Moraga (Eds.), *Third woman: The sexuality of Latinas* (pp. 73–79). Berkeley, CA: Third Woman Press.

ESPÍN, O. M. (1985). Influences on sexuality and Hispanic/Latin women. In C. S. Vance (Ed.), *Pleasure and danger: Exploring female sexuality* (pp. 149–164). Boston: Routledge & Kegan Paul.

ESPÍN, O. M. (1987). Issues of identity in the psychology of Latina lesbians. In Boston Lesbian Psychologies Collective (Ed.), *Lesbian psychologies* (pp. 35–55). Chicago: University of Illinois Press.

FLORES-ORTIZ, Y. G. (1995). Psychotherapy with Chicanas at midlife: Cultural/clinical considerations. In J. Adleman & G. Enguídanos (Eds.), *Racism in the lives of women: Testimony, theory, and guides to antiracist practice* (pp. 251–259). New York: Harrington Park Press.

GONZALEZ, J. T. (1988). Dilemmas of the high-achieving Chicana: The double-bind factor in male/female relationships. *Sex Roles, 18*, 367–380.

HURTADO, A., HAYES-BAUTISTA, D. E., BURCIAGA VALDEZ, R., & HERNANDEZ, A. (1992). *Redefining California: Latino social engagement in a multicultural society.* Los Angeles: UCLA Chicano Studies Research Center.

KLINE, A., KLINE E., & OKEN, E. (1992). Minority women and sexual choice in the age of AIDS. *Social Science and Medicine, 34*, 447–457.

LEADLEY, K., CLARK, C. L., & CAETANO, R. (2000). Couples' drinking patterns, intimate partner violence, and alcohol-related partnership problems. *Journal of Substance Abuse, 11*, 253–263.

MARKIDES, K. S., RAY, L. A., STROUP-BENHAM, C. A., & TREVIÑO, F. (1990). Acculturation and alcohol consumption in the Mexican American population in the southwestern United States: Findings from the HHANES 1982–1984. *American Journal of Public Health, 80*, 42–46.

PADILLA, A. M., & BAIRD, T. L. (1991). Mexican American adolescent sexuality and sexual knowledge: An exploratory study. *Hispanic Journal of Behavioral Sciences, 13*, 95–104.

PADILLA, E. R., & O'GRADY, K. E. (1987). Sexuality among Mexican Americans: A case of sexual stereotyping. *Journal of Personality and Social Psychology, 52*, 5–10.

RAMIREZ, R. R., & DE LA CRUZ, G. P. (2002). *The Hispanic population in the United States: March 2002.* (Current Population Report No. P20–545.) Washington, DC: U.S. Census Bureau.

SCOTT, C. S., SHIFMAN, L., ORR, L., OWEN, R. G., & FAWCETT, N. (1988). Hispanic and Black American adolescents' beliefs relating to sexuality and contraception. *Adolescence, 23*, 667–688.

SORENSON, S. B., & SIEGEL, J. M. (1992). Gender, ethnicity, and sexual assault: Findings from a Los Angeles study. *Journal of Social Issues, 48*, 93–104.

SORENSON, S. B., & TELLES, C. A. (1991). Self-reports of spousal violence in a Mexican-American and non-Hispanic White population. *Violence and Victims, 6*, 3–15.

STRAUS, M. A., & GELLES, R. J. (1990). *Physical violence in American families: Risk factors and adaptations to violence in 8,145 families.* New Brunswick, NJ: Transaction.

TRUJILLO, C. (Ed.). (1991). *Chicana lesbians: The girls our mothers warned us about.* Berkeley, CA: Third Woman Press.

U.S. CENSUS BUREAU. (2004a). *Current population survey, annual social and economic supplement. Table 15.1, Poverty status of families in 2003 by family type, and by Hispanic origin and race of householder: 2004.* Retrieved May 30, 2006, from http://www.census.gov/population/socdemo/hispanic/ASEC2004/2004CPS_tab15.1.pdf

U.S. CENSUS BUREAU. (2004b). *The Hispanic population in the United States: 2004 detailed tables. Table 6.1, Educational attainment of the population 25 years and over by sex, Hispanic origin, and race: 2004.* Retrieved May 30, 2006, from http://www.census.gov/population/www/socdemo/hispanic/cps2004

U.S. CENSUS BUREAU. (2004c). *Current population survey, annual social and economic supplement. Table 10.1, Occupation of the employed civilian population 16 Years and over by sex, Hispanic origin, and race: 2004.* Retrieved May 30, 2006, from http://www.census.gov/population/socdemo/hispanic/ASEC2004/2004CPS_tab10.1c.pdf

U.S. CENSUS BUREAU. (2005a, June). *Population division. Table 4, Annual estimates of the population by age and sex of Hispanic or Latino origin for the United States: April 1, 2000 to July 1, 2004.* Retrieved May 30, 2006, from http://www.census.gov/popest/national/asrh/NC-EST2004/NC-EST2004-04-HISP.xls

U.S. CENSUS BUREAU. (2005b, June). *Population division. Table 4, Annual estimates of the population by age and sex of White alone not Hispanic for the United States: April 1, 2000 to July 1, 2004.* Retrieved May 30, 2006, from http://www.census.gov/popest/national/asrh/NC-EST2004/NC-EST2004-04-WANH.xls

U.S. CENSUS BUREAU. (2005c). *Facts for features. Hispanic heritage month 2005.* Retrieved May 30, 2006, from http://www.census.gov/Press-release/www/releases/archives/facts_for_features_special_editions/005338.html

U.S. DEPARTMENT OF EDUCATION. (2003, August). *National center for educational statistics. Higher education general information survey (HEGIS). Table 270, Doctor's degrees conferred by degree-granting institutions, by racial/ethnic group and sex of student: Selected years, 1976–77 to 2001–02.* Retrieved May 30, 2006, from http://www.ed.gov

WILLIAMS, N. (1988). Role making among married Mexican American women: Issues of class and ethnicity. *Journal of Applied Behavioral Science, 24*, 203–217.

ZAVELLA, P. (1993). Feminist insider dilemmas: Constructing ethnic identity with "Chicana" informants. *Frontiers, 13*, 53–76.

*S*UGGESTED READINGS

ANZALDÚA, G. (Ed.). (1990). *Making face, making soul, haciendo caras: Creative and critical perspectives by feminists of color.* San Francisco: Aunt Lute Books.

FLORES-ORTIZ, Y. (1998). Voices from the couch: The co-creation of a Chicana psychology. In C. Trujillo (Ed.), *Living Chicana theory* (pp. 102–122). Berkeley, CA: Third Woman Press.

HURTADO, A. (2003). *Voicing Chicana feminisms: Young women speak out on sexuality and identity.* New York: New York University Press.

TRUJILLO, C. (Ed.). (1991). *Chicana lesbians: The girls our mothers warned us about.* Berkeley, CA: Third Woman Press.

*A*NGELA **R.** *G*ILLEM *is Professor of Psychology at Arcadia University and is a licensed clinical psychologist. She previously taught psychology of women at The Pennsylvania State University and was a Distinguished Scholar in Residence there during the summer of 1996. She is committed to integrating issues of gender and other aspects of human diversity into her teaching, writing, and clinical practice.*

17

Triple Jeopardy in the Lives of Biracial Black/White Women

❖

Biracial women who are the offspring of one African American parent and one European American parent are the focus of this lecture. Although more has been written about biracial people and about African American women's issues in recent years than in the past (more than 80 percent of articles listed in PsycINFO about Black/White biracial people have been written since 1990), very little has been done to explore the interface of gender and race as it impacts biracial women and girls. In fact, a search of PsycINFO from 1900 through 2005 turned up only 33 articles about biracial women and girls, all of which have been published since 1992. Ten are about Black/White women (Bing, 2004; Buckley & Carter, 2004; Constantine & Gainor, 2004; Gillem, 2000; Henriksen & Trusty, 2004; Rockquemore & Brunsma, 2004; Scales-Trent, 1995; Shorter-Gooden, 2000; Streeter, 1996; Williams, 1999), and three are about Black/White biracial girls (Fields, 1996; Harrison, 1997; Vagas, 1992). Five of these 13 articles are found in one edited volume (Gillem & Thompson, 2004).

This lecture will consider whether biracial women are in multiple jeopardy, being Black (according to the "one-drop rule" that governs how race is constructed

I would like to thank those students and friends who, through their candid, joyous, and often painful sharing, helped me to begin in my exploration of what it is to be biracial. I especially want to thank Erica Freeman, Joy Zarembka, April Brown, Cambria Throne, and Cynthia Sloan-Miller. I would also like to acknowledge those friends and colleagues who have spent their valuable time and energy in helping me to develop my ideas and express them understandably, particularly Ruth Hall, Beverly Greene, Maria Root, and Cathy Thompson.

269

in the United States), female, and the product of a union of members of two antagonistic groups. Given the dearth of research specific to biracial women, I will attempt to construct an answer to this question through a discussion of the relevant theory and research on African American women, biracial people, biracial women and girls, and the social construction of race. Drawing on the paradigm of triple jeopardy that has been proposed by Greene (1994b) to describe the multiple oppressions experienced by Lesbians of Color, I will describe a similar paradigm that may apply to the multiple oppressions that biracial women must manage in their lives. I will also incorporate Root's (1999) ecological construction of racial identity that "explicitly consider[s] the interactive role of geographic history, gender, class, sexual orientation, or generation on the construction of racial or ethnic identity" (p. 67). Recognizing that multiple oppressions have more than an additive effect on people's lives, I will call my paradigm triple jeopardy.

THE DOUBLE JEOPARDY OF AFRICAN AMERICAN WOMEN

In 1904, Mary Church Terrell stated that "not only are colored women... handicapped on account of their sex, but they are almost everywhere baffled and mocked because of their race. Not only because they are women, but because they are colored women" (quoted in King, 1988, p. 42). Greene (1994a) echoed this sentiment when she stated that "gender and race constitute two major dimensions around which most people organize themselves and which influence both their understanding of the world and of their relative place in it" (p. 131). Smith and Stewart (1983) developed a model that suggests that racism and sexism provide contexts for each other that produce not only cumulative or parallel effects on Black women's lives but also interactive effects. This phenomenon has been referred to as "double jeopardy" by a number of authors (Fleming, 1983; King, 1988; Smith & Stewart, 1983). The interaction of these two oppressions may lead to the development of psychological strengths to cope with adversity in some areas of Black women's lives, but in other areas there may be negative effects, accounting, for example, for Black women's low socioeconomic status and proneness to depression. Thus, Smith and Stewart (1983) suggested that this complex interaction of oppressions might produce a qualitative difference between the effects of racism on Black men and those on Black women and between the effects of sexism on Black women and those on White women.

Fleming (1983) and Allen (1992) observed the double-jeopardy phenomenon in Black college women. Fleming found that the racially adverse conditions of predominantly White colleges were related to self-reliance and enhanced coping and survival skills, articulateness, Black ideological consciousness, and assertiveness in African American women, but they were also related to lower academic performance and greater negative feelings and dissatisfaction with their college experience. On the other hand, she found that the academically supportive atmosphere of Black colleges was related to academic motivation, confidence, and perform-ance, but apparently the presence of large numbers of African American men may have encouraged passivity, reduced social assertiveness, and increased shyness, submissiveness, and fear of confrontation—all stere-otypical, and often problematic, "feminine" characteristics. These findings have been fairly consistent across a number of studies that involve Black college women (Allen, 1992; Fleming, 1983; Smith, 1982). In comparison, Allen (1992) found that it has been consistently advantageous, both aca-demically and psychologically, for Black men to attend Black colleges.

Further, despite higher scholastic achievement than Black men in high school and overall lower fear of success than White women (Smith, 1982), Black women had lower career aspirations in college than did Black men. Most aspired to stereotypical female jobs with less prestige and power and lower pay (Allen, 1992; Smith, 1982) than their Black male counterparts were seeking. These lower aspirations lead Black women to the bottom of the occupational pyramid in low-status service jobs (Fleming, 1983), where they earn a median income of $3,120 less than Black men and $5,044 less than White women for full-time work (U.S. Bureau of Labor Statistics, 2005). Over 60 percent of African American women hold jobs in the serv-ice and sales economy (e.g., waitresses, store clerks) with little chance of advancement (Matlin, 1996; U.S. Bureau of Labor Statistics, 2005). It's no wonder, then, that Black women report lower psychological well-being than Black men and White men and women and are two to three times more likely than Black men to experience depression in their lives (Matlin, 1996). In contrast, Smith (1982) has found that Black women have a positive sense of themselves despite the double jeopardy of racism and sexism. It would appear then, that Black women develop strength in the face of racial adversity but pay a high price for it academically and profes-sionally. On the other hand, they gain academically in a racially support-ive atmosphere but lose strength in their relationships with Black men, as White women do with White men.

The strengths that Black women display in some contexts often lead to stereotypes of them as domineering matriarchs. Because of this stere-otype, African American women have been blamed for everything from the deterioration of the Black family (the "normal" role of dominance being reserved, of course, for men) to the "castration" of Black boys and men, which ultimately leads to their imprisonment and endangerment. Black women have also been stereotyped as not being in need of the kind of emotional support and physical help that White women supposedly deserve. This was eloquently addressed in Sojourner Truth's famous "Ain't I a Woman?" speech. Fleming (1983) concluded that the concept of the Black matriarchy is a myth despite the strength that many African American women evidence in some contexts. Instead, Fleming interpreted this strength not in terms of Black women being more domineering than Black men, but in terms of Black women being less passive and dependent than White women because of a long history of self-reliance and an orientation toward serving the family. One ought not confuse strength with dominance (Ladner, 1971, cited in Smith, 1982).

Thus, theory and research point to the existence of double jeopardy for African American women with regard to the interaction of the dual oppressions of racism and sexism, as well as in their adaptive and maladaptive responses to those oppressions. I suspect that many biracial women are subject to similar jeopardy, particularly if they self-identify as Black or are perceived as Black because of physical appearance. Research on biracial people in general may provide a clue to yet a third level of oppression that may interact with race and gender oppression to enhance the social and psychological jeopardy of biracial women.

BIRACIAL RESEARCH AND THE SOCIAL CONSTRUCTION OF RACE

I became interested in issues concerning biracial people as a result of my interaction with a group of biracial college students during a prefreshman orientation program for Students of Color. During an extended discussion with students of mixed heritage, I learned of both the joys and the sorrows of growing up biracial in the United States. I heard them speak of feeling "torn," "split," guilty, and without a community. But I also heard them speak of feeling more sensitive, unique, and happy in their inherent diversity; challenged and lucky at having two cultural heritages; and pleased to represent a "coming together of differences," "a point of connection, a link." Thus, in spite of the challenges associated with making their way in a racialized society, these young people have been able to harness the richness of their dual heritages as a resource in their lives. This was explored more fully by Edwards and Pedrotti (2004), who suggested a strengths-based approach to biracial people's experiences based on positive psychology.

Much of what has been written about biracial people has been related to racial identity and self-concept. These have been of interest to many researchers primarily because of the way that race is constructed in our society. Root (1990) suggested that racial identity development and self-concept can be especially difficult for biracial people because of the tension between the two racial components of the self, and she asserted that rejecting part of their heritage most likely reflects racial discrimination within the nuclear and/or extended families. This also represents internalized oppression for biracial people. Sebring (1985) said that adopting a monoracial identity can lead to "massive guilt" and "feelings of disloyalty" (pp. 6–7), and many biracial people themselves have indicated that being forced to adopt a monoracial identity is emotionally damaging and feels like a betrayal of the self (Watts, 1991; Williams, 1999). To understand this potential for damage, we need to consider the racial history of the United States. The practice of monoracial assignment of biracial people in the census is rooted in a history of discrimination against people of African descent. According to the one-drop rule, anyone with "one drop" of African blood is considered Black (Davis, 1991; Spickard, 1992). This hierarchical typology of race, which was developed by Europeans, places White people, Asians, Native Americans, and Africans, respectively, in descending order of evolutionary development (Curchack, 1991; Spickard, 1992). The majority of scientists now agree, however, that the concept of race is itself a myth and that all human populations are racially mixed and have been mixing for thousands of years (Curchack, 1991; Davis, 1991). Thus, this typology has been used to create and justify boundaries between races that are based on phenotype (physical appearance), not genotype (genetic inheritance) (Davis, 1991). For biracial people, this has meant being assigned exclusively to the racial group with the lowest social status. Spickard (1992) suggested that this has been done so that Whites could maintain absolute and undiluted economic, social, and political power in the United States. Thus, the one-drop rule is simply a social fiction with no biological legitimacy. Its use continues to benefit Whites at the expense of Blacks by maintaining a social, political, and economic hierarchy. As the Reverend Joseph Lowery has stated, "What's implied in labeling everybody black [sic] who has any black blood . . . is that you are contaminated" (quoted in Watts, 1991, p. A10).

This social fiction and the historical antagonism of Whites toward Blacks in the United States have given rise, in many African American communities, to a range of strict rules for determining who is Black and who is not. One of these rules is reflected in a "you're either with us or against us" attitude. Negative experiences with Black people, including criticism for identity choices, challenges regarding racial loyalties, and distrust because of Anglicized physical appearance, have been well documented in the biracial literature (e.g., Gillem, Cohn, & Throne, 2001; Rockquemore & Brunsma, 2002; Thompson, 1999; Williams, 1999). Pressure is placed on those who are biracial to identify as Black in order to expand numbers, to increase political strength, and to avoid dilution of what little political power Blacks have managed to gain. In this context, claiming an exclusively Black identity is presumed to establish racial loyalty, and claiming a biracial identity is deemed suspect. However, imposing a Black monoracial identity on biracial persons carries the danger of perpetuating the one-drop rule and not respecting the dual heritage of biracial people.

I am not saying that Black and biracial people should not join forces politically. However, to be unified, they need not be the same. In fact, making sameness a requirement of unity only denies the reality of the diversity of Black people and pressures biracial persons to denounce half of their heritage. This may be psychologically damaging as it imposes an additional layer of racial discrimination from members of a group that should be their allies. Thus, I agree with Root (1994), who has concluded that "multiraciality poses no inherent type of stress [or threat] that would result in psychological maladjustment [or political division]; any distress [or threat] related to being multiracial is likely to be a response to an environment that has internalized racist beliefs" (p. 456).

The difference between the social context of miscegenation in the late 1800s and the context of interracial relationships today is important in further understanding this potential for psychological jeopardy. In the 1800s, most of those who were biracial were mixed race as the result of sexual exploitation of Black women by White slave owners (Davis, 1991; Williamson, 1984). Thus, rejection of their White heritage was consistent with rejection of the illicit, immoral, exploitative means by which it usually occurred and, thus, was adaptive. Today, however, biracial offspring are most often the result of a consensual union between a Black person and a White person based on mutual attraction. (A discussion of whether or not social or economic exploitation exists in these relationships is beyond the scope of this lecture.) Thus, for children of a consensual interracial union, compulsory rejection of a part of their racial heritage may, to them, represent rejection or betrayal of the parent of that race; conversely, a child's racial rejection of either parent may be a reflection of the child's rejection of that racial part of herself. Thus, taking on a monoracial identity may be maladaptive for biracial people.

Root (1990) asserted that, because of racial inequality in our society, biracial people "begin life as marginal people" (p. 185) and experience severe stress in identity development. If parents don't openly talk with each other and their children about racial issues, identity problems could result and contribute to that sense of marginalization. Buckley and Carter (2004) reported that their participants, who were poorly socialized by their families about race, tended to minimize, intellectualize, or deny the salience of race, which could negatively affect their ability to deal with challenges to their racial identity. Their data are consistent with Root's (2001) Biracial Sibling Project findings of problematic family approaches to racial dialogue that leave biracial people without skills to deal effectively with racial issues. One of these is the colorblind approach, in which the parents naively assume that "race is not important" (p. 146). Another is minimization of race by parents who are ill equipped to deal with race themselves.

Sommers (1964) found that identity problems in biracial people tend to result from lack of a secure parental relationship, from society's messages about their parents' social status (for example, that the Black parent has lower status), and from conflicting social and cultural loyalties. These conflicting loyalties can arise out of societal pressures to identify with the "race" of only one parent. When that one parent is Black, and there is little affirming dialogue about race in the family, developing a positive self-concept is even more complex because of the negative information and stereotypes about Black people that are both expressed and implied by our society's treatment of race (Brandell, 1988; Gibbs, 1989; Lyles, Yancey,

Grace, & Carter, 1985). Some of that negative information may even come from the White parent who raises the biracial child (Rockquemore, 2002). Thus, Arnold's (1985) research indicated that biracial children with a Black identity had lower self-concept scores than those with White or biracial identities. Also, Field (1996) found that her White-identified biracial participants who expressed negative feelings about their Black heritage had lower self-concept scores than her Black or biracially identified participants. Thus, for some biracial people, a monoracial identity, whether Black or White, can be a reflection of internalized racism, which involves the acceptance and incorporation of idealized constructions of European Americans and devalued constructions of African Americans.

Conversely, for Storrs's (1999) mixed race participants, a monoracial non-White identity was "psychologically fulfilling" and gave them meaning and a sense of belonging. These women constructed Whiteness as stigmatized and spoiled: "normative, empty, and bland but also as oppressive, prejudicial, and discriminatory" (p. 194) and, thus, something with which they avoided identifying. At the same time, they idealized their non-Whiteness as culturally positive and as providing a home; they established their non-White identities by emphasizing the biological markers of their difference from Whites and by behaving in ways culturally consistent with their non-White heritage. Although Storrs (1999) characterized these essentialist notions as challenging racial boundaries, it seems more like these women were caving in to the status quo essentialist notions of race that have been characterized as problematic in the psychological literature. These women have developed monoracial "oppositional identities," much as did Gillem, Cohn, and Throne's (2001) participant who denigrated Whiteness and idealized Blackness.

As an alternative to forcing a choice between Black and White heritage, current research and theory suggest that we might do better to support the identification of biracial people with both sides of their heritage in order to have a positive biracial identity and healthy psychological adjustment. Those who identify as biracial have been found to have fewer emotional and psychological problems; to have a stronger, more positive sense of identity; and to have greater self-confidence than those who adopt a monoracial label (Arnold, 1985; Watts, 1991). Research has also shown that being raised in interracial families that provide minority status consciousness (Lyles et al., 1985; Miller & Miller, 1990; Wardle, 1987), parental support with regard to encounters with racism (Brandell, 1988; Gibbs & Hines, 1992; Thompson, 1999), and interracial self-labeling (Jacobs, 1978; McRoy & Freeman, 1986; Thompson, 1999) is associated with positive self-concept and identity in biracial people. In addition, Thompson's (1999) participants indicated that their connection to both Black and White sides of their families strongly influenced their decision to identify as biracial and helped them to feel positive about it: "Asserting a biracial identity is one way to recognize and honor the people who were responsible for making them who they are" (p. 144).

However, Rockquemore and Brunsma (2002, 2004) warned against the shortsightedness of privileging biracial identity as an ideal for biracial people. They encouraged an expansion of the discourse on biracial identity by focusing on the multidimensionality and complexity of identity development. They proposed a dynamic model based on interactional validation of identity. Based on their data from 177 survey participants and 25 interviews, they suggested four variations on identity resolution for Black/White biracial people: singular identity, which involves choosing only one racial background; border identity, which blends Black and White and is referred to by most as biracial identity (may be validated or unvalidated in social interaction); protean identity, which changes with life circumstances, much like Root's (1996, 2001) situational identity; and transcendent identity, which involves refusing to have a racial identity, similar in some ways to Root's (2001) symbolic race/ethnicity, in which race or ethnicity is acknowledged without any cultural competence or attachment to the group(s). Like Shorter-Gooden (2000), who contended that the meaning of a biracial identity develops through the interaction between internal experience and the external world of family, community, and society, Rockquemore and Brunsma concluded that interactional validation and invalidation, the push and pull in social relations with Blacks and Whites, are critical in understanding identity resolution in biracial Black/White people.

Root (1990) suggested that, however biracial people identify, they must always accept both sides of their heritage, make their own uncoerced choices, and develop ways to deal with others' perceptions and reactions to them. They need to learn to adjust and function within mainstream society without sacrificing the integrity of their cultural identities (Brown, 1990). Many have suggested that, by doing so, biracial people become more tolerant and less biased individuals (Brandell, 1988; Thompson, 1999) and develop the ability to function within diverse, and even antagonistic, cultural environments (Sebring, 1985; Thompson, 1999; Wardle, 1987). We must remember, however, that our society has not yet gotten beyond racial hierarchy and the one-drop rule. Those who are biracial must often struggle to attain the level of personal integrity that these authors prescribe. Williams (1999) coined the term "simultaneity" to refer to the biracial experience of being in several stages of racial identity at one time, both White identified and Black identified. She was referring to "a combined consciousness that is very difficult to reconcile with existing social constructions of race and racial identity development theory" (p. 34). For example, one biracial woman reported that, despite the fact that her upbringing fits the described ideal, she still always feels that, in both Black and White settings, she is "adopting experiences that are not her own." She reported that, "if I try to be rooted in either culture, my perceptions are never totally genuine" (personal communication, August 17, 1994). She believes that she is both but neither.

BIRACIAL GIRLS AND WOMEN: TRIPLE JEOPARDY?

Sandoval (quoted in Root, 1992) placed the racial hierarchy into a gendered context, in which "the final and fourth category [after White men, White women, and Men of Color in descending order] belongs to Women of Color who become survivors in a dynamic which places them as the final 'other' in a complex of power moves" (p. 5). Root (1992) suggested that biracial men and women would be fifth and sixth, respectively, in this power hierarchy. However, as suggested by Smith and Stewart's (1983) model discussed earlier, multiple oppressions have more than just an additive effect; they have very complex interactive effects on people's lives. For example, Johnson (1992) explained that "the biracial child has a dual minority status both within the larger society as a member or partial member of a devalued racial group and often within the African American community due to perceived lack of 'full' affiliation" (p. 45). The experience of being caught between two antagonistic cultural worlds—not being either, but being both—would seem to compound for biracial women the double jeopardy found in Black women's lives in which the oppressions of racism and sexism have a multiplicative and interactive, not merely additive, relationship (King, 1988).

Jeopardy is multiplied by the stereotypic characterizations of biracial women as exotic, passionate, sexually promiscuous, "Anglicized" versions of Black women (Nakashima, 1992). Root (1990) suggested that biracial women may be less of a threat to Whites than monoracial (Black) women, perhaps because of assumptions of Anglicization. Thus, we see Madison Avenue and Hollywood "diversifying" their ads by using lightskinned or biracial models and actresses to represent Black women, virtually ignoring the other end of the skin color spectrum among Black women. For example, the first Black woman to receive the Best Actress award in the history of the Academy of Motion Pictures is Halle Berry, a biracial woman who played a Black woman in relationship with the White man who executed her Black husband. This often makes biracial women the target of resentment from darker-skinned Black women. "[C]ombined with gender biases such as the unequal distribution of power to women, women being viewed as sex objects, and a woman's worth assessed through her physical appearance, [this has] ... put the multiracial woman at a particular disadvantage" (Root, 1994, p. 457).

Gibbs's (1989) clinical discussion of biracial adolescent girls indicated that they were especially likely to feel ashamed of their Black physical traits and were more likely than boys to feel anxiety about social acceptance. She also found that biracial adolescent girls felt culturally different and rejected by Boys of Color whom they saw as constituting their dating pool (Gibbs & Moskowitz-Sweet, 1991). Similarly, Phillips (2004), in a study that compared biracial Black/White, Asian/White, and Hispanic/White adolescent girls with their monoracial female peers, found that Black/White girls who identified as White appeared to suffer some of the lowest levels of overall well-being among their biracial and mono-racial peers, and they had the lowest levels of global self-esteem and perceived physical attractiveness. However, their biracial Black/White counterparts who identified as Black had among the highest self-esteem, social acceptance, and perceived physical attractiveness. Phillips suggested that the disparity between White identifiers and Black identifiers may have to do with the White standard of beauty in our society and "[t]he degree to which a biracial adolescent girl resembles a typical member of the ethnic group with which she identifies, [which] could easily influence both her level of acceptance by that group and her feelings of self-regard." I suspect that the pressure in our society on all Girls and Women of Color to live up to a White standard of beauty, which, as we all know, is often unrealistic even for White women, may cause some biracial women and girls to be more prone to reject the Black part of their heritage. One biracial college woman, who had resisted rejecting her Black heritage and who reported having achieved a good level of self-esteem, wondered why other Blacks didn't value their hair and skin color as much as they did hers. She eventually "realized that people valued my hair and skin because it is 'good' or closer to White. Of course it was easy for me to accept myself when everybody always told me how beautiful I was and when everybody wanted to play in my hair" (personal communication). She was learning through socialization that her "White features" were especially valuable, whereas "Black features" were not as valuable. It was on this socialization that her good level of self-esteem was based. Thus,

> the outcomes associated with biracial status are not a function of race or ethnicity, per se, but rather of the relationship between individuals and social groups and, in particular, of the cognitions and emotions that individuals have regarding that relationship. That is to say, biracial girls who don't fit in fail to do so not because they are, say, Black and White, but, rather, because the relationship between Blacks and Whites in their society is tension-ridden, and this tension produces a host of other negative sequelae. (Phillips, 2004)

Root (1994) suggested that biracial adolescent girls in some groups have "double lower status" (p. 460) related to being female and racially ambiguous-looking. In recent research (Rockquemore, 2002; Rockquemore & Brunsma, 2004; Thompson, 1999) that supports this idea, both male and female participants had negative interactional experiences with Black people in their lives. However, these experiences were significantly more likely and especially powerful in the lives of biracial Black/White women. Their negative encounters were with Black women and usually centered on their ambiguous physical appearance and the advantage it gave them on the dating scene with Black men, who were seen as an increasingly scarce commodity. They were often accused of thinking they were better than other Blacks. This led many to develop strong anti-Black sentiments, which complicated their racial identity development. Funderburg (1994) suggested that the overvaluing of skin color and physical features in our society makes biracial people especially prized by some as romantic partners; however, the exoticized and Anglicized perception of biracial women can have a negative impact on dating experiences. Many have reported feeling used or mistreated by Black men, as did Jeana Woolley, "to reinforce their legitimacy in terms of the majority population" (quoted in Funderburg, 1994, p. 193) and to get revenge against White men who, many Black men think, have deprived them of power and self-respect. In this sense, as Sandy Shupe suggested, biracial women become a trophy in the struggle between Black and White men (Funderburg, 1994). It is interesting that Rockquemore and Brunsma's (2004; Rockquemore, 2002) male participants received positive attention from women and no negative interactions with men regarding their ambiguous physical features.

Root (1992, 1994) suggested that dating for biracial women may be difficult both because of the sexual stereotypes and Anglicized perceptions and because all dating for biracial women is interracial dating. For example, Thompson's (1999) female participants, more than the male participants, found that their dating pool was limited despite their willingness to date people from a variety of backgrounds. In Roberts-Clarke, Roberts, and Morokoff's (2004) study of how racial identity impacts the dating practices of biracial women, many participants, despite feeling more attractive and interesting to potential partners because they were biracial, felt as if they were in an interracial relationship and somewhat of a cultural outsider, no matter whom they dated. An incident in the early 1990s at a high school in Alabama exemplifies this dilemma. When the principal of the high school attempted to ban interracial couples from the prom, a biracial student, Revonda Bowen, asked him, "Who am I supposed to go with?" He responded that she was a " 'mistake' he wanted to prevent others from making" (Smothers, 1994, p. A16).

Other biracial women have reported being perceived as White and resented by Blacks when they date Blacks (Funderburg, 1994), or they are perceived as trying to pass when dating Whites. Whites often reject biracial women's involvement with White men, particularly if they "appear Black," because they are violating the taboo against interracial dating. Sonia Trowers, who was raised to identify as mixed, attended a predominantly White school and started having problems only when dating became an issue among her all-White set of friends: "I just knew that these White guys in this group I associated with wouldn't have any interest in me" (quoted in Funderburg, 1994, p. 37). When her friends actually started dating, she decided to transfer to a more racially mixed public school to escape the uncomfortable feeling of being left out.

Finally, Thompson (1999) found a difference in the way that her male and female participants responded to negative social interactions about being biracial. The women were more likely to internalize the negativity as indicating that something was wrong with them, and their self-doubts lasted longer after the confrontation. The men tended to let it roll off their backs, externalizing the negative interaction and attributing it to the other person's jealousy or ignorance. She concluded that the women's more relational style seemed to be a significant factor in how they dealt with negative interactions.

CONCLUSION

Research has shown that the multiple oppressions that biracial women face may have a negative effect on their self-esteem, psychological adjustment, social relations, and identity formation. They are routinely confronted with racism and sexism from White-supremacist society. They encounter sexism and internalized racism within the Black community. They may experience guilt about rejecting their White heritage, and their White parent, if they submit to the one-drop rule. On the other hand, they may experience lowered self-esteem and conflicts about rejecting Black heritage, and their Black parent, if they identify as White. They may elicit invalidation in the form of confused, distrustful, or even hostile reactions from the Black community if they adopt a biracial, mixed, or multicultural identity. Thus, there is strong support for the conclusion that biracial women may be in triple jeopardy with regard to both the types of discrimination that they experience and their responses to that discrimination (see also Rockquemore & Brunsma, 2004).

In conclusion, we must consider the possibility that many women who identify themselves as Black in clinical and research settings (often because of a forced choice that does not allow other than a monoracial identity) are, in fact, biracial. When we fail to consider this phenomenon, we lose a sense of the richness of their diverse experiences, we ignore their experiences of invalidation, and we lose accuracy in our data. Furthermore, we need to understand the clinical implications of different life experiences, special stressors and vulnerabilities in biracial women, and their effects on their functioning. This is exemplified in Shorter-Gooden's (2000) case study in which her client's biracial identity issues were not immediately apparent because she identified as African American and socialized almost exclusively with African Americans. However, the impact of racial issues on her life as a biracial Black/White woman was significant in her ability to experience genuine intimacy.

Finally, we need to develop models of healthy racial identity development for biracial women that take their unique statuses into account. As race and gender interact in complex ways in Black women, we need to know more about how they interact in equally complex, and perhaps different, ways in biracial women who may be caught between the rock of gender and the hard place of race.

REFERENCES

ALLEN, W. R. (1992). The color of success: African-American college student outcomes at predominantly White and historically Black public colleges and universities. *Harvard Educational Review, 62*(1), 26–44.

ARNOLD, M. C. (1985). The effects of racial identity on self-concept in interracial children. *Dissertation Abstracts International, 45*(9–A), 3000.

BING, V. M. (2004). Out of the closet but still in hiding: Conflicts and identity issues for a Black-White biracial lesbian. In A. R. Gillem & C. A. Thompson (Eds.), *Biracial women in therapy: Between the rock of gender and the hard place of race* (pp. 185–201). New York: Haworth Press.

BRANDELL, J. R. (1988). Treatment of the biracial child: Theoretical and clinical issues. *Journal of Multicultural Counseling and Development, 16*(4), 76–187.

BROWN, P. M. (1990). Biracial identity and social marginality. *Child and Adolescent Social Work, 7*(4), 319–337.

BUCKLEY, T. R., & CARTER, R. T. (2004). Biracial (Black/White) women: A qualitatives study of racial attitudes and beliefs and their implications for therapy. In A. R. Gillem & C. A. Thompson (Eds.), *Biracial women in therapy: Between the rock of gender and the hard place of race* (pp. 45–64). New York: Haworth Press.

CONSTANTINE, M. G., & GAINOR, K. A. (2004). Depressive symptoms and attitudes toward counseling as predictors of biracial college women's psychological help-seeking behavior. In A. R. Gillem & C. A. Thompson (Eds.), *Biracial women in therapy: Between the rock of gender and the hard place of race* (pp. 147–158). New York: Haworth Press.

CURCHACK, M. P. (1991, November). *Race, language, and culture: Some forgotten anthropological lessons.* Paper presented at the conference on The Inclusive University: Multicultural Perspectives in Higher Education, Oakland, CA.

DAVIS, F. J. (1991). *Who is Black? One nation's definition.* University Park: Pennsylvania State University Press.

EDWARDS, L. M., & PEDROTTI, J. T. (2004). Utilizing the strengths of our cultures: Therapy with biracial women and girls. In A. R. Gillem & C. A. Thompson (Eds.), *Biracial women in therapy: Between the rock of gender and the hard place of race* (pp. 33–43). New York: Haworth Press.

FIELD, L. D. (1996). Piecing together the puzzle: Self-concept and group identity in biracial Black/White youth. In M. P. P. Root (Ed.), *The multiracial experience: Racial borders as the new frontier* (pp. 211–226). Thousand Oaks, CA: Sage.

FIELDS, R. H. (1996). Friendship patterns and peer relations of biracial girls. *Dissertation Abstracts International: Section B: The Sciences and Engineering, 57*(6–B), 4054.

FLEMING, J. (1983). Black women in Black and White college environments: The making of a matriarch. *Journal of Social Issues, 39*(3), 41–54.

FUNDERBURG, L. (1994). *Black, White, other: Biracial Americans talk about race and identity.* New York: William Morrow.

GIBBS, J. T. (1989). Biracial adolescents. In J. T. Gibbs & L. N. Huang (Eds.), *Children of color: Psychological interventions with minority youth* (pp. 322–350). San Francisco: Jossey-Bass.

GIBBS, J. T., & HINES, A. M. (1992). Negotiating ethnic identity: Issues for Black-White biracial adolescents. In M. P. P. Root (Ed.), *Racially mixed people in America* (pp. 223–238). Thousand Oaks, CA: Sage.

GIBBS, J. T., & MOSKOWITZ-SWEET, G. (1991). Clinical and cultural issues in the treatment of biracial and bicultural adolescents. *Families in Society, 72*(10), 579–592.

GILLEM, A. R. (2000). Beyond double jeopardy: Female, biracial, and perceived to be Black. In J. C. Chrisler, C. Golden, & P. D. Rozee (Eds.), *Lectures on the psychology of women* (2nd ed., pp. 199–209). New York: McGraw-Hill.

GILLEM, A. R., COHN, L. R., & THRONE, C. (2001). Black identity in biracial Black/White people: A comparison of Jacqueline who refuses to be exclusively Black and Adolphus who wishes he were. *Cultural Diversity and Ethnic Minority Psychology, 7*(2), 182–196.

GILLEM, A. R., & THOMPSON, C. A. (Eds.). (2004). *Biracial women in therapy: Between the rock of gender and the hard place of race.* New York: Haworth Press.

GREENE, B. (1994a). African American women: Derivatives of racism and sexism in psychotherapy. In E. Tobach & B. Rosoff (Eds.), *Challenging racism and sexism: Alternatives to genetic explanations* (pp. 122–139). New York: Feminist Press.

GREENE, B. (1994b). Lesbian women of color: Triple jeopardy. In L. Comas-Diaz & B. Greene (Eds.), *Women of color: Integrating ethnic and gender identities in psychotherapy* (pp. 389–427). New York: Guilford Press.

HARRISON, P. M. (1997). Racial identification and self-concept issues in biracial girls. *Dissertation Abstracts International: Section B: The Sciences and Engineering, 58*(4–B), 2123.

HENRIKSEN, R. C., JR., & TRUSTY, J. (2004). Understanding and assisting Black/White biracial women in their identity development. In A. R. Gillem & C. A. Thompson (Eds.), *Biracial women in therapy: Between the rock of gender and the hard place of race* (pp. 65–83). New York: Haworth Press.

JACOBS, J. H. (1978). Black/White interracial families: Marital process and identity development in young children. *Dissertation Abstracts International, 38*(10–B), 5023.

JOHNSON, D. J. (1992). Developmental pathways: Toward an ecological theoretical formulation of race identity in Black-White biracial children. In M. P. P. Root (Ed.), *Racially mixed people in America* (pp. 37–49). Thousand Oaks, CA: Sage.

KING, D. K. (1988). Multiple jeopardy, multiple consciousness: The context of a Black feminist ideology. *Signs, 14*(1), 42–72.

LYLES, M. R., YANCEY, A., GRACE, C., & CARTER, J. H. (1985). Racial identity and self-esteem: Problems peculiar to biracial children. *Journal of the American Academy of Child Psychiatry, 24*(2), 150–153.

MATLIN, M. W. (1996). *The psychology of women* (3rd ed.). Fort Worth, TX: Harcourt Brace.

McROY, R. G., & FREEMAN, E. M. (1986). Racial-identity issues among mixed-race children. *Social Work in Education, 8*(3), 164–174.

MILLER, R. L., & MILLER, B. (1990). Mothering the biracial child: Bridging the gaps between African-American and White parenting styles. *Women and Therapy, 10*(1–2), 169–179.

NAKASHIMA, C. L. (1992). An invisible monster: The creation and denial of mixed-race people in America. In M. P. P. Root (Ed.), *Racially mixed people in America* (pp. 162–178). Thousand Oaks, CA: Sage.

PHILLIPS, L. (2004). Fitting in and feeling good: Patterns of self-evaluation and psychological stress among biracial adolescent girls. In A. R. Gillem & C. A. Thompson (Eds.), *Biracial women in therapy: Between the rock of gender and the hard place of race* (pp. 217–236). New York: Haworth Press.

ROBERTS-CLARKE, I., ROBERTS, A. C., & MOROKOFF, P. (2004). Dating practices, racial identity, and psychotherapeutic needs of biracial women. In A. R. Gillem & C. A. Thompson (Eds.), *Biracial women in therapy: Between the rock of gender and the hard place of race* (pp. 103–117). New York: Haworth Press.

ROCKQUEMORE, K. A. (2002). Negotiating the color line: The gendered process of racial identity construction among Black/White biracial women. *Gender and Society, 16*(4), 485–503.

ROCKQUEMORE, K. A., & BRUNSMA, D. L. (2002). *Beyond Black: Biracial identity in America.* Thousand Oaks, CA: Sage.

ROCKQUEMORE, K. A., & BRUNSMA, D. L. (2004). Negotiating racial identity: Biracial women and interactional validation. In A. R. Gillem & C. A. Thompson (Eds.), *Biracial women in therapy: Between the rock of gender and the hard place of race* (pp. 85–102). New York: Haworth Press.

ROOT, M. P. P. (1990). Resolving "other" status: Identity development of biracial individuals. *Women and Therapy, 9*(1–2), 185–205.

ROOT, M. P. P. (1992). Within, between, and beyond race. In M. P. P. Root (Ed.), *Racially mixed people in America* (pp. 3–11). Newbury Park, CA: Sage.

ROOT, M. P. P. (1994). Mixed-race women. In L. Comas-Diaz & B. Greene (Eds.), *Women of color: Integrating ethnic and gender identities in psychotherapy* (pp. 455–478). New York: Guilford Press.

ROOT, M. P. P. (1996). *The multiracial experience: Racial borders as the new frontier.* Thousand Oaks, CA: Sage.

ROOT, M. P. P. (1999). The biracial baby boom: Understanding ecological constructions of racial identity in the 21st century. In R. H. Sheets & E. R. Hollins (Eds.), *Racial and ethnic identity in school practices: Aspects of human development* (pp. 67–89). Mahwah, NJ: Erlbaum.

ROOT, M. P. P. (2001). *Love's revolution: Interracial marriage.* Philadelphia: Temple University Press.

SCALES-TRENT, J. (1995). *Notes of a White Black woman: Race, color, community.* University Park: Pennsylvania State University Press.

SEBRING, D. L. (1985). Considerations in counseling interracial children. *Journal of Non-White Concerns in Personnel and Guidance, 13*(1), 3–9.

SHORTER-GOODEN, K. (2000). Finding the lost part: Identity and the Black/White biracial client. In L. C. Jackson & B. Greene (Eds.), *Psychotherapy with African American women: Innovations in psychodynamic perspective and practice* (pp. 194–207). New York: Guilford Press.

SMITH, A., & STEWART, A. J. (1983). Approaches to studying racism and sexism in Black women's lives. *Journal of Social Issues, 39*(3), 1–15.

SMITH, E. J. (1982). The Black female adolescent: A review of the educational, career, and psychological literature. *Psychology of Women Quarterly, 6*, 261–288.

SMOTHERS, R. (1994, March 16). Principal causes furor on mixed-race couples. *New York Times*, p. A16.

SOMMERS, V. S. (1964). The impact of dual-cultural membership on identity. *Psychiatry, 27*(4), 332–344.

SPICKARD, P. R. (1992). The illogic of American racial categories. In M. P. P. Root (Ed.), *Racially mixed people in America* (pp. 12–23). Thousand Oaks, CA: Sage.

STORRS, D. (1999). Whiteness as stigma: Essentialist identity work by mixed-race women. *Symbolic Interaction, 22*(3), 187–212.

STREETER, C. A. (1996). Ambiguous bodies: Locating Black/White women in cultural representations. In M. P. P. Root (Ed.), *The multiracial experience: Racial borders as the new frontier* (pp. 305–320). Thousand Oaks, CA: Sage.

THOMPSON, C. A. (1999). Identity resolution in biracial Black/White individuals: The process of asserting a biracial identity. *Dissertation Abstracts International: Section B: The Sciences and Engineering, 59*(12–B), 6498.

U.S. BUREAU OF LABOR STATISTICS. (2005). *Labor force statistics from the current population survey.* Retrieved May 25, 2006, from http://www.bls.gov./cps/home.htm#weekearn

VAGAS, R. J. (1992). The psychological and social functioning of latency age Black/White biracial girls from intact interracial families. *Dissertation Abstracts International, 52*(10–B), 5571–5572.

WARDLE, F. (1987). Are you sensitive to interracial children's special identity needs? *Young Children, 42*(2), 53–59.

WATTS, R. A. (1991, January). Not Black, not White, but biracial. *Atlanta Journal and The Atlanta Constitution,* pp. A1, A10.

WILLIAMS, C. B. (1999). Claiming a biracial identity: Resisting social constructions of race and culture. *Journal of Counseling and Development, 77*(1), 32–35.

WILLIAMSON, J. (1984). *New people: Mulattoes and miscegenation in the United States.* New York: New York University Press.

SUGGESTED READINGS

FUNDERBERG, L. (1994). *Black, White, other: Biracial Americans talk about race and identity.* New York: William Morrow.

GILLEM, A. R., & THOMPSON, C. A. (Eds.). (2004). *Biracial women in therapy: Between the rock of gender and the hard place of race.* New York: Haworth Press.

ROCKQUEMORE, K. A., & LASZLOFFY, T. A. (2005). *Raising biracial children.* Lanham, MD: Rowman & Littlefield.

ROOT, M. P. P. (2001). *Love's revolution: Interracial marriage.* Philadelphia: Temple University Press.

*C*AROLYN M. WEST *is Associate Professor of Psychology and the Bartley Dobb Professor for the Study and Prevention of Violence in the Interdisciplinary Arts and Sciences Program at the University of Washington at Tacoma. Dr. West has taught courses on the psychology of women since 1986. She is editor of the book* Violence in the Lives of Black Women: Battered, Black, and Blue *and is best known for her research on violence in ethnic minority families and on images of African American women in popular culture.*

18

Mammy, Jezebel, Sapphire, and Their Homegirls

Developing an "Oppositional Gaze" Toward the Images of Black Women

❖

I collect Black memorabilia such as movie posters and cookie jars that depict images of fat, Black Mammies and Aunt Jemimas. Like other collectors (Motley, Henderson, & Baker, 2003), I am able to look past the distorted physical features and feel the warmth and resilience of my Southern relatives. These items also remind me to recognize and challenge oppressive images on a daily basis. I learned this lesson after attending a large professional convention for psychologists. As I was leaving the hotel restaurant, a White woman asked me to show her to a table. She had mistaken me for a waitress.[1] I was stunned and confused. It ruined my day.

As a feminist psychologist and researcher, I wondered why I, rather than the older White gentleman who was standing next to me, was mistaken for the server. Scholars have discovered that some stereotypes have been activated so frequently, for example through media exposure, that they can occur nonconsciously in the mere presence of a stereotyped group member. If an individual chooses to accept a stereotype, or if he or she simply does not think about it, then the image can influence the way in which they perceive African American women in social situations (Givens & Monahan, 2005). In other words, it is likely that my fellow diner had encountered more Black female servants than Black female university professors, which made it easier for her to assume that I was a waitress, although my dark blue power suit and armful of books suggested otherwise.

[1]This is a disturbingly common event. Many Black women professors have been mistaken for clerical staff and even prostitutes (Byrd & Solomon, 2005; Thomas, Speight, & Witherspoon, 2004).

This incident also raised a second question: Why do I care that a stranger assumes that I am a waitress? Perhaps it was an honest mistake. In any case, I could simply gather my books and move on. However, for me, this event illustrates how stereotypes can become institutionalized and sometimes internalized by Black women. For example, with few employment opportunities after slavery, many African American women worked as domestic servants well into the twentieth century. Because they were overrepresented in these fields, it appeared that Black women were inherently suited to work as domestics and caregivers. This belief can become institutionalized when powerful individuals create social policies and situations, such as job training programs, that discourage higher education and redirect Black women into such low-paying jobs like daycare provider and home health aide. As a result, Black women's formal education opportunities become circumscribed, effectively limiting their occupational options (Davis, 2004). Fortunately, Mozell, my hardworking grandmother, used her experience as a domestic servant to encourage me to stay in school, which enabled me to pursue my professional goals. Other Black women are less fortunate and may lower their academic aspirations.

In addition to caregiving Mammies, African American women are often portrayed as sexually irresponsible, promiscuous Jezebels and as angry, combative Sapphires (Collins, 2000; Jewell, 1993). If you do not believe that these images still exist, spend an afternoon watching television. Although many marginalized groups are stereotyped, including women from all ethnic backgrounds, poor people, and sexual minorities, oppressive images can be more damaging for some groups because there are fewer positive or realistic images to counter these negative representations (Hudson, 1998).

According to bell hooks (1992), a Black feminist scholar, we should take an "oppositional gaze" toward the images of Black women. This requires us to critically examine, challenge, and ultimately deconstruct these images to reflect more positive and accurate representations. This is what I will do in my lecture. First, I will discuss why the Mammy, Jezebel, and Sapphire images were created, why they persist, and how they have evolved into contemporary images of, among others, the strong Black woman, freak, and gangsta girl. These images are rooted in history; shaped by structural inequalities such as race, gender, and class oppression; and further reinforced by the scientific, popular, and social science literature as well as the media, politics, and the law (Collins, 2000; Stephens & Phillips, 2003). Second, researchers have documented a link between the internalization of negative stereotypes and chronic health problems, psychological distress, and low self-esteem (Thomas, Speight, & Witherspoon, 2004). Accordingly, I will discuss how the Mammy image can contribute to role strain, which is the challenge of balancing multiple roles, and to concerns about physical features, including skin color, hair texture, and weight. Next, I will discuss how the Jezebel image shapes perceptions of Black women's sexuality and victimization. Finally, I will explore how Black women's expression of anger is shaped by the Sapphire image.

MAMMY

The Mammy image, which originated in the South after slavery, is one of the most pervasive images of Black women. Christian (1980) described her as

> black in color as well as race and fat with enormous breasts that are full enough to nourish all the children in the world; her head is perpetually covered with her trademark kerchief to hide the kinky hair that marks her as ugly. Tied to her physical characteristics are her personality traits: she is strong, for she certainly has enough girth, but this strength is used in the service to her white master and as a way of keeping her male counterparts in check; she is kind and loyal, for she is a mother; she is sexless... (pp. 12–13)

There is little historic evidence to support the existence of a subordinate, nurturing, self-sacrificing Mammy figure. Enslaved women often were beaten, overworked, and raped. In response, they ran away or helped other slaves escape, fought back when punished, and, in some cases, poisoned slave owners. In order to deal with this uncomfortable reality, historians and authors rewrote history to create the image of the loyal, happy Mammy. After all, if we could believe that Mammy in Margaret Mitchell's novel *Gone with the Wind* was content with her life, we could believe that slavery was a humane institution (Collins, 2000; Jewell, 1993).

Of course, Mammy has not retired. We encounter her in our daily life, for example, as the smiling Aunt Jemima, an icon that has appeared on breakfast products for more than a century. In the 1990s, the Quaker Oats Company removed her trademark red bandana and eliminated her slave dialect. She no longer declared, "Honey, it's easy to be the sweetheart o' yo family. Yo know how de men folks' and de young folks all loves my tasty pancakes." Despite Aunt Jemima's makeover, the Mammy sightings continue. Consider the Pine-Sol lady, a dark-skinned, slightly overweight, motherly figure who smilingly announced, "Honey, it's rain clean Pine-Sol." Are we seeing things? In research conducted by Fuller (2001), college students clearly saw the legacy of the Aunt Jemima image. One student remarked, "They're giving an up-to-date Aunt Jemima image to Black women that clean" (p. 128).

Professional status and education cannot protect Black women from the Mammy image. In 1998, John Gray, an author and psychologist, appeared on the Oprah Winfrey talk show. In response to an audience member's distress, he instructed Ms. Winfrey, one of the most powerful women in the television industry, to give the woman a hug. He went on to say, "Oprah's going to be your mommy... She's the mother of America. That's why she didn't have time for her own kids. She's taking care of all the other lost children" (Burrelle's Transcripts, 1998, p. 8). Jewell (1993) concluded that like many high-achieving Black women, Ms. Winfrey has the additional burden of being a chronic caregiver as she struggles to function as a competent professional.

Role Strain

I do not want to give the impression that caretaking, nurturing, and service to others are negative characteristics. By exhibiting these traits, Black women have contributed to the survival of the African American community. I also do not want to imply that role strain is unique to Black women. Regardless of ethnicity, many women face the challenge of managing the multiple roles of mother, worker, and intimate partner. However, on average, Black women earn less money, have lower levels of education and job status, and are more likely to be single parents than their White peers. As a result, African American women must often perform multiple roles without economic security or partner support (Brown, 2003).

The Mammy image exacerbates role strain by reinforcing the belief that Black women happily seek multiple roles rather than assuming them out of necessity, that they effortlessly meet their many obligations, and that they have no desire to delegate responsibilities to others. Extreme caretaking by African American women has been referred to as *Mammy-ism* (Abdullah, 1998). Hip-hop feminist Joan Morgan (1999) coined the term *strongblackwoman* to describe this image. This spelling implies that *strong, black,* and *woman* are inseparable parts of a seemingly cohesive identity. Both conditions are characterized by a woman's personal sacrifice within her family, community, or workplace, at the expense of her own mental and physical health.

Performing strength as one's identity, in conjunction with role strain, can contribute to depression. For example, in a study of 100 middle-class Black women, Warren (1997) discovered that increased work responsibilities, in the absence of a strong social support system, was related to depression. Again, these feelings may be exacerbated by adherence to the Mammy image. In her memoir, Meri Danquah (1998), a young, single mother who was struggling with depression, wrote that "Black women are supposed to be strong—caretakers, nurturers, healers of people—any of the twelve dozen variations of Mammy" (p. 19). It is not surprising that this expectation made it more difficult for her to seek treatment for her depression.

In some cases, it may be undesirable or emotionally unhealthy to completely abandon important roles, such as nurturer, mother, partner, or activist. On the other hand, endless working, loving, volunteering, organizing, protecting, and saving others, while neglecting one's own needs, can be equally unhealthy. So, what are some solutions to Black women's role strain? As a larger society, it is necessary to address the economic and social inequalities that leave Black women more vulnerable to role strain. This means challenging social and political policies that assume Black women don't need community or government support in the form of social services, such as child support and daycare centers (Harris-Lacewell, 2001). At the individual level, Black women must learn to nurture themselves as well as they nurture others, set boundaries and learn to refuse unreasonable requests, and seek and accept social support. They must give themselves permission to move from superhuman to merely human, which will allow them to express the doubts, fears, depression, and frustration that accompany the hardships they face (Morgan, 1999).

Skin Color and Hair Texture

Recall that Mammy was portrayed as a large, dark-complexioned, bandanna-clad Black woman. The devaluation of Mammy's physical features reinforced a beauty standard that valued white-/light-colored skin; straight, preferably blond hair; and thinness. Collins (2000) reminded us that these physical features "could not be considered beautiful without the Other—Black women with African features of dark skin, broad noses, full lips, and kinky hair" (p. 89). The portrayal of Black women as unappealing Mammies made it easier to deny sexual abuse in plantation households. However, rape and miscegenation, or race mixing, were common occurrences in the antebellum South, which created a variety of skin colors and hair textures among African Americans.

Slaveholders used these physical features to create a hierarchy of beauty and social status within the enslaved community. Bondmen and women with African physical features were considered less attractive and intelligent and thus more suitable for field labor.[2] In contrast, Blacks with lighter skin and straighter hair, often the offspring of White slave owners, were sometimes given more education, less strenuous physical labor, and better housing. These privileges continued after emancipation. In the early 1900s, consistent with the color discrimination perpetuated in the larger society, some Black community members used European physical features to determine admission to schools, churches, and social organizations. For example, in some affluent organized clubs, preference was given to African Americans who were lighter than a paper bag. During the 1960s and early 1970s, the "Black is beautiful movement" was at its height and celebrated African physical features, such as natural hairstyles and dark skin. Yet *colorism*, a discriminatory economic and social system that values light-skinned over dark-skinned people, continues to exist (Hunter, 2005).

Although many Black women are generally happy with their complexion and appearance, particularly if they have strong racial identities and family support, others sometimes feel ashamed and unattractive (Hesse-Biber, Howling, Leavy, & Lovejoy, 2004). These emotional wounds and life restrictions often begin early in life. For example, Marita was playing outside and enjoying the summer afternoon, when her mother yelled, "Come on in the house—it's too hot to be playing out here. I've told you don't play in the sun. You're going to have to get a light-skinned husband for the sake of your children as it is" (p. 4). Other restrictions quickly followed: Don't

[2]Researchers continue to link skin color to intelligence. African Americans who rated their skin color as "light" performed better on a 10-word vocabulary test, and Lynn (2002) concluded that "the level of intelligence in African Americans is significantly determined by the proportion of Caucasian genes" (p. 365).

go swimming because your hair will revert back to its curly texture. Don't wear bright colors, like red or yellow, which are unflattering on darker skin tones (Golden, 2004). During adolescence, this message is reinforced when girls encounter some young men who prefer to date women with more European physical features. One teenager reflected on a high school crush:

> It was obvious and evident that most if not all of the black boys in my school wanted nothing to do with black girls, which was sort of traumatizing.... In the final analysis, I ended up feeling that there was something wrong with him, but it was hell getting there. (Carroll, 1997, pp. 131–132)

The consequences of colorism become more pronounced in adulthood. On average, darker-skinned African American women have lower salaries, less education, and are more likely than their lighter-skinned counterparts to marry less educated men (Hunter, 2005). Although darker-skinned Black women who are educated and financially successful evaluate themselves as positively as their lighter-skinned peers do, their impoverished peers, dark-skinned African American women who most resemble Mammy, report the lowest levels of self-esteem (Thompson & Keith, 2004). In an effort to increase their economic and social opportunities, some Black women use skin lightners and hair relaxers. These products can cause adverse reactions, including severe acne, skin discoloration, and hair breakage when they are misused (Golden, 2004).

Although light-skinned Black women appear to enjoy more privileges, they are sometimes the victims of misdirected hostility. For instance, one Black woman recalled the fights she had with classmates. She wrote: "High yella culud girls with long hair were moving targets for their darker-hued sisters. When girls went after whuppin' your butt, hair was the first thing they went after" (Muse, 1994, p. 127). These rivalries can continue into adolescence as young women compete for men's attention. Although it seems that they enjoy an advantage in the dating game, they also may be highly sexualized or find themselves wondering if partners are more attracted to their physical appearance than to their personalities. In adulthood, their racial identities may be challenged by Whites who discount their Black heritage, whereas Blacks may be suspicious of their commitment to the African American community. They may be accused of trying to "pass" for White or using their physical features to gain unearned opportunities. In response, light-skinned Black women may feel isolated, guilty, and unfairly targeted. Despite these challenges, many light-skinned Black women develop a sense of pride and healthy racial identities (Hunter, 2005).

According to Patton (2006), it is time for African American women to begin their own "Black Beauty Liberation" movement to stop the pain, shame, and competition around skin color and hair texture. Simply changing our language might help. For example, we can challenge ourselves when we refer to wavy or straight hair as "good" hair and curly or kinky hair as "bad" hair. In addition, the media should reflect the diversity of Black beauty by valuing dark skin and kinky hair, physical features that are typically associated with the Mammy image, as much as lighter skin and straight hair. As we broaden our definition of beauty, "African American women begin the process of renaming their beautiful characteristics, not as eye color and hair color, but as pride, intelligence, perseverance and solidarity with one another" (Hunter, 2005, p. 122).

Eating Disorders

Despite their higher rates of obesity, Black women generally report more positive body images than their White counterparts do. In fact, many young Black women celebrate their curves and express great pride in being described as *thick, healthy,* or *phat.* Acceptance of larger body sizes in the Black community and rejection of restrictive White beauty standards may enable some Black women to maintain body satisfaction (Alleyne & LaPoint, 2004; Hesse-Biber et al., 2004). Of course, these cultural factors do not protect all Black women. Some women develop eating disorders, such as anorexia, a syndrome of self-induced weight loss in which a person attempts to become thinner despite the unhealthy consequences. Others are vulnerable to bulimia, an eating disorder characterized by binge eating followed by various forms of purging, including self-induced vomiting or laxative abuse (O'Neill, 2003).

A Black woman's economic situation may interact with the Mammy image to shape the type of eating disorder for which she is at risk. For example, unlike the fictional fat, happy Mammy, Black women who work in low-status jobs are often unhappy. Overeating provides an escape, albeit fleeting, from the stress associated with poverty and emotional deprivation (Beauboeuf-Lafontant, 2003). One impoverished Black woman explained how her oppression contributed to overeating:

> I work for General Electric making batteries, and I know it's killing me. My old man is an alcoholic. My kid's got babies. Things are not well with me. And one thing I know I can do when I come home is cook me a pot of food and sit down in front of the TV and eat it. And you can't take that away from me until you're ready to give me something in its place. (Avery, 1994, p. 7)

If they believe that obesity is culturally normative for poor Black women, healthcare providers may overlook their weight gain and possible eating disorder. As a result, treatment for eating disturbances in this population may be delayed (O'Neill, 2003).

Conversely, in their effort to assimilate into White-dominated school and work environments, upwardly mobile Black women may be pressured to conform to the dominant cultural standards of thinness. A "Mammy-like" appearance would be deemed unattractive, slovenly, and unprofessional. Despite her achievements, Margaret Bass (2000) explained that "my fat belies my new 'white' middle-class status, and I am keenly aware of that each time I enter a room" (p. 225). Her fear of reinforcing the Mammy image made this awareness more painful because "my fat signifies the perpetuation of a stereotype... I look like 'mammy' without her bandanna" (p. 230). Consequently, some Black women engage in excessive dieting in their attempt to distance themselves from the Mammy image.

To conclude, many Black women appreciate their large hips, rounded backside, and ample thighs, especially if they have strong racial identities, reject mainstream beauty standards, and receive favorable comments about their appearance from partners, family, and community members (Hesse-Biber et al., 2004). On the other hand, African American women do not differ significantly from White women in their risk for bulimia and binge-eating disorder (O'Neill, 2003). Furthermore, obesity and its associated health risks, including diabetes and heart disease, are epidemic among Black women. The challenge is to reduce obesity and its health consequences without creating negative body images and unhealthy eating patterns. This requires culturally sensitive programs to meet the health needs of African American women (Alleyne & LaPoint, 2004). In addition, we must attend to Black women's unmet emotional needs, which may lead them to binge eat or engage in restrictive dieting, as well as cultural factors, such as adherence to the emotionally strong Mammy image, which also can contribute to eating problems (Beauboeuf-Lafontant, 2003).

JEZEBEL

In 1619, the first ship loaded with enslaved Africans arrived in Jamestown, Virginia. Upon arrival, bondwomen were placed on the auction block, stripped naked, and examined to determine their reproductive capacity. Once sold, they were coerced, bribed, induced, seduced, ordered, and, of course, violently forced to have sexual relations with slaveholders, their sons, male relatives, and overseers. Sexual terrorism did not end with slavery. During nighttime raids, vigilante groups, such as the Ku Klux Klan, whipped African Americans, destroyed their property, and savagely raped Black women. The Jezebel stereotype, which branded Black women as sexually promiscuous and immoral, was used to rationalize these sexual atrocities. This image gave the impression that Black women could not be rape victims because they always desired sex. Consequently, perpetrators faced few legal or social sanctions for raping Black women (West, 2006).

Referred to as "hoochies," "freaks," "hoodrats," or "chickenheads," contemporary Jezebels can be found jiggling and gyrating in hip-hop music videos. Their scantly clad bodies are often draped over expensive cars or fondled by male rappers. In some hardcore gangsta rap these women are lyrically raped, mutilated, and murdered (for sample song lyrics, see Adams & Fuller, 2006). When the cameras are turned off, the life of a "video vixen" is far less glamorous (Steffans, 2005). Furthermore, characteristics that are associated with the Jezebel image may be projected onto Black women, even when they do not engage in sexually explicit behavior. For example, when exposed to sexually provocative videos, followed by slides of unknown, well-dressed women, White undergraduates more often described the Black women who were depicted in these photos as indecent, promiscuous, sleazy, and sluttish. The researchers concluded that the "perceived traits and conduct of a rather small sample of female Black rappers were generalized to other members of the population, namely Black women, but not to members of alternative populations, such as White women" (Gan, Zillman, & Mitrook, 1997, p. 397).

The Jezebel stereotype also can influence our perceptions of rape survivors. In a date rape scenario, college students were less likely to define the hypothetical incident as rape, believe that it should be reported to the police, and hold the assailant accountable when the victim was Black (Foley, Evanic, Karnik, King, & Parks, 1995). According to the researchers, "racial history and rape myths thus make African American women more vulnerable to forced sexual encounters while simultaneously making accusations of rape more difficult for them" (p. 15). As a result, Black women may receive a "double dose" of cultural rape myths, those that target all survivors and those that claim that Black women are especially deserving of sexual assault. In one study, Black rape survivors who internalized beliefs that were consistent with the Jezebel image, such as "People think Black women are sexually loose," reported more victim blaming, which in turn was related to lower self-esteem (Neville, Heppner, Oh, Spanierman, & Clark, 2004). Acknowledgment of the influence of this image on the mental health of African American survivors may increase their willingness to disclose rape and seek assistance (West, 2002).

How do contemporary Black women create a healthy sexuality in a society that depicts them as oversexed and unrapeable, an image that is now broadcast around the world in the form of 24-hour music videos? Some artists have created alternative beauty standards and a self-possessed sexuality to counter negative images. For example, in her song *Video*, India.Arie asserted, "I'm not the average girl from your video/And I ain't built like a supermodel/But I've learned to love myself unconditionally" (Golden, 2004, p. 104). Other artists have attempted to "reclaim and revise the controlling images, specifically 'the Jezebel,' to express sexual subjectivity" (Emerson, 2002, p. 133) by depicting Black women's sexuality as positive and enjoyable, as, for example in the Salt-n-Pepa song *Let's Talk About Sex*. The difficulty, however, lies in telling the difference between representations of Black women who are sexually liberated and those who are sex objects. Are rappers like Lil' Kim and Foxy Brown victims of the hip-hop industry, examples of repackaged Jezebels, or savvy business women who freely exploit their sexuality for personal financial gain?

SAPPHIRE

During slavery, the "cult of true womanhood" required upper-middle class White women to adhere to a standard of femininity that was characterized by passivity, frailty, and domesticity. In contrast, the traditional standards of womanhood were not applied to Black women. They were characterized as strong, masculinized workhorses who labored with Black men in the fields or as aggressive women who drove their children and partners away with their overbearing natures. The reality is that slaveholders sold Black women's children and husbands away, which caused unimaginable grief and understandable anger. In addition, the absence of their partners compelled African American women to assume traditional men's roles, such as financial providers. Yet, social scientists claimed that Black women's dominance and matriarchal status within their families, rather than discriminatory social policies and economic inequalities, were responsible for the unemployment and the emasculation of Black men, which ultimately resulted in poverty, single parenthood, and the production of criminally inclined, academically low-achieving Black children (Collins, 2000).

The image of the hostile, nagging Black woman was personified by the character Sapphire on the 1940s and 1950s *Amos 'n' Andy* radio and television shows. After years of complaints, the show was taken off the broadcast schedule in 1953 (Jewell, 1993). However, we see traces of this angry sister with an "attitude," such as Omarosa on Donald Trump's *The Apprentice,* and other reality shows and recent movies (Millner, Burt-Murray, & Miller, 2004). Popularized in hip-hop music and urban fiction, Sapphire has now become the "gangsta girl" who is equally as violent as her male peers (Stephens & Phillips, 2003). Sapphire also provides comic relief as Tyler Perry's character Medea (a southern term for "mother dear"). She is a pistol-packing grandmother who is frequently depicted rolling her neck, with both hands on her hips, telling off the person who has just offended her. If this conflict resolution strategy fails, she recommends, "'Take your earrings off!' This is the Black woman's national anthem. She's getting ready to fight" (Perry, 2006, p. 238). The Sapphire image implies that Black women's anger, their justifiable response to societal injustice, is dangerous or funny.

The Sapphire image has the potential to influence how anger is expressed and experienced. Although some Black women perceive this image as powerful, they may be using an angry, self-protective posture to shield themselves from discrimination, victimization, and disappointment. Displays of anger can become dangerous when they reach the "Sapphire level," defined by Childs and Palmer (2001) as a response "that takes an argument to the extreme, which includes losing the perspective of the situation, becoming verbally or physically abusive, throwing things, and venturing into tactics that are below the belt" (p. 5). By lashing out and alienating others, African American women may unwittingly undermine their support system, which leaves them without emotional support. Other African American women fear reinforcing the Sapphire stereotype. In their attempt to appear nonthreatening, they avoid appropriate expressions of anger (Thomas et al., 2004).

What can be done? I believe that we need fewer tongue-in-cheek, humorous accounts of Black women's anger (e.g., Millner et al., 2004; Perry, 2006) and more research should be focused on Black women's daily experiences with anger, which is often fueled by racism and lack of power, control, and respect (Fields et al., 1998). Second, assertiveness training can help some African American women to learn more appropriate ways to manage their anger. Finally, anger can be used to spark change. For example, after viewing Nelly, the rapper, run a credit card through the "crack" of a young Black woman's buttocks, the students at Spelman College, a historically Black women's college in Atlanta, began a "take back the music" protest in response to objectionable song lyrics and videos. These young activists conducted community forums, wrote articles, and lobbied the music industry to change these images (Holsendolph, 2005).

CONCLUSION

In this lecture, I provided a historical overview of three images of Black women (Mammy, Jezebel, and Sapphire). These images were derived from historically constructed conditions; were shaped by structural inequalities, such as racism and sexism; and continue to exist today. They can influence the psychological functioning of many African American women. By taking an "oppositional gaze," as bell hooks (1992) suggested, we can see, name, question, resist, and ultimately transform these and other oppressive images.

REFERENCES

ABDULLAH, A. S. (1998). Mammy-ism: A diagnosis of psychological misorientation for women of African descent. *Journal of Black Psychology, 24,* 196–210.

ADAMS, T. M., & FULLER, D. B. (2006). The words have changed but the ideology remains the same: Misogynistic lyrics in rap music. *Journal of Black Studies, 36,* 938–957.

ALLEYNE, S. I., & LaPOINT, V. (2004). Obesity among Black adolescent girls: Genetic, psychosocial, and cultural influences. *Journal of Black Psychology, 30,* 344–365.

AVERY, B. (1994). Breathing life into ourselves: The evolution of the National Black Women's Health Project. In E. C. White (Ed.), *The Black women's health book: Speaking for ourselves* (pp. 4–10). Seattle, WA: Seal Press.

BASS, M. K. (2000). On being a fat Black girl in a fat-hating culture. In M. Bennett & V. D. Dickerson (Eds.), *Recovering the Black female body: Self-representations by African American women* (pp. 219–230). New Brunswick, NJ: Rutgers University Press.

BEAUBOEUF-LAFONTANT, T. (2003). Strong and large Black women? Exploring relationships between deviant womanhood and weight. *Gender & Society, 17,* 111–121.

BROWN, D. R. (2003). A conceptual model of mental well-being for African American women. In D. R. Brown & V. M. Keith (Eds.), *In and out of our right minds: The mental health of African American women* (pp. 1–19). New York: Columbia University Press.

BURRELLE'S TRANSCRIPTS (1998, July 9). John Gray on loving again [Television series episode]. In Harpo Productions (Producer), *The Oprah Winfrey Show.* Chicago, IL.

BYRD, A., & SOLOMON, A. (2005). *Naked: Black women bare all about their skin, hair, hips, lips, and other parts.* New York: Penguin.

CARROLL, R. (1997). *Sugar in the raw: Voices of young Black girls in America*. New York: Crown.

CHILDS, F., & PALMER, N. (2001). *Going off: A guide for Black women who've just about had enough*. New York: St. Martin's Press.

CHRISTIAN, B. (1980). *Black women novelists: The development of a tradition: 1892–1976*. Westport, CT: Greenwood Press.

COLLINS, P. H. (2000). *Black feminist thought: Knowledge, consciousness, and politics of empowerment*. New York: Routledge.

DANQUAH, M. (1998). *Willow weep for me: A Black woman's journey through depression*. New York: W. W. Norton.

DAVIS, D. (2004). Manufacturing Mammies: The burdens of service work and welfare reform among battered Black women. *Anthropologica, 46*, 273–288.

EMERSON, R. A. (2002). "Where my girls at?" Negotiating Black womanhood in music videos. *Gender & Society, 16*, 115–135.

FIELDS, B., REESMAN, K., ROBINSON, C., SIMS, A., EDWARDS, K., McCALL, B., SHORT, B., THOMAS, S. P. (1998). Anger of African American women in the South. *Issues in Mental Health Nursing, 19*, 353–373.

FOLEY, L. A., EVANCIC, C., KARNIK, K., KING, J., & PARKS, A. (1995). Date rape: Effects of race of assailant and victim and gender of subjects on perceptions. *Journal of Black Psychology, 21*, 6–18.

FULLER, L. (2001). Are we seeing things? The Pine-Sol lady and the ghost of Aunt Jemima. *Journal of Black Studies, 32*, 120–131.

GAN, S., ZILLMANN, D., & MITROOK, M. (1997). Stereotyping effects of Black women's sexual rap on White audience. *Basic and Applied Social Psychology, 19*, 381–399.

GIVENS, S. M., & MONAHAN, J. L. (2005). Priming Mammies, Jezebels, and other controlling images: An examination of the influence of mediated stereotypes on perceptions of an African American woman. *Media Psychology, 7*, 87–106.

GOLDEN, M. (2004). *Don't play in the sun: One woman's journey through the color complex*. New York: Doubleday.

HARRIS-LACEWELL, M. (2001). No place to rest: African American political attitudes and the myth of Black women's strength. *Women & Politics, 23*, 1–33.

HESSE-BIBER, S. N., HOWLING, S. A., LEAVY, P., & LOVEJOY, M. (2004). Racial identity and the development of body image issues among African American adolescent girls. *Qualitative Report, 9*, 49–79.

HOLSENDOLPH, E. (2005, March 24). "Taking back the music": Spelman students combat hip-hop's negative portrayal of Black women. *Black Issues in Higher Education, 22*, 8–9.

HOOKS, B. (1992). *Black looks: Race and representation*. Boston: South End Press.

HUDSON, S. V. (1998). Re-creational television: The paradox of change and continuity within stereotypical iconography. *Sociological Inquiry, 68*, 242–257.

HUNTER, M. L. (2005). *Race, gender, and the politics of skin tone*. New York: Routledge.

JEWELL, K. S. (1993). *From Mammy to Miss America and beyond: Cultural images and the shaping of US social policy*. New York: Routledge.

LYNN, R. (2002). Skin color and intelligence in African Americans. *Population and Environment, 23*, 365–375.

MILLNER, D., BURT-MURRAY, A., & MILLER, M. (2004). *The angry Black woman's guide to life*. New York: Plume.

MORGAN, J. (1999). *When chickenheads come home to roost . . . my life as a hip hop feminist*. New York: Simon & Schuster.

MOTLEY, C. M., HENDERSON, G. R., & BAKER, S. M. (2003). Exploring collective memories associated with African American advertising memorabilia: The good, the bad, and the ugly. *Journal of Advertising, 32,* 47–57.

MUSE, D. (1994). The Bob—Not an Afro, but still a liberating do. In E. Featherston (Ed.), *Skin deep: Women writing on color, culture, and identity* (pp. 125–132). Freedom, CA: Crossing Press.

NEVILLE, H. A., HEPPNER, M. J., OH, E., SPANIERMAN, L. B., & CLARK, M. (2004). General and culturally specific factors influencing Black and White rape survivors' self-esteem. *Psychology of Women Quarterly, 28,* 83–94.

O'NEILL, S. K. (2003). African American women and eating disturbances: A meta-analysis. *Journal of Black Psychology, 29,* 3–16.

PATTON, T. O. (2006). Hey girl, am I more than my hair?: African American women and their struggle with beauty, body image, and hair. *NWSA Journal, 18,* 24–51.

PERRY, T. (2006). *Don't make a Black woman take off her earrings: Medea's uninhibited commentaries on love and life.* New York: Riverhead Books.

STEFFANS, K. (2005). *Confessions of a video vixen.* New York: Amistad.

STEPHENS, D. P., & PHILLIPS, L. D. (2003). Freaks, gold diggers, divas, and dykes: The sociohistorical development of adolescent African American women's sexual scripts. *Sexuality & Culture, 7,* 3–49.

THOMAS, A. J., SPEIGHT, S. L., & WITHERSPOON, K. M., (2004). Internalized oppression among Black women. In J. L. Chin (Ed.), *The psychology of prejudice and discrimination: Bias based on gender and sexual orientation* (Vol. 3, pp. 113–132). Westport, CT: Praeger.

THOMPSON, M. S., & KEITH, V. M. (2004). Copper brown and blue black: Colorism and self-evaluation. In C. Herring, V. M. Keith, & H. D. Horton (Eds.), *Skin deep: How race and complexion matter in the "color-blind" era* (pp. 45–64). Chicago: University of Illinois Press.

WARREN, B. J. (1997). Depression, stressful life events, social support, and self-esteem in middle-class African American women. *Archives of Psychiatric Nursing, 11,* 107–117.

WEST, C. M. (2002). *Violence in the lives of Black women: Battered, black, and blue.* Binghamton, NY: Haworth Press.

WEST, C. M. (Ed.). (2006). *Sexual violence in the lives of African American women: Risk, resilience, and response.* National Online Resource Center on Violence Against Women. http://www.vawnet.org

SUGGESTED READINGS

BYRD, A., & SOLOMON, A. (2005). *Naked: Black women bare all about their skin, hair, hips, lips, and other parts.* New York: Penguin.

COLLINS, P. H. (2004). *Black sexual politics: African Americans, gender, and the new racism.* New York: Routledge.

JONES, C., & SHORTER-GOODEN, K. (2003). *Shifting: The double lives of Black women in America.* New York: Harper Collins.

THOMPKINS, T. (2004). *The real lives of strong Black women: Transcending myths, reclaiming joy.* Chicago: Agate.

*S*UZANNA *M. R*OSE *is Director of Women's Studies and Professor of Psychology at Florida International University. Dr. Rose has taught courses on the
psychology of women, female sexuality, and women and mental health at
Florida, the University of Missouri–St. Louis, and University of Pittsburgh since
1974. Her current research focuses on how gender, race, and sexual orientation
affect the development of friendships and romantic relationships.*

19

Crossing the Color Line in Women's Friendships

❖

As a White woman interested in building friendships across race, I've often reflected on the wisdom of the advice given by African American lesbian poet Pat Parker (1978, p. 68):

> For the white person who wants to know
> how to be my friend
> The first thing you do is to forget that i'm Black.
> Second, you must never forget that i'm Black.
> ——Pat Parker, "For the White Person Who
> Wants to Know How to Be My Friend"
> from *Movement in Black*,
> Firebrand Books, Ithaca, New York.
> Copyright © 1978 by Pat Parker.

The deep truth expressed in this poem is that, in order to cross the color line in friendship, White people simultaneously need to see the other person's individuality free of racial prejudice while always being aware that people of other races have a unique identity that reflects their racial heritage and experiences with racism. A cross-race friendship is not likely to succeed if one person cannot see beyond the other's race. However, it is not sufficient to be "color-blind" in friendship. This denies the Person of Color the reality of her or his life as a member of a racial group with its own cultural values and as a target of racism; it also ignores the history of privileges the White friend has had. A similar point may be made concerning cross-cultural friendships. Women from different cultures, such as American and Arabic or Chinese and Liberian, confront a fundamental Otherness (Bell & Coleman, 1999). A recognition of these differences may be needed before a common ground or empathy can occur and lead to friendship.

Cross-race friendships are significant because understanding women's relationships is important within the realm of the psychology of women. Building alliances among women has been one of the feminist principles that guides research in the field. The idea that "sisterhood is powerful" rests on the assumption that affiliations among women who differ in terms of race, class, culture, sexual orientation, and ability can be developed. The strong racial tensions present in the United States also suggest there is a need for greater racial tolerance. In the near future, one of three Americans will be a member of an ethnic minority, and this will increase the need for racial understanding. In addition, ethnic and cultural prejudices that resulted from the terror attack on the World Trade Center in 2001 point to the need for greater cross-cultural awareness. Cross-race friendships might aid in this process. Having a cross-race friend—as opposed to merely knowing someone of another race as a neighbor or co-worker—is associated with more positive racial attitudes and has been shown experimentally to reduce racial prejudice (Pettigrew, 1997; Wright, Aron, McLaughlin-Volpe, & Ropp, 1997).

Despite the great importance of interracial relationships, little research has been done specifically on cross-race friendship. Hypothetically, transcending the race barrier might be easier for women than men. First, women tend to be more intimate and affectionate with their friends than men are (Duck, 1991). This capacity for intimacy perhaps would enable them to empathize easily with women of other races. Women's stronger orientation toward interpersonal connection may be partly responsible for the positive racial attitudes they express. In a national survey of high school seniors, both Black and White women more than men of those races indicated a willingness to be friends with people of other races (Johnson & Marini, 1998). Intergroup contact in real-world situations also may reduce prejudice. Intergroup contact had a positive and significant effect on the attitudes toward Hispanics of Whites living in an area with a high concentration of Hispanics (Stein, Post, & Rinden, 2000). Second, women of all races share a common oppression based on gender, which, if acknowledged, may enhance a sense of sisterhood.

Contrary to expectation, women and girls do not have more cross-race friends than do men and boys (Smith & Schneider, 2000; Way & Chen, 2000). Little is known about why this occurs. Recently, researchers have begun to ask questions about how same-sex friendships vary across races and cultures. Cultural blueprints for friendship exist that specify who can and cannot be friends, what friends are supposed to do together, and how intimate the friendship will be (McCall, 1988). Discomfort or conflict might occur if the friendship deviates from what is expected. The friendship blueprints of different cultures are just beginning to be explored.

The blueprint in the United States is that friendships typically occur between those who are alike in terms of race, age, sex, social class, sexual orientation, and culture. As a friendship develops, the personality of the friend, as well as similar interests, attitudes, and values, becomes increasingly important. Friends also are expected to be considerate, affectionate, self-disclosing, and companionable (Hays, 1984). In addition, all friendships require trust (Holmes & Rempel, 1989). As friends get to know each other better, they become more vulnerable to one another. Trust is based on the belief that friends will be responsive to one's intimate communications, as well as sometimes make sacrifices to help, if necessary. Once formed, close or best friendships are regarded as virtually self-maintaining (Rose & Serafica, 1986).

The idea of friendship as an intimate, personal, spontaneous, and private relationship between two people reflects a Western, White middle-class notion of friendship. Many cultures do not share the individualism of European and North American societies (Bell & Coleman, 1999). Thus, women from other cultures may hold different values about friendships. For instance, in the United States, friendships are regarded as important, but have no public recognition. In contrast, friendships in South Korea are influenced by Confucianism, which identifies friendship as one of the five basic relationships required for a stable society (French, Bae, Pidada, & Lee, 2006). The word *cheong* describes the intimacy that exists between friends (and family members); it refers to the merging of individuals into a new collective unit. Obligations of the relationship are outlined and incorporate elements of unconditional acceptance, trust, and intimacy, Extremely close Korean friendships imply a sharing of one's life that requires a level of intimacy and merging of identities to a degree that is not reflected in U.S. concepts of friendship.

The blueprints of West African and North American friendships also differ. In Ghana, West Africa, social norms dictate that friendships should be approached with caution. One poem sighted on a Ghanian truck intoned: "Beware of friends. Some are snake under the grass. . . . Some are just no good; Beware of friends (cited in Adams & Plaut, 2003, p. 333). North American norms of friendship are quite different; friends are considered to be "good medicine," and many people want to win friends. The differences may be due to cultural expectations of obligations toward others. The interdependence of West African society may make it more difficult for people to turn down requests for help from a friend, whereas in North America, the obligations of friendship are light, which makes it easy for people to escape from undesirable friendships. Whatever the reason, Ghanaians are more likely than North Americans to say that it is foolish or naïve to have many friends, that one should be cautious or suspicious toward friends, and that friends should provide material and practical support and advice. On the other hand, North Americans value having more friends, think that having no friends would be sad or regrettable, and expect trust and respect from friends (Adams & Plaut, 2003).

Cross-race friendships develop similarly to any other friendship but may also entail additional responsibilities and rewards not associated with same-race relations. My goals in this lecture are to illustrate the barriers to cross-race friendship and examine how those barriers might be overcome, particularly in women's same-sex friendships. Three experiential exercises shown in Table 1 accompany this lecture: (a) a guided fantasy about being a person of another race; (b) an experiential assignment aimed at exposing students to areas of cultural difference; and (c) an essay assignment in which students reflect on cross-race friendships. Responses given by students to Exercise 3 in Psychology of Women classes I have taught are used as examples in the following *discussion*.

TABLE 1

Experiential Exercises on Cross-Race Friendship

Exercise 1: Guided Fantasy on Being a Person of Another Race

Imagine it is morning and you are just waking up. If you are a Person of Color, you will be White when you wake up. If you are White, you will wake up as an African American (or select the minority race that is most represented in your region). As your eyes open, you see your hand against the sheets. What is the color of your skin? You rise and enter the bathroom. You look in the mirror. What do you see? Examine your face. Look down and imagine your body. How does it look and feel to you?

You go into the kitchen and greet the rest of your household. How do they respond to you? How does it feel to be____in this environment? You go outside to get the newspaper. Your neighbors see you. How do they react to you?

You get dressed for school. What do you do to get ready (e.g., hair, clothes)? How do you look? You enter the class. Where do you sit? How does it feel? The professor is talking about race. All the other students are a different race from you. How do you feel?

Later, you go to see a White male teacher about your grade in a course. You believe you deserve a higher grade on an exam. You show the professor where you got your information. How does this situation make you feel? What is the outcome?

You meet your girlfriend/boyfriend at a cafe. How comfortable is the situation? How comfortable is your girlfriend/boyfriend? How does the server treat you? How do other customers and passersby respond? Now you go to meet your friends. How do you feel with them? What do you do together?

Next, you apply for a job that you want. You ask the personnel director for an application. How do you feel? How does she/he respond? What do you think your chances are of getting the job?

You go home and go to bed. You close your eyes. When you open them again, you will slowly come out of the fantasy. Hold onto the feelings you had. We will discuss them.

Discussion Questions
1. What were the advantages and disadvantages of being another race?
2. How comfortable was your world (family, neighborhood, friends) to a person of another race? How might this affect your ability to form interracial friendships?
3. What was your social world like as a person of another race?
4. How did you feel being the majority/minority race in an academic and job setting? What privileges did you have as a White person? As a Person of Color, how were you treated by White people?
5. What was the most important thing you learned from the race reversal fantasy?

TABLE 1 *(continued)*

Exercise 2: Increasing Race Awareness

Participate in one of the following assignments and write a three-page essay about the experience.

1. Examine the children's section at any bookstore. What is the availability of books with African American, American Indian, Latina/Hispanic, or Asian American children as main characters at the preschool level and from Grades 1 to 6? To what extent are girls vs. boys of different races represented? What content or themes are explored? Discuss what messages are conveyed to girls of different races about themselves by the books or lack of books. What messages are conveyed to White children?

2. Read an issue of *Essence* or *Ebony* or another magazine catering to Women/People of Color. How easy or difficult is it to buy these magazines in your neighborhood? What articles or topics reflect concerns not represented in White-oriented magazines? What did you learn about the women of the race represented in the magazine?

3. It has been said that the most segregated hour in the United States is 11 A.M. Sunday morning. Places of worship are highly race-segregated. Cross the race barrier by attending services at a place of worship that is predominantly for a race not your own. Discuss your reactions to the experience.

4. Compare an issue of the main local paper with an issue of a newspaper aimed primarily at another race (e.g., African American), if you live in a large urban area. What concerns are expressed in the newspaper for People of Color that are not expressed in the White newspaper? To what extent did either paper educate you concerning what it means to be a *woman* of that race?

Exercise 3: Whom to Let In and Whom to Keep Out: Thinking About Friendship

People tend to have friends who are a lot like themselves. As Minnie Bruce Pratt pointed out in her essay *Rebellion,* very early in life we are taught "who to let in and who to keep out" (1991, p. 19). For example, Pratt described how her parents taught her to be cordial to Blacks but never to invite them into the house. In response to the following questions, write a three-page essay about what you have learned about drawing or crossing the color line in friendship.

1. How interested are you in having a same-sex friend of another race? What influence has your family had on your attitudes? How many cross-race close friendships do you have now, if any? What race(s) are they?

2. What is your "friendship potential" as a cross-race friend? How knowledgeable are you about people of other races? (Refer to Exercises 1 and 2.) Generally, White people are less informed about the concerns of People of Color than vice versa. If you are a Person of Color, how much responsibility are you willing to assume in order to educate a White person who has friendship potential about your racial concerns? If you are White, what do you "bring to the table" in terms of contributing to/understanding the concerns of a person of another race? How could you educate yourself about other races, so that you would have more to contribute in a cross-race friendship?

Continued

TABLE 1 (concluded)

3. If you are a Person of Color, what would *inhibit* you from pursuing a same-sex friendship with someone White? If you are White, what would inhibit same-sex friendships with someone of another race?

4. What would *motivate* you to establish a cross-race friendship?

5. Would someone of another race want to be friends with you? Why or why not?

6. What problems might arise in a cross-race friendship that are not likely to occur in a same-race friendship?

7. What benefits are there to having cross-race friendships?

8. What is the likelihood that you would pursue a cross-race friendship in the future? (1 = not at all likely; 7 = highly likely)

9. Specify your race, age, gender.

BARRIERS TO CROSS-RACE FRIENDSHIP

Numerous barriers to cross-race friendship exist. A few that will be covered in this lecture include (a) racism and prejudice, (b) racial segregation of neighborhoods and schools, (c) the expectation by Whites that People of Color must assimilate into a White social world for such friendships to occur, and (d) peer influences.

Racism and Prejudice

Racism and prejudice are the most powerful barriers to establishing cross-race friendship. Prejudice against Black people is predominant in the United States, possibly due to the unique history and subhuman treatment of Africans brought to the colonies as slaves (Amodio & Devine, 2005). However, prejudices exist against many different ethnic groups in American society. Although many White people today consciously reject racist beliefs and assert that everyone should be treated equally regardless of skin color, a majority of Whites hold negative attitudes toward other races, particularly Blacks (e.g., Schuman, Steeh, Bobo, & Krysan, 1997). In one study, 25 to 74 percent of White people selected the following traits to describe Black people: lazy, athletic, rhythmic, low in intelligence, poor, criminal, hostile, and loud (Devine & Elliott, 1995). Sometimes these beliefs are communicated directly by parents, as illustrated by the comments of one White woman student:

> I used to go to bake sales with my mother when I was six. The black people would bring in beautiful pies and cakes, but after they left the church, people threw all of the desserts in the trash. My grandmother told me they were dirty people. . . . My mother also told me that my brother and I were not allowed to walk home from school with a black boy we knew because the neighbors were complaining. Everyone had to stay on their own side of the tracks.

At other times, they are communicated indirectly, as another White woman explained:

> My grade school was considered progressive. It was a mixture of children of university faculty and children from, as my mother euphemistically said, "the other side of town" (black children). While I never heard or saw my mother saying anything overtly racist—indeed, she proclaimed that we were getting a "better education" because we were "exposed to different people"—she was always very condescending toward the mothers of the black girls, taking particular care to explain in a simple way how to fill out the forms to award [Girl Scout] badges. She also made a point of telling me how fortunate I was to "have these experiences." Now, looking back, I realize she was drawing the line between "them" and "us." I also see that in my daily interactions I am still very aware of the line drawn in part by my mother. . . . I am careful with people of other races, take more time to be warm and helpful. . . . Now that I examine those expressions, I'm afraid they are a bit too close to the attitude my mother used to take.

In terms of Black women specifically, Weitz and Gordon (1993) found that White college students ascribe more negative traits to Black women than to American women in general. Almost all (95 percent) described Black women as threatening (argumentative, loud, stubborn, bitchy, or dishonest). About 28 percent endorsed "welfare mother" traits as describing Black women (for example, too many children, fat, and lazy). Only 19 percent selected traits associated with a good mother/wife/daughter image (for example, intelligent, family-oriented, loyal to family ties). In contrast, traits selected by the White women and men for "American women in general" were uniformly more positive, including intelligent, sensitive, attractive, sophisticated, emotional, ambitious, career-oriented, independent, talkative, imaginative, and kind. Similar negative stereotypes about Asian, Latina, and American Indian women exist among Whites and may result in White women rejecting Women of Color as possible candidates for friendship. These stereotypes then may be perceived as "differences" that cannot or should not be transcended, as indicated by a 19-year-old White woman's remark:

> I am not particularly interested in having a friend of another race. If they lived in an entirely black neighborhood, I would be uncomfortable visiting their home. . . . I am more likely to pursue a friendship with those African-Americans who display ambition in business and who try to speak in a well-modulated voice. You might say I [would be willing to be] friends with blacks whom other blacks would refer to as "Uncle Toms," those blacks who show the traits of my white friends. . . . My friends have told me I am a racist and I suppose that I may seem that way to some.

Many White Americans today are not consciously or deliberately prejudiced. Public expressions of racism are discouraged, and many people have a sincere belief that people should be treated equally. Although overt prejudice is less accepted, unconscious or implicit racial biases appear to be quite prevalent. For instance, Whites tend to associate Black faces more strongly with negative words (e.g., awful, repulsive) and to associate White faces more strongly with positive words (e.g., appealing, delightful), which demonstrates an implicit race bias against Black people (Fazio, Jackson, Dunton, & Williams, 1995). This illustrates that deep-seated negative attitudes may be activated when Whites interact with Blacks and other People of Color. These unconscious attitudes may cause them to avoid interactions with people of other races.

Even when a White person does not engage in overtly racist acts, Whites benefit from White racism toward other races. The inadvertent benefits of being White are referred to as "White privilege." For example, a White person with less experience might be able to get a job more easily than a Black person with more experience if the employer thinks that Whites are smarter. The White person is "privileged" over the Black person simply because of skin color.

Do People of Color hold racist views of Whites that result in Whites being perceived as undesirable as friends? According to the definition of racism, People of Color can be *prejudiced* against Whites but cannot accurately be labeled *racist*. "Prejudice" refers to unreasonable or hostile feelings, opinions, or attitudes directed against a racial, religious, or national group or behaviors that discriminate against individual members of such a group. In contrast, racism has two components: (1) the *belief* that one's race is superior and has the right to rule others and (2) a *policy* of enforcing such rights or a *system of government* based on them (Mallon, 1991, p. 115). White people have the power in the United States to put their racial prejudices into action in terms of governmental and institutional policies as specified by this definition; people of other races do not. Moreover, White people benefit from White racism even if they do not support racist policies. For instance, Whites have easier access to mortgages than African Americans in many cities because some banks apply different criteria to Whites who wish to obtain a loan than they do to Blacks. This policy, called *red-lining*, is illegal but widely practiced (e.g., Janofsky, 1998; "Subtle but Odious," 1998).

People of Color who are prejudiced against Whites often develop racial hostility in response to the racism they experience. They frequently operate from three major assumptions (Sue, 1990). First, there is a common saying among Black Americans and other People of Color: "If you really want to know what White folks are thinking or feeling, don't listen to what they say, but how they say it" (p. 427). A second assumption held by many People of Color is that all Whites are racist because they actively or passively participate in racist institutions and benefit from them. Third, many believe that most Whites will go to great lengths to deny that they are racist or biased. These suspicions may make People of Color wary of becoming friends with Whites.

In summary, many White people hold negative attitudes toward People of Color that are likely to inhibit cross-race friendships. People of Color, in turn, may not be very motivated to establish friendships with Whites who do not regard them as peers or who deny that racism exists.

Racial Segregation

Racism has had a profound effect on race relations through the practice of racial segregation within neighborhoods, schools, religious institutions, and the workplace in the United States. Due to school segregation prior to the 1960s, most women over 55 today did not expect to become friends with someone of another race while growing up (Wilson & Russell, 1996). For a short period of time in U.S. history, court-ordered integration in urban areas introduced Whites and Blacks to each other in school settings. However, the nationwide dismantling of school busing programs in the 1980s and 1990s once again reduced opportunities for cross-race friendships between girls.

In racially segregated neighborhoods and schools, cross-race friendships are not an option. In addition, racial segregation can contribute to racial hostility when the only interracial contact that People of Color have is with White people in positions of power and authority over them. As one Black woman explained:

> Growing up, the only Caucasians that I remembered coming into my neighborhood were the bill collectors and the police. The bill collectors came to collect and then were gone. The police came under the guise of law enforcement. I remember some of the Caucasian officers shoving, kicking, and hitting several Black men. . . . It was clear to me that the Caucasian officers were the aggressors, since the Black men were handcuffed and the Black officers stood around without saying a word or stepping in to stop their fellow officers' aggression. Seeing the brutality of those police officers solidified an existing uneasiness [in me] of the Caucasian people. I believe this is the "why" I used to avoid building friendships with other races.

Racially integrated schools are more likely to facilitate cross-race friendships, particularly in the early grades; however, interracial friendships have been found to decline during the teen years. For instance, among third graders in an integrated school, 24 percent of White students named a Black student as a best friend, and 37 percent of Black children named a White child as a best friend in research conducted by Singleton and Asher (1979). These percentages dropped dramatically in high school, when about 8 percent of White 10th graders named a Black student as a best friend, and only 4 percent of Black students named a White student as a best friend. A 19-year-old Black woman student in the Psychology of Women class described how her cross-race friendships were affected as she got older:

> As a young African-American child, I was never given the option to let certain people in or out of my life. Economic segregation decided for me. It decided that I was going to only let my own people into my life. It made me realize at an early age that friends like myself were easy to obtain and very comfortable to have. [Then] we moved to a desegregated neighborhood. . . . Many of the whites in the neighborhood were those who could not afford to make the

suburban exodus [away from blacks]. Our next door neighbors were a very nice white family, except for the father. My sister and I became very close to the children. . . . As we grew older, things changed. . . . The father was very racist and he would do things to make me realize that cross-race friendships were going to be difficult to maintain and rare in my life.

Although integration of predominantly White schools increases the likelihood of cross-race friendship between White and ethnic minority girls, it does not guarantee it. Even in an integrated environment, cross-race friendships may be inhibited by the social segregation of children by race in classrooms and playgrounds (e.g., Black girls playing jump rope, White girls playing hopscotch). Similarly, social class differences between middle-class and low-income children might reinforce racial and cultural divides. School integration also does not guarantee that girls of different racial or ethnic minority groups, such as Latina and Asian, will befriend each other. Hamm (2000) observed an interesting pattern in a racially diverse high school that included African American, Asian American, Latina/o, and European American students where Whites were the majority group. Cross-racial friendships were found among 41 percent of the Asian Americans, 19 percent of the African Americans, and 19 percent of the European Americans (data on Latinas/os were not reported). The typical cross-race friendship constellation was comprised of one White and one racial/ethnic minority student. Friendships among Asian American, African American, and Latina/o students were very rare. Thus, the integration of predominantly White schools appears to encourage cross-race friendships with White girls but may not facilitate friendships between girls from different racial minorities.

Expectation of Assimilation

In discussions of cross-race friendship, White people often assert that they would be glad to have a cross-race friend if they only could find a Person of Color who fit into their social world. In other words, the expectation is that a cross-race friendship will occur only if the Person of Color assimilates into the White person's social group (i.e., knows and conforms to the norms of the White group). This sentiment was directly expressed by one White woman, who indicated that she had never had a friend of another race:

I pursue friendship when I have something in common with the other person. If I met a Black woman who I enjoyed being with . . . I wouldn't hesitate to become friends . . . [if] each of us had the same set of values and lifestyle . . . [but] I can't think of any black people who have the same values and lifestyles as I do. . . . It's not because they're different from me, but because of their values.

There are several possible reasons for White people's reluctance to move outside a White social world. First, because a majority of people in the United States are White, Whites have many individuals of their own race from whom to choose friends. Second, White racism contributes to the attitude that Whites should "stick with their own kind," as well as the belief that People of Color are very different from themselves. Also, many Whites have had little exposure to People of Color on an interpersonal level, as opposed to a formal level, such as boss-employee, and are unfamiliar or uncomfortable with the interests, customs, or styles of interaction with people of other races. Last, White people may believe they have little to gain or learn from a cross-race friendship.

White attitudes such as those described may result in inequities in cross-race friendships, when People of Color are expected to assimilate into White culture, but White people do not reciprocate. For example, Serafica, Weng, and Kim (2000) described how several groups of Asian American women, including Filipinas, Japanese Americans, and Chinese Americans, were accepted as friends and invited into White women's social circles only after they became assimilated, or came to share the norms, values, and attitudes of the White majority. Similarly, Taiwanese students in the United States who had knowledge of American culture had more friendships with Americans than did students who were less assimilated (Ying, 2002).

Language difficulties were reported to be one of the most challenging barriers to cross-race friendship for Asian international women students (Constantine, Kindaichi, Okazaki, Gainor, & Baden, 2005). Limited English skills and unfamiliarity with the U.S. educational system made it a struggle for the Asian Indian, Japanese, Korean, and Vietnamese women to earn the trust and respect of American students. The Asian women also experienced conflict between the traditional gender roles valued in their culture and the expectation for independence and interpersonal assertiveness that was expected of women in the United States. One Korean student noted that: "You have to do almost everything for yourself here [in the United States in order to survive] . . . Relying on people to help you is seen as a weakness [rather than a sign of strength]" (p. 169).

Expectations for emotional support in friendship also may be culturally based. For instance, White women appear to have higher expectations for emotional support in friendship than do Black or Asian women. Cross-race friendships could be impeded if women are not aware of the cultural differences. For instance, White, Black, and Asian American women college students were asked to read about a hypothetical situation in which a close, same-sex friend was experiencing a breakup with a long-term boyfriend (Samter, Whaley, Mortenson, & Burleson, 1997). Then they rated which of nine messages would be most effective in that situation. White American women indicated that highly comforting statements like "That's awful. One minute you think everything's cool, and the next minute you get dumped" would be most effective in helping a same-sex friend. Black and Asian American women also endorsed the highly comforting messages but rated them less highly than White women did. However, Black women also said that low-comfort messages would be helpful, such as: "You are my friend, so I have to be honest with you. You're acting like this is the end of the world, not the end of a relationship."

Messages that White women considered to be "low comfort" or "cold comfort" also were rated more highly by Black women in a study of what type of support from friends was considered to be most helpful (Holmstrom, Burleson, & Jones, 2005). In response to a hypothetical situation, Black women were more likely to say that friends were helpful if they told their friend how to act in a situation, advised the friend to forget about the problem, suggested that there "were more important things in this world" to think about, or otherwise challenged the legitimacy of the friend's perspective. White women rated the preceding behaviors as not helpful and preferred instead a friend who would acknowledge the friend's feelings, indicate that the feelings were understandable, offer to talk about the feelings, and suggest alternative ways to view the situation.

One implication of these results is that cross-race friendships between Black and White American women and between Asian and White American women may be more difficult to establish and maintain than same-race friendships. White women friends view friends as important sources of emotional support and prefer to discuss feelings more than to solve problems. In contrast, emotional support is less central to Black women in friendships, and both Black and Asian American women interpret less comforting types of support to be valuable. Messages from a friend that White women might consider to be "cold comfort" actually may be quite appreciated, and even preferred, by Black women. The different expectations for friendship easily could contribute to feelings of discomfort in cross-race interactions that might inhibit friendships.

Other Women of Color may find the effort to enter a White world to be too great, as one Black woman indicated:

> I am very limited in the amount of time I have to spend cultivating relationships. There are no white people in the places that I enjoy going for recreation such as rollerskating, softball games, and get-togethers with family and friends. . . . White people I know seem to like golfing, tennis, skiing, surfing, bowling, iceskating, and soccer. . . . So, the likelihood of my developing a close relationship with a white person would be dependent upon the amount of effort I put into going outside my boundaries and into an environment which includes whites.

Peer Influences

Opposition from peers is another reason cross-race friends are driven apart at puberty, if not earlier (Wilson & Russell, 1996). Friends may ridicule or reject girls who develop attachments outside their racial group. For example, Black girls who socialize with White girls might be labeled a "UT," or

Uncle Tom. White girls might be called a "wigger," a pejorative term for a White person who acts Black. In some instances, intense social sanctions are enacted against cross-race friendships, including verbal and physical attacks or ostracism, to name a few. Some of this pressure may be fueled by the concern that cross-race mixing even among the same sex may eventually lead to interracial dating. These pressures cause many girls to turn away from cross-race friendships in adolescence, as indicated by a Black woman student:

> I was accepted into the cliques that existed in my private predominantly white elementary school. I felt comfortable being one of the very few black children there. [Then] after attending a predominantly black public school, I saw hostilities that I had not seen or had not noticed before between whites and blacks. . . . My white friends from my previous school would call my mom to ask if I could sleep over at their homes and I would immediately whisper to my mom, "Does her mom know that I am black?" I have preconceived notions that her mom would not want me to sleep over if she knew that I was black. . . . I became unable to relate to my white friends as I had done before. Unconsciously, I was accepting my black peers as my exclusive circle of friends.

A second reason that cross-race friendships drop off in the teen years may have to do with the maturation rates of girls of different races (Wilson & Russell, 1996). For example, more Black than White girls develop breasts or pubic hair by age 8. Black girls also menstruate earlier than White girls, on average. Girls who mature early receive a lot of sexual attention from boys, which draws the girls away from their former activities and derails their friendships with less physically mature girls. As girls enter their teens and young adulthood, issues of beauty and style subvert their cross-race friendships in ways that do not affect men's interracial friendships. In the United States, White women with pale, creamy skin and long, blond, straight hair are widely regarded as the most beautiful; women with deeper shades of skin and dark, kinky hair are placed at a disadvantage in terms of the beauty standard. In adulthood, the economic advantages that accrue to White women due to White skin privilege and through their association with White men further divide women along racial lines.

In summary, the discussion of barriers to cross-race friendship presented here suggests that mutually satisfying and fully reciprocal cross-race friendships may be difficult to establish. A White woman's insensitivity toward racism or unconsciously prejudiced remarks may offend the Woman of Color; conversely, the Woman of Color may not want to assume the extra burden of educating a White woman about racial matters in order to make friends with her. Lack of contact due to racial segregation of schools and neighborhoods also prevents the racial mixing necessary to form friendships. Furthermore, Whites may not extend themselves to People of Color who are not assimilated into White culture. If friendships happen to be formed across the color line, hostile reactions from peers and competition for men or jobs may drive cross-race friends apart.

PROMOTING WOMEN'S CROSS-RACE FRIENDSHIPS

Is it possible for Women of Color and White women to be friends, given the barriers to interracial friendship? Hall and Rose (1996) reported that cross-race friendships between Black and White feminists were most successful when several conditions were met. First, the White woman usually had to initiate the friendship because Black women were hesitant to approach White women as friends due to previous negative experiences with Whites. Second, the friends had to act consciously to establish trust around racial matters. This was accomplished by socializing, not just at work or school, but in each other's homes. Third, the friendships were stronger when White women educated themselves about race and acted as allies against racism in both public and private settings. In return for the extra effort that cross-race friendships seemed to require, the women cited numerous rewards. The insights cross-race friendships provided into another culture were highly valued; examples ranged from being exposed to different types of food or activities to making feminist political work more meaningful. Furthermore, the friendships were often seen as more solid than same-race ones because they were forged more consciously.

It is clear that, once established, cross-race friendships can yield ample benefits to participants. However, interracial relationships are more likely to evolve if certain preconditions are met. Three that will be discussed include (a) contact with people of other races, (b) transformative experiences that challenge prejudiced attitudes, and (c) the willingness of White people to act as allies to People of Color.

Contact

Contact between women of different races is one necessary precondition for the development of cross-race friendships. For women who seldom interacted with someone of another race while growing up, the first place interracial contact is likely to be made is in work, college, or sports settings. These interactions have the potential to lead either to conflict or to friendship. However, there is reason to believe that sustained cross-race contact under certain circumstances will facilitate friendships and racial tolerance toward other members of the friends' respective racial groups (e.g., Thomas, 1995; Wright et al., 1997). Interracial contact provides opportunities where prejudiced attitudes and beliefs can be tested and changed. This is most likely to happen when the two people have equal status (i.e., where both are students) and when the contact is sustained and cooperative (Thomas, 1995). For instance, cross-race friendships among elementary school children in a mixed-race school were similar to those in a same-race school in terms of friendship functions such as loyalty and emotional security (Aboud, Mendelson, Purdy, & Mendip, 2003).

Several women students described having their prejudices disproved by intimate contact with women of another race. Being assigned a Black college roommate who was from the Chicago projects was the impetus for one White woman to face her racial biases. Another woman noticed her own covert stereotyping and racism when she defended to her family a friendship she had with a Black woman: "I responded by saying, 'She's different. She's very educated.'" Similarly, a Black woman who had grown up and lived in a mostly Black environment explained how an intimate disclosure by a White women challenged her preconceived notions about Whites. One day, the White woman asked her for help and confided that she had been sexually abused as a child and was now having marital problems. The Black woman recounted:

> I sat and listened to B— with amazement and disbelief . . . surprised that she trusted me enough to talk openly about her pain . . . and disbelieving that a Caucasian woman could experience any of the things B— had just described to me, especially after seeing the happy-all-the-time June Cleaver depictions on television.

Although still wary of Whites, this personal experience made the woman more willing to respond to those Whites who approached her with personal sincerity.

An added benefit of cross-race friendships is that they appear to increase racial tolerance in those who witness the friends' positive interactions. College students who observed cross-race friends complete a task together became significantly more positive in their attitudes toward the friends' respective racial groups than did observers who watched a neutral or hostile cross-race interaction (Wright et al., 1997). Thus, cross-race friendships may have the potential to affect race relations positively among the friends' extended social network.

Transformative Experiences regarding Race

Consciously sought or serendipitous events concerning race or other experiences of discrimination also may serve as catalysts for challenging racial prejudice and promoting cross-race friendships. Several of the White women interviewed by Hall and Rose (1996) indicated that they consciously and deliberately chose to learn more about race; they educated themselves through reading and talking with both White and Black women. One White woman spoke of the importance of White people "not coming empty to the table" in the discussion concerning race. This relieved the Black women from having to assume the role of educator, a responsibility that was often resented because it reinforced stereotyped roles of the Black woman as the nurturing mother figure (e.g., Mammy) to Whites. For instance, undergraduate Women of Color, including African American, Latina, and Asian American women, indicated that they felt ambivalent about the constant demand to educate Whites about racial matters (Martinez Aleman, 2000). On one hand, they recognized the need to help their White peers who lacked personal experience with racial prejudice and discrimination. On the other hand, they said that the need to educate others took time away from their own personal and intellectual growth.

Other types of transformative experiences may be built on a person's decision that racial prejudice is morally wrong. For example, one 21-year-old White woman had serious arguments with her father about race:

> My father thinks that other races are the reasons this country is in such bad shape. He was an active member of the KKK for a short period of time. . . . Most of his animosity was directed toward blacks. He tried to drill into my head that blacks were bad. . . . But I just knew my father was wrong. . . . [Often] I argued with him about it. . . . I've just never had the prejudice in me.

Similarly, a 35-year-old White woman expressed guilt about her failure to continue friendships with Black women from work outside the work setting. Even though she had been invited to parties and dances by Black co-workers, she had never attended, citing safety as a factor. She pondered whether this was an honest reason or "an excuse not to take the risk to really get to know those who are different." Other White women struggled with having received one message from parents to "love thy neighbor" and treat all people equally and an opposite message when the families deliberately fled from racially mixed neighborhoods and schools.

Transformations in racial attitudes also may develop from empathy related to incidents of discrimination that were not racially based. One 21-year-old woman thought that prejudice directed at her because she was overweight had made her reluctant to judge others based on race. According to a 34-year-old White woman, her family's racial tolerance was expanded by empathy for gay issues:

> The summer of my freshman year, my older brother announced that he was gay. Mike's lover was a black man. . . . That year I discovered how cruel prejudice and fear could be. . . . [There were] nasty phone calls from neighbors. . . . I heard the hushed voices of my parents late into the night . . . [and] was surprised by the cruelty of [his peers]. . . . I often felt his pain. . . . [Then] my brother died of AIDS and I discovered another world of untouchables. . . . In the later years, Mike's partner became a member of our family. . . . We mourned together. . . . When we gathered for dinner in a few months after Mike's death, my father said, "People realize how little differences in color and lifestyles matter when they gotta rally together to survive." His words were profound. As a family, we have come a long way in recognizing our prejudices.

Sometimes the challenge to race prejudice results from a class or lecture such as this one. After completing the three exercises from this lecture, one White woman student wrote:

> Why, now, do I feel uncomfortable when I read the questions in this exercise [on cross-race friendship]? I think that I try very hard to be open-minded,

unprejudiced, nonjudgmental, and I feel disappointed in myself when I am brought face-to-face with my shortcomings in this area. The reality is that intellectually I see similarities between races more than differences, but on a gut level my fear of the differences outweigh rationality.

Another White women who participated in the exercises in this lecture was extremely upset during a discussion of White privilege. She argued that she treated everyone fairly and that she did *not* benefit from institutional racism. However, an event occurred during the semester that forced her to challenge her assumption. In her friendship essay, she had described an incident at work where the cook, a Black male co-worker, had cursed her and mentioned her race. She was shocked at what she labeled "reverse racism" and reported the incident to the White owner of the restaurant. Her view of the situation had changed drastically a few days later, when she presented me with a supplement to the essay. The cook had apologized to her. She learned that he had been forced to do so by the owner, who angrily told him, "You picked the wrong White girl to mess with." The event caused her perception of the situation to shift. She wrote:

> I felt very confused and upset about this. It made me realize that racism really is prejudice + institutional power. The cook may have been prejudiced against me or even angry with all whites. However, I realized that he couldn't have been racist even if he wanted to. He was "put in his place" and made to apologize, not because of our argument, but because he is black and I am white. It was no longer "our" argument. It had become bigger than that and I began to feel like the one to blame. I felt like something had been turned around and I was on the wrong side.

In sum, the intervention by the boss served to reinforce racist values (e.g., "White is right").

For other women, the transformative experience may result from a lifetime of dealing with racism, as suggested by one Black woman:

> At this stage of my life, I don't feel the need to prove anything to anyone. I have broken through enough color barriers and am well aware of my abilities and attributes. If the intended friend is receptive to change, pliable, and willing to ignore possible long-held stereotypes, prejudices, and discriminatory practices, I am more than willing to educate, befriend, evolve, and grow with them.

The ability to look beyond race as suggested by Pat Parker in the opening poem, while simultaneously never forgetting about race, provides an important blueprint for establishing a cross-race friendship, as one Black woman explained:

> I would like to understand the blanket hatred deeply rooted in many Caucasians and be given the opportunity to explain my own deeply embedded anger. If we could come to grips with our inner feelings, bring them to the surface, face and deal with them intelligently, then work toward solving our problems, then we could begin to develop a friendship. . . . There are benefits

to having cross-race friendship. . . . You may share ideas, compare lifestyles, negate the bad, build on the good, break down/shatter barriers, and possibly change the world.

Transformative experiences concerning race suggest that racist attitudes can be unlearned by listening to each other's ideas, learning to disagree with respect instead of derision, working for common goals, and viewing people of other races as "like me" or "insiders," instead of "different" or "outsiders" (Fishbein, 1996).

Becoming an Ally

An ally is "a person who is a member of the 'dominant' or 'majority' group who works to end oppression in his or her personal and professional life through support of, and as an advocate with and for, the oppressed population" (Washington & Evans, 1991, p. 195). According to this definition, becoming an ally around race requires that White women first take the experiences and analyses of Women of Color seriously, then use our race privilege to help change the economic conditions, institutions, and cultural traditions that oppress them (Christensen, 1997). Often, a White woman's first step toward being an ally is likely to occur in the context of peer interaction, when she is confronted with a choice between gaining acceptance by other Whites or supporting a friend of another race. This alliance builds trust in a cross-race friendship. For example, one 22-year-old woman chose to become an ally to a Black friend after she took the friend to a party aboard a boat in an affluent White community. The boat owner, a close White male friend, made comments about how much his property value was being lowered by having someone Black on the boat. She chose to drop the White man as her friend. Her willingness to incur interpersonal losses to resist racism cemented the friendship with the Black friend.

Crossing the line to become an ally is not without its risks (Christensen, 1997). This threat is one faced by Women of Color all of their lives. An excellent historical example of the extreme cost of racism for African Americans is shown in a documentary by Spike Lee, *Four Little Girls*. The film depicts the circumstances surrounding the murder of four Black girls in a church bombed by White supremacists in Birmingham, Alabama, during the civil rights era.

White women who begin to do serious antiracist work may experience negative emotional consequences, such as rejection by peers and family. Their personal safety may also be threatened by White people who turn to violence in order to defend White privilege. By accepting a portion of the violence for crossing the race line, White women are able to stand in solidarity with Women of Color. An example of how one White woman came to be an ally of a Black woman is illustrated in *The Long Walk Home*, a movie starring Whoopi Goldberg as Odessa, a Black maid, and Sissy Spacek as her

White employer, Ms. Thompson. When Odessa joins the 1956 bus boycott organized by Blacks to protest racial segregation of public facilities, Ms. Thompson is faced with a moral decision concerning whether to help her Black employee or to side with White segregationists. The costs and rewards of her eventual choice to act as an ally to Odessa are vividly portrayed.

White people who become allies generally do so after developing a strong understanding of their own racial identity and the consequences of White racism for People of Color. Cross-race friendships are then sought out as opportunities for growth. Such a friendship is movingly illustrated in *Passion Fish*, one of the few films that has addressed the issue of interracial friendship between women.

CONCLUSIONS

The discussion presented here concerning what inhibits and promotes women's cross-race friendships suggests that, although difficult to establish and maintain, such relationships provide numerous interpersonal benefits. In addition, close interracial same-sex relations enhance racial tolerance among the friends' social circles. However, the ability for Women of Color and White women to join together in sisterhood depends, to a large extent, on White women's willingness to confront their own racial prejudices and take the initiative in forming such relationships. Conversely, cross-race friendships require that Women of Color be open to knowing and socializing with White allies.

Last, the friendships are strongest when the relationship is able both to encompass race and to go beyond it. Although friendships have their serious side, the companionship and enjoyment friends provide are highly valued. In other words, as Pat Parker (1978, p. 68) concluded in her poem "For the White Person Who Wants to Know How to Be My Friend": "If you really want to be my friend—*don't* make a labor of it."

REFERENCES

ABOUD, F. E., MENDELSON, M. J., PURDY, K. T., & MENDIP, F. (2003). Cross-race peer relations and friendship quality. *International Journal of Behavioral Development, 27*, 165–173.

ADAMS, G., & PLAUT, V. C. (2003). The cultural grounding of personal relationship: Friendship in North American and West African worlds. *Personal Relationships, 10*, 333–347

AMODIO, D. M., & DEVINE, P. G. (2005). Changing prejudice: The effects of persuasion on implicit and explicit forms of race bias. In T. C. Brock & M. C. Green (Eds.), *Persuasion: Psychological insights and perspectives* (2nd ed., pp. 249–280). Thousand Oaks, CA: Sage.

BELL, S., & COLEMAN, S. (Eds.). (1999). *The anthropology of friendship.* New York: Berg.

CHRISTENSEN, K. (1997). "With whom do you believe your lot is cast?" White feminists and racism. *Signs, 22,* 617–648.

CONSTANTINE, M. G., KINDAICHI, M., OKAZAKI, S., GAINOR, K. A., & BADEN, A. L. (2005). A qualitative investigation of the cultural adjustment experiences of Asian international college women. *Cultural Diversity and Ethnic Minority Psychology, 11,* 162–175.

DEVINE, P. G., & ELLIOTT, A. J. (1995). Are racial stereotypes really fading? The Princeton Trilogy revisited. *Personality and Social Psychology Bulletin, 21,* 1139–1150.

DUCK, S. (1991). *Understanding relationships.* New York: Guilford Press.

FAZIO, R., JACKSON, J., DUNTON, B., & WILLIAMS, C. (1995). Variability in automatic activation as an unobtrusive measure of racial attitudes: A bona fide pipeline? *Journal of Personality and Social Psychology, 69,* 1013–1027.

FISHBEIN, H. (1996). *Peer prejudice and discrimination.* Boulder, CO: Westview.

FRENCH, D. C., BAE, A., PIDADA, S., & LEE, O. (2006). Friendships of Indonesian, South Korean, and U.S. college students. *Personal Relationships, 13,* 69–81.

HALL, R., & ROSE, S. (1996). Friendships between African-American and White lesbians. In J. S. Weinstock & E. D. Rothblum (Eds.), *Lesbian friendships: For ourselves and each other* (pp. 165–191). New York: New York University Press.

HAMM, J. V. (2000). Do birds of a feather flock together? The variable bases for African American, Asian American, and European American adolescents' selection of similar friends. *Developmental Psychology, 36,* 209–219.

HAYS, R. B. (1984). The development and maintenance of friendship. *Journal of Social and Personal Relationships, 6,* 21–37.

HOLMES, J. G., & REMPEL, J. K. (1989). Trust in close relationship. In C. Hendrick (Ed.), *Close relationships* (pp. 187–220). Newbury Park, CA: Sage.

HOLMSTROM, A. J., BURLESON, B. R., & JONES, S. M. (2005). Some consequences for helpers who deliver "cold comfort": Why it's worse for women than men to be inept when providing emotional support. *Sex Roles, 53,* 153–172.

JANOFSKY, M. (1998, February 23). Report finds bias in lending hinders home buying in cities. *New York Times,* p. A13.

JOHNSON, M. K., & MARINI, M. M. (1998). Bridging the racial divide in the United States: The effect of gender. *Social Psychology Quarterly, 61,* 247–258.

MALLON, G. L. (1991). Racism: The White problem. In G. L. Mallon (Ed.), *Resisting racism: An action guide* (pp. 115–118). San Francisco: National Association of Black and White Men Together.

MARTINEZ ALEMAN, A. M. (2000). Race talks: Undergraduate Women of Color and female friendships. *Review of Higher Education, 23,* 133–152.

McCALL, G. J. (1988). The organizational life cycle of relationships. In S. Duck (Ed.), *Handbook of personal relationships: Theory, research, and interventions.* (pp. 467–486). New York: Wiley.

PARKER, P. (1978). For the White person who wants to know how to be my friend. In *Movement in black: The collected poetry of Pat Parker, 1961–1978* (p. 68). Ithaca, NY: Firebrand Books.

PETTIGREW, T. F. (1997). Generalized intergroup contact effects on prejudice. *Personality and Social Psychology Bulletin, 23,* 173–185.

PRATT, M. B. (1991). *Rebellion: Essays, 1980–1991.* Ithaca, NY: Firebrand.

ROSE, S., & SERAFICA, F. C. (1986). Keeping and ending casual, close, and best friendships. *Journal of Social and Personal Relationships, 3,* 275–288.

SAMTER, W., WHALEY, B. B., MORTENSON, S. T., & BURLESON, B. R., (1997). Ethnicity and emotional support in same-sex friendship: A comparison of

Asian-Americans, African Americans, and Euro-Americans. *Personal Relationships, 4,* 413–430.

SCHUMAN, H., STEEH, C., BOBO, L., & KRYSAN, M. (1997). *Racial attitudes in America: Trends and interpretations.* Cambridge, MA: Harvard University Press.

SERAFICA, F. C., WENG, A., & KIM, H. (2000). Asian-American women's friendships and social networks. In J. L. Chin (Ed.), *Asian American women in relationships* (pp. 151–180). Washington, DC: American Psychological Association.

SINGLETON, L. C., & ASHER, S. R. (1979). Racial integration and children's peer preferences: An investigation of developmental and cohort differences. *Child Development, 50,* 936–941.

SMITH, A., & SCHNEIDER, B. H. (2000). The inter-ethnic friendships of adolescent students: A Canadian study. *International Journal of Intercultural Relations, 24,* 247–258.

STEIN, R. M., POST, S. S., & RINDEN, A. L. (2000). Reconciling context and contact effects on racial attitudes. *Political Research Quarterly, 53,* 285–303.

SUBTLE BUT ODIOUS. (1998, March 31). *Washington Post,* p. A16.

SUE, D. W. (1990). Culture-specific strategies in counseling: A conceptual framework. *Professional Psychology, 21,* 424–433.

THOMAS, C. B., JR. (1995). Cross-racial interpersonal relations and job satisfaction. *Social Behavior and Personality, 23,* 345–368.

WASHINGTON, J., & EVANS, N. J. (1991). Becoming an ally. In N. J. Evans & V. Wall (Eds.), *Beyond tolerance: Gays, lesbians, and bisexuals on campus* (pp. 195–203). Alexandria, VA: American College Personnel Associations.

WAY, N., & CHEN, L. (2000). Close and general friendships among African American, Latino, and Asian American adolescents from low-income families. *Journal of Adolescent Research, 15,* 274–301.

WEITZ, R., & GORDON, L. (1993). Images of Black women among Anglo college students. *Sex Roles, 28,* 19–34.

WILSON, M., & RUSSELL, K. (1996). *Divided sisters: Bridging the gap between Black women and White women.* New York: Anchor Books.

WRIGHT, S. C., ARON, A., McLAUGHLIN-VOLPE, T., & ROPP, S. A. (1997). The extended contact effect: Knowledge of cross-group friendships and prejudice. *Journal of Personality and Social Psychology, 73,* 73–90.

YING, Y. (2002). Formation of cross-cultural relationships of Taiwanese international students in the United States. *Journal of Community Psychology, 30,* 45–55.

SUGGESTED READINGS

KATZ, J. H. (1989). *White awareness: Handbook for anti-racism training.* Norman: University of Oklahoma Press.

KIVEL, P. (1995). *Uprooting racism: How White people can work for racial justice.* Gabriola Island, BC: New Society Publishers.

MATHIAS, B., & FRENCH, M. A. (1996). *40 ways to raise a nonracist child.* New York: HarperPerennial.

WILSON, M., & RUSSELL, K. (1996). *Divided sisters: Bridging the gap between Black women and White women.* New York: Anchor Books.

PATRICIA **D. R**OZEE is Professor of Psychology and Women's Studies at California State University at Long Beach. Dr. Rozee has taught courses on the psychology of women since 1983 and conducts research on violence against women, including sexual assault and rape resistance.

20

Women's Fear of Rape

Cause, Consequences, and Coping

❖

Aset of collector prints called "The Four Freedoms" by well-known artist Norman Rockwell was recently advertised in a popular magazine. Rockwell's four freedoms, as immortalized in these Americana prints, are freedom of speech, freedom from want, freedom of worship, and freedom from fear. The artist's message is that these are the freedoms Americans hold most dear. This lecture is concerned with the last of these—freedom from fear. For women in American society, freedom from fear, especially from fear of rape, is far from the present reality. Without freedom from fear, the other three freedoms are not possible. How can you have freedom of speech and worship if you are afraid to leave your house? How can you have freedom from want if your economic opportunities are limited by fear of night work, bad neighborhoods, and aggressive co-workers? In fact, many writers have pointed out that the threat of sexual assault has essentially closed the door on women's freedom. As one therapist expressed it, "I have come to realize that fear is the last remaining enslaver of women" (Leland-Young & Nelson, 1987, p. 203). Women may fear a number of things—getting older, not being thin—but many theorists point out that the fear of rape unites all women (Koss et al., 1994, p. 157).

Feminist theorists Susan Brownmiller (1975) and Susan Griffin (1979), among others, have held that the fear of rape is universal among women. Susan Griffin expressed the feelings of many women when she wrote: "I have never been free of the fear of rape. From a very early age I, like most women, have thought of rape as part of my natural environment—something to be feared and prayed against like fire or lightning" (p. 3). "The fear of rape keeps women off the streets at night. Keeps women at home. Keeps women passive and modest for fear that they be thought provocative" (p. 21).

Both theorists and researchers have considered the fear of rape to be a means of social control, a way to keep women in their place: at home or under male protection. Several studies have shown that, indeed, fear of rape is quite prevalent among women, as are self-imposed restrictive behaviors intended primarily to avoid rape (Riger & Gordon, 1981; Warr, 1985).

In a study of fear of rape among urban women, Mark Warr (1985) found that rape is feared more than any other offense (including murder, assault, and robbery) among women under age 35. Two-thirds of the young women in his study were classified as fearful of rape. One-third of the entire sample reported the highest possible levels of fear (10 on a scale of 0 to 10). When asked to what extent they thought getting raped would be devastating to their lives, nearly half of the women in one of my studies marked the highest possible agreement levels (Rozee-Koker, Wynne, & Mizrahi, 1989). Think about your own fear of rape: How would you rate yourself on the preceding items?

Women's fear of rape is disproportionate to their actual likelihood of being raped (Day, 1999). This has led many researchers to examine social norms for appropriate behavior for women and men. Such norms severely restrict women's full and equal access. Social rules in most cultures convince both women and men to internalize values that restrict women's behavior much more than they do men's behavior. Women, in fact, are expected to self-restrict their behavior or be accused of "asking for trouble" (Day, 1999). Kristin Day (1999), a researcher on urban issues at the University of California, pointed out the way in which such social expectations on college campuses reinforce erroneous notions of comparative risk as well as reinforce the social control of women:

> To the extent that danger of sexual assault on campus is constructed as exclusively stranger related, outdoors, at night, especially without evidence of greater risk under these conditions, universities and individuals reinforce patriarchal domination of public space. (p. 290)

Women's fear of crime, especially rape, results in their use of more precautionary behaviors than men (Riger & Gordon, 1981; Rozee-Koker, 1987). Fear of rape is also the best predictor of the use of isolation behaviors, such as not leaving the house (Riger, Gordon, & LeBailly, 1982), and of assertive behaviors (Rozee-Koker, 1987; Rozee-Koker et al., 1989). Assertive behaviors include "street-savvy" tactics intended to reduce risks in dangerous situations, such as wearing shoes that allow one to run and being aware of whom one sits near on the bus, as well as physical self-defense tactics. Stephanie Riger and Margaret Gordon (1981) conducted in-person interviews with women and found that 41 percent used isolation tactics all or most of the time or fairly often, and 74 percent reported frequent use of street-savvy tactics. Women's fears were most likely to result in avoidance of discretionary activities, those activities they enjoy most, such as visiting friends or going out for evening entertainment.

Although these are disheartening findings in terms of women's free-dom, it occurred to me that the frequent use of active strategies or street savvy by about three-quarters of the women in Riger and Gordon's study could also be looked at in a more positive way. These women are not just sitting around being timid and fearful; they are actively engaged in manipulating a dangerous environment for their own protection. These women are not victims—most women take a great many actions to pre-vent victimization. Later, I will discuss specific avoidance and prevention strategies used by women. But first, let's examine the sociocultural context in which fear develops, including the prevalence of rape worldwide and the factors that put women at risk for rape. We will also examine how and why the fear of rape develops among women and girls.

RAPE PREVALENCE AND RISK FACTORS

Rape is prevalent all over the world. The estimated prevalence among industrialized societies is 21 percent to 27 percent (Koss, Heise, & Russo, 1994). Rough estimates put the prevalence of all kinds of rape at between 43 percent and 90 percent of nonindustrial societies (Rozee, 1993). Heise, Ellsberg, and Gottenmoeller (1999) concluded that rape is the most preva-lent and least recognized human rights issue in the world today.

In the United States, rape prevalence studies find that the current rate of rape has remained the same at 15 percent over the last quarter of a cen-tury (Rozee & Koss, 2001). Eighty-four percent of rape survivors knew their assailants (Koss, Gidycz, & Wisniewski, 1987). Despite these facts, women still fear stranger rape more and take more precautions against it than against acquaintance rape. This is true even when women know acquaintancerape is more common and estimate themselves to have a higher probability of being raped by an acquaintance than by a stranger (Hickman & Muehlenhard, 1997). It is likely that women have a greater sense of control over the circumstances of acquaintance rape, whereas encounters with strangers are frightening (Hickman & Muehlenhard, 1997).

Many researchers have looked at possible behaviors and experiences that may put some women more at risk than others. Known risk factors include use of alcohol, multiple sexual partners, prior victimization, men-tal health issues, and insecurities about relationships with men (Greene & Navarro, 1998). However, the most important finding from these studies is that most rape survivors have *no known risk factors* (Greene & Navarro, 1998) except their gender—being women (Rozee & Koss, 2001).

Rape is a gendered crime—that is, the vast majority of all rapes are perpetrated by men, against women (Rozee & Koss, 2001). Even when sex-ual orientation is taken into account, Moore and Waterman (1999) found that, whether one is male or female, the primary risk factor for acquaint-ance rape is dating men.

DEVELOPMENT OF FEAR OF RAPE

Studies that attempt to explain women's fear of rape have come to a number of conclusions. Women fear rape because women worldwide are the primary victims of rape and other forms of male sexual violence, women perceive a high likelihood of becoming victimized, women are socialized to be vulnerable to rape and to fear it, women are encouraged to believe rape resistance is both futile and dangerous, and the social and institutional systems reinforce fear of rape by placing blame on the victim. Through these mechanisms, women come to fear rape and distrust other people, especially men. In fact, some writers have asserted that the fear of rape is essentially the fear of men (Stanko, 1993).

FEMALE VICTIMIZATION AND ASSESSMENT OF LIKELIHOOD

Early studies repeatedly documented women's greater fear of crime, especially rape. Women report levels of fear three times higher than men's (Stanko, 1993). Women's apparently lower levels of crime victimization compared with those of men in crime victim surveys may lead people to believe that somehow women's fears are not objectively based. But some authors have pointed out the "hidden" forms of victimization of women (Smith, 1988) and the fact that such victimization takes place in a pervasive atmosphere of sexual threat to women (Stanko, 1993). Crime victim surveys frequently do not ask about the forms of victimization most prevalent in women's lives. Women's assessment of the risk for rape is based on a background of other experiences of victimization, from harassment by men on the street and in the office, to obscene phone callers and flashers, to rape by trusted intimates (that is, date, acquaintance, incestuous, and marital rapes) and woman battering. Most women who are beaten and raped are not attacked by strangers but by trusted male intimates. A majority of women who are murdered are murdered by husbands or boyfriends (Barnett & LaViolette, 1993). Elizabeth Stanko (1993) put this sense of sexual danger most succinctly:

> Women gather information about potential personal danger and violence throughout their lifetime (Stanko, 1993). Direct involvement with violence; the "but nothing happened" encounters; observations of other women's degradation; the impact of the media and cultural images of women; and shared knowledge of family, friends, peers, acquaintances and co-workers all contribute to assessments of risk and strategies for safety. (p. 159)

From these observations, women assess their level of sexual vulnerability, and from this assessment comes their level of fear.

There is a strong relationship between experiences of sexual intrusion and fear of rape. Alina Holgate (1989) found that all the women in her sample had experienced fear-inducing sexual intrusions or harassment and that such intrusions were significantly related to reported fear of rape. Every woman had been honked at, whistled at, leered at, propositioned, and commented upon sexually. Nearly all the women (two-thirds or more) reported that they had been followed, physically restrained, pressured for sex, hassled by men in hotels, rubbed against, grabbed, or fondled; they had received obscene phone calls, witnessed a flasher or masturbator, or been in a likely rape situation. The most fearful women were those who had been followed (71 percent) or been in a likely rape situation (62 percent).

Situational or environmental factors can also elicit fear of rape. Research indicates that the physical environment is one of the strongest factors in exacerbating fear of rape and enacting protective strategies among women (Riger & Gordon, 1984). The most fearful situation for the working women in my study was being harassed on the street by men (Rozee-Koker et al., 1989). The strong, negative psychological effects of street harassment reported here belie the common myth among men that women enjoy such attentions and take them as compliments.

Among professional working women, situational factors in the workplace, such as poor lighting, lack of security in parking areas, and sexual harassment contribute to women's fear of rape (Rozee-Koker et al., 1989). The most fearful work-related situations tend to be associated with working late or being in unfamiliar surroundings. Fears directly pertaining to professional travel are the fear of arriving late at night in a distant city, working in unfamiliar parts of town, and fear of travel in rural areas. Working overtime when no one else is around is also fear-inducing for many women. Other major fear-inducing situations are having to be in poorly lighted areas, being alone and having strangers pay unwanted attention to you, being around physically aggressive people, and having to use underground or isolated parking areas.

Women who perceive themselves as having a high likelihood of being raped report more fear of rape (Riger, 1981; Rozee-Koker, 1987). In addition to previous victimization experiences, another way that women assess the likelihood of rape concerns the way rape is represented in the mass media. Media depictions of women as the victims of all manner of brutal sex crimes heighten women's perception of the likelihood of rape. Recently, a number of television commercials sponsored by home security companies and cellular phone companies have capitalized on women's fear of rape in order to sell products. The National Rifle Association has also capitalized on women's increasing fears by offering their particular brand of solution—automatic weapons (Neuborne, 1994). And it has worked. Women are buying guns in unprecedented numbers, despite a threefold increase in the risk of being killed or having someone in one's family killed when there is a gun in the house (Jones, 1994). (See *Ms.* magazine, May/June 1994, for an excellent issue on women and guns.)

The way in which the news media report rape leaves one with the impression that it happens all the time and that women have little or no chance of escaping a would-be rapist. This couldn't be further from the truth. In fact, most women *do* escape. The random-sample survey of households conducted by the National Crime Victim Survey (NCVS, 1987) for the Census Bureau found that there are four attempted rapes for every completed rape (a ratio of 4 to 1). But the press covers only one attempted rape for every 13 completed rapes. This gives the false impression that there are far more completed rapes than attempted rapes, whereas the reverse is actually true (Riger & Gordon, 1989). Why is this important? Because an attempted rape is a rape in which the victim fought back, escaped, and was *not raped*. Women are four times more likely to fight back and escape their would-be rapists than they are to be raped. Who would not be scared if they believed media reports that women are 13 times more likely to be raped than to escape rape? What a terrible disservice this kind of sensationalist reporting is to women! It exaggerates women's helplessness, increases fear of rape among women, and instills a lack of confidence in our ability to fight back.

One lesson that can be learned from the pervasive fear-inducing effects of media presentations of rape is that firsthand experience with rape is not needed to instill a fear of rape among women. In societies where rape is classified as rare, even the concept of rape as communicated through folk tales (for example, when a fictional person is punished by being raped) is effective in keeping women in their place and fearful (Rozee, 1993).

In addition, the racist portrayal by the media of rapists as disproportionately Black men, as well as the greater frequency of arrests of Black men due to inequities in the criminal justice system, leads White women to fear Black men in particular. In truth, most violent crimes are intraracial, occurring primarily between people of the same race and socioeconomic class (Amir, 1971; O'Brien, 1987). When one also considers that many unreported sexual assaults are within families (incestuous or marital rapes), the probability of being sexually assaulted by a person of the same race becomes even greater.

We can conclude, then, that women experience a wide variety of sexual intrusions throughout life, as well as media images of women as ineffective at stopping such intrusions. Women's fear of rape is thus based on an accurate assessment of the risk of sexual intrusion coupled with a wide variety of prior victimization experiences and media reinforcement of the victim image of women.

SOCIALIZATION OF FEAR

Many authors have pointed to the socialization practices of U.S. society and the tendency to encourage girls to be weak and passive and boys to be strong and aggressive. Many women are still raised to defer to men, to support men in their goals, and to expect men to take care of them and protect them. Girls are expected to be ladylike, timid, dependent, and quiet and never to embarrass anyone by making a scene. Many of these socialized traits are in direct opposition to being able to defend oneself successfully. They may also leave women with negative perceptions of their physical competence and a lack of physical strength and endurance. I have seen women at the gym lifting tiny 5-pound weights, one in each hand, and saying to the trainer, "I don't want to get big muscles." A friend told me recently that her former partner used to admonish her to stop working out so much because she was getting too muscular. Why are we socialized to believe that physical strength is a negative trait? Women's negative perceptions of physical competence may play a part in their levels of fear and precaution (Riger, 1981).

In addition, there is a social expectation that women will, and should, have a man to protect them, yet how can women feel safe in the company of men when most rapes are committed by male dates and acquaintances? Still, I have heard female students ask a male stranger (a fellow student) in the class to walk her to her car rather than risk walking with a female friend!

Fear of rape seems to develop early in life. The women in our sample remembered receiving parental warnings between the ages of 2 and 12 years old about avoiding strangers (Rozee-Koker et al., 1989). The nervousness of some parents about this issue is illustrated by the fact that, the *earlier* a girl received warnings about such things as avoiding strangers, the *more often* she was warned to avoid them.

Women receive warnings about various dangers throughout their lives. The warnings come from a number of sources, including parents, boyfriends, friends, and, of course, the media. Martha Burt and Rhoda Estep (1981) described the way in which such warnings communicate a sense of danger among women.

> If warnings reflect other people's expectations that someone needs protecting, the present data on warnings suggest that adult males are perceived as able to take care of themselves, while adult females and children of both sexes received warnings which assume they are in some danger. (p. 516)

Warnings from adult friends and family are a strong predictor of fear of rape. In an effort to be protective, such social contacts share warnings, experiences of crime and fear, and crime rumors and news (Valentine, 1992). Pranks by male friends often reinforce social control through fear. According to Day (1999), women students told her in interviews that male students often do such things as jump out of the bushes at night as a supposedly harmless prank. But the women students reported increased feelings of vulnerability to strangers and often restricted their behavior following such pranks.

RESISTING RAPE

Some parents encourage their young daughters to fight back if ever confronted by a threatening situation. In their book *Stopping Rape: Successful Survival Strategies*, Pauline Bart and Patricia O'Brien (1985) reported the results of in-depth interviews with 94 women volunteers from an urban community who were either raped or who had avoided rape. They found significant racial and ethnic differences in childhood socialization to fight back. A majority of Black women were advised by parents to fight back, whereas Jewish women were least likely of all groups to receive such parental advice. The authors noted that, although verbal skills are prized in traditional Jewish families, physical fighting is considered "un-Jewish." Discussion of rape was reportedly more common among Black families. The Black women in their study seemed to learn how to deal with violence in concrete ways rather than developing a somewhat abstract fear of rape. Black women who were accosted used more kinds of strategies than did other women, and, even though they often faced weapons or multiple offenders, their strategies were more likely to fend off an attacker.

It is interesting that 51 percent of rape avoiders in the Bart and O'Brien study said that fear of rape and/or the determination not to be raped was their main thought in the rape situation, compared with only 7 percent of raped women. Women who were raped were more concerned about avoiding physical injury or death. They reasoned that if they went along with the rape they would reduce the chances of physical injury or death.

Contrary to popular belief, researchers have found that, by physically resisting immediately, women reduce both the chances of being raped and the amount of injury (Bart, 1981; Brown, 1995; Furby & Fischhoff, 1986; Kleck & Sayles, 1990; Koss & Mukai, 1993; Ullman, 1997; Ullman & Knight, 1991, 1992, 1993, 1995; Ullman & Siegel, 1993; Zoucha-Jensen & Coyne, 1993). There is considerable conflict between common cultural myths about rape resistance and the results of published research studies. Cultural myths suggest that rape resistance is both ineffective and dangerous. The first myth is that, if you are accosted by a rapist, it is unlikely that you will be able to escape or fight him off. I mentioned earlier that the National Crime Victim Survey found that there are four attempted rapes for every completed rape (Riger & Gordon, 1989). This means that, for every woman who was raped, four fought off their attacker, escaped from him, or in some other way avoided being raped. The most comprehensive information on rape resistance to date is found in a review article by Sarah Ullman (1997). After reviewing all published studies on rape resistance, she concluded that forceful physical resistance by the victim is consistently related to rape avoidance. Furby and Fischhoff (1986), who conducted an earlier review of the literature, found the same results.

The second myth is that if you try to resist your attacker you are more likely to get hurt. Would it surprise you to know that you are *no* more likely to be hurt by fighting back than you are if you do not resist? Virtually all women who do not resist are raped (Bart, 1981). This is self-evident. What may not be self-evident is that those who fight back are far less likely to be raped and no more likely to be hurt (Bart, 1981; Bart & O'Brien, 1985; Furby & Fischhoff, 1986; Kleck & Sayles, 1990; Ullman, 1997). Brown (1995) pointed out that many police officers and even some rape investigators share the common myth that if you fight back you will be hurt worse. She noted that these myths persist despite a 1989 FBI study that found no correlation between victim resistance and physical injury. When victims are hurt, they are more likely to be hurt before they resist than after. In fact, a large-scale study using a representative sample from the National Crime Surveys from 1979 to 1985 found that resistance was not significantly related to higher rates of injury because the attack against the victim provoked the victim resistance rather than the reverse (Kleck & Sayles, 1990).

An associated myth is that physical resistance provokes increased violence in particular types of rapists, such as sadists (see Groth, 1990). Ullman and Knight (1995) conducted a study based on a random sample of incarcerated rapists. They showed that, overall, the efficacy of women's resistance strategies for avoiding sexual abuse and physical injury did not vary by rapist type. Women who fought in response to sadistic rapists were no more likely to experience physical injury than women who did not. Ullman and Knight admonished people for issuing warnings against physical resistance to sadistic rapists in the absence of any empirical data to support such claims. They also pointed out the futility of advising women to assess the "type" of rapist before determining whether or not to resist.

Taken in sum, resistance studies show a consistent pattern of results: (1) Women who fight back and fight back immediately are less likely to be raped than women who do not; (2) women who fight back are no more likely to be injured than women who do not fight back (victim resistance often occurs in response to physical injury); (3) pleading, begging, crying, and reasoning are ineffective in preventing rape or physical injury; (4) women who fight back experience less postassault symptomology (both physical and psychological) due to avoidance of being raped; (5) women who fight back have faster psychological recoveries whether or not they are raped; and (6) fighting back strengthens the physical evidence should the survivor decide to prosecute for rape or attempted rape. Thus, we can conclude that traditional advice from authorities who tell women to refrain from resisting not only is unsupported by virtually every research study on the topic but also has the unintended effect of increasing the number of completed rapes.

Even if she does not fight back, it is important to remember that each woman makes the best decision she can under such circumstances; no woman should be blamed for being raped if she chooses *not* to defend herself.

SOCIETAL AND INSTITUTIONAL FACTORS

Joyce Williams (1984) cited public attitudes about rape as a source of the secondary victimization of women; she maintained that the pervasive atmosphere of victim blaming in our society adds to the trauma of a rape victim. Although both women and men engage in victim blaming, researchers find consistent gender differences, with women less likely than men to blame the victim for her rape. On our campus, a female student was raped at knife point on a Sunday afternoon while she worked on a project in the art studio. I heard students talking about the case. They asked, "What was she doing on campus alone?" "Why was she there on a Sunday?" "Didn't she scream—surely there were others somewhere around?" According to the just-world theory, people blame the victim because of their belief that the world is a just place where bad things happen only to bad people. By distancing themselves from the victim in this way, they can feel safer.

The social tendency to blame and restrict women while excusing men's behavior extends to so-called solutions to the social problem of violence against women. Golda Meir, the late prime minister of Israel, upon hearing that the Parliament was considering a curfew on women in order to stop violence against women called into question the androcentric (male-centered) assumptions inherent in such a solution. She pointed out that, if you really want women to be safe on the streets, you need to put a curfew on *men!* Indeed, some students at Brigham Young University (BYU), prompted by an on-campus attack of a female student, proposed such a curfew. BYU admonished women not to walk alone on campus at night, thus effectively putting a curfew on women. Women students claimed that violence against women would stop immediately if men, not women, had such a curfew (Corbin, 1991). They hung flyers all over campus that said,

> Due to the increase in violence against women on BYU campus, a new curfew has been instated. Beginning on Wednesday, November 20, men will no longer be allowed to walk alone or in all-male groups from 10 PM until 6 AM. Those men who must travel on or through campus during curfew hours must be accompanied by two women in order to demonstrate that they are not threatening. Provisions have been made for men who need to be escorted home. (p. 6)

The action by the women on campus was itself empowering. By refusing to be restricted in their behavior, they at least opened a dialogue among students about the inherent assumptions in such restrictions. The men seemed to understand restrictions of *their* rights; one man stated, "You can't curb our rights just to give someone else rights" (p. 6).

Other ways in which social and institutional forces tend to engender fear of rape include the "revictimization" of rape victims by police, hospitals, and the courts. In fact, the criminal justice system, the state, and the individual men with whom women live have been termed "the collective male protection system" (Hanmer & Saunders, cited in Smith, 1988.) It is a male-controlled system that *regulates* violence against women in the guise of protecting women (Rozee, 1993). All women are taught to be dependent for protection on the very system that enables violence against women to go essentially unpunished.

To summarize, there are a number of ways in which the fear of rape is instilled in women, starting at an early age and continuing throughout adulthood. Socialization practices, personal experiences with male violence, media representations of women, societal ideas about female incompetence in defending themselves, and social and institutional supports for women's fear of rape ensure that women will perceive a high likelihood of being raped and thus a heightened level of fear of rape.

COPING WITH FEAR

Many women are beginning to challenge the institutions that keep them in fear. Rape crisis centers and hot lines are banding together with police, district attorneys, and hospital staff to form sexual assault response teams (SART), safe places for women to report rape and receive treatment for injuries. The processing of rape complaints has improved greatly in cities with SART teams. Many women's groups are pressuring legislators, government and university officials, and corporate leaders to make changes in the situations that create fear.

Many writers have focused on the role of men and male-controlled institutions in stopping rape (see Funk, 1993; Riger & Gordon, 1989; Rozee & Koss, 2001; Warshaw, 1994). Prevention specialists are thus focusing on the only ones (i.e., men) who can actually stop rape (Funk, 1993; Rozee & Koss, 2001; Warshaw, 1994). Such efforts are likely to net better results than prevention efforts focused on the behavior of the victims of rape. This is a positive step in the direction of curbing rape in our society. In the meantime, though, women must cope with the threat of rape every day of their lives. How do they cope with the fear that this engenders?

From childhood on, women develop certain coping mechanisms and behaviors to reduce fear. Behaviorally, women may cope with fear of rape by taking some kind of personal, social, or political action. Most women have a multitude of methods for easing fear. In my class on the psychology of women, I ask women to call out the daily precautions that they take while I write them all on the chalkboard. The number of individual precautions most women take every day is staggering. The men in my classes are usually astonished at the lists. One female student told me that, while we were constructing this huge list of strategies, her boyfriend whispered to her, "You don't do all these things, do you?" She was as amazed by the question as he was by the answer, "Yes, of course, I do." Men lead very different existences with regard to safety; they find it hard to believe that women live this way. You might take five minutes to jot down a list of the precautions you take every day. Share your list with a male friend.

Nicole Gavey (2005) reported that often women in her study coped with male violence by giving in to forced sex in order to prevent being raped; they reported that giving in was a way to avoid the unambiguous conclusion that they had no control. By going along they kept some measure of control and felt like they had avoided actually being raped.

As mentioned earlier, taking a self-defense class and using those skills to protect oneself in a rape situation is the best prevention method available to women. Women who defend themselves against a would-be rapist are less likely to be raped, and no more likely to be hurt, than those who do not. Of course, if and how women decide to take action must be determined by each woman based on her individual needs and skills (Rozee, Bateman, & Gilmore, 1992).

Some women have made major job sacrifices in order to reduce fear and increase perceived safety, refusing job opportunities in bad areas, making longer commutes to work in order to live in safer neighborhoods, and refusing jobs for reasons of personal safety. Jan Leland-Young and Joan Nelson (1987) had a particularly powerful way of expressing how fear of rape affects women's education and career development:

> No matter how many reforms were accomplished, if women were in danger and in fear of utilizing those reforms, they were useless. It seemed to me that our society, by ignoring and often condoning violence against women, had very successfully found a way to make women oppress and limit themselves. It was not necessary to forbid women to go to school or work. With the fear of rape, women would avoid certain jobs, locations, libraries, buildings, even cities. (Leland-Young & Nelson, 1987, p. 204)

No matter how you look at it, the fear of rape has profound effects on the freedoms experienced by most women. Clearly, women are taking every precaution to protect themselves. One wonders about the psychological stress produced as a result of having to enact such a vast array of protective strategies.

Successful reductions of women's fear of rape will require a multifaceted approach. First, as Leland-Young and Nelson pointed out, the internalization of fear and its concomitant self-enforced behavioral restrictions must be addressed. The socialization of girls' and boys' roles in the victim-victimizer scenario must be challenged. In addition, changes must be made to ensure women's safety, such as improvement of physical environments, education of the public as well as members of the criminal justice system, enforcement of existing rape laws, and creation of new antirape policies.

Combatting fear of rape and empowering women require solutions aimed at *changing* the dangerous situations first (such as adding security in parking areas) rather than only focusing on helping women *adapt* to dangerous situations (as in learning to walk assertively). The physical environment is especially in need of attention by installing more and better lighting, more accessible and patrolled parking, escort service, and other measures designed to relieve women of the entire burden of self-protection. Next, educational programs need to be set up for men with regard to sexual harassment, sexually aggressive behavior, and sexual remarks and pictorial displays. Explicit enforcement of antisexual harassment policies are necessary. Institutions need to become more mindful of their role in preventing rape. After changes have been enacted in the *situational* factors that contribute to reduced perception of safety, the *empowerment* of women can be served by free or low-cost self-defense classes and rape prevention trainings. Women must be given accurate information about the benefits of rape resistance and encouraged to fight back against their attackers. Prevention efforts must have a much greater focus on the prevention of date and acquaintance rape because it is estimated that they comprise the majority of sexual assaults. Education of women to potential hazards, as well as training in protective responses, can be helpful after situational causes of fear have been addressed.

Expression of concern for and action toward women's safety are in themselves empowering. Many actions that are not costly themselves increase the perception of a safer environment (for example, sexual harassment workshops) and thus reduce fear. Public policies and practices aimed at fear reduction and empowerment may give women a first step toward enjoying *all* of the four freedoms.

REFERENCES

AMIR, M. (1971). *Patterns in forcible rape.* Chicago: University of Chicago Press.

BARNETT, O. W., & LaVIOLETTE, A. D. (1993). *It could happen to anyone: Why battered women stay.* Newbury Park, CA: Sage.

BART, P. (1981). A study of women who both were raped and avoided rape. *Journal of Social Issues, 37,* 123–137.

BART, P. B., & O'BRIEN, P. (1985). *Stopping rape: Successful survival strategies.* New York: Pergamon Press.

BROWN, M. (1995, July 13). Should you fight? No easy answers. *Sacramento Bee,* p. A10.

BROWNMILLER, S. (1975). *Against our will: Men, women and rape.* New York: Simon & Schuster.

BURT, M. R., & ESTEP, R. E. (1981). Apprehension and fear: Learning a sense of sexual vulnerability. *Sex Roles, 7,* 511–522.

CORBIN, B. (1991, December). Women's group proposes curfew for men. *National NOW Times,* p. 6.

DAY, K. (1999). Strangers in the night: Women's fear of sexual assault on urban college campuses. *Journal of Architecture and Planning Research, 16,* 289–312.

FUNK, R. E. (1993). *Stopping rape: A challenge for men.* Philadelphia: New Society Publishers.

FURBY, L., & FISCHHOFF, B. (1986). *Rape self-defense strategies: A review of their effectiveness.* Eugene, OR: Eugene Research Institute.

GAVEY, N. (2005). *Just Sex? The Cultural Scaffolding of Rape.* NY: Routledge.

GREENE, D. M., & NAVARRO, R. L. (1998). Situation-specific assertiveness in the epidemiology of sexual victimization among university women: A prospective path analysis. *Psychology of Women Quarterly, 22,* 589–604.

GRIFFIN, S. (1979). *Rape: The power of consciousness.* San Francisco: Harper & Row.

GROTH, A. N. (1990). *Men who rape: The psychology of the offender.* New York: Plenum Press.

HEISE, L., ELLSBERG, M., & GOTTENMOELLER, M. (1999). Ending violence against women. *Population Reports, 27,* 1–43.

HICKMAN, S. E., & MUEHLENHARD, C. L. (1997). College women's fears and precautionary behaviors relating to acquaintance rape and stranger rape. *Psychology of Women Quarterly, 21,* 527–547.

HOLGATE, A. (1989). Sexual harassment as a determinant of women's fear of rape. *Australian Journal of Sex, Marriage and Family, 10,* 21–28.

JONES, A. (1994, May/June). Living with guns, playing with fire. *Ms. Magazine,* pp. 38–45.

KLECK, G., & SAYLES, S. (1990). Rape and resistance. *Social Problems, 37,* 149–162.

KOSS, M. P., GIDYCZ, C. A., & WISNIEWSKI, N. (1987). The scope of rape: Incidence and prevalence of sexual aggression and victimization in a national sample of higher education students. *Journal of Consulting and Clinical Psychology, 55,* 162–170.

KOSS, M. P., GOODMAN, L. A., BROWNE, A., FITZGERALD, L. F., KEITA, G. P., & RUSSO, N. G. (1994). *No safe haven: Male violence against women at home, at work, and in the community* (pp. 157–176). Washington, DC: American Psychological Association.

KOSS, M. P., HEISE, L., & RUSSO, N. F. (1994). The global health burden of rape. *Psychology of Women Quarterly, 18,* 509–537.

KOSS, M. P., & MUKAI, T. (1993). Recovering ourselves: Frequency, effects, and resolution of rape. In F. L. Denmark & M. A. Paludi (Eds.), *Psychology of women: A handbook of issues and theories* (pp. 477–512). Westport, CT: Greenwood Press.

LELAND-YOUNG, J., & NELSON, J. (1987). Prevention of sexual assault through the resocialization of women: Unlearning victim behavior. *Women & Therapy, 6,* 203–210.

NEUBORNE, E. (1994, May/June). Cashing in on fear: The NRA targets women. *Ms. Magazine,* pp. 46–50.

MOORE, D. E., & WATERMAN, C. K. (1999). Predicting self-protection against sexual assault in dating relationships among heterosexual men and women, gay men, lesbians, and bisexuals. *Journal of College Student Development, 40,* 132–140.

O'BRIEN, R. M. (1987). The interracial nature of violent crimes: A reexamination. *American Journal of Sociology, 92,* 817–835.

RIGER, S. (1981). Reactions to crime: Impacts of crime on women. *Sage Criminal Justice System Annuals, 16,* 47–55.

RIGER, S., & GORDON, M. (1981). The fear of rape: A study in social control. *Journal of Social Issues, 37*(4), 71–94.

RIGER, S., & GORDON, M. (1984). The impact of crime on urban women. In A. Rickel, M. Gerrard, & I. Iscoe (Eds.), *The social and psychological problems of women* (pp. 139–156). Washington, DC: Hemisphere.

RIGER, S., & GORDON, M. (1989). *The female fear.* New York: The Free Press.

RIGER, S., GORDON, M., & LeBAILLY, R. (1982). Coping with urban crime: Women's use of precautionary behaviors. *American Journal of Community Psychology, 10,* 369–386.

ROZEE, P. (1993). Forbidden or forgiven: Rape in cross-cultural perspective. *Psychology of Women Quarterly, 17*, 499–514.

ROZEE, P., BATEMAN, P., & GILMORE, T. (1992). The personal perspective of acquaintance rape prevention: A three-tier approach. In A. Parrot & L. Bechhofer (Eds.), *Acquaintance rape: The hidden crime* (pp. 337–354). New York: John Wiley.

ROZEE, P. D., & KOSS, M. P. (2001). Rape: A century of resistance. *Psychology of Women Quarterly, 25*, 295–311.

ROZEE-KOKER, P. (1987, March). *Effects of self-efficacy, fear of rape and perceived risk on intention to take a self-defense class.* Paper presented at the meeting of the Midwest Society for Feminist Studies, Akron, OH.

ROZEE-KOKER, P., WYNNE, C., & MIZRAHI, K. (1989, April). *Workplace safety and fear of rape among professional women.* Paper presented at the meeting of the Western Psychological Association, Reno, NV.

SMITH, M. D. (1988). Women's fear of violent crime: An exploratory test of a feminist hypothesis. *Journal of Family Violence, 3*, 29–38.

STANKO, E. (1993). Ordinary fear: Women, violence, and personal safety. In P. Bart & E. Moran (Eds.), *Violence against women: The bloody footprints* (pp. 155–165). Newbury Park, CA: Sage.

ULLMAN, S. E. (1997). Review and critique of empirical studies of rape avoidance. *Criminal Justice and Behavior, 24*, 177–204.

ULLMAN, S. E., & KNIGHT, R. A. (1991). A multivariate model for predicting rape and physical injury outcomes during sexual assaults. *Journal of Consulting and Clinical Psychology, 59*, 724–731.

ULLMAN, S. E., & KNIGHT, R. A. (1992). Fighting back: Women's resistance to rape. *Journal of Interpersonal Violence, 7*, 31–43.

ULLMAN, S. E., & KNIGHT, R. A. (1993). The efficacy of women's resistance strategies in rape situations. *Psychology of Women Quarterly, 17*, 23–38.

ULLMAN, S. E., & KNIGHT, R. A. (1995). Women's resistance stragies to different rapist types. *Criminal Justice and Behavior, 22*, 263–283.

ULLMAN, S. E., & SIEGEL, J. M. (1993). Victim-offender relationship and sexual assault. *Violence and Victims, 8*, 121–134.

VALENTINE, G. (1992). Images of danger: Women's source of information about the spatial distribution of male violence. *Area, 24*, 22.

WARR, M. (1985). Fear of rape among urban women. *Social Problems, 32*, 238–250.

WARSHAW, R. (1994). *I never called it rape: The Ms. report on recognizing, fighting and surviving date and acquaintance rape* (2nd ed.). New York: Harper & Row.

WILLIAMS, J. E. (1984). Secondary victimization: Confronting public attitudes about rape. *Victimology: An International Journal, 9*, 66–81.

ZOUCHA-JENSEN, J. M., & COYNE, A. (1993). The effects of resistance strategies on rape. *American Journal of Public Health, 83*, 1633–1634.

*S*UGGESTED READINGS

FUNK, R. E. (1993). *Stopping rape: A challenge for men.* Philadelphia: New Society Publishers.

GAVEY, N. (2005). *Just Sex? The Cultural Scaffolding of Rape.* NY: Routledge.

RIGER, S., & GORDON, M. (1989). *The female fear.* New York: The Free Press.

WARSHAW, R. (1988). *I never called it rape: The Ms. report on recognizing, fighting and surviving date and acquaintance rape.* New York: Harper & Row.

BRITAIN A. SCOTT is Associate Professor of Psychology at the University of St. Thomas. Dr. Scott has taught courses on the psychology of women since 1995 at St. Thomas and the University of Minnesota. She is a social psychologist whose primary scholarly interests include the psychological and social implications of women's sexual objectification.

21

Women and Pornography

What We Don't Know Can Hurt Us

❖

In 1983, at the request of the Minneapolis, Minnesota, city council, feminist activist Andrea Dworkin and legal scholar Catherine MacKinnon drafted an Antipornography Civil Rights Ordinance. Their ordinance was not about censorship, but about providing women some legal recourse when they had been harmed by pornography; that is, women would be able to sue when they had been coerced into pornography, had pornography forced upon them, been assaulted because of particular pornography, or been defamed though pornography. In addition, the ordinance declared that the production, sale, exhibition, or distribution of pornography is sex discrimination and thereby allowed any individual to file a complaint against pornographers for subordination of women. In MacKinnon's (1997) words, "Its point [was] to hold those who profit and benefit from that injury accountable to those who are injured. It [meant] that women's injury—our damage, our pain, our enforced inferiority—should outweigh their pleasure and their profits, or sex equality is meaningless" (p. 405). The ordinance was passed twice by the Minneapolis city council and vetoed both times by the mayor. Why did Dworkin and MacKinnon consider pornography to be a violation of women's civil rights? The answer lies in their definition of pornography.

WHAT IS PORNOGRAPHY?

Dworkin and MacKinnon (1988) included a very specific definition of pornography in their ordinance:

> Pornography is the sexually explicit subordination of women, graphically depicted, whether in pictures or in words, that also includes one or more of the following:

(i) women are presented dehumanized as sexual objects, things, or commodities; or (ii) women are presented as sexual objects who enjoy pain or humiliation, or (iii) women are presented as sexual objects who experience sexual pleasure in being raped; or (iv) women are presented as sexual objects tied up or cut up or mutilated or bruised or physically hurt; or (v) women are presented in postures or positions of sexual submission, or (vi) women's body parts—including but not limited to vaginas, breasts, or buttocks— are exhibited such that women are reduced to those parts; or (vii) women are presented as whores by nature; or (viii) women are presented being penetrated by objects or animals; or (ix) women are presented in scenarios of degradation, injury, abasement, torture, shown as filthy or inferior, bleeding, bruised, or hurt in a context that makes these conditions sexual. (p. 101)

The important thing about this definition is that it does *not* define as pornography all sexually explicit material. Although the general public tends to label all sexually explicit material as pornographic (e.g., Lottes, Weinberg, & Weller, 1993), Dworkin and MacKinnon focused on material that combines sex and degradation or sex and violence. Dworkin and MacKinnon are not the only scholars to emphasize this distinction. Philosopher Helen Longino (1994) described pornography as "...verbal or pictorial explicit representations of sexual behavior that...have as a distinguishing characteristic the degrading and demeaning portrayal of the role and status of the human female as a mere sexual object to be exploited and manipulated sexually" (p. 154), and sociologist Diana Russell (1993) described it as "material that combines sex and/or the exposure of genitals with abuse or degradation in a manner that appears to endorse, condone, or encourage such behavior" (p. 3). According to these definitions, not only is some sexually explicit material not pornographic, but some material may be pornographic without being "X-rated."

Can you think of examples of sexually explicit material that *would not* fit these definitions of pornography? Examples include instructional videotapes used by sex therapists to help couples improve their love making skills and erotic photographs that celebrate the beauty of the human body and the joy of sex without degrading or objectifying the persons pictured.

Can you think of examples of less explicit material that *would* fit these definitions? Many R-rated Hollywood films mesh sex and violence in scripts that show harassment, stalking, voyeurism, prostitution, rape, or murder of women. These films are often marketed as "erotic thrillers." Pornographic themes have been pandemic in music videos since the inception of MTV in the early 1980s. More recently, images of sexualized violence have become commonplace in fashion photography and in advertising for numerous products, including jeans, alcohol, and computer games. I challenge you to begin looking critically at the images that surround you every day on billboards, in magazines, on posters in your campus bookstore, in movie advertisements, on television commercials, in unsolicited e-mail messages, and so on. (For examples collected by other critical consumers, see the "No Comment" page in every issue of *Ms.* magazine or go to www.about-face.org.)

"PORNOGRAPHY" VS. "EROTICA"

At this point, you may be wondering whether the distinction between sexually explicit materials and materials that combine sexual themes with violence or degradation is based solely on feminist theory or whether it is also supported by research findings. If we consider the impact that exposure to these materials may have on attitudes and behavior, there is empirical evidence that favors this distinction. Some of the research evidence was reviewed by Daniel Linz, Edward Donnerstein, and Steven Penrod (1987) who stated:

> The research...has demonstrated, for the most part...that sexually explicit images, per se, do not in the short run facilitate aggressive behavior against women, change attitudes about rape, or influence other forms of antisocial behavior. Instead, the research indicates that it is the violent images embedded in some forms of pornography, or even the violent images alone, that account for many of the antisocial effects observed in experimental studies. (p. 97)

For example, in one of their own studies, Linz, Donnerstein, and Penrod (1984) exposed male college students to 10 hours of R-rated or X-rated movies (two hours a day for five days). Some of the men saw films that were sexually explicit and portrayed sexual assault; some saw films that were sexually explicit but portrayed consenting sex; and the rest saw films that were less sexually explicit but portrayed violence against women within a sexual context. At the end of the five days, the three groups of men, along with a control group who had not seen any films, were asked to watch a re-enactment of a rape trial and to make several judgments about the case. Compared with the control group and the group that had seen the X-rated nonviolent films, the two groups who had seen violent films judged the rape victim's injury to be less severe and rated her significantly more worthless as a person. The pattern of results in this study corresponds to the definitions previously presented; negative effects were observed for material that combined violence and sexual themes, regardless of the level of sexual explicitness, but no negative effects were observed for the sexually explicit nonviolent material.

With few exceptions, other experiments have yielded similarly disturbing findings. Exposure to sexually violent material increases men's sexual callousness toward women and lowers their support of sexual equality (e.g., Zillmann & Bryant, 1982), desensitizes men to violence against women and increases men's acceptance of rape myths such as "all women secretly want to be raped" (e.g., Malamuth & Check, 1981), and increases aggression toward women in the laboratory (e.g., Donnerstein & Berkowitz, 1981).

Meta-analysis reveals a reliable association between frequent use of violent pornography and men's sexually aggressive behavior, especially when the men are predisposed to aggression (Malamuth, Addison, & Koss, 2000).

More recent experiments have focused on the distinction between sexually degrading and non-degrading material in the absence of violent content. "Degrading" films are operationally defined as those that contain male dominance, female availability, penis worship, female insatiability, and the objectification of women; "non-degrading" films contain mutual respect, affection, and sexual pleasure (Cowan & Dunn, 1994). Researchers have found that male college students exposed to a sexually explicit and degrading film clip behave differently in a subsequent interaction with a woman than do men exposed to a sexually explicit but non-degrading film clip. One study showed that highly gender-typed men who had viewed a sexually degrading scene underestimated the woman's intellectual competence and overestimated her sexual interest in them (Jansma et al., 1997). In another study, the less gender-typed men were more impacted by the degrading film in that they displayed more dominance behavior in the subsequent interaction (Mulac, Jansma, & Linz, 2002). Men who have viewed video segments that sexually degrade women—whether explicit or not—exhibit more rape-supportive attitudes than do men who have viewed non-degrading segments (Golde, Strassberg, Turner, & Lowe, 2000).

The bulk of social science research on the effects of pornography has focused exclusively on *men's* attitudes and behaviors. Because pornography historically has been produced for and by men, researchers have directed their efforts accordingly; however, these studies of men suggest that pornography may be harmful, at least indirectly, to women. Legal scholar Kathleen Lahey (1991) has argued that an "alternative, feminist way [to conduct research on potential harmful effects of pornography] is to listen to women" (p. 118). Recently, a few researchers have included women participants in their studies; some have conducted traditional correlational or experimental studies, and others have done what Lahey advocated by collecting women's accounts about their experiences with pornography.

EXPERIMENTAL RESEARCH ON WOMEN AND PORNOGRAPHY

Few researchers have directly investigated women's responses to sexually explicit material. Some early work conducted in the 1970s and 1980s looked at whether women are aroused by visual depictions of graphic sex. The general consensus among researchers was that women are not particularly aroused by visual sex. We cannot tell from these studies whether the materials used were pornographic in the sense described previously, but we can be confident that the stimuli used were produced by and for men.

In the past decade, there has been an increase in sexually explicit material geared toward women. For example, former-porn-star-turned-director, Candida Royalle, produces sexually explicit videos under the *Femme* label. Her videos portray nonviolent, nondegrading, consensual sex within a romantic context. With new materials such as these films available, several researchers have designed studies to address the question of whether women respond differently to material designed for women and material designed for men.

In most of these investigations, researchers have focused on *sexual arousal* in response to the films. For example, Donald Mosher and Paula MacIan (1994) randomly assigned female and male undergraduates to watch one of six X-rated videos, three intended for men and three for women. Then, they measured sexual arousal, affective response, absorption in the material, and subsequent sexual behavior. They found that men had a more positive response than women did to all of the videos, but especially to the videos designed for men, which elicited a negative emotional reaction from the women. Compared with the women who had seen the videos designed for men, women who had seen the videos designed for women reported more sexual arousal, more positive affect, more absorption, and increased subsequent sexual activity. In a study that employed only women participants, Ellen Laan, Walter Everaerd, Gerdy van Bellen, and Gerrit Hanewald (1994) found that "woman-made, female-initiated, and female-centered" erotic films were considered more arousing than "man-made, male-initiated, and male-centered erotic films." The men's films also evoked feelings of shame, guilt, and aversion. In addition to asking for women's *subjective* reports of arousal, these researchers also measured sexual arousal *objectively* with a vaginal photoplethysmograph. This device, about the size of a tampon, is inserted into the vagina to record vasocongestion (i.e., blood flow to the vagina); the greater the vasocongestion, the more physiologically aroused the woman is. It is interesting that physiological arousal measured in this way did *not* differ between the group who watched the women's films and the group who watched the men's films. In a combination experimental-correlational study, Sara Pearson and Robert Pollack (1997) showed women undergraduates either a female-oriented *Femme* video or a traditional male-oriented video and then collected subjective reports of arousal. They also correlated arousal with measures of previous experience with sexually explicit material, masturbatory experience, and sex guilt. Pearson and Pollack found that women reported greater subjective arousal in response to the *Femme* video and that greater arousal was associated with more previous experience with sexually explicit materials, more masturbatory experience, and less sex guilt.

At this point, you may be thinking, "This is all very interesting, but are these studies really about pornography?" Perhaps not. Most likely, the material designed specifically for women and labeled "erotica" would not fit the definitions of pornography offered earlier. The material designed for men might constitute pornography, but the researchers did not explicitly say so. There are, however, some studies in which the researchers have intentionally used violent or degrading pornography as experimental stimuli. For example, Charlene Senn and Lorraine Radtke (1990) exposed women undergraduates to one of three sets of sexually explicit slides: erotica (with a focus on mutual pleasure between consenting partners), nonviolent porn (with the implication of violence or submission), or violent porn (with explicit violence or its aftereffects). As predicted, women rated erotica positively, nonviolent porn negatively, and violent porn more negatively—and both types of porn decreased women's moods. Participants who reported having experienced sexual coercion in the past evaluated the pornography even more negatively, and the erotica more positively, than did participants with no self-reported history of sexual coercion. Jack Glascock (2005) exposed both women and men undergraduates to either erotic or nonviolent but degrading pornographic video clips and then collected subjective reports of sexual arousal. Men's and women's arousal did not differ significantly in the erotica condition. In the degrading pornography condition, however, men reported significantly more arousal than women did—and the men's arousal in this condition was slightly (though not significantly) higher than in the erotica condition, whereas women's was lower than in the erotica condition.

Laboratory studies tend to be stripped down versions of reality; therefore, some researchers have explored whether situational factors present when women encounter pornography outside the laboratory might affect women's reactions to pornography. Charlene Senn and Serge Desmarais (2004) addressed the social context in which women encounter pornography; they asked women participants accompanied by either a female friend or a male partner to view erotic, sexist, or violent sexually explicit images and then discuss them with the friend or partner. Women experienced more agreement with female friends than with male partners regarding evaluations of the slides (the men viewed them all more positively than the women did, especially the sexist set), but regardless of whether the discussion was with a friend or partner, women generally reported that discussing the slides improved their moods.

As a whole, the experimental research on women and pornography does not have much to say about how pornography might directly harm women (besides putting them in a bad mood). Take a minute to brainstorm other dependent measures that might better capture the effects of pornography on women. These could include measures of body image, self-esteem, the sexual self-concept, fear of sexual assault, relationship distress, women's behavior toward other women, and...?

L*ISTENING TO WOMEN*

Several researchers have investigated the link between pornography and harm to women by soliciting accounts from battered women regarding the use of pornography by their abusers and the role of pornography in the abuse episodes. For example, Evelyn Sommers and James Check (1987) interviewed 44 battered women from shelters and 32 women from a "mature university population." Thirty-nine percent of the battered women (compared with 3 percent of the other women) said that their partners had upset them by trying to get them to do something seen in pornographic pictures, movies, or books. The battered women also reported more sexual aggression from their partners than did the other women. Elizabeth Cramer and Judith McFarlane (1994) surveyed 87 women who were filing criminal charges against their male partners for battery. Forty percent of the women reported that their batterers used pornography, and use was significantly associated with these women being asked or forced to participate in violent sex, even rape.

Janet Shope (2004) collected information from 271 women in a New York battered women's program. She found that women whose batterers used pornography, in contrast to women whose partners did not, were nearly twice as likely to have experienced sexual abuse from their batterers.

Sexual assault and battery happens to women in all walks of life, including to those walking the streets. Mimi Silbert and Ayala Pines (1984) set out to study the sexual abuse of prostitutes without regard to pornography, but found that nearly one-quarter of the victims in 193 rape cases spontaneously described their rapists' allusions to porn. One victim quoted her attacker as saying, "I know all about you bitches, you're no different; you're like all of them. I seen it in all the movies. You love being beaten" (p. 864). Similar anecdotes surfaced in prostitutes' testimonies at the Minneapolis Antipornography Ordinance hearings (MacKinnon & Dworkin, 1997). For example, a former prostitute, Ms. S., claimed that women prostitutes "were forced constantly to enact specific scenes that men had witnessed in pornography" (p. 116). One woman was told by a man holding a picture of a beaten woman, "I want you to look like this. I want you to hurt" (p. 118). Ms. S. claimed that another prostitute was burned with cigarettes, had clips attached to her nipples, and was continuously raped and beaten for 12 hours by a group of men brandishing sadomasochistic pornography.

What can we conclude from accounts such as these? Can we conclude that pornography causes male violence against women? No. In fact, even if all of the battered women reported that their partners used pornography, and even if all of the cases of assault on prostitutes involved pornography, we still could not conclude that the pornography was the cause of the violence. What we *can* conclude, however, is that pornography is associated with many cases of sexual violence and that from the perspective of these women, pornography suggested ways to harm the women and was, itself, part of the harm inflicted upon them.

Recently, Raymond Bergner and Ana Bridges listened to women in nonabusive relationships who believed that they, too, have been harmed by their partners' use of pornography. In their first study (Bergner & Bridges, 2002), the researchers analyzed postings to Internet discussion boards by women distressed by what they perceived to be heavy use of pornography by their male partners. These women felt traumatized by their discovery of their partners' porn usage and described negative effects on their relationship, their feelings of self-worth and sexual desirability, and their views of their partner. Based on these accounts, the researchers developed a 50-item Pornography Distress Scale (PDS) that they administered to a sample of 100 women (Bridges, Bergner, & Hesson-McInnes, 2003). Although the overall attitudes of women in the sample were neutral rather than negative, 42 percent reported that their partner's use of pornography made them feel insecure, 41 percent felt less attractive and desirable since discovering their partner's porn usage, and 34 percent said that their self-esteem had suffered.

THE "WHY" AND "HOW" OF FUTURE RESEARCH ON WOMEN AND PORN

I think it is imperative for researchers to conduct more studies on pornography and women. The study of pornography is one example among many in the field of psychology where women have been relatively absent as researchers and research participants, and where women's perspectives have not been fairly represented in theory and research design. Without more studies to rectify this neglect of women's experiences, psychologists cannot hope to offer a complete picture of pornography's possible effects to those involved in the social and legal debates about it.

It is important for psychologists to conduct more studies on pornography and women in order to bring some diversity to the discussion. We need diversity of participants, not just regarding gender but also in terms of characteristics such as race/ethnicity, age, sexual orientation, and ability. We need diversity in the research methods used, so that women's perspectives are represented as more than group averages in experimental or correlational studies. We need diversity in what we consider "pornography," so that we are not limited to studies about X-rated films or *Playboy* centerfolds. Finally, we need diversity in our ideas about what effects pornography might have on women; we need to consider more than just sexual arousal and mood.

Diversity of Women

I am advocating not only including women from a variety of demographic categories in studies of pornography, but also addressing how various demographic characteristics are integrated into pornography itself. Women of Color must be included in the study of pornography, not only as research participants, but also as part of the theoretical understanding of what pornography is. Patricia Hill Collins (1997) suggested that

> the treatment of Black women's bodies in nineteenth-century Europe and the United States may be the foundation upon which contemporary pornography as the representation of women's objectification, domination, and control is based. (p. 396)

She noted that the "image of Black women in pornography is almost consistently one featuring them breaking from chains" (p. 397). Black women are portrayed as (sexual) slaves and savages whose animal sexuality must be tamed. Collins also made reference to how Asian women in pornography are often portrayed being tortured. In her very disturbing collection of visual pornography, Russell (1993) included examples from a 1984 *Penthouse* photo essay that featured young Asian women trussed in ropes and, in one instance, hung from a tree. Russell also included anti-Semitic pornography that portrays women as concentration camp victims in such publications as *Swastika Snatch*. These are only a few examples of how women's race and ethnicity are integrated into pornography.

Most research on pornography has addressed heterosexual men's and women's experiences with heterosexually oriented material. The voices of lesbian women have been largely absent. It is important for researchers to hear from lesbian women regarding erotica and pornography designed for their own consumption and regarding pornography for heterosexual men in which lesbianism is exploited and distorted into a fantasy for the male viewer. Todd Morrison and Dani Tallack (2005) conducted focus groups on these issues with a sample of lesbian and bisexual women. To spark discussion, they first showed the participants explicit film clips of "ersatz lesbian" material for men and material for lesbian women (without identifying which was which). The participants reported that, in contrast to the genuinely lesbian-oriented film clip, the scene from *Lesbian Cheerleader Squad 2* presented an unrealistic portrayal of lesbian sexuality that lacked emotional intimacy and featured performers whose bodies conformed to a heterosexual ideal. Still, there was not uniform agreement about which film clip was "better," and the women generally did not find either clip threatening or offensive. Morrison and Tallack (2005) advocated, therefore, that researchers explore the variety of reactions women may have to pornography and move beyond an exclusive focus on harm.

Current global politics dictate that we must consider the diverse experiences of women worldwide. Since the infiltration of the "free market" into the former Soviet Union, the production and distribution of pornography there have hugely increased. Some commentators have dismissed this surge as an expected reaction to the lifting of Communist restrictions on such materials; others have sounded the alarm about what the increase in sex trafficking of women and children means for the status of women under the new political structure. Only time will tell what will happen with regard to pornography in Afghanistan after the fall of the Taliban regime in 2002. Might the pendulum swing from one extreme of women's sexuality completely muted under the burka to women being exposed and exploited as sexual commodities? We cannot afford an ethnocentric perspective when it comes to pornography. This is a global phenomenon, and it is facilitated in large part by the World Wide Web.

Diversity of Pornography

Most of you have probably experienced the unwelcome appearance of pornographic messages or images in your e-mail inbox. Some of you likely have explored pornographic sites on the Internet. Do you have a sense of what is out there? Unlike print media and video, Internet forms of pornography are very difficult to monitor and control. Child pornography, which is illegal in the United States, is widely available online. In fact, pornography catering to just about any taste is available somewhere in the electronic universe. In my own online research, I have encountered shocking photographs of women with their breasts nailed to boards, sickening text that glorifies the brutal anal rape of "teen schoolgirls," and sites dedicated to mutilation in a sexual context. Jennifer Gossett and Sarah Byrne (2002) analyzed the content of 31 Web sites that included "rape" or "forced sex" in their titles, text, or Internet addresses. Twenty-one of the sites included visuals accompanied by captions such as "These teenagers' hell is your pleasure. They are stretched, whipped, raped, and beaten. Their tits are crushed, twisted, pierced, thrashed, and tortured...they scream, cry, and plead" (p. 696). Fourteen of the sites described victims with derogatory terms such as "bitch," "pussy," "whore," and "slut." Four of the sites bragged that they featured documentation of actual rape, and several invited viewers to participate in sexual violence (e.g., by downloading a "cyberslave" whom the viewer can "torture" and "abuse" as he pleases). Martin Barron and Michael Kimmel (2000) conducted a comparative analysis of violent content in pornographic magazines, videos, and Internet newsgroups. They found that about 5 percent of the sexual scenes in videos and magazines contained violence or coercion, compared to 26 percent of the scenes posted on the Internet.

Some of the most common sexually oriented Web sites feature women who have no idea that their bodies are being objectified online: women captured by hidden cameras or cell phones in locker rooms or public restrooms, and women whose partners post pictures or video of them without their consent. And, with the increases in digital technology, when real women are not available, the skilled graphic artist can create and post whatever type of image his mind can conjure up. The Internet makes pornography available in unprecedented volume and variety.

Graphic artists also use their skills in the video/computer game genre. These games are marketed almost exclusively to teenage boys and young adult men. Violence is a pervasive theme, and much of that violence is sexualized. Sexualized violence in video games is not a new phenomenon. For example, in 1982, a company called Mystique produced an Atari-compatible game called "Custer's Revenge." The goal of the game was for the player (Custer) to wend his way across the screen, avoiding cacti and arrows, to reach the nude Native American "maiden" tied to a post. Once there, he was to rape her as many times as possible with his crudely animated, but clearly erect, penis (see www.atariguide. com/3/320.htm). More recently, national media attention was directed at the highly popular *Grand Theft Auto* series of video games in which the player assumes the role of a criminal who engages in a variety of antisocial and violent behavior (e.g., stealing cars, dealing drugs, shooting police officers, and running over pedestrians). *Grand Theft Auto III* offered the player the opportunity to have sex with a prostitute and then to kill her to get his money back. Meta-analysis of research on the effects of violent video games shows a clear association with aggressive thinking and behavior (Anderson et al., 2004).

*P*ORNOGRAPHY AND THE FIRST AMENDMENT

My hope for future research on pornography and women is that it will illuminate the ongoing debate about whether the production of pornography should be protected as "free speech" or whether it should be legally restricted or penalized in some way.

There is a wide range of opinions, even among feminists, about what constitutes pornography. Some people consider all sexually explicit material to be "obscene" and "pornographic" and draw no distinction between material that portrays consensual sex and material that shows real women experiencing real abuse. Some people *do* see a difference between instructional videos designed to help couples improve their lovemaking skills and magazines that feature photographs of tortured women being gang-raped at knife point. Even those who make distinctions, however, often think that protecting "free speech" is more important than protecting the women in the photographs, the women who see the photographs, or the women whose partners masturbate to the photographs. I am intentionally being provocative here because I personally do not agree that material that endorses, condones, or encourages the sexual abuse and degradation of half the human population should be defended as "free speech." At the same time, I think that many anticensorship feminists make important points, particularly regarding the potentially negative impact of censorship on women's sexuality.

Would Restricting Pornography Restrict Women's Sexuality?

At a 1993 conference entitled "Women, Censorship, and "Pornography," sex therapist and President of the International Academy of Sex Research Leonore Tiefer argued that women benefit from access to sexually explicit materials. She claimed that such materials enhance women's ability to develop their sexualities, a challenging process in a culture that has traditionally suppressed female sexual exploration and expression (National Coalition against Censorship, 1998). Given that the estimated rate of inorgasmia (inability to achieve orgasm) among women in the United States is 30 percent (Palace, 1995), I find this a persuasive point. I agree that an important function is served by many sexually explicit materials. For example, sex therapist Betty Dodson produced a video, *Selfloving*, which graphically documents her hands-on workshops on female masturbation. Her intent is to benefit women. Women might benefit similarly from exposure to sexually graphic woman-oriented erotica, such as the *Femme* films I described earlier. I, however, see a clear distinction between materials like this (which I do not consider pornography) and pornographic periodicals such as *Take That, Bitch!* and *Black Tit and Body Torture* (Russell, 1993); it is difficult for me to imagine how photographs of women enduring extreme pain and physical injury inflicted by sexually aroused men would assist women in developing a healthy and fulfilling sexuality.

Some anticensorship feminists have argued that restricting pornography might especially limit lesbian women's sexual expression; they believe that some of the first materials to go would be lesbian and gay erotica because they would be viewed by some as unconventional or obscene (e.g., Strossen, 1995). This position gained momentum in the wake of the Canadian Supreme Court's (1992) *Butler* decision. Donald Butler was a pornographer who had been prosecuted under Canada's obscenity laws, which defined as obscene the undue exploitation of sex or sex and violence (MacKinnon & Dworkin, 1994). Butler argued that this obscenity law violated his rights to free speech under the new Canadian constitution. This new constitution, the Charter of Rights and Freedoms, also included sexual equality rights, rights that the Women's Legal Education and Action Fund (LEAF) had argued were violated by pornography. The Supreme Court agreed with LEAF that it is constitutional to restrict materials that harm women if that restriction promotes sex equality.

There is a striking similarity between the Dworkin and MacKinnon Ordinance, which considered pornography a violation of women's civil rights, and the Canadian Supreme Court determination that pornography can represent a violation of sex equality. Shortly after the *Butler* decision, there were widespread reports about Canadian Customs using the decision as justification for stopping gay and lesbian material at the border. Due to the resemblance between the theme of the *Butler* decision and the Antipornography Ordinance, these reports eventually metamorphosed into allegations that Canada had adopted the Antipornography Ordinance and was using it to ban lesbian and gay erotica. In a 1994 press release, MacKinnon and Dworkin clarified that, although the *Butler* decision was based on an equality approach to pornography, Canada had not adopted their Antipornography Ordinance or their civil (as opposed to criminal) approach. They also claimed that Canadian Customs had a long history of "homophobic seizures," but under the new constitution these are illegal (this is actually supported by the *Butler* decision, which stated that it *is* unconstitutional to restrict materials on a *moral* basis). Indeed, the Antipornography Ordinance does not contain any language that would condemn lesbian or gay materials on the basis that they portray homosexuality; however, material that promotes the degradation, humiliation, or pain of women—whether homosexual or heterosexual—would fit the Ordinance definition of pornography.

Pornography as "Free Speech"

The American Civil Liberties Union (ACLU), an organization that defends pornography as free speech, states on its Internet site that

> the First Amendment exists precisely to protect the most offensive and controversial speech from government suppression. The best way to counter obnoxious speech is with more speech. Persuasion, not coercion, is the solution. (ACLU)

Do you think that "offensive and controversial speech" is a sufficient label for the pornography that I have described? If not, in what ways do you think pornography differs from other forms of protected speech? Should some forms of pornography be censored?

In her book *Defending Pornography*, former president of the ACLU, Nadine Strossen (1995), offered a compelling argument about censorship being a "slippery slope" (p. 239). Like many anticensorship feminists, she warned that, if we restrict some material, we will open the door to restrictions on anything anybody happens to find offensive, including art, literature, scholarly works, and educational materials. Strossen believes that threats to the First Amendment threaten women in that

> freedom of speech consistently has been the strongest weapon for countering misogynistic discrimination and violence, and censorship consistently has been a potent tool for curbing women's rights and interests. Freedom of sexually oriented expression is integrally connected with women's freedom, since women traditionally have been straitjacketed precisely in the sexual domain, notably in our ability to control our sexual and reproductive options. (p. 30)

In my opinion, Strossen's points are good ones. I would characterize myself as a "prosex, proerotica, antipornography feminist," so where do I stand on censorship of pornography? Like the 119 National Organization for Women newsletter recipients surveyed by Gloria Cowan in 1992, my views of pornography could probably be predicted by my beliefs about the importance of protecting free speech and my beliefs about the harmful effects of pornography. I do believe that the right to free speech is an important one to protect and that censorship is a dangerous practice. I am not, however, very troubled by the idea of restricting material that is, in fact, a documentation of actual illegal sexual violence. Some anticensorship feminists argue that, because there already exist laws prohibiting sexual violence, we do not need more laws to address pornographic documentation of such violence (Strossen, 1995). My response to this argument is to point out that, if current laws were preventing the sexual violence, it could not be documented and sold as entertainment.

Clearly, there are no easy answers here. Were Dworkin and MacKinnon on the right track with their Antipornography Civil Rights Ordinance? These feminists recognized the value of protecting free speech and so were not proposing the criminalization of pornography. They were not advocating censorship. They were suggesting, however, that pornography is propaganda that promotes and maintains the subordinate status of women in our culture and, as such, should be considered a violation of women's civil rights. They proposed their ordinance because they believe a clear distinction can, and should, be made between material that is simply sexually explicit and material that is potentially harmful to women and men. For the most part, I agree. I recognize, however, that even the detailed definition offered by Dworkin and MacKinnon leaves room for subjective interpretation.

Psychological research cannot determine whether pornography should be considered a violation of women's civil rights. Psychological research can, however, yield information about potentially harmful effects of pornography on women, men, and social relationships. I am a social psychologist who is motivated by the belief that the best research findings are those that have practical applications. I think that questions about pornography are ones that cannot be answered without the continued input of social science researchers.

*R*EFERENCES

American Civil Liberties Union. Free Speech. Retrieved from http://www.aclu.org/freespeech/index.html

ANDERSON, C. A., CARNAGEY, N. L., FLANAGAN, M., BENJAMIN, A. J., JR., EUBANKS, J., & VALENTINE, J. C. (2004). Violent video games: Specific effects of violent content on aggressive thoughts and behavior. *Advances in Experimental Social Psychology, 36,* 199–249.

BARRON, M., & KIMMEL, M. (2000). Sexual violence in three pornographic media: Toward a sociological explanation. *Journal of Sex Research, 37,* 161–168.

BERGNER, R. M., & BRIDGES, A. J. (2002). The significance of heavy pornography involvement for romantic partners: Research and clinical implications. *Journal of Sex & Marital Therapy, 28,* 193–206.

BRIDGES, A. J., BERGNER, R. M., & HESSON-MCINNIS, M. (2003). Romantic partners' use of pornography: Its significance for women. *Journal of Sex & Marital Therapy, 29,* 1–14.

COLLINS, P. H. (1997). Pornography and Black women's bodies. In L. L. O'Toole & J. R. Schiffman (Eds.), *Gender violence: Interdisciplinary perspectives* (pp. 395–399). New York: New York University Press.

COWAN, G., & DUNN, K. F. (1994). What themes in pornography lead to perceptions of the degradation of women? *Journal of Sex Research, 31,* 11–21.

CRAMER, E., & MACFARLANE, J. (1994). Pornography and abuse of women. *Public Health Nursing, 11,* 268–272.

DONNERSTEIN, E., & BERKOWITZ, L. (1981). Victim reactions in aggressive-erotic films as a factor in violence against women. *Journal of Personality and Social Psychology, 41,* 710–724.

DWORKIN, A., & MACKINNON, C. A. (1988). *Pornography and civil rights: A new day for women's equality.* Minneapolis, MN: Organizing against Pornography.

GLASCOCK, J. (2005). Degrading content and character sex: Accounting for men's and women's differential reactions to pornography. *Communication Reports, 18,* 43–53.

GOLDE, J. A., STRASSBERG, D. S., TURNER, C. M., & LOWE, K. (2000). Attitudinal effects of degrading themes and sexual explicitness in video materials. *Sexual Abuse: Journal of Research and Treatment, 12,* 223–232.

GOSSETT, J. L., & BYRNE, S. (2002). "CLICK HERE": A content analysis of Internet rape sites. *Gender & Society, 16,* 689–709.

GROSSMAN, D. (1996). *On killing: The psychological cost of learning to kill in war and society.* Boston: Little, Brown.

JANSMA, L. L., LINZ, D. G., MULAC, A., & IMRICH, D. J. (1997). Men's interactions with women after viewing sexually explicit films: Does degradation make a difference? *Communication Monographs, 64,* 1–24.

LAAN, E., EVERAERD, W., VAN BELLEN, G., & HANEWALD, G. (1994). Women's sexual and emotional responses to male- and female-produced erotica. *Archives of Sexual Behavior, 23,* 153–169.

LAHEY, K. A. (1991). Pornography and harm: Learning to listen to women. *International Journal of Law and Psychiatry, 14,* 117–131.

LINZ, D., DONNERSTEIN, E., & PENROD, S. (1984). The effects of long-term exposure to filmed violence against women. *Journal of Communication, 34,* 130–147.

LINZ, D., DONNERSTEIN, E., & PENROD, S. (1987). Sexual violence in the mass media: Social psychological implications. In P. Shaver & C. Hendrick (Eds.), *Review of Personality and Social Psychology: Vol. 7. Sex and gender* (pp. 95–123). Newbury Park, CA: Sage.

LONGINO, H. (1994). Pornography, oppression, and freedom: A closer look. In A. M. Jaggar (Ed.), *Living with contradictions: Controversies in feminist social ethics* (pp. 154–160). Boulder, CO: Westview Press.

LOTTES, I., WEINBERG, M., & WELLER, I. (1993). Reactions to pornography on a college campus: For or against? *Sex Roles, 29,* 68–89.

MacKinnon, C. (1997). Pornography, civil rights, and speech. In L. L. O'Toole & J. R. Schiffman (Eds.), *Gender violence: Interdisciplinary perspectives* (pp. 400–413). New York: New York University Press.

MacKinnon, C., & Dworkin, A. (1994, August 26). Statement by Catherine A. MacKinnon and Andrea Dworkin regarding Canadian customs and legal approaches to pornography [Press release].

MacKinnon, C., & Dworkin, A. (Eds.). (1997). *In harm's way: The pornography civil rights hearings.* Cambridge, MA: Harvard University Press.

Malamuth, N., Addison, T., & Koss, M. (2000). Pornography and sexual aggression: Are there reliable effects and can we understand them? *Annual Review of Sex Research, 11,* 26–91.

Malamuth, N., & Check, J. V. P. (1981). The effects of mass media exposure on acceptance of violence against women: A field experiment. *Journal of Research in Personality, 15,* 436–446.

Mayerson, S. E., & Taylor, D. A. (1987). The effects of rape-myth pornography on women's attitudes and the mediating role of sex-role stereotyping. *Sex Roles, 17,* 321–338.

Morrison, T. G., & Tallack, D. (2005). Lesbian and bisexual women's interpretation of lesbian and ersatz lesbian pornography. *Sexuality & Culture, 9,* 3–30.

Mosher, D. L., & MacIan, P. (1994). College men and women respond to X-rated videos intended for male or female audiences: Gender and sexual scripts. *Journal of Sex Research, 31,* 99–113.

Mulac, A., Jansma, L. L., & Linz, D. G. (2002). Men's behavior toward women after viewing sexually-explicit films: Degradation makes a difference. *Communication Monographs, 69,* 311–328.

National Coalition against Censorship. (1998). The sex panic: A conference report [Online]. Available from www.ncac.org/sexpanic.html

Palace, E. (1995). Modification of dysfunctional patterns of sexual response through autonomic arousal and false physiological feedback. *Journal of Consulting and Clinical Psychology, 63,* 604–615.

Pearson, S. E., & Pollack, R. H. (1997). Female response to sexually explicit films. *Journal of Psychology and Human Sexuality, 9,* 73–88.

Russell, D. E. H. (1993). *Against pornography: The evidence of harm.* Berkeley, CA: Russell.

Senn, C. Y., & Desmarais, S. (2004). Impact of interaction with a partner or friend on the exposure effects of pornography and erotica. *Violence and Victims, 19,* 645–658.

Senn, C. Y., & Radtke, H. L. (1990). Women's evaluations of and affective reactions to mainstream violent pornography. *Violence and Victims, 5,* 143–155.

Shope, J. H. (2004). When words are not enough: The search for the effect of pornography on abused women. *Violence Against Women, 10*(1), 56–72.

Silbert, M. H., & Pines, A. M. (1984). Pornography and sexual abuse of women. *Sex Roles, 10,* 857–868.

Sommers, E. K., & Check, J. V. (1987). An empirical investigation of the role of pornography in the verbal and physical abuse of women. *Violence and Victims, 2,* 189–209.

Strossen, N. (1995). *Defending pornography: Free speech, sex, and the fight for women's rights.* New York: Anchor Books.

Zillman, D., & Bryant, J. (1982). Pornography, sexual callousness, and the trivialization of rape. *Journal of Communication, 32,* 10–21.

SUGGESTED READINGS

DONNERSTEIN, E., & MALAMUTH, N. (1997). Pornography: Its consequences on the observer. In L. B. Schlesinger & E. Revitch (Eds.), *Sexual dynamics of antisocial behavior* (2nd ed., pp. 30–49). Springfield, IL: Charles C Thomas.

MACKINNON, C., & DWORKIN, A. (1997). *In harm's way: The pornography civil rights hearings.* Cambridge, MA: Harvard University Press.

RUSSELL, D. E. H. (1993). *Against pornography: The evidence of harm.* Berkeley, CA: Russell.

STROSSEN, N. (1996). *Defending pornography: Free speech, sex, and the fight for women's rights.* Garden City, NJ: Anchor Books.

*G*ERALDINE **B.** S*TAHLY* is *Professor of Psychology at California State University at San Bernardino, where she has been teaching psychology of women since 1980. Dr. Stahly has written and lectured widely on women's experiences of relationship violence. She frequently conducts training sessions on domestic violence for the police and judiciary and has testified as an expert witness in cases involving battered women.*

22

Battered Women

Why Don't They Just Leave?

❖

Violence against women is a problem of international proportions, and nowhere is a woman in greater danger than in her own home (Walker, 1999). In 1995, I attended the United Nations Fourth World Conference on Women in Beijing, China, and I met women from all over the world who were working with victims of domestic violence. The final report of the conference included a declaration, which stated: "In all societies . . . women and girls are subjected to physical, sexual and psychological abuse that cuts across lines of income, class and culture" (United Nations Fourth World Conference on Women, 1995, paragraph 112). The World Bank (2001) tracked data on family violence as an indicator of social development and reported the percentage of the total population of women that are victims of intimate partners; every continent of the world was represented. Here is a sample: 48 percent in Puerto Rico, 34 percent in Egypt, 29 percent in Canada, 28 percent in Nicaragua, 23 percent in Australia, 22 percent in the United States, 19 percent in Colombia, 16 percent in South Africa, and 13 percent in Switzerland.

No nation in the world is without family violence, and advocates for battered women point out that the reported statistics are much lower than the actual occurrence of violence (Walker, 1999). In the United States, the Violence against Women Grants Office of the U.S. Department of Justice (1997) indicated that a little more than 1 million women made reports of violence in a year, but another department of the U.S. Department of Justice estimated that intimate partners beat 2.1 million women each year, more than twice the reported number (Langer & Innes, 1986). Perhaps even more telling, FBI statistics indicated that battered women account for one-quarter of all women who are murdered each year (U.S. Department of Justice, Federal Bureau of Investigation, 1996), and more American women are injured by their partners than suffer injury due to muggings, rapes, and automobile accidents combined (O'Reilly, 1983).

The tragedy of violence extends beyond the physical and emotional injuries to the woman. Children of violent homes are at increased risk of both physical and emotional abuse. Even if the battering husband does not physically injure the children, they live in an environment of terror. Children of battered women who have never been physically abused show all the characteristics of battered children (APA Presidential Task Force, 1996). As the director of a shelter in the late 1970s, I observed the effects on children firsthand. Hardly a night went by without several children waking up screaming with night terrors. Children as young as 10 had high blood pressure and even ulcers. The damaging effects on the children's emotional and behavioral well-being were also clear. Little boys often hit their mothers to get attention, and one day several little girls hid in terror when a man came to repair the house.

Empirical studies have confirmed the serious effects of family violence on children that I observed in the shelter. Boys who have witnessed their fathers beating their mothers are 24 times more likely to commit sexual assault than are boys with nonviolent fathers; they are 74 percent more likely to commit violent crimes in general. Girls and boys who witness their mothers beaten are six times more likely to commit suicide, and the girls are more likely to engage in teenage prostitution (Jaffe, Wolfe, & Wilson, 1990). Ultimately, the son may try to protect his mother from violence, and as a result 63 percent of males between the ages of 11 and 20 who are in jail for homicide are there for killing their mother's batterer. Tragically, these young men who went to prison for protecting their moms may well become batterers of their own intimate partners because sons who witness their mother's battery are three times more likely to become batterers than are sons of nonviolent fathers (Hotaling & Sugarman, 1986). In my work (Stahly, 1987), I have found what may be part of the attitudinal base of the intergenerational transmission of partner battering. Male college students who had witnessed their mothers being battered had the most negative attitudes toward women—and were significantly more antifeminist than men in general, even more so than men who reported being emotionally or physically abused by their mothers (Stahly, 1987). Clearly, it's time to stop blaming the mothers for men's hatred of women! In the violent home, the boy learns not only the behaviors of violence but also the misogynist attitudes that support and justify the abuse of women.

Given the tremendous toll of violence on the lives of women and their children, it is probably not surprising that the question people most often ask of battered women and their advocates is: Why does a battered woman stay? Over the course of the more than 30 years I have been working in the area of domestic violence—first as a shelter director beginning in 1977 and later as a social psychologist doing research—I have been asked this question hundreds of times. Sometimes, the question is asked in a hostile and victim-blaming tone—as at a men's service club meeting, where a member suggested to me that women who stay must like being battered. Sometimes, the question is asked factually, in an attempt to understand

and craft interventions, as it was by now Senator Barbara Mikulski when I testified before Congress in support of the first national domestic violence legislation in 1979 (a bill vetoed by Ronald Reagan as one of his early acts in office). Sometimes, the question is asked in agony, as it was by a mother who called me in the middle of the night after her daughter had been murdered by her husband, despite the mother's best efforts to help her daughter leave and stay away.

However it is asked, it is a question worth answering. In this lecture, we will explore some of the answers to this question from a number of different perspectives. Perhaps we can put to rest the question "Why does she stay?" and begin to ask more clearly and forcefully the most appropriate question: Why should a woman and her children have to leave home in order to live in peace?

HISTORICAL PERSPECTIVE

A dog, a wife, and a cherry tree, the more ye beat them the better they be.
Anonymous

This old English rhyme of unknown origin captures the traditional attitude toward violence against women in the context of the patriarchal family. Historically, women have rarely had the option of leaving a battering relationship. Under common law, the married woman and the children she bore were the property of the man. He was obliged to control and discipline them, and violence was an accepted method to accomplish this end. Evidence of a man's beating of his wife or children had no place in any court of law and was accepted as a matter of privacy and due course (Liss & Stahly, 1993). The home was the man's castle, and abuse of either children or spouse was no one else's business (Aries, 1970).

There were some limits put on the man's exercise of his privilege of violence against family members; under common law, the "rule of thumb"—a term we still use today to indicate a standard of behavior—dictated that a man should not beat his wife or children with a stick thicker than his thumb (Calvert, 1974). Needless to say, this standard did little to ensure the peaceful resolution of family disputes, and a battered woman was left with little recourse but to endure her husband's violence.

The tolerant attitude toward a man's violence against his spouse continued for more than 100 years after the official demise of the rule of thumb (Calvert, 1974). The criminal justice system continued, until very recently, to view most of the violence against women in relationships as matters of "privacy" and "civil disturbances" not appropriate for criminal proceedings. Women who wanted to leave a violent relationship could expect little assistance from the police or the courts, and only in recent decades have shelters been available for battered women and their children.

RACE AND CLASS EXPLANATIONS OF FAMILY VIOLENCE

An early, and probably the most complete, statement of the sociology of violence is the subculture-of-violence hypothesis (Wolfgang, 1958; Wolfgang & Ferracutti, 1967; Stahly, 1978). According to this theory, rather than being deviant, a violent act may be a response to subcultural values, attitudes, and rituals that define violent behavior as normative. Wolfgang offered this subcultural explanation of violence after he conducted a study in which he observed that most of the men convicted of homicide in Philadelphia over several years in the 1950s were poor and minority (Black and Puerto Rican in his sample). These men felt justified in their violent responses as a defense against what they perceived as threats to their masculine identity—behavior by the victim that they considered demeaning, demasculinizing, or disrespectful. The notion that battering men were predominately poor and minority was based on observing only the men in jail. The bias of this sample reinforced existing stereotypes about violence and people of poverty and of Color. As a result, domestic violence continued for nearly three more decades to be ignored as a problem of women of all classes and races.

The social perception that violence is "normative" only for certain stigmatized groups served to discourage women from leaving violent relationships. Women of poverty and Color who experienced the "subculture of violence" often believed the violence was an inevitable part of male privilege. Several woman in the shelter told me that they had not left their batterer sooner because they feared "going out of the frying pan into the fire," or "the next man will just be the same." On the other hand, the associations of domestic violence with stigmatized groups left White and middle-class women often feeling shame and isolation because the violence against them was denied by the larger society. Because middle-class violence was not considered normative, the White, middle-class woman often thought the violence against her was highly unusual, and to acknowledge it would bring shame and a loss of social standing on her partner and herself.

Although poor people and People of Color are more likely to be arrested and incarcerated for violent behavior, the notion that these groups are more prone to woman battering has probably never been true. An early survey of attitudes about interpersonal violence found no significant differences by race or class in acceptance of wife battering (Stark & McEvoy, 1970). A comparison of domestic violence calls between police precincts with different racial and socioeconomic demographics found no difference in the reported occurrence of violence, but poor and minority men were more likely to be arrested and incarcerated (Bard & Zacker, 1971). More recently, as arrests for partner battering have become mandatory in many jurisdictions, the bias toward arresting poor and minority men has been reduced. Arrested batterers now come from all races and income groups and include nationally known celebrities and politicians.

PSYCHOLOGICAL THEORIES AND VICTIM BLAME

Freud provided the earliest psychological theory of aggressive behavior; his explanations were intrapsychic and clinical (Freud, 1925/1974). Freud's theory of psychosexual development delineates gender differences in violence and suggests that sadism is an inevitable characteristic of normal male development and masochism of normal female development (Deutsch, 1945). Although the sadistic nature of males is rarely used to explain general male violence, the masochism of females became the defining feature of femininity and has been used extensively by psychiatry to blame women victims (Masson, 1984). According to the intrapsychic perspective, the battered woman stays in the violent relationship because of her unconscious need to be hurt and punished for her sexual feelings. This view of the battering relationship as rooted in female masochism is unfortunately not an anachronism—it is alive and well today. The continuing pathologizing of battered women by a significant number of mental health professionals is a form of victim blame, and it discourages serious analysis of the social forces that create violent men and trap battered women.

Another, more recent intrapsychic explanation of family violence is found in family systems theories. These theories suggest that all family members play roles in maintaining a status quo (homeostasis), even in violent and destructive families. The battered woman is seen as "equally" participating in the violence against her because of her intrapsychic needs (probably based on her own dysfunctional family experiences) and her secondary gains (she gets to be "right" when she "makes" the man hit her) (Lawson, 1989; Weitzman & Dreen, 1982). By attributing violence to the woman's prior personality style and provocative behavior, family systems theorists diminish the responsibility of the perpetrator and perpetuate the victimization of women. Feminist psychologists have been highly critical of family systems theory. For example, Hansen (1993, p. 81) stated: "Only when we recognize that battering is 'solely the responsibility of the man,' that 'no woman deserves to be beaten,' and that the social/political context has a direct impact on the maintenance of the behavior, is the family system likely to change."

A popular model that describes the alcoholic family takes the notion of "coresponsibility" even further and suggests that the partner plays a role in maintaining the dysfunctional family system by "enabling" the alcoholic behavior. This "enabling" individual (usually the woman) is seen as "codependent"—that is, facilitating the destructive behavior of the alcoholic to meet some intrapsychic needs of her own. This model of codependency has been extended to explain the behavior of a wide range of victims, including women who stay in violent relationships, although there appears to be no empirical data to support such a generalization (Cooley & Severson, 1993). The codependence model takes victim blame to the logical extreme of intrapsychic explanations of victimization; that is, the battered woman is "addicted" to violent relationships and therefore "finds" a man to abuse her. Like Freud's masochistic woman who "wants" to be beaten, the codependent woman "needs" the violent relationship to play out her internal script of "victim" or "rescuer."

Although the reversal of responsibility in violent families defies common sense and may seem ludicrous, such psychological theories of victim blame have real-world consequences. While conducting training for court mediators, I was told of a judge who routinely gave custody of children to the father in domestic-violence cases. The judge's bizarre rationale, apparently based on his cursory "understanding" of psychology, was that, because battered women always sought violent relationships, it was better for the children to be with their own violent father than to be subjected to the violence of the men in their mother's future relationships! I wish I could say that no psychologist, even those who endorse the concepts of family systems theory or codependency, would make such an absurd judgment. Unfortunately, I have worked on several custody cases in which a consulting psychologist has testified that the father's violent behavior was not significant and/or was "caused" by the mother's pathology.

FEMINIST THEORIES

Feminists come from a variety of theoretical backgrounds and may use parts of the traditional theories from sociology and psychology, but the aspect that best characterizes feminist analysis is the central position of gender and power as the fundamental issues in the explanation of violence within relationships (Bograd, 1990; Crowell & Burgess, 1996; Dobash, Dobash, Cavanagh, & Lewis, 1998; Walker, 1989). Intimate relationships are based on a value structure that assumes an unequal distribution of power between the man and woman. The man is a member of the dominant class, and he has greater access to resources and social power (Bograd, 1984). Regardless of race, socioeconomic status, or the details of their personal relationship, the woman is devalued relative to the man. In a patriarchal society, both partners learn that masculinity is superior. The masculine is defined by all that is "not feminine," and physically, cognitively, psychologically, and emotionally the male is normative. Patriarchal men share a sense of entitlement to respect and service from women based on the superiority of their sex alone. Feminist theorists view violence against women as, first and foremost, political acts of terrorism designed to maintain the privilege and power of men and the structure of patriarchy at whatever cost to women and children (Bograd, 1984, 1990; Dobash et al., 1998; Yllo & Bograd, 1988).

To understand why women stay in abusive relationships, feminists note that social institutions, including most religions, the criminal justice system, and the mental health establishment function within the rules and assumptions of patriarchy. These institutions, like marriage itself, generally support the right of men to dominate women, ignore or trivialize violence against women, and blame the victims. The woman who is battered has traditionally been discouraged from leaving by a combination of social forces that ignore her plight and deny her resources (APA Presidential Task Force, 1996; California Judicial Council, 1991; Ullrich, 1986). Feminists stress the practical reasons that women stay in dangerous relationships—for example, economic disadvantage in the workplace (women still earn nearly 30 percent less than men), fear of men's threats of retaliation, fear of losing their children, and lack of protection afforded by the police and the court system.

The Three-Stage Cycle of Violence

The classic work of Lenore Walker (1979) gave the first detailed analysis of the psychosocial forces that may trap a woman in a battering relationship. Based on clinical observations and a detailed questionnaire filled out by hundreds of battered women, Dr. Walker concluded that the battering relationship is cyclic, with an escalating and reinforcing nature that both isolates and traps the woman. The three stages of the "cycle of violence" were identified as the tension-building phase, the acute episode, and the loving reconciliation.

During the tension-building phase, the woman becomes aware of the man's increasing tension, as he becomes edgy and lashes out in anger. The woman often reports feeling that she is "walking on eggshells." The man's demands and accusations may be exaggerated and unreasonable. One battered woman with whom I worked was accused of trying to sabotage an important business meeting by forgetting to pick up her husband's suit from the cleaners.

The man shatters the woman's self-esteem and self-confidence. He may criticize her appearance or call her stupid or incompetent. (The businessman I mentioned previously told his wife that, if she were his secretary, he would fire her!). As the woman tries to anticipate the man's needs and "keep a lid on" the situation, she is taking responsibility for making him feel better. When eventually the batterer explodes in violence despite her best effort, she usually feels partially responsible and looks for ways she could have "tried harder."

As the man's unreasonable demands and threats increase, the woman may withdraw emotionally and even physically. Or the woman may try even harder to please and placate the man, only to find that he explodes, anyway. Other women may be accused of provoking the violence when they are finally "fed up" and "talk back," or even explode themselves at the men's excesses, giving the men a rationale for battering. Whether or not the woman knows what triggered the violence, she generally thinks she has failed and tries desperately to figure out what she could have done to prevent it.

The tension-building phase ends in an explosion of violence that is the second stage, the acute battering episode. The incident that sets off the man's violence is often trivial or unknown. Although people often ask the woman, "What did you do to make him so angry?" assuming that there must be some relationship between the offensiveness of the woman's behavior and the severity of the man's violence, I have rarely found this to be the case. On the contrary, the events that generally trigger violence are often mundane and even absurd. In one case I know of, a wealthy professional man broke his wife's jaw when he discovered that the large palm plant in the foyer of their mansion was dry; in another case, when a construction worker's wife served him "sunny-side up" eggs that had broken and run into his toast, he threw the plate across the room and then cut her face with the broken glass. Some women even report that behavior that pleases their man one day may cue his rage on another, leaving them desperately confused and feeling very helpless. For example, a woman in the shelter had been accused by her husband of not being interested in sex; when she bought a sexy negligee and behaved romantically to please him, he accused her of being demanding and a "whore."

During the violent beating, the woman may try to defend herself. If she manages to scratch or kick the man, he will often claim later that she started the violence or that she is as violent as he is. Women may actually be arrested for defending themselves!

The period following the battering is the third stage, the loving reconciliation. This stage is one of great relief for the woman—the tension that has been building is finally released, and the beating is over. The woman may initially be very frightened or angry; she may cooperate with the police and seek shelter with friends or relatives (she may even go to a battered women's shelter if there is one in her area that's not full). However, within hours or days of the beating the loving reconciliation begins. The man is often sorry and frightened that this time he may lose the relationship. He begins an intense campaign to "win her back," showering the woman with apologies, gifts, and loving sentiments. The man's attention helps repair the woman's shattered sense of herself as competent and lovable. The couple may appear to be on a "second honeymoon." Lenore Walker calls this the "love bond" that is reinforced as the cycle of tension and pain is followed by closeness. The battered woman may believe that the way the man behaves during the loving reconciliation is her "real" partner—and he could be this way all the time if they could just solve this problem or that. If the man has been arrested and charged with battery, the woman may beg the district attorney to drop the charges against her husband. If the case goes forward, the woman may testify in the man's defense, sometimes even contradicting her statements to the police and perjuring herself.

Not all battered women defend their batterers out of love—they may also defend them out of fear. When the district attorney's office has a policy that allows women to drop the charges—and some still do—the criminal justice system is, in effect, making the woman responsible for the outcome of the case and putting her in a terribly dangerous dilemma. If she testifies, the batterer will blame her and retaliate; if she doesn't testify, the violence will continue and she will blame herself for not following through and be less likely to call for help in the future.

The loving reconciliation can also be isolating for the woman. Helpers or friends may be unwilling to overlook the seriousness of the violence; friends will often reject the couple, and helping professionals will be dismissed by them. When the violence recurs, the woman finds she has fewer places to turn for support. Her isolation increases and, over time, the reinforcing nature of the cycle of violence may lead to escalation, trapping the woman in an ever-more violent and abusive relationship (Stahly, 1980).

Learned Helplessness and Learned Hopefulness

Studies of animal behavior indicate that, when an animal is repeatedly prevented from escaping punishment, it will eventually stop trying to escape (Seligman & Maier, 1968). Most animals can learn in one trial to escape from the white to the black side of a cage to avoid electric shock. But once an animal has been repeatedly prevented from escaping, it "learns to be helpless." Once this learning occurs, it may take as many as 100 trials with the experimenter literally dragging the animal to the safe side of the cage before it will finally escape on its own. Studies of learned helplessness in animals have been used to explain the reactions of humans caught in chronically abusive situations (Seligman, 1975; Walker, 1977–1978).

The experience of battered women is certainly different from that of the trapped animals in these studies. The woman is not just punished unconditionally but is specially punished for behavior that asserts her independence from the batterer. Further, she is rewarded for behaviors that make it more difficult for her to leave—for example, for passivity, compliance, and dependence. Hope that things may change and the gestures of kindness and concern that the man shows during the loving reconciliation stage may also play a role in keeping the woman in the violent relationship. This model has been called learned hopefulness, and elements of both the learned helplessness and learned hopefulness models fit the violent relationship (LaViolette & Barnett, 2000).

Early in the relationship, the woman often tries many different ways to stop the violence or escape. She changes the behavior the man criticizes, but in spite of her best efforts the beatings eventually come. She calls the police for help, only to find they do not respond effectively. The woman may turn to clergy and be told to be a better wife, to pray, or to be more submissive. She may try to follow this advice, but the violence continues. The woman may turn to her doctor, who tells her she needs to relax; the doctor may give her pills and she may become addicted to tranquilizers, but the violence still escalates. (I found that over 75 percent of the women entering Womenshelter in Long Beach, California, brought prescription tranquilizers or sleeping pills with them.) Other women may self-medicate, using alcohol or drugs to try to escape the tension and fear and reduce the pain.

If the woman leaves after a beating to stay with friends or relatives, the man follows her with threats or promises. She returns to him, often to find herself an unwelcome guest at that home the next time violence occurs. The list of experiences is nearly endless, but the result is the same. Eventually, the woman may become so depressed and feel so helpless that, even if alternatives to leave the situation are offered, it will be difficult for her to believe escape is possible and even more difficult for her to take action.

It is perhaps ironic that learned hopefulness may trap women in a violent relationship just as effectively as learned helplessness. Unrealistic hope is fed by many aspects of the culture—friends, relatives, the media, love songs, even religions encourage women to believe that they can save and change their partners (LaViolette & Barnett, 2000). The popular notion that "behind every good man is a woman" implies that it is women's role to change men and make them "good" and that the abusive husband presents a challenge. In one study, 73 percent of shelter residents returned to their abusive partners because they believed they would change (Pagelow, 1981). Learned hopefulness and learned helplessness both played a powerful role in keeping women trapped: The number one reason given by women for staying with the abuser was the hope he would change; the number two reason was fear of revenge (LaViolette & Barnett, 2000).

The Hostage Syndrome and Traumatic Bonding

Psychologists who study hostage situations have identified a pattern of behavior that emerges when individuals find their survival depends on placating a violent, hostile, unpredictable aggressor. After an initial period of shock and numbness, the hostages begin to communicate with the person threatening them. The abuse may be intermittent, interspersed with pleasant moments and even acts of consideration by the aggressor. A bond of sympathy, even friendship, may emerge.

Some psychologists consider the hostage's positive feelings toward the aggressor to be the result of a traumatic bond that appears to develop in chronic, intermittent abusive situations (Dutton & Painter, 1981; Graham, 1994). Even studies of animal behavior indicate that intermittent punishment and reward appear to strengthen the power of attachment. In studies of puppies' attachment to humans, it was found that a puppy that is intermittently punished and treated kindly shows 2 1/3 times greater orientation to humans than the consistently indulged puppy (Dutton & Painter, 1993). Similar findings appear in the study of attachment of infants to caregivers. Researchers have concluded: "The data show that inconsistent treatment (that is, maltreatment by, and affection from, the same source) yield an accentuation of attempts to gain proximity to the attachment object" (Rajecki, Lamb, & Obmascher, 1978, p. 425). Unlike puppies or infants, the battered woman's thinking as well as her feelings are distorted by the power the abuser has over her. Battered women who explain and defend their batterers' behaviors may be showing cognitive distortions created by the survival demands of their situations. They learn to survive by taking the point of view of the person who presents a threat to their survival. Battered women and battered children often love their abuser and try to survive by anticipating the abuser's needs and satisfying his wants—that is, by learning to think like the abuser.

The victims view themselves through the abuser's eyes and find fault with themselves and excuses for the abusers. This strategy may reduce the abuser's anger and may have important survival value for the woman or child while they are under the abuser's control. However, the perspective of the batterer cannot be easily abandoned, even when the victim is safely away from the battering situation. Battered women may go to court to testify in defense of their abusers, and at the time of a divorce, battered children may actually ask to live with the abusive parent. Sometimes, this behavior reflects cognitive distortion, and the victim really has taken the abuser's perspective. On the other hand, the woman and the child know they will have to deal with the abuser long after the court trial is over, and anticipating what the batterer would want them to say may be a way of trying to survive in the long run.

Effects on Self-Esteem

Because women have been reinforced for relationships more than for achievement, psychologists have found that women, more than men, depend on their primary love relationship for self-esteem and self-confidence. Many battered women adhere to traditional stereotypes of femininity and may consider their roles as wives and mothers central to their identity. The woman may believe it is her primary responsibility to make a happy home. When her partner beats her, it is "proof" that she has failed in this most important role. If she cannot please her man, she feels worthless and unlovable.

The battered woman is often socially isolated by her partner. He may restrict her activities and embarrass friends who visit until she is literally alone. She may get little feedback from people or activities outside her home. On the other hand, the battered woman's isolation may be more subtle. I worked with a very successful attorney who was also a battered woman. In court, the woman was a defense attorney who fought hard and successfully for her clients. At home at night, she was expected to prepare her husband's dinner, and if he was displeased with her cooking, her appearance, or even her conversation, he would hit her. No one in her public life could have guessed that this assertive woman would play such a traditional, subservient role at home. This woman reported that she felt competent and strong at work, but she believed that if she couldn't please her husband she was not really a successful woman. Like many battered women, she hid the violence against her in shame and embarrassment.

Whether the battered woman is literally imprisoned by her batterer or finds herself isolated from others by shame and silence, she gets little feedback from others. The batterer becomes the primary source of her information about her attractiveness, competence, and worth. As the battering and isolation continue, women report that it becomes harder and harder for them to remember "who I was" before the battering began. During the loving reconciliation, the man often rebuilds the woman's shattered self-esteem with his love and praise. It is not surprising that it is very difficult for her to leave him when he is meeting such a desperate need and easy for her to believe that somehow this time it is different and things will be better.

Passive and Dependent Behavior

As we have seen, the batterer is usually very jealous and controlling. The woman learns that to appear to be too independent or assertive will increase his anger and invite violence. The woman's passive and dependent behavior makes the man feel powerful and in control; it reassures him and sometimes postpones the violence. Thus, the passive-dependent behavior of the woman is adaptive, a survival strategy that is rewarded within the battering relationship. Unfortunately, such behavior helps to trap the woman in the relationship. Passivity and dependence increase her sense of helplessness and make it more difficult for her to gather the courage and resources she needs in order to leave.

Guilt and Shame

One aspect of the cognitive distortion we have discussed is the victims' belief that they can control the violence by changing their own behavior. The woman may accept the man's explanations for the violence as well as the common social attitude that "no man beats a good woman." The woman feels ashamed that she has failed to be "good enough." Accepting blame for her situation may actually be the woman's attempt to combat the sense of despair and helplessness she feels. She holds onto the hope that a change in her behavior will stop the violence.

Hope notwithstanding, nothing the woman does can ultimately control the man's violence. She may cook perfect meals, look like a Barbie doll, and agree with everything the man says, yet she will still be beaten. It is the abuser who is in control, not the victim. Ultimately, the woman finds herself with a painful choice between guilt and despair. When she believes she has the power to control the violence, she escapes the feelings of total helplessness and despair. However, by accepting responsibility for the man's violence, she is also accepting the man's blame of her. The double bind can be devastating. If the woman realizes that she has no control over the violence, then she may not feel guilt, but her feelings of fear, despair, and powerlessness may be immobilizing, and she may find it difficult to act to protect herself or leave. On the other hand, if she feels responsible and believes she has some control, then the guilt keeps her in the relationship trying to change her behavior to stop the violence. Either way, she is trapped.

While working in the shelter, I found that battered women were very relieved to learn about the cycle of violence and the social-psychological theories of victim response. For the first time, many felt less isolated and "crazy"— their behavior in forgiving the man and staying in the relationship made sense to them, and they were not alone. Ironically, women may find that they can stay away once they stop blaming themselves for staying so long.

WHEN THE BATTERED WOMAN LEAVES

The U.S. Department of Justice included questions about domestic violence in the National Crime Survey for the first time in 1986. This scientific poll questions a stratified sample of more than 800,000 Americans and is the basis for the FBI's estimates of the frequency of crime in the country. When this huge sample of people were asked about crime in relationships, a phenomenal statistic emerged. The U.S. Department of Justice found that 70 percent of domestic violence happened *after* the women had left the relationship (U.S. Department of Justice, Bureau of Justice Statistics, 1986a, b).

The battering man's need for power and control are increased when the woman leaves him, and the result is increased harassment and violence. When California enacted a law against stalking in the early 1990s—after a series of assaults on movie stars by berserk fans—the primary beneficiary became battered women because most stalkers turned out to be former husbands and boyfriends. National statistics confirm the link; in the 12 months preceding the 1997 U.S. government report on domestic violence and stalking, more than 1 million women reported having been stalked, 58 percent by a current or former intimate partner. Further, the same crime survey found that "among victims of violence committed by intimates, the victimization rate for women separated from their husband was . . . 25 times higher than for married women" (Violence Against Women Grants Office, U.S. Department of Justice, 1997, p. 20).

Studies of partner homicide have also revealed that the time of a woman's leaving is the most deadly, for both the woman and the man. Some critics of the feminist view of family violence have used homicide statistics to suggest that women are nearly as violent as men; the most recent findings suggest that over 40 percent of partner homicides are men killed by women (Hirshman, 1994; Sherven & Sniechowski, 1994). These critics overlook an important gender difference in partner homicide: Battered women kill defending themselves and trying to leave; battering men kill the women who are trying to leave or have succeeded in doing so.

Violence is not the only strategy the battering man uses to keep the woman from leaving or to force her to return. In discussions in the literature of the reasons women stay in or return to violent relationships, the women's fears for their children's safety and well-being have been generally overlooked. Threats of child kidnapping, custody battles, or violence against the children are significant factors in keeping the women in violent relationships (Lemon, 2000; Reihing, 1999; Stahly, 1999a, b). I conducted a pilot study (Stahly, Oursler, & Takano, 1988) of 94 women in shelters who reported that their batterers had tried to keep them from leaving by threatening the children with physical harm (25 percent), kidnapping (25 percent), or legal actions for custody (35 percent). In this sample, 20 percent of the women reported returning to the batterer at least once because of his threats to hurt or take away the children.

In a larger survey of the problems battered women face when they leave the batterer, staff members from 37 shelters in California completed a survey to describe the experiences of their clients (Stahly, 1990). During a one-year period, these shelters reported serving 6,034 women and 8,550 children as resident clients and 14,637 women and 4,204 children as nonresident clients and providing hot line counseling to an additional 87,378 women. The shelter staff were asked to reconstruct from their case files and staff logs information regarding the problems their clients experienced with custody and visitation. Their reports were astonishing. Of more than 100,000 women with whom the shelter staff had contact, 34 percent had children threatened with kidnapping, and 11 percent of the batterers had actually kidnapped a child—a total of 10,687 kidnappings in California in one year! Most of these kidnappings were never reported to the police, and the father returned the children after hours or days, but the point was made. The women were on notice that, if they did not return to their batterer or give him whatever he wanted, he would take the children and she might never see them again!

Fathers also used court action to intimidate and control the women, with 22,813 fathers (23 percent) threatening custody action and 7,168 fathers filing actions for sole custody. It is disturbing that the shelter staff reported that the batterers who had not directly abused their children actually won full custody less often (1,844) than fathers who were physically (2,997) or sexually abusive (2,262). This finding is consistent with the observation that mothers who report child abuse during custody proceedings are not only ignored but are sometimes seen as "vindictive" and are actually punished by the court (Chesler, 1986). Also disturbing is the tendency of courts to ignore violence and abuse in orders regarding visitation. In 25 percent (24,719) of the cases, the batterer used court-ordered visitation as an occasion to continue verbal and emotional abuse, and in 10 percent (9,512) of the cases, the mother was physically abused during the father's visits.

When the father makes good his threat to dispute custody, he is surprisingly successful. In the 1980s, an extensive clinical and case history study of women's experiences with custody found that "good enough" mothers lost custodial challenges 70 percent of the time, often to fathers who were abusive of the woman and children (Chesler, 1986). In the 1990s, the situation worsened with the introduction of an unfounded theory called parental alienation syndrome (Gardner, 1989). Mothers who raise allegations of sexual or physical abuse of their children or themselves are labeled "alienators," and the courts award full custody to the alleged abuser. Although the theory of parental alienation has little empirical support and appears to be unfounded (Faller & DeVoe, 1995), it has been widely disseminated among custody evaluators and court personnel. The practice of discounting allegations and evidence of sexual abuse and domestic violence raised during custody disputes is now well established in family courts across the United States, and it has begun to spread to other countries as well (Busch & Robertson, 2000; Dalton, 1999; Jaffe & Geffner, 1998; Lemon, 2000; Reihing, 1999; Stahly, 1999a, 1999b).

In several studies of randomly selected court records conducted in 1990, 1995, and 2000, a colleague and I found that violent fathers were twice as likely as nonviolent fathers to dispute the mother's custody of the children (Liss & Stahly, 1993; Stahly, 1999a, 1999b; Suchanek & Stahly, 1991). The courts apparently did not consider the history of violence important because the violent fathers won custody as often as the nonviolent fathers—or the mothers. The violent fathers were also more likely to want custody of sons than daughters, and they were more likely *not* to be paying court-ordered child support (a fact that seemed not to influence the judges' assessment of their parental fitness). The findings regarding custody disputes and woman battering seem to support the feminist analysis of battering men as motivated by power and control needs—and by misogyny.

CONCLUSION

We have discussed a number of explanations of why a battered woman stays in a violent relationship. Many different theories have been advanced to explain the woman's behavior. This reinforces the notion that the problem of family violence could be solved by convincing the woman to leave. Early on, feminists focused their energy on developing alternatives for battered women, including working to establish shelters and to change the policies of the criminal justice system and social-welfare systems that discouraged a woman from leaving and staying away.

I found that at every speech I gave as a shelter director, someone would ask some variation of the question: "Why doesn't she just leave?" I would do my best as a social psychologist and a women's advocate to help the audience understand and sympathize. I often asked the question I posed earlier: Why should a woman and her children have to leave home to be safe? Then after working 10 years on the issue of battered women, something dramatic happened to my thinking about the issue of leaving. I read the National Crime Survey of the Department of Justice previously cited, indicating that 70 percent of domestic violence crime happened after the woman left. I realized that asking "Why does she stay?" was begging the question! The fallacy of victim blame informed the question: We assumed that leaving would end the violence, and therefore the woman was made culpable for staying.

Now we know the terrible truth. Leaving the relationship does not end the violence for thousands of battered women. Not only does the violence continue, but it often escalates when the woman leaves. The feminist theory of battering as political—based on the man's power and control needs—is validated by the fact that the man is even more likely to assault and even kill the woman *after* she leaves. The reality of the battered woman's situation is not only that she is often trapped in the relationship, but even when she escapes that trap she is still prey to the violent, possessive man. It is important to understand the factors that discourage women from leaving, but the real dilemma is how to protect women who do find the courage and resources to leave.

In the final analysis, the best answer to the question "Why don't they just leave?" is simply that they can't. Battered women don't stay because of love, or dependency, or even economics; too often, they stay from the sheer terror that leaving will be even more dangerous than staying. A declaration of the United Nations (1995, paragraph 117) stated: "High social, health and economic costs to the individual and society are associated with violence against women. . . . [It] is one of the crucial social mechanisms by which women are forced into a subordinate position compared with men." We, as a world society, will not effectively address the tragedy of family violence and the fundamental issues of economic and social justice until we stop asking questions about the victim's character and behavior and demand instead that the abuser be held responsible.

REFERENCES

APA PRESIDENTIAL TASK FORCE. (1996). *Violence and the family: Report of the APA Presidential Task Force on Violence and the Family.* Washington, DC: American Psychological Association.

ARIES, P. (1970). *Centuries of childhood: A social history of family life.* New York: Knopf.

BARD, M., & ZACKER, J. (1971). The prevention of family violence: Dilemmas of community intervention. *Journal of Marriage and the Family, 33,* 677–683.

BOGRAD, M. B. (1984). Family systems approaches to wife battering: A feminist critique. *American Journal of Orthopsychiatry, 54*(4), 558–568.

BOGRAD, M. B. (1990). Why we need gender to understand human violence. *Journal of Interpersonal Violence, 5*(1), 132–135.

BUSCH, R., & ROBERTSON, N. (2000). Innovative approaches to child custody and domestic violence in New Zealand. *Journal of Aggression, Maltreatment and Trauma, 3*(1), 269–299.

CALIFORNIA JUDICIAL COUNCIL. (1991). *Gender bias in the courts.* Sacramento: State of California.

CALVERT, R. (1974). Criminal and civil liability in husband-wife assaults. In S. Steimetz & M. Straus (Eds.), *Violence in the family* (pp. 88–90). New York: Harper & Row.

CHESLER, P. (1986). *Mothers on trial*. New York: McGraw-Hill.

COOLEY, C. S., & SEVERSON, K. (1993). Establishing feminist systemic criteria for viewing violence and alcoholism. In M. Hansen & M. Harway (Eds.), *Battering and family therapy: A feminist perspective* (pp. 217–225). Newbury Park, CA: Sage

CROWELL, N., & BURGESS, A. (1996). *Understanding violence against women*. Washington, DC: National Academic Press.

DALTON, C. (1999). When paradigms collide: Protecting battered parents and their children in the family court system. *Family and Conciliation Courts Review, 37,* 273–296.

DEUTSCH, H. (1945). *The psychology of women: A psychoanalytic interpretation* (Vol. 2). New York: Grune & Stratton.

DOBASH, R., DOBASH, R., CAVANAGH, K., & LEWIS, R. (1998). Separate and intersecting realities: A comparison of men's and women's accounts of violence against women. *Violence Against Women, 4,* 382–414.

DUTTON, D. G., & PAINTER, S. (1981). Traumatic bonding: The development of emotional attachments in battered women and other relationships of intermittent abuse. *Victimology: An International Journal, 1*(4), 139–155.

DUTTON, D. G., & PAINTER, S. (1993). Emotional attachments in abusive relationships: A test of traumatic bonding theory. *Violence and Victims, 8*(2), 105–120.

FALLER, K. C., & DeVOE, E. (1995). Allegations of sexual abuse in divorce. *Journal of Child Sexual Abuse, 4*(4), 1–25.

FREUD, S. (1925/1974). Some psychical consequences of the anatomical distinction between the sexes. In *The standard edition of the complete psychological works of Sigmund Freud* (Vol. 19). London: Hogarth Press and the Institute of Psycho-Analysis.

GARDNER, R. A. (1989). *The parental alienation syndrome and the differentiation between fabricated and genuine child sexual abuse*. Cresskill, NJ: Creative Therapeutics.

GRAHAM, D. L. R. (1994). *Loving to survive*. New York: New York University Press.

HANSEN, M. (1993). Feminism and family therapy: A review of feminist critiques of approaches to family violence. In M. Hansen & M. Harway (Eds.), *Battering and family therapy: A feminist perspective* (pp. 69–81). Newbury Park, CA: Sage.

HIRSHMAN, L. (1994, July 31). Scholars in the service of politics. *Los Angeles Times,* p. M5.

HOTALING, G. T., & SUGARMAN, D. B. (1986). An analysis of risk markers in husband to wife violence: The current state of knowledge. *Violence and Victims, 1,* 101–124.

JAFFE, P. G., & GEFFNER, R. (1998). Child custody disputes and domestic violence: Critical issues for mental health, social service, and legal professionals. In G. W. Holden & R. Geffner (Eds.), *Children exposed to marital violence: Theory, research, and applied issues* (pp. 371–408). Washington, DC: American Psychological Association.

JAFFE, P. G., WOLFE, D. A., & WILSON, S. K. (1990). *Children of battered women: Issues in child development and intervention planning*. Newbury Park, CA: Sage.

LANGER, P., & INNES, C. (1986, August). *Preventing violence against women* (Bureau of Justice Statistics Special Report). Washington, DC: U.S. Department of Justice.

LAVIOLETTE, A. D., & BARNETT, O. W. (2000). *It could happen to anyone: Why battered women stay* (2nd ed.). London: Sage.

Lawson, D. M. (1989). A family systems perspective on wife battering. *Journal of Mental Health Counseling, 11*(4), 359–374.

Lemon, N. (2000). Custody and visitation trends in the United States in domestic violence cases. *Journal of Aggression, Maltreatment and Trauma, 3*(1), 329–343.

Liss, M. B., & Stahly, G. B. (1993). Domestic violence and child custody. In M. Harway & M. Hansen (Eds.), *Battering and family therapy: A feminist perspective* (pp. 175–187). Newbury Park, CA: Sage.

Masson, J. M. (1984, February). Freud and the seduction theory. *The Atlantic,* p. 12.

O'Reilly, J. (1983, September 5). Wife beating: Silent crime. *Time*, pp. 30–32.

Pagelow, M. D. (1981). *Women battering: Victims and their experiences.* Beverly Hills, CA: Sage.

Rajecki, D. W., Lamb, M., & Obmascher, P. (1978). Toward a general theory of infantile attachment: A comparative review of aspects of the social bond. *Behavioral and Brain Sciences, 3,* 417–464.

Reihing, K. M. (1999). Protecting victims of domestic violence and their children after divorce: The American Law Institute's model. *Family and Conciliation Courts Review, 37,* 393–410.

Seligman, M. E. (1975). *Helplessness: On depression, development and death.* San Francisco: Freeman.

Seligman, M. E., & Maier, S. F. (1968). Failure to escape traumatic shock. *Journal of Experimental Psychology, 78,* 340–343.

Sherven, J., & Sniechowski, J. (1994, June 21). Women are responsible too. *Los Angeles Times,* p. B7.

Stahly, G. B. (1978). A review of select literature of spousal violence. *Victimology, 2*(3–4), 591–607.

Stahly, G. B. (1980, August). *Psychosocial aspects of wife abuse: A theory of the spiralling effect of marital violence.* Paper presented at the meeting of the American Psychological Association, New York, NY.

Stahly, G. B. (1987, March). *Roots of misogyny: Long-term effects of family violence on children's attitudes.* Paper presented at the meeting of the Association for Women in Psychology, Denver, CO.

Stahly, G. B. (1990, April). *Battered women's problems with child custody.* Paper presented at the annual meeting of the Western Psychological Association, Los Angeles, CA.

Stahly, G. B. (1999a). Domestic violence and custodial challenges. In E. St. Charles & L. Crook (Eds.), *Expose: The failure of family courts to protect children from abuse in custody disputes: A resource book for lawmakers, judges, attorneys, and mental health professionals.* Los Gatos, CA: Our Children Our Future Charitable Foundation.

Stahly, G. B. (1999b). Women with children in violent relationships: The choice of leaving may bring the consequences of custodial challenge. In K. C. Faller, (Ed.), *Maltreatment in early childhood: Tools for research-based intervention.* New York: Haworth Press.

Stahly, G. B., Oursler, A., & Takano, J. (1988, April). *Family violence and child custody: A survey of battered women's fears and experiences.* Paper presented at the annual meeting of the Western Psychological Association, San Francisco, CA.

Stark, R., & McEvoy, J., III. (1970, November). Middle-class violence. *Psychology Today,* pp. 30–31.

SUCHANEK, J., & STAHLY, G. B. (1991, April). *The relationship between domestic violence and paternal custody in divorce.* Paper presented at the meeting of the Western Psychological Association, San Francisco, CA.

ULLRICH, V. H. (1986). Equal but not equal: A feminist perspective on family law. *Women's Studies International Forum, 9*(1), 41–48.

UNITED NATIONS FOURTH WORLD CONFERENCE ON WOMEN. (1995). *Report of the Fourth World Conference on Women, Beijing, China.*

U.S. DEPARTMENT OF JUSTICE, BUREAU OF JUSTICE STATISTICS. (1986a). *National crime survey.* Washington, DC: U.S. Government Printing Office.

U.S. DEPARTMENT OF JUSTICE, BUREAU OF JUSTICE STATISTICS. (1986b). *Preventing domestic violence against women: Special report.* Washington, DC: U.S. Government Printing Office.

U.S. DEPARTMENT OF JUSTICE, FEDERAL BUREAU OF INVESTIGATION. (1996). *Crimes in the United States: Uniform crime report.* Washington, DC: U.S. Government Printing Office.

VIOLENCE AGAINST WOMEN GRANTS OFFICE, OFFICE OF JUSTICE PROGRAMS, U.S. DEPARTMENT OF JUSTICE. (1997, July). *The second annual report to Congress under the Violence Against Women Act.* Washington, DC: U.S. Government Printing Office.

WALKER, L. E. A. (1977–1978). Battered women and learned helplessness. *Victimology, 2*(3/4), 525–534.

WALKER, L. E. A. (1979). *The battered woman.* New York: Springer.

WALKER, L. E. A. (1989). Psychology and violence against women. *American Psychologist, 44,* 695–702.

WALKER, L. E. A. (1999). Psychology and domestic violence around the world. *American Psychologist, 54,* 21–29.

WEITZMAN, J., & DREEN, K. (1982). Wife beating: A view of the marital dyad. *Social Casework, 63,* 259–265.

WOLFGANG, M. E. (1958). *Patterns of criminal homicide.* Philadelphia: University of Pennsylvania Press.

WOLFGANG, M. E., & FERRACUTTI, F. (1967). *The subculture of violence: Towards an integrated theory of criminology.* New York: Tavistock.

WORLD BANK. (2001, April). *World development indicators.* Washington, DC: Development Data Center, The World Bank.

YLLO, K., & BOGRAD, M. (Eds.). (1988). *Feminist perspectives on wife abuse.* Newbury Park, CA: Sage.

*S*UGGESTED READINGS

AMERICAN PSYCHOLOGICAL ASSOCIATION PRESIDENTIAL TASK FORCE. (1996). *Violence and the family: Report of the APA Presidential Task Force on Violence and the Family.* Washington, DC: American Psychological Association.

LAVIOLETTE, A. D., & BARNETT, O. W. (2000). *It could happen to anyone: Why battered women stay.* (2nd ed.). London: Sage.

WALKER, L. E. (1989). *Terrifying love: Why battered women kill and how society responds.* New York: Harper & Row.

YLLO, K., & BOGRAD, M. (Eds.). (1988). *Feminist perspectives on wife abuse.* Newbury Park, CA: Sage.

MARY GERGEN is Professor Emerita of Psychology and Women's Studies at Pennsylvania State University-Delaware County, where for many years she taught courses on the Psychology of Women. She is co-editor of the Positive Aging Newsletter, *an international e-publication, which is designed to challenge stereotypes about aging. Her interests include narrative psychology, adult development and aging, and qualitative research methods.*

23

Positive Aging for Women

❖

Unlike most other demographic characteristics, such as sex, race, sexual orientation, and ethnicity, stable qualities that usually last a lifetime, being old is one that is eventually acquired by anyone who lives a long time. Thus, whether you are 19 or 29, chances are good that you will someday be an old woman or an old man. This fact of life is one that is frequently overlooked by young people, and, when alluded to, is often suppressed. In American culture, no one wants to get old. In fact, being old is considered so negative that most "older" people refuse to define themselves as such (Friedan, 1993). This is especially true of women because, of all the stereotypes in society today, "old woman" is probably the worst and the most pervasive. What do we think of when we hear the phrase "old woman"? We may think "unattractive, out of shape, unfashionable, unhealthy, slow, dull," and perhaps even "demented." For many people, old women are so socially useless that they might as well disappear. As it is they often are eased from the public eye into some state of oblivion. No wonder no one wants to imagine what they will be like at that age. No wonder we all but disappear (Gergen, 2001).

*N*ON-WESTERN VIEWS OF OLDER WOMEN: *A GLIMPSE*

This story of female obsolescence is primarily a Western one. Many non-Western cultures hold older women in much higher regard than Western cultures do. Let us highlight a few examples. Old women have an important role in Native

377

American religious pantheons. The Lakota offer prayers to Grandmother and Grandfather, as the deities connected to the Earth and the Sky. The Navajo's Changing Woman is responsible for all new life and crop growth. Among the Cheyenne, the Old Woman of the Spring has knowledge and power to restore the buffalo. Grandmother Spider brought fire to the world after the young men failed. Wise old women are also the bearers of medical knowledge in many tribes (Plaskow & Christ, 1989; Wall, 1993). Among some African cultural groups, girls go on a retreat to learn from the wise older women how to cook, to heal, and to bring children into the world. They know about poisonous and dangerous plants, and so older women are often not only respected, but feared. Among the Gusii people of West Kenya, "Seniority is associated with respect, obedience, prestige and social esteem," according to anthropologist Richard Sweder (1998, pp. 58).

In this lecture, we will be primarily concerned with the lowly position of the older woman in Western societies. Our goal will be to shake up this negative stereotype and to suggest that the last one-third of life might well be the best one of all. What would it take to make that seem convincing? It would, first of all, require that we challenge many of the pervasive myths about aging. Second, it would suggest that new kinds of information and perspectives would have to replace these tired old myths and misassumptions, and, third, it would require that younger people, such as yourselves, take the risk of creating a lifestyle that will sustain you for the next 50, 60, 70, or 80 years. (The number of centenarians now alive exceeds 100,000, and the number who will be alive in 80 years is astounding; you may well be among them (Gollop, 1997) .

DISMANTLING THE MYTHS OF THE "OLD WOMAN"

One of the reasons that older women are seen as unfit is that the gerontological literature, including physical and mental health research, focuses on the central notion of deficit. What is interesting to researchers about older people is what they lose: health, cognitive abilities, reproductive potential, mobility, occupational capacities, physical skills, and social connections. A look at gerontological journals and books reveals titles related to Alzheimer's disease, broken bones from falls, cancer, depression, early onset dementia, forgetfulness, gout, heart disease, incontinence, and so on down the alphabet to widowhood, xenophobia, youth-envy, and Zzzzzzzzz—sleep disorders. Although I do not want to suggest that older people never have physical and mental problems, it is surprising how these problems are overestimated and how often the attributes and advantages of older adulthood are overlooked. Imagine, for example, that one lives happily for 87 years, as my mother-in-law did, and then after two weeks of being ill, dies. Should we only focus on her relatively brief demise and forget the blessings of the 87 years that preceded her decline?

I don't think so. Although it may seem foolish to be so focused on her life as it is ending, there are many reasons for this emphasis on deficit. They include our general tendency to see the world as problem-centered, to want to make lives better by changing what is wrong, and to be in a profession that caters to people who need us. For feminists there is also the political strategy of emphasizing the mistreatment of women and girls in order to create the grounds for broad social change.

Many myths are perpetuated that fulfill the stereotype that aging for women is a downward trajectory that leads to the grave. Among them are four common ones: the myth of menopause as disease; the myth of the loss of sexual interest; the myth of the empty nest; and the myth of feebleness. Let us disabuse ourselves of these myths as quickly as we can.

The Myth of Menopause as Disease: Going Crazy at 50

One of the prominent myths of women as they age is that they must pass through the period of menopause, during which time they become mentally and physically ill (Avis, 2003). This point of view is called the medical model of menopause, and it suggests that all women become (or should become) patients. This is the last hurdle of female development, from certain points of view; this perspective posits that after a crazy-making, disturbed 3–5-year-period, during which time women are often impossible to live with and should be medicated, they enter into a peaceful backwater of existence. After menopause women are believed to have lost their good looks, their meaning in life as productive creatures, and their femininity. This is almost never a true story of women's lives during menopause, and it need not be the case that every woman should become a patient or worry about her saga of menopause (Gergen, 1989). Yet, there is a near hysteria about menopause in current medical and social science writings. For example, psychologist Margaret Matlin (2000) reported that between 1990 and 2000, biological "retirement" was the topic of psychological research in 21,000 published articles, whereas only 116 articles were about women's retirement from paid employment. Yet, this latter type of retirement is also a life transition that is worthy of attention.

One of the interesting observations to make about this supposedly dire life event for every female of the species is that there are cross-cultural differences in what the experience of menopause is like and how it is regarded. For example, research in Japan has demonstrated how women's views of menopause are dependent on the cultural milieu in which they live (Gullette, 1997). The symptoms that Japanese women experience during their transition to menopause are different from those American women describe. They do not report having "hot flashes," a common complaint of American women, but rather muscular stiffness. In contrast to the stereotypes, U.S. women who no longer menstruate

often feel liberated from the "curse." Their moods often are more positive than before (Matthews, Wing, Kuller, Costello, & Caggiula, 1990).
Based on interviews with 65 American post-childbearing women, Emily
Martin (1997) found that the vast majority of women saw menopause
in a positive light, as an end to discomforts and worries associated with
menstruation and to fears of pregnancy, as well as a time of greater happiness and feelings of energy and strength. The medical community
needs to recognize the impact of the deficit model on the well-being
of patients and work toward a less pathologizing framework to help
women (Muhlbauer & Chrisler, 2007).

The Myth of the Loss of Sexual Interest

In many cultures strong connections are made between youth, beauty, and
sexuality. Opportunities for sexual contact are often dependent upon these
qualities. Yet sexual desire is not confined to the young or the beautiful.
In fact, for women, the development of sexuality often is a long-term
affair, with great variations in women's sexual preferences, desires, and
experiences. Leonore Tiefer (1995), a psychologist and author of *Sex Is Not
a Natural Act*, has suggested that sexual activity should be considered akin
to a hobby, enjoyable for many, not a necessity of life for everyone. Women
should feel a freedom to be sexual at any age, and also feel a freedom to
tailor a lifestyle that has little or no sexual content. Different strokes for
different folks, so to speak.

This diversity of desire was born out in a study regarding the sex
lives of over 400 older women in the United States, who were either interviewed or participated in focus groups with psychologists (Kliger &
Nedelman, 2006). About 40 percent of these women said that their sexual
desire was the same or greater than it had ever been; often the increased
sexuality was related to their increased appreciation for other sensual
things, such as perfumes, flowers, soft fabrics, music, and massage. For
many, their 50s, 60s, and 70s were the decades when they finally gave
themselves permission to explore creative impulses and try new outlets,
from glassblowing to playing the drums. They found that taking the time
to indulge in these forms of expression could lead to newfound sources
of pleasure, including sexual pleasure. Also important for sexual desire
to flourish among these women was the belief that one has the right,
as a woman past her reproductive years, to express her sexuality as she
chooses. For many women, having a partner often increased dormant
desires at every age. Having no sexual partner was the most important
reason given for a reduced interest in sexual activity.

There is a scarcity of research on sex among older women, and almost
all of it focuses on heterosexual women. Available research suggests that
among lesbian couples of all ages, as compared to heterosexual couples,
sexuality is much more a whole person experience than a genital activity,

focused on intercourse. Lesbians engage in longer lasting sexual encounters than heterosexuals do ("quickies" are not encouraged); they are more concerned that both partners are experiencing pleasure, and they include a wider variety of sensual techniques in sex play (Iasenza, 2002). In a rare case study of two older Lesbians of Color, researchers found that both continued to be sexually active women into their 70s (Hall & Fine, 2005). As Lesbians of Color, they believed that they had a sexual advantage over heterosexual women, who are more strictly bound by social conventions (Minnigerode & Adelman, 1978). Although "marginalized" by mainstream culture, these women considered themselves lucky to be so free.

The Myth of the Empty Nest

As long as mothering is considered the major accomplishment of a woman, and her children as the centerpiece of her life, then when these children leave home, a woman is presumed to be bereft. The meaning of her life is gone. This idea, called the "empty nest syndrome," surfaced in the 1970s in the United States and became a popular formulation for describing a woman's life. Although many women were inculcated with some feelings of trepidation at the advancing ages of their children, recent research has tended to question the reality of the empty nest syndrome. Rather, what seems to be the case is that, although mothers may deeply love their children, the great majority are happy to see them grow up and eventually leave home. For most parents, the empty nest is a place where they can again return to their own comforts, their own relationships with their partners, and their own personal priorities. Of course, the separation is never as complete as the myth describes. Children keep coming home again for holidays, vacations, or for laundry privileges; some even decide to return home for long periods of time. Contrary to the notion that mothers are delighted to have their children back under their roofs again, the friction of newly independent children residing in their parental homes can be a source of discomfort for both parties. It now seems clear that the "empty nest" was an empty problem for most women (Dennerstein, Dudley, & Guthrie, 2002).

Myth: Old Ladies Are Weak, Dependent, and Senile

The myth of the crazy old lady is alive and well in the United States. Old ladies are thought to be weak, dependent, and senile. This stereotype comes from a mixture of truth and fiction. The truth is that prior to the expansion of Social Security benefits, including cost of living raises and federal healthcare benefits to the elderly, the oldest people in the United States were the poorest (Morris, 1996). Today much has changed, and the average 70-year-old is richer than the average 30-year-old. Although there are many poor older women, this is often the result of earlier career and family circumstances. They may have had low-paying jobs or taken time off to raise children; they may have been single or lesbian, and, thus, have fewer or no rights to partner pensions; they may be minority group members who have been discriminated against racially or immigrants without the legal papers that would provide them welfare or other public benefits.

The poorest of the poor are "never-married-elderly-African-American women," but the generalization that old women are all weak, dependent, and mentally deficient is simply a myth. Even among the poorest Black women, research suggests that being an active member of a church is extremely powerful in helping these women to feel secure and happy (Larson, Sherrill, & Lyons, 1999). Money isn't the only source of comfort in an economically bleak world. Interviews with older African American women about healthcare suggests that they have more important things to do than be sick. "Some of the nice little old ladies that many people think they know can also be described as fiercely independent, unorthodox, and adventurous" (Gollop, 1997, p. 155).

There are great variations in the fates of older women, and age, per se, may not be the best predictor of whether or not they are satisfied with their lives. In a German study, Steverink and colleagues (2001) concluded that age is not a central factor in how satisfied or emotionally rich one's life is. Psychological factors and social resources, especially friends, are more important. Even physical decline was not a powerful predictor of life satisfaction. The researchers suggested that many physical changes are seen "as trivial…a normal part of the aging process" (p. 371). Many old people cannot run up a flight of stairs anymore, and almost all of them couldn't care less. But then there are a few who decide that they can and will run a marathon, even into their 70s and 80s.

One of the most powerful and debilitating myths of old age is that sooner or later everyone becomes senile. Yet the notion that all old women have some form of dementia, such as Alzheimer's disease, is greatly exaggerated. Even into the oldest of ages, the majority of people still have most, if not all, of their faculties. What does change is the speed with which older people process some materials, such as written texts. Younger people are quicker at most cognitive tasks, but not always more accurate. In certain kinds of intellectual activities, on average, older people are "smarter" than younger ones. The types of tests in which this is true tend to be ones where various solutions can be measured against each other. According to research by Paul Baltes and Ursula Staudinger (2000), lifespan developmental psychologists, when faced with a variety of dilemmas related to the "good life," older people are rated as the wisest in their views. In the case of wisdom, the tortoise is wiser than the hare.

Recent research also suggests that the brain, like the leg muscles, gains by exercise. Marian Diamond (2003), a psychologist who has studied how novelty increases brain capacity in rats, has suggested that if we do mental gymnastics, such as play Scrabble or Sudoku, read newspapers, magazines, and books, and have intellectual conversations, we will do for our minds what workouts in the gym do for our calves. Supporting her point of view is a massive study of elderly nuns, who have been given tests of mental ability for the past 20 years (Snowdon, 2001). These nuns have agreed to donate their brains to scientific study when they die, and to date 520 have been collected. Overall, according to David Snowdon, the results of cognitive tests and autopsies suggest that the nuns who have led a life rich in intellectual and social activities do not tend to have Alzheimer's disease when they die (often at very old ages). This perspective suggests that the better educated we are and the more we develop our cognitive skills throughout our lives, the better prepared we will be for a vibrant old age, mentally speaking (Schaie, 2005).

THE SOCIAL CONSTRUCTION OF AGE: CHANGING THE TEMPLATE

What motivates me, besides my age and gender, to challenge these myths and to create new ways of exploring what it means to be an old woman? My perspective on aging is guided by social constructionist theory, which endorses the possibility that people can co-create social change through their ways of making meaning together. This has been particularly important to me as a feminist concerned about reductions in life options for women at any age (Gergen, 2001). From a constructionist standpoint, descriptions and explanations of the world are not demanded by the nature of the world itself. The world, in an important sense, is speechless. Rather, it is when people communicate together that understandings about the world are constructed (K. Gergen, 1999; Gergen & Gergen, 2004). This capacity to "make meaning together" is not done through conscious decision-making nor through democratic processes. No, it is done mostly without our awareness. As we learn our native tongues from parents and teachers, we also acquire ways of knowing the world. When we use certain phrases, engage in particular gestures, and interact in our social and physical worlds, we create our realities. For example, as a teenager, you may have shared a language with your friends that was so private and distinctive that only your inner circle could understand it. Your social group was constructing its own reality. So too, gerontologists, doctors, therapists, professors, cosmetic salespeople, attorneys, and physical trainers have their own special ways of constructing the world, one that gives them a certain reality in which to practice their professions.

With regard to the concept of aging, a social constructionist point of view unsettles the widespread tendency within the social and biological sciences to declare "the truth" that human capacities begin to decline in middle age (Gergen & Gergen, 2000). From a constructionist perspective, the meaning of *aging* is the collaborative accomplishment of various parties, such as medical authorities, gerontologists, advertisers, and social scientists (Gubrium, Holstein, & Buckholdt, 1994). The myths of the aging woman that were described earlier are the result of past conversations that put older women in their place. Yet there is nothing about changes in the human body that requires a concept of aging or of decline. Because this image of aging is so strong within our culture, it is difficult to disregard it. Too much of our common sense (that is, our shared constructions) rejects this possibility. The rules of society are especially hard on aging women. There is a double standard that allows men to be much freer and more highly regarded, no matter what age, but especially after 50. As women lose their youthful beauty, their social currency seems to flag, according to the most superficial, yet powerful, cultural standards. In Hollywood movies, for example, it is not uncommon for the leading man to be 30 years older than his leading lady, but the reverse is almost never true.

There are serious and negative consequences of accepting the traditional narrative of inevitable and lengthy decline over the life span. One can view this scientific "story" as imposing an unhappy ending on older women's lives. This notion of a downward spiral can stifle optimism, variability, and creativity. Older women often learn to police themselves in such a way as to enact the very stereotypical images of aging that oppress them. They may behave in ways that support the view of themselves as undesirable, dependent, and demented as they fade into the background in business and social settings and let others take risks and try new things. They have learned that one should act one's age!

The path ahead would certainly be dark if the myth of decline in the last one-third of life went unchallenged. When we reject this bleak future, we are also opening up ways to construct new futures and new ways to become old. If we take a social constructionist position, we may ask: How can we create better futures for older women? What possibilities exist for the cultural transformation of aging? With this constructionist orientation in place, let us consider the grounds for viewing aging as a generative period of life for women.

RECONSTRUCTING THE LAST ONE-THIRD OF LIFE AS GENERATIVE

For the past several years many psychologists have tried to redress this negative view of aging. I have been among those deeply engaged in developing a perspective called "positive aging" and providing resources that may facilitate this refocus (see www.positiveaging.net). In the next section, research that has profound implications for living well across the life span is discussed.

Researching the Positive Potentials in Women's Lives

In reviewing gerontological research, I have discovered a rich array of materials that support the notion that older ages can be a wonderful period of life. Often, research is done with both genders, yet the majority of the participants are women because women are more prevalent in the older age ranges. I will indicate, if possible, differences that were found when women and men were studied together.

Relational resources. Family and friends are powerful influences on our well-being. They can help us to live well at all ages. Among older lesbian women, for example, friendship is extremely important to one's satisfaction in life because often one's sexual orientation has led to rejection by family members (Gabbay & Wahler, 2002; Hall & Fine, 2005). Friends are also very important when a spouse dies, even more so than family members (Stroebe & Stroebe, 1996). Studies indicate that people with numerous social contacts are more likely to feel supported and cared for; they are also less likely to become depressed (Pierce, Frone, Russell, Cooper, & Mudar, 2000). One of the strongest predictors of happiness over the life span is a good marriage (Myers, 1993). The so-called gender gap, the view that marriage makes men happier and women less so has not been confirmed, although, in general, single men are not as happy as single women, and men are more prone to depression than women if their spouse dies (Gove et al., 1990). Wood, Rhodes, and Whelan (1989) performed a meta-analysis of gender differences in happiness from a comprehensive set of studies, and found that women reported experiencing more happiness than did men and that marriage was associated with increased well-being for both genders; however, marriages were happiest during the honeymoon, at older ages, and, in most cases, after the children had left (Argyle, 1999).

Mental health resources. How older women experience life, how they make sense of it, and how optimistic and enthusiastic they are also contributes to their well-being. As women age, they regard themselves as better able to cope with their environments and relationships with others. Many older women see themselves on an upward trajectory psychologically, having internalized the idea of progress in their life narratives (Greene, 2003). Each year they believe that they are getting "better," not simply "older." Investigators increasingly believe that positive mental states may lead to better states of physical health. Argyle's (1999) summary of the literature indicates that the older a woman becomes, the more likely it is that she will feel happy and contented more often and depressed and upset less often. She will also be somewhat more likely to feel satisfied with her life than she did when she was younger (Krause & Shaw, 2000). In the longitudinal study of Catholic nuns in their 80s (mentioned earlier), researchers found a strong relationship between mortality and the kinds of emotions the nuns had expressed in diaries written when they were adolescents. Of those nuns who had expressed few positive emotions in their diaries, 54 percent had died by the age of 80. Of those who had expressed a high number of positive emotions, only 24 percent had died by age 80 (Danner, Snowdon, & Friesen, 2001).

Overall, it appears that older people have accomplished the task of the famous adage that one should change what is changeable, accept what is inevitable, and know the difference between the two.

Activities as resources. Relevant research indicates that the more older women are active, mentally and physically, the better their lives are (Prenda & Lachman, 2001). In one study, engaging in low-impact aerobic dance classes three times a week for 12 weeks improved the flexibility, muscle strength, body agility, and balance in women aged 57–77 (Hopkins, Murrah, Hoeger, & Rhodes, 1990). Greater involvement in religion, such as attending church and participating in church activities, is also positively related to life satisfaction among older women. Within the African American community, especially for older women, the church is an extremely important source of life satisfaction. As Larson, Sherrill, and Lyons (1999) found, among African American women, religious involvement is associated with physical health and psychological well-being. Other activities, such as volunteering, also are positively related to physical health (Van Willigen, 2000).

Aging, Mood, and Quality of Life

Recently, many gerontologists have found evidence that older women enjoy a great deal of autonomy and pleasure in their senior years. This may be a well-guarded secret, but one of the earliest such claims was made by the feminist scholar Bernice Neugarten (1968), who found that older women rated their quality of life as high, in part because they relished the freedom offered to them as they escaped the constraints of the traditional feminine gender role. Similarly, Carol Ryff (1985) found that, as they aged, older women valued achievement or success in the eyes of others less, and valued having a sense of freedom and being happy more (regardless of what others think). Research on personality traits over the life span shows that, as they age, women become less and less "neurotic," according to the "Big Five" personality indicator terminology (McCrae & Costa, 1990), and more emotionally stable (Srivastava, John, Gosling, & Potter, 2003). In terms of "agreeableness" and "openness," women are generally higher on these scales than men are, and become increasingly agreeable with age (Weiss et al, 2005).

WALKING THE TALK: PREPARING FOR POSITIVE AGING

From the moment of our birth we are all aging. In our culture, we celebrate aging primarily in childhood. The decade birthdays of 30 to 60 become times of anxiety of varying magnitudes, depending on our achievements and expectations in life. Forty is a time I once described as the point when a woman is considered "finished"—washed-up, no longer of interest (Gergen, 1990). Today, that societal scale has changed, and we think of 50 as the new 40, and 60 as the new 50, etc. The slide rule of time has given us 10 more "good" years. There are many reasons for this: better healthcare, "the pill," the workplace equality advanced by the feminist movement, and an increasing standard of living in the Western world. Also important, as Baby Boomers age, they challenge the negative stereotypes that now apply to them.

There are many choices to make about how one wishes to age. To experience positive aging for yourself, the most important move you can make at a younger age is to reduce your own prejudices against aging. What else might be done to have a wonderful last one-third of life? To apply what much gerontological research tells us, we can engage in certain important practices. First, if we fear aging and reject thinking about it, we are not off to a very good start. Rather, one can decide to meet the challenges of growing older head on. As one powerful resource, you can develop talents now that you can call on for the rest of your life. Educating yourself can be a lifelong pursuit, whether it is in a college, an art studio, or at home on your own. In terms of livelihood and civic engagement, fulfilling employment, community involvement, and leadership roles are physically and mentally stimulating. It is vital that you cherish your close relationships, as they are a source of nurturance and connection. Finding playful activities that keep you in motion is good, as is laughing as often as possible. Engaging in sensual pleasures (e.g., smelling the flowers, petting dogs and cats, and cooking a good soup) is life-giving. For some women, the desire for fun and freedom has encouraged them to join the Red Hat Society, which allows them to engage in spirited encounters with other women, usually while wearing a red hat, and perhaps a purple dress (Cooper, 2004; www.redhatsociety.com). Meeting people from different cultural and social groups enriches your life with new foods, languages, and styles of living. These are all good ways to age positively.

In terms of personal traits, optimism is helpful to well-being, so we should cultivate the capacity to see the glass as half-full, rather than half-empty. Developing a spiritual life is also very important for many, as is finding ways to relax and replenish your body and soul. Investing in a long and lovely retirement requires some planning and forethought, so don't wait until you are old to get started. Although all of these recommendations are seen as ways to lead a good life in old age, they are not so different from what facilitates an ideal lifestyle at any age. It's just easier to do it when you are old.

Social Policy to Enhance Positive Aging

To enhance the lives of older women, the most important goals are to improve their economic well-being, provide easily accessible medical care, and eliminate ageism in public and private realms. Without adequate funds for basic living needs, getting old can be a depressing and frightening period of life. Proposals to provide economic security for older women are especially relevant to African American women, who have the highest rate of poverty in the United States. A society that did not promote ageism in its communicative systems would be on the path to becoming a great society. Through political activism, with the support of educational, religious, and for-profit organizations, an era of positive aging can become a reality for us all (Belle & Doucet, 2003).

REFERENCES

ARGYLE, M. (1999). Causes and correlates of happiness. In D. Kahneman, E. Diener, & N. Schwarz (Eds.), *Well-being: The foundations of hedonic psychology* (pp. 353–374). New York: Russell Sage.

AVIS, N. E. (2003). Depression during the menopausal transition. *Psychology of Women Quarterly, 27*, 91–100.

BALTES, P. B., & STAUDINGER, U. M. (2000). Wisdom: A metaheuristic (pragmatic) to orchestrate mind and virtue toward excellence. *American Psychologist, 55*, 122–136.

BELLE, D., & DOUCET, J. (2003). Poverty, inequality, and discrimination as sources of depression among U.S. women. *Psychology of Women Quarterly, 27*, 101–113.

COOPER, S. E. (2004). *The Red Hat Society: Fun and friendship after 50*. New York: Warner Books.

DANNER, D. D., SNOWDON, D. A., & FRIESEN, W. V. (2001). Positive emotions in early life and longevity: Findings from the nun study. *Journal of Personality and Social Psychology, 80*, 804–813.

DENNERSTEIN, L., DUDLEY, E., & GUTHRIE, J. (2002). Empty nest or revolving door? A prospective study of women's quality of life in midlife during the phase of children leaving and reentering the home. *Psychological Medicine, 32*, 545–550.

DIAMOND, M. (2003). Forward. In S. Cusack & W. Thompson, *Mental fitness for life: A 7-step guide to healthy aging*. New York: Porter Books.

FRIEDAN, B. (1993). *The fountain of age*. New York: Simon and Schuster.

GABBAY, S. F., & WAHLER, J. J. (2002). Lesbian aging: Review of a growing literature. *Journal of Gay and Lesbian Social Services, 14,* 1–21.

GERGEN, K. J. (1999). *An invitation to social construction.* Thousand Oaks, CA: Sage.

GERGEN, K. J., & GERGEN, M. (2000). The new aging: Self construction and social values. In K. W. Schaie (Ed.), *Social structures and aging* (pp. 281–306). New York: Springer.

GERGEN, K. J., & GERGEN, M. (2004). *Social construction: Entering the dialogue.* Chagrin Falls, OH: Taos Institute Publications.

GERGEN, M. (1989). Talking about menopause: A dialogic analysis. In L. E. Thomas (Ed.), *Research on adulthood and aging: The human sciences approach* (pp. 65–87). Albany, NY: State University of New York Press.

GERGEN, M. (1990). Finished at forty: Women's development within the patriarchy. *Psychology of Women Quarterly, 14,* 451–470.

GERGEN, M. (2001). *Feminist reconstructions in psychology: Narrative, gender, and performance.* Thousand Oaks, CA: Sage.

GOLLOP, C. J. (1997). Where have all the nice old ladies gone? Researching the health information-seeking behavior of older African American Women. In K. M. Vaz (Ed.), *Oral narrative research with Black women* (pp. 143–155). Thousand Oaks, CA: Sage.

GOVE, W. R., STYLE, C. B., & HUGHES, M. (1990). The effect of marriage on the well-being of adults: A theoretical analysis. *Journal of Family Issues, 11,* 4–35.

GREENE, S. (2003). *The psychological development of girls and women: Rethinking change in time.* London: Routledge.

GUBRIUM, J. F., HOLSTEIN, J. A., & BUCKHOLDT, D. R. (1994). *Constructing the life course.* Dix Hills, NY: General Hall.

GULLETTE, M. M. (1997). Menopause as magic marker: Discursive consolidation in the United States and strategies for cultural combat. In P. Komesaroff, P. Rothfield, & J. Daly (Eds.), *Reinterpreting menopause: Cultural and philosophical issues* (pp. 176–199). London: Routledge.

HALL, R. L., & FINE, M. (2005). The stories we tell: The lives and friendship of two older black lesbians. *Psychology of Women Quarterly, 29,* 177–187.

HOPKINS, D. R., MURRAH, B., HOEGER, W. W. K., & RHODES, R. C. (1990). Effect of low-impact aerobic dance on the functional fitness of elderly women. *Gerontologist, 30,* 189–192.

IASENZA, S. (2002). Beyond "lesbian bed death": The passion and play in lesbian relationships. In S. M. Rose (Ed.), *Lesbian love and relationships* (pp. 111–120). New York: Harrington Park Press.

KLIGER, L., & NEDELMAN, D. (2006). *Still sexy after all these years? The 9 unspoken truths about women's desire beyond 50.* New York: Penguin/Perigee.

KRAUSE, N., & SHAW, B. A. (2000). Role-specific feelings of control and mortality. *Psychology and Aging, 15,* 617–626.

LARSON, D. B., SHERRILL, K. A., & LYONS, S. S. (1999). What do we really know about religion and health among the aging populations? In J. S. Levin (Ed.), *Religion in aging and health* (pp. 183–199). London: Sage.

MARTIN, E. (1997). The woman in the menopausal body. In P. Komesaroff, P. Rothfield, & J. Daly (Eds.), *Reinterpreting menopause: Cultural and philosophical issues* (pp. 239–254). New York: Routledge.

MATLIN, M. (2000). *The psychology of women* (4th ed.). Fort Worth, TX: Harcourt Brace.

MATTHEWS, K. A., WING, R. R., KULLER, L. H., COSTELLO, E. J., & CAGGIULA, A. W. (1990). Influences of natural menopause on psychological characteristics and symptoms of middle-aged healthy women. *Journal of Consulting and Clinical Psychology, 58,* 345–351.

McCRAE, R. R., & COSTA, P. T. (1990). *Personality in adulthood.* New York: Guilford

MINNIGERODE, F. A., & ADELMAN, M. R. (1978). Elderly homosexual women and men: Report on a pilot study. *Family Coordinator, 27,* 451–456.

MORRIS, C. R. (1996). *The AARP: American's most powerful lobby and the clash of generations.* New York: Random House.

MUHLBAUER, V., & CHRISLER, J. C. (2007). *Women over 50: Psychological perspectives.* New York: Springer.

MYERS, D. G. (1993). *The pursuit of happiness.* New York: Avon.

NEUGARTEN, B. (1968). Adult personality: Toward a psychology of the life course. In B. Neugarten (Ed.), *Middle age and aging* (pp. 3–37). Chicago: University of Chicago Press.

PIERCE, R. S., FRONE, M. R., RUSSELL, M., COOPER, M. L., & MUDAR, P. (2000). Social contact, depression and alcohol. *Health Psychology, 19,* 28–38.

PLASKOW, J., & CHRIST, C. P. (Eds.). (1989). *Weaving the visions: New patterns in feminist spirituality.* New York: Harper & Row.

PRENDA, J. M., & LACHMAN, M. E. (2001). Planning for the future: A life management strategy for increasing control and life satisfaction in adulthood. *Psychology and Aging, 16,* 206–216.

RYFF, C. D. (1985). The subjective experience of life span transitions. In A. Rossi (Ed.), *Gender and the life course* (pp. 97–113). New York: Aldine.

SCHAIE, K. W. (2005). *Developmental influences on adult intellectual development: The Seattle Longitudinal Study.* New York: Oxford University Press.

SHWEDER, R. (Ed.) (1998). *Welcome to middle age! (and other cultural fictions).* Chicago: University of Chicago Press.

SNOWDON, D. (2001). *Aging with grace: What the nun study teaches us about leading longer, healthier, and more meaningful lives.* New York: Bantam.

SRIVASTAVA, S., JOHN, O. P., GOSLING, S. D., & POTTER, J. (2003). Development of personality in early and middle adulthood: Set like plaster or persistent change? *Journal of Personality and Social Psychology, 84,* 1041–1053.

STEVERINK, N., WESTERHOF, G. J., BODE, C., & DITTMANN-KOHLI, F. (2001). The personal experience of aging, individual resources, and subjective well-being. *Journal of Gerontology, 56,* 364–373.

STROEBE, W., & STROEBE, M. (1996). The social psychology of social support. In E. T. Higgins & A. W. Kruglanski (Eds.), *Social psychology: Handbook of basic principles* (pp. 597–621). New York: Guilford Press.

TIEFER, L. (1995). *Sex is not a natural act.* Boulder, CO: Westview Press.

VAN WILLIGEN, M. (2000). Differential benefits of volunteering across the life course. *Journal of Gerontology, 55,* S308–S318.

WALL, S. (Ed.) (1993). *Wisdom's daughters: Conversations with women elders of Native America.* New York: HarperCollins.

WEISS, A., COSTA, P. T., KARUZA, J., DUBERSTEIN, P. R., FRIEDMAN, B., & McCRAE, R. R. (2005). Cross-sectional age differences in personality among medicare patients aged 65 to 100. *Psychology and Aging, 20,* 182–185.

WOOD, W., RHODES, N., & WHELAN, M. (1989). Sex differences in positive well-being: A consideration of emotional styles and marital status. *Psychological Bulletin, 106,* 249–264.

SUGGESTED READINGS

CLASSEN, C. (2005). *Whistling women: A study of the lives of older lesbians.* Binghamton, NY: Haworth Press.

GREENE, S. (2003). *The psychological development of girls and women.* New York: Routledge.

KOMESAROFF, P., ROTHFIELD, P., & J. DALY (Eds.) (1997). *Reinterpreting menopause: Cultural and philosophical issues* (pp. 176–199). New York: Routledge.

MUHLBAUER, V., & CHRISLER, J. C. (2007). *Women over 50: Psychological perspectives.* New York: Springer.

MAUREEN **C**. **M**C**H**UGH is Professor of Psychology at Indiana University of Pennsylvania. Dr. McHugh has taught psychology of women and related courses in diverse settings since 1974. She is a social psychologist and has published extensively on her work on feminist research methods, gender roles and gender differences, women and achievement, and violence against women.

24

A Feminist Approach to Agoraphobia

Challenging Traditional Views of Women at Home

❖

What is free will if you can't walk down your own road, if the idea of going to the market makes you so nauseated you have to lie down? You would trade your soul for a cigarette, which unfortunately you can't have because you can't get to the store.
— *Vonny, in* Illumination Night *by Alice Hoffman, 1987*

AGORAPHOBIA "EXPLAINED"

Diagnostic Criteria

Agoraphobia is defined by fear of public places and by the fear of being away from home. Fears of going places such as crowded stores or restaurants are frequently reported. People with agoraphobia often experience panic attacks when traveling, including driving and riding on public transportation. The agoraphobe may fear either closed-in spaces, such as elevators or tunnels, or open spaces, such as fields and empty streets, or both. Going to strange and unfamiliar places and being alone when away from home are the two most common fears reported. The agoraphobic woman may avoid any situation in which an easy retreat to safe and familiar

This lecture is dedicated to the memory of Marjorie Gelfond, feminist psychologist and researcher, whose work first challenged my thinking about agoraphobia. She died of breast cancer in 1992.

territory is not possible. Normal activities become increasingly restricted. Some agoraphobes are housebound; others may travel when escorted by a "safe person," often a specific companion.

Typically, the agoraphobic individual has experienced an attack in one or more public situations. The attack may have been medical in nature (e.g., asthma) but is more typically reported as panic. The panic attacks involve shortness of breath, heart palpitations, dizziness, nausea, weakness in the limbs, and the threat of bladder or bowel incontinence. These attacks are often accompanied by a sense of doom and a fear that one will die, become insane, faint, or otherwise lose control. Today the disorder is officially viewed as a subcategory of panic disorder; the agoraphobe is defined as an individual who has experienced an attack with four or more symptoms and has increasingly restricted her or his activities as a result (American Psychiatric Association, 2000).

Agoraphobia is the most common of the phobias. Over 50 percent of the individuals who report phobic distress are diagnosed as agoraphobic. Moreover, clinicians have described agoraphobia as the most distressing, disabling, and all-consuming of the phobias (Goldstein, 1987; Sable, 1991). Agoraphobes represent about 6.7 percent of the population, according to a national study (Magee, Eaton, Wittchen, McGonagle, & Kessler, 1996). Research has focused on White, middle-class populations, but some evidence indicates that there may be more agoraphobia in minority groups, and among the poor, than had been previously assumed (Michelson, 1987). Agoraphobic individuals are believed to exist across all classes and ethnic groups (Fleming & Faulk, 1989).

A Case Study

My grandmother was an agoraphobe. For the six years before she died, she only left her apartment in downtown Pittsburgh on a handful of occasions. These occasions diminished in frequency so that for the last year of her life she was completely apartment-bound. On one occasion, I coaxed her to ride the elevator of her high-rise apartment down 16 floors to the Muffin Burger on the ground floor. She raised her usual objections: She wasn't dressed right. She would have to "do" her hair. She might have an asthma attack. I don't know why, on that particular day, I was able to convince her when numerous other attempts had failed.

I visited her in her apartment regularly. Usually, I took a bus from another part of town where I was attending graduate school. I was one of her "suppliers." My mother and my aunts also helped to keep Grandma supplied with fresh milk, bread, and groceries. It was difficult for my mother, who did not drive. I had to make my visits during the day because that section of town with its adult bookstores and bars was not safe at night. On weekdays, the streets were crowded and we couldn't park; on weekends the streets were deserted and scary. As a healthy and strong woman in my twenties, I was sometimes afraid in downtown Pittsburgh. Question: *Was my grandmother's fear of leaving her apartment an irrational one?*

My grandmother was moved to this downtown apartment by her children. After she became a widow, the house that she lived in for her adult life was sold, and living with my aunt had created conflict, so at the age of 73 she was moved into this "comfortable" urban high-rise. My mother and her siblings thought their mother would like living downtown because downtown was the only place she would go unescorted (by public transport) in her adult years. Like many women of her generation, she did not drive and had never been employed outside the home. I can remember seeing my grandmother away from her home (at our house, for example) on only a few occasions. Usually, we visited her at her house. She lived on a steep hill. As a fat woman and an asthmatic, she could not easily walk anywhere. Question: *When did her staying at home become a "condition"?*

Even looking back, I can't say when her condition would qualify as agoraphobia, and at the time I didn't recognize the problem. But it did become more noticeable, and more inconvenient for others, after she moved downtown. Question: *Did she feel trapped in her apartment? Did she yearn to travel, to visit us, to shop in the downtown department stores?*

My grandmother, like most agoraphobes, was never diagnosed as such, yet in many ways her case is a classic one. She was a woman with a medical or physical condition; she was afraid she would experience an attack in public. She couldn't shop. The onset was related to role transition, to physical relocation, and to loss of autonomy.

I now have a better understanding of my grandmother's experience and that of many other women like her, which I would like to share with you. In this lecture, I will briefly present the current treatment approaches to agoraphobia and the feminist critique of traditional theories and treatments. Several alternative feminist perspectives on why some women are afraid of the marketplace and public streets are presented.

Traditional Approaches

Behavioral and pharmaceutical approaches have replaced the original psychodynamic interpretations of agoraphobes (Fodor, 1992). Historically, agoraphobia was attributed to fixation, regression, projection, or displacement of sexual and aggressive feelings (Sable, 1991). Agoraphobics were viewed as dependent personalities; the focus was on deep-seated individual psychopathology (Andrews, 1966; Deutsch, 1929; Weiss, 1964). One current psychodynamic approach is to view agoraphobic individuals as experiencing anxious attachment (Bowlby, 1988; Sable, 1991); the concepts of attachment and separation may be used to guide therapy. Brief psychodynamic therapy has been shown to be an effective short-term treatment, but there may be a high rate of relapse at follow-up (Hoffart & Martinsen, 1990).

Contemporary treatment of agoraphobia typically involves medication and behavior therapy. Agoraphobes may be prescribed antianxiety or antidepressive medication. Most anxious patients are using benzodiazepines (Craske, 1999), drugs that have a high addiction potential (Julien, 2000). Pharmacological treatment is not always effective; more than one-fourth of individuals do not respond to antidepressant medication, and there are high drop-out and relapse rates reported (van Balkoom, deBeurs, Keole, Lange, & Van Dyke, 1997). An underlying, usually unstated assumption of the medication approach is that something is wrong with the basic organism—for example, the brain, brain functions, or the endocrine system (Fodor, 1992). Frequently, biological models emphasize the role of genetics in agoraphobia; some people are seen as biologically predisposed to respond to stress with panic (e.g., Barlow, 1988). Other biological models examine the role of chemicals in the brain, including norepinephrine and serotonin, in producing panic (Coupland & Nutt, 1995).

Behaviorists view phobias as the result of the association (through classical conditioning) of anxiety with certain situations or stimuli. The avoidance of the feared situations or stimuli eliminates the anxiety and is reinforced physiologically and socially. Behavior therapy typically attempts to reduce the anxiety associated with the feared situation through systematic desensitization. The client is supported and reinforced through a series of approximations to the feared situation. For example, the agoraphobe may first be escorted to the store but not go in. This is followed by several trips in which she goes in and walks through increasing portions of the store quickly and without purchase. The desensitization is built up until she can shop alone under normal or even crowded conditions. Success rates for systematic desensitization are reported to be anywhere from two-thirds to 87 percent of clients (Fava, Zielezny, Savroon, & Grandi, 1995), but may subsequently entail substantial relapse and drop-out rates (Barlow & Brown, 1996).

Today most of the behavioral treatments include some attention to cognitive variables. The therapy explores the "irrational" nature of catastrophic thinking and other anxiety-provoking cognitions (Beck & Emery, 1985). The client is taught to combat such thinking or to substitute productive thinking. For example, Clark (1986) proposed that individuals with panic disorders attend to and misinterpret benign bodily sensations as dangerous. Panic patients interpret bodily sensations as signs of impending physical or mental danger (Clark et al., 1997). Barlow (2002) emphasized the factor of perceived control in his model of agoraphobia. Support for this model has been demonstrated. Patients who are fearful of the physical symptoms of anxiety and who perceive themselves as having little control over situations exhibit more phobic avoidance behavior (White, Brown, Somers, & Barlow, 2006). Cognitive-behavioral models have been refined and validated (Beck & Zebb, 1994) and have been shown to be effective in both brief and extended forms (Clark et al., 1999).

Neither the biologically based nor the cognitive-behavioral approaches to agoraphobia address explicitly the reason that 75 percent of agoraphobes are women (Fodor, 1992). For many individuals working with agoraphobia, the gender issue remains a mystery (Barlow, 1988).

A GORAPHOBIA AND GENDER

By all accounts, agoraphobia is related to gender in some way. In the United States, it is estimated that 75 to 95 percent of individuals diagnosed as agoraphobic are women. (For a review, see Craske, 1999.) This result is also commonly found in other parts of the globe (Barlow, 1988). Women are more likely than men to experience general anxiety (Wittchen, Zhao, Kessler, & Eaton, 1994) and are twice as likely to experience panic (APA, 2000). According to the American Psychiatric Association, panic disorder without agoraphobia is diagnosed twice as often in women as in men, and panic disorder with agoraphobia is diagnosed three times as often in women as in men (APA, 2000). More important, women are three times more likely than men to demonstrate the avoidant behaviors associated with agoraphobia (APA, 2000). Women are especially overrepresented at the most severe levels of the disorder (Turgeon, Marchand, & Dupuis, 1998). Ninety percent of individuals with severe agoraphobia are women, as are 70 percent of those with mild agoraphobia (Sanderson, Rapee, & Barlow, 1987).

Not only are the experiences of anxiety, panic, and agoraphobia more likely for women than for men, but women and men experience these problems differently. Some research suggests that the clinical course and outcomes of these disorders differ for men and women. For example, there appear to be gender differences in the onset of panic. In a Scandinavian sample, women more often than men reported that the panics resulted from a precipitating life event, often a family conflict and/or separation (Barzega, Maina, Venturello, & Bogetto, 2001). Girls similarly reported the experience of more stressful life events than boys in a study of gender differences in anxiety disorders of U.S. adolescents (Lewinsohn, Gotlib, Sieley, & Allen, 1998). Women with panic disorder are more likely than their male counterparts to develop avoidance (Reich, Noyes, & Troughton, 1987). Men with agoraphobia show less avoidance and more alcohol use. Barlow (1988) noted that men tend to self-medicate for anxiety with alcohol and suggested that men may turn to alcohol to help them through situations in which panic might occur. Women with agoraphobia are more likely than men to restrict their mobility and to require a companion or safe person to be with them when they go outside (Starcervic, Djordjevic, Latas, & Bogojevic, 1998). Women also suffer more recurrences and relapses than men do (Yonkers et al., 1998) and have poorer treatment outcome (Chambless & Mason, 1986). For women, especially, agoraphobia is a serious, chronic, recurring illness (Yonkers et al., 1998). (One way to interpret these findings is to view current treatment approaches as inadequate, especially for women.)

Given the greater prevalence in women, and the research that demonstrates the different experiences of men and women, isn't it likely that the experience of agoraphobia is related to gender and/or gender roles? Shouldn't the theories about the causes of agoraphobia and the intervention strategies employed to treat agoraphobia incorporate some form of gender analysis or sensitivity? That agoraphobia is more common in women than in men is acknowledged in the *Diagnostic and Statistical Manual of Mental Disorders* (*DSM IV-TR*, American Psychiatric Association, 2000). The relevance of gender to the incidence of agoraphobia is not explained by most theories or interventions, yet gender-based expectations figure significantly in the diagnosis of agoraphobia in terms of the rationality or pathology of the women's fears (McHugh & Cosgrove, 2004). Mental health professionals are likely to attend to agoraphobic symptoms when women cannot perform their traditional roles; not being able to carry out home-making responsibilities, such as grocery shopping and taking children to the doctor, are specifically mentioned in the *DSM* (APA, 2000). Further, current diagnostic approaches conceive agoraphobia as pathology that resides within the patient (as presented in the *DSM*, for example), and this conception results in a failure to recognize agoraphobia as a reaction to the everyday experiences of women that make them feel unsafe (McHugh & Cosgrove, 2004). Until we can answer the questions about the relationship between gender and psychological disorders, we will not be able to understand the problems of women, and we will not be able to move to a more proactive, preventative approach to women's mental health.

The feminist perspective asks what gender has to do with it. How is the fact that a person is a woman or a man related to her or his likelihood of experiencing anxiety or panic and of developing a phobia about leaving home? Feminists urge us to consider the sociohistorical context of women's experience (of anxiety or of agoraphobia). A feminist approach might see agoraphobia as a form of oppression in women's lives (Mohlman, 2000) that leads to immobility, excessive fear, increased dependency, and perceptions of helplessness. The feminist perspective includes an analysis of how cultural gender roles and sexual inequality create stress for women or affect the ways in which women react to stress. In an empirical demonstration of the impact of stress on women's mental health, university women who experienced frequent sexism had significantly more symptoms of anxiety, depression, and somatic symptoms than college men did, whereas women who did not report the experience of sexism did not differ from college men (Klonoff, Landrine, & Campbell, 2000). A feminist explores the possibility that women's problems in general, and an individual's problems in particular, may be rooted in gender roles and in gender inequalities. Thus, a feminist analysis of why most agoraphobes are women is part of a larger social movement to place women's mental health problems in a cultural context and to develop a structured, societal, and preventative approach to such problems.

Agoraphobia is identified as one of several mental health problems that are more prevalent among women (Fodor, 1992; Franks, 1986; Lott, 1994). Depression and eating disorders are similarly connected to gender, yet feminist therapists and researchers have not given agoraphobia the same attention that eating disorders, depression, and posttraumatic stress have received (Fodor, 1992). A feminist approach to treating agoraphobia has not been explicated (Mohlman, 2000). However, Mohlman (2000) suggested ways that a feminist perspective would inform our understanding and treatment of agoraphobia. She argued for a greater understanding of the role of culture in the development and maintenance of agoraphobia and called for therapy to focus on relational and social issues. Shouldn't the theories about the causes of agoraphobia and the intervention strategies employed to treat agoraphobes incorporate some form of gender analysis or sensitivity?

*F*EMINIST APPROACHES TO AGROPHOBIA

"The disorder of agoraphobia is a quintessential women's issue" (Fodor, 1992, p. 189). Fodor's (1992) conclusion is based on the same observation made by Seidenberg and DeCrow (1983) that agoraphobia in women is related to the ways in which all women are socialized to relate to the world.

Agoraphobia as a Cultural Construct

In many historical periods and cultures, women were not allowed to participate or were discouraged from participating in the public spheres of society. Remaining at home or being afraid to enter public streets would not be considered pathological in such a context. For example, women who remain at home in Islamic cultures are not considered agoraphobic. Thus, labeling the anxiety associated with participation in public spheres as "pathology" is related to the changing conception of what is appropriate behavior for women in our culture. The disorder agoraphobia was first named in 1871, at a point in Western society when women's roles were beginning to change (Fodor, 1992).

Gelfond (1991) argued that the assumption that the agoraphobe's fears are unrealistic or irrational needs to be closely examined. The phobic's anxiety is only unrealistic to the extent that the streets are objectively safe and that public places are comfortable for women. She suggested that many women who are not overtly phobic lead environmentally restricted lives. Women generally restrict their behaviors and avoid certain locations because they fear rape (Rozee, Chapter 20, this volume); who decides which fears are realistic or rational? Similar observations about women's comfort in public spaces have been made by others (Matrix, 1984). In their analysis, restrictions on mobility are taught to girls along with a fear of men. Societal inability to police the behaviors of (some) men means that women are forced to resort to remedial behaviors, such as not going out, going out escorted by a man, or staying in and around safe spaces (Matrix, 1984).

In her research, Gelfond (1991) compared agoraphobic women with two other groups: highly independent women and average women. (She recruited snowball samples and used an autonomy scale and the Brief Symptom Inventory by Derogatis and Spencer, 1982, to determine the groups.) She reported that 55 percent of the average women scored at or near the clinical range for agoraphobia. The average women also resembled the agoraphobes in their negative attitudes toward traveling alone, limited way-finding skills, and infrequent use of cultural, social, and recreational activities. Similarly, Brown and Cash (1990) found avoidance behaviors to be common among a normal sample of college students, and one-fourth of the sample reported a history of panic. Meyer (1987) described a group of women in the community who met the criteria for agoraphobia but who forced themselves to override their anxiety and continue to function. These women were less phobic and had fewer panic attacks than the matched agoraphobic controls.

This line of research questions traditional conceptions of agoraphobia as a distinct clinical entity and challenges traditional clinical research that fails to incorporate appropriate comparison or control groups. Both Gelfond (1991) and Fodor (1992) argued that agoraphobia might be more appropriately viewed as one end of a continuum; agoraphobes can be seen as sharing characteristics and behaviors with much of the female population. Gelfond (1991) questioned whether the opposing end of the continuum would be fear of being at home (domiphobia) or being comfortable at home. In her research, she employed highly independent women as a third point of comparison.

The Gendering of Public Spaces

Both Gelfond (1991) and Fodor (1992) suggested that public environments may not be safe or comfortable for women, especially for women who are unescorted. There are environments in U.S. society from which women are excluded or are strongly discouraged. Some examples are football games, military academies, coal mines, and Wall Street. Women who are anxious about going to a pool hall or who are afraid to run for U.S. Congress are not viewed as suffering from a disorder. Gelfond (1991) suggested that our understanding of agoraphobia, and our understanding of the female experience in general, would be assisted by viewing agoraphobia in relation to women's reluctance to enter public places unescorted.

I would like to illustrate Gelfond's (1991) point with a personal example. Although I am an independent woman who currently travels 100 miles a day to work at a university, I have a history of avoiding gas stations. I had an aversion to gas stations, which I initially viewed as a personal idiosyncratic neurosis. But based on Gelfond's (1991) analysis, I reexamined my discomfort with gas stations. I never had a traumatic experience at a gas station, but I perceived them as distinctly male environments in which women were unwelcome and were likely to be ridiculed or exploited. This is especially true of certain stations and was more true in the past than now, so I deliberately began to purchase gas at more female-friendly stations, ones that were clean, were well lit, or had women pumping gas. This analysis was confirmed for me when a large gas company called me as part of a national market survey. It was interested in what influenced women (a growing share of the market) to frequent particular service stations. I now see the redesign of service stations to include convenience stores and to exclude mechanical services as a response to women's stated preferences for a clean environment and one in which they could simultaneously perform another (women's) task. This example suggests that a serious societal response to women's anxieties, including those of agoraphobes, would be to analyze and potentially redesign many of our public spaces to make them female-friendly. We should inquire into whether or not public environments do present real dangers for women and whether or not unescorted women are made to feel safe and welcome (Gelfond, 1991).

Women at Home

Gelfond (1991) suggested that our understanding of agoraphobia could be enhanced not only by an examination of the experience of public spaces but also by a consideration of the meaning of home to women in general and to agoraphobes in comparison. Home, and a sense of place in general, may play a greater role in women's psychic lives than in men's. In a study of the meaning of home, women described home as a place for family, self-expression, and security (Churchman & Sebba, 1985). In a study of young couples, wives described the home as an expression of their identity; in contrast, the husbands described the home as a physical space (Hayward, 1977). Men are more likely to view home in terms of status and achievement, whereas women are more likely to view home as a haven or source of protection (Sommerville, 1997). In Gelfond's study, highly independent women as well as phobic and average women stayed home when disturbed. "From this perspective, women's reluctance to leave home can be seen to result from the control, status, identity, and personal meaning embedded in the place and concept of home" (Gelfond, 1991, p. 253). In an extension of Gelfond's research (Sagee & McHugh, 2006) both agoraphobic and non-agoraphobic community women described their homes as a place to retreat to when they feel stressed.

As an interesting extension of this reasoning, Gelfond reported on her home visits. She described the homes of the phobics as highly personalized, reflecting a "life compressed into a limited space" (Gelfond, 1991, p. 257).

Agoraphobes were likely to be collectors, especially of dollhouses or miniatures, and their homes created a feeling of enclosure and separation from the outside world. In contrast, the homes of the average women were "pleasant, yet unremarkable," and the homes of the highly independent women were functional, "bereft of expressions of the self" (p. 257). Thus, it appears that these women differed not only in their comfort with public environments but in their relationships to their homes as well.

Agoraphobia in Relation to Women's Roles

Today, women's roles often require them to leave home and frequent public spaces. Even the traditional role of homemaker includes public travel, such as shopping and community involvement. An analysis of agoraphobia might begin with what tasks or activities agoraphobic women avoid. In what context did they originally experience a panic attack?

Mary, a friend of mine, experienced a classic but mild form of agoraphobia. She was a suburban homemaker with two young children. She was not employed outside the home. She experienced a panic attack when taking her children to visit her in-laws. As a result of this attack, she was afraid to chauffeur her children to their many activities. This represented a problem for the family. When women cannot perform their traditional roles, when their anxieties inconvenience family members—that is, when they can no longer shop or chauffeur their children—then we design a label and an intervention for their fears. Mary was prescribed an antianxiety medication. Eventually, she resumed more limited chauffeuring duties. Today, she is employed as a school bus driver. There are two big differences between her original chauffeuring and being a school bus driver—autonomy and salary—that may be instructive in our consideration of the dynamics of agoraphobia. In my grandmother's case, it was her aversion to shopping that was considered the most indicative of a problem, not her refusal to take a vacation, to be active in community organizations, or to attend sports or cultural events.

Seidenberg and DeCrow (1983) offered a political analysis of agoraphobia. They suggested that the agoraphobic woman is "a living and acting metaphor, making a statement, registering a protest, effecting a sit-in strike" (p. 209). In their analysis, agoraphobia calls our attention to the limitations placed on women and to women's limited participation in the decisions of the world by exaggerating or caricaturing women's limited roles.

Gender Role Socialization

Agoraphobia runs in families. Most researchers in the area of agoraphobia agree that agoraphobics learn a dependent-avoidant pattern in childhood and that their families promote dependency and mistrust of the outside world while inhibiting the desire to move away (Fodor, 1992). Parental overprotection has been observed (Andrews, 1966). Fodor (1992) reported that in her clinical experience agoraphobics are likely to have families that promote traditional values, including that the woman's place is in the home. She observed that her clients come frequently from first-generation, working-class and middle-class Italian American, Greek American, Puerto Rican, and Jewish families.

Gelfond (1991) called our attention to studies that demonstrate that girls are more restricted and supervised and are given less encouragement to explore their environments (Block, 1978; Maccoby & Jacklin, 1974). Possibly as a result of these messages, girls and women have a less developed sense of direction than boys and men and are less able to form cognitive maps (Bryant, 1982; Koslowski & Bryant, 1977; Saegert & Hart, 1978). In her study (Gelfond, 1991), the independent women were found to be more geographically competent than the agoraphobic and average women. She reported that the independent women in her study were given more opportunity as children to be alone, both indoors and outdoors, than were the phobic and average women. For example, they were more likely to have attended overnight camp and to have gone downtown unchaperoned. Gelfond (1991) contended that this research should be extended. We should examine how women, agoraphobic and nonagoraphobic, have been socialized to adapt to private and public environments.

Franks (1986) remarked on the similarity between agoraphobic behavior and gender role stereotypes. In our culture, girls are socialized to express fear, whereas boys are encouraged to become independent and to fend for themselves. Women have traditionally been allowed to express fears and anxieties and to withdraw from feared activities in ways that men have not been. Among clients with an anxiety disorder, women are less likely than men to expose themselves to fear-inducing situations (Bekker, 1996). Chambless (1982) suggested that passively avoiding a feared situation rather than facing it may be more typical of women in our society.

Fodor (1974) explored the relationship between societal expectations for women and the helplessness and dependency that is characteristic of agoraphobia. She argued that agoraphobia is an exaggeration of the female role. Agoraphobic women are viewed as being oversocialized into the female role, receiving overdoses of femininity training to be fearful, emotional, avoidant, nonassertive, and nonadventuresome. Other theorists have adopted similar arguments that the gender role training of women leads to their socialization into a prescribed role that promotes fearfulness (Brehoney, 1983; Wolfe, 1984). However, when Schmidt and Koselka (2000) evaluated the popular belief that differences in "courage" explain the greater occurrence of agoraphobia in women, male and female participants did not differ in courage. Further, courage, as measured in the study, did not relate to phobic avoidance for either men or women.

Studies designed to examine femininity have not demonstrated that agoraphobic women are noticeably more feminine than other women

(Chambless & Mason, 1986). Similarly, Gelfond (1991) found that agoraphobic women and homemakers demonstrated very similar patterns of behavior. Women's feminine "nature" continues to be investigated as a cause of psychological disorders. In a recent study, for example, the researchers characterized the women as "overly expressive" and concluded that "they neglect their own wishes and needs, are too generous, are likely to be influenced by the wishes of others, and are unable to set boundaries" (Sachs, Amering, Berger, & Katschnip, 2002, p. 123). These women were viewed as being too easily exploitable. Are the men who exploit them viewed as having any pathology or responsibility?

Some researchers have argued that, rather than being too feminine, women with agoraphobia are insufficiently masculine (Chambless & Mason, 1986; Hafner & Minge, 1989; McCarthy & Shean, 1989). For example, in a comparison of women with agoraphobia and women who did not demonstrate a clinical disorder (normals), Chambless and Mason (1986) found that the agoraphobic women demonstrated lower masculinity scores—that is, they reported themselves to be less instrumental, active, and assertive. Hafner and Minge (1989) also found agoraphobic women to be less autonomous than controls. In a comparison of agoraphobic individuals and evening college students (controls), McCarthy and Shean (1996) found that controls demonstrated higher levels of agency than agoraphobic individuals (that is, they were more active and independent). Further, in each of these studies (Chambless & Mason, 1986; Hafner & Minge, 1989; McCarthy & Shean, 1996), higher levels of fear and anxiety in the participants coincided with lower levels of masculinity or autonomy. This is consistent with the general finding that in our culture masculinity is correlated with psychological well-being—for both men and women (Whitley, 1985). Both Fodor (1974, 1992) and Chambless and Mason (1986) argued that agoraphobia is connected to traditional gender roles in the United States, roles that promote dependency, deemphasize autonomy and mastery for girls and women, at the same time as they emphasize independence and instrumental behavior for boys and men. Although support for the relationship between feminine traits and agoraphobia has not been demonstrated at the individual level (see discussion above and Arrindell, Kolk, Pickersgill, & Hagemen, 1993), the gender role hypothesis was interpreted by Arrindell and his associates (Arrindell et al., 2003) as suggesting that social gender roles and agoraphobic fears are connected at the cultural level. In a test of the association of the cultural emphasis on traditional gender roles and incidence of reported agoraphobic symptoms at the cultural level, Arrindell and colleagues studied 11 cultures/countries, and found that in cultures that make clear distinctions between roles for men and women, and emphasize toughness for men, agoraphobic symptoms are high relative to the anxiety levels reported in cultures with less traditional gender roles.

One interpretation of the research is that women in general are taught to be anxious, fearful, and dependent and to restrict their mobility in varied ways. However, women with agoraphobia do not have the countervailing tendencies of agency, assertion, and autonomy to the degree that some other women do. Agoraphobic women's lack of autonomy and agency and demonstrated dependency are viewed as especially important within the context of their interpersonal relationships with men who are domineering. Although we do not want women to remain "trapped" in proscribed gender roles, feminists should also question the equation of competence, confidence, and autonomy with masculinity and the devaluation of generosity and nurturance that is implicit in this approach to agoraphobia (Mohlman, 2000).

Agoraphobia, Interpersonal Relationships, and Conflict

Traditionally, the agoraphobic patient has been a young married woman, and the onset of agoraphobia often occurs soon after her marriage (Chambless, 1982; Fodor, 1987). Marriage represents a change in identity, in status, and often in geographical location. Moving to a new home frequently means not only unfamiliar surroundings but also separation from one's friends and family. Research suggests that not only marriage, but also separation, divorce, death, and change in employment status are all role transitions related to the experience of panic and anxiety (Wittchen et al., 1994). Alternatively, marital roles and conflict are viewed as precipitating factors in the development of agoraphobia (Chambless et al., 2002; Craske & Zoellner, 1995; Fodor, 1974; Goldstein & Chambless, 1978; McCarthy & Shean, 1996). A recent review of the literature suggests that marital and interpersonal conflict are one type of stress that sometimes precedes and may trigger agoraphobic symptoms, but there are other equally likely stressful life events (e.g., relocation, new employment, or loss of employment) reported by individuals with panic disorder with agoraphobia (Marcaurelle, Belanger, & Marchand, 2003).

Beck and Emery (1985) presented an illuminating discussion of the way in which the married individual develops agoraphobia. The agoraphobic individual is suppressed by another person on whom he depends for support. Domination by the spouse erodes his confidence in his ability to function independently. He wants to receive support from his partner, yet be free and autonomous. The individual suppresses his expression of autonomy because it may alienate his spouse.

Notice that the use of the male pronoun in the preceding observations makes them nonsensical. The authors, Beck and Emery (1985), did not use the male generic; they employed the female pronouns even though their analysis is supposedly gender-neutral; that is, they did not address the question of why agoraphobes tend to be women, yet their analysis about the effects of suppressed autonomy and domination within marriage (on women) is very revealing. Their analysis cannot be presented using the generic masculine pronouns because the logic of their analysis rests upon our understanding that *women* cannot remain autonomous in marriage. Their analysis specifically discusses the way in which the husband's domination reduces the agoraphobic wife's confidence and increases her dependence, yet the problem is located within the woman; the husband's domination is not challenged or seen as pathological.

Similarly, Fodor (1987) discussed agoraphobia in married women as stemming from a feeling of being trapped in marriage, a feeling of being dominated with no outlet for expression of assertiveness. Agoraphobia assists the individual in avoiding autonomy, assertion, and conflict.

Fodor's analysis, however, explicitly concerns the way that gender role expectations create a strain for some married women. Other feminist theorists have similarly suggested that traditional gender roles within marriage can make women sick (Bernard, 1972; Chesler, 1972; Seidenberg & DeCrow, 1983).

Many of us might hope that marital patterns have changed and that fewer marriages reflect the traditional gender roles of dominant husbands and submissive wives. However, researchers continue to describe the marriages of agoraphobes as involving conflict and traditional patterns of domination and dependency. Prolonged marital conflict was reported as the main stress factor preceding agoraphobia by 84 percent of the respondents in one study (Kleiner & Marshall, 1987). Issues of domination and assertion were described, and respondents expressed a desire to separate from their controlling partners (Kleiner & Marshall, 1987). In another account, agoraphobic women rated themselves as passive and nonconfident, described their relationships as conflicted and unsatisfactory, and said that their husbands provided little emotional support (McCarthy & Shean, 1996). Women agoraphobes continue to be seen as experiencing marital conflict due to their "psychosocial disabilities" of being nurturant and generous (Sachs et al., 2002). Impaired problem solving, extended negative interchanges, and negative nonverbal behavior were observed in couples with an agoraphobic wife (Chambless et al., 2002).

Some view the relationship conflict and dissatisfaction as the result of the agoraphobia; the woman's symptoms are seen as the cause of marital conflict and distress (Emmelkamp & Gerlsma, 1994; Vose, 1981). Other reviews have led to the conclusion that relationship conflict is not significantly different for women with agoraphobia than for other women (Arrindell, 1987). Although many women other than agoraphobic women may have bullying husbands and severe marital conflict, that does not mean that marital conflict is not a problem in the lives of women with agoraphobia and not a factor in their distress.

Other reports in the literature suggest that marital distress and conflict occur in reaction to the patient's treatment and recovery. Unstable or unsatisfactory marriages get worse as the agoraphobe gets better. Marital disharmony increased in 60 percent of the couples studied during the course of treatment by Milton and Hafner (1979). Similarly, Hand and Lamontagne (1976) reported exacerbation of marital problems in married couples after exposure therapy. Hafner (1977, 1979, 1982, 1986) and his colleagues (Milton & Hafner, 1979) have carefully attended to the impact of treatment on the marital relationships of agoraphobes. Often, marital discord or dissatisfaction increases as the wife improves (Hafner, 1984). They reported, for example that, in some cases, the spouses experienced depression, anxiety, sexual disorders, jealousy, and extreme weight loss in response to the wife's recovery. Hafner (1986) described two relationship patterns that occurred in response to treatment. Six months after treatment, about one-half of the couples were having conflict over the wife's autonomy; however, these couples had adapted by the end of the year. In contrast, the more traditional couples experienced very limited conflict over the first six months, but significant conflict emerged later. Others have similarly noted that treatment dropout, treatment failure, and relapse following treatment are predicted by the features of the marriage (Carter, Turovsky, & Barlow, 1994; Chambless & Steketee, 1999; Dewey & Hunsley, 1990). In particular, the degree to which family members (generally spouses) express criticism of and hostility toward the agoraphobic patient predicts treatment outcome (Chambless & Steketee, 1999).

The connection between the quality of the marital relationship and subsequent treatment outcomes is an important consideration in designing interventions (Daiuto, Baucom, Epstein, & Dutton, 1998). In cognitive-behavioral treatments, the spouse is often recruited to act as a co-therapist. Such spouse-assisted exposure treatments are assumed to improve compliance in the patient, to enhance the spouse's support of treatment goals (Daiuto et al., 1998), and even to be useful in modifying husbands' negative reactions to their wives' autonomy. However, the positive (or negative) effects of such an approach are not well documented (Daiuto et al., 1998; Dewey & Hunsley, 1990; Sable, 1991). Such approaches may unwittingly perpetuate the dependency of the wife and the power imbalance in the relationship (Emmelkamp, 1982; Mohlman, 2000). Based on their review, Daiuto and his colleagues (1998) concluded that couples with healthy interactions are the best candidates for partner-assisted exposure. They recommended couples-focused therapy as an intervention strategy for couples who report conflict or marital distress. In cases in which marital conflict contributes to the problem, and husbands dominate or bully their wives, having the husband assist the therapist and escort the woman as she seeks more autonomous movements may be detrimental. Mohlman's (2000) recommendations for making cognitive-behavioral interventions with agoraphobic women consistent with feminist approaches to therapy include not using spouse-assisted exposure when it will maintain women's dependency and traditional power imbalances.

Marriages can and do break up once the agoraphobe has regained freedom of movement. For example, Goldstein (1973) presented a case in which the married female patient described her husband as a tyrant who constantly ridiculed her. When she needed emotional support, he was likely to make fun of her or become explosively angry with her. After therapy, she acquired sufficient self-confidence to initiate separation and divorce, and her symptoms disappeared.

In other cases, marital conflict is significantly associated with relapse after treatment (Milton & Hafner, 1979; Lazarus, 1966). The partner may undermine the agoraphobe's recovery. Goldstein and Swift (1977) reported three cases in which the patient's recovery was jeopardized by the spouse. Each of the patients had a husband who believed that control and authority over his wife was essential to his masculine image. Hafner (1982) also presented some illuminating case studies of the effect of intervention on marital discord. These cases include instances of attempted suicide and acute behavior disturbance of the husband. Also described are threats of hospitalization, abnormal jealousy, interrogation of the client after she returned home, verbal abuse, and intense disagreements. A family systems therapist would note how successful treatment of the agoraphobe has in each case upset the family system.

Agoraphobia and Violence

The first time I read through the case studies presented by Hafner (1982), I was upset by the images of agoraphobic women being dominated and intimidated "back" into illness by their husbands. I was also struck by the similarity between these descriptions of marital discord and a different set of cases with which I was familiar, those of battered women.

In particular, the jealousy, interrogation, and surveillance behaviors of the husbands are very similar to the spouse behaviors reported by battered women (e.g., Frieze & McHugh, 1993). Male batterers typically maintain control by limiting the wife's geographical and temporal mobility and by restricting her social interactions with her family and friends. In some cases, the agoraphobic client reported feeling isolated. Often, the onset is after physical relocation away from family and friends.

Social and physical isolation are also typical in a battering relationship. This similarity, combined with the researchers' report of psychological forms of intimidation such as attempted suicide and verbal abuse, convinced me that some of the marriages being described involved battering. The current evidence that many U.S. marriages involve physical violence suggests that some of the marriages of agoraphobes in treatment are probably violent; the fact that marital conflict is common in this population increases the likelihood of wife beating among these cases. The following is an example of this that one of my students recorded in her journal (used by permission):

> I personally feel that I was suffering from agoraphobia while involved in an abusive relationship. . . . Fear was an everyday, consistent, permanent emotion. . . . I was terrified that something would happen to harm my physical well-being. . . . I did not feel strong enough to defend myself against an act of physical or sexual violence, and my partner always reminded me of that fact. . . . I never went anywhere alone. He would accompany me everyplace. . . .

The agoraphobic reaction of this student made it difficult for her to leave her abusive boyfriend, although eventually she did flee to a shelter. If she had sought help for panic attacks, what type of treatment might she have received? Her description sounds very similar to the way that agoraphobic women are often escorted through life by the "safe person." Would her boyfriend be enlisted to help in assisted exposure treatment? What happens if the safe person is not safe?

A careful examination of the literature on agoraphobia has not yielded a single reference by any author to the possibility of woman battering. In a review of 24 studies of the relationship between marital problems and agoraphobia, Byrne and his colleagues (Byrne, Carr, & Clark, 2004) concluded that the research findings are inconsistent. A critical review of marital relationships and treatment of panic disorder conducted by Marcaurelle and his colleagues (Marcaurelle, Belanger, & Marchand, 2003) concluded that the research to date is insufficiently rigorous and the results are inconsistent. More important, the incidence of intimate partner violence in couples where one partner has agoraphobic symptoms was not addressed in either of these two reviews or in any of the included studies, even though marital conflict was the focus of the research. Despite references to specific forms of psychological abuse (e.g., tyrannical, making fun of her, explosive anger, vigorous arguments), none of the authors have addressed the question of whether these marriages involve physical, sexual, or psychological abuse. Further, I have been unable to find any assessment or investigation of the incidence of violence in the marriages or families of origin of agoraphobes. It is surprising and distressing that, so many years after my initial discussion (McHugh, 1989) of the possibility that violence is a precipitating or maintaining factor in agoraphobia, it remains uninvestigated. Recent articles on marital conflict in agoraphobia do not address the assessment of violence and abuse. Even without the extensive literature that documents marital discord and male domination in agoraphobia, one might anticipate certain levels of abuse to occur in these relationships, given the prevalence of intimate abuse generally (McHugh & Bartoszek, 2000). Individuals with a mental disorder are at higher risk of being a victim of domestic violence (Bohn & Holz, 1996). In one study of psychiatric patients, 64 percent had a history of domestic violence (Jacobson & Richardson, 1987).

Others have recognized that abuse and trauma can precipitate agoraphobia. Agoraphobia was found to be an early predictor of posttraumatic stress disorder (PTSD) in rape victims (Darves-Bornoz et al., 1998). Fodor (1992) reported incidents of panic disorder and an increase in fearfulness and anxiety that occurs following rape. Panic is also discussed as a feature of posttraumatic stress disorder (Steketee & Foa, 1987). Fodor (1992) concluded that real-life experiences of trauma may contribute to the development of agoraphobia. Agoraphobia was among the reactions of the 26 percent of a representative community sample of teenagers who indicated that they had been physically abused (Flisher, Kramer, Hoven, & Greenwald, 1997).

This analysis is distressing on several levels. It points to the need for better education of therapists, so that questions about physical violence get asked. Therapists who are not trained to deal with the answers are especially unlikely to ask questions about violence. Currently, there is no suggestion in the literature that encourages the therapist or the researcher to consider or assess the possibility that violence has occurred or is occurring in the marriages of agoraphobes.

Can we continue to ignore the possibility that violence is occurring, and can we identify those who are at risk for serious physical or psychological harm?

*C*ONCLUSION

Why doesn't she just leave? This is the question most often asked about battered women (McHugh, Frieze, & Browne, 1993; Stahly, Chapter 22, this volume), and it might also be asked about agoraphobic women. Elsewhere, I have argued that this question places the responsibility for the solution to societal problems on the shoulders of individual women and absolves men, and society in general, of any culpability or responsibility (McHugh, 1993; McHugh et al., 1993).

Therapeutic practices that focus on the individual woman and make it possible for her to leave do not solve the underlying problems. The batterer goes on to beat another woman; the dominating husband continues to dominate the agoraphobe or dominates someone else. Anxiety and fearfulness are still engendered in girls and women. Public streets and other settings remain dangerous or inhospitable for women who must have a "safe" companion to escort them. Women are expected to fulfill traditional roles. Individualistic approaches are thus viewed as ineffective and inefficient. A feminist analysis calls for structural or societal changes, such as Gelfond's (1991) call for a preventative approach to agoraphobia.

The feminist perspective encourages us to view agoraphobia (and other gender-linked disorders) not as individual pathology but in relation to women's experiences in general. The panic experienced by the agoraphobe is compared to the fearfulness experienced by most women in public settings. The phobic reaction of some women is compared to other women's responses to battering, domination, and marital conflict. Traditional clinical research methods that fail to include comparison or control groups are thus seen as flawed. Questions are raised concerning what are appropriate comparison groups (Gelfond, 1991).

The feminist analysis also offers insight into some novel practices that could be incorporated into traditional therapy approaches. Mohlman (2000) provided suggestions for incorporating feminist therapy principles into a cognitive-behavioral treatment of agoraphobia: Especially because (male) dominance and (female) nonassertiveness may be relationship issues, the feminist therapist would not establish another imbalanced relationship but enter into an active collaboration with the client that respects the client's goals and choices, including more traditional choices, such as staying in a conflicted relationship. Feminist therapists might try to help agoraphobic women transcend their prior socialization into the feminine gender role (including anxiety and dependency) and to develop a new set of behaviors that is not "based on essentialist ideas of what is masculine and feminine" (Mohlman, 2000, p. 33). In contrast to the individual focus typical of cognitive-behavioral therapy, there would be an emphasis on gender roles and the cultural context of relationships. The therapy would encourage women to become fully human and agents of change, at least in their own lives. Agoraphobic women may be deficient in map-reading and way-finding skills (Gelfond, 1991), which suggests that skill building in these areas could be part of the solution. Therapists and researchers may explore the meaning of home to agoraphobes or examine the fears that women have about specific public settings. I have argued that therapists need to question the agoraphobic client about her experiences of violence both within the home and outside of it.

Feminists have argued for a thorough examination of the sociological, historical, cultural, economic, political, and psychological factors that affect and limit women's choices. Women's experiences and problems are seen as occurring in a sociocultural context, as affected by gender socialization and as limited by gender roles. In contrast to contemporary treatment approaches, a feminist analysis of agoraphobia explores how these factors influence women to "stay home."

REFERENCES

AMERICAN PSYCHIATRIC ASSOCIATION (APA). (2000). *Diagnostic and statistical manual of mental disorders* (4th ed.). Washington, DC: Author.

ANDREWS, J. D. (1966). Psychotherapy of phobias. *Psychological Bulletin, 66,* 455–480.

ARRINDELL, W. A. (1987). *Marital conflict and agoraphobia: Fact or fantasy?* Delft, Netherlands: Eburon.

ARRINDELL, W., EISEMANN, M., RICHTER, J., OEI, T., CABALLO, V., VAN DER ENDE, J., et al. (2003). Masculinity-femininity as a national characteristic and its relationship with national agoraphobic fear levels: Fodor's sex role hypothesis revitalized. *Behavior Research and Therapy, 41,* 795–807.

ARRINDELL, W., KOLK, A. M., PICKERSGILL, M. J., & HAGEMAN, W. J. (1993). Biological sex, sex role orientation, masculine sex role stress, dissimulation, and self reported fears. *Advances in Behavior Research and Therapy, 15,* 103–146.

BARLOW, D. H. (1988). *Anxiety and its disorders: The nature and treatment of anxiety and panic.* New York: Guilford Press.

BARLOW, D. H. (2002). *Anxiety and its disorders: The nature and treatment of anxiety and panic* (2nd ed.) New York: Guilford.

BARLOW, D. H., & BROWN, T. A. (1996). Psychological treatments for panic disorder and panic disorder with agoraphobia. In M. R. Mavissakalian & R. F. Prien (Eds.), *Long-term treatments of anxiety disorders* (pp. 241–250). Washington, DC: American Psychiatric Press.

BARZEGA, G., MAINA, G., VENTURELLO, S., & BOGETTO, F. (2001). Gender-related differences in the onset of panic disorder. *Acta Psychiatrica Scandinavica, 103,* 189–195.

BECK, A. T., & EMERY, G. (1985). *Anxiety disorders and phobias: A cognitive perspective.* New York: Basic Books.

BECK, J. G., & ZEBB, B. J. (1994). Behavioral assessment and treatment of panic disorder: Current status, future directions. *Behavior Therapy, 25,* 581–611.

BEKKER, M. H. J. (1996). Agoraphobia and gender: A review. *Clinical Psychology Review, 16,* 129–146.

BERNARD, J. (1972). *The future of marriage.* New York: World.

BLOCK, J. (1978). Another look at sex differentiation in the socialization behaviors of mothers and fathers. In J. Sherman & F. Denmark (Eds.), *The psychology of women: Future directions of research.* New York: Psychological Dimensions.

BOHN, D., & HOLZ, K. (1996). Sequelae of abuse: Health effects of childhood sexual abuse, domestic battering, and rape. *Journal of Nurse-Midwifery, 6,* 442–456.

BOWLBY, J. (1988). *A secure base.* New York: Basic Books.

BREHONEY, K. A. (1983). Women and agoraphobia: A case for the etiological significance of the feminine sex role stereotype. In V. Franks & E. D. Rothblum (Eds.), *The stereotyping of women: Its effects on mental health* (pp. 112–128). New York: Springer.

BROWN, T. A., & CASH, T. F. (1990). The phenomenon of nonclinical panic: Parameters of panic, fear, and avoidance. *Journal of Anxiety Disorders, 4*(1), 15–29.

BRYANT, K. (1982). Personality correlates of sense of direction and geographical orientation. *Journal of Personality and Social Psychology, 43,* 1318–1324.

BYRNE, M., CARR, A., & CLARK, M. (2004). The efficacy of couples-based interventions for panic disorder with agoraphobia. *Journal of Family Therapy, 25,* 105–125.

CARTER, M. M., TUROVSKY, J., & BARLOW, D. H. (1994). Interpersonal relationships in panic disorder: A review of empirical evidence. *Clinical Psychology: Science and Practice, 1,* 25–34.

CHAMBLESS, D. (1982). Characteristics of agoraphobics. In D. L. Chambless & A. J. Goldstein (Eds.), *Agoraphobia: Multiple perspectives on theory and treatment* (pp. 1–18). New York: Wiley.

CHAMBLESS, D. L., FAUERBACH, J., FLOYD, F. J., WILSON, K. A., REMEN, A. L., & RENNEBERG, B. (2002). Marital interaction of agoraphobic women: A controlled behavioral observation study. *Journal of Abnormal Psychology, 11,* 502–512.

CHAMBLESS, D. L., & GOLDSTEIN, A. (1980). Anxieties: Agoraphobia and hysteria. In A. M. Brodsky & R. Hare-Mustin (Eds.), *Women and psychotherapy: An assessment of research and practice* (pp. 113–134). New York: Guilford Press.

CHAMBLESS, D. L., & MASON, J. (1986). Sex, sex-role stereotyping, and agoraphobia. *Behavior Research and Therapy, 24,* 231–235.

CHAMBLESS, D. L., & STEKETEE, G. (1999). Expressed emotion and behavior therapy outcome: A prospective study with obsessive-compulsive and agoraphobic outpatients. *Journal of Consulting and Clinical Psychology, 67,* 658–665.

CHANG, V. N. (1996). *I just lost myself: Psychological abuse of women in marriage.* Westport, CT: Praeger.

CHESLER, P. (1972). *Women and madness.* New York: Doubleday.

CHURCHMAN, A., & SEBBA, R. (1985). Women's territoriality in the home. In M. Safir, M. T. Mednick, D. Israeli, & J. Bernard (Eds.), *Women's worlds* (pp. 31–37). New York: Praeger.

CLARK, D. M. (1986). A cognitive approach to panic. *Behaviour Research and Therapy, 24,* 461–470.

CLARK, D. M., SALKOVSKIS, P. M., HACKMANN, A., WELLS, A., LUDGATE, J., & GELDER, M. (1999). Brief cognitive therapy for panic disorder: A randomized controlled trial. *Journal of Consulting and Clinical Psychology, 67,* 583–589.

CLARK, D. M., SALKOVSKIS, P. M., OST, L. G., BREITHOLTZ, E., KOEHLER, K. A., WESTLING, B. E., JEAVONS, A., & GELDER, M. (1997). Misinterpretations of body sensations in panic disorder. *Journal of Consulting and Clinical Psychology, 65,* 203–213.

COUPLAND, N. J., & NUTT, D. J. (1995). Neurobiology of anxiety and panic. In J. Bradwejn & E. Vasar (Eds.), *Cholecystokinin and anxiety: From neuron to behavior* (pp. 1–32). Austin, TX: R. G. Landes.

CRASKE, M. G. (1999). *Anxiety disorders: Psychological approaches to theory and treatment.* Boulder, CO: Westview Press.

CRASKE, M. G., & ZOELLNER, L. A. (1995). Anxiety disorders: The role of marital therapy. In N. S. Jacobson & A. S. Gurman (Eds.), *Clinical handbook of couples therapy* (pp. 394–410). New York: Guilford Press.

DAIUTO, A. D., BAUCOM, D. H., EPSTEIN, N., & DUTTON, S. S. (1998). The application of behavioral couples therapy to the assessment and treatment of agoraphobia: Implications of empirical research. *Clinical Psychology Review, 18,* 663–687.

DARVES-BORNOZ, J. M., LEPINE, J. P., CHOQUET, M., BERGER, C., DEGIOVANNI, A., & GAILLARD, P. (1998). Predictive factors of chronic posttraumatic stress disorder in rape victims. *European Psychiatry, 13,* 281–287.

DEROGATIS, L., & SPENCER, P. (1982). *Brief symptom inventory: Administration, scoring and procedures manual* (Vol. 1). Baltimore, MD: Clinical Psychometric Research.

DEUTSCH, H. (1929). The genesis of agoraphobia. *International Journal of Psychoanalysis, 10*(1), 51–69.

DEWEY, D., & HUNSLEY, J. (1990). The effects of marital adjustment and spouse involvement on the behavioral treatment of agoraphobia: A meta-analytic review. *Anxiety Research, 2,* 69–83.

EMMELKAMP, P. M. G. (1982). In vivo treatment of agoraphobia. In D. L. Chambless & A. J. Goldstein (Eds.), *Agoraphobia: Multiple perspectives on theory and treatment* (pp. 43–76). New York: Wiley.

EMMELKAMP, P. M. G., & GERLSMA, C. (1994). Marital functioning and the anxiety disorders. *Behavior Therapy, 25,* 407–429.

FAVA, G. A., ZIELEZNY, M., SAVROON G., & GRANDI, S. (1995). Long-term effects of behavioral treatment for panic disorder with agoraphobia. *British Journal of Psychiatry, 166,* 87–92.

FLEMING, B., & FAULK, A. (1989). Discriminating factors in panic disorder with and without agoraphobia. *Journal of Anxiety Disorders, 3*(4), 209–219.

FLISHER, A., KRAMER, R. A., HOVEN, C. W., & GREENWALD, S. (1997). Psychosocial characteristics of physically abused children and adolescents. *Journal of the American Academy of Child and Adolescent Psychiatry, 36,* 123–131.

FODOR, I. G. (1974). The phobic syndrome in women: Implications for treatment. In V. Franks & V. Burtle (Eds.), *Women in therapy* (pp. 132–168). New York: Brunner/Mazel.

FODOR, I. G. (1987). Cognitive/behavior therapy for agoraphobic women: Towards utilizing psychodynamic understanding to address family beliefs systems and enhance behavior change. In M. Braude (Ed.), *Women, power, and therapy: Issues for women* (pp. 103–123). New York: Haworth Press.

FODOR, I. G. (1992). The agoraphobic syndrome: From anxiety neurosis to panic disorder. In L. Brown & M. Ballou (Eds.), *Personality and psychopathology: Feminist reappraisals* (pp. 177–205). New York: Guilford Press.

FRANKS, V. (1986). Sex role stereotyping and diagnosis of psychopathology: The dynamics of feminist therapy [Special issue]. *Women & Therapy, 5*(2–3), 219–232.

FRIEZE, I. H., & McHUGH, M. C. (1993). Power and influence strategies in violent and nonviolent marriages. *Psychology of Women Quarterly, 16,* 449–465.

GELFOND, M. (1991). Reconceptualizing agoraphobia: A case study of epistemological bias in clinical research. *Feminism & Psychology, 1*(2), 247–262.

GOLDSTEIN, A. J. (1973, September). *Learning theory insufficiency in understanding agoraphobia: A plea for empiricism.* Paper presented at the European Association for Behavior Therapy and Behavior Modification, Munich, Germany.

GOLDSTEIN, A. J. (1987). *Overcoming agoraphobia.* New York: Viking.

GOLDSTEIN, A. J., & CHAMBLESS, D. L. (1978). A reanalysis of agoraphobia. *Behavior Therapy, 9,* 47–59.

GOLDSTEIN, R. K., & SWIFT, K. (1977). Psychotherapy with phobic patients: The marriage relationship as the source of symptoms and focus of treatment. *American Journal of Psychotherapy, 31*(2), 285–292.

HAFNER, R. J. (1977). The husbands of agoraphobic women and their influence on treatment outcome. *British Journal of Psychiatry, 131,* 289–294.

HAFNER, R. J. (1979). Agoraphobic women married to abnormally jealous men. *British Journal of Medical Psychology, 52,* 99–104.

HAFNER, R. J. (1982). The marital context of the agoraphobic syndrome. In D. L. Chambless & A. J. Goldstein (Eds.), *Agoraphobia: Multiple perspectives on theory and treatment* (pp. 77–118). New York: Wiley.

HAFNER, R. J. (1984). The marital repercussions of behavior therapy for agoraphobia. *Psychotherapy, 21,* 530–542.

HAFNER, R. J. (1986). *Marriage and mental illness: A sex-roles perspective.* New York: Guilford Press.

HAFNER, R. J., & MINGE, P. J. (1989). Sex role stereotyping in women with agoraphobia and their husbands. *Sex Roles, 20,* 705–711.

HAND, I., & LAMONTAGNE, Y. (1976). The exacerbation of the interpersonal problems after rapid phobia removal. *Psychotherapy: Theory, Research, and Practice, 13,* 405–411.

HAYWARD, G. (1977). *Psychological concepts of home among urban middle class families with young children.* Doctoral dissertation, Environmental Psychology Program, City University of New York Graduate Center.

HOFFART, A., & MARTINSEN, E. W. (1990). Exposure-based integrated vs. pure psychodynamic treatment of agoraphobia inpatients. *Psychotherapy, 27,* 210–218.

HOFFMAN, A. (1987). *Illumination night.* New York: Fawcett Press.

JACOBSON, A., & RICHARDSON, B. (1987). Assault experiences of 100 psychiatric inpatients: Evidence for the need for routine inquiry. *American Journal of Psychiatry, 144,* 908–912.

JULIEN, R. M. (2000). *A primer of drug action.* New York: Worth.

KLEINER, L., & MARSHALL, W. L. (1987). The role of interpersonal problems in the development of agoraphobia with panic attacks. *Journal of Anxiety Disorders, 1,* 313–323.

KLONOFF, E. A., LANDRINE, H., & CAMPBELL, R. (2000). Sexist discrimination may account for well known gender differences in psychiatric symptoms. *Psychology of Women Quarterly, 24,* 93–99.

KOSLOWSKI, L. T., & BRYANT, K. (1977). Sense of direction, spatial orientation, and cognitive maps. *Journal of Experimental Psychology: Human Perception and Performance, 3,* 590–598.

LAZARUS, A. (1966). Broad-spectrum behavior therapy and the treatment of agoraphobia. *Behavior Research and Therapy, 4,* 95–97.

LEWINSOHN, P. M., GOTLIB, I. H. M., SIELDY, J. R., & ALLEN, N. B. (1998). Gender differences in anxiety disorders and anxiety symptoms in adolescents. *Journal of Abnormal Psychology, 107,* 109–117.

LOTT, B. (1994). *Women's lives: Themes and variations.* Pacific Groves, CA: Brooks/Cole.

MACCOBY, E. E., & JACKLIN, C. N. (1974). *The psychology of sex differences.* Stanford, CA: Stanford University Press.

MAGEE, W. J., EATON, W. W., WITTCHEN, H. U., McGONAGLE, K. A., & KESSLER, R. C. (1996). Agoraphobia, simple phobia, and social phobia in the national comorbidity survey. *Archives of General Psychiatry, 53,* 159–168.

MARCAURELLE, R., BELANGER, C., & MARCHAND, A. (2003). Marital relationship and the treatment of panic disorder in agoraphobia: A critical review. *Clinical Psychology Review, 23,* 247–276.

MATRIX. (1984). Women and public space. In Matrix (Ed.), *Making space-women and the man-made environment* (pp. 37–54). London: Pluto Press.

McCARTHY, L., & SHEAN, G. (1996). Agoraphobia and interpersonal relationships. *Journal of Anxiety Disorders, 10,* 477–487.

McHUGH, M. C. (1989, March). *Rethinking agoraphobia.* Paper presented at the meeting of the Association for Women in Psychology, Tempe, AZ.

McHUGH, M. C. (1993). Studying battered women and batterers: Feminist perspectives on methodology. In M. Hansen & M. Harway (Eds.), *Battering and family therapy: A feminist perspective* (pp. 54–68). Newbury Park, CA: Sage.

McHUGH, M. C., & BARTOSZEK, T. A. (2000). Intimate violence. In M. Biaggio & M. Hersen (Eds.), *Issues in the psychology of women* (pp. 115–144). New York: Plenum Press.

McHUGH, M., & COSGROVE, L. (2004). Agoraphobia. In P. Caplan & L. Cosgrove (Eds.), *Bias in psychiatric diagnosis* (pp. 177–181). New York: Jason Aronson.

McHUGH, M. C., FRIEZE, I. H., & BROWNE, A. (1993). Research on battered women and their assailants. In F. Denmark & M. Paludi (Eds.), *Psychology of women: A handbook of issues and theories* (pp. 513–552). Westport, CT: Greenwood Press.

MEYER, R. (1987). *The relation of cognition and affect in agoraphobics with differing avoidance patterns.* Unpublished doctoral dissertation, New York University, New York, NY.

MICHELSON, L. (1987). Cognitive-behavioral assessment and treatment of agoraphobia. In L. Michelson & L. M. Ascher (Eds.), *Anxiety and stress disorders* (pp. 213–279). New York: Guilford Press.

MILTON, F., & HAFNER, R. J. (1979). The outcome of behavior therapy for agoraphobia in relation to marital adjustment. *Archives of General Psychiatry, 36,* 807–811.

MOHLMAN, J. (2000). Taking our housebound sisters to the mall: What can a feminist perspective add to CBT for panic and agoraphobia? *Behavior Therapist, 23*(2), 30–34.

MYERS, J., WEISSMAN, M., & TISCHLER, G. (1984). Six-month prevalence of psychiatric disorders in three communities. *Archives of General Psychiatry, 41,* 959–967.

REICH, J., NOYES, R. J., & TROUGHTON, E. (1987). Dependent panic disorder association with phobic avoidance in patients with panic disorder. *American Journal of Psychiatry, 144,* 323–326.

SABLE, P. (1991). Attachment, anxiety and agoraphobia. *Women & Therapy, 11*(2), 55–69.

SACHS, G., AMERING, M., BERGER, P., & KATSCHNIP, H. (2002). Gender related disabilities in panic disorder. *Archives of Women's Mental Health, 4,* 121–127.

SAEGERT, S., & HART, R. (1978). The development of environmental competence in girls and boys. In M. Salter (Ed.), *Play: Anthropological perspectives* (pp. 157–175). West Point, NY: Leisure Press.

SAGEE, P., & McHUGH, M. C. (2006). *Agoraphobia and the meaning of home.* Unpublished manuscript, Indiana University of Pennsylvania.

SANDERSON, W. C., RAPEE, R. M., & BARLOW, D. H. (1987, November). *The DSM-III—Revised anxiety disorder categories: Description and patterns of comorbidity.* Paper presented at the meeting of the Association for the Advancement of Behavior Therapy, Boston, MA.

SCHMIDT, N. B., & KOSELKA, M. (2000). Gender differences in patients with panic disorder: Evaluating cognitive mediation of phobic avoidance. *Cognitive Therapy and Research, 24,* 533–550.

SEIDENBERG, R., & DECROW, K. (1983). *Women who marry houses: Panic and protest in agoraphobia.* New York: McGraw-Hill.

SOMMERVILLE, P. (1997). The social construction of home. *Journal of Architectural and Planning Research, 14,* 226–241.

STARCERVIC, V., DJORDJEVIC, A., LATAS, M., & BOGOJEVIC, G. (1998). Characteristics of agoraphobia in women and men with panic disorder with agoraphobia. *Depression and Anxiety, 8,* 8–13.

STEKETEE, G., & FOA, E. B. (1987). Rape victims: Post-traumatic stress responses and their treatment. *Journal of Anxiety Disorders, 1,* 69–86.

TURGEON, L., MARCHAND, A., & DUPUIS, G. (1998). Clinical features in panic disorder with agoraphobia: A comparison of men and women. *Journal of Anxiety Disorders, 12,* 539–553.

VAN BALKOOM, A. L. J. M., DEBEURS, E., KEOLE, P., LANGE, A., & VAN DYKE, R. (1997). Long-term benzodiazepine use is associated with smaller treatment gain in panic disorder with agoraphobia. *Journal of Nervous and Mental Disease, 184,* 133–145.

VOSE, R. H. (1981). *Agoraphobia.* London: Faber.

WEISS, E. (1964). *Agoraphobia in light of ego psychology.* New York: Grune & Stratton.

WHITE, K. S., BROWN, T. A., SOMERS, T. J., & BARLOW, D. H. (2006). Avoidance behavior in panic disorder: The moderating influence of perceived control. *Behaviour Research and Therapy, 44,* 147–157.

WHITLEY, B. (1985). Sex role orientation and psychological well-being: Two meta-analyses. *Sex Roles, 12,* 207–225.

WITTCHEN, H. U., ZHAO, S., KESSLER, R. C., & EATON, W. W. (1994). DSM-III-R generalized anxiety disorder in the national comorbidity survey. *Archives of General Psychiatry, 51,* 355–364.

WOLFE, B. E. (1984). Gender ideology and phobias in women. In C. S. Wisdom (Ed.), *Sex roles and psychopathology* (pp. 51–72). New York: Plenum Press.

YONKERS, K. A., ZLOTNICK, C., ALLSWORTH, J., WARSHAW, M., SHEA, T., & DELLER, M. B. (1998). Is the course of panic disorder the same in women and men? *American Journal of Psychiatry, 155,* 596–602.

SUGGESTED READINGS

BROWN, L., & BALLOU, M. (Eds.). (1992). *Personality and psychopathology: Feminist reappraisals.* New York: Guilford Press.

GELFOND, M. (1991). Reconceptualizing agoraphobia: A case study of epistemological bias in clinical research. *Feminism & Psychology, 1*(2), 247–262.

SEIDENBERG, R., & DECROW, K. (1983). *Women who marry houses: Panic and protest in agoraphobia.* New York: McGraw-Hill.